RELATIVE VALUES

Reconfiguring Kinship Studies

Edited by Sarah Franklin & Susan McKinnon

© 2001 Duke University Press,
except "Kinship, Controversy, and the
Sharing of Substance: The Race/Class
Politics of Blood Transfusion,"
© 2001 Kath Weston
All rights reserved
Printed in the United States of
America on acid-free paper ∞
Designed by Amy Ruth Buchanan
Typeset in Minion by Tseng
Information Systems Inc.
Library of Congress Cataloging-
in-Publication Data appear on the
last printed page of this book.

CONTENTS

ILLUSTRATIONS

ACKNOWLEDGMENTS

This volume is the result of the Wenner-Gren international symposium New Directions in Kinship Study: A Core Concept Revisited, which took place from 27 March to 4 April 1998 in Palma de Mallorca. We wish to thank the Wenner-Gren Foundation for the rare gift that their international symposium program provided: nine days to think and talk about a topic of common concern in an elegant setting. We are especially grateful to Sydel Silverman for her support and encouragement, as well as the remarkable depth and breadth of her vision about the nature of anthropology; to Laurie Obbink for her brilliant organization of the conference (and for being so calm); to Mark Mahoney for his spirited assistance on site in Mallorca; and to Cori Hayden for her remarkable rapporteurial ricochets. Above all, we thank the participants for their tremendous energy and enthusiasm, their keen and provocative papers, and their good humor, graciousness, and warm congeniality. For comments on earlier drafts of our introduction, we would like to thank Mary Bouquet, Janet Carsten, Charis Thompson, Carol Delaney, Jonathan Marks, Martine Segalen, Verena Stolcke, Marilyn Strathern, and Kath Weston. We are also grateful to Susannah Bowyer and Kim Haslinger for preparing a bibliography of recent work on kinship; to Elizabeth Vann for her superb editorial assistance in preparing the manuscript; and to Charles Kaut for creating the kinship diagrams for Martine Segalen's paper. Finally, we wish to express our appreciation of the Wenner-Gren Foundation's generous support for the production of this volume.

Sarah Franklin and Susan McKinnon

INTRODUCTION

Relative Values: Reconfiguring Kinship Studies
Sarah Franklin and Susan McKinnon

At the core of social and cultural anthropology for decades, and arguably one of the discipline's most distinctive theoretical innovations, the study of kinship is itself symbolic of the anthropological tradition. Like all traditions, it has also undergone periodic reinventions, and it is currently in the midst of a revival that has entailed significant reconfigurations within a range of sites — from rural China to fertility clinics to cyberspace. The new uses of kinship theory, and the novel sites and locations where kinship study is being pursued, open up new possibilities for understanding the age-old question, What is kinship all about? It allows us to look both forward and back — ahead to the as yet little explored worlds of kinship-in-the-making, and back across a rich and varied history of scholarship on kinship and social life.

The chapters in this volume take seriously the challenge to kinship studies posed by new topics such as reproductive technology, international adoption, global capitalism, and virtual life. Kinship study takes on an altered significance in the context of the Human Genome Project or genetic screening programs, and it is to such empirical and theoretical challenges that the contributors to *Relative Values* have responded. These responses are as varied as their author's disparate interests, but they share in common the effort to begin to articulate a vocabulary of kinship analysis that bridges the unique legacy of historical debate about this concept and its ongoing prominence as a feature of social life.

Kinship is investigated in this volume both as a theoretical concept and a social category, and it is the tension between the two that generates many of our central questions. On the one hand, kinship remains a central concept within anthropology despite having undergone many transformations: indeed, this historical legacy gives the idea of kinship its sustained appeal and enduring flexibility. On the other hand, kinship remains a contested analytic concept. Like all epistemic devices, kinship helps to constitute what it describes so that even imagining its purchase on sets of phenomena, whether in Western societies or elsewhere, may be seen as ideological or circular, and thus complicit with an unreconstructed version of the anthropological project. Interrogating kinship, then, continues to precipitate lively debate concerning not only what kinship is "all about" but also how its uses index wider changes within anthropology as well as within the societies of which anthropologists are a part.

ON THE "NATURE" OF KINSHIP

The reflexive critique of kinship as a Western preoccupation, or as an imposition of Western ontological categories onto other peoples and cultures, is most often associated with David Schneider's 1984 *A Critique of the Study of Kinship*.[1] Schneider describes the two most prominent assumptions within kinship theory as the "Doctrine of the Genealogical Unity of Mankind," which "states that genealogical relations are the same in every culture," and "the assumption that Blood is Thicker Than Water," which "makes kinship or genealogical relations unlike any other social bonds" (1984, 174). Kinship, according to these assumptions, is seen to be an aftereffect of the natural facts of sexual reproduction. For Schneider, such a formulation produces a tautology:

> The notion of a "base in nature" creates a self-justifying and untestable definition of kinship: "kinship" as a sociocultural phenomenon is, in the first instance, defined as entailing those "natural" or "biological" facts which it is at the same time said to be "rooted in" or "based on." The phenomena which are shown by analysis to be related are already related by definition. (138)

It is not so much the biologism per se of such depictions that concerns Schneider, however, but the extent to which they reproduce "the more general characteristic of European culture toward what might be called 'biologistic' ways of constituting and conceiving human character, human nature, and human behavior" (175). The reproduction of this biologism is thus evidence of how "the study of kinship derives directly and practically unaltered from the ethnoepistemology of European culture" (175). In other words, occupied more with the general charge of ethnocentrism than the culturally specific form of the biologism, Schneider's critique foregrounds his key complaint that the privileging of kinship rests on a tautology.

Schneider was not alone in making this argument: Schneider's (1968, 1972) claim that the theoretical categories of Euro-American kinship study are informed and shaped by Euro-American understandings of kinship was shared by Ernest Gellner (1957) and Rodney Needham (1960). Such criticisms contributed to the rejection of structural-functionalist understandings of kinship as a core social structure—as espoused by A. R. Radcliffe-Brown, Bronislaw Malinowski, E. E. Evans-Pritchard, and Meyer Fortes—and allowed for more varied interpretations of the significance of kinship (as, for instance, in Leach 1967). Moreover, Schneider's 1984 *Critique* was exemplary of a broad shift within anthropology in the 1970s and 1980s toward more self-critical and reflexive approaches (see Marcus and Fischer 1986; Clifford and Marcus 1986), and a rejection of objectivist models in favor of more hermeneutical ones (see Geertz 1973; Rabinow and Sullivan 1979; Wagner 1975).

Schneider was also not the only theorist to identify kinship as a primary site of many of anthropology's most "biologistic" and thus Eurocentric concepts. This point had been extensively argued since the 1970s by feminists, such as Gayle Rubin (1975), who were critical of the latent biologism of both structural-functionalist and structuralist models. Nicole-Claude Mathieu's 1973 critique of the nature-culture models employed in Edwin Ardener's analysis of gender asymmetry (1972) was a major impetus behind the influential volume *Nature, Culture, and Gender* (MacCormack and Strathern 1980), in which the specificity of post-Enlightenment European culture was closely examined. According to this critique, both kinship and gender had for too long been presumed to be based on "natural facts" in a manner that was both essentialist and obfuscating, as well as ethnocentric. This contention directly paralleled Schneider's insistence that "the notion of a pure, pristine state of biological relationships 'out there in reality' which is the same for all mankind is sheer nonsense" (1965, 97).

The critique of "natural facts" that had been a prominent feature of Schneider's critique of kinship was thus widely articulated across a range of anthropological debates from the 1960s onward. Marilyn Strathern's synthetic account of this critique in 1980 cites numerous exponents of this view, including Marshall Sahlins (1976, 52, 101), Roy Wagner (1975, 1978), Jack Goody (1977, 64), and Jean-Marie Benoist (1978, 59) as well as Mathieu (1973). These critiques of the ethnocentrism of Western ideas of the natural and their codification as a nature-culture opposition by Claude Lévi-Strauss as a central tenet within structuralist anthropology significantly reshaped the study of both kinship and gender. Hence, although Schneider has often been singled out as being responsible for the "death of kinship" within anthropology, a more contextual reading of his work demonstrates that his arguments concerning the problematic status of natural facts were shared by others.

Jane Collier and Sylvia Yanagisako's anthology *Gender and Kinship: Essays toward a Unified Analysis* (1987) offered the first major extension of the critique of natural facts set out in *Nature, Culture, and Gender*. As Yanagisako and Collier observe in their assessment of kinship:

> Much of what is written about the atoms of kinship [Lévi-Strauss 1969], the axiom of prescriptive altruism [Fortes 1958, 1969], the universality of the family [Fox 1967], and the centrality of the mother-child bond [Goodenough 1970] is rooted in assumptions about the natural characteristics of women and men and their natural roles in sexual procreation. The standard units of our genealogies, after all, are circles and triangles about which we assume a number of things. Above all, we take for granted that they represent two naturally different categories of people and that the natural difference between them is the basis for human reproduction and, therefore, kinship. (Yanagisako and Collier 1987, 32)

Arguing that such naturalized differences cannot be presumed as the prediscursive, universal, and timeless basis for kinship, gender, or reproduction, Yanagisako and Collier propose a model of kinship that does not "begin by taking 'difference' for granted and treating it as a presocial fact" (29) but instead tries "to unpack the cultural assumptions embodied in [such concepts], which limit our capacity to understand social systems informed by other cultural assumptions" (34).

Since Collier and Yanagisako's challenging reassessment of kinship and gender, other theorists have extended this project still further. In *Naturalizing Power* (Yanagisako and Delaney 1995a), the argument that naturalization is a *symbolic* activity is widened to demonstrate how profoundly *productive* it is of social inequalities. Moving beyond Schneider's normative account of biology, the contributors to *Naturalizing Power* examine the productive effects of biological discourse, demonstrating how "inequality and hierarchy come already embedded in symbolic systems" and are "elaborated through contextualized material practices" (ix–x). By critically examining the power of naturalizing discourses to secure or authenticate an "order of things," the essays in *Naturalizing Power* challenge the ways in which hierarchical differences are legitimated as "natural," "biological," or "genetic" through categories such as "sex," "gender," "race," "reproduction," and "the family." [2] Insofar as "kinship" has been thoroughly imbricated within such essentialized categories, the critique of *naturalization as power* has advanced the analysis both of kinship as a concept and the types of sociocultural practices it is used to describe.

Similarly, the analysis of *naturalization as knowledge* has greatly broadened the scope of kinship study, particularly in the work of Marilyn Strathern, whose accounts of kinship in *After Nature* (1992a) and *Reproducing the Future* (1992b) reconfigure the critique of nature and natural facts as an exegesis of knowledge production more generally. For Strathern, naturalizations are cultural practices that domain knowledge, produce comparisons, and ground contexts for meaning specific to Euro-Americans. Kinship provides a useful example of naturalization as knowledge because of the way in which kin ties are seen to be constituted out of primordial natural facts. As Strathern notes:

> Kinship was regarded as an area of primordial identity and inevitable relations. It was at once a part of the natural world that regenerated social life and provided a representation of this relationship between them. Anthropologists, in turn, apprehended kinship as a symbolic construction that took after the natural facts on which society imagined itself based, a microcosm of the relationship between nature, society and symbol. (1992a, 198)

The naturalization of kinship within a reproductive model—where kinship is a "hybrid" institution, connecting nature and culture—depended on the way in which nature could provide not only a grounding function, or context, for society but indeed a model for context itself. Nature, Strathern maintains, "itself provided the very model for domaining" (1992a, 177). This has consequences not only for how one understands what kinship is, means, and does but also for how kinship can be seen to illustrate culturally specific features of what a Euro-American "understanding" is comprised of in itself. Such a view both expands widely what "kinship" can be used to analyze (for instance, knowledge practices) and opens up a whole new dimension of interpretive possibility for how kinship can be applied within a specific context (for example, reproductive technologies; see Edwards et al. 1999).

Writing of kinship in relation to the new reproductive technologies, Strathern suggests that the capacity for nature to be seen as a separate and distinct domain has increasingly been lost because its technological modification in the name of consumer choice exposes its contingency: "Nature as a ground for the meaning of cultural practices can no longer be taken for granted if Nature itself is regarded as having to be protected and promoted" (1992a, 177). Nature has been "flattened" and "no longer provides a model or analogy for the very idea of context," Strathern concludes (195).

It is thus possible to trace a challenge to the model of kinship as "based on" or "derived from" a set of natural facts from the 1950s onward, which, far from waning, has continued to gain momentum. Some might assert that such a view of kinship "weakens" its analytic hold, by "deconstructing" its very meaning. In contrast, we argue it is misleading to claim that kinship studies within British and U.S. anthropology have suffered or declined precipitously as a result of these critical interventions. As this volume demonstrates, kinship studies within anthropology have been productively reconfigured and indeed revitalized by the many critical interventions through which they have been transformed.[3] Contesting some of the taken-for-granted bases of kinship study has enabled it not only to become more flexible and mobile but also more precise. In turn, kinship theory can address a much wider range of contexts in a more complex and multidimensional way that is, at the same time, more rigorous as a result of being more reflexive. Kinship study has not reawakened, like some disciplinary Sleeping Beauty waiting to be rescued: rather, it has been steadily reinventing itself and, in the process, has undergone a substantial makeover.

As such, *Relative Values* contributes to a tradition of critical attention to both the concept and practice of kinship that has its roots in feminist anthropological debates about nature, culture, and gender in the 1980s, and their parallels in the reevaluation of kinship in the overlapping period. Building on the work of MacCormack and Strathern (1980), Collier and Yanagisako (1987), and Yanagisako and Delaney (1995b), this volume extends the critique of naturalization by using several contexts of comparison to reconfigure kinship study. By using historical and contemporary case studies from both established and nontraditional ethnographic sites, this volume stresses the increasing contemporary uncertainty surrounding ideas about kin relatedness, while attempting also to demonstrate their enduring centrality to various forms of social organization. The question of how kinship may be conceived of outside its ruling sign of biology has been powerfully explored in recent studies of "house societies" (McKinnon 1991; Carsten and Hugh-Jones 1995; Carsten 1997), gay and lesbian kinship (Weston 1991), adoption (Modell 1994), and surrogacy (Ragoné 1994). Both the effort to explore "cultures of relatedness" beyond what kinship has traditionally been used to represent (Carsten 2000) and the project of reimagining what kinship can connect through unfamiliar uses of genealogy (Helmreich 1998) enact the project of "making strange" what kinship means and does, even as the frame of kinship studies is greatly widened.

In bringing these diverse perspectives together and into collision, *Relative Values* challenges the claims of those who advocate a return to more traditional approaches to kinship that assert, as Robert Parkin does, that "all human societies have kinship" because "they all impose some privileged cultural order over the biological universals of sexual relations and continuous human reproduction through birth" (1997, 3).[4] At the same time, this volume rejects the Schneiderian axiom that "insofar as the comparative study of kinship is tenable or a legitimate endeavor, it must be assumed that kinship is a unitary phenomena. . . . [For] if kinship is not comparable from one society to the next, then it is self-evident that comparative study is out of the question" (Schneider 1984, 177). Seeking instead to open up the category of kinship and examine how it can be put to use in ways that destabilize the "obviousness" of its conventional referents, while expanding the scope of its purchase as well, *Relative Values* (as the title suggests) attempts to shift the terms of anthropological debate about kinship onto more contingent and productive terrain.

The Wenner-Gren international symposium, New Directions in Kinship Study: A Core Concept Revisited, brought together twenty-one scholars researching kinship within cultural anthropology, cultural studies, science studies, and biological anthropology.[5] The explicit aims of the conference were threefold: to reassess the widely noted displacement of kinship studies from the center of anthropological inquiry; to bring together for the first time new ethnographic, theoretical, and methodological approaches to kinship study that have emerged at the intersection of anthropology and cultural analyses of science, gender, race, sexuality, nationalism, and transnational political economy; and to examine a diverse range of new ethnographic sites of kinship studies. In looking back to past configurations of kinship study within anthropology, the symposium provided the opportunity to reexamine analytic concepts and contrast different national traditions (primarily U.S., British, and French). In addressing emergent reconfigurations of kinship and kinship studies, the symposium focused on the transformations of familiar concepts as they are refracted through a range of novel sites of kinship production.

The results of the symposium clearly indicate that kinship studies have neither declined nor been displaced from the center of anthropological inquiry: they have instead been transformed and revitalized. Kinship studies continue to be crucial to the discipline, not in spite of having been subject to a thoroughgoing critique but precisely because they no longer look quite the same. Thus, while the study of kinship has altered, it not only continues to be pivotal to a wide range of anthropological concerns but has begun to be more widely used in other areas of study (see, for example, Maynes et al. 1996).

RESITING KINSHIP STUDIES

One of the lasting contributions of the 1982 Wenner-Gren conference on feminism and kinship theory was the critique of the concept of analytic "domains," which had relegated kinship study to specific "types" of society and to differentially gendered "domains" of society (Collier and Yanagisako 1987; for critiques of analytic domaining practices in anthropology, see Kelly 1977; Yanagisako 1979, 1987; Comaroff 1987; Strathern 1992b; Carsten 1997; Ginsburg and Rapp 1995; Yanagisako and Delaney 1995a; McKinnon 2000). In both evolutionary and structural (functional) theory, kinship was largely studied in non-Western settings, within "primitive," small-scale, and "prestate" societies. And as Martine Segalen's essay in this volume documents, when kinship was studied in Europe, it was often among rural peasant communities or the urban working class, and was closely tied to the study of folklore and regional identities along with topics such as consanguinity and ethnicity.

A number of works in this volume—such as Segalen's on French grandparents—bring kinship studies back into not only the West but also the heart of urban, cosmopolitan, middle-class families—indeed, often into anthropologists' own families. There is a sense from such studies that kinship has come to again rest among the anthropologists themselves, much as it did for Lewis Henry Morgan, for whom—as Gillian Feeley-Harnik so vividly recounts—the kinship dilemmas of his own family life were ever-present in his theoretical writings. Going still further, in other chapters—such as Signe Howell's on Norwegian transnational adoption—the analytic separation between Euro-American and other kinship formations collapses altogether in the cultural compressions of transnational movements.

Not only have kinship studies escaped their confinement to non-Euro-American societies (and subordinate groups within Europe and the United States) but they have also, importantly, escaped their confinement to the domestic domain: new sites of kinship production include the biogenetics lab, the transnational adoption agency, and cyberspace. Consequently, it is clearer than ever before that the meaning of kinship can be understood only by reading *across* different cultural domains (Yanagisako and Delaney 1995a). *Relative Values* amply demonstrates that cultural understandings of kinship are shaped by—and, in turn, contribute to the shaping of—the political dynamics of national and transnational identities, the economic movements of labor and capital, the cosmologies of religion, the cultural hierarchies of race, gender, and species taxonomies, and the epistemologies of science, medicine, and technology. In essays focusing on these topics, it is evident that the work of making kinship in such contexts is both prominent and deliberate. There is a corresponding sense, in settings such as the in vitro fertilization (IVF) laboratory or genetic counseling session, that the foundational units or assumptions about what creates kinship are being made explicit—as Marilyn Strathern describes in her work on ideas of the natural in English kinship (1992a), Helena Ragoné shows in the context of surrogacy (1994), Susan Kahn details in her account of Jewish Orthodox debates over assisted conception in Israel (1995, 2000), or Sarah Franklin argues in her analysis of IVF practices in England (1997; see also Edwards et al. 1999; Franklin and Ragoné 1998). Such studies foreground a simultaneous multiplication and division of the substantial-codings from which kinship can be assembled, and an associated self-consciousness about what will count as kinship and how it is brought into being.

Although such familiar contingencies of kinship negotiation may be newly visible in unfamiliar contexts such as genetic medicine, where groups of people brought together by shared bodily substance form kin associations of a very contemporary kind, these settings establish important bases of comparison with other kinds of kinship work-in-progress. For instance, changes in the global economy make it possible to adopt or marry not only locally but across a wide range of national, geographic, cultural, sexual, and ethnic boundaries, as well as across various economic, political, and religious fault lines. While this is hardly a novel phenomenon, the increased intensity and frequency of the movements and migrations involved make kin relations such as those established through transnational adoption more familiar to ever-increasing numbers of people in various parts of the world. In this sense, kinship can be said to be subject to the same globalizing effects that are transforming definitions of the nation-state, through an intensification of transnational flows of labor, capital, information, and media (see Glick Schiller, Basch, and Blanc-Szanton 1992). The new hybridities often associated with global culture are noticeable not only in the West but in countries such as China, where Yunxiang Yan describes a decreasing emphasis on traditional patrilineal forms of kinship and an increasing reliance on nonkin (such as friends, fellow villagers, and work associates) in forms of traditional exchange (*guanxi*). As Yan demonstrates, the changing conditions of the Chinese political economy and the de-traditionalization of Chinese society have produced innovative techniques of relation making, which, in turn, demand of the anthropologist new kinds of analytic self-consciousness.

These new contexts of kinship and kinship study reveal a highly diverse range of interrelated phenomena of markedly different scales — from the gene to the body, to the family or species, to the commodity form and cyberspace. One of the challenges of the new kinship studies will be to trace the connections and conceptual crossovers between phenomena at these vastly different scales of embodiment.

WHAT SIGNIFIES KINSHIP

One important achievement of this volume is the exploration and complication of anthropological understandings of the symbolic density of the substances and codes that come to signify kinship, and their relation to the formation of kinship and other ties. In considering a range of analytic and cultural understandings of the substantial-codings of kinship (to use a formulation provoked by Janet Carsten's chapter), we find that they are as thick and dense with meanings as their negotiations are delicate and subtle.

Substantial-Codings: From Blood to Hypertext

In a detailed historical exegesis of the connection between Morgan's work on kinship and on the American beaver, Feeley-Harnik documents how he relied not on modern notions of biology but on a thick layering of connections among linguistic, zoological, geologic, and hydrologic flows and formations. It was in a deeply spiritual sense that Morgan tracked between biblical, indigenous Native American (Iroquois) and evolutionary frameworks through which his "channels of blood" linked together ideas about land, animals, water, railroads, indigenous peoples, their languages, and the afterlife. Moving from the late nineteenth to the late twentieth century, both Carsten and Franklin probe what we mean analytically and ethnographically by the terms *substance* and *biology,* respectively, arguing that these have been operating as broad and often poorly defined categories in kinship analysis. Carsten makes a valuable contribution by demonstrating the ambiguity and multivocality of the term *substance* as it is used analytically and as it has been deployed in the different ethnographic contexts of Melanesia, Malaysia, and India. In the process, she shows how profoundly other cultural understandings can interrogate and de-familiarize Euro-American cultural and analytic presuppositions about what constitutes kinship, and about the relation between nature and culture, substance and code. Franklin, in a similar fashion, traces the complexities of the varied understandings of biological "facts" in the context of the new biologies of commercial biotechnological innovation. Exploring the geneticization of biology and, in particular, the commodification of genetic information as intellectual property, she challenges the fixity of the notion of biological "substance."

Following the threads of Euro-American kinship analogies—from biology to blood to genes to code to information—it becomes evident that in late-twentieth-century Euro-American cultures, the substantial-codings that might signify kinship include a diverse range of phenomena—including genetic disease syndromes, the "informatics" of computer programming, and family photography. The chapter by Rayna Rapp, Deborah Heath, and Karen-Sue Taussig shows how a shared gene—for Down's syndrome, Marfan's syndrome, or achondroplasia—becomes the basis for new forms of kinship biosociality emerging out of genetic disease support groups. Providing a striking example of the analogic unfolding of what signifies kinship, Stefan Helmreich explores how artificial life scientists read genes as "information" and "code," which then allows them to read the "information" and "coding" of computer programs as equivalent to "life itself." The running of computer programs is seen by these scientists to be equivalent to the evolutionary unfolding of kinship relations over time. Likewise, Mary Bouquet's piece invites reflection on the ways in which the generic conventions of family photography have become one of the primary substantial-codings of kinship relations in both Euro-American cultures and ethnographic representations.

In the end, it is clear that not only what we mean by terms such as *substance* and *biology* is much richer and more diverse than we thought but also that what count as the substantial-codings of kinship have undergone significant historical transformation. As understandings of the "substances" of kinship change—from the Bible's transubstantiation of divinity through Abraham's seed, to Morgan's transubstantiated kinship across rivers of water and blood, to modern biology's definition of human nature and kinship in terms of genetic codes—so too is the capacity to make and unmake kinship out of them transformed. For example, as genes are described as a code, so kinship has acquired the capacity to become informatic, in the form of virtual genealogies linking lineages of algorithmic progeny in the laboratories of Artificial Life scientists. As informatic relation "overflows substance," Helmreich argues, it becomes possible to draw new "genealogical" connections between humans, animals, and machines.

Kinship Negotiations: What's Biology Not/Got to Do with It?
Given the multiplication, division, and fluidity of what might count as kinship in late-twentieth-century Euro-American cultures—and indeed, in many other cultures as well—it becomes imperative to examine the processes through which potential kinship ties are both assembled and disassembled. The chapters in this volume make significant contributions to understanding the mechanisms by which possible lines of relation are brought into being or erased by foregrounding and backgrounding various substantial connections and cultural codings. While agency, "choice," and negotiation become foci of scrutiny, the authors are careful to frame their use of such terms by an analysis of the complex historical and sociocultural forces that produce the possibility (or negation) of agency and choice.

In considering the decisions made in the context of the unprecedented combinatory practices of the new reproductive technologies in infertility clinics, Charis Thompson provides an account of the divergent biological and social models mobilized to decide which of several possible mothers—genetic, gestational, social—will be recognized as the "real" mother of a child. Arguments that foreground one possible line of relationality simultaneously background and erase other potential avenues to the creation of kinship ties. For instance, the same shared tie through genetic substance might be foregrounded to connect a mother to her child through her daughter's egg, but effaced when such close physical links threaten conjugal integrity or look too much like incest. Similarly, Kath Weston's piece shows how a range of shifting solidarities is established by foregrounding the same shared bodily substance —blood—in different contexts to create lines of "transfusion" across racial or class divisions. In other contexts, however—for example, blood banks— the disembodiment, standardization, and commodification of blood both obscure tensions and close down possibilities for solidarities and alliances across race and class lines. In her essay on transnational adoption, Howell offers a different perspective on the tensions between various strategies of creating kinship ties by illustrating how Norwegians move between contradictory explanatory frames that naturalize adoptive relations in biological terms, stress social nurturance, and biologize culture as a form of heredity.

Novel recombinatory possibilities are conspicuous not only in what are most evidently the "new" contexts of kinship—such as transnational adoption or reproductive technologies—and not only in Western or Euro-American contexts. As Yan observes in his account of new "privatized" family formations in rural northern China, changes in both customary exchange relations (guanxi) and the wider commercial economy in China have introduced new forms of "practical kinship" that foreground more egalitarian links between friends, affines, fellow villagers, and religious associates while backgrounding more traditional, hierarchical patrilineal relations. More flexible, these practical networks are more suited to the changing realities of economy, class, and the influence of cultural tradition. Examining changing kinship patterns in France—in particular, the "recomposed families" resulting from multiple divorces and remarriages—Segalen describes how the emergence of an active, healthy, grandparental "third age" has altered the intergenerational flow of resources (inheritance, property), sociality, and child care within newly flexible urban families. Grandparenting relationships, Segalen contends, are an important site for reinscribing filial stability into increasingly unstable family configurations, even as the flexibility of third-generation relationships is itself an expression of an emphasis on individual choice that contributes to family instability to begin with.

These chapters compel us to consider how kinship is created in ways that coexist with, push against, complement, contradict, erase, and make explicit divergent means of connection and disconnection—that is, they prompt us to "connect less familiar dots," as Weston urges. It is not simply that kinship must always be created, negotiated, and brought into being in practice, as Yan and others argue. It is also that the lines between kinship and other forms of relationality are fluid (see Carsten 2000). On the one hand, friends, villagers, religious associates, "racialized" others, and strangers can be made into kin, while mothers, grandparents, and patrilineal relations can be made into strangers, or "just" friends. On the other hand, the same substance (blood, genes, eggs, sperm) that is mobilized to create kinship ties in one context, will in different institutional contexts—given different historical, political-economic, and religious forces as well as different individual perspectives— be made to create other kinds of relations, or no relation at all. Kinship is not a preexisting thing but rather something "congealed," and all these essays address, in varying ways, the question that Weston poses at the end of her piece: "Congealed how, for whose benefit, and from what?"

Moving across Cultural Registers:
The Traffic between "Science" and "Culture"
Schneider drew attention to the manner in which scientific—specifically bio-genetic—representations are privileged in the United States in the determination of "what kinship is all about" (1968, 1972, 1984). Nevertheless, he did not consider either how biological/scientific representations came to have such a hold on Euro-American cultural understandings of kinship or how those biological/scientific representations are themselves shaped by cultural understandings—including those relating to kinship. In the period since Schneider's work, a burgeoning field of cultural studies of science has made evident both the cultural context within which scientific knowledge is created and the cultural content of scientific ideas, theories, and practices (for a review of science studies, see Franklin 1995). The chapters in this volume take up this issue of the traffic between different cultural registers as ideas about kinship travel in and out of the scientific lab and through a multiplicity of other cultural contexts. Thus, Jonathan Marks and Stefan Helmreich show how specifically Euro-American cultural ideas about kinship—including paternity, maternity, descent, genealogy, marriage, bounded and unbounded groupings—shape scientific research on the human genome and artificial life, respectively. Carsten and Bouquet examine how cultural tropes of relatedness concerning substance and the visual-substantial representations of family, respectively, have had a specific history and particular consequences for the disciplinary discourse within the "science" of anthropology. Franklin's investigation of the concept of biology traces the complex crisscrossing of cultural registers in the historical transformation of this crucial idea. The essay by Rapp, Heath, and Taussig is especially rich in its exploration of the multi-directional traffic between scientific and other cultural registers: not only do tropes of kinship and genealogy organize the relations and production of scientific ideas about genetic diseases but the latter are mobilized by people with genetic diseases in the creation of new kinship formations based on shared genetic traits. Moreover, their chapter also points to the productive possibilities of a close, critical, and mutually respectful relationship between scientists and those with whom they are working. By contrast, the potential for scientific representations to be used to define, control, subordinate, and exploit human populations in a variety of contexts is addressed in Jonathan Marks's

account of genetics and the Human Genome Diversity Project and in Melbourne Tapper's history of the colonial uses of medical research on sickling in Africa. As Daniel Segal noted in his summary comments at the symposium, the question is not primarily whether the science here is good or bad (although that is certainly something to consider) but rather how to understand the complex traffic between different cultural registers, including that of science. This is essential in order to comprehend not only the inseparability of science and other cultural registers as mutually constituting discourses but also the peculiar authority and hold that science is granted—at least in Euro-American societies—in defining and naturalizing the modalities of human relations.

WHAT KINSHIP SIGNIFIES

Kinship systems, like gender, have often been theorized as classification systems and even as grammars. In turn, such social technologies of naming and classifying, or of sorting and dividing, are seen to be generative of the kinds of material, relational, and cultural worlds that are possible, and for whom. As a classificatory technology, kinship can be mobilized to signify not only specific kinds of connection and inclusion but also specific kinds of disconnection and exclusion—as well as the boundary-crossing trickster movements that confound such classifications. Since relations of power are central to the articulation of such classificatory boundaries and movements, kinship is also utilized to articulate the possibilities for social relations of equality, hierarchy, amity, ambivalence, and violence. In so doing, it becomes evident that kinship's classificatory maneuvers can be mobilized to bring into being *other* categories of relationality—including genders, sexualities, races, species, machines, nature, and culture. In what follows, we explore some of the signifying characteristics of kinship in Euro-American cultures. We do so, however, without losing sight of the fact that the cultural specificity of these Euro-American understandings of kinship are only made visible through comparative work (both theoretical and ethnographic) that simultaneously opens windows onto other cultural visions of relationality.

Nature, Culture, and the Properties of Kinship
In her recent work, to which the concept of kinship is primary, Donna Haraway defines kinship as "a technology for producing the material and semiotic effect of natural relationship, of shared kind" (1997, 53). Yet as Strathern points

out, kinship's naturalizing function is two-way. For Euro-Americans, kinship is a "hybrid" between nature and culture, or biology and society (Strathern 1992b, 16–17). It therefore becomes a cultural technology not only for naturalizing relationships but also, and at the same time, for the reverse — for transforming naturalized relations into cultural forms. *"Kinship thus connects the two domains"* (Strathern 1992b, 17) and works in both directions — moving back and forth between what counts as natural/given and cultural/created. In the process, kinship becomes the site for producing what will count as the *difference* between nature and culture.

In the Euro-American tradition, this difference is often additive: culture, for example, is configured as "after nature" (Strathern 1992a), as "something more" added to and transformative of nature. It is for this reason that definitions of property, enterprise, paternity, and their formal configurations as patent, copyright, or commodity — which all depend on the idea of adding something more to nature — become key to the narratives of kinship that articulate the origins of culture and significance of scientific invention. Analyzing these linkages, McKinnon's and Franklin's chapters look at the relationship between kinship, property, and paternity in the anthropological stories of the origin of culture and the contemporary stories of scientific progress, respectively. Both sets of narratives outline a developmental trajectory marked by the "enterprising up" (Strathern 1992b; Haraway 1997) of naturalized kinship relations into the property relations that signal both cultural and scientific progress. Examining two contrasting "origin stories" in the work of Morgan and Lévi-Strauss, McKinnon considers how — despite different (indeed opposite) starting points — both theorists imagine the development of culture as the transformation of naturalized forms of kinship (maternal, female, consanguineal) into transcendent cultural forms marked by the simultaneous discovery and coalescence of paternity and property (whether conceptualized in terms of inheritance or exchange). The paternal enterprise that is the mark of civilization is thus nearly indistinguishable from the enterprise that creates relations of property out of more naturalized forms of kinship. Similarly, in her discussion of the changing meanings of biological facts in the context of the new genetics and biotechnology, Franklin explores the significance of commercial propriety in the generation of new life-forms, such as transgenic animals and cloned sheep. Asking whether biological facts are doing the same kind of naturalizing work when they have become commercial transactions marketed under trademarks, she expands the linkages examined by McKinnon, Haraway, and Strathern between property, paternity, and enterprise as they occur in the context of the new biologies.

'R' Genes US? Genetics and the Uses of Gene/alogies

The use of the concepts of blood, genes, genetics, and genealogy to produce social classifications and definitions of the "family of man" is not a recent phenomenon. The chapters in this volume, however, take critical steps in advancing our understanding of how the acceleration of scientific and medical research into human phylogeny and disease comprises a powerful force in society, in relation to which kinship definitions are actively reconstructed in a range of contexts. Together, these essays provide a contrastive frame in which it is possible to theorize the multiple uses of gene/alogy—as it can be mobilized both in the service of discrimination and subordination, and as the basis for new communities of shared concern.

Several works address the scientific-political uses of kinship in the production of naturalized or racialized types and discriminations. Marks traces the naturalization of the idea of "isolated" and "pure" human populations—which draw clear lines of exclusion and inclusion—through various scientific studies of genes and race up to and including the Human Genome Diversity Project (HGDP). In the process, he warns of the consequences of the unexamined classificatory maneuvers deployed by the HGDP, especially in light of those of an earlier era that distinguished populations subject to eugenic interventions and were a means for establishing hierarchical control over genetic resources. Similarly, Tapper's historical reading of the scientific construction of sickle cell anemia in Africa demonstrates how colonial scientists and administrators used sickling rates to naturalize tribal relations as biogenetic categories. Mapping racial categories "in the blood" reshaped not only the practice of medicine but also, through it, the structures of government by means of which African people became racialized tribes subject to colonial subordination and control.

By contrast, other chapters investigate the innovative uses of the analogies of kinship to create new forms of inclusiveness and egalitarian community. For instance, Rapp, Heath, and Taussig show how the scientific identification of genetic mutations has enabled the renegotiation of the meaning of disease and disability, and has provided the basis for the creation of genetic genealogies and kinship communities, which have arisen in the context of genetic disease support groups. Although some of these communities have, at different times, reinscribed hierarchies based on the relative valuation of ge-netic differences, others have focused on shared genetic inheritance to create communities based on equality rather than hierarchy, inclusion rather than exclusion.

From Amity to the Ambivalence and Violence of Kinship

One of the purposes of this book is to explore the ways in which ideologies of kinship become embedded in and signifiers of relations of power that draw lines of hierarchy and exclusion, bring about relations of dominance and sub-ordination, and generate a range of violences in the heart of kinship. While these are as central to kinship as "amity" or "diffuse enduring solidarity," the emphasis on kinship as a form of connection has often led to a neglect of its equally important constitution out of acts of disconnection or rupture (see Dominguez 1986; Martinez-Alier 1974; Strathern 1981; Williams 1995).

Returning to the biblical story of Abraham, Carol Delaney traces the ways in which ideas about paternity entail ideas about ownership and inheritance that have multiple consequences for who is included and excluded in the gene-alogy of Abraham. The father has rights (here, the right to sacrifice) over his children that are not accorded to the mother; and genealogical lines are drawn to include the children of some mothers (married) but not others (unmar-ried), and some children (male) but not others (female). The entailments of religious ideas about paternity in the Abraham story, Delaney contends, not only place an act of violence (the willingness to sacrifice one's child) at the heart of kinship but also explicitly delineate which forms of relation will and will not count as kinship. As such, kinship becomes a signifier of the power relations, inclusions, and exclusions that are definitive of religious faith and community. In a similar fashion, Pauline Turner Strong delves into the ways in which extra-tribal adoptions of Native American children, undertaken in the so-called best interests of the child, are experienced by Native Americans as a violent assault on their identity and culture—one that also makes evi-dent the relations of power as well as the cultural differences between Native Americans and the dominant political-social-economic order of the United States.

Once the focus of inquiry includes both inclusions and exclusions, both the amity and the violence at the core of kinship, and both the egalitarian and hierarchical lines of relation, ambivalence emerges as an important ave-nue for understanding the complexities of kinship relations. In his chapter, Michael G. Peletz argues that an emphasis on ambivalence yields insights into the nature of kinship as it is shaped by the tensions and contradictions between differential relations of power and resistance, individual agency and desire, and diverse rights, demands, and obligations. And as Peletz, Howell, and Yan all note, attention to ambivalence and emotional valences produces a different perspective not only on kinship and family but also on the meaning of social structure and the means of theorizing its determining influence. In this way, the self-conscious shift toward the use of practice theory in both Yan's and Peletz's accounts reveals again how close the connection is between the ways kinship is signified analytically and what shows up as kinship as a result.

Cultures of Inclusion and Exclusion: Fixing and Crossing Boundaries
If, as has been argued, kinship has long been used to conceptualize ideas about the bounded integrity of nations (Schneider 1969; Heng and Devan 1992; Delaney 1995), races and castes (Williams 1995; Haraway 1997), species (Haraway 1992, 1997), and bodies and machines (Haraway 1991; Helmreich 1998), it has also been and, especially now, has increasingly become a medium through which both the fixing and crossing of boundaries between these categories is signified. For example, while Delaney (1995) has shown how the bounded integrity of the Turkish nation-state is conceptualized through the figures of paternity and maternity, Veena Das (1995) demonstrates how the partition of India in 1947 was negotiated and literally embodied through the boundary-crossing kidnapping and marriage of Indian and Pakistani women by their respective enemies as well as through their subsequent repatriation. In this latter case, affinal relations became a primary figure through which to articulate not only the bounding but also the crossing and subsequent uncrossing of political and religious identities. The chapters in this volume explore various ways in which kinship is mobilized to articulate these kinds of bounding and boundary-crossing effects.

With regard to ideas about *race,* Tapper's essay illustrates how discourses concerning blood (and specifically sickling) could be used in the colonial context to bring into effect rigid distinctions between "races" and "tribes," while Weston's chapter explores how discourses concerning blood transfusions could bring into relief both racial fears of miscegenation and narratives of the cross-racial kinship solidarity of common blood. With regard to ideas about *culture* and *nation,* Strong's piece shows how adoptions of Native American children by Euro-American couples take place in a context of differential power and operate under a hegemonic definition of what constitutes a family—thereby working to effect the exclusion and erasure of nondominant forms of family relation. In the process, distinct lines between two cultures (and nations) are drawn by reference to different understandings of what counts as family. From a different perspective, Howell examines the ways in which Norwegians who have adopted Korean children work hard to create unambiguously Norwegian children at the same time that they effect a kind of bridging between the two cultures and nations — as Norwegians travel to Korea to find their children's so-called roots and as they attempt to re-create Korean culture in Norwegian meeting halls. With regard to *species,* Franklin's work investigates the emerging terrain of transgenic species boundary crossing, while Helmreich pushes the frontiers of kinship into human-machine hybridities that extend out into cyberspace. In all these examples, kinship becomes a medium through which to think about, configure, and articulate the shape and consequences of such boundary crossings and boundary enforcement as well as their respective embodiments.

RECONTEXTUALIZING KINSHIP STUDIES

The trajectory of kinship studies described by the chapters in this volume directly challenges those outlined in recent books on kinship by Robert Parkin (1997) and Linda Stone (1997), in which the distinction between biological and social facts is defended, a return to more traditional approaches to kinship is advocated (Parkin 1997, 137–38), and the critique of the concept of kinship offered by Yanagisako and Collier (1987) is rejected (Stone 1997, 4). In the midst of ongoing debates within anthropology — including those concerning the scientific authority of the discipline or the relationship of anthropology to cultural studies — it is likely that the study of kinship will continue to register broader currents of the discipline, much as it has always done.

For the authors in this book, Ladislav Holy's observation in his astute review of anthropological perspectives on kinship is aptly succinct: "New insights into kinship have been gained, as they are always gained, through shift[s] in contextualization" (1996, 6). Indeed, we have argued here that a number of shifts in contextualization, both theoretical and ethnographic, have produced new insights into what signifies kinship and what kinship signifies.

In contemplating the consequences of these shifts for transforming kinship studies, the authors in *Relative Values* have been confronted with multiple tasks. As much as we are concerned to trace the new lines of recombinatory logic — which produce kinship in the unfamiliar contexts of patented or artificial life-forms, transspecies hybrids, and local-global compressions — we are concerned to avoid both overestimating the novelty of such phenomena and overly celebrating their transgressiveness. While responsive to what is distinctive about the emergent "hybrid" possibilities associated with biotechnology, for example, we think it equally important to map out the points where such combinations and fusions are prohibited, suppressed, or unacknowledged, and for whom new technologies are put to use. As much as we are intrigued by the ways in which boundaries — of nations, cultures, species, races, persons, bodies, cells — have been breached, we are equally concerned to draw attention to the ways in which such ruptures become occasions to reestablish and reinforce familiar normative categories (see Cannell 1990). As much as we focus on the destabilization of foundational certainties, we also highlight the ways in which categories such as the natural and human continue to be used to signify what is certain, essential, and given in the nature of things. As much as we turn to the role of process, negotiation, and choice, we are also attentive to the restrictions that make them possible for some people in some contexts but not for others. And as much as we wish to map out new directions in kinship studies, we are deeply mindful of the complex ways in which older directions and questions become newly relevant by the recontextualization of kinship studies.

NOTES

1 Mary Bouquet (1993) demonstrates that it is impossible to characterize the analytic categories of kinship study as generically "Western": her study of the difficulties of teaching kinship theory in Portugal make evident the peculiarly "British" nature of many of the categories used in kinship analysis (see also Kahn 2000).

2 The critique of naturalization outlined by Sylvia Yanagisako and Carol Delaney foregrounds the importance of scientific discourse, in particular, as a form of reproducing inequalities. For example, the use of scientific racial categories is cited as "a system of social categories constructed *in terms of biological difference*" (1995a, 20). Although we do not discuss the more recent debates within the anthropology of science or "science as culture" here in this introduction, the links between the critique of natural facts in anthropology and the reexamination of Western scientific knowledge more generally are explored in several chapters below.

3 For reviews of contemporary kinship studies, see Faubion 1996; and Peletz 1996.

4 Similarly, Linda Stone asserts that "a male/female difference in reproduction is universal (however varied the cultural constructions of this difference might be) and that on the basis of this 'fact' we can begin to make meaningful cross-cultural comparisons" (1997, 4). Stone's bracketing of "this 'fact'" expresses precisely the instability

of its place at the center of her proposed model of kinship study, in a somewhat paradoxical recapitulation of its uncertainty even as she claims it as a "basis" for "meaningful cross-cultural comparisons."

5 The participants in the symposium included Mary Bouquet (University of Utrecht), Janet Carsten (University of Edinburgh), Charis Thompson (Harvard University), Carol Delaney (Stanford University), Gillian Feeley-Harnik (University of Michigan), Sarah Franklin (Lancaster University), Christine Gailey (University of California, Riverside), Corinne Hayden (University of California, Santa Cruz), Stefan Helmreich (New York University), Signe Howell (University of Oslo), Jonathan Marks (University of North Carolina, Charlotte), Susan McKinnon (University of Virginia), Michael Peletz (Colgate University), Rayna Rapp (New York University), Daniel Segal (Pitzer College), Martine Segalen (University of Paris X, Nanterre), Sydel Silverman (Wenner-Gren Foundation), Verena Stolcke (Universidad Autonoma, Barcelona), Marilyn Strathern (University of Cambridge), Pauline Turner Strong (University of Texas, Austin), Melbourne Tapper (independent scholar), Kath Weston (Harvard University), and Yunxiang Yan (University of California, Los Angeles).

REFERENCES

Ardener, Edwin. 1972. Belief and the Problem of Women. In *The Interpretation of Ritual*, edited by Jean S. La Fontaine. London: Tavistock.

Benoist, Jean-Marie. 1978. *The Structural Revolution*. London: Weidenfeld and Nicholson.

Bouquet, Mary. 1993. *Reclaiming English Kinship: Portuguese Refractions on English Kinship Theory*. Manchester, U.K.: Manchester University Press.

Cannell, Fenella. 1990. Concepts of Parenthood: The Warnock Report, the Gillick Debate, and Modern Myths. *American Ethnologist* 17, no. 4:667–86.

Carsten, Janet. 1997. *The Heat of the Hearth: The Process of Kinship in a Malay Fishing Community*. Oxford: Clarendon Press.

————, ed. 2000. *Cultures of Relatedness: New Approaches to the Study of Kinship*. Cambridge: Cambridge University Press.

Carsten, Janet, and Stephen Hugh-Jones, eds. 1995. *About the House: Lévi-Strauss and Beyond*. Cambridge: Cambridge University Press.

Clifford, James, and George E. Marcus, eds. 1986. *Writing Culture: The Poetics and Politics of Ethnography*. Berkeley: University of California Press.

Collier, Jane F., and Sylvia J. Yanagisako, eds. 1987. *Gender and Kinship: Essays toward a Unified Analysis*. Stanford, Calif.: Stanford University Press.

Comaroff, John L. 1987. *Sui Generis:* Feminism, Kinship Theory, and Structural "Domains." In *Gender and Kinship: Essays toward a Unified Analysis,* edited by Jane F. Collier and Sylvia J. Yanagisako. Stanford, Calif.: Stanford University Press.

Das, Veena. 1995. National Honor and Practical Kinship: Unwanted Women and Children. In *Conceiving the New World Order: The Global Politics of Reproduction*, edited by Faye D. Ginsburg and Rayna Rapp. Berkeley: University of California Press.

Delaney, Carol. 1995. Father State, Motherland, and the Birth of Modern Turkey. In *Naturalizing Power: Essays in Feminist Cultural Analysis,* edited by Sylvia J. Yanagisako and Carol Delaney. New York: Routledge.

Dominguez, Virginia. 1986. *White by Definition: Social Classification in Creole Louisiana.* New Brunswick, N.J.: Rutgers University Press.

Edwards, Jeanette, Sarah Franklin, Eric Hirsch, Frances Price, and Marilyn Strathern. 1999. *Technologies of Procreation: Kinship in the Age of Assisted Conception.* 2d ed. London: Routledge.

Faubion, James D. 1996. Kinship Is Dead, Long Live Kinship: A Review Article. *Comparative Studies in Society and History* 38, no. 1: 67–91.

Fortes, Meyer. 1958. Introduction to *The Development Cycle in Domestic Groups,* edited by Jack Goody. Cambridge: Cambridge University Press.

———. 1969. *Kinship and the Social Order: The Legacy of Lewis Henry Morgan.* Chicago: Aldine.

Fox, Robin. 1967. *Kinship and Marriage.* Middlesex, U.K.: Penguin.

Franklin, Sarah. 1995. Science as Culture, Cultures of Science. *Annual Review of Anthropology* 24:163–84.

———. 1997. *Embodied Progress: A Cultural Account of Assisted Conception.* London: Routledge.

Franklin, Sarah, and Helena Ragoné, eds. 1998. *Reproducing Reproduction: Kinship, Power, and Technological Innovation.* Philadelphia: University of Pennsylvania Press.

Geertz, Clifford. 1973. *The Interpretation of Cultures.* New York: Basic Books.

Gellner, Ernest. 1957. Ideal Language and Kinship Structure. *Philosophy of Science* 24: 235–42.

Ginsburg, Faye D., and Rayna Rapp, eds. 1995. *Conceiving the New World Order: The Global Politics of Reproduction.* Berkeley: University of California Press.

Glick Schiller, Nina, Linda Basch, and Cristina Blanc-Szanton, eds. 1992. *Towards a Transnational Perspective on Migration: Race, Class, Ethnicity, and Nationalism Reconsidered.* New York: New York Academy of Sciences.

Goodenough, Ward H. 1970. *Description and Comparison in Cultural Anthropology.* Chicago: University of Chicago Press.

Goody, Jack. 1977. *The Domestication of the Savage Mind.* Cambridge: Cambridge University Press.

Haraway, Donna J. 1991. *Simians, Cyborgs, and Women: The Reinvention of Nature.* New York: Routledge.

———. 1992. The Promises of Monsters: A Regenerative Politics for Inappropriate/d Others. In *Cultural Studies,* edited by Lawrence Grossberg, Cary Nelson, and Paula Treichler. New York: Routledge.

———. 1997. *Modest_Witness@Second_Millennium.FemaleMan©_Meets_Onco Mouse™.* New York: Routledge.

Helmreich, Stefan. 1998. *Silicon Second Nature: Culturing Artificial Life in a Digital World.* Berkeley: University of California Press.

Heng, Geraldine, and Janadas Devan. 1992. State Fatherhood: The Politics of Nationalism, Sexuality, and Race in Singapore. In *Nationalisms and Sexualities,* edited by

Andrew Parker, Mary Russo, Doris Sommer, and Patricia Yaeger. New York: Routledge.

Holy, Ladislav. 1996. *Anthropological Perspectives on Kinship*. London: Pluto Press.

Kahn, Susan. 1995. Jewish Sperm and Spinster Ova: Rabbinic Recipes for Reproduction. Paper presented at the Meetings of the American Anthropological Association, 17 November 1995, Washington, D.C.

———. 2000. *Reproducing Jews: A Cultural Account of Assisted Conception in Israel*. Durham, N.C.: Duke University Press.

Kelly, Raymond. 1977. *Etoro Social Structure: A Study in Structural Contradiction*. Ann Arbor: University of Michigan Press.

Leach, Edmund. 1967. Virgin Birth. In *Proceedings of the Royal Anthropological Institute of Great Britain and Ireland for 1966*. London: Royal Anthropological Institute of Great Britain and Ireland.

Lévi-Strauss, Claude. 1969. *The Elementary Structures of Kinship*. Boston: Beacon Press.

MacCormack, Carol, and Marilyn Strathern, eds. 1980. *Nature, Culture, and Gender*. Cambridge: Cambridge University Press.

Marcus, George E., and Michael M. J. Fischer. 1986. *Anthropology as Cultural Critique: An Experimental Moment in the Human Sciences*. Chicago: University of Chicago Press.

Martinez-Alier, Verena. 1974. *Marriage, Class, and Colour in Nineteenth-Century Cuba: A Study of Racial Attitudes and Sexual Values in a Slave Society*. Ann Arbor, Mich.: University of Michigan Press.

Mathieu, Nicole-Claude. 1973. Homme-Culture et Femme-Nature? *L'Homme* 13:101–41.

Maynes, Mary Jo, Ann Waltner, Birgitte Soland, and Ulrike Strasser, eds. 1996. *Gender, Kinship, Power: A Comparative and Interdisciplinary History*. New York: Routledge.

McKinnon, Susan. 1991. *From a Shattered Sun: Hierarchy, Gender, and Alliance in the Tanimbar Islands*. Madison: University of Wisconsin Press.

———. 2000. Domestic Exceptions: Evans-Pritchard and the Creation of Nuer Patrilineality and Equality. *Cultural Anthropology* 15, no. 1:35–83.

Modell, Judith S. 1994. *Kinship with Strangers: Adoption and Interpretations of Kinship in American Culture*. Berkeley: University of California Press.

Needham, Rodney. 1960. Discussion: Descent Systems and Ideal Language [Response to Gellner]. *Philosophy of Science* 27:96–101.

Parkin, Robert. 1997. *Kinship: An Introduction to Basic Concepts*. Oxford: Blackwell.

Peletz, Michael G. 1996. Kinship Studies in Late Twentieth-Century Anthropology. *Annual Review of Anthropology* 24:343–72.

Rabinow, Paul, and William Sullivan, eds. 1979. *Interpretive Social Science: A Reader*. Berkeley: University of California Press.

Ragoné, Helena. 1994. *Surrogate Motherhood: Conception in the Heart*. Boulder, Colo.: Westview Press.

Rubin, Gayle. 1975. The Traffic in Women: Notes on the "Political Economy" of Sex. In *Toward an Anthropology of Women*, edited by Rayna R. Reiter. New York: Monthly Review Press.

Sahlins, Marshall. 1976. *Culture and Practical Reason*. Chicago: University of Chicago Press.

Schneider, David M. 1965. Kinship and Biology. In *Aspects of the Analysis of Family Structure,* edited by Ansley J. Coale. Princeton, N.J.: Princeton University Press.

———. 1968. *American Kinship: A Cultural Account.* Englewood Cliffs, N.J.: Prentice-Hall.

———. 1969. Kinship, Nationality, and Religion in American Culture: Toward a Definition of Kinship. In *Forms of Symbolic Action,* edited by Victor Turner. Seattle: American Ethnological Society.

———. 1972. What Is Kinship All About? In *Kinship Studies in the Morgan Centennial Year,* edited by Priscilla Reining. Washington, D.C.: Washington Anthropological Society.

———. 1984. *A Critique of the Study of Kinship.* Ann Arbor: University of Michigan Press.

Stone, Linda. 1997. *Kinship and Gender: An Introduction.* Boulder, Colo.: Westview Press.

Strathern, Marilyn. 1980. No Nature, No Culture: The Hagen Case. In *Nature, Culture, and Gender,* edited by Carol MacCormack and Marilyn Strathern. Cambridge: Cambridge University Press.

———. 1981. *Kinship at the Core: An Anthropology of Elmdon, Essex.* Cambridge: Cambridge University Press.

———. 1992a. *After Nature: English Kinship in the Late Twentieth Century.* Cambridge: Cambridge University Press.

———. 1992b. *Reproducing the Future: Anthropology, Kinship and the New Reproductive Technologies.* New York: Routledge.

Wagner, Roy. 1975. *The Invention of Culture.* Englewood Cliffs, N.J.: Prentice-Hall.

———. 1978. *Lethal Speech.* Ithaca, N.Y.: Cornell University Press.

Weston, Kath. 1991. *Families We Choose: Lesbians, Gays, Kinship.* New York: Columbia University Press.

Williams, Brackette. 1995. Classification Systems Revisited: Kinship, Caste, Race, and Nationality as the Flow of Blood and the Spread of Rights. In *Naturalizing Power: Essays in Feminist Cultural Analysis,* edited by Sylvia J. Yanagisako and Carol Delaney. New York: Routledge.

Yanagisako, Sylvia J. 1979. Family and Household: The Analysis of Domestic Groups. *Annual Review of Anthropology* 8:161–205.

———. 1987. Mixed Metaphors: Native and Anthropological Models of Gender and Kinship Domains. In *Gender and Kinship: Essays toward a Unified Analysis,* edited by Jane F. Collier and Sylvia J. Yanagisako. Stanford, Calif.: Stanford University Press.

Yanagisako, Sylvia J., and Jane F. Collier. 1987. Toward a Unified Analysis of Gender and Kinship. In *Gender and Kinship: Essays toward a Unified Analysis,* edited by Jane F. Collier and Sylvia J. Yanagisako. Stanford, Calif.: Stanford University Press.

Yanagisako, Sylvia J., and Carol Delaney. 1995a. Naturalizing Power. In *Naturalizing Power: Essays in Feminist Cultural Analysis,* edited by Sylvia J. Yanagisako and Carol Delaney. New York: Routledge.

———, eds. 1995b. *Naturalizing Power: Essays in Feminist Cultural Analysis.* New York: Routledge.

PART I

Substantial-Codings:

From Blood to Hypertext

CHAPTER 1

Substantivism, Antisubstantivism, and
Anti-antisubstantivism
Janet Carsten

This essay explores the uses of the term *substance* in the anthropological literature on kinship. I begin with the varied meanings of substance in English. The very breadth of this semantic domain, I suggest, has been central to the fruitfulness of analyses of kinship that have employed the term. And this is amply attested to elsewhere in this volume, where substance is used not only to refer to blood (see Weston) and other bodily fluids but also to information (Helmreich), rivers and railways (Feeley-Harnik), and family photographs (Bouquet). But the ambiguities of *substance,* which seem to have gone largely unexamined in the literature, also raise problems—particularly for the analytic rigor of any comparative endeavor.

The Oxford English Dictionary (*OED*) lists twenty-three separate meanings for *substance* covering three full pages. Several of these meanings clearly overlap or are closely related to each other. Nevertheless, there are some important distinctions between substance as essential nature or essence; a separate distinct thing; that which underlies phenomena; matter or subject matter; the material of which a physical thing consists; the matter or tissue composing an animal body part or organ; any corporeal matter; a solid or real thing (as opposed to appearance or shadow); a vital part; what gives a thing its character; and the consistency of a fluid. I have selected just some of the *OED*'s long list of meanings—those that, it seems to me, have relevance for an examination of the uses to which substance has been put in the anthropological study of kinship. The *OED*'s list of meanings might be further reduced to four broader categories: vital part or essence; separate distinct thing; that which underlies phenomena; and corporeal matter. All of these distinct meanings have some bearing on anthropological understandings. Indeed, I maintain that the utility of substance as a term is due in large measure to the very breadth of the meanings that I have delineated.

This ambiguity emerges clearly in David Schneider's deployment of substance in *American Kinship: A Cultural Account* (1980). In tracing the passage of substance, from Schneider's original application of it in 1968 in the analysis of American kinship, to India, and from India to Melanesia, I attempt to highlight some of these discrepancies of meaning. It would be quite impossible to present a thorough examination of all the uses to which substance has been put. I have selected a few of the more prominent instances in order to make explicit the analytic work that is being done. It should be clear that I am more interested in what substance *does* than what it *is*. I focus on how substance has been employed in the analysis of kinship, rather than on what it means within any one particular culture. This is part of a larger project to study critically what kinship itself does for anthropologists (see Carsten 2000).

This chapter offers a critique "from within." The work that I discuss here has been highly influential and fruitful in the analysis of kinship and personhood over the past twenty years. Substance has undoubtedly been "good to think with," yet partly because of a lingering dissatisfaction with my own use of substance in the study of Malay kinship, it seemed worth exploring its ambiguities. Finally, therefore, I turn to my own study of Malay relatedness to see whether "making things explicit" actually achieves an advance on previous ways of understanding indigenous relatedness.

SUBSTANCE IN AMERICAN KINSHIP

Schneider was one of the first anthropologists to use substance as an analytic term in relation to kinship. As is well-known, Schneider argues that "relatives" are defined by "blood," and that "the blood relationship, as it is defined in American kinship, is formulated in concrete, biogenetic terms" (1980, 23). Each parent contributes half of the biogenetic substance of their child. "The blood relationship is thus a relationship of substance, of shared biogenetic material" (25). Schneider notes two crucial properties of such relationships. First, blood endures and cannot be terminated: blood relationships cannot be lost or severed. Even if parents disown their children, or siblings cease to communicate, the biological relationship remains unaltered. Blood relatives remain blood relatives. Second, "kinship is whatever the biogenetic relationship is. If science discovers new facts about biogenetic relationship, then that is what kinship is and was all along, although it may not have been known at the time" (23).

Schneider's analytic strategy, then, moves between blood and biogenetic substance—also rendered as "natural substance." Hence he writes, "Two blood relatives are 'related' by the fact that they share in some degree the stuff of a particular heredity. Each has a portion of the natural, genetic substance" (24). Blood is the symbol for biogenetic substance (24). But what is remarkable in this rendering of American kinship is that blood and biogenetic substance are quite unexplored as symbols—one could, after all, easily imagine a whole book on American notions of blood. Elsewhere in this volume, Kath Weston demonstrates the potential fruitfulness of such a line of inquiry by comparing two highly specific and politically charged "moments" in U.S. history when the symbolic imagery of transfers of blood is vividly elaborated. The links between blood and race, and the contrast Weston sketches between discourses about blood transfers in a novel set in 1930s' rural Georgia and a blood drive for Betty Shabazz in 1990s' Harlem, are highly suggestive of the potential scope of an anthropology of blood in American culture.

Further, Schneider's shift from blood to biogenetic substance (in other words, the relationship between the symbol and what is allegedly symbolized) is also unexamined. It is, for example, not at all clear that biogenetic heredity, or substance, is not itself a symbol in American culture. It may be that recent scientific and popular discourses in which the biogenetic components of heredity have been particularly prominent have made Schneider's shift from blood to heredity, and from heredity to genetic substance, appear less than self-evident. If that is the case, this only underlines the point that there is something worth studying here.

Jeanette Edwards's observations from northwest England about what is transferred from mother to child through the placenta are suggestive in this context. Her informants speculate on the effect on a baby of being nurtured in an artificial womb in the laboratory. Such a baby would not be connected to its mother or her feelings.

> Somebody somewhere must be creating this artificial womb. A baby re-
> acts to what you're feeling—if your heartbeat is faster then the baby's
> heartbeat is faster. It could be fed on just vegetables—how would it react
> then, through the placenta—not what you fancy like crisps, or salad, or
> chewitts on the bus, like cravings at different times—vegetables, sweets,

alcohol whatever it takes to make a baby. It will have no feelings because no feelings are going through it. (Edwards 1992, 59)

The image of a baby born without feelings because it was never connected to maternal emotion, never received the effects of maternal cravings in the form of a packet of crisps, or a glass of beer, indicates something rather different from scientific discourse on biogenetic heredity. It is beyond the scope of the present essay to explore the meanings of blood and biogenetic substance in American culture. As Charis Thompson (this volume) shows through her analysis of practices and discourses in infertility clinics, "biological" kinship can be configured in a remarkable number of ways, as can the connections that are made between "social" and "biological" kinship. Her conclusion that there is no "unique template" for biological kinship implies that the relationship between blood and biogenetic substance is less straightforward than Schneider appears to assume.

Schneider's analysis also asserts that American kinship is a product of two elements: relationship as natural substance and relationship as code for conduct. These elements are themselves derived from the two major orders of American culture: the order of nature and that of law (Schneider 1980, 29). Certain relationships exist by virtue of nature alone — for example, the natural or illegitimate child. Others, like husband and wife, are relatives in law alone. The third class of relatives are those defined by blood. These include father, mother, brother, sister, son, and daughter, as well as aunt, uncle, niece, nephew, grandparent, grandchild, cousin, and so on. These derive from both nature and law, substance and code. Schneider's analysis thus not only suggests the combinatory power of substance and code in the category of so-called blood relations but also posits obvious, strong boundaries between substance and code, and the two cultural orders from which they are derived: nature and law. Each can be clearly defined, and legitimacy is derived either from one or the other, or from both together — but one can attribute aspects to either one domain or the other. As Schneider himself puts it,

> It is a fundamental premise of the American kinship system that blood is a substance and that this is quite distinct from the kind of relationship or code for conduct which persons who share that substance, blood, are supposed to have. It is precisely on this distinction between relationship as *substance* and relationship as *code for conduct* that the classification of relatives in nature, relatives in law, and those who are related in both nature and in law, the blood relatives, rests. . . . [T]hese two elements,

substance and code for conduct, are quite distinct. Each can occur alone or they can occur in combination. (1980, 91)

It is this seemingly unproblematic distinction between the order of nature and that of law, and between natural substance and code for conduct, that I question here.

I have already cited a case from northwest England that makes the distinction between substance and code — between a biological basis for heredity and maternal cravings for crisps or chewitts on a bus — rather difficult to draw. My questioning comes with other recent ethnographic examples from Britain and the United States in mind. The first is from Gerd Baumann's portrait of the mixed ethnic setting of the London suburb of Southall. Baumann describes how young Sikhs, Hindus, and Muslims, as well as Afro-Caribbeans, and whites in Southall emphasize "cousin" relations to a remarkable degree — and often in the absence of specific genealogical ties. Young people make claims to cousinship for a variety of reasons, saying "cousins are friends who are kin and kin who are friends" (Baumann 1995, 734). It is precisely the coincidence of nature and choice in the discourse about cousins that Baumann underscores. Cousins are sufficiently related to owe solidarity to each other, but distant enough to require a voluntaristic input. This explicit blurring of the boundaries between the natural and social orders bears some similarities to Weston's depiction of gay American kinship ideology (1991, 1995). Gay coming-out stories stress the traumatic experience of disruption to bonds of kinship that are supposed to be about "diffuse enduring solidarity." Weston's informants emphasize the enduring qualities of friendship in the face of an experience of kinship that involves the severance of "biological" ties. Reversing the terms of the dominant discourse of kinship, ties that last are here defined as those of kinship. Once again, this discourse suggests an explicit attempt to "muddle" the distinction between two cultural orders. Weston openly challenges the traditional anthropological ascription of one set of ties as "fictive," while Marilyn Strathern has underlined how the critique of gay kinship makes plain "the fact that there always was a choice as to whether or not biology is made the foundation of relationships" (1993, 196, cited in Hayden 1995, 45). And this point is amply substantiated by Thompson's ethnography of the way discourses about biology are deployed in infertility clinics (this volume).

I would not claim that these examples rule out the possibility of analyzing kinship in Schneider's terms — indeed, both Baumann and Weston fruitfully discuss their material in terms of Schneider's analysis. But such cases do, I think, indicate that the categorical separation, or even opposition, of the two orders, and of substance and code, is worthy of further examination. That much remains to be said about substance, and the relationship between substance and code, is all the more critical when one begins to trace what happened to substance when it was transferred from American kinship to India. For the relationship between substance and code was very much at issue when anthropologists compared India to the United States, or "the West."

SUBSTANCE IN INDIA

On the one hand, it seems as though the promise of substance as an analytic term lies to a considerable extent in its flexibility, which can be attributed to its multiple meanings in English. On the other hand, the separation or opposition of substance and code, which Schneider proposes, imposes a startling rigidity on the analysis of kinship undertaken in these terms. This rigidity becomes clear when one looks at the way substance came to be understood in the context of Indian notions of kinship and personhood. What is perhaps even more significant is that both the flexible and rigid aspects of substance as an analytic term remain quite implicit and unexplored.

The ethnosociological model of India offered by McKim Marriott, Ronald Inden, R. W. Nicholas, and others explicitly follows the logic of Schneider's analysis and utilizes the same terms. On the first page of an article titled "Toward an Ethnosociology of South Asian Caste Systems," Marriott and Inden write, "The aims of this chapter are inspired by the results of a cultural style of analysis exemplified in Schneider's book *American Kinship*" (1977, 227). Similarly, in "Hindu Transactions: Diversity without Dualism," Marriott (1976, 110) proposes a model of Indian transaction and personhood that specifically refers to Schneider's model. What these authors assert, however, is a radical opposition between American understandings (Marriott 1976, 110) — or "Western" or "Euro-American" ones (Marriott and Inden 1977, 228) — and those of Indian actors.

Instead of the dual categories of nature and law, substance and code, that Schneider postulates, Indian thinking displays a "systematic monism" (Marriott 1976, 109). Here code and substance are inseparable — a point that Marriott emphasizes by using the forms "code-substance" or "substance-code" (1976, 110). Bodily substance and code for conduct are not only inseparable, they are also malleable: "Actions enjoined by these embodied codes are thought of as transforming the substances in which they are embodied" (Marriott and Inden 1977, 228). Conduct alters substance, and all interpersonal transactions (for example, sex, sharing food or water, coresidence) involve the transfer of moral and spiritual qualities of those involved. Gift giving not only transmits these qualities of the person from donor to recipient but also the physical aspects of gifts. In other words, there is no radical disjunction between physical and moral properties of persons, or between body and soul. This, of course, had profound implications for understandings of personhood and caste, and particularly the significance of food transactions across caste boundaries (see Marriott and Inden 1977, 229).

The ethnosociological model has an appealing clarity about it and appears to make sense of a wide range of phenomena. But it has also been criticized on a number of counts. The most obvious of these is its tendency to over-systematize (see, for example, Barnard and Good 1984, 178–82; Good 1991, 179–82). Anthony Good (2000) argues that to present these ideas as a consistent and coherent philosophical system is not only misleading in the face of marked divergencies between informants and localities; it also omits any sociological account of how such knowledge is deployed in practice, the ways in which it can be used to further particular actors' interests, and the different contexts in which this is done. Ethnographic data from different areas in south Asia have produced rather different versions of indigenous notions of personhood, including those in which body and "spirit," or blood and "spirit" are separately derived (see Barnett 1976; McGilvray 1982). Such data suggest that dualism is not totally absent from Indian thought — an issue that I will return to below. Even within one area or village, different informants often have divergent views on the quite esoteric subjects under examination in these studies.[1]

More serious, perhaps, is the degree of difference proposed in this model between Indian and American or, as it tends to be glossed, Indian and Western categories. This radical opposition implies limits to the comparability of ideas about the person between India and the West. On this count, Good (2000) maintains that the ethnosociological model represents an extreme form of orientalism. In an illuminating article on the body in India, Jonathan Parry (1989) makes a number of key points about the contrast proposed between Western dualism and Indian monism. The monist view is one in which body and soul are merged, and persons are not discrete, bounded individuals composed of immutable substance as they are in the West but instead are "divisible" and constantly changing (see Marriott 1976, 112).

Parry observes, first, that these notions of personhood do "not altogether accord with the quite robust and stable sense of self" of his own acquaintances, and second, that it is difficult to see how they would square with the notion of the equivalence of members of the same caste:

> How, one wonders, could such equivalence be sustained in a world in which *each* actor's substance-code is endlessly modified and transformed by the myriad exchanges in which he is *uniquely* involved? How, indeed, could anybody ever decide with whom, and on what terms, to interact? (1989, 494)[2]

Noting the radical implications of such a contrast in ideas about the person between the West and India, Parry proposes a more complex model in which the kind of ideas documented by the ethnosociologists coexist with another strand of thought more familiar to westerners — one in which a degree of dualism can be discerned. He also notes that Western ideology is not as thoroughly dualistic as the ethnosociologists have assumed. He suggests, in other words, that both monism and dualism are present in the West and India, and that to miss this point is also to miss the role of monist ideas as an ideological buttress to caste ranking in India.

These assertions are all highly pertinent to my argument here. But before leaving India, I want to return for a moment to the term *substance*. In the second edition to *American Kinship,* Schneider explicitly comments on the use of the opposition between substance and code outside the American context. He states unequivocally,

> I myself make only one limited claim for this opposition; it is an important part of American culture. I make no claims for its universality, generality, or applicability anywhere else. (1980, 120)

If the use of these terms by Indianist anthropologists is compared with the original use made of it by Schneider, some striking anomalies emerge. While Marriott insists on the hyphenated form *substance-code* to underline a contrast with the West, other writers in the same tradition simply employ *substance* while still emphasizing the same contrast (see, for example, Daniel 1984). There is something rather odd, though, in using one term to refer to two explicitly opposed sets of meanings. Schneider, as we saw, argues that blood or natural substance is unalterable and indissoluble in the context of American kinship. In India, it is precisely the mutability, fluidity, and transformability of substance that underpins a contrasting set of notions about the person and relations between persons (see Daniel 1984, 2–3).

There are, however, differences in the way substance is deployed even within a small group of seemingly like-minded scholars of south Asia. Steve Barnett, for example, distinguishes his own use of substance as remaining close to Schneider's—in contrast to the more culturally specific usages of, for example, Inden and Nicholas (1977). According to Barnett, biogenetic substance and code for conduct are not to be regarded as universal categories but are particularly relevant in a comparison of India and the West. They should not be reduced "to biology or to monism or to some simple generative mechanism (innateness or particles)" (Östör, Fruzetti, and Barnett 1982, 228). In a volume devoted to the comparison of personhood, kinship, caste, and marriage in India, Ákos Östör, Lina Fruzetti, and Steve Barnett are at pains to differentiate how these terms are utilized:

> In fact, the use of substance and code in these very different analytical approaches has led to a number of premature attempts to suggest that these approaches all derive from a single school. (1982, 228)

Nonspecialists in the complexities of caste and kinship in India might be forgiven for finding all this somewhat confusing. And these confusions are apt to become more serious when the comparative focus switches to yet another region—as we shall see when we turn to anthropological writings on substance in Melanesia.[3]

To sum up, in the comparison of the West with India, different understandings of substance are being posited as underlying quite different notions of the person. A clear recognition of the analytic significance of using this term is therefore crucial. The problem with substance lies partly in the opposition to code for conduct, which Schneider uses in his analysis of American data. Following Parry's argument, it might be said that the strong demarcation between these two orders fits neither the Indian nor the Western case. But another problematic aspect of using this term arises from quite a different source: the multiple meanings of substance in English that I sketched at the beginning of this chapter. Substance, as we saw, can denote a separate thing (that is, a person or body part); a vital part or essence of that thing or person; and also corporeal matter more generally, the tissue or fluid of which bodies are composed. This conflation becomes particularly critical when it is precisely the relation between persons—the discreteness or relative permeability of persons, flows of bodily fluids, exchanges of corporeal matter—that is at issue. Where one term can mean the discrete thing, its essence, and the matter of which it is composed, the use of that term as an analytic category is, at the very least, likely to be a confusing basis for achieving a comparative understanding of the relations between personhood, essences, and bodily matter.

SUBSTANCE IN MELANESIA

These issues are at the heart of analyses of kinship in terms of flows of substance in Melanesia. Significantly, the migration of substance as an analytic category to Melanesia is roughly contemporaneous with its appearance in studies of India. But although the Indianists I cite above refer directly to Schneider's work on American kinship, they make no mention of Melanesian studies. Later commentators, however, note the connection. Arjun Appadurai observes that Marriott's rendering of Indian ideas "looks more Melanesian, than say, Chinese" (1988, 755; cited in Spencer 1995). In contrast, the examples I will cite from Melanesia make more explicit reference to understandings of substance in India than to Schneider's use of substance versus code.

Before examining the rather complex Melanesian examples in detail, it may be helpful to signal in advance the direction of my argument. In tracing the passage of substance from America to India, and from there to Melanesia, I am struck by how the same term takes on quite different meanings. In the Melanesian cases, not only do analysts drop the reference of substance to code, which was central to Schneider's depiction of American kinship and retains a presence in the analyses of India, but they describe substance itself as something *inherently* transmissible and malleable. In American kinship, Schneider emphasizes the immutability of substance as well as its distinction from code. It is the inseparability in India of substance and code that apparently confers malleability. In Melanesia, in the instances I mention, what is stressed is the "analogizing" capacity of substance — the way it can be substituted by detachable "things" such as meat, women, or pearl shells. Considerably influenced by depictions of personhood and substance in India, and in direct contrast to America, what is *not* malleable (that is, not analogized in a range of other substances) and *not* transmitted comes to be described in Melanesia as, *by definition*, not substance. As we shall see, however, some of the analytic moves involved in the development of this contention are more explicit than others.

My first example is taken from Roy Wagner's discussion of "analogic kinship" (1977) among the Daribi. Wagner begins with the proposition that kinship may be viewed as a process of differentiating relational categories so as to bring about a flow of relatedness among them. In other words, kinship does not begin from prior, genealogically defined, difference but is itself about the *creation* of socially significant difference in a broad context where all kinds of human relationships can be considered as analogous to each other. From this vantage point, the work of kinship is in the maintenance of categorical distinctions to ensure the proper "flow of similarity" (Wagner 1977, 623). As Wagner writes,

> The "relational" aspect of kinship is thus always understandable as a kind of analogic "flow"—that is what we mean by "being related," and this flow is always the consequence of kin differentiation. (624)

He goes on to describe Daribi kinship in terms of flows of male and female substance. Daribi consider maleness to be an effect of seminal fluid and femaleness an effect of maternal blood. Both are necessary to create an embryo, but while the mother's component of blood is self-sufficient, the male component of seminal fluid requires constant replenishment from the juice and fat of meat. Meat, then, is "the partible and portable accessory to masculine continuity" (624). The primary concern of wife givers and wife takers is the retention and replenishment of male substance. While wife givers regard the giving of women and their subsequent reproduction as its own flow of male substance, the wife takers perceive the flow of lineal substance of the wife givers as one of blood or female substance.

Wagner claims that the giving of male and female wealth objects at a betrothal and marriage is not "merely symbolic" but the "very substance" of the interdict between a man and his wife's mother that is central to the relation between wife givers and wife takers (629). He explains that after the presentation of the bride-price, the bride is no longer regarded as linked to her natal group through paternal and maternal substance but by a single tie—regarded as maternal substance by the groom's side and as paternal substance by the bride's. The wife givers are therefore compensated for their perceived loss of male flow.

Two points from Wagner's analysis deserve emphasis: the centrality of ideas about substance to gender differentiation, a prominent theme in subsequent analyses of Melanesian cultures and one that I will return to below; and his understanding of "flows" of substance to connote what he calls "analogic relations."

> We can understand a kind of analogy to be manifest between the givers and takers of souls, women, and pearlshells, and this analogy can indeed

> be said to relate them. Yet the terms of the interdict are such that this kind
> of analogy is not embodied in internal substantial "flow," but in the kinds
> of "detached" or "detachable" things (souls, women, pearlshells) that are
> being presented and accepted. For it is these detachable things, *used as
> mediators in lieu of substantial flow,* that are used socially to "mark" and
> confirm, to establish and substantiate, the setting up of parallel substan-
> tial flows. (631)

Wagner suggests that the analogies between bodily substance and particular
kinds of detachable male and female wealth objects allow for the creation of
analogous relationships between wife givers and wife takers. His use of substance is inextricably bound up with this capacity for analogy. Substance is
the kind of stuff that can be detached from persons, flows between people,
and creates the possibility for relationships founded on analogy. One might
say there is a play on the conflation of at least two meanings of substance here:
substance as corporeal matter and as opposed to form—in other words, the
content of relations.

Wagner also notes that restrictions and distinctions in the exchange of detached, partible objects recall the elaborate food restrictions at the core of the
caste system in India (although he cites Louis Dumont rather than the ethnosociologists of India whose work I have drawn on here). If the restrictions and
exchanges are observed, then the sociality and its analogies of substantial flow
will follow. In this sense, "the 'flow' of controlled analogy through exchange
is thus constitutive of the whole relational matrix" (631).

Marilyn Strathern's comparative analysis of Melanesian relationships and
substance in *The Gender of the Gift* is clearly influenced by Wagner's approach
(see, for example, Strathern 1988, 278). Strathern also explicitly draws on Marriott's model of the "dividual" person:

> Far from being regarded as unique entities, Melanesian persons are as
> dividually as they are individually conceived. They contain a generalized
> sociality within. Indeed, persons are frequently constructed as the plural
> and composite site of the relationships that produced them. The singular
> person can be imagined as social microcosm. (1988, 13)

In the footnote to this passage, Strathern quotes the following passage from
Marriott as "pertinent":

> Persons—single actors—are not thought in South Asia to be "indivi-
> dual," that is, indivisible, bounded units, as they are in much of Western

social and psychological theory as well as in common sense. Instead, it appears that persons are generally thought by South Asians to be "dividual" or divisible. To exist, dividual persons absorb heterogeneous material influences. They must also give out from themselves particles of their own coded substances—essences, residues, or other active influences—that may then reproduce in others something of the nature of the persons in whom they have originated. (Marriott 1976, 111; cited in Strathern 1988, 348)

While others have concentrated on the contrast Strathern paints between Melanesian and Western personhood, gender, and society (see, for example, Busby 1997), I want to focus particularly on aspects of her analysis of substance. The quote from Marriott provides a useful starting point. Like Wagner, Strathern is concerned with flows of substance between people and the reproductive capacity of substances.

In a chapter on "Forms Which Propagate," Strathern discusses at length the connections made in the Trobriands between a woman, her child, her husband, and her brother (1988, 231–40). Anthropologists have long been familiar with the much-disputed claim that Trobriand fathers have no physiological connection with their children. Strathern has gone further in suggesting that Trobriand mothers are also not connected to their children by ties of substance. She asserts this in spite of Bronislaw Malinowski's insistence on the Trobriand assertion that "without doubt or reserve, . . . the child is of the same substance as its mother" (Malinowski 1929, 3; cited in Strathern 1988, 235). Malinowski quotes the following Trobriand statements: "'The mother feeds the infant in her body. Then, when it comes out, she feeds it with her milk.' 'The mother makes the child out of her blood'" (1929, 3). I am intrigued by such a stark contradiction. How does Strathern come to deny Malinowski's straightforward claim with such force? What work is the idea of substance doing here?

Basing her alternative rendering of the Trobriand material on Annette Weiner's (1976) account, Strathern suggests that a Trobriand woman does not feed the fetus within her:

Blood is simply the counterpart already in the mother of the spirit children who will be brought her by matrilineal ancestral beings; it is not to be thought of as food at all. Malinowski's error, if we can call it that, comes from mistaking form for substance. (1988, 235)

As we shall see, the relationship between form and substance is crucial to Strathern's argument. A Trobriand brother and sister cannot overtly exchange with each other. The sister produces children, the brother produces yams. These are "analogically equivalent" items that "each must make the other yield" (235–36). The brother has an interest in the production of his sister's children, but since he cannot interact directly with the sister, his harvest yams go to her husband, who then "opens the way" (236) for the entry of the spirit child at conception. In other words, the crucial act of the husband here is the creation of the woman's body as container for a body that is distinct from her own. The brother's gift of yams thus coerces his sister's husband into creating this separation between the mother and child. It is the father's *activity,* rather than his bodily emissions, that have this effect. The "work . . . of molding the fetus . . . gives the child its bodily form, as an extraneous and partible entity" (236).

The activities of molding the fetus and, after birth, feeding the child, give the child a form that is different from its mother's, and in this way separate the child from its mother. The fetus is a "contained entity within the mother . . . herself composed of *dala* blood" (237), and while the father creates its external form, its internal form is dala blood—that is, blood of the matrilineal subclan. "Mother and child are thus internal and external homologues for one another" (237). As I understand it, it is this homologous relationship—the fact that substance is neither transformed food nor has it been *exchanged*—that is at the root of Strathern's assertion that "Trobriand mother and child are not connected through ties of substance" (237). This, however, appears to be a very particular interpretation of the meaning of substance.

Crucially, while the child's blood replicates that of the mother and the mother's brother,

> the mother does not "give" this blood to the fetus as though it were food, any more than the brother impregnates his sister or sister and brother exchange gifts between themselves. And only most indirectly does the mother's brother feed it; the feeding is mediated by the sister's husband's vital act as nurturer. It cannot be the case, then, that the fetus is an extension of the mother's bodily tissue and that the mother "makes" it in this sense. (238).

Strathern contends that for Trobrianders, the feeding and growing of children are contrasting activities. A Trobriand father feeds food, which is considered as a form of mediating wealth item, to his child and his wife, but this food does not contribute to internal substance (251); the mother's brother "grows" yams, partly for his sister, just as the sister "grows" the child. But "since yams and children are 'the same,' the brother's yams cannot be conceptualized as directly feeding the sister's child, for they are analogs of the child" (239). The growth of the child is here a consequence of the relationship between mother and child—it is not mediated by the feeding or transmission of substance.[4]

So, to return to the original question, it is worth considering for a moment just why Strathern is suggesting that the Trobriand mother and child are not connected through ties of substance. It would seem that in this version, substance must have two properties, which can both be linked to Wagner's earlier account. One property of substance is that it is transmitted—and this underlines the link with Wagner's analysis of "substantive flows" between persons; and the second is the substitutability or analogizing capacity of substance. Trobriand blood is not analogized in a range of other substances, such as milk, semen, or food (as it is elsewhere in Melanesia; see Strathern 1988, 240–60), and this, as I understand it, is what makes it not a substance. The capacity for analogy is linked to a further property of substance: that it gives content to form. As such, Strathern comments on paternal feeding in the Trobriands "where substance remains on the surface"—that is, it is not an inner condition—and "what is within has no substance" (251). Once again, there is a play on several meanings of substance: corporeal matter, substance as opposed to form, inner essence.

If one looks at this last transformation of substance in comparative terms, some surprising twists are discernible. I noted above that one of the properties of substance that Schneider points to in *American Kinship* is its immutability. It is the crucial distinction between this version of substance and more malleable Indian versions of bodily substance that Marriott underlines by using the term *substance-code* or *coded substances*. Other writers on India, however, are less punctilious in their usages and perhaps unwittingly contribute to a general, if largely implicit, view among anthropologists that an inherent property of bodily substance is malleability. Hence, Strathern's commentary on the Trobriand material, in which what is not transmittable and malleable is not substance, appears to make sense from an Indian point of view.

From the perspective of *American Kinship,* though, in which immutability is seen as a key property of blood, it might be thought surprising that what is not malleable could *therefore* not be considered as substance. It is also worth mentioning that in its passage to Melanesia, the relationship of substance to code seems to have been lost. This was perhaps predictable given the nature of the larger arguments being made about Western versus non-Western categories, which I discuss below. One effect of this, however, was that substance itself came to encompass an even less specific domain of meaning than Schneider had originally delineated. Strathern's attempt to limit the use of substance may perhaps be understood as a way of introducing greater analytic rigor to a usage that had become highly unspecific. But it is also worth noting that the emphasis placed on the "analogizing capacity" of substance in Melanesia, and on its flow between persons or persons and things, indicated that substance was *inherently* relational whereas the dictionary definitions with which I began this essay do not attribute a relational quality to substance. On the contrary, they refer to something more or less material within which qualities or essences are located.[5]

MELANESIAN AND INDIAN SUBSTANCE AND PERSONHOOD COMPARED

Strathern's discussion of notions of substance is, of course, part of a wider analysis of gender and personhood in Melanesia. The model she proposes is broadly comparative: persons are "partible" or "dividual" in contrast to the individuality of Western personhood. Partible persons are composite mosaics, composed of elements of female and male substance. Gender has to be performed and elicited rather than, as in Western notions, being an inherent property of personhood.

Cecilia Busby (1997) provides an incisive comparison of these ideas with Indian ones based on her own fieldwork in Kerala. In spite of some obvious similarities, Busby notes important divergences between the south Indian and Melanesian cases. Briefly, she suggests that instead of partible persons, composed of elements of male or female substance, persons in Kerala are permeable and connected. I will explain her contrast between permeable and partible persons shortly. Here, gender is essentialized rather than being performed or elicited. And it resides, crucially, in what are perceived to be essentially male and female substances—semen and male blood, or womb and breast milk. The concerns and anxieties of her informants were thus expressed over the proper separation and transmission of these substances, particularly through marriage to the correct category of relative and through the birth of children. The flow of female substance connects mothers to their children, and the flow of male substance connects fathers to their children.

Busby highlights the distinction between an internally whole person with fluid and permeable body boundaries in south Asia, and an internally divided and partible person in Melanesia. In India, transmitted substances merge and, within the body, they become indistinguishable; bodies cannot be divided according to male and female substantive components. In Melanesia, male and female substances are commonly associated with different parts of the body. Bodies are internally divided into differently gendered parts, and gender is unstable; it must be made known, often in ritual performances (Busby 1997, 270–71). Hence, in Melanesia, men and women may alternate their perceived gender through specific kinds of transactions with male or female things. In India, by contrast, gender is concerned with bodily essences — men and women can only act in male or female ways, respectively, and their activities arise out of bodily differences between men and women.

These distinctions, as Busby points out, are connected to a focus on relationships in Melanesia and one on persons in south India. Strathern argues that in Melanesia, the body "is a microcosm of *relations*" (1988, 131; cited in Busby 1997, 273), whereas in south India, the flows of substances between persons "always refer to the persons from whom they originated: they are a manifestation of persons rather than of the relationships they create" (Busby 1997, 273). Persons are both connected through substantive flows and complete in themselves — they are not microcosms of relations. And here substance itself is differently conceived: "Substance may connect persons in India and in Melanesia, but it is substance as a *flow from* a person compared with substance objectified as part of a person" (Busby 1997, 276).

Clearly, this is not a matter of a simple opposition between Western immutable substance and Melanesian or Indian mutability. It seems to me that in all the examples I have discussed, there are discernible elements of immutability and mutability — essences and mixing. Indeed, one might consider these as instances of a kind of cultural speculation on the effects of sedimenting essences, processes of detachment and separation, and the merging and mixing of flows between people. This recalls Gillian Feeley-Harnik's sensitive discussion (this volume) of Morgan's preoccupation with "the channels of the blood," which as she demonstrates, was not rooted in biology as Schneider and other mid- or late-twentieth-century analysts of kinship have understood it. And it recalls, too, Parry's earlier discussion of ideas about the body in India, and his emphasis on contrastive strands of thought within both India and the West. With such contrastive themes in mind, I now revisit my own material on Malay bodily substance.

MALAY SUBSTANCE

In earlier work, I described conversations I had with Malay people on the island of Langkawi about the relationship between food (particularly rice), breast milk, and blood in the body (Carsten 1995; 1997, 107–30). Blood has a central place in ideas about life itself and relatedness. I was told repeatedly that people are both born with blood and acquire it through life in the form of food, which is transformed into blood in the body. Death occurs when all the blood leaves the body.

Blood is transformed food, as is breast milk. But breast milk is also understood as converted blood, a kind of "white blood." And it has a special power because it is thought to carry emotional as well as physical properties from the mother. Indeed, mothers and their children are thought to be especially closely connected because a child is fed on the mother's blood in the womb and on her milk after birth. Those who eat the same food together in one house also come to have blood in common, and this is one way in which foster children and affines become connected to those they live with.

The status of semen in these ideas about convertibility is somewhat unclear. Some people told me that while the child gets blood from the mother, the father's contribution, the seed, is "just a drop" and less important. In some respects, it appears that semen is viewed as another form of white blood, rather like breast milk. Yet semen is also associated with bone—in particular, the head, from where it originates, and the backbone, to which it makes its way before conception can occur. In any case, what made a most vivid impression on me in these discussions was the centrality of ideas about blood to the constitution of the body and relations of kinship. I was forever hearing about illnesses in terms of imbalances in the blood; I was endlessly listening to comments on the effects of different kinds of food on the blood, on the problems of transfusions, on blood pressure, even on the proper color of blood. (My own was regarded with approval as being healthily red.)

One theme that constantly recurred was convertibility. It was not just the conversion of food, milk, and blood that concerned people but direct transfers of blood as well. I have already mentioned a concern about transfusions. Blood groups were much discussed, too, and generally blood group O was thought to be particularly good because of its possibilities for transfer. Vampire spirits are a well-known theme in Malay beliefs. Fears about the illicit taking of blood were expressed in stories about one such spirit, Langsuir, who is strongly attracted to postpartum women because of the smell of blood.

Murderers, the illicit takers of life, can make themselves invincible by consuming their victim's blood.

As in the Indian and Melanesian cases, Malay ideas about bodily substance can also be linked to personhood. Like corporeal substance, the identity of the Malay person could be said to be partly given at birth and partly acquired through life along with kin relations, which are likewise given and acquired. There is also a sense in which Malay personhood can be shown to express both ideas about connectedness and separateness. Connectedness is emphasized in the form of siblingship, which through the existence of spirit siblings, predates birth. Ideas about the relative permeability of the body, revealed in discourses about sickness, display a considerable concern over the boundaries of the body. The boundedness of individuals is qualified by the strength of bonds between siblings, both spiritual and actual. One might view Malay kinship as partly a speculative process on the possibilities of boundedness and unboundedness, difference and similarity, between persons. I have described it largely in terms of processes of making similarity.

It should be obvious why I could hardly ignore the extensive discourse about blood, and why it seemed tempting to render the Malay for blood, *darah,* as substance. Substance seemed to capture the centrality of blood to Malay ideas about relatedness. It nicely evoked the idea of blood as a vital essence, necessary for life, as well as the stress on mutability between food, blood, and breast milk. Like other anthropologists, I could play on several meanings of substance: content, vital essence, corporeal matter. In truth, until challenged, I didn't think much of the elision of blood and substance. And when challenged, I simply added a note to the effect that this usage seemed in keeping with the force of the Malay ideas I was portraying (Carsten 1997, 108).

Nevertheless, I think it is worth giving further consideration to the suitability of substance to convey Malay ideas about blood. Quite simply, I was not translating a Malay term when I used substance. I think the same is also likely to be true of other anthropologists who have used the term elsewhere (see Thomas 1999). In fact, given the wide semantic domain of substance in English, it seems rather unlikely that an exact equivalent to it would be found in non-European languages.

On the positive side, substance apparently captured quite neatly certain qualities of blood in Malay ideas: mutability, transferability, vitality, essence, content. It also captured a tension between the givenness of inherited characteristics and the acquisition of identity through life, which is a major theme in the ideas I was discussing. Blood was partly given at birth, partly acquired and mutable. Crucially, it played a key role in the *transformation* of acquired characteristics into given ones, and vice versa, through the postulated relations between blood, birth, and feeding. Blood did not fit neatly into the kind of analytic categories that have been central to the analysis of kinship — the given and the acquired, the biological and the social, substance and code, nature and nurture. In fact, it could be used to destabilize these dichotomies.

USES AND ABUSES OF SUBSTANCE

It should not be surprising that quite subtle shifts in how the composition of the body is perceived may carry implications for personhood and gender. What is notable in all the literature to which I have referred is that the English term substance apparently easily accommodates a remarkable range of indigenous meanings, including bodily matter, essence, and content in opposition to form, as well as differences in degrees of mutability and fluidity. I want to return here to the analytic work to which substance has been put — to what substance *does* for kinship.

This work of substance bears some resemblance to the analysis of personhood with which it is so closely connected. Strathern has recently maintained that the analytic significance of personhood for anthropologists in the 1980s lay in its capacity to "force the reconceptualization of what we might mean by kinship, so that it fed back into the existing assumptions about kinship, provided a new focus of critique" (1997, 8). This is an effect of the way personhood drew together "what anthropologists previously distributed in different ways" (8) — procreation, reproduction, and kinship relations.

One might say something rather similar about substance. Like concepts of the person, substance could be shown to be highly variable in different cultures. The examples I have discussed demonstrate that it was impossible to speak of substance without bringing together a whole range of other themes, including procreation, relations between kin, bodies, personhood, gender, and feeding. Undoubtedly, this has contributed to a critique of the way kinship has been conceived of by anthropologists. But there are also some differences between the way personhood and substance have been analytically deployed. One of these is the degree of explicitness about the analytic status of the terms used. Whereas the study of the person, from its inception, explicitly distinguished different kinds of personhood analytically (such as the self and individual), such distinctions have been rather implicit in discussions of substance. Indeed, I have tried to show how a blurring of distinctions — for instance, between bodily matter, essences, vital parts, and content — was a key element in its fruitfulness for opening up the study of persons, bodies, and their relationships.

This has inevitably led to ambiguity, to the obscuring of differences, as well as the opening up of fresh possibilities. I would suggest that it is not the range of meanings itself that has been problematic; rather, it is the unexamined nature of this range. In all the non-Western examples utilized here, it might be said that conduct, feeding, living in houses, and growing things in the soil may transform bodily substance. These connections nicely evoke those forgotten links between geology, hydrology, linguistics, politico-economics, and zoology in the work of Morgan to which Feeley-Harnik (this volume) draws attention.

The usefulness of substance as an analytic term has been partly as a means to express transformability. To again return to the dictionary definitions with which I began this piece, however, it is notable that the meanings of substance, although they include corporeal matter and the consistency of a fluid, do not specify malleability, transformability, or relationality as inherent properties of substance.[6] Yet these properties have been important aspects of the analytic work achieved by substance in the non-Western examples I have cited.

If in the non-Western cases mentioned here substance has been used to convey meanings that, in some respects, are more or less the opposite of either its dictionary definition or its use in Schneider's original analysis, this may suggest that it was doing a particular kind of analytic work. The co-optation of substance to express mutability and transformability, the flow of objects or bodily parts between persons, and the capacity to stand for the relations between those persons, indicates a gap in the analytic vocabulary of kinship. The analysis of kinship, in its mid-twentieth-century forms, tended to separate and dichotomize the biological and social domains, nature and nurture, substance and code. But in some non-Western cases, indigenous discourses highlighted processes of conversion, transformation, and flow between the very domains that anthropological analysis distinguished (see Carsten 2000). Substance seemed an appropriate term in descriptions of such processes partly because of the breadth of meanings it encompassed. Simultaneously, substance could be used to destabilize the dichotomizing practices on which the analysis of kinship was based. And this is one way of summing up the way in which substance was deployed in the analysis of Melanesian or Indian material.

But this analytic strategy also involved, as we have seen, setting up another dichotomy—this time not within the terms that defined kinship but between "the West" and "the rest." Dividual non-Western persons in India or Melanesia could be opposed to the Western individual; substance in India or Melanesia, which was fluid and subject to transformation, could be contrasted to substance in the West, which was permanent and immutable. One purpose of this essay has been to argue against such a stark contrast between Western and non-Western categories. At the beginning of this chapter I suggested that in the context of kinship in Britain or America, Schneider's original opposition between substance and code seems unnecessarily rigid and restrictive in light of the material I cited from Edwards, Baumann, and Weston, as well as that of Thompson and others in this volume. These examples should encourage an investigation not just of blood as "biogenetic substance" but also of the relationship between substance and code, and the degree to which these domains are clearly distinguished and separate—in other words, there is a need to interrogate closely the combinatory power of substance and code, which according to Schneider, was at the heart of the category of "blood" relative.

If the analytic vocabulary of kinship apparently lacked a means to express mutability and relationality in terms of flows between persons or persons and things, and substance neatly filled that gap, this may have had more to do with the particular history of the academic study of kinship than with European or American folk discourses about kinship. The separation of nature from nurture, the biological from the social, substance from code, was central to a particular juncture in the anthropological analysis of kinship. But it remains to be investigated whether local practices and discourses of kinship in the West privileged the separation of these elements to the same extent, or in the same way, as did the midcentury academic discourse. In this volume, Signe Howell and Charis Thompson suggest that in very different ways—and in the very different contexts of transnational adoption and infertility clinics—the boundaries between what is considered social and what is biological are far from being stable or set in stone. In fact, considerable effort goes into the elaboration of processes of conversion between one domain and the other. At the start of the twenty-first century, perhaps those interested in the study of kinship in the West are beginning to see the significance of Schneider's lead and will take seriously the combinatory potential of these elements.

What attracted me about substance as a way to convey Malay ideas about blood was precisely the way it captured the simultaneous boundedness and unboundedness of Malay personhood, and the capacity to transform characteristics that are acquired into those that are given. In these respects, Malay, Indian, Melanesian and even North American discourses of kinship have a considerable amount in common, even as they reveal some quite subtle differences.

NOTES

It should be obvious that I have found the works of David Schneider, Jonathan Parry, and Marilyn Strathern (who generously made available to me unpublished material) particularly inspiring. Celia Busby's comparative critique has helped enormously to clarify my understandings. Jonathan Spencer has encouraged me for several years to rethink substance. I am very grateful to Sarah Franklin, Tony Good, Susan McKinnon, and Jonathan Spencer for their comments on a previous version of this essay.

1 Outside the Indian context, the tendency of anthropologists to oversystematize procreation beliefs has been noted by Maurice Bloch (1993) and Philip Thomas (1999) in reference to Madagascar.

2 In fact, some of Parry's own work on priests in Benares (for instance, Parry 1980, 1985) suggests people contemplate such problems with considerable anxiety. I am grateful to Tony Good for pointing out that in everyday contexts, the extremely small modifications to substance caused, for example, by eating, defecating, and menstruating can be redressed by other everyday acts of bathing and purification. More serious modifications — say, that resulting from a woman having sex with someone of a lower caste — would formerly have led to expulsion from the family or death, and thus put an end to further interaction.

3 Although, from an external view, the Indianists seemed closely linked to Schneider, it appears that in fact the Chicago school was deeply divided. In his later writings, Marriott emphasized his differences with Schneider and his opposition to a universal substance-code distinction, which he understood Schneider to espouse (in spite of Schneider's published disavowal). Barnett appears to have been more closely aligned to Schneider. I am indebted to Tony Good for making available to me a personal communication from Marriott on these points (see also Good 2000).

4 Tony Good, in a personal communication, suggests that according to the above description, substance is in fact transmitted, but all at once, and not exchanged thereafter. This point highlights the significance of a *flow* of substance to its generative capacity.

5 I am grateful to Tony Good for bringing this to my attention.

6 I am grateful to both Tony Good and Susan McKinnon for this point.

REFERENCES

Appadurai, Arjun. 1988. Is Homo Hierarchicus? *American Ethnologist* 15:745–61.

Barnard, Alan, and Anthony Good. 1984. *Research Practices in the Study of Kinship.* London: Academic Press.

Barnett, Steve. 1976. Coconuts and Gold: Relational Identity in a South Indian Caste. *Contributions to Indian Sociology* 10:133–56.

Baumann, Gerd. 1995. Managing a Polyethnic Milieu: Kinship and Interaction in a London Suburb. *Journal of the Royal Anthropological Institute* (n.s.) 1:725–41.

Bloch, Maurice. 1993. Zafimaniry Birth and Kinship Theory. *Social Anthropology* 1:119–32.

Busby, Cecilia. 1997. Permeable and Partible Persons: A Comparative Analysis of Gender and Body in South India and Melanesia. *Journal of the Royal Anthropological Institute* (n.s.) 3:261–78.

Carsten, Janet. 1995. The Substance of Kinship and the Heat of the Hearth: Feeding, Personhood, and Relatedness among Malays of Pulau Langkawi. *American Ethnologist* 22, no. 2:223–41.

———. 1997. *The Heat of the Hearth: The Process of Kinship in a Malay Fishing Community.* Oxford: Clarendon Press.

———. 2000. Introduction to *Cultures of Relatedness: New Approaches to the Study of Kinship,* edited by Janet Carsten. Cambridge: Cambridge University Press.

Daniel, E. Valentine. 1984. *Fluid Signs: Being a Person the Tamil Way.* Berkeley: University of California Press.

Edwards, Jeanette. 1992. Explicit Connections: Ethnographic Enquiry in North-West England. In *Technologies of Procreation: Kinship in the Age of Assisted Conception,* edited by Jeanette Edwards et al. Manchester: Manchester University Press.

Good, Anthony. 1991. *The Female Bridegroom: A Comparative Study of Life Crisis Rituals in South India and Sri Lanka.* Oxford: Clarendon Press.

———. 2000. Power and Fertility: Divine Kinship in South India. In *Culture, Creation, and Procreation,* edited by Monika Bock and Aparna Rao. Oxford: Berghahn Books.

Hayden, Corinne. 1995. Gender, Genetics, and Generation: Reformulating Biology in Lesbian Kinship. *Cultural Anthropology* 10, no. 1:41–63.

Inden, Ronald, and Ralph Nicholas. 1977. *Kinship in Bengali Culture.* Chicago: University of Chicago Press.

Malinowski, Bronislaw. 1929. *The Sexual Life of Savages in North-Western Melanesia.* London: Routledge and Kegan Paul.

Marriott, McKim. 1976. Hindu Transactions: Diversity without Dualism. In *Transactions in Meaning,* edited by Bruce Kapferer. Philadelphia, Pa.: ISHI Publications.

Marriott, McKim, and Ronald Inden. 1977. Toward an Ethnosociology of South Asian Caste Systems. In *The New Wind: Changing Identities in South Asia,* edited by Kenneth David. The Hague: Mouton.

McGilvray, Dennis B. 1982. Mukkuvar Vannimai: Tamil Caste and Matriclan Ideology in Batticaloa, Sri Lanka. In *Caste Ideology and Interaction,* edited by Dennis B. McGilvray. Cambridge: Cambridge University Press.

Östör, Ákos, Lina Fruzetti, and Steve Barnett. 1982. Conclusion to *Concepts of Person: Kinship, Caste, and Marriage in India,* edited by Ákos Östör, Lina Fruzetti, and Steve Barnett. Cambridge: Harvard University Press.

Parry, Jonathan. 1980. Ghosts, Greed, and Sin: The Occupational Identity of the Benares Funeral Priests. *Man* (n.s.) 15:88–111.

———. 1985. Death and Digestion: The Symbolism of Food and Eating in North Indian Mortuary Rites. *Man* (n.s.) 20:612–30.

———. 1989. The End of the Body. In *Fragments for a History of the Body, Part Two,* edited by Michel Feher. New York: Zone.

Schneider, David M. 1980. *American Kinship: A Cultural Account.* 2d ed. Chicago: University of Chicago Press.

Spencer, Jonathan. 1995. Occidentalism in the East: The Uses of the West in the Politics and Anthropology of South Asia. In *Occidentalism: Images of the West,* edited by James Carrier. Oxford: Oxford University Press.

Strathern, Marilyn. 1988. *The Gender of the Gift.* Berkeley: University of California Press.

———. 1993. Weston, Kath, *Families We Choose: Lesbians, Gays, Kinship. Man* (n.s.) 28, no. 1:195–96.

———. 1997. Marilyn Strathern on Kinship (Interview). *EASA Newsletter* 19:6–9.

Thomas, Philip. 1999. No Substance, No Kinship? Procreation, Performativity, and Temanambondro Parent-Child Relations. In *Conceiving Persons: Ethnographies of Procreation, Fertility, and Growth,* edited by Peter Loizos and Patrick Heady. London: Athlone Press.

Wagner, Roy. 1977. Analogic Kinship: A Daribi Example. *American Ethnologist* 4:623–42.

Weiner, Annette B. 1976. *Women of Value, Men of Renown: New Perspectives in Trobriand Exchange.* Austin: University of Texas Press.

Weston, Kath. 1991. *Families We Choose: Lesbians, Gays, Kinship.* New York: Columbia University Press.

———. 1995. Forever Is a Long Time: Romancing the Real in Gay Kinship Ideologies. In *Naturalizing Power: Essays in Feminist Cultural Analysis,* edited by Sylvia J. Yanagisako and Carol Delaney. New York: Routledge.

CHAPTER 2

The Ethnography of Creation:
Lewis Henry Morgan and the American Beaver
Gillian Feeley-Harnik

In the systems of relationship of the great families of mankind some of the oldest memorials of human thought and experience are deposited and preserved. They have been handed down as transmitted systems, through the channels of the blood, from the earliest ages of man's existence upon the earth; but revealing certain definite and progressive changes with the growth of man's experience in the ages of barbarism. — Lewis Henry Morgan, *Systems of Consanguinity and Affinity of the Human Family*

This essay explores how American ideas and practices concerning blood relations in the mid–nineteenth century contributed to the definition of kinship in the nascent field of anthropology. I focus on the works and lives of Lewis Henry Morgan, his family, and their contemporaries. Morgan's *Systems of Consanguinity and Affinity of the Human Family* ([1871] 1997) is credited with inventing the anthropological study of "kinship" from a comparative perspective (Trautmann 1987). Since Émile Durkheim's (1898) critique of *Systems*, scholars have claimed Morgan's "consanguinity" simply reduced kinship to biology, in keeping with Anglo-American cultural assumptions about blood relations given in nature. David Schneider (1984, 187–88) went further, arguing that even anthropologists who agreed with Durkheim's alternative, that "kinship is social or it is nothing," still retained the assumption that kinship involved the socialization of biological processes, yet now it was hidden and unexamined. Schneider (1984, 67–92, 199–201) urged anthropologists to concentrate on the vernacular categories of the people they study. Anthropologists should also scrutinize their own analytic categories, as Schneider did in *American Kinship* (1968, 21–29), where he claimed that cultural conceptions of kinship in the United States could be understood in terms of contrasts between what—in his abstractions from the vernacular—he called "natural substance" and "code for conduct."

This study attempts to do both by focusing on "American kinship" in the mid–nineteenth century, mainly in the years between the Revolutionary War and Civil War. "American" was being radically redefined during this time, and as Morgan himself stated, "the permanence of species" and "the special creation of man" were "the question of questions in modern science" (1872, 354). How did Americans understand their blood relations and marriages then? And how, if at all, did Morgan incorporate his and their understandings of these relations into his conception of *Systems of Consanguinity and Affinity of the Human Family*, which so influenced the study of kinship worldwide?

Using archival and field research, I have tried to get beyond verbal testimonies, which were Schneider's main evidence in *American Kinship*, to a broader ethnographic approach, as exemplified in Marilyn Strathern's (1992) and Mary Bouquet's (1993) studies of how English sociality has contributed to kinship theory. Although I will allude to the importance of Morgan's early work in geology, archaeology, and ethnology, I will concentrate especially on the relationship between Morgan's kinship research and the work on animal behavior that he did concurrently from roughly 1855 to 1870.[1] *The American Beaver and His Works* ([1868] 1996) and *Systems of Consanguinity and Affinity of the Human Family*, published about the same time, are the fruits of this work.[2] My basic question is, How do Morgan's explorations of "the channels of the blood" encompassing the globe relate to his inquiries into the riverine communities of beavers living around Marquette, Michigan?

Like his contemporary Charles Darwin, Morgan had a global vision of "descent as the hidden bond of connection," to use Darwin's recurrent phrase in *On the Origin of Species* ([1859] 1964). Although Morgan did not voyage around the world, he sent out questionnaires to traders, missionaries, and other travelers asking for information about how the people around them reckoned their genealogies. The greatest contribution of his research on kinship terminologies in the 1850s and 1860s was to establish from the systems of consanguinity and affinity, which he inferred from the terminologies, that all the people of the earth were, as he said, one "human family." Yet Morgan's vision, like Darwin's, also derived from his study of local ways of life. Darwin viewed the world in part through the eyes of the English animal breeders around him. Morgan saw the American wilderness from the perspectives of the dwindling number of Iroquois who still lived around the Finger Lakes, where his grandfather settled in the 1790s, and later through the polyglot communities of the frontier shifting ever further west. My purpose in exploring these relations is not to abstract a new general definition of kinship but rather to grasp more fully how Morgan and his contemporaries understood consanguinity and affinity, thus providing a broader foundation for looking at their "family resemblances" (Needham 1975) from a comparative perspective.

"BLOOD RELATIONS" IN AMERICAN KINSHIP

The place of blood relations in contemporary American kinship is hotly contested, as many of the papers in this volume show. What are blood relations? How do they contribute to relationships? Are they central, marginal, or irrelevant to creating a "family"? These are all open questions. In retrospect, it might be asked how sanguine people in the United States were about natural substance and code for conduct in the midst of the Vietnam War and radical social movements of the 1960s, when Schneider researched and published *American Kinship*. If one looked to Morgan for historical perspective — supposing that he took for granted the basis of kinship in blood ties, and that "for the earlier workers like Morgan and [John Ferguson] McLennan the actual, natural, biological state of affairs remained constant and given" (Schneider 1984, 189) — one would be forced to ask: What did blood relations ever mean, or biology for that matter? On close inspection, Morgan's consanguinity proves to be fraught with contradictions. Debates about the degenerative effects of mixing bloods in marriage — consanguinity *with* affinity — encompassed not only miscegenation, a term coined in 1864 toward the end of the Civil War (Grossberg 1985, 136), but also "consanguineous marriages," such as Morgan's own marriage to his first cousin — his mother's brother's daughter — in 1851.

From the mid-1850s to the late 1860s, while Morgan was working on his genealogy of the human family, Morgan's fourth cousin once removed, Nathaniel Harris Morgan of Hartford, Connecticut, was compiling the *Morgan Genealogy*. In his introductory notes on "Consanguinei," Nathaniel supports the idea that "the direct tendency of such [consanguineous] marriages is to deteriorate, and not to improve the blood." Yet he ridicules the notion of "pride of blood" as "a baseless, shallow conceit, without a shadow of foundation for its support," addressing his work to "Kinsmen of the Name" (1869, 2, 16).

There is an error in the popular notion that the transmission of a family name transmits also its peculiar kinship, or corresponding relation by blood, or family stock. We say, that we are of the Morgan lineage and blood. True! as to the mere name—but not at all true, as to the Morgan blood. It may seem a little ungracious to explode this pleasant fallacy, but the truth is, that we inherit no more of this blood than we do that of a thousand other bloods of different names. (12)

Lewis Henry Morgan, like fellow New Yorkers who have kept first-cousin marriages legal to this day, despite its illegality in a growing number of U.S. states (now thirty-one), would have disputed Nathaniel's views on consanguineous marriages. Yet his statements about channels of the blood in his account of the human family seem to indicate he supported precisely the "baseless, shallow conceit" that his cousin so ridiculed. Michael Grossberg (1985, 140–52) and Martin Ottenheimer (1996, 31–41, 56) show that increasing legislation against consanguineous marriages and miscegenation, especially after the Civil War, were among the several signs of an increasingly biological view of "domestic relations," to use the phrase that became common among U.S. lawyers by 1870 (Grossberg 1985, 28). Given these complexities, it is important to remember that Morgan's contributions to these issues included not only the work he did on the human family but also his concurrent studies of the beaver communities around Marquette, Michigan.

Having grown up in Vermont where (as in much of the United States) *beaver* is still common slang for women's private parts, I have long wondered how the human family and the American beaver are related. Perhaps the nocturnal beavers and their watery habitats were where Morgan and his contemporaries explored their unspoken thoughts about the intimate lives of human beings hidden within the numerical tabulations of the channels of the blood in *Systems*. Much in the tumult of the fur trade and its aftermath in American consanguinity and affinity might ultimately support such a hypothesis. Yet to leap directly to the beavers' allusive relations with human beings would do violence to Morgan's efforts to understand the "Mutes" (as he called them) in their own terms.

Morgan's questions about kinship and affinity, outlined in *Systems*, encompassed the full scope of humans' generative acts from "primitive promiscuity" to "monogamy." Yet his deepest question about "all animated existences" was, as Morgan outlined most clearly in *The American Beaver*, the "mystery" of "life in all its forms" ([1868] 1996, 256). It might be argued that Morgan's very interest in the mutual relations of humans and animals, like Darwin's, derived from and contributed to the trend toward biological reductionism following the Civil War. Yet close examination of both their work suggests rather that they were interested in shifting the study of life processes from dead to living creatures. They sought the broadest possible range of creatures, precisely in order to achieve a closer understanding of the hidden bond of connection among them and the elements around them, in which some Providence, if not denominational God, might be included. Thus, as Morgan stated in the introduction to his beaver book, his purpose was not an "exposition limited to the frigid details of anatomical structure . . . dead rather than . . . living forms" but rather "a minute exposition of their artificial works, where such are constructed; of their habits, their mode of life, and their mutual relations" ([1868] 1996, 6), what might fairly be called an ethnography of creation. More discussion of Morgan's early life and work will help to clarify and substantiate that assertion.

While Nathaniel's branch of the Morgan family remained back in Connecticut, near where their Welsh forebear had settled in the 1650s, Lewis's grandfather headed west in 1792 to claim land around the Finger Lakes of western New York State. The U.S. government had taken this land from the Iroquois and granted parcels to soldiers who had fought in the Revolutionary War (Morgan 1869, 59). Lewis Morgan was born in 1818 on one of the family farms south of Aurora on Lake Cayuga, where his father had some 570 acres devoted to the cultivation of cattle, horses, and at least 1,200 merino sheep, as well as wheat, according to Jedediah Morgan's will, admitted to probate on 28 April 1827 (Morgan Papers, ms. 108).

As in England during these years (Ritvo 1987; Franklin 1997), Anglo-Americans seem to have borrowed freely from the language, if not yet the practices, of livestock breeding in their considerations of human relationships. In a letter of 2 February 1850 to William Seward, then senator of New York, Morgan urged Seward to vote against Henry Clay's resolutions on slavery and the Fugitive Slave Act, which favored southern states, in order to "fix some limits to the Reproduction of this black race among us [because] in the south while the blacks are property, there can be no assignable limit to their reproduction" (Seward Papers, correspondence). Throughout his life, Morgan used "breed," "cross," "half-breed," and "quarter-breed" as if he were talking about his family's herd of wool bearers, taking up the language of Robert Livingston's *Essay on Sheep: Their Varieties* (1813), one of the earliest entries in his library list, most likely inherited from his father. His language also seems to imply that he, like Darwin and the English breeders with whom Darwin worked, regarded these creations as no more than clay in a builder's hands. Indeed, Leslie White (1944, 219, 226) describes Morgan as a man "for Science," in contrast to "Morgan's wife . . . a very narrow, devout, and strict Presbyterian," just as most scholars have contrasted Darwin with his wife, Emma. Yet closer examination suggests otherwise.

Morgan's kin were churchgoing Presbyterians. His cousin, Mary Elizabeth Steele, would have joined her brother as a missionary in the South Seas if she and Lewis had not married in 1851. The library list, which they kept from their marriage until shortly before their deaths in 1881 and 1883, begins with the family Bible where they kept their genealogies, followed by six more Bibles and Testaments, and the first fifteen volumes of the *Natural History of New York* (New York 1842–94). The list ends with editions of Frances Ridley Havergal's religious poems and the *Daigaku* (calendar) for Tokyo University, with a comparable mixture in between (Trautmann and Kabelac 1994, 62–95). The common list reveals that their "friendship and mutuality of life" was not limited to their sharing the same bed and table—the "American" practices to which Morgan so proudly attributed the intimate equity of spousal life in the United States when he visited Europe in 1870–1871 (Morgan Papers, journal of a visit to Europe, 2:62). Books on religious subjects with Lewis's signature and endnotes include Cardinal Wiseman's 1837 *Twelve Lectures on the Connexion between Science and Revealed Religion,* purchased in April 1864. In short, although Morgan never publicly confessed his faith, as his friend and pastor, Reverend Joshua Hall McIlvaine, hoped he would, I would argue that he never stopped deliberating on matters of faith and reason as they were then understood, most especially in matters of creation and regeneration.[3]

Elsewhere, I have contended that Morgan's early study of geology in 1841 (Morgan Papers, ms. 2), which contributed to his later interests in iron mining, was critical not only in pointing to a new chronology for thinking about history, as Trautmann (1992) argues, but also as a means of exploring the earthy-watery substance of creation as described in *Genesis* (Feeley-Harnik 1999). Both Morgan and Darwin focused especially on creatures that crossed over the geologic, hydrologic, and zoological realms, either because like corals, it was not clear for centuries whether they were animal, vegetable, or mineral, or because like corals, and also earthworms and beavers, these creatures were such phenomenal transmuters of land and water, virtually creating new worlds. While Darwin (1881, 139) described earthworms as the corals of the temperate zones, one of his English contemporaries, Reverend John George

Wood (1866, 436) compared "Beaver-dams and Coral-reefs," based on their astonishing capacity to spawn new life. Morgan's early studies of animals— "Mind or Instinct" (1843) — were related in concentrating on phenomena like "instinct" that had been taken to be the inchoate grounds of animate behavior, analogous to the unmoving "darkness . . . upon the face of the deep" (Gen. 1.2) before God's quickening words. His early archaeological and ethnographic work on the Iroquois began in 1844 and culminated in *League of the Ho-de'-no-sau-nee, or Iroquois* (1851). Here, he documented his growing awareness that these generative processes in earth and water could not be abstracted from the political and economic conflicts over the land as property.

Morgan's research on the human family and the American beaver perhaps best exemplifies how he could envision that "some of the oldest memorials of human thought and experience are deposited and preserved [and] handed down as transmitted systems, through the channels of the blood" ([1871] 1997, xxii). I will focus here especially on Morgan's work with the mutes. I will try to show, at least in outline, the relationship between his geo-hydrological and genealogical interests, and how these in turn might have contributed to his understanding of the significance of land as property in generating, maintaining, and destroying relations among kin.

GREAT LAKES

In 1855, the year that Darwin started raising pigeons at Down, south of London, Morgan made his first trip from Rochester, New York, where he was working as a lawyer, to Marquette, Michigan, on the south shore of Lake Superior (Morgan Papers, journal 2:8:225–26) (see figure 2.1). In this area where his close friend, Reverend McIlvaine, saw vestiges of the biblical flood, Morgan hoped to invest in the Ely family's railroad venture. Morgan had already done legal work for the Ely family when they were flour millers back in Rochester. The Ely family had turned from flour milling to railroads because the Genessee River falls and millraces that supported the political economy of Rochester were failing. Morgan had just completed his report of 30 June 1855 to the U.S. commissioner of patents on "The Flour Mills and Flour Manufacture in Rochester, N.Y. [1 July 1854–30 June 1855]." The report showed why the Genessee River had begun to run too low in the harvest period of August to November, when the millers' needs for waterpower were greatest (Morgan Papers, box 2:1; reproduced in Kosok 1946). Morgan later dedicated *The American Beaver* to his close friend, Samuel P. Ely.

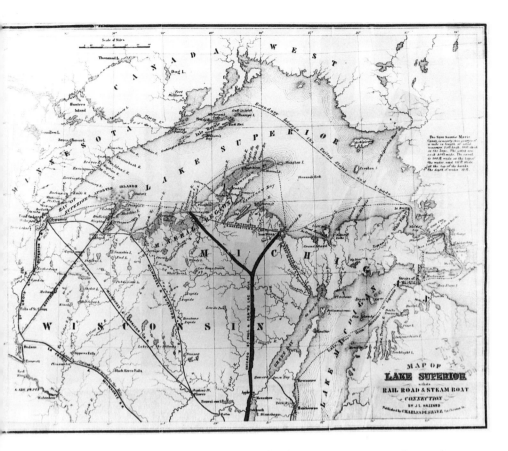

FIG. 2.1 "Map of Lake Superior with Its Rail Road and Steam Boat Connection." Entered according to an act of Congress in the year 1857 by Charles Desilver in the Clerk's Office of the District Court of the Eastern District of Pennsylvania. Courtesy of Marquette County Historical Society.

Morgan does not mention in his journals or the beaver book that Marquette had been called "Indian Town" before the entrepreneur Peter White started mining operations in the area in the 1840s. Long before the iron miners, railroad workers, and canal builders were to turn northern Michigan into the center of an international iron trade, this region of the Great Lakes was the heart of an international fur trade focusing on the beaver. The fur trade had moved west only after the colonialists' victory in the Revolutionary War destroyed the fragile political equality that had sustained relations among the various groups of Native Americans and Europeans up to that point.

Back in New York, the fur trade on the western frontier supported the utopian Oneida Perfectionists' transformation in the 1850s and 1860s from a horticultural economy, based on fruit trees, to an industrial one. The key was their invention of an improved iron trap to catch beavers, then a line of traps for animals ranging in size from otters to moose. Morgan ([1868] 1996, 229, fig. 23) reproduces a catalog illustration of "Newhouse's Trap" in *The American Beaver.* In northern Michigan, the Ojibwa (also called "Chippaway") had been allotted reserves too small for hunting and trapping. They were moving into menial jobs in the railroad and mining camps as suppliers of fish, meat, and fuel, and as laborers, or as "guides," "camp masters," "explorers," "porters," and "cooks" for businesspeople like Morgan who hunted and fished for sport (Morgan Papers, journal 2, 4, 6 passim). Beaver had long since become money in name and kind, and it was partly through debts to trade stores owned by the American Fur Company that the Ojibwa were forced to sell land. The treaty of Prairie du Chien in 1825–1826, and subsequent land cession treaties in 1837, 1842, and 1854, became the basis for bitterly fought struggles with and among the increasingly numerous mining and railroad companies in the area. Morgan's main legal work for the Ely family's railroad was to establish their rights to land according to the U.S. land law in this region.

In *The American Beaver,* Morgan describes the Marquette region from his Anglo-American perspective as "an uninhabited wilderness" ([1868] 1996, 7, 81). Morgan may have gotten this impression because of its striking difference to the already deforested land and dwindling streams he had left in New York (see, for example, Morgan Papers, journal 1:14:241 [12 August 1846]). When Morgan came to northern Michigan, he found "a dense forest overspreads the land," broken only by the beavers' meadows, the miners' camps, and the Indians' trails. "No one but an experienced woodman" is capable of getting around ([1868] 1996, 80, 81). Back east, the Iroquois, "situated upon the headwaters of the Hudson, the Delaware, the Susquehanna, the Ohio and the St. Lawrence flowing in every direction to the sea, . . . held within their jurisdiction, as it were, the gates of the country, and could, through them, descend at will upon any point" (Morgan 1851, 40). Here too, the rivers were "the gates of the country," as elsewhere throughout the North American continent up into the mid–nineteenth century. Although the Great Lakes area had "a pattern of land trails approximating the modern highway system, waterways were the main thoroughfares. These water routes are the key to understanding Great Lakes history" (Tanner et al. 1987, 6). Thus, in carrying out his kinship and beaver research, Morgan drew on the knowledge of waterways and relations between people and animals that generations of local trappers and traders had accumulated through the fur trade. Yet this was a time when current workers were being transformed into a rural proletariat and the animals driven off or killed out.

Morgan's first trip in July–August 1855 was taken up with the commercial interests that brought him to Marquette. He toured several of the already famous iron mines (see figure 2.2). Then, as he recorded in his journal on 16 August 1855, became "engaged quite unexpectedly to myself in assisting Mr. [Samuel] Ely in taking testimony in four cases he is now presenting and defending in his railroad and iron business" (Morgan Papers, 2:8:299). Morgan's journal picks up again three years later with his second visit to Marquette in the summer of 1858, staying as usual with Samuel Ely and his family. On 13 July 1858, he records a vocabulary "through William Cameron Jr. from his mother a Chippewa woman [Morgan also inserted: 'and an old Chippewan']. Cameron was absent fishing. He is a Scotsman and disowned by his family" (2:10:310). The vocabulary begins with "God, Devil, Man, Woman, Boy, Girl," and includes a list of animals, starting with "Beaver." When William Cameron Sr. returns, Morgan goes "over again the whole subject of their law of descent" (2:10:346). Although the languages of the Algonquian-speaking Ojibwa and the Iroquois-speaking Seneca are different, the Ojibwa "law of descent . . . is the same essentially as that of the Iroquois" (2:10:346). Morgan confirms this by returning to the Seneca at Tonawanda in November (2:11:357–420).

Morgan used this data as the basis of a circular in January 1859 asking for information on "systems of consanguinity among tribes of North American Indians." Receiving data suggesting that his hypothesis of an Asian origin of the North American Indians might be confirmed, he did a revised circular in October 1859, on "systems of consanguinity among peoples of Asia, Africa, Islands of the Pacific, Mexico and South America," which Thomas Trautmann (1987, 98, 113) considers a kind of *Systems* in embryo. Morgan's own field-work, documented in his journals (3, 4, 5, 6) included several trips to the western frontier between 1858 and 1862, and at least seven return visits to Marquette between 1860 and 1866. Morgan traveled by railroad, then steamship up the Missouri River into Kansas and Nebraska, in May–June 1859 and again in May–June 1860; by railway, then steamship up the Mississippi and Minnesota Rivers and the Red River of the north to Pembina and then Fort Garry in July–August 1861; returning by railroad, then steamship up the Missouri River, through Kansas and Nebraska into the foothills of the Rocky Mountains in May–July 1862; and returning to Tonawanda at least one more time

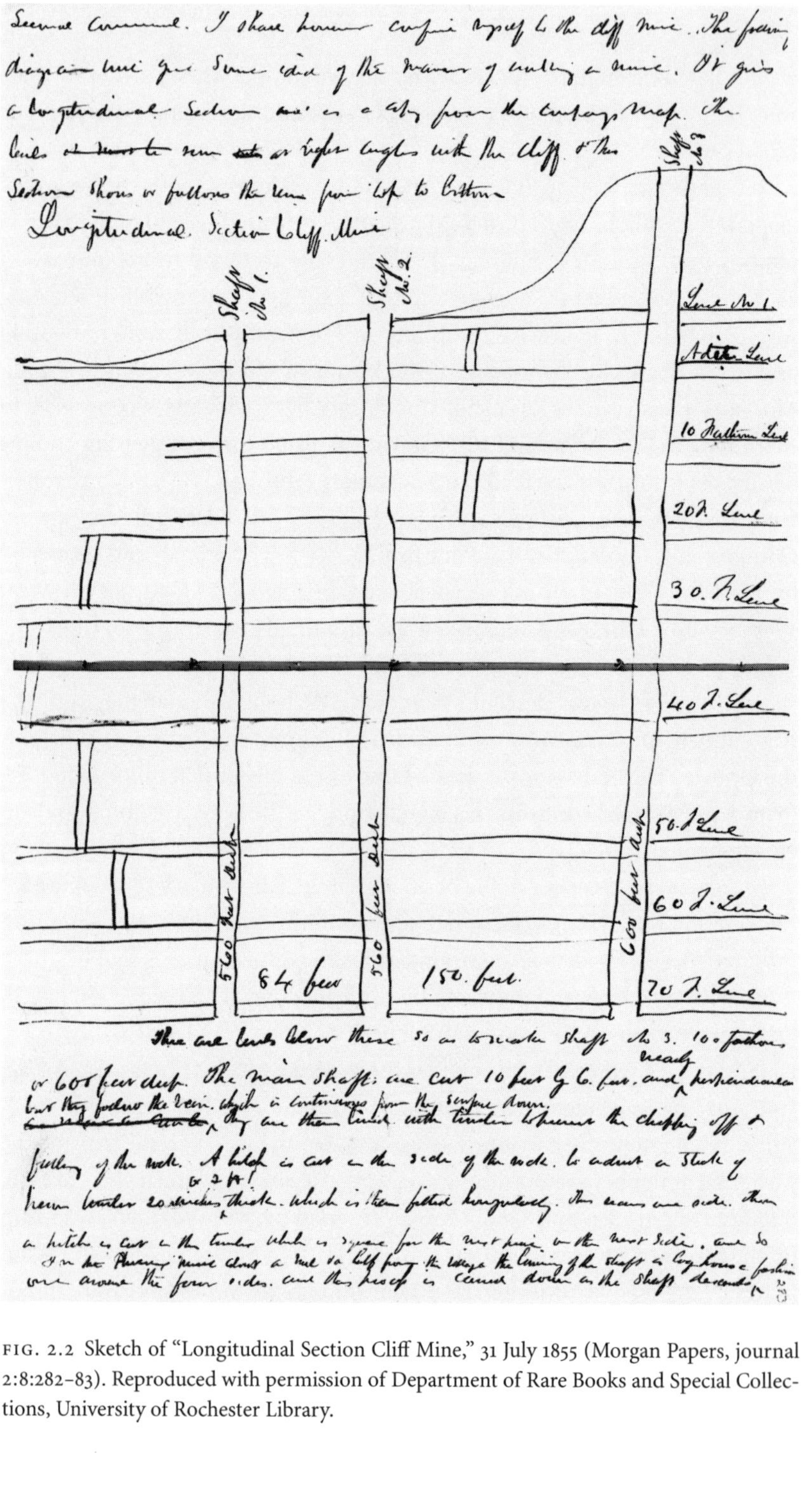

FIG. 2.2 Sketch of "Longitudinal Section Cliff Mine," 31 July 1855 (Morgan Papers, journal 2:8:282–83). Reproduced with permission of Department of Rare Books and Special Collections, University of Rochester Library.

in 1865. In Morgan's trips to the western frontier, he found himself in communities so wholly organized around the fur trade that John Jacob Astor's American Fur Company was the main intermediary of the U.S. government. In 1860, Morgan started a file he called "Newspaper Articles and Anecdotes of Animals," which he kept into 1872 (Morgan Papers, box 27:11). Back in Marquette, beginning in 1860, he began focusing on the "American beaver."

THE ARCHITECTURAL MUTES

The common BEAVER has earned a world-wide reputation by the wonderful instinct it displays, independently of its very great value in producing costly fur and perfume. — James G. Wood, *Illustrated Natural History: Mammalia*

The American beaver was not simply a zoological species, "one of the oldest of living mammals," and a variant of a single species, *Castor fiber,* that once spanned the European and North American continents, as Morgan ([1868] 1996, 44–45) hoped to prove. The beaver embodied the continent, having a huge range extending from the Arctic Circle to the Rio Grande, larger than the range of any other mammal in North America (besides human beings, as many early explorers had observed). Furthermore, the beaver was by far the most valuable animal in the fur trade, "probably the single most important factor in the early exploration of North America" (Naiman 1996: vi), dominating the international political economy of the region since the mid-1600s.

"Beavers abound here. . . . Their works meet the eye at almost every point on the numerous streams with which it [the area] is covered as with a network" (Morgan [1868] 1996, 81), like the network of Iroquois, English, Dutch, French, and German names in New York State from which Morgan had just come. Morgan's sketch-map of Township no. 47 made in August 1860 shows where he did most of his research: the mining district southwest of Marquette at the crest of the mountains dividing the drainages of Lakes Superior and Michigan (Morgan Papers, journal 4:2:246–47) (see figure 2.3). He is already plotting the river courses against the U.S. geologic surveyors' grid lines made just six years earlier. He shows the Carp River flowing into Lake Superior, the Ely Branch of the Esconauby (now Escanaba) River flowing into Lake Michigan, and the numerous lakes of the region, intertwined with the railroads connecting the three most famous iron mines (Jackson, Cleveland, and Lake Superior).

Morgan reproduces this map in his beaver book to show "how completely

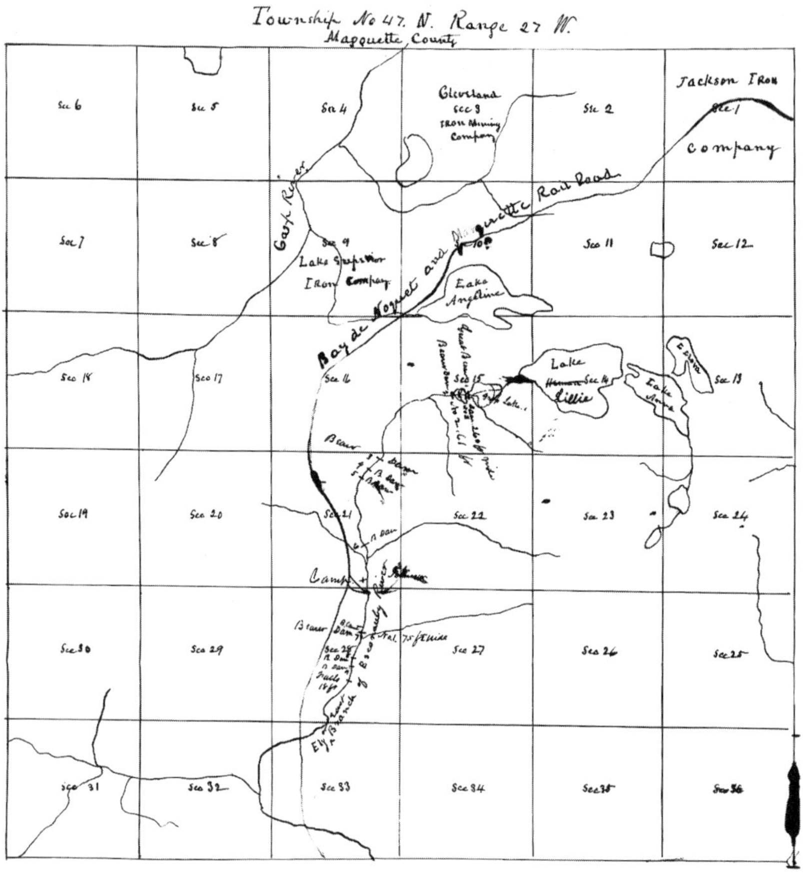

FIG. 2.3 Sketch of "Township No. 47 N. Range 27 W., Marquette County," August 1860 (Morgan Papers, journal 4: insert between 246–47). Reproduced with permission of Department of Rare Books and Special Collections, University of Rochester Library.

they occupy a given district as their numbers increase," and "the relations of their dams and other erections to each other" ([1868] 1996, 80). On the finished version, published in *The American Beaver* (83–84), he has extended the relations of the beavers more systematically so that they include relations between beavers and people. This map was drawn by engineers employed by the railroad company. Although just a fragment of the area Morgan studied, it shows sixty-three beaver dams and other beaver works (not counting the smallest) interspersed among the two human settlements of Negaunee and Ishpeming, nine named iron mines, and several unnamed ones.

Of these, his favorite was the dam at Grass Lake, the sixth of a chain of lakes issuing from one of the highest of the iron-bearing hills in the area (see figure 2.4). The Grass Lake dam, together with other constructions, exemplifies several distinctive features of the beavers' works. First is their astonishing size. Morgan describes Grass Lake dam as "by far the largest and most extraordinary Beaver structure I have seen and perhaps is not exceeded by any in the country" (Morgan Papers, journal 4:2:223). Second, they are built to relate to the local topography. Third, they are built to relate to other structures, including the beavers' lodge, other dams immediately above and below, and channels for reaching more distant sources of food (see figure 2.5). Fourth, the beavers' building techniques are adapted to different circumstances — for example, bank dams and bank burrows to larger, deeper streams. Fifth, the beavers' works are amazingly strong. Morgan says of a bank dam on the Esconcauby River: "It is . . . a solid bank on which a beaver and a man may walk with ease and but for the open work at the opening at which the water was discharged a horse and wagon might be driven across the river upon the top level of the dam" (4:2:200). Historical work has confirmed that the colonialists in New England turned beavers' bank dams into their roadbeds (see figure 2.6).

Sixth, the beavers must "supervise" their works daily: "It is clear enough that the Beaver work at their dams daily, or nightly rather as they are nocturnal animals, and make their condition a matter of constant supervision" (4:2:229). Furthermore, they must persist in their skilled labors not only throughout their own lifetimes but pass on their skills to the next generation. Morgan infers from the nature of the related structures — dams, lakes, lodges, meadows, and canals — that they are centuries old: "The entire extermination of the trees except in the most shallow parts of the pond is evidence that it is some hundreds of years old, or rather that a Beaver dam has been maintained at this precise point for some hundreds of years at least" (4:2:224). Pollen deposits

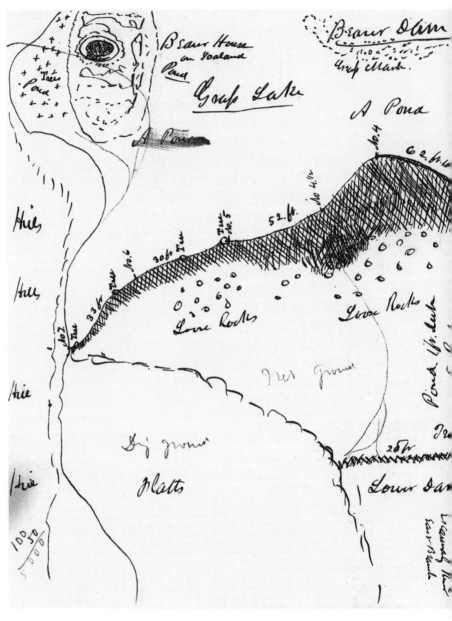

FIG. 2.4 Sketch of "Beaver Dam 3 . . . Grass Lake," August 1860, in section 15 of "Township" map (Morgan Papers, journal 4:216–17). Reproduced with permission of Department of Rare Books and Special Collections, University of Rochester Library.

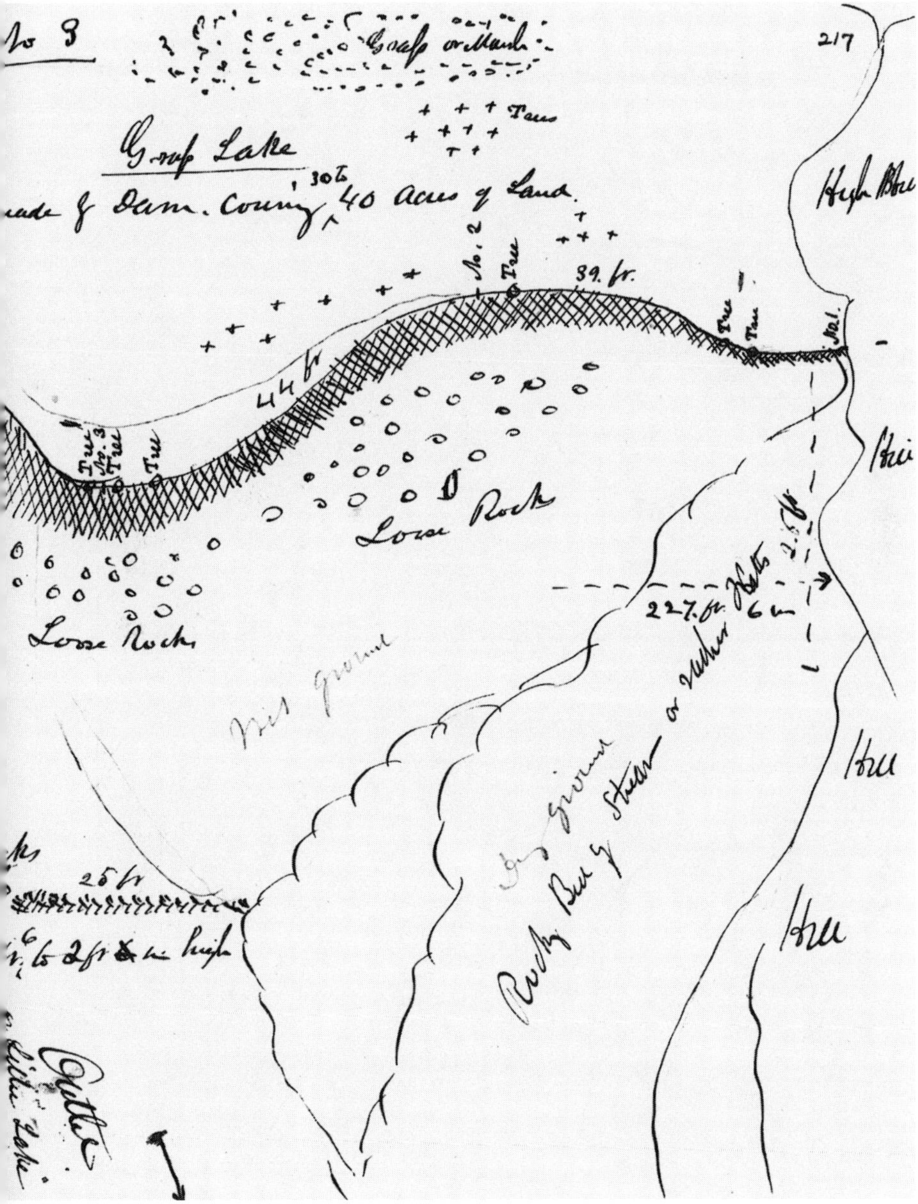

No 3

Grass or Marsh

217

Grass Lake

...ade of Dam. Coning 306 40 Acres of Land.

Trees

No 2 Tree

39 ft

High Bl...

44 ft

Tree 3 Tree Tree

Loose Rock

Loose Rocks

Wet ground

227 ft 6 in

Dry ground Rocky Bed of Stream or rather flats 15 ft

Hill

Hill

25 ft

6 to 2 ft & in high

Outlet of Grass Lake

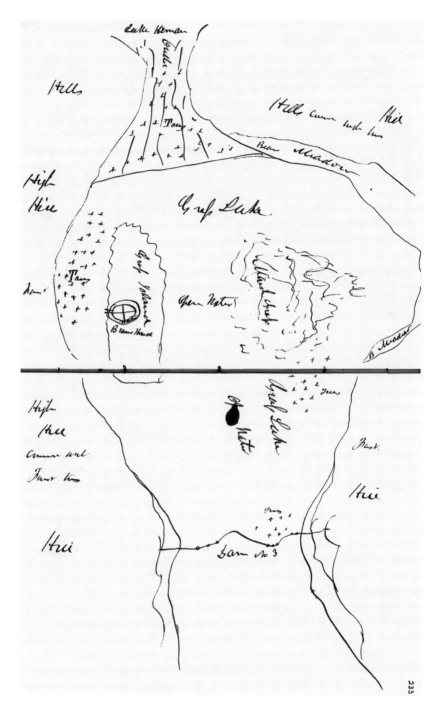

FIG. 2.5 Sketch of "Grass Lake," August 1860 (Morgan Papers, journal 4:232–33). Reproduced with permission of Department of Rare Books and Special Collections, University of Rochester Library.

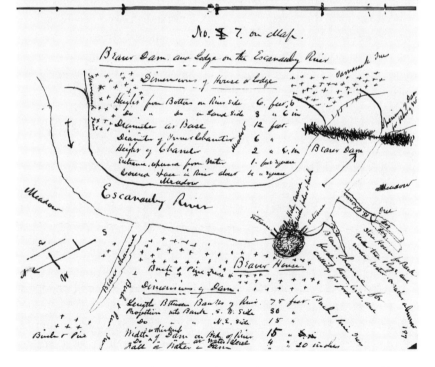

FIG. 2.6 "Beaver Dam and Lodge on Escanauby River," August 1860, in section 28 of "Township" map (Morgan Papers, journal 4:196–97). Reproduced with permission of Department of Rare Books and Special Collections, University of Rochester Library.

analyzed in the 1980s showed that a beaver dam forming Echo Lake on nearby Grand Island was about seven hundred years old (Graham 1995, 12).

Morgan returned to Grass Lake every year until 1865, when the dam showed signs of neglect, suggesting that "after centuries of use and maintenance by unnumbered generations of beavers, this interesting and remarkable structure was about to be abandoned by its natural proprietors" ([1868] 1996, 94). Yet it is a testimony to their great works that Grass Lake still remains, although now almost surrounded by strip mines that have replaced the shaft mines in the Marquette area. The pile of "waste rock" from the adjacent open-pit mine, which rises up above the trees southeast of the lake, was expected to reach 1,950 feet by December 1997, which would then be the highest point in northern Michigan (Feeley-Harnik 1997).

The creation and maintenance of these regional networks of constructions over centuries suggests to Morgan that these "humble, but most industrious mute[s]" ([1868] 1996, 6) possessed culture and social organization, and were capable of transmitting their skills down the generations. I think Morgan was helped to come to this conclusion by the Ojibwa Indians who were his guides. Just as they provided Morgan with information about Native American kinship patterns, so they expanded the scope of his research to include animals whom they saw as sentient beings. Thus, for example, Morgan states in his journal for August 1860:

> They eat the bark so a Chippeway Beaver hunter told me yesterday. . . . (Morgan Papers, journal 4:2:231)

> The beaver do their work in the night as near as I can learn. They are rarely seen in the day time. They live in pairs of two each or in families of from six to ten so an old Indian informed me. . . . (4:2:241)

> Have just seen my old friend Cameron again and have had a Beaver talk with him and Rosean [who he later identifies as Roussein]. Cameron is an old trapper. He says the Beaver always marry or live in pairs and never in companies made of different pairs. The first year they build a Lodge or Wigwam and a Dam and raise two young beavers. The second year they raise four. They are born in May. This makes the second year a family of 8, which he calls the old pair the half grown and the young ones. (4:2:244–45)

Putting the names together, it gradually becomes evident that the same people who are explaining human kinship and labor practices to Morgan are also telling him about beaver kinship and labor practices. In the preface to *The American Beaver* ([1868] 1996, 11), he thanks four "Ojibwa trappers" by name: William Cameron, William Bass, Paul Pine, and Jack La Pete.

Whereas Cameron was "a Scotsman disowned by his family" (Morgan Papers, journal 2:10:310) for marrying an Ojibwa woman (or so Morgan thought when he first met him), La Pete enters Morgan's journals as a "Frenchman," the local name for the descendants of Ojibwa-French unions. When Morgan knew La Pete (also known as Jacques LePete, Jacques LePique, and perhaps Buk-kau-kau-duz), La Pete was working as a trapper and trader for the American Fur Company on Grand Island near Marquette, and also serving as an interpreter, guide, and camp master. His given name, as Morgan notes on 5 September 1862 in his journal, was Francis Nolin (6:1:30). By his own account in the 1890s, his father's father, born in Ireland, was orphaned in France, adopted by a French couple, emigrated to Canada when they died, became a fur trapper and trader, and married an Ojibwa woman in Sault Ste. Marie (see Kawbawgam, Kawbawgam, and LePique 1994, 139–40). Jacques LePique was born and raised among Cree Indians in Canada. Following his grandfather and father into the fur trade, he married an Ojibwa woman and traveled extensively, learning several languages, including Cree, Ojibwa, Canadian French, and fluent English. LePique's critical role as an interpreter encompassed not only his linguistic prowess in moving back and forth among these languages but also his ability to *parler sauvage* in the broadest sense of the local idiom. According to Homer H. Kidder, who recorded some of his stories and employed him as an interpreter in recording the stories of Charlotte and Charles Kawbawgam, his in-laws and close friends, LePique was "steeped in Ojibwa lore" (cited in Kawbawgam, Kawbawgam, and LePique 1994, 140). In his stories and those of the Kawbawgams, people and animals understand each other, often with the help of interpreters, address each other by common sets of kin terms, and take each other's shapes in the course of their life and death struggles.

As Trautmann (1987, 58–83, 263–65) points out about Morgan's analysis of kinship terminologies, Morgan was influenced by the methods of philology current in his time, but he went beyond the conventionally debated alternatives of historical reconstruction based on vocabulary or grammar to examine their semantic patterns and relations. The beaver research was an explanation of these relations among creatures who did not have human kinds of languages. Morgan shows that the beavers' dams, lodges, and channels do not exist in isolation but in relation to each other and the structures around them.

The beavers' works are related semantically, not by accident or coincidence. Their relations derive from systems of social relationships, in particular the "marriage relation," which for Morgan epitomized more than any other relation the distinctive sociality of people and certain mutes. Huge dams, like Grass Lake, had been imagined to be the work of large numbers of beavers, working collectively and living in great multistoried houses, as Morgan (1843) himself had argued earlier, following Georges Louis Leclerc Buffon. Morgan proves that these structures acquire their enormous stature, so closely integrated with the land around them, only after repeated repairs and refinements. Generations of beavers, couples and small families, construct them bit by bit. Finally, these mutes are capable of extending their systems of relationships, through their creations, over much wider areas of land than previously recognized, once encompassing the continent and possibly even the ancient landmass once joining America, Europe, and Asia.

Morgan had to create new methods of representation to get at these relations. At first, he seems to use his measurements of the beavers' works as if he were an interpreter, trying to make them sufficiently commensurate with human works so that people who have never lived and worked among the architectural mutes will also grasp the intelligence in their making. His numerical measurements of the beavers' dams, canals, and lodges are like his kinship tables, where words describe numerical degrees of proximity or distance in human generational relationships. The counterpart to the "Tables of Consanguinity and Affinity" in *Systems* are his annotated drawings of the measured spatial relations among the beavers' dams, lodges, and canals, later made into engravings. Finally, he resorts to photographs. Yet just as he broke through the beavers' lodges to measure their insides, so he was perfectly willing to make his photographs by cutting down obscuring vegetation and having beavers killed in order to use them as lifelike props. Morgan enlisted the help of his friend Dr. William Watson Ely to dissect some of the dead beavers that he sent to him and to write the chapter on "Beaver Anatomy" and the appendix on their private parts.

Morgan's matter-of-factness in having beavers killed so he could pose them in his photographs is the strongest evidence of his not anthropomorphizing. Yet precisely here, in his efforts to grasp the structural significance of the pieces of wood, stones, and earth put together in these dams and lodges, he understands them increasingly as signs in a communicative system involving beavers and humans. He documents special qualities particular to beavers, evident in both their behavior and anatomy—for example, their acute senses of hearing and smell, far superior to those of humans, and the ways they signal with their tails. But he also notes again and again what he clearly sees as intercommunication between beavers and humans. Each appears to be using their knowledge of the others' distinctive ways of communication, what the trappers themselves called "signs."

Partly, Morgan's sensitivity to these signs seems to come from his personal sensibilities and his convictions about biblical, geologic, legal, and commercial interconnections between land and living beings that I have briefly discussed. Partly, his sensitivity to these relations seems to come directly from the people with whom he worked — notably, the Ojibwa trappers who were his principal informants around Marquette. Morgan's arguments about relations between animals and people rest on his efforts to relate human vocal-auditory speech with other sign systems through living creatures' "artificial works . . . their habits, their mode of life, and their mutual relations," which taxonomists had heretofore rejected as "immaterial and transient" ([1868] 1996, 5, 6). Words, put together in letters, journals, books, and libraries, had their structural analogues in sticks, stones, and earth, put together in houses, tombs, lodges, dams, and channels. Through the communicative practices of people and animals, they become organically integrated with each other as well as with the land and water where they live and die over time.

As Morgan does his research on human and animal communities ever further west, he becomes ever more sensitive to the polylingualism of life in the riverine fur-trading communities of the frontier, growing explosively through channels of consanguinity and affinity forbidden back east. Eventually, in his journal entries in 1864, he begins to document examples of human sign language. The linguistic virtuosity that Morgan encounters in frontier communities is clearly associated with new forms of sociality among groups that rarely mingled back east. Although I cannot properly substantiate this claim here, I believe that Morgan's research in northern Michigan and further west was critical in transforming his conceptions of "breeds" and "crosses." The marriage relation seemed especially potent in radically changing relations among creatures, not only among beavers but also humans, and not only for Morgan but also for the people with whom he worked. In the polyglot communities of the frontier, so-called "mixed marriages" were commonplace, not exceptional. Herein lie the sources of the beavers' allusive relations with humans, historically rooted in the sociality of generations in the international fur trade. Morgan drew on the insights of polymaths in mutual relations — the Camerons and Le Pique in northern Michigan, Joseph Tesson, Mrs. Chouteau, and

Mrs. Graham Rogers in Kansas and Nebraska, among many others — to document the deep history and transcontinental scope of Native American, and European, life associated with their common pursuit of the wily, imaginative architectural mutes. In the process, Morgan was recording the astonishing creative ferment of new life at the outermost limits of society as he knew it (Morgan 1993).

In May and June 1862, during the most distant of these trips, which took Morgan into the foothills of the Rocky Mountains, the Morgans' two young daughters, aged six and two, died within three weeks of each other of scarlet fever. My hypothesis is that these catastrophic events led the Morgans, and Lewis Henry Morgan in his research, to focus ever more acutely on forms of communication extending so far beyond human speech as to connect the living to the dead. This was a major issue for many Rochesterians at this time, whether or not they were spiritualists. Morgan hoped to dedicate *Systems* to his dead daughters. As he explains in a 21 February 1867 letter to Joseph Henry, secretary of the Smithsonian: "I have ever felt that I lost my children, in some sense by following this investigation, and I cannot divest my mind of the sense of justice which prompts the dedication. It shall be unobjectionable in form: but I hope and trust you will concede the point to me" (Morgan Papers, box 4:1).

Henry refused to print Morgan's dedication on the grounds that it was not appropriate to a scientific work. The drafts that Morgan carefully saved show that *Systems* was to have been "an offering upon their tomb" because it was "equally their contribution and mine to the Science of the Families of Mankind." In concluding, he addressed the dead "Mary & Helen" directly by name, following an Iroquois practice that Ely S. Parker had earlier recorded as "no longer in vogue," but in fact still practiced (Morgan Papers, journal 1:1:4a; see 1851:175–76). Then he added, "No voices answer, from beneath their heavy covers, our mute appeals; and yet they seem to say 'We are not here! We are waiting for you in the Spirit Land!' May it be our infinite joy again to meet and know them there." (Morgan Papers, box 12:2). Morgan designed a tomb around their coffins to bear their message in Latin on the facade: "*Non Hic Sumus*" ("We Are Not Here"). *Systems of Consanguinity and Affinity*, tracking back almost to the original unity of "the Human Family" that Morgan was sure lay in ancient streams of communication just beyond human speech, was also to have brought their voices back from beyond the grave.

"THE WHOLE SURFACE OF THE EARTH MADE PROPERTY"

In Morgan's later work, he seems to shift from his geohydrologic inquiries into the multifarious, open-ended channels of communication of humans and animals to the codification of the direction of human progress. As he outlines toward the end of *Ancient Society*, "field agriculture" marked a key point in this historical process:

> When field agriculture had demonstrated that the whole surface of the earth could be made the subject of property owned by individuals in sev-eralty, and it was found that the head of the family became the natural center of accumulation, the new property career of mankind was inaugu-rated. ([1877] 1963, 554)

A "feeble impulse" among the savages became a "tremendous passion" among the barbarians, inaugurating the time when "monogamy, having assured the paternity of children, would assert and maintain their exclusive right to in-herit the property of their deceased father" (554). This assumed, of course, that the children would not die before the father. But how exactly did Mor-gan understand this process, the "accumulation" of generational flows em-bedded in the very earth itself? How might Morgan and his contemporaries have understood the inheritance of "property" in relation to their various views about the inheritance of vitality and morbidity? To conclude this brief study of Morgan's ethnography of creation, I want to return to his consider-ations of consanguinity and affinity to show how these questions might be addressed.

Morgan and his contemporaries were involved in intense debates about the physiology of life and death. Bloodletting, the dominant method of ther-apy, was nevertheless criticized for being violent and invasive. Homeopaths, like the Morgan's close friend Dr. Gerard Arink, considered herbal and min-eral remedies for cleansing and restoring blood to be far more effective. Yet Dr. William Andrus Alcott, in his widely read *Lectures on Life and Health; or, The Laws and Means of Physical Culture,* scorned the idea of "renovating or purifying the ever-changing mass of blood" on the grounds that

> the blood of to-day will not be the blood of to-morrow. . . . You might as well think of changing the character of the mass of waters that con-stitute the mighty Mississippi. But who does not know that if he could change the Mississippi of to-day, it would not reach the Mississippi of to-

morrow, and that his work must be repeated daily, without end? (1853, 196)

Indeed, hydrotherapy—bathing, drinking, steaming, soaking, sweating, douching, wet packing, sponging, plunging—was another important alternative, especially for women's reproductive ailments. The Morgans' closest friends included practitioners in all these areas whom they sought out at different times for different purposes throughout their lives. It seems plausible—although I have not yet confirmed this directly—that they shared some common ground with their contemporaries in assuming that "every part of the body was interrelated with other parts [and] that the environment (climate and seasons) could affect the working harmony of these parts, that health or disease was the state of the entire system" (Cayleff 1987, 6).

Thus, when Morgan himself wrote about the channels of the blood, I would argue that he was not reducing human kinship to biology, as it would now be understood, but neither was he being metaphorical—that is, using these terms figuratively to compare domains he considered separate. Earth and water, soil and river, provided Morgan and his contemporaries with language for talking about life and life's blood because they were inseparable in practice. Theologically, the watery earth was the matrix of life where knowledge about creative processes could be found. Therapeutically, land and body were the common matrix of everyday living. Earth and soil had bodily dimensions, in which, to quote from Morgan's copy of Ebenezer Emmons's *Agriculture of New-York,* a treatise on "agricultural geology" written by a medical doctor, "the rocks are the parents of the present soil" (1846). Similarly, the human body, derived from and returning to dust, was a kind of land that could be drained, watered, cultivated, channeled, and fertilized.

Morgan unquestionably shared the hope that he was examining long-term historical trends in the "improvement" of human life, in exactly the same way that farmers like his father Jedediah had "improved" their land by clearing, organizing, channeling, and crossing. This view of people and land, and their common potential for improvement, is expressed explicitly in the "new edition" of Francis Smith Eastman's *History of the State of New York,* published in 1832, not long after Jedediah Morgan's death in 1826. Indeed, Eastman's revised edition of his 1831 work included "many important alterations, which, it is hoped, will be considered as improvements" (1832, 5). Eastman begins his "View of the Country at the Time of Its Discovery by Hudson" with these words:

At the period of Hudson's discovery, the country was mostly in an un-improved state. From its general appearance, and from the traditions of its inhabitants, we infer, that it had previously continued in this situation for a long succession of ages.

No traces of recent civilization enlivened the dreary waste. A few scat-tered villages, comprising a limited number of habitations, of the most imperfect construction, and some feeble and ill-directed attempts at agri-culture, announced the more frequented haunts of savage life; but by far the greater part of this extensive territory was covered by an unbroken wilderness. . . .

The luxuriance of vegetation evinced the fertility of a soil, which re-quired only the hand of art to render it in the highest degree subservient to the wants of man. But the country was inhabited by a race averse to improvement, rude and uncultivated at the scenery around them. (1832, 60–61)

This is, in fact, precisely the approach to the management of reproduction and generation of wealth that now dominates today's handling of domestic animals and people and also "wildlife management," in which, as it happens, profitable furbearers, like beavers, have a leading role. Morgan's beaver re-search shows how the generative imagery of land and water was incorporated into the new landforms associated with the railway. James Hodges, an English worker on Canada's Grand Trunk Railroad, explained the U.S. perspective to his English employer, Thomas A. Brassey, when Brassey visited the railroads in Canada and northern Michigan in the mid-1850s. In his words, "In America, a railway is like a river, and is regarded as the natural channel of civilization" (cited in Helps 1873, 188). Hodges would probably not be surprised that in their industrialization of agriculture over the past century, U.S. breeders of livestock have turned from extensive accumulation, based on the cultivation of additional land, to forms of intensive accumulation, based on restructur-ing the "interior geographies" of animals (Ufkes 1995) in which their acreage is concentrated.

Morgan witnessed the sociohistorical process of so-called improvement firsthand. He documented and actively participated in it, accumulating some 256,169.80 acres of land for railroad companies in Marquette by the time the U.S. General Land Office finally certified his land lists in 1865 (see Benison 1954, 237). Indeed, following the advice of his friend, the Reverend McIlvaine, in transforming *Systems* from an account of Indian origins and migrations into a "conjectural solution" to the ultimate origins of the descriptive and classificatory systems in "primitive promiscuity" (Trautmann 1987, 148–78), he collaborated in projecting this vision of cultivation and improvement onto human history as a whole. Still, Morgan was irrevocably changed as a result, concluding with deeply ambivalent views on the process and especially his personal contributions to it. The letters he saved are proof of this. For example, Samuel Ely wrote to Morgan on 17 February 1880, the year before Morgan died, berating him for not investing in silver mines in Utah: "It bothers me a little that I cannot make you apprehend the difference between developing, exploiting, producing and speculating" (Morgan Papers, box 9:1). His written works provide further evidence — for instance, his claim in the conclusion to *Ancient Society* that "the dissolution of society bids fair to become the termination of a career of which property is the end and aim; because such a career contains the elements of self-destruction." He can hope only that future generations will revive the equitable mutuality of the Iroquois ([1877] 1963, 561–62).

With these end points in mind, the latter-day observer goes back and finds the seeds of doubt in Morgan's earliest work. Perhaps for Morgan, too, the deposits, accumulations, and shifting channels were clearer to him in retrospect than they ever were at the time. Yet his daughters' deaths were unquestionably critical, incomprehensible in any progressive way, except possibly as sacrifices. As such, they might be like "the annual sacrifice of animal life to maintain human life," the "frightful" subject with which he closed *The American Beaver* ([1868] 1996, 283), or like "the struggles, the sufferings, the heroic exertions and the patient toil of our barbarous, and more remotely, of our savage ancestors," to whom we owe "our present condition," as he insists at the end of *Ancient Society* ([1877] 1963, 563). But insofar as he felt himself wholly to blame for his daughters' sacrifices, I think he questioned the redemptive value of the deadly appropriation of vital flows of earth, water, and blood that the "property career" seemed to entail.

Morgan's language might sometimes seem quaint, but his interests are entirely continuous with present-day concerns. In some ways — for example, in his assessment of what is now called "animal intelligence," in his recognition and analysis of the intimately entwined fates of human and other creatures, and in his phenomenology of communicative practices — he might still be considered ahead of the times. Yet his work also keeps open questions about the directionality of science, the relationship between science and religion now construed popularly, if not in anthropology, as a relationship between science and culture, and the relationship of both of these to capitalism.

NOTES

This paper is based on continuing research in the archives of Morgan's papers and related materials in the Department of Rare Books and Manuscripts, Rush Rhees Library, University of Rochester, Rochester, New York, in October 1994, July 1996, and July 1998; in the historical archives at the John M. Longyear Research Library, Marquette County Historical Society, Marquette, Michigan, in July 1997; and on ethnographic research on iron mining in northern Michigan in July 1997. Karl Kabelac and Amy Burnam, curators of the Morgan archives, and Linda Panian, librarian at the John M. Longyear Research Library, helped me enormously. I have also benefited from correspondence with Faye Swanberg at the Alger County Historical Society, Munising, Michigan. I am grateful to fellow participants in the Wenner-Gren conference, New Directions in Kinship Study, for their comments in March–April 1998, and especially to Sarah Franklin and Susan McKinnon for their inspiring work throughout.

1 For a discussion of Morgan's early work and a more substantial account of the arguments summarized here, see Feeley-Harnik 1999. Thanks to the editors of *Comparative Studies in Society and History* for permission to cite some passages from this article.

2 Although *Systems* was not published until 1871, it was, as noted on the title page, "accepted for publication, January, 1868." Morgan published *The American Beaver and His Works* in the same year. Five years after he finished them, he also saved a memento of their common creation: a gold pen with a short wooden shank chewed at the tip. He sewed the pen to the back of a card (an invitation, dated 14 April 1873, to a talk at his scholars' club), then wrote around it:

> This Pen, first put in use in May 1863, wrote,
> and rewrote "Systems of Consanguinity and Affinity
> of the Human Family," including the Tables. 590.
> pp.2to. and all the correspondence connected with it
>   [pen sewed to card]
> after that date. It also wrote, and rewrote "The
> American Beaver & His Works" 330.pp6to. and is still
> a good Pen. The brand seems to be Ford & Co: LH. Morgan
>   May 15, 1873   1873
> (Morgan Papers, box 27:6)

Following Morgan's son's death in 1905, Morgan's papers and collections were delivered to the University of Rochester, according to the terms of his will. This bit of chewed wood was kept with his beaver collection—two stuffed beavers, beavers' bones, and cuttings of winter wood—which went to the university's Museum of

Natural History. In 1934, when the museum was merged with the zoology department, the pen was transferred to the Department of Rare Books and Manuscripts. Morgan's beaver collection has since disappeared.

3 For more discussion, see Feeley-Harnik 2001.

REFERENCES

Alcott, William Andrus. 1853. *Lectures on Life and Health; or, The Laws and Means of Physical Culture.* Boston: Phillips, Sampson and Co.

Benison, Saul. 1954. *Railroads, Land, and Iron: A Phase in the Career of Lewis Henry Morgan.* Ann Arbor, Mich.: University Microfilms International.

Bouquet, Mary. 1993. *Reclaiming English Kinship: Portuguese Refractions of British Kinship Theory.* Manchester, U.K.: Manchester University Press.

Cayleff, Susan E. 1987. *Wash and Be Healed: The Water-Cure Movement and Women's Health.* Philadelphia, Pa.: Temple University Press.

Darwin, Charles. [1859] 1964. *On the Origin of Species by Means of Natural Selection, or the Preservation of Favoured Races in the Struggle for Life.* Reprint, with an introduction by Ernst Mayr, Cambridge: Harvard University Press.

Darwin, Charles. 1881. *The Formation of Vegetable Mould, Through the Action of Worms with Observations on Their Habits.* London: John Murray.

Durkheim, Émile. 1898. [Review of] Prof. J. Kohler. — *Zur Urgeschichte der Ehe: Totemismus, Gruppenehe, Mutterrecht.* (Contribution l'histoire primitive du mariage. Totémisme, mariage collectif, droit maternel.) *L'Année Sociologique* 1:306–19.

Eastman, Francis Smith. 1832. *A History of the State of New York, from the First Discovery of the Country to the Present Time: With a Geographical Account of the Country, and a View of Its Original Inhabitants.* Rev. ed. New York: A. K. White.

Emmons, Ebenezer. 1846. *Agriculture of New-York: Comprising an Account of the Classification, Composition, and Distribution of the Soils and Rocks, and the Natural Waters of the Different Geological Formations, together with a Condensed View of the Climate and Agricultural Productions of the State.* Vol. 1. Albany, N.Y.: C. Van Benthuysen and Co.

Feeley-Harnik, Gillian. 1997. Field notes, Marquette, Michigan, July.

———. 1999. "Communities of Blood": The Natural History of Kinship in Nineteenth-Century America. *Comparative Studies in Society and History* 41, no. 2:215–62.

———. 2001. "The Mystery of Life in All Its Forms": Religious Dimensions of Culture in Early American Anthropology. In *Religion and Cultural Studies,* edited by Susan L. Mizruchi. Princeton, N.J.: Princeton University Press.

Franklin, Sarah. 1997. Dolly: A New Form of Transgenic Breedwealth. *Environmental Values* 6:427–37.

Graham, Loren R. 1995. *A Face in the Rock: The Tale of a Grand Island Chippewa.* Washington, D.C.: Island Press.

Grossberg, Michael. 1985. *Governing the Hearth: Law and the Family in Nineteenth-Century America.* Chapel Hill: University of North Carolina Press.

Helps, Arthur. 1873. *Life and Labours of Mr. Brassey, 1805–1870.* 4th ed. London: Bell and Daldy.

Kawbawgam, Charles, Charlotte Kawbawgam, and Jacques LePique. 1994. *Ojibwa Narratives of Charles and Charlotte Kawbawgam and Jacques LePique, 1893–1895.* Recorded with notes by Homer H. Kidder. Edited by Arthur P. Bourgeois. Detroit: Wayne State University Press.

Kosok, Paul. 1946. Lewis Henry Morgan on the Flour Mills and Water Power of Rochester. *Rochester Historical Society Publications* 23:109–27.

Livingston, Robert R. 1813. *Essay on Sheep: Their Varieties: Account of the Merinoes of Spain, France, &c.: Reflections on the Best Method of Treating Them, and Raising a Flock in the United States.* Concord, N.H.: Daniel Cooledge and I. and W.R. Hill.

Morgan, Lewis Henry. 1843. Mind or Instinct: An Inquiry concerning the Manifestation of Mind by the Lower Orders of Animals. *Knickerbocker* 22, no. 5:414–20; 22, no. 6:507–15.

———. 1851. *The League of the Ho-de'-no-sau-nee, or Iroquois.* Rochester, N.Y.: Sage and Bros.

———. [1868] 1996. *The American Beaver: A Classic of Natural History and Ecology by Lewis Henry Morgan.* [Reprint of *The American Beaver and His Works.*] Mineola, N.Y.: Dover.

———. [1871] 1997. *Systems of Consanguinity and Affinity of the Human Family.* Reprint, with an introduction by Elisabeth Tooker, Lincoln: University of Nebraska Press.

———. 1872. *The Human Race, by Louis Figuier. Nation* 15, no. 387:354.

———. [1877] 1963. *Ancient Society, or Researches in the Lines of Human Progress from Savagery through Barbarism to Civilization.* Reprint, with an introduction by Eleanor Burke Leacock, Cleveland, Oh.: World.

———. 1993. *The Indian Journals, 1859–62. Lewis Henry Morgan.* Edited with an Introduction by Leslie A. White. Mineola, N.Y.: Dover.

———. Papers. Department of Rare Books and Manuscripts, Rush Rhees Library, University of Rochester.

Morgan, Nathaniel Harris. 1869. *Morgan Genealogy: A History of James Morgan, of New London, Conn., and His Descendants; From 1607 to 1869 (13 Illustrative Portraits), with an Appendix, Containing the History of His Brother, Miles Morgan, of Springfield, Mass.; and Some of His Descendants.* Hartford, Conn.: Case, Lockwood and Brainard.

Naiman, Robert J. 1996. Introduction to the Dover Edition. In *The American Beaver: A Classic of Natural History and Ecology by Lewis Henry Morgan.* Mineola, N.Y.: Dover.

Needham, Rodney. 1975. Polythetic Classification: Convergence and Consequences. *Man* 10, no. 3:349–69.

New York (State) State Museum, Albany. 1842–94. *Natural History of New York.* 30 vols. Albany, N.Y.: C. Van Benthuysen.

Ottenheimer, Martin. 1996. *Forbidden Relatives: The American Myth of Cousin Marriage.* Urbana: University of Illinois Press.

Ritvo, Harriet. 1987. *The Animal Estate: The English and Other Creatures of the Victorian Age.* Cambridge: Harvard University Press.

Schneider, David M. 1968. *American Kinship: A Cultural Account*. Englewood Cliffs, N.J.: Prentice-Hall.

———. 1984. *A Critique of the Study of Kinship*. Ann Arbor: University of Michigan Press.

Seward, William Henry. Papers. Department of Rare Books and Manuscripts, Rush Rhees Library, University of Rochester.

Strathern, Marilyn. 1992. *After Nature: English Kinship in the Late Twentieth Century*. Cambridge: Cambridge University Press.

Tanner, Helen Hornbeck, Adele Hast, Jacqueline Paterson, and Robert J. Surtees, ed. 1987. *Atlas of Great Lakes Indian History*. Cartography by Miklos Pinther. Norman: University of Oklahoma Press.

Trautmann, Thomas R. 1987. *Lewis Henry Morgan and the Invention of Kinship*. Berkeley: University of California Press.

———. 1992. The Revolution in Ethnological Time. *Man* 27, no. 2:379–97.

Trautmann, Thomas R., and Karl Sanford Kabelac. 1994. *The Library of Lewis Henry Morgan and Mary Elizabeth Morgan*. Vol. 84, parts 6 and 7, of *Transactions of the American Philosophical Society*. Philadelphia, Pa.: American Philosophical Society.

Ufkes, Frances M. 1995. Lean and Mean: U.S. Meat-Packing in an Era of Agro-Industrial Restructuring. *Environment and Planning D: Society and Space* 13:683–705.

White, Leslie A. 1944. Morgan's Attitude toward Religion and Science. *American Anthropologist* 46, no. 2:218–30.

Wiseman, Nicholas Patrick Stephan. 1837. *Twelve Lectures on the Connexion Between Science and Revealed Religion*. Andover, N.Y.: Gould and Newman.

Wood, James G. 1865. *Illustrated Natural History: Mammalia*. London: George Routledge.

———. 1866. *Homes Without Hands. Being a Description of the Habitations of Animals, Classed According to Their Principle of Construction*. London: John Murray.

CHAPTER 3

Making Kinship, with an Old Reproductive Technology
Mary Bouquet

Even a single photograph can provoke multilayered insights into the life of an individual and the ethos of an age. . . . Here too lies the fascination of family photographs, which provide such a powerful starting point for wider investigations of how the everyday narratives we construct for them are shaped by currents of culture, ideology and history. — James Ryan, *Picturing Empire*

The institution of the family and the institution of art are implicated in the same rhetorical, aesthetic, and social structures. They promulgate a dream of coherence and unity against which the second kind of family stands, the family that admits the disruptive forces from outside into the space of the post-modern family. — Henry Sayre, *The Object of Performance*

This essay was instigated by a press photograph. In the split second that it takes to turn the page of a newspaper, the mind's eye registers what seems to be a family photograph. The caption and accompanying article reveal, however, a complicated story of contemporary kinship. In considering how different kinds of photography are used to constitute kinship, I introduce some of the complexities of photographic seeing and knowing raised by the newspaper photograph; I pursue this issue by focusing on some of the sixty-two black-and-white photographic illustrations in Meyer Fortes's classic anthropological kinship studies *The Dynamics of Clanship among the Tallensi, Being the First Part of an Analysis of the Social Structure of a Trans-Volta Tribe* (1945) and *The Web of Kinship among the Tallensi* (1949). Finally, I discuss photographs that although invisible to the reader, work with the same forensic force as if they were there. Photographic images in prose are deeply embedded in the novel *Behind the Scenes at the Museum* (Atkinson 1995), where they are engaged in making, breaking, and reinventing an English family during the twentieth century. The "invisible" photographs work as a kind of reverse case against which to ground the other two.

The crosscurrents present in these various examples underscore the workings of what I consider to be the visual rhetoric of kinship. Cameras go with family life, as Susan Sontag (1977, 8) famously put it. She imagined families as making portrait chronicles of themselves—portable kits of images bearing witness to their connectedness. The content of these images was more or less immaterial, as long as photographs were taken and cherished. Sontag argued that photography became a family ritual at the very moment that the family was undergoing radical transformation in the industrializing countries of Europe and the United States. She saw the nuclear family as being carved out of much larger family aggregates, and understood photography as serving to memorialize, to restate symbolically, the fragile continuity and depleted extension of family life.

A quarter of a century on, Sontag's vision of photography as somehow reconstituting the reduced family seems less straightforward than when she wrote it. Recomposed families (see Segalen 1998), nuclear families (see Simpson 1994), and families we choose (see Weston 1997) are complex without being nostalgic (see Weston 1999). And a family portrait that seems to attest to the connectedness of an archetypal nuclear family may be much more complicated than it appears (see Spence and Holland 1991). Photographic seeing, Sontag contends, turns out to be mainly the practice of a dissociative kind of seeing: intense and cool, solicitous and detached (1977, 97–99). My argument is that family photography can also be *associative:* persuasive, rhetorical. While the act of photographing requires a degree of dissociation, it also involves making or unleashing connections between people: think of the wedding photograph (see Segalen 1972) or family albums (see Mavor 1997; Arrans 1998). Photographs are material objects (see Porto 2001), and both their taking and what happens to them once they have been printed are subject to conventions—such as the pose, consignment to or exclusion from the album, reproduction or destruction. Such conventions (making and showing albums, exchanging prints, consignment to drawers and boxes, mutilation or even destruction) bear comparison with the Schneiderian kinship code. David Schneider's (1968, 21–29) distinction between shared "biogenetic substance" (nature) and "code of conduct" (culture) in his study of American kinship suggests a distinction between photographs as a form of material culture and the ways people deploy and invest them with meaning, although the nature/culture dichotomy is not sustainable. But what of the substance of photography? In what sense do these material objects constitute a kinship substance (see Carsten, this volume)? And could Sarah Franklin's assertion that "new reproductive and genetic technology is increasingly seen as commensurate with the generative power of life itself" (1997, 211) be extended to an old reproductive technology such as (family) photography?

Family photography is constituted both by conventions of production (such as pose, camera angle, portraiture conventions) and consumption (what is in the eye of the beholder: interpretation, decoding). Furthermore, the way photography circulates as a material object or signifier is also shaped by established conventions of placement or display. The question is both how photographs circulate as a kind of substance that parallels other constitutive substances of kinship and how this is doubled by anthropology's conventions concerning what kinship "is" or "looks like." This raises a question about the ways in which family photographic conventions may appear in, and inform, anthropological representations of kinship.

This essay considers the way the family photograph, posed and unposed, unpacks in the three very different sources I bring together here: press photography, ethnographic plates, and a novel. And I will explore in a preliminary manner the links between the compositional conventions of family photography (vernacular and anthropological) and the diagrammatic representation of genealogical connection as they are used to make kinship.

WHAT A PICTURE!

The photograph in figure 3.1 shows the Italian gynecologist, Dr. Severino Antinori, holding "his" child Donalda aloft on the steps of the national monument in Amsterdam, together with Donalda's mother, Anita Blokziel. "Isn't it a picture?" quips the caption, rephrasing Blokziel's own rhetorical question originally referring to Donalda (Snoeijen 1997).

At one level, this photograph appears to be a perfect example of what Pierre Bourdieu called "barbarous taste" (1965), typical of family photographs, where the appeal of the image relies on charm and emotion rather than classical notions of "the beautiful." Yet the inverted commas around "his" in the photographic caption already announce that this family portrait may be more than it seems. Pride in the achievement of Donalda's assisted conception is evident: Antinori's gesture in putting the child on his shoulders is triumphant. Blokziel proudly clutches at his midriff. Donalda appears to

FIG. 3.1 The caption reads: "Dr. Severino Antinori visiting Amsterdam on the third birthday of 'his' child Donalda. Together with her 59-year-old mother at the Dam. 'Isn't it a picture?'" (Photo: Persbureau Peter Smulders, *NRC Handelsblad*, 31 May 1997).

be blissfully unaware of what she represents — the child that Dutch gynecologists said could never be. The fact that this is a professional press photograph, part of the publicity surrounding Blokziel as the oldest mother in the Netherlands and Antinori as the successful specialist (rather than the father), does not annul the genre to which it belongs. It could certainly go into the family album, celebrating as it does a high point of family life, but it is simultaneously public property circulating around the imagined communities of newspaper readers. Such a studied intimacy, designed for a wider audience, is reminiscent of the tradition of family portraiture going back to the Dutch Golden Age.

Henry Sayre (1989) contends that seventeenth-century Dutch family portraits were intended to elevate the bourgeois institution of marriage by placing it in a larger frame of reference. He refers to the public mask of decorum in Rembrandt's marriage portraits. Is there a public mask of decorum assumed in the Donalda portrait, too? The photograph evokes the familiar — placing it in the public, indeed national domain — in a way that is similar to seventeenth-century portraits that associated conjugality (virtue and moderation) with citizenship. It is worth looking more closely at the family portrait as a rhetorical device.

Sayre traces how these early bourgeois portraits, with their poise and self-assertion borrowed from Renaissance courts, gave way to the more casual and intimate portraiture of Jan Vermeer, and by the eighteenth century, the conversation piece. The depiction of the family in simple everyday surroundings helped to define the individuality of the patrons: "Their homes, their country-house, their place of work, or their form of recreation — for the first time were deemed worthy of inclusion in the family portrait" (Sayre 1989, 49). The democratization of the portrait through photography in the nineteenth century had the intriguing effect of reformalizing the pose (along the lines of the early Dutch portrait) among the newly enfranchised. Quietude and calm became associated with photographic decorum — as Alice Barker's portrait exemplifies in the third part of this essay.

A second look at Donalda's photograph brings some of its artifice to light: there is something about Blokziel's beringed left hand as it fingers Antinori's lapel that doesn't quite fit. It is an awkward gesture in its mimicry of intimacy. There is something about the way Antinori holds Donalda's right wrist — the limpness of her hand perhaps — to support her on his shoulders that is unrequited by her left hand, the forefingers of which, instead of grasping his hair for support, seek quizzically her own mouth in a gesture that is almost a question. Antinori's left hand, with its wedding and signet rings, encircles Blokziel's neck, but stiffly: the left forefinger is raised — as if pointing, thereby avoiding too close contact with Blokziel's hair and ear. Blokziel's right arm is probably by her side and not around the back of Antinori, thus hunching her back, and this is partly what gives the picture away.

But *what* does it give away? What is this image that it is not? Hoisting Donalda above the parents upends the conventional family group triangle — on some steps, for example, grandparents at the top, parents in the middle, cascading down to the grandchildren on the lower levels (compare Ripert and Frere-Michelat 1976) — and yet it continues to evoke ironically and provocatively something familiar. Backgrounding this portrait against the national monument in Amsterdam, site of sleep-ins and other protests during the 1960s, politicizes it, mocking (through this memorial to those who died during the German occupation of the Second World War) those now responsible for the nation's life (Dutch politicians and gynecologists). A *lieu de mémoire*, turned symbol of protest and the permissive society, makes a fitting backdrop for this sociolegal struggle. Indeed, hoisting a child up onto (usually) the father's shoulders is surely one of those triumphant gestures of parenthood (fatherhood?): look, this is mine, it seems to say. Fatherland would in this case, however, seem to be Italy rather than the Netherlands. Yet as Blokziel herself remarks in the newspaper article, she carried and bore Donalda after implantation with a fertilized egg (from an Italian woman who was "exactly my type," thereby reducing the alterity of the operation) in Antinori's clinic in Rome. Donalda, Blokziel asserts, is a "copy of herself." Donalda has her flesh and blood; Blokziel carried her. Blokziel minimizes the significance of "that tiny little egg" when set beside what disappears into Donalda's tummy: mother and daughter are drinking coffee and milk, respectively, in a café whilst being interviewed (Snoeijen 1997). In this way, Donalda is rendered emphatically Dutch, without denying the assistance of an enlightened Italian, and so the visible embodiment of complex contemporary Dutch life.

The interaction between painterly and photographic traditions of portraiture, on which Sontag (1977, 95) has remarked, is an important element of seeing all these complex threads when looking at Donalda's picture. In this respect, it is not too far-fetched to uncover a family resemblance between one of the most famous seventeenth-century court paintings and the Donalda photograph. Ernst Gombrich notes the photographic quality of Diego Rodríguez de Silva Velázquez's painting *Las Meninas,* or *Maids in Waiting* (1656) (see figure 3.2): "I like to fancy that Velázquez has arrested a real moment of time long before the invention of the camera" (1989, 323). Velázquez's main task at the court of Philip IV was to paint the portraits of the king and other members of the royal family.

The premonition of photography to which Gombrich refers is brilliantly developed in Michel Foucault's (1970) analysis of the visual system of *Las Meninas.* Foucault interprets this painting of the artist at work on a canvas that we cannot see depicting a subject we cannot see, in the presence of a princess with her entourage and a visitor, all of whom are looking at an invisible scene before them. He identifies the faint reflections in the mirror on the wall behind the figures as those of the sovereign and his wife, whose gaze coincides with what the artist saw as he painted the canvas, the scene before the sovereigns themselves and that available to the spectator. Foucault suggests that this painting contains the representation of classical representation, at the center of which there is "an essential void: the necessary disappearance of that which is its foundation — of the person it resembles and the person in whose eyes it

FIG. 3.2 Velázquez's *Las Meninas*. Madrid, Prado.

is only a resemblance" (1970, 16). The elision of the subject in this way frees representation from the relation that was impeding it so that it can "offer itself as representation in its pure form" (16). The painting can thus be interpreted as visualizing the transition from the classical to the modern episteme, and the collection of paintings on the walls behind pointing to the future "displacement, in the art gallery, of the king by the citizen as the archnarrator and metanarrator of a self-referring narrative" (Bennett 1995, 38).

Another way of looking at *Las Meninas* is as the premonition of a family portrait within a court scene. The Infanta Margarita forms, together with the reflections of the two sovereigns in the mirror, yet another geometric variation on those analyzed by Foucault. However weak this triangular form—for the Infanta Margarita occupies center stage—it is nonetheless there, at the heart of all the complex changes to sovereignty and citizenship of the seventeenth century.

Las Meninas has been compared with the Delft painter Vermeer's *Music Lesson* (see Blankert 1988, 124–26). The still-life quality of Vermeer's portraits from around the same time in the Netherlands are not so far from the scene at the court of the Spanish king as might at first be surmised. Vermeer's depiction of homely Dutch domesticity had its own staged quality. Like other

Delft painters, he was greatly preoccupied with the problem of creating spatial volume and perspective on a two-dimensional canvas, and may have used a camera obscura for establishing the perspectival vanishing point. Many of the props used in Vermeer's paintings (furniture, hangings, drapes, clothing) are borrowed from a richer social class (see his *The Art of Painting,* 1666–1667). The absence of children in Vermeer's paintings has led one art historian to hint at the repression of violent family circumstances in these images of perfection (see Montias 1988, 49). Vermeer married a Catholic, and they lived together with his mother-in-law and violent brother-in-law, who insulted his mother and attacked his sister when pregnant. Despite or perhaps because of these outbursts, Vermeer continued to paint a peaceful vision of the world. John Michael Montias suggests, however, that the three paintings of apparently pregnant women (*Woman Holding a Balance, Woman in Blue Reading a Letter,* and *Woman with a Pearl Necklace*—1662–1664) celebrated the serene dignity of the woman with child, unruffled by violence. This might mean that "the sidereal calm of Vermeer's painting may be viewed as an idealized transposition of an everyday reality that itself was sordid to a degree. Vermeer, who lived and worked surrounded by the tribe of his offspring, never places a child prominently in one of his pictures; perhaps that can be explained by a similar phenomenon of repression" (Montias 1988, 49).

Donalda's elevation onto the shoulders of the man who facilitated her birth to a mother beyond childbearing years inverts the usual order of the generations, which is faintly visible even in *Las Meninas.* The Infanta's seeming occupation of center stage in a world order (of absolute monarchy) that was about to collapse is indeed comparable to a photographic vision in a further constitutive sense to the one proposed by Gombrich. The painting makes visible the relations of kinship through a complex system of reflections and conventions, which are not simply given but have to be externally represented. The photograph of Donalda performs in our time a comparable operation. Donalda is constituted as the child of this unusual couple—who are not monarchs but citizens of modern states—against the unblinking backdrop of the national monument. It is the modern state system, with its idiosyncratic national stonewalling and loopholing, that constitutes in this portrait of Donalda an uncanny resemblance with the Infanta of another time and place. Certainly the new world, represented by the Dutch republic, involved its own sordid violence at the domestic level, which would in turn be excluded by a painterly tradition that immortalized coherent-looking groups (compare Sayre 1989, 51). The photographic solemnization of family groups continues

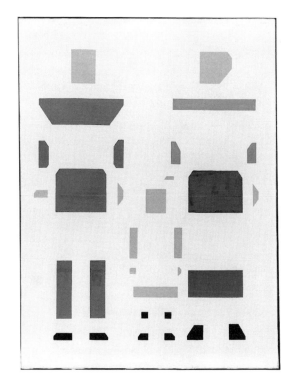

FIG. 3.3 Van der Leck's
Gezin. Kröller-Müller
Museum, Otterloo.

apace—as does popular genealogy.[1] This, then, suggests that disruption and
violence actually encourage people to cling to and/or (re)constitute what they
can in the way of tangible evidence of meaningful relations.[2]

Seen in this way, the break with the figurative tradition brought about
by abstraction in twentieth-century modern art and the democratization of
photography had much less impact on family portraiture than might have
been predicted (see Duncan 1995). The triangular shape found in Bart van der
Leck's 1921 painting, *Gezin (The Family)*, is an extreme example: the figures are
reduced to the simple shapes of primary colors associated with the artist Piet
Mondriaan and the De Stijl movement (see figure 3.3). It is, in fact, astonishing that a man, woman, and child—a girl—are discernible in these thirty-one
patches of color. The title is obviously crucial. Yet the clues are there: three yellow heads (which together form a triangle); whereas father's and daughter's
faces are depicted head-on, the mother's face is oriented toward the father
and child. The red (female) and blue (male) symbolism, the two vertical rect-
angles (man's trousers), and the horizontal red rectangle (woman's skirt; yellow horizontal rectangle for daughter's skirt) are among the other signs that

FIG. 3.4 Galán's *The Family*. Collection Stedelijk Museum, Amsterdam.

enable recognition of a family portrait. The mother touches her daughter's head with her yellow right hand while she looks at the father. It is yellow — in the shapes of the mother's right hand, the daughter's head, and the father's left hand (plus the other areas of yellow) — that subtly binds the three together. Not to mention the row of gray feet.

The point is that however simple it is to reveal the artifice of such family images, that is exactly their power. Even when the constituents do not seem to add up to a "biological family," they manage effortlessly to evoke one, while simultaneously adding a new dimension to the original form. The way abstraction introduced a new visual vocabulary, yet accomplished this by reworking recognizable forms, is a case in point. Mondriaan's treatment of both natural (trees, the sea) and architectural (a pier) forms is among the best-known examples (see below). While abstraction seemingly undoes recognizable forms, it at the same time testifies to their strength by restating them. This observation is not limited to abstract art.

The Mexican artist Julio Galán (born 1959) painted *The Family* in 1986 (see figure 3.4). Galán's work has been compared to that of the surrealists such as

René Magritte and Max Ernst, as well as to pop artists such as Andy Warhol (see Verlichak 1999). Galán often uses his own portrait in his work, and indeed his own face as a little boy is at the center of *The Family*. This painting bears the title *Familie*—meaning extended kin group, in Dutch, as distinct from the *gezin* (elementary or nuclear family) exemplified in van der Leck's painting. The family members here are different species, which serves to gender the figures. At the center of the painting is the artist as a child, with terrifying pinpoint eyes that seem to look within rather than out. Of the two parental figures, the dog contrives to be the father and the cat is the mother, using the facial characteristics of domestic species to differentiate parental roles in a way comparable to van der Leck's use of color, shape, and disposition. The bodies are apparently swathed like mummies: the child is individually swaddled; there is some ambiguity about the two adult animal figures' swaddling since their child obscures their connection (or separation). The swathes of material in which they are bound, which look like spaghetti bandages, allow for either interpretation. This group could, in one way, scarcely be further removed from van der Leck's family; yet it persuades the viewer that it *is* a family, by reworking the basic form. One significant difference rests with the ancestral figures who occupy the space normally taken up by the sky: the rear end of a dog (or horse?), whiskered humans in various states of undress (vaguely Greek in attire, one is strumming a lyre), and the forked lightning of the gods.

The animal heads could easily be masks, and Galán's use of this convention bears comparison with Ralph Meatyard's photographs in the *Family Album of Lucybelle Crater* (1974). Marianne Hirsch argues that this text succeeds in "laying bare and challenging the most obvious conventions and rituals of family photography," which she identifies "in the pretense of snapshot photography . . . maintained through the unvarying perspective and distance of the camera: the figures always face frontally, filling the frame. The poses are deliberate and naïve" (1997, 94). This is what Hirsch terms the "familial gaze": she claims that "in the context of the conventions of family-snapshot photography . . . we wear masks, fabricate ourselves, according to certain expectations and are fabricated by them" (98). This way of visually constituting kinship underlines what I referred to earlier as the associative or rhetorical aspect of family photography. We see what we have learned to see out of unfamiliar elements, as Donalda's portrait demonstrates. This suggests that it is not simply a question of *finding* ready-made families but also a matter of making them *appear*.

The kinship, connection, and shared substance in family photographs are narrative devices for unifying and making sense of situations that might otherwise remain alien. This is exactly what the family portrait of Donalda achieves. There is, of course, a commercial sense in which Blokziel and Antinori are bound together: the fees for her treatment at his clinic were waived because he understood very well that, if successful, the publicity she would provide would remunerate him many times over. He assists some one hundred Dutch couples annually at his clinic in Rome. They are also bound together in a symbolic sense against the Dutch gynecologists and Dutch state, which does not permit women beyond the age of forty to receive fertility treatments. The accompanying article is subtitled, "Those unable to fulfill their desire for children in the Netherlands, go over the border." Antinori is quoted as saying: "Italy is a liberal state that permits the use of advanced techniques *because they are beneficial to human beings*" (Snoeijen 1997).

So at one level, the pose can be interpreted as a rebellious gesture aimed at Dutch gynecologists, one of whom told Blokziel that she might as well chuck her money in the Amstel (river) as attempt to bear a child at her age. Her determination to go ahead (and Antinori's collusion) *despite* the advice of her local specialists was motivated by the death of Blokziel's (adult) son some ten years earlier. But there is a further moral dimension to this photograph: Blokziel now wants a sibling for Donalda and more free treatment (Snoeijen 1997). So looking into the camera's eye, she is somehow contemplating her own death, which will leave Donalda "alone." She is anticipating when she will become herself a memory for the viewer. She wants to provide for Donalda in mourning. The pose she adopts expresses something of her moral desperation. Although her head is turned toward the camera, her body is in a three-quarters pose: a variation on van der Leck's woman's posture. Her left hand, clutching at Antinori's lapel, is emphatic to a degree. He represents her only hope in a project that has produced this solitary child, whose elevation onto Antinori's shoulders accentuates the exceptional nature of her existence, defying, as it does, generational time and order. The exchange of looks in this contemporary portrait becomes as complex in its way as that in *Las Meninas*, analyzed by Foucault. And those who remain outside the frame (the murdered son, the Dutch state, Dutch gynecologists, the egg and sperm donors, the nursing staff) figure a scene as complex as the violent family relations encircling Vermeer.

What will Donalda see forty years from now when she looks into her mother's eyes? The memory of her dead brother? The prememory of a not-yet-living sibling? Or will her gaze be motivated by a search for her "real" mother and father in Italy? The photograph mimics the biological family while actually depicting highly complex commercial, technical, and emotional ties, plus an added desire. The translation of relational complexity into visual simplicity captures the essence of the journey required to reach this achievement of maternity. The lengths to which people will go to achieve this "natural" state of affairs are extraordinary: one Dutch specialist is quoted as saying that would-be parents would allow themselves to be rocketed to the moon if they thought that that would deliver them a child (see Snoeijen 1997; compare Franklin 1997).

The preliminary analysis of this single photograph of Donalda provides insight on the complexity of the genre: the conventions that link it to art history and family portraiture as a rhetorical device. Given the contemporary ubiquity—indeed imperatives—of family photography, could it be that the new reproductive technologies are partially designed to meet the imperatives of old reproductive technologies?

THE EFFECTIVE MINIMAL LINEAGE

Once upon a time, Robin Fox's classic *Kinship and Marriage* could assume that middle-class England was a "relatively 'kinshipless' society" (1967, 14). Paradoxically, the study of kinship elsewhere became a central component of British twentieth-century anthropology: "Kinship is to anthropology what logic is to philosophy or the nude is to art" (Fox 1967, 10). The comparison with the nude in art is particularly apposite for the present discussion. Visual representation of kinship relations in the form of genealogical diagrams was central to the way kinship came to be construed as synonymous with "the basic facts of life . . . 'birth, and copulation, and death'" (Fox 1967, 27). The extraordinary power of genealogical diagrams lay in their way of showing kinship relations, of illustrating (making visible) how persons are related to one another. And as representations, genealogical diagrams were part of a dual process to which Howard Morphy (1994, 666) refers: the representation partly constituting the object it represents. The objectification of relations in genealogical form is seen as evidence of being related. In the case of kinship, this meant prioritizing procreative relations and, more particularly, "seeding," at the expense of all the hard work of kinship that goes on after the event ("feeding"; see Carsten 1995). Lives were assumed to follow the substance that genealogies reified.

The cultural-historical form to which kinship theorists had recourse was the family tree, which had been deployed to represent relations through historical, biblical, and geological time. Once an aristocratic prerogative, the family tree has by now been democratized as a commodity item. But it was also engaged in nineteenth-century phylogenetic trees, such as Ernst Haeckel's or Charles Darwin's, enabling one to visualize the connectedness between all forms of life. Before this, trees of Jesse depicted the earthly ancestry of Christ (see Bouquet 1996).

The moment that the genealogical diagram entered the anthropological instrumentarium, during the second decade of the twentieth century, coincided with the transition from figuration to abstraction in Western art. Carol Duncan contends that the "pursuit of abstraction . . . becomes the supreme sign of an artist's liberation from the mundane and commonplace" (1995, 108–9). This transition is exemplified in the passage from Mondriaan's still recognizable *Trees Along the River Gein* (1907–1908), through the cubistic *Gray Appletree* (1912) and *Flowering Appletree* (1912), to the abstract compositions dating from 1914 onward (see Blotkamp 1994). Abstraction, for Mondriaan, involved a long search for a deeper reality behind the appearances of things, which he expressed especially through the use of interdependent horizontal and vertical lines.

W. H. R. Rivers's formalization of the genealogical method, which included visualization in diagrammatic form, took even longer than the evolution of Mondriaan's abstraction. First developed during the Torres Strait Expedition of 1898, and later among the Todas, Rivers formalized what he saw as a scientific method in a 1910 paper. The genealogical diagram can be tracked not only in the well-known ethnographies produced until midcentury—by Raymond Firth ([1936] 1983), Meyer Fortes (1945), E. E. Evans-Pritchard (1940), and Edmund Leach (1961)—but also *after* that (see Bouquet 1993, 51–93). A description of the kinship system became a routinized part of competent ethnographic fieldwork from the 1960s. The "unconscious optics" of the genealogical diagram—essentializing and purifying kinship relations to the horizontal lines of generation and the vertical lines of descent, intersecting in the procreative union—were fundamental in constituting kinship as an anthropological field.

Ethnographic photographs were sometimes used in tandem with genealogical diagrams, apparently testifying to empirical reality and thereby substantiating abstract theory. Fortes combined the diagram, in its supposed abstraction, with the photograph, in its supposed indexicality, in his ethnographic account of Tallensi kinship. The question is, To what effect? Fortes

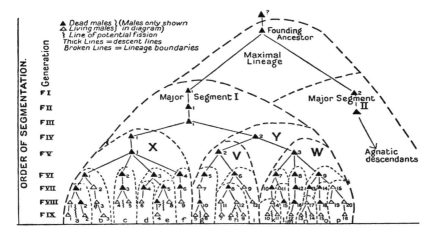

FIG. 3.5 "Diagram Illustrating the Paradigm of the Lineage System" from Meyer Fortes, *The Dynamics of Clanship among the Tallensi, Being the First Part of an Analysis of the Social Structure of a Trans-Volta Tribe* (London: Oxford University Press, 1945), 34. Reproduced with permission of the Fortes estate.

reproduces his "Diagram Illustrating the Paradigm of the Lineage System" (see figure 3.5) from page 34 of *The Dynamics of Clanship among the Tallensi* (1945) and again on page 8 of *The Web of Kinship among the Tallensi* (1949). Both volumes contain thirty-one black-and-white photographs, and in each case they come at the end—when the ethnography, analysis, and theoretical part of the work are complete. Photographs therefore seem to illustrate what is already known. And this is particularly striking in the photograph with the caption, "The effective minimal lineage" (1949, plate 12a; see figure 3.6). The paradigm, which shows males only, suddenly becomes an empirically documented reality at the level of the effective minimal lineage. We see what we are told we are being shown.

Fortes's photography may be comparable to that of Rivers, who according to Paul Hockings (1992), staged many of the Toda photographs to suggest a parallel between the priests of Nemi (familiar to Rivers as they were to all British anthropologists of the time) and those of the Todas. The issue is not raised in *Anthropology and Photography* (Edwards 1992), which stops at 1920, almost as if modern ethnographic photography left such setups behind after fieldwork became established empirical practice in the 1920s. Marcus Banks and Howard Morphy (1997) allege, however, that photography missed out on the "fieldwork revolution" partly because of its association with evolutionary theorists, for whom it was an important technique. So although photographs were certainly used to illustrate post-1920 monographs, there was little comment on their use beyond the *Notes and Queries on Anthropology*'s (British Association 1929) instructions about taking photographs.

Or is it an issue of framing? Of seeing what we expect to see, and in this respect, a question of the familial gaze in action? The photographs in figures 3.7 and 3.8 complicate the apparently illustrative fit between the effective minimal lineage and the dynamics of clanship. It is instructive to compare the photographs of the effective minimal lineage (see figure 3.6) and the domestic family party (see figure 3.7). While the caption for the latter refers to a "homestead in the background," the caption for the former invokes more abstractly being "out on the farm for the day." The unconscious optics at work in these backgrounds are not trivial—as the analysis of the Donalda photograph showed. Fortes has to persuade us that agnatic ties are decisive beyond the domestic domain; unlike the domestic family party, the effective minimal lineage is not visibly tied to any homestead. Yet his own ethnography is

FIG. 3.6 "The effective minimal lineage" from Meyer Fortes, *The Web of Kinship among the Tallensi* (London: Oxford University Press, 1949), plate 12a. Reproduced with permission of the Fortes estate.

FIG. 3.7 "The domestic family is the matrix of kinship" (Fortes 1949, plate 2a).
Reproduced with permission of the Fortes estate.

against him for, as he says, the uterine line can be thought of as "traveling" from clan to clan with the generations; and uterine kinship enabled people to travel outside their normal range of contacts and so build up social relations with members of clans usually inaccessible to their own clanspeople (Fortes 1949). These observations make the argument about the "centrifugal, sundering force of matrilateral kinship" one-sided, to say the least. The plates should convince one of the empirical veracity of Fortes's analytical distinction between lineage "dynamics" and kinship "webs." Fortes (1949, 9) reports that the effective minimal lineage forms the basis of a domestic family, which usually constitutes a single unit of food production and consumption:

> The domestic family is the matrix of all the genealogical ties of the individual, the contemporary mechanism for ever spinning new threads of kinship, and the focal field of new social relations based on consanguinity. In it we can observe the working of the nuclear patterns of kinship and the formation of the ideas and values which steer the individual in all his genealogical relationships. In the domestic family we get the sharpest picture of the interaction between cognatic kinship and agnatic or lineage ties. We have there the elementary ties of cognatic kinship linking parent to child and sibling to sibling, and we also have the agnatic tie which

FIG. 3.8 "Kinship patterns are not specific in public etiquette or domestic intercourse" (Fortes 1949, plate 10a). Reproduced with permission of the Fortes estate.

sets apart males as the nucleus of the lineage. We can see the centrifugal, sundering force of matrilateral kinship counterbalancing the centripetal, uniting pull of patrimony. In the context of family life we can see the play of conflict and compromise in the working out of the primary equilibrium of Tale social organisation, due to the interaction of these two sectors of social life. (14–15)

The reference to "the sharpest picture" and the inclusiveness of "we can see" in this passage invite the reader to look at the photographs as evidence of what is, in fact, an abstract assertion about social organization. Fortes refers to the ambivalence of intrafamilial, weblike kinship (being both cognatic and agnatic), which he contrasts with the solidarity of extrafamilial, dynamic lineage bonds. But what makes the minimal lineage "effective"? It does not look particularly productive. Why is the family party the matrix of kinship, when it is so clearly also an effective production unit? It is the way these photographs are framed and captioned, combined with what is already known from the text (including the diagram of the paradigm), that turns them into evidence for a theory.

The caption to figure 3.8, "An unposed group having a rest in the middle of the day," is also striking. Does the reference to "unposed" mean that other photos, such as "the effective minimal lineage" and "the domestic family is the matrix of kinship" were posed? For if they were, this would certainly suggest that still photography had a much more constitutive role in midcentury anthropological theory than has been acknowledged to date.

These examples have been used to scrutinize how photographs combined with genealogical(-type) diagrams *constituted kinship* in a highly specific sense (domestic, nonpolitical). I maintain that just as Rivers democratized pedigree and at the same time turned it into a scientific tool for studying others' kinship, so the democratization of photography (the production of the first cheap modern camera by Kodak in 1888 is the usual benchmark) had profound implications for the conduct of participant observation. The combination of these two visual techniques, from apparently opposite ends of the spectrum of figuration and abstraction, were in fact powerful constituents of vision — both in the field and the text — and hence of kinship.

Fortes would have read in the 1929 edition of *Notes and Queries* that portraits are the most important anthropological pictures and that group shots were to be avoided as far as possible (British Association 1929, 376). Clearly, Fortes did not follow this advice, and (some of) his pictures are of artistic as well as scientific interest (see British Association 1929, 375). One of the few pictures where the subject looks really unhappy and uncomfortable is a portrait of a mother and child (Fortes 1949, plate 1), bearing the caption, "The relationship of mother and child is the root of the uterine (*soog*) tie" (see figure 3.9). As the comment on the unposed group suggests, and many of the photographs demonstrate, Fortes was sensitive to composition. Was he then following implicit practices of family photography rather than the (already outdated) prescriptions of *Notes and Queries*? As J. David Sapir has observed, "Fieldwork . . . falls into the category of experience that, as Bourdieu shows, calls for photographs to 'solemniz[e] and immortalize the high points of family life,' where the family extends out to the community of fieldwork" (1994, 882).

Posed groups, engaged in all kinds of mundane tasks or dignified in court style, were and are both options within family portraiture (as discussed in the first section). The deliberately unposed group (see figure 3.8) does not look like a family photograph in the easily identifiable style of Donalda's group. The caption explains: "Kinship patterns are not specific in public etiquette or domestic intercourse." This seems to mean, "Don't expect a family photo-

FIG. 3.9 One of the few portraits in *The Web of Kinship* (Fortes 1949, plate 1). Reproduced with permission of the Fortes estate.

graph, even though the domestic family is the matrix of kinship." This unspecifiable web, which starts out from the relationship depicted in that unhappy-looking portrait of an anonymous naked mother and child, contrasts sharply with the dignified portrait of "Na Naam Bion, Chief of Tongo (d. 1941), wearing his red fez (*mun*) the chief emblem of his office, and clad in his finest ceremonial robes" (Fortes 1945, plate 16; see figure 3.10).

The placing of these two striking portraits—the chief as the last plate in *The Dynamics of Clanship,* and the mother and child as the first plate of *The Web of Kinship*—cannot be accidental. The camera angle in the case of the chief is from below, enhancing the bearing and stature of the figure against the sky; the mother and child sitting on the ground, by contrast, are taken from above. What better way of imaging the hierarchical relation between the public domain of men (and the lineage) and the domestic domain of women (and kinship)?

James Faris asks, "What . . . are the rhetorics of the Western photographic

FIG. 3.10 Another portrait from *The Dynamics of Clanship* (Fortes 1945, plate 16). Reproduced with permission of the Fortes estate.

projects, the figures that allow us to recognize master portrayals that forecast, that indicate something of the optical unconscious?" (1996, 19). He argues that these projects are quite limited in number, with the same gestures reappearing across time. Fortes clearly drew on a genre of photography to substantiate his analysis. While this was a completely logical step on his part, the way that these photographs seem to pass unnoticed into the ethnography is of considerable interest for the present discussion.

Photography has never been a neutral or objective technology in anthropological studies, as many have noted (see Edwards 1992). My proposal is that photography stands in the same sort of relation to its cultural origins as does the genealogical method. The genealogical diagram freezes procreative relationships, prioritizing conception as the decisive moment of kinship and marriage as its main conduit. The photograph frames its object, cutting out all that goes into constituting the frame. The photographic surface *looks* natural enough, certainly when compared with the genealogical diagram, where complex reality seems to be abstracted to its finest and most elegant form. In fact, poses, backgrounds, and conventions make photographic coherence as contrived as any diagram. When harnessed together by their captions, the two ostensibly different forms supply, especially in the case of photographs, meaning for images that might otherwise work against the text.

The ethnographic kinship photograph finds its source of inspiration in the family photograph. Yannick Geffroy indeed sees the family photographers he studied in southern France as "the first visual anthropologists of family photography" (1990, 407). Is seeing anthropologists as extending the range of the family lens (compare Sapir 1994) perhaps the other side of the coin? Considering how often anthropologists have been adopted by the people they study, this is not so surprising. One could scarcely wish for better evidence of how kinship categories and practices could absorb even foreign bodies such as these than in the photographs they took. In taking their subjects' photographs, anthropologists were also engaged in making kinship. The practice of providing people with prints of themselves as gifts has entered the folk wisdom of anthropological reciprocity toward "the field." The generative, kinshiplike quality of photography becomes extremely convoluted when, as a fieldwork technique, it yields still photographs purporting to depict kinship.[3]

Various kinds of kinship, then, are made to materialize through the visual techniques and conventions of family portraiture. Quite a limited set of formal conventions — such as the triangular shape, perspective and distance from the viewer, and frontal pose — constituted not only familiar family groups but also quite *un*familiar ones, such as Donalda's. These conventions were recycled in works of twentieth-century art as diverse as those of van der Leck, Galán, and Meatyard. Figurative (photographic) conventions were used together with abstract genealogical diagrams to visualize scientific theories of kinship elsewhere. The combination of abstract diagrams and photographic plates made a powerful visual case for notions developed in the text. This example demonstrates the unacknowledged centrality of often quite implicit visual techniques in making anthropological kinship.

THE REAL GREAT-GRANDMOTHER

The power of the visual techniques I have discussed can be further elaborated in a literary text, from which family photographs, although physically absent, are repeatedly conjured up. One way of describing *Behind the Scenes at the Museum* (Atkinson 1995) would be as a fictional portrait of an English family during the twentieth century. Much of the narrative is held together by the trajectories of a set of photographs of a mother and her children, taken by a traveling professional photographer toward the end of the nineteenth century. The first photograph is introduced quite early in the book when Ruby Lennox first sees a portrait of her great-grandmother, brought home by Bunty—her mother—on the death of her Uncle Tom. This photograph is later contrasted with another in distinguishing who is the "real" mother and "true" bride:

> The photograph is in a silver frame, padded with red velvet with an oval of glass in the middle from behind which my great-grandmother regards the world with an ambiguous expression.
>
> She stands very straight, one wedding-ringed hand resting on the back of a *chaise-longue.* In the background is the typical studio backdrop of the time, in which a hazy Mediterranean landscape of hills drops away from the *trompe-l'oeil* balustraded staircase which occupies the foreground. My great-grandmother's hair is parted in the middle and worn in a crown of plaits around her head. Her high-necked, satin dress has a bodice that looks as trimmed and stuffed as a cushion. She wears a small locket at her throat and her lips are half-open in a way that suggests she's waiting for something to happen. Her head is tilted slightly backwards but she is staring straight at the camera (or the photographer). In the photograph her eyes look dark and the expression in them is unfathomable. She seems to be on the point of saying something, although what it could be I can't possibly imagine. (Atkinson 1995, 27)

Ruby is surprised because the woman in the photograph seems to have changed a lot: "She's ugly and fat in that photograph you've got—the one taken in the back yard at Lowther Street with all the family" (28). This brings forth a second photograph:

> This was a photograph Bunty had with '1914, Lowther Street' written on the back in watery-blue ink and it shows my great-grandmother with her whole family gathered around her. She sits, big and square, in the middle of a wooden bench and on one side of her sits Nell (Bunty's mother), and on the other is Lillian (Nell's sister). Standing behind them is Tom and squatting on the ground at Rachel's feet is the youngest brother, Albert. The sun is shining and there are flowers growing on the wall behind them. (28)

Bunty dismisses the identity of the two women, explaining that the woman in the Lowther Street photograph is Rachel — "their step-mother, not their *real* mother. She was a cousin, or something" (28).

Two photographic images suddenly testify to the distinction between the "real" great-grandmother, Alice, and the "unreal" Rachel. What is extraordinary about this watershed are the indexical terms in which it is made: posed, silver-framed Alice is designated as real, while Rachel — surrounded by her whole family on a loose print — is unreal. Author Kate Atkinson subsequently deconstructs this indexicality by telling the stories of how these images were made and trafficked from the perspectives of several different protagonists.

She first zooms in on the very afternoon that Alice's photograph was taken, introducing the traveling photographer, Monsieur Jean-Paul Armand, and describing the way the portrait was set up. She evokes the photographer as a magician, transporting his strange props — the collapsible Mediterranean backcloth, the ornate brass pot holding a palm with stiffened cotton leaves, the velvet drapes, the extraordinary camera — in his cart (36–37). This is a brilliant variation on the encounter between the rural and modern urban cultures analyzed by Geffroy (1990, 379 ff.). Alice herself was born into an urban middle-class family that went down in the world, becoming a teacher in a village school and marrying a local farmer. She was horrified by the way her children grew up rough and wild in the country. Enter Armand, who persuades Alice to allow him to take their photographs: they are smartened up and photographed in various combinations: Ada with Albert; Albert, Tom, and Lawrence together; Ada with baby Lillian; and so on (Atkinson 1995, 37).

Alice herself squeezed her several months' pregnant figure into her best dress and did up her hair for her portrait. The combination of hot weather and the time taken by the photographer perspiring under his black cloth may have been responsible for the enigmatic expression on Alice's face. Armand, however, is taken by this "unexpected rural Madonna" (46), and resolves to run away with her when he returns with the photographs: Alice is consigned to eternity with a flash, an explosion of chemicals, to Armand's satisfaction — "Lovely!" he purrs in the parlance of photographers down the ages (46).

The other photograph, of the unreal great-grandmother Rachel with the children Alice had abandoned for Armand, was taken sixteen years later in 1914. It was Tom's idea to take the "whole family together" (53), perhaps with the premonition that this would be for the last time. A keen amateur photographer friend came by one sunny afternoon and posed them all in the backyard at Lowther Street (53–54).

Much later in the novel, the reader returns to Rachel putting Armand's framed photographs of the children on the mantelpiece on either side of a clock. The children never looked at them, reminders as they were of the last time they ever saw their mother. The unframed prints were put into a drawer. Tom, however, had discovered — and purloined — the two framed portraits of their mother left behind on the kitchen table. When he finally lets them in on his secret, "the three oldest children exclaim[ed] over the photograph of Alice — the beautiful (albeit ambiguous) expression on their missing mother's face and the plush extravagance of the silver and red velvet frame" (132). The photograph resurfaces in Tom's adult life, and he confides to Mabel — his new young wife — about his childhood in the Dales and how awful he felt when his mother died. Mabel takes care of the photograph throughout their married life, sighing as she dusts, "'Poor woman,' which, if Tom happened to overhear, gave him a funny tight feeling in his throat" (220).

Tom's sister Lillian meanwhile emigrates to Canada, where she marries Pete Donner, with whom she has a son, Edmund, who marries Tina. Now an old woman, Lillian invites Tina (who lives close, and of whom she is very fond) over one day to give her the photograph of her dead siblings. It is an emotional moment since Tina realizes that "Lillian wasn't kidding when she said she was going to die" (312). This complex photographic transaction, far removed in time and space from the one between Alice and Armand, underlines the generative rather than the staying power of family photographs in making kinship.

But what of Alice, her photographer, and the photographs of her children? Toward the end of the novel, the reader learns what happened when Armand returned with the photographs. Three were framed. The one of the pouting Alice, which was the photographer's (and as we have seen, also Tom's) personal favorite, was in the most expensive frame. Alice herself prefers the portraits of her children, struck by how much more attractive they appear frozen into immobile poses (339). After their elopement, she persuades Armand to print a new set, placed in "expensive tooled-leather travelling frames that closed securely, enabling Alice to hug her children — fixed for ever in time — to and fro across the continent" (345). Alice dies in 1940, tragically surrounded by her photographs and a collection of plaster saints. Yet the kinship consequences of her action on those she thought to leave behind extended, as we have seen, far beyond the photographic memories that accompanied her own literal demise. Atkinson neatly weds photographic with genealogical kinship manufacture in the unlikely person of Ruby's sister, Patricia, who (after running away from home and settling in Australia) is the one to commission a family tree — "a huge chaotic arboretum," causing her to correspond with "sawn-off branches" (381). Visits are arranged, reuniting relatives who have never met, and using as currency the photographic prints of common ancestors stemming from Alice's misdemeanor.

Atkinson's explorations of the meanings of death and kinship through photography leave little doubt about how this old reproductive technology has intervened in family life since at least 1898. The fact that these are textual photographs attests to how deeply photographic vision has penetrated family life. And the fact that it would be quite redundant to show "real" photographs says a great deal about the visual imagination of readers. The author — clearly correctly — assumes that readers can "see" the images in their mind's eye: readers are on such intimate terms with the substance and code of family photography that it seems to have colonized language itself, becoming indissociable from what is thought of as the very fiber of kinship. Ruby's assertion that "words are the only things that can construct a world that makes sense" (382), neglects the intervening power of photographic images. Where would the family arboretum (that includes Armand and a host of others) be without those absent images? Such a family tree would be something like Fortes's diagrams and ethnography without his photographic plates.

KINSHIP WITH PHOTOGRAPHY

Atkinson's novel reveals photographic reproduction as a powerful means of establishing and cutting genealogical relationship. So powerful indeed that Armand is granted a place in the family tree — recognizing a decisive intervention in his subjects' worlds. Armand bears comparison, in this respect, with Antinori: photographer and specialist are both implicated — albeit differently — in photographic magic. Photographs were decisive in Ruby's identification of the unknown Alice as her real great-grandmother and the familiar Rachel as an impostor. The sleekly framed portrait of a pouting woman with an enigmatic expression and the rumor of a romantic "death" was a more attractive proposition than the print of Rachel, struggling with the tribe of children Alice had abandoned. Armand's photographs of these children were, in their turn, so much more attractive to Alice — before and after her elopement — than the children themselves, becoming indeed her children as she entered solitary old age. The original set of photographs that was left behind with the children get scattered around the world, becoming one of the technically assisted substances they use to make contact, to make kinship, with one another.

As both Donalda's and Alice's portraits reveal, however, photographic evidence may not be quite what it seems — and not only in newspaper accounts and novels. Fortes's photograph of the "effective minimal lineage" or his portrait of mother and child demonstrate how anthropological intervention with the camera also created images that are as staged and complex as those of Donalda and Alice. Family photographic vision, harnessed to the project of mid-twentieth-century anthropological studies of kinship, created a persuasive vision of kinship "rooted" in a "matrix" that fell outside the "paradigm of the lineage system." The interpolation of photographic *evidence* of the genealogical ties that count and those that may be discounted is telling. It exposes the store that is set by what are taken to be the visual traces of a relation, posed or unposed, that somehow *become* part of that relation. The way photographs *somehow become* the relations that are cherished or neglected (see Mavor 1997; Hirsch 1997; Geffroy 1990), finds an analogue in the selection and arrangement processes of anthropological photography during that fascinating period after the 1920s, when the subject matter purportedly changed from "an observable world to the more abstract notions of social structure" (Sapir 1994, 869).

Donalda's photograph, Fortes's plates, and Atkinson's evocation of photographs share, despite differences in their respective functional contexts, properties that are simultaneously and mutually constitutive. The photographic instant viewed as some kind of truthful capture of a moment echoes the procreative moment viewed as some sort of definitive moment of kinship. The attraction of still photography resembles the moment of birth as one of revelation. The lives that people and prints lead after their respective "explosions of chemicals" are so complex and tangled, so substantial, that the photographic possibility of referring back to still, intelligible images is a coveted one. The substantial codes of kinship must therefore include photographic images, which render particular relations and groups visible through the kinds of conventions that have been discussed.

Recent studies of kinship have devoted much attention to the new reproductive technologies without considering how old reproductive technologies, such as photography, might articulate with the desire for children. This essay has explored how the conventions of family photography corset very differently constituted relations into recognizable forms. Starting from an analysis of a single photograph involving the new reproductive technologies, family photography can be connected to earlier forms of family portraiture (see Bouquet 2000). Even when twentieth-century art abandoned the project of trying to create spatial volume and perspective on two-dimensional surfaces, abstract artists such as Mondriaan stripped the appearances of trees, family groups, and piers back to their "essence," reworking visual conventions in experiments with line and color. There is a historical coincidence between abstraction in art and scientific visualization of abstract relations, such as the genealogical diagram, in anthropology. Nonetheless, this was the end of neither figurative art nor illustrative plates in ethnographies: just as abstract art gains by juxtaposition with selected figurative works in art galleries (see Duncan 1995, 111 ff.), so does abstract argument and diagrammatic representation benefit from "illustrative" plates.

Photographic imagery, by contrast, permeates the language in which *Behind the Scenes at the Museum* (Atkinson 1995) is written to such a degree that Foucault's (1970, 44) assertion about literature compensating for the signifying function of language in the modern age, seems to overlook the intervening role of photography in language and literature. This neglect is similar to that of anthropologists, who appear to have ignored the doubly constitutive role of photography in their ethnographic studies of kinship. For if kinship came to be significantly constituted through camera lenses during the twentieth century, then anthropologists have been active participant-observers in this process. The pervasiveness of family photography—whether in a rapidly leafed newspaper, a closely read kinship classic, or a novel meant for distraction— suggests an extremely rich source for exploration in future studies.

NOTES

I am indebted to Sarah Franklin and Susan McKinnon for their invitation to take part in the Wenner-Gren symposium held in Mallorca, March/April 1998, and their continuing encouragement and help while rewriting this essay. Grateful thanks to Rayna Rapp for her stimulating discussion of the Mallorca version; and to Gillian Feeley-Harnik, Kath Weston, Martine Segalen, and Nuno Porto for providing me with further literature.

1 There are hundreds of stories attesting to the contemporary explosion of interest in popular genealogy. Two recent examples include a cover story, "How to Search for Your Roots," that graced the 19 April 1999 issue of *Time* magazine. A subtitle explained, "Genealogy is America's Latest Obsession. And Thanks to the Computer, It's As Easy As One, Two . . . Tree!" Inside there were pieces on "Roots Mania" (Hornblower 1999), "How to Map Your Heritage" (Prato 1999), "A Visit to the National

Archives, the American People's Library" (Mitchell 1999), and "How to Program Your Family History" (Jackson 1999). A similar story, although more soberly presented, appeared in the Dutch *NRC Handelsblad* in 1998 under the title, "Searching for Roots Together" (Bergeijk 1998).

2 Reports during the 1999 war in Kosovo substantiate this assertion. Both the confiscation of photographs by Serbian troops from Kosovan refugees as they were driven out of Kosovo and smuggled videos (such as the one shown on the BBC nine o'clock news, 27 May 1999) show not only ethnic cleansing but also the remains of another, normal life. It was the fleeting glimpse of a birthday party, rather than the filmed ordeal of their escape, that reduced two Kosovan sisters to tears as they viewed their video together with the BBC correspondent in a refugee camp.

Stories of the dead and the photographs they leave behind them, such as Vivien Butler's "I Remember Mama" in the *Washington Post* (3 May 1999), indicate the enormous emotional cargo of these images of order and stability.

3 Fortes does not state in either of these two books who the photographer was. He does dedicate *The Web of Kinship* (1949) to "My wife and fellow-worker Sonia L. Fortes," and certainly she seems likely to have taken at least plate 3a, "Elders of a Maximal Lineage assemble to sacrifice to their Founder" (Fortes 1945), where Fortes himself appears to be seated on a chair at the back watching the proceedings.

REFERENCES

Arrans, Frank. 1998. The Memory Keepers: Women Gather to Create Family Albums and Friendships. *Washington Post,* 22 July, D11.

Atkinson, Kate. 1995. *Behind the Scenes at the Museum.* London: Transworld Publishers.

Banks, Marcus, and Howard Morphy, eds. 1997. *Rethinking Visual Anthropology.* New Haven, Conn.: Yale University Press.

Bennett, Tony. 1995. *The Birth of the Museum: History, Theory, Politics.* London: Routledge.

Bergeijk, Jeroen van. 1998. Samen op zoek naar wortels. *NRC Handelsblad,* 12 August.

Blankert, Albert. 1988. Vermeer's Work. In *Vermeer,* edited by Albert Blankert, John Michael Montias, and Gilles Aillaud. New York: Rizzoli.

Blotkamp, Carel. 1994. *Mondriaan: Destructie als Kunst.* Zwolle, Netherlands: Waanders Uitgevers.

Bouquet, Mary. 1993. *Reclaiming English Kinship: Portuguese Refractions of British Kinship Theory.* Manchester: Manchester University Press.

———. 1996. Family Trees and Their Affinities: The Visual Imperative of the Genealogical Diagram. *Journal of the Royal Anthropological Institute* 2, no. 1:43–66.

———. 2000. The Family Photographic Condition. *Visual Anthropology Review* 16, no. 1:2–19.

Bourdieu, Pierre. 1965. *Un art moyen: Essai sur la photographie.* Paris: Editions de Minuit.

British Association for the Advancement of Science, ed. 1929. *Notes and Queries on Anthropology.* London: Royal Anthropological Institute.

Carsten, Janet. 1995. The Substance of Kinship and the Heat of the Hearth: Feeding, Personhood, and Relatedness among Malays in Pulau Langkawi. *American Ethnologist* 22, no. 2:223–41.

Duncan, Carol. 1995. *Civilizing Rituals: Inside Public Art Museums.* London: Routledge.

Edwards, Elizabeth. 1992. Introduction to *Anthropology and Photography, 1860–1920,* edited by Elizabeth Edwards. New Haven, Conn.: Yale University Press.

Evans-Pritchard, Edward Evans. 1940. *The Nuer: A Description of the Modes of Livelihood and Political Institutions of a Nilotic People.* Oxford: Oxford University Press.

Faris, James. 1996. *Navajo and Photography: A Critical History of the Representation of an American People.* Albuquerque: University of New Mexico Press.

Firth, Raymond. [1936] 1983. *We, the Tikopia: A Sociological Study of Kinship in Primitive Polynesia.* Reprint, Stanford, Calif.: Stanford University Press.

Fortes, Meyer. 1945. *The Dynamics of Clanship among the Tallensi, Being the First Part of an Analysis of the Social Structure of a Trans-Volta Tribe.* London: Oxford University Press.

———. 1949. *The Web of Kinship among the Tallensi.* London: Oxford University Press.

Foucault, Michel. 1970. *The Order of Things: An Archaeology of the Human Sciences.* London: Tavistock Publications.

Fox, Robin. 1967. *Kinship and Marriage: An Anthropological Perspective.* Harmondsworth, U.K.: Penguin.

Franklin, Sarah. 1997. *Embodied Progress: A Cultural Account of Assisted Conception.* London: Routledge.

Geffroy, Yannick. 1990. Family Photographs: A Visual Heritage. *Visual Anthropology* 3:367–409.

Gombrich, Ernst H. 1989. *The Story of Art.* London: Phaidon.

Hirsch, Marianne. 1997. *Family Frames: Photography, Narrative, and Postmemory.* Cambridge: Harvard University Press.

Hockings, Paul. 1992. The Yellow Bough: Rivers's Use of Photography in *The Todas.* In *Anthropology and Photography, 1860–1920,* edited by Elizabeth Edwards. New Haven, Conn.: Yale University Press.

Hornblower, Margot. 1999. Roots Mania. *Time,* 19 April, 55–59.

Jackson, David. 1999. How to Program Your Family History. *Time,* 19 April, 58–59.

Leach, Edmund. 1961. *Pul Eliya, a Village in Ceylon: A Study of Land Tenure and Kinship.* Cambridge: Cambridge University Press.

Mavor, Carol. 1997. Collecting Loss. *Cultural Studies* 11, no. 1:111–37.

Mitchell, Emily. 1999. A Visit to the National Archives, the American People's Library. *Time,* 19 April, 67.

Montias, John Michael. 1988. Chronicle of a Delft Family. In *Vermeer,* edited by Albert Blankert, John Michael Montias, and Gilles Aillaud. New York: Rizzoli.

Morphy, Howard. 1994. The Anthropology of Art. In *Companion Encyclopedia of Anthropology,* edited by Tim Ingold. London: Routledge.

Porto, Nuno. 2001. Picturing the Museum: Photography and the Work of Mediation in the Third Portuguese Empire. In *Academic Anthropology and the Museum: Back to the Future,* edited by Mary Bouquet. Oxford: Berghahn Books.

Prato, Rodica. 1999. How to Map Your Heritage. *Time,* 19 April, 63–65.

Ripert, Aline, and Claude Frere-Michelat. 1976. Images corporelles de la triade familiale: Le discours photographique du magazine Parent. *Ethnographie Française* 3–4:265–78.

Ryan, James R. 1997. *Picturing Empire: Photography and the Visualization of the British Empire.* London: Reaktion Books.

Sapir, J. David. 1994. On Fixing Ethnographic Shadows. *American Ethnologist* 21, no. 4: 867–85.

Sayre, Henry M. 1989. *The Object of Performance: The American Avant-Garde since 1970.* Chicago: University of Chicago Press.

Schneider, David M. 1968. *American Kinship: A Cultural Account.* Englewood Cliffs, N.J.: Prentice-Hall.

Segalen, Martine. 1972. Photographie de noces, mariage et parenté en milieu rural. *Ethnologie Française* 11, nos. 1–2:123–40.

———. 1998. The Filiation Dilemmas and the Shift of Kinship Studies in France from Anthropology to Sociology: The Case of Grandparenting. Paper prepared for the Wenner-Gren symposium, New Directions in Kinship Study, Mallorca, Spain, March 27–April 4.

Simpson, Bob. 1994. Bringing the "Unclear" Family into Focus: Divorce and Remarriage in Contemporary Britain. *Man* 29:831–51.

Snoeijen, Monique. 1997. De laatste-kansouders. *NRC Handelsblad,* 31 May, Z1.

Sontag, Susan. 1977. *On Photography.* Harmondsworth, U.K.: Penguin.

Spence, Jo, and Patricia Holland, eds. 1991. *Family Snaps: The Meanings of Domestic Photography.* London: Virago.

Verlichak, Victoria. 1999. ?Quien es Julio Galán? Http://www.proa.org.ar/exhibicion/galan/quien-galan.html.

Weston, Kath. 1997. *Families We Choose: Lesbians, Gays, Kinship.* 2d ed. New York: Columbia University Press.

———. 1999. Introduction: Capturing More Than the Moment: Lesbian/Gay Families in the Making. In *Love Makes a Family: Portraits of Lesbian, Gay, Bisexual, and Transgender Parents and Their Families,* edited by Peggy Gillespie, photographs by Gigi Kaeser. Amherst: University of Massachusetts Press.

CHAPTER 4

Kinship in Hypertext: Transubstantiating Fatherhood and Information Flow in Artificial Life

Stefan Helmreich

I want to introduce to you a unique device for recording the flow of a family history: Bailey's Family Ancestral Album (fifth edition), patented by the Reverend Frederic W. Bailey in 1915 and in use in the United States at about the same time. Its somewhat complex operation is explained and depicted in figures 4.1 and 4.2. Briefly, the device allows a person to record paternal and maternal lines of ancestry in a kind of hypertext book, with links between pages furnished by strategically placed cutaways. An examination of figure 4.2, the first page of a genealogy for George and Martha Washington, illustrates the technique.

KINSHIP IN HYPERTEXT 1

Imagine for a moment that you are Martha Washington. Your husband's line of forefathers is traced up the left side of figure 4.2, matched, on the right side, with their corresponding wives—all, with the exception of George's mother, foremothers of George on his father's side. To trace your own ancestry, you must turn to the page corresponding to your maiden name, Dandridge. It turns out that the Washington page is linked to Dandridge through a cutaway rectangle just to George's right, the rectangle through which you can see your own full maiden name. Poking your finger through this cutaway and lifting the intervening pages brings you to the Dandridge page, which is organized somewhat like the Washington page. Here, you will find your father's patriline as well as cutaways leading to your mother's patriline and those of your paternal foremothers.

By this point you will have noticed that learning about lineages of foremothers in Bailey's odd contrivance requires traveling through the time-space

Bailey's Photo=Ancestral Record

OR

Family Ancestral Album

"THE RECORD OF MY ANCESTRY"

Fifth Edition, Enlarged and Improved

(PATENTED)

Showing Pages 6 and 7 of Bailey's
Ancestral Record filled. (2d Edition.)

DIRECTIONS

To begin your Ancestral Record, turn to page 7 and there, in the lowest left hand square—top line—write (if a married man) your own Christian name.

If a single man or woman, write therein the Christian name of your father.

If a married woman, write therein the Christian name of your husband, while the surname in each case is to be written in the vignette at top and center of the page.

The date of birth and locality follow on line indicated in the square; and to the right of the name add the date and place of marriage; and still farther to the right in the upper line of the square (on page 39) you will write the *full maiden name* of the wife. Now add the names and dates of the birth of the children in space between and below (page 7) and you have a generation recorded.

It is well to complete page 7 as far as possible before attempting any of the others; and so, now proceed to fill the left hand square above the first one already written in. Herein write the Christian name of his father with birth, death, locality; when and where married; and then, over to the right as before, the full maiden name of his wife (on page 23).

Please note here that as we are recording ancestors only, no wife's name is to appear in **any square** except she be the mother of the succeeding generation and your own ancestress. All the children are to be recorded in the space designed for them and if, of several mothers, their names written at the head of each group; but remember that only your maternal occupies the square opposite your paternal. Proceed thus with page 7 upward from square to square, generation to generation till as far as possible the page is made complete and with all the details supplied. The Washington chart herewith will well illustrate the method of the page.

You will now perceive that to every maternal is devoted a separate page of the book on which to carry back her individual ancestry in the same way as on page 7. Each page arranged for the surname at the top; and with a continuation of cuttings to provide for other maternals farther back.

Proceed now to fill the first maternal page (39), that of your wife or your mother, according as you have begun your book. After recording her birth in square as indicated, write in the lowest left hand square of page 39, the Christian name of her father, and add his surname at top and center of that page. Then as before add his birth and marriage; and over to the right, through the cutting in page, the full maiden name of his wife. Their children will appear on page 39 and will include the name repeated of that daughter in whom you are especially interested.

With this beginning one needs but little additional instruction in the use of the book other than the suggestions noted in detail therein.

The Supplement for attachment to the top of each page where required for a record of the more remote ancestors will be found very useful, though sometimes it may be as well, where only one or two generations are to be recorded, to employ the upper division of the left hand page. Space there is also afforded for a brief account of the early origin of the family and other interesting matter.

We would also call attention to the Appendix at the back of the book. Its sections will be of service for the record of distant maternal lines, which, named in one or other of the upper right hand squares of the book, must by reference be continued here.

Note also that a maternal name appearing in a square thus and referred back, would then be written under the head of the "Children" in the lowest space.

☞ The photographic features of the book deserve special mention. No other ancestral record provides in any way for such an opportunity. And yet, we feel free to say, that if there is a branch of ancestral study more fascinating, it lies here in the gathering of ancestral pictures of persons, homesteads, gravestones, coats of arms, historic scenes, etc., and their preservation as provided for. Oil paintings, silhouettes, daguerreotypes, photographs, likenesses of any kind can be reduced or enlarged to uniform size at very small expense, and unmounted, inserted herein. Space for photographs of the collateral lines with notes is provided in the continued divisions of the left hand pages. And as the faces, etc., of each generation are preserved, no more valuable heir-loom can be found in any family. We are pleased to learn that many Records are used in this way for a Pictorial Family History.

Do not fail to make use of the Index page and there gather together for ready reference all the surnames found in the book.

In proof of your recorded statements add the references in every case. A place is provided. It will make your work more valuable and authoritative.

Use photographers' paste only and good ink always.

The writer, appreciating the popular favor in which the Record is held and desirous of making it of the greatest practical benefit to its possessors, would be pleased to hear from anyone seeking further explanation or suggestion.

FREDERIC W. BAILEY,

September, 1915.   33 Harvard Street, Worcester, Mass.

FIG. 4.1 Instructions for Bailey's Family Ancestral Album.

The ANCESTRY OF GEORGE WASHINGTON, As arranged on Page 7 of Bailey's famous 4th Ed., Photo- Ancestral Record, "Record of My Ancestry." NOTE—Your own family records with all maternal lines may be as clearly arranged for permanent preservation by using Bailey's popular Record. Prices $10, $5, $3. For sale by Brentano or Putnam's Sons or Dutton Co., New York, or send direct to the publisher—Frederic W. Bailey, Worcester, Mass.

[OVER]

FIG. 4.2 First page of genealogy for George and Martha Washington. Used as an example by Bailey's Family Ancestral Album.

corridors that link mothers to patrilines. If you want to satisfy your curiosity about George's ancestry on his mother's side, for example, you need to turn back to the Washington page and follow the wormhole that leads to Mary Ball and her patriline, recorded on a page leaved somewhere between Washington and Dandridge. Though somewhat cumbersome, this format is meant to allow the tracing of matrilines, often lost in forests of patronyms. As ad copy for Bailey's book puts it, "Every man living has many fathers and mothers great and grand, and he ought to keep a personal record of them and not trust it all to memory or to someone else to keep for him. To be sure it is a complicated problem, especially when it comes to the many mothers every man has who are just as worthy as the many fathers" (Bailey 1915). Bailey's device for tracing Euro-American kinship intends to preserve matrilines through employing something akin to hypertext: a database format in which interconnections between documents can be represented and accessed from within documents themselves, leading the reader into a dense, proliferating net of overlapping and sometimes recursive connections between texts. But even if Bailey means well, his book fortifies the logics by which women's lineages are subordinated to patrilines. Caught between patrinominalism and the bilateralism of a recently rediscovered Mendelian genetics, Bailey's book affirms the flow of blood down lines of fathers.

As a logic and practice, hypertext finds its most recent resonances in computing, in the ways that links are forged between bundles of information on, say, the package of Internet services known as the World Wide Web. In the life worlds of turn-of-the-millennium computing, relationships of shared connection materialize in configurations far messier than those of Euro-American genealogy. But not always. In this essay, I examine how genealogical tales like George and Martha's — tales that focus on fathers — often get downloaded into the work of computer scientists who seek to model populations of real and virtual organisms in cyberspace simulations.

In the mid-1990s, I conducted fieldwork among scientists in the field of Artificial Life, a new science devoted to mimicking the logic of biology in computers. My work was centered at the Santa Fe Institute (SFI) for the Sciences of Complexity in New Mexico, an interdisciplinary research center organized around the notion that computer simulation can provide new tools for theory and experiment in fields ranging from evolutionary biology to economics. Artificial Life researchers claim that life is a property of the formal organization of matter, and they hold that this makes sensible the attempt to model vitality in a computer. Many have found this assertion so compelling that they maintain that alternative, real, artificial life-forms can exist in a computer, and some hope that the creation of computer life will expand biology's purview to include not just *life-as-we-know-it,* but also *life-as-it-could-be.* They hope that through creating swarms of self-replicating entities in virtual worlds, they might add to the dominion of life a new kingdom of organisms existing in the universe of cyberspace.

It is a wish powered in large part by the science-fiction-inspired imagination that many of these relatively young scientists, mostly Euro-American men, possess. SFI is a magnet for scientists who imagine themselves as unorthodox, maverick thinkers; many have histories of participation in the 1960s' counterculture and 1970s' hacker culture, and are attracted to Santa Fe's image as a frontier town, as a place to do pioneering art and science. Unlike nearby Los Alamos National Laboratory with which it once maintained strong links of personnel (SFI was founded by semiretired physicists from the lab), the much smaller institute (only about forty people are in residence at any one time) promotes unclassified research. Its funding from the public-sector National Science Foundation and Department of Energy is joined by moneys from the MacArthur Foundation, private companies, and philanthropic agencies; many locals have quipped that it is meant to be a site for producing technologies of life rather than death. The institute promotes this image, and encourages researchers' speculations on virtual worlds and the realities that might unfold within them (for more on the anthropology of SFI and Artificial Life, see Helmreich 1998).

I argue here that the desire that "life" might emerge through the replication of information structures in cyberspace depends crucially on understandings of genealogy particular to secularized Judeo-Christian patriarchal culture, especially in an age when life has been compressed into genes and genes have become synonymous with information. The digital creations of Artificial Life scientists are linked to their creators through a kind of informatic paternity. "Information" is the shared substance that produces a kinship bond between these scientists and their program progeny. But if information can be used to cement rather conservative narratives of kinship, it can also unglue these stories in surprising ways. Information has properties of its own that contort the landscapes of geneaology and patrilineality, as I hope to show toward the end of this essay.

```
InstExec  = 0,005911  Cells =   7    Genotypes =    1 Sizes =   1

Extracted =

InstExeC        =        0  Generations   =        0  Mon May  9 21:08:29 1994

    NumCells =        1  NumGenotypes  =        1  NumSizes  =        1

    AvgSize  =       80  NumGenDG      =        1  NumGenRQ  =        1

    RateMut  =     3191  RateMovMut    =      640  RateFlaw  =     9600
```

FIG. 4.3 Tierra simulator display.

ARTIFICIAL LIFE CREATION STORIES AND MASCULINE MONOGENESIS

Let me introduce Artificial Life through one of its canonical artifacts: a popular computer program that acts as a model of evolutionary dynamics in populations. This system, crafted by biologist Tom Ray, is called "Tierra," and consists of a large program containing packs of small self-replicating programs. To use Tierra, one must first "inoculate" the system with an "ancestral" self-replicating program. To demonstrate how this works, I narrate the creation in Tierra as it appeared to me when I used the system myself.

To use the Tierra simulator, the user types "tierra" at the prompt. As soon as this word of creation is entered, the user is presented with a display like that in figure 4.3, which includes information about the history of the world as it unfolds. When Tierra is running, these numbers are constantly updating, showing the user how many instructions have been executed, how many generations have been cycled through, how many creatures exist, what the average size of a Tierran organism is, and so on.

The screen text frozen in figure 4.3 is taken from the beginning of a run and reports information sampled from the dawn of a Tierran history. Studying this text, we can see that we are at generation zero and that there is only one digital organism in existence, indicated by NumCells = 1. This is the self-replicating program Ray created from scratch, the program he used and provides to start up the system. Ray explains what we are seeing: "Evolutionary runs of the simulator are begun by inoculating the soup of 60,000 instructions with a single individual of the 80 instruction ancestral genotype" (1992a, 382).

Ray calls this individual the "ancestor" and describes it as a "'seed' self-replicating program" (1992b, 37). Seed is a common word in computer science, usually used in the phrase "random number seed," referring to a pseudo-random number employed as a starting point for a set of computational processes. Ray's phrase echoes this, but also evokes the meaning of seed as a germinal entity that has latent within it the potential to develop into a living thing capable of producing more seeds. Yet the use of the word seed does more than this. Carol Delaney has argued that in cultures influenced by Judeo-Christian narratives of creation and procreation, using the word seed to speak of the impetus of creation summons forth gendered images. In the creation tales of these traditions, God, imagined as masculine, sparks the formless matter of earth to life with a kind of divine seed: the word of creation or *logos spermatikos*. In tales of procreation, males made in the image of a masculine god plant their active "seed" in the passive, receptive, yielding, and nutritive "soil" of females, "fertilizing" them (see Delaney 1986, 1991). Creation and procreation in these narratives are "monogenetic," generated from one source, symbolically masculine. Man and God take after one another. I suggest that the creation in Tierra—and note that Tierra means "soil" as well as "Earth" in Spanish—symbolically mimics the story of creation in the Bible. The programmer is akin to a masculine god who sets life in motion with a word—a word that plants a seed in a receptive computational matrix; a seed that in its search for nourishment, organizes an initially undifferentiated "soup." We might see in Tierra images of a symbolically "male programmer mating with a female program to create progeny whose biomorphic diversity surpasses the father's imagination" (Hayles 1994, 125).

Chris Langton, the computer scientist who gave the field of Artificial Life its name, has claimed that Artificial Life is about "the attempt to abstract the logical form of life in different material forms" (cited in Kelly 1991, 1), a definition that holds that formal and material properties can be usefully partitioned, and that what matters is form. But form and material, like seed and soil, also have gendered valences for those of us swimming down the stream of Western natural philosophy and life sciences. Aristotle proclaimed in his *Generation of Animals* that in procreation, "the male provides the 'form' and the 'principle of movement,' the female provides the body, in other words, the material" (1979, I.XX.729a). Images of form and seed easily overlap in Artificial Life when practitioners make analogies between computer codes (information) and genetic codes. When Ray writes of single-handedly creating digital life in Tierra with a seed, when he remarks that this "digital life exists in a logical, not material, informational universe" (1994, 183), and when he asserts that he occupies the position of God with respect to Tierra, it is hard not to hear echoes of a masculine monogenetic creation. Certainly this language is playful, especially as most Artificial Life researchers are ardent atheists and enjoy poking fun at institutionalized religion. But it is also essential. The God imagery allows programmers to indulge in the notion that they have created life one moment and to imagine themselves as objective observers, as digital naturalists, the next. Theological and evolutionary language are both needed to bring artificial life-forms to life.

The masculine imagery of seed shows up again and again in Artificial Life, with several programmers going so far as to call their seeds "Adam." Imagery of a masculine creation also surfaces in researchers' casual comments, jokes, and occasionally, confessions about why they do Artificial Life at all. The links between masculinity, paternity, and the creation of Artificial Life worlds were evoked for me one day when, at an institute workshop, a male researcher claimed to have a "grandfatherly pride" in a program he had had the inspiration for, yet had not himself programmed. The symbolically masculine creation of silicon life is a theme some men in Artificial Life explicitly play with; some joke that their wives take care of the kids while they take care of the virtual creatures. Craig Reynolds, in acknowledgments for an article in *Artificial Life IV*, writes, "Special thanks to my wife Lisa and to our first child Eric, who was born at just about the same time as individual 15653 of run C" (1994, 68). Ray quotes his wife, Isabel Ray, in one epigraph: "I'm glad they're not real, because if they were, I would have to feed them and they would be all over the house" (1994, 202). Journalist Steven Levy's pop description of Ray's "creation of life" reruns a Frankensteinian tale of male creation: "On January 3 [1990], working at night on a table in the bedroom of his apartment while his wife slept, Ray 'inoculated' the soup with his single test organism, eighty instructions long. He called it the 'Ancestor'" (1992b, 221). This story also illustrates the way that scientific invention is often understood as analogous to fathering (see Franklin 1995).

In spite of the fathering motifs quilted into Artificial Life talk and programming, some people I interviewed wondered whether Artificial Life might be seen as an expression of male researchers' birth envy. As one biologist told me:

> Women create things, right? We have babies and we certainly know the role of males in that, but it's not clear how much men feel that role, and maybe that's what Artificial Life is. Maybe men would like to give birth to something, and here it is, this is it. They're saying to us, "We're going to beat you guys. We're going to create entire worlds."

One male computer scientist, after several beers, confessed to me that he created artificial worlds in part because he felt frustrated he was not a woman and could not create "naturally" (by birthing). Another person suggested that if pressed to account for the fact that there were more men in Artificial Life than women, he would "propose the theory that men are more frustrated in the urge to create life than women, and that Artificial Life gives an outlet to this frustration." At one conference, I met a young man who had a remarkable set of reflections on this topic:

> In the Middle Ages, male alchemists tried to come up with ways to by-pass women in reproduction. I was thinking that Artificial Life research could very easily be just another way of being a surrogate, for males to bear children knowing that they actually can't. It reminds me of something which no one has yet asked me, but which I have thought about — and I still haven't come up with an answer — which is: why it is that I'm interested in Artificial Life and how I can reconcile that with the fact that I'm gay. Of course, the mistake that many people make is that they assume that anyone who is other than straight is going to incorporate their sexuality into everything they do. I am interested in the idea of evolution and reproduction. I've never particularly been interested in *sexual* reproduction. I don't know if that's an artifact of my sexuality or not. [But] it's amusing to think that Artificial Life is overrun by males because it's their way of having babies.

This man's ironic and reflexive musings reveal an intriguing inconsistency. Artificial Life is figured as a practice in potential dissonance with (normatively nonreproductive) gay masculinity, but it is simultaneously construed as something in which men in general — and perhaps gay men in particular — should be interested.

In all these pronouncements, male creation is imagined as fundamentally artificial and female creation as fundamentally natural. Men create artificial life, while women create natural life. There is a curious contradiction here. On one side, females supposedly create naturally and birthing is conflated with reproduction, with males vanishing from the scene. On the other, males are the sole creative force in creation and procreation, with feminine contributions regarded as simply supportive. Female birthing is everything at one moment and nothing in the next — so much nothing that reproduction can proceed without women, can even be pristinely transferred to a different vessel — the computer. Some Christians believe that the pure and uncorrupted Virgin Mary was the perfect vessel for the seed of God, birthing a child who was not half-God, half-Mary, but all God. Computers might be seen as capable of the same clean conception as Mary, bearing faithfully those formal self-reproducing seed programs that are the conceptions of Artificial Life scientists.

Stories of masculine creation usurping or bettering female creation can be found in many scientific narratives. Physicist Brian Easlea (1983) has written of how male nuclear weapons scientists often speak of the bombs they produce as babies, and has interpreted this as bespeaking the desires of a masculine science to appropriate and transcend female reproductive abilities. Hugh Gusterson (1996), in his ethnographic study of weapons scientists, has argued that while there is something notable in how mostly male researchers use this language, it is ultimately unconvincing as a key to their psychology. After all, women can easily use this language, and sometimes do. This language does not reference subconscious motives—like supposed male birth envy— so much as it draws on shared imagery to provide a lexicon for producing artifacts. This is not to say the language is strictly utilitarian; it also reproduces essentialized notions of gender difference. In an effective way, masculine God imagery allows researchers to imagine themselves engaged in fathering new, improved forms of life.

FATHERING ARTIFICIAL LIFE THROUGH THE FIGURE OF INFORMATION

The "vitality" of Tierran "organisms" is not simply or only the effect of narratives of masculine monogenetic creation. The popular and scientific conceit that organisms are merely the readout of a "genetic code" makes possible a collateral collapse of "life" into "program." The kinship that Artificial Life researchers have with their coded creations—the paternity they claim for their virtual organisms—is mediated through their intellect, through the abstraction of information. In fact, some scientists have called artificial life-forms "mind children" (Moravec 1988). This is not surprising given that in Euro-American kinship epistemology, as Marilyn Strathern has observed, "thoughts can be conceived as children are" (1998, 3).

Many researchers I interviewed felt that the near future will see an efflorescence of many new, mostly artificial life-forms, engineered (initially) by humans. Life will exist as pure information in computer networks, as robots, and as genetically engineered organisms. To one researcher, it seemed that the evolutionary process that created humans was continuing as we humans manufacture via artificial means our own evolutionary successors. To be afraid of this process, he said, was perhaps understandable, but was also anthropocentric. There were plenty of things wrong with humans that might be improved or done away with, and he would not be sad to see something "better" emerge, though he admitted that it might take getting used to the idea that "life, instead of being generally mushy and carbon based, like fuzzy teddy bears, could be shiny and metallic." In a way, he felt we humans "owed it to the evolutionary process that created us" to continue its evolutionary work.

Computer scientist Danny Hillis, in a published interview with Steven Levy, put similar thoughts this way:

> I guess I'm not overly perturbed by the prospect that there might be something better than us that might replace us. Because as far as I'm concerned we've just kind of recently crawled out of the muck. We've got a lot of bugs, sort of left over history back from when we were animals. And I see no reason to believe that we're the end of the chain and I think better than us is possible. (cited in Levy 1992a, 39)

In his work, Hillis envisions himself as taking after God in making intelligent computational systems—systems that may potentially, eventually, overtake or surpass him:

> If I put a system inside some future Connection Machine that's the right fertilizer, and I give it the seed of human intelligence by talking to it and interacting with it and telling it what I know, and it grows and flowers into a living being, an intelligent being or something like that, then I created it in exactly the same sense that I've created [a] flower [from planting a seed]. I've made it possible for it to exist, and I've nurtured it, but I didn't make up the rules that made it possible for such a thing to exist. I mean that's a sense in which it's mystic, I mean that's what God did. God made it possible to do that. (cited in Levy 1992a, 41)

The seeds Hillis speaks of are oddly immaterial. They are seeds made of information, the unearthly stuff through which Artificial Life researchers produce their paternity of virtual creatures; it is an updated version of Aristotle's form (see Oyama 1985). Information is understood as a spiritual, masculinized force that can transcend the material, feminized world. With this inflection, quite against the grain of most biological evolutionary theory, Artificial Life stories read as narratives of progress. Evolution reaches into a more perfect future in Artificial Life as information flows down lines of fathers. In this sense, the evolutionism of Artificial Life actually looks more like the progressivist social evolutionism of nineteenth-century theorists such as Lewis Henry Morgan (see McKinnon, this volume).

Like George Washington, popularly known as the "father" of that transcendent entity known as the United States of America, Artificial Life researchers see themselves as progenitors of abstractions, as fathers of creations that express and embody more elevated, more noble purposes than their own. George Washington came from a line of illustrious fathers, but was transported onto a higher plane when he fathered the nation. So Artificial Life researchers, sprouting from the branches of biological evolution, hope to find their true calling, their true fame, in fathering the next stage of evolution.

KINSHIP IN HYPERTEXT 2

This vision of paternity as primary, as eclipsing all other flows of substance, is central in Euro-American systems of patronymic inheritance. It is codified in such genealogical tools as Bailey's Family Ancestral Album as well as in its late-twentieth-century descendants—like Family Tree Maker 4.0, a program produced by Broderbund Software, Inc., that allows users to create family tree Web pages and link these pages via hypertext to the similarly constructed pages of on-line relatives (see www.familytreemaker.com). The family tales told within these webs are messy, but bend persistently to the logics of paternity.

More informal Web links between people and their relatives exist, and I want to look at just one example here: the link between Artificial Life scientist Ray's Web page and a page constructed by Ray for his toddler daughter, Ariel Ivy Ray. Tom Ray's page affords links to a variety of sites he feels are important, including a host of pages that detail the workings of his Tierra system. But amid this thicket of hypertext links, there is also one leading to a page documenting his family tie to his only child. This page, containing a collection of baby photos, is narrated by Ray in the voice of his daughter:

> I began in August of 1993 when I was conceived by my parents in Santa Fe, New Mexico, where my father was working at the Santa Fe Institute. . . . While I was in my mother's womb, my father spoke to me and played music for me. I like to hear him and I moved when he spoke to me. Then one day I stopped moving, even when he spoke to me. . . . The next morning I arrived by surprise. They called my father at work and

told him to come to the hospital. He met me in the elevator because they had already taken me out. When I was born, the nurses wrapped me in a blanket. But my father loosened the blanket and freed my arms. He said that he wanted his daughter to be free to feel and manipulate the world. (www.hip.atr.co.jp/-ray/ariel/ivy.html, January 1996)

What jumps out of this text, of course, is Ray's focus on himself as Ariel Ivy's father and his almost complete erasure of Ariel's mother, who appears as a body with virtually no agency. We might well ask how Isabel Ray, named only at the top of this Web page, figures in this story. Perhaps she occupies the same place as Ray's Tierran computer: the nurturing though not generative site for reproduction. After all, as the narrative indicates, Ariel Ivy's life begins at the moment of conception, the moment of the planting of the seed, the point where Ray begins his story. Leaping through hypertext and hyperspace to learn about Ray's human daughter, one sees an affirmation of the logic of paternity.[1]

But this, of course, makes the story too simple. Artificial Life workers are hardly ignorant of the logic of bilateral, biogenetic inheritance. As Ray notes, in an article contending that Artificial Life should not be seen as a sublimation of a "religious" desire to achieve immortality,

I prefer to achieve immortality in the old-fashioned organic evolutionary way, through my children. I hope to die in my patch of Costa Rican rain forest, surrounded by many thousands of wet and squishy species, and leave it all to my daughter. Let them set my body out in the jungle to be recycled into the ecosystem by the scavengers and decomposers. I will live on through the rain forest I preserved, the ongoing life in the ecosystem into which my material self is recycled, the memes spawned by my scientific works, and the genes in the daughter that my wife and I created. (1994, 204)

In contrast to the monogenetic God Ray played in Tierra, here he is coshareholder in the genetic endowment of his child. Kinship through informatic connection is obviously not essentially monogenetic—or necessarily bilateral or biological, since Ray identifies several streams of informatic transmission—even if the focus is still on transcendence.[2] There are manifold sorts of inheritance that information can underwrite. More than this, though, there are possibilities in the substance of information that quite exceed even Ray's polyglot picture of multiple geneaologies, as I will try to demonstrate below.

RECOMBINATION AND REPRODUCING THE FUTURE

Many Artificial Life scientists are keen to produce evolutionary models that contain sexual recombination, and so, in several simulations, virtual organisms can "mate." Because Artificial Life organisms are made of information, mating really refers to the mutual exchange of computer code.

Mating is usually accomplished though a "genetic algorithm"—a computational procedure that can "evolve" solutions to complex problems by generating populations of possible solutions, and by treating these solutions metaphorically as individuals that can "mate," "mutate," and "compete" to "survive" and "reproduce." In Artificial Life systems, solutions stand for different variants of a kind of program organism. Individuals in the genetic algorithm are represented ultimately as strings of zeroes and ones, and they can produce so-called offspring using a procedure called crossover, thought of as analogous to "sexual recombination." As the inventor of the genetic algorithm puts it, "Biological chromosomes cross over one another when the two gametes meet to form a zygote, and so the process of crossover in genetic algorithms does in fact closely mimic its biological model" (Holland 1992, 68). Algorithmist Lawrence Davis writes, "In nature, crossover occurs when two parents exchange parts of their corresponding chromosomes. In a genetic algorithm, crossover recombines the genetic material in two parent chromosomes to make two children" (1991, 16) (note that the use of familiar language papers over the disanalogy concealed in the example: "in nature," such recombination would not often produce two children). The terms "parents" and "children" are routinely used to refer to genetic algorithm bit strings' "generational" relation to one another: "In reproduction, we use the parent selection technique to pick two *parent* chromosomes. The Reproduction Module applies the one-point crossover and mutate operator to those two parents to generate two new chromosomes, called *children*" (Davis 1991, 12).

There are a number of ways one might understand the exchange of code between programs, but the metaphor of productive heterosexual coupling is consistently emphasized by most researchers. Computer scientist David Goldberg observes, "With an active pool of strings looking for mates, simple crossover happens in two steps: (1) strings are mated randomly, using coin tosses to pair off the happy couples, and (2) mated string couples cross over, using coin tosses to select the crossing sites" (1989, 16). John Holland, the inventor of the procedure, maintains, "As the genetic algorithm proceeds, strong rules mate and form offspring rules that combine their parents' building blocks"

(1992, 71). In a popular account in *Artificial Life,* Steven Levy tells us that "next, the strings mated. In a mass marriage ceremony worthy of Rev. Moon, each string was randomly paired with another" (1992b, 163). A notable algorithmist once said at SFI that he thought intuitively about crossover in the genetic algorithm by "thinking about what it means to recombine my genes and my wife's genes." In these descriptions, monogamous heterosexual marriage (even if pairs are randomly selected) is considered a productive template for natural processes of sexual coupling for reproduction. The commonsensicality of male-female procreative couplings is a resource for thinking about how crossover works in the genetic algorithm. Cultural assumptions and biological reductionisms, even as they sometimes contradict one another, are both enlisted to craft this computational procedure.

In the folk kinship constructs of middle-class Euro-America, the act of heterosexual intercourse that "produces" children is thought to be the generative knot that produces "families" and makes people "related" (Schneider 1968). In Artificial Life, the relatedness of digital organisms is produced through couplings fashioned after this model. The people I interviewed were overwhelmingly Euro-Americans, and David Schneider's reflections on American kinship are directly relevant here: "In American cultural conception, kinship is defined as biogenetic. This definition says that kinship is whatever the biogenetic relationship is. If science discovers new facts about biogenetic relationship, then this is what kinship is and was all along" (1968, 23). For Artificial Lifers, who inhabit a world in which genetics has become an information science, kinship is becoming fundamentally informatic. It should be no surprise that Artificial Life researchers can speak of the "relatedness" of the information structures they think of as organisms. In short, it is no wonder that information has become a kind of shared substance, since as Strathern notes, "in popular parlance [genes] are both substance (the 'blood' that is inherited) and information (codes for saying how cells will develop)" (1998, 19). In an age of genetic fetishism—when genes encode the secret of life itself—this sort of silicon transubstantiation of kinship is not far behind.

But there is something fishy (bacterial?) about the way genetic algorithm bit strings "reproduce." Although people routinely invoke human heterosexual coupling to talk about what goes on in the genetic algorithm, there is no "sexual" difference between genetic algorithm bit strings. The idea that mating can happen between structurally identical entities recalls what Evelyn Fox Keller has labeled the masculine bias of mathematical population genetics. In this discourse, all individuals are structurally equal, all just bags of genes. As Keller remarks,

> Effectively bypassed with this representation were all the problems entailed by sexual difference, by the contingencies of mating and fertilization that resulted from the finitude of actual populations and also, simultaneously, all the ambiguities of the term reproduction as applied to organisms that neither make copies of themselves nor reproduce by themselves. (1992, 132)

Sex becomes an informational affair; no disorderly bodies intervene, and everything is reduced to the all-important seed. Evidence of the popular currency of this definition of sex can be found in conflicting claims to parental custody in some cases of surrogacy and in vitro fertilization, where "parenthood" is sometimes proved by the out-of-body donation of an "essence" of reproduction, genes, that turns mothers into "father-equivalents" (Rothman 1989). Or as one male Artificial Life researcher put it to me, in a sentence that is iconic of the ways genetic relatedness has been culturally isolated as the essential connection between organisms: "Pregnancy is merely an implementation problem."

When virtual organisms reproduce, they do so in artificial worlds that have been provided with a sort of computational imitation of natural selection; in this way, they "evolve." Under this regime, parent programs are understood to be eugenically fit, and productive of offspring that are different from and fitter than they. Computer scientist John Koza writes that "the crossover operation produces two offspring. The two offspring are usually different from their two parents and different from each other. Each offspring contains some genetic material from each of its parents" (1992, 23). Holland continues, "The algorithm favors the fittest strings as parents, and so above-average strings will have more offspring in the next generation" (1992, 68). Computer scientists Larry Eshelman, Richard Caruana, and J. David Schaffer assert that "two parents are selected according to fitness and material between them is exchanged to produce two children which replace them" (1989, 11). And Koza says, "The genetic process of sexual reproduction between two parental computer programs is used to create new offspring computer programs from two parental programs selected in proportion to fitness" (1992, 74–75). Figure 4.4 shows two parental programs from Koza's book, poised to exchange subroutines and create a new, perhaps more effective program.

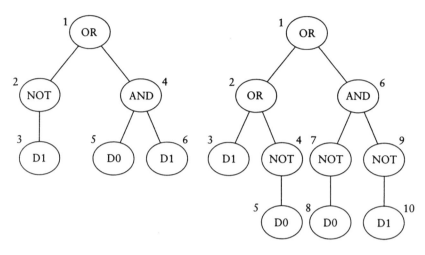

FIG. 4.4 Parent programs from John Koza, *Genetic Programming: On the Programming of Computers by Means of Natural Selection* (Cambridge: MIT Press, 1992), fig. 6.5. Reprinted by permission.

This commitment to the proposition that children should be better off than their parents relies in part on an understanding of kinship as a system that continually generates future possibilities. Marilyn Strathern describes this English and Euro-American view of the future: "Increased variation and differentiation invariably lie ahead, a fragmented future as compared with a communal past. To be new is to be different. Time increases complexity" (1992a, 21). Strathern maintains that for Euro-Americans, "kinship delineated a developmental process that guaranteed diversity, the individuality of persons and the generation of future possibilities" (39). In this system, children are "new" "individuals" that emerge from parental relations. She argues that the Euro-American reproductive model is itself an algorithm for the generation of future possibilities—something of great use to those who would write programs that produce new programs.[3] The synopsis Strathern provides of a child's genetic "individuality" might equally well be applied to the brave new organisms of Artificial Life and genetic algorithms:

> The child's guarantee of individuality lies in genetic origin: its characteristics are the outcome of a chance combination from a range of possibilities.... Genetic potential ... maintains an array of possible characteristics from which an entity might emerge; the future is known ... by its unpre-

dictability, and one would not necessarily wish to anticipate it. (1992b, 172)

All this talk of ever newer and fitter organisms reproduced by recombination in artificial worlds suggests that not all recombinations are equal. There is a strong eugenicist charge to this digital Darwinism. In my survey of the genetic algorithm literature, I found declarations that programs should be prevented from crossing with programs *too similar* to themselves — an operation that could stall the generation of new solutions. To accomplish this, one set of researchers has proposed the installation of an "incest taboo" in their system (Eshelman and Schaffer 1991). And in an effort to keep populations of genetic algorithm individuals "evolving" toward better solutions, some researchers have proposed regulating the kinds of individuals that can cross, introducing what they call "marriage restrictions" (see Goldberg 1989). They reason that crosses between strings that are *too different* might disrupt a population's accumulation of useful and potentially optimal genetic combinations. In discussions around this strategy, researchers often employ highly racialized imagery. For instance, in an Artificial Life system named PolyWorld, restrictions can be enforced in order to encourage the divergence of populations (as genetically interbreeding groups) using a tool called the

> "miscegenation function" (so dubbed by Richard Dawkins), that may be used to probabilistically influence the likelihood of genetically dissimilar organisms producing viable offspring; the greater the dissimilarity, the lower the probability of their successfully reproducing. (Yaeger 1994, 272)

Miscegenation is, of course, a loaded term, referring not to mixing between species or incipient species but to mixing between so-called races. The racial and eugenic logics skittering below the surface of genetic algorithms are made explicit here, and key one into a notion of races as distinct genetic groups, rather than socially constructed groupings. Genetic difference, coded here as biological race, is to be handled carefully, with one population kept pure of information contamination from others. In the universes of Artificial Life, sexual recombination, which produces new combinations of traits, must be kept within boundaries, lest lineages lose their vigor. Donna Haraway has suggested that "racial hygiene and its typological syntax are not supported by genome discourse, or by artificial life discourses in general" (1997, 248). This is not always true; early-twentieth-century notions of race can still shape the biology of bits and bytes.

Artificial Life scientists see themselves as ushering in a new stage of evolution, one in which new life-forms will be birthed through scientific conceptions that lead to self-reproducing computer programs. They view biological reproduction and the machinic reproduction they are engineering as parts of a larger evolutionary story, and see themselves as "in the employ" of evolution, creating new life-forms that will unchain themselves from carbon chemistry, perhaps traveling off-planet in the silicon splendor of robot bodies. Artificial Life researchers can claim that organic biological reproduction can be subsumed, transcended, and devoured by new techno-biological reproduction because they participate in a culture that uses the word reproduction to refer to both the perpetuation of practices and ideas and the generation of new organic beings (see Harris and Young 1981). This is how Artificial Life has become thinkable.

Strathern has commented that the Euro-American reproductive model "makes us greedy for both change and continuity, as though one could bring about momentous (episodic) change while still being regarded as the continuous (evolutionary) originators of it" (1992b, 177). These words illuminate the cultural logic beneath Artificial Life researchers' contentions that the manufacture of Artificial Life is both novel and evolutionarily inevitable. When Christopher Langton writes, "The creation of life is not an act to be undertaken lightly. We must do what we can to ensure that the future is equally bright for both our technological and our biological offspring" (1992, 22), we learn that reproduction is the real fuel for Euro-American time travel into the future.

MUTATING KINSHIP IN THE AGE OF INFORMATION

But reproduction can never be counted on to work perfectly, to copy faithfully its objects and subjects indefinitely. As Strathern notes, "The ideas that reproduce themselves in our communications *never reproduce themselves exactly.* They are always found in environments or contexts that have their own properties or characteristics" (1992b, 6). Reproduction always reconfigures the kinship structures in which it works. And kinship, in the age of recombinant information, is no longer so easy to delineate.

In traditional anthropology, kinship has often been defined as the social organization of "the facts of life," as a social arrangement modeled after and attentive to genealogical, biogenetic connection. Recent anthropological reconsiderations, however, have reoutfitted kinship as a concept that refers to how people make sense of social connection in general; kinship may make reference to biogenetics, but may also implicate political, class, caste, racialized, sexualized, and religious affiliations (see, for example, Stack 1974; Geertz and Geertz 1975; Yanagisako and Collier 1987; Weston 1991). Contemporary practices of genetic engineering, new reproductive technology, and information science force still further changes in accountings of kinship, especially since "biology" still haunts the landscape of relatedness (see, this volume, Thompson; Franklin). In *Modest_Witness@Second_Millennium.Female Man©_Meets_OncoMouse™*, Haraway provides some useful remappings of this mutated terrain. She argues that kin are "tied to each other by the passage of bodily substance" (1997, 22), but notes that where the passage of bodily substance once referred exclusively to the flow of blood or genes down generations, it now enfolds multiple kinds of connections between such entities as humans, transgenic organisms, and machines. OncoMouse™, the transgenic rodent that reliably develops breast cancer, is kin, is sister, to the human females with whom she shares a particular kind of tumor-producing gene. As Haraway observes, "Transgenic creatures, which carry genes from 'unrelated' organisms, simultaneously fit into well-established taxonomic and evolutionary discourses and also blast widely understood senses of natural limit. What was distant and unrelated becomes intimate" (56). And in an era when genes have become information, transgenic creatures are also kin to other sorts of text-based creations, like the various genome projects' databases, which provide information enabling new sorts of organisms to be intellectually and corporeally conceived.

As information becomes a conduit for thinking kin connection, it enters into confluence and interference with the concept of "substance." Janet Carsten (this volume) points out that substance — a word that has referred to that which anchors "natural" relatedness in U.S. kinship — is a notoriously ambiguous term. It "accommodates a remarkable range of indigenous meanings, including bodily matter, essence, and content in opposition to form, as well as differences in degrees of mutability and fluidity" (Carsten, this volume). In so doing, substance oscillates between essence and corporeal matter, and sometimes seems to mean both. When substance is filtered through the lens of information, this oscillation is intensified. Information has historically had two primary meanings. The first is simply a quantitative measure of the complexity of a linear code or message and has nothing to do with what the code or message means. How *much* information is there? The second, associated with computer programming, attaches to the concept of instruction or program, for which meaning is of the utmost concern (see Keller 1995). Information, then, like substance, sometimes refers to abstract form and sometimes to content.[4] But information also overflows substance because what it can contain as content or meaning is so ambiguous — information can be "about" anything (Oyama 1985), which is one reason it can connect entities such as humans, transgenic mice, and digital organisms.

Carsten says that she is "more interested in what substance *does* than what it *is*." I have the same curiosity about information. I think that what information *does* when it becomes a kind of shared substance is to both solidify and disturb the neatness of lineage. Kinship in the age of informatically enabled transubstantiation is no longer only or so cleanly about family trees or roots.[5] Transgenic tomatoes containing genes from flounders are a sign that lines of kinship are becoming rhizomatic — webbing together in new formations that not only ramify but rejoin and connect in recursive ways. Under the sign of information, we get hybrids of the natural and artificial, the organic and technological, and the fictional and factual. Chimerical creatures like OncoMouse™ and the FlavrSvr tomato become possible, the spawn of technologies of genetics and informatics. In this regime, the stability of such concepts as lineage, paternity, or racial purity is decidedly at risk. Though it has a hypertext format, Bailey's Family Ancestral Album is tailored to patrilineal tales and would be hard-pressed to contain all the new sorts of connection that informatics makes possible.

What else about information might destabilize tales of patrilineal inheritance, even against the apparent efforts of some Artificial Life scientists to download such stories into the future? What else does information *do*? Because it also carries the meaning of "instruction" or "code," it resonates with "code for conduct" as well — the item that in Schneiderian kinship theory at least, is often contrasted with substance. While substance refers to natural connection, code refers to relationships by law. "Blood relations" materialize in Euro-American kinship when substance and code are conjoined by heterosexual intercourse and the legitimating institution of marriage. When information replaces blood as that which ties substance and code together, different sorts of relationships become thinkable. To begin with, the close connection between kinship and gender that post-Schneiderian theory assumes (see Yanagisako and Collier 1987) becomes unfastened — extending the unbraiding of sex, gender, and reproduction highlighted in recent discussions of new reproductive technologies as well as lesbian and gay kinships (see, for example, Strathern 1992b; Weston 1991; Hayden 1995). Because information as a substance is less sexualized than blood or genes as it is differently embodied/materialized (Franklin 1995), the kinship it underwrites may have quite different implications for gender. Mothers, fathers, women, and men may morph, mix, and meet new sorts of kinship agencies and entities—like multinationals with legal rights and interests in patented genes or transgenic creatures. Novel sorts of corporate bodies could attain the status of "in-laws," as witnessed by the government of Iceland's recent decision to sell the rights to its national genome—the genetic sequence data of its citizenry—to a private pharmaceutical company that hopes to "mine" it for useful therapeutic information. In a world where genomes are for sale, the claims of so-called mothers and fathers to their children are being renegotiated.

The presence of law and capital on the scene should signal that property persists as an important player in kinship. What Johann Jakob Bachofen, Lewis Henry Morgan, and Friedrich Engels saw as a crucial ingredient in the consolidation of patrilineality and patriarchy now points away from systems of consanguinity toward corporate affinities. Charles Darwin argued that "natural classification" must follow and reflect genealogical history, the history of the transmission of hereditary properties in ramifying family lineages ([1859] 1964, 411–34). These days, mapping the socionatural terrain of "life" requires knowing who owns what. In Haraway's terms, we are witnessing a transition from a concern with natural kinds to a concern with brands—generic marks, new sorts of genres, genders, typologies, and typographies of kinship categories. The Motorola corporation now offers "DigitalDNA™," an embedded microchip that "breathes life into products, from simple things such as a coffeemaker to complex things like a computer" (Motorola 1998). DigitalDNA™, suffused with the public relations and protocols of Artificial Life technology, naturalizes the commodity fetishism that allows corporations and their customers to see products as the animate entities that struggle to exist in the Darwinian marketplace.

KINSHIP IN HYPERTEXT 3

Haraway has contended that hybrid creations like OncoMouse™ are kinds of tricksters—vampires polluting "the lineage of nature itself—transforming nature into its binary opposite, culture" (1997, 60), and she maintains that the currency that enables this transformation, this exchange of logics, is

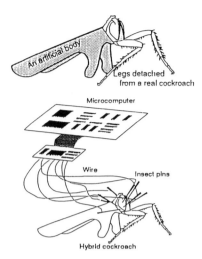

FIG. 4.5 A hybrid cockroach robot from Hirofumi Miura, Takashi Yasuda, Yayoi Kubo Fujisawa, Yoshihiko Kuwana, Shoji Takeuchi, and Isao Shimoyama, "Insect-Model Based Microrobot," in *Artificial Life V,* ed. Christopher G. Langton and Katsunori Shimohara (Cambridge: MIT Press, 1997), fig. 7. Reprinted by permission.

information. Information is the stuff that allows some scientists to contemplate splicing carbon-based life-forms to silicon-based computer systems, to think of making not only transgenic organisms but what I would call "transinformatic" creatures—like the hybrid cockroach robot reproduced in figure 4.5, created by Artificial Life researcher Hirofumi Miura and his Tokyo team (1997). This creation—a compound of paper body, insect legs, and microcomputer—is an artificial life-form that is neither virtual nor transgenic, nor more bizarrely, living or dead.[6] Mixing signals from nature and culture, it is the result of a new sort of AI: Alchemical Informatics, not Artificial Intelligence. The kinship that this artificial insect has with other things in the world looks more like hypertext than genealogy. Its kinship network extends into a worldwide web of computer science, biology, and capital. Asking after its "parents" lands one in a net of techno-scientific relationships, none of which can be reduced to the traditional descent categories of Euro-American kinship.

Paul Edwards has characterized hypertext as a mode of connection that relentlessly brings together elements from widely different and sometimes contradictory domains. According to Edwards, "Hypertext is fundamentally unstable, open for constant revision" (1994, 232). A never finished set of connections between an often heterogeneous set of entities, it demands ever-mutating reading practices. In the techno-scientific worlds of Artificial Life, tales of fathering are linked to a net of beliefs about monogenetic creation, progress, purity, and genius. But because these stories are told in the tongue of information—a language capable of making surprising connections between radically different orders of things—they are ever in danger of dissolving. Kinship, in the age of Artificial Life, threatens and promises to run away into the rhizomatic world of hyperactive hypertext—a world that may be difficult to contain within the frames of masculine monogenesis and patrilineality.

I think some sense may be made of this proliferation of connection and definition by returning to the concept of kinship within anthropology. Artificial Life and anthropology are both enmeshed in modernity's vexed project of self-examination and self-critique, and both are in transformation as their most paradigmatic objects of investigation—life and kinship—are under stress as coherent categories. Life occupies the same position in Artificial Life as kinship has in anthropology. Artificial Life assumes that the category of life can be universalized to both carbon and silicon creations, but this ignores that life is not only a contingent fact of the history of biology on earth but also, as Michel Foucault taught in *The Order of Things* (1966), a contingent category of the history of natural philosophy. Life only emerged as a force or principle unifying living things because of formalist commitments in taxonomy. Similarly, traditional anthropology assumed that kinship was a universal formation connecting the order of nature to the order of culture, but failed to recognize the cultural specificity of social and symbolic valuations of genealogy and blood. All this is not to say that biologists or anthropologists should discard life or kinship as categories. Rather, it must be recognized that these terms have histories that inform any possible attempts to redefine them. The denaturalization of kinship available through the logic of information is a challenge to take up the work of articulating relationships in ways that accent shared responsibility and risk, not just shared substance.

NOTES

I would like to thank Sarah Franklin and Susan McKinnon for inviting me to the Wenner-Gren conference, for which this paper was developed, and for pressing me through various revisions of this essay. I also express my gratitude to the Wenner-Gren Foundation for a fabulously memorable gathering, and my appreciation to all the participants in Mallorca for their warm collegiality and commentary. I thank Heather Paxson, who made invaluable suggestions at all stages of this work, as well as Nick DeGenova, Cori Hayden, and Ritty Lukose.

1   An affirmation that, as Mary Bouquet (this volume) might remind us, is reinforced by the display of the family photo, a kind of technologically materialized substance that helps make kinship ties "real." When people put baby photos on-line, often on their

"home page," they assert and even advertise what they believe their kin connections to be.

2 Note, too, that while Ray's image of his body as compost for "life" acknowledges matter as crucial for vitality, this matter is primarily coded as dead stuff in need of recycling.

3 This sort of Artificial Life practice contrasts with the fashioning of patented lab animals in which stopping the evolutionary process and holding reproduction constant is the goal (see Haraway 1997; Franklin, this volume).

4 Strathern (1998) has argued that Euro-Americans believe that information about biogenetic relationships is identical to those relationships themselves, and Bouquet (this volume) has shown how artifacts such as family photos can act as informational substances that solidify normative notions of family.

5 It should be noted, of course, that "blood" was never a completely neat way of signaling genealogical flows; blood can run in pathways that cut across the grain of lineal relations (see Weston, this volume).

6 Informatics is also responsible for blurring this boundary between life and death in other domains, especially as it becomes technologically possible to mine and revive the genes of organisms long dead. Of course, Euro-American kinship has long been predicated on symbolically linking the living to the dead, as Gillian Feeley-Harnik (this volume) argues in her astonishing account of the ways Lewis Henry Morgan's theories of consanguinity were inspired by his desire to communicate with and feel connected to his prematurely departed daughters. Morgan's obsession with railroads may have emerged in part from his regret that he could not come sooner to his dying daughters' sides; train tracks, laid alongside the North American rivers that Morgan compared to the channels of blood linking human families, could be crucial technologies in kinship networks. Many decades later, telephone lines—first set alongside these same railroad tracks—would become the conduits for which information theory would be developed (helping predict the communication capacity of these filaments), and would themselves become pathways for reinforcing old and new kinship relations (telephones were also early technologies through which the living tried to contact the dead [see Ronell 1989]).

REFERENCES

Aristotle. 1979. *Generation of Animals.* Translated by A. L. Peck. Cambridge: Harvard University Press.
Bailey, Frederic. 1915. Bailey's Family Ancestral Album advertisement. Worcester, Mass.: Frederic Bailey.
Darwin, Charles. [1859] 1964. *On the Origin of Species by Means of Natural Selection, or the Preservation of Favoured Races in the Struggle for Life.* Reprint, with an introduction by Ernst Mayr, Cambridge: Harvard University Press.
Davis, Lawrence, ed. 1991. *Handbook of Genetic Algorithms.* New York: Van Nostrand Reinhold.

Delaney, Carol. 1986. The Meaning of Paternity and the Virgin Birth Debate. *Man* 21, no. 3:494–513.

———. 1991. *The Seed and the Soil: Gender and Cosmology in Turkish Village Society.* Berkeley: University of California Press.

Easlea, Brian. 1983. *Fathering the Unthinkable: Masculinity, Scientists, and the Arms Race.* London: Pluto Press.

Edwards, Paul. 1994. Hyper Text and Hypertension: Post-Structuralist Critical Theory, Social Studies of Science, and Software. *Social Studies of Science* 24:229–78.

Eshelman, Larry J., Richard A. Caruana, and J. David Schaffer. 1989. Biases in the Crossover Landscape. In *Proceedings of the Third International Conference on Genetic Algorithms,* edited by J. David Schaffer. San Mateo, Calif.: Morgan Kaufmann Publishers.

Eshelman, Larry J., and J. David Schaffer. 1991. Preventing Premature Convergence in Genetic Algorithms by Preventing Incest. In *Proceedings of the Fourth International Conference on Genetic Algorithms,* edited by Richard K. Belew and Lashon B. Booker. San Mateo, Calif.: Morgan Kaufmann Publishers.

Foucault, Michel. 1966. *The Order of Things: An Archaeology of the Human Sciences.* New York: Random House.

Franklin, Sarah. 1995. Romancing the Helix: Nature and Scientific Discovery. In *Romance Revisited,* edited by Lynne Pearce and Jackie Stacey. London: Lawrence and Wishart.

Geertz, Hildred, and Clifford Geertz. 1975. *Kinship in Bali.* Chicago: University of Chicago Press.

Goldberg, David E. 1989. *Genetic Algorithms in Search, Optimization, and Machine Learning.* Reading, Mass.: Addison-Wesley.

Gusterson, Hugh. 1996. *Nuclear Rites: A Weapons Laboratory at the End of the Cold War.* Berkeley: University of California Press.

Haraway, Donna J. 1997. *Modest_Witness@Second_Millennium.FemaleMan©_Meets_OncoMouse™: Feminism and Technoscience.* New York: Routledge.

Harris, Olivia, and Kate Young. 1981. Engendered Structures: Some Problems in the Analysis of Reproduction. In *The Anthropology of Pre-Capitalist Societies,* edited by Joel S. Kahn and Josep R. Llobera. London: Macmillan Publishers Ltd.

Hayden, Corinne. 1995. Gender, Genetics, and Generation: Reformulating Biology in Lesbian Kinship. *Cultural Anthropology* 10, no. 1:41–63.

Hayles, N. Katherine. 1994. Narratives of Evolution and the Evolution of Narratives. In *Cooperation and Conflict in General Evolutionary Processes,* edited by John L. Casti and Anders Karlqvist. New York: John Wiley and Sons.

Helmreich, Stefan. 1998. *Silicon Second Nature: Culturing Artificial Life in a Digital World.* Berkeley: University of California Press.

Holland, John. 1992. Genetic Algorithms. *Scientific American* 267, no. 1:66–72.

Keller, Evelyn Fox. 1992. *Secrets of Life, Secrets of Death: Essays on Language, Gender, and Science.* New York: Routledge.

———. 1995. *Refiguring Life: Changing Metaphors of Twentieth-Century Biology.* New York: Columbia University Press.

Kelly, Kevin. 1991. Designing Perpetual Novelty: Selected Notes from the Second Artificial Life Conference. In *Doing Science: The Reality Club,* edited by John Brockman. New York: Prentice-Hall.

Koza, John. 1992. *Genetic Programming: On the Programming of Computers by Means of Natural Selection.* Cambridge: MIT Press.

Langton, Christopher G. 1992. Introduction to *Artificial Life II,* edited by Christopher G. Langton, Charles Taylor, J. Doyne Farmer, and Steen Rasmussen. Redwood City, Calif.: Addison-Wesley.

Levy, Steven. 1992a. A-Life Nightmare. *Whole Earth Review* 76:34–47.

———. 1992b. *Artificial Life: The Quest for a New Creation.* New York: Pantheon.

Miura, Hirofumi, Takashi Yasuda, Yayoi Kubo Fujisawa, Yoshihiko Kuwana, Shoji Takeuchi, and Isao Shimoyama. 1997. Insect-Model Based Microrobot. In *Artificial Life V,* edited by Christopher G. Langton and Katsunori Shimohara. Cambridge: MIT Press.

Moravec, Hans. 1988. *Mind Children: The Future of Robot and Human Intelligence.* Cambridge: Harvard University Press.

Motorola. 1998. Ad for DigitalDNA™.

Oyama, Susan. 1985. *The Ontogeny of Information: Developmental Systems and Evolution.* Cambridge: Cambridge University Press.

Ray, Tom. 1992a. An Approach to the Synthesis of Life. In *Artificial Life II,* edited by Christopher G. Langton, Charles Taylor, J. Doyne Farmer, and Steen Rasmussen. Redwood City, Calif.: Addison-Wesley.

———. 1992b. Natural Evolution of Machine Codes: Digital Organisms. In *SFI Proposal for a Research Program in Adaptive Computation.* Santa Fe, N.M.: SFI

———. 1994. An Evolutionary Approach to Synthetic Biology: Zen and the Art of Creating Life. *Artificial Life* 1, nos. 1–2: 179–210.

Reynolds, Craig. 1994. Competition, Coevolution, and the Game of Tag. In *Artificial Life IV,* edited by Rodney Brooks and Pattie Maes. Cambridge: MIT Press.

Ronell, Avital. 1989. *The Telephone Book: Technology, Schizophrenia, Electric Speech.* Lincoln: University of Nebraska Press.

Rothman, Barbara Katz. 1989. *Recreating Motherhood: Ideology and Technology in a Patriarchal Society.* New York: W. W. Norton.

Schneider, David M. 1968. *American Kinship: A Cultural Account.* Englewood Cliffs, N.J.: Prentice-Hall.

Stack, Carol. 1974. *All Our Kin: Strategies for Survival in a Black Community.* New York: Harper and Row.

Strathern, Marilyn. 1992a. *After Nature: English Kinship in the Late Twentieth Century.* Cambridge: Cambridge University Press.

———. 1992b. *Reproducing the Future: Anthropology, Kinship and the New Reproductive Technologies.* New York: Routledge.

———. 1998. Thought Experiments. Paper distributed at New Directions in Kinship Study: A Core Concept Revisited, Wenner-Gren Foundation for Anthropological Research conference, 27 March–4 April, Mallorca, Spain.

Weston, Kath. 1991. *Families We Choose: Lesbians, Gays, Kinship.* New York: Columbia University Press.

Yaeger, Larry. 1994. Computational Genetics, Physiology, Metabolism, Neural Systems,

Learning, Vision, and Behavior or PolyWorld: Life in a New Context. In *Artificial Life III,* edited by Christopher G. Langton. Redwood City, Calif.: Addison-Wesley.

Yanagisako, Sylvia J., and Jane F. Collier. 1987. Toward a Unified Analysis of Gender and Kinship. In *Gender and Kinship: Essays toward a Unified Analysis,* edited by Jane F. Collier and Sylvia J. Yanagisako. Stanford, Calif.: Stanford University Press.

PART II

Kinship Negotiations: What's Biology Not/Got to Do with It

CHAPTER 5

Kinship, Controversy, and the Sharing of Substance:
The Race/Class Politics of Blood Transfusion
Kath Weston

Once upon a time, not too many years ago, an esteemed and devoted colleague was called on to assume the expert position. "Contemporary Families"
would be the theme for an upcoming evening of original dance compositions.
Would he like to join an interdisciplinary panel following the performance?
Professor Esteemed A. Devoted accepted the invitation, believing as he did
in the importance of taking anthropology's message to a wider public. When
the evening came, he took care to tailor his comments to a general audience.
"Anthropologists have a hard time defining what a family is," he began, a note
of apology creeping into his voice, "but rest assured that we know one when
we see one." From my balcony seat, I could see universalism taking relativism
to the mat on the very spot where, moments before, a troupe of dancers had
attempted to evoke the contours of an interracial relationship.

A SHORT HISTORY OF THE CRITIQUE OF KINSHIP

In the years after David Schneider (1984) developed his celebrated critique of
kinship, one might have thought that *he* thought he had laid all such foolish-
ness to rest. In his view, the dangers of drawing false assurance from a claim
to know-one-when-we-see-one extended well beyond garden-variety ethnocentrism. Certainly any ethnographer who clings to unexamined assumptions
about what makes a family will have a hard time recognizing families that are
constituted along different lines. But Schneider had argued (more radically)
that it was dangerous to presume that anything so coherent as "families" or
"kinship" exists, either as an existential object for investigation or an ideo-

logical universal, much less as a "natural fact." For Schneider, the habit of placing an inordinate amount of social significance on biogenetic connection was just one way of reckoning belonging, and a culturally specific one at that.

On the face of it, the critique of kinship approach dealt a serious blow to kinship studies. There no longer appeared to be any reason to traverse the globe in relativist fashion, seeking "variants" of a non-thing called kinship. If kinship turned out to be a figment of Anglo-European modes of understanding attachment, rather than a powerful tool with transcultural applicability, that would seem to narrow the scope for investigation considerably. All those hours spent penciling in genealogies, chasing after cross-cousins, and for what? Kinship assumed a new status as an amalgam of practices and beliefs made meaningful only by and through a "Western" analytic apparatus. Think of it as totemism for the next generation.

Of course, the critique of kinship approach cannot assume full credit (blame? responsibility?) for the partial eclipse of kinship studies within North American anthropology. As Sarah Franklin and Susan McKinnon (this volume) have noted, the demise of structural-functionalism undermined kinship's position as a regularized division in the structural-functionalist compendium of politics, economics, kinship, religion, and the like. Neither was the fate of kinship studies an isolated product of succession disputes in the ivory tower, with the organic divisions of structural-functionalism giving way in turn to structuralism and poststructuralism. Back in the "outside" world (which on many campuses begins just outside the window), the department store lost ground first to designer-label discount chains, which marketed the mythemes of fashion to Everywoman, then to the poststructuralist (albeit carefully targeted) eclecticism of the mail-order catalog and the outlet mall. However loosely construed these parallels, it clearly no longer suffices to send students to the "kinship department" of the library or course schedule to think through even the simplest problems in social organization and belonging.

When *Families We Choose* (1997), my book on lesbian/gay kinship ideologies in the United States, first came out, Schneider greeted its publication with more than a hint of dismay. Over lunch at an American Anthropological Association meeting, he pushed pasta around his plate by way of getting to the question that troubled him. Why would I be interested, he wondered, in advocating for this historically destructive conception called family? Later he became magnanimous, profuse, almost anxious in his apologies, having read the book and concluded that "it's just good ethnography." As long as people "in the field" were living with and through conceptions of kinship, it made sense to him to study them. In this instance, Schneider found himself willing to concede the smallest of grounds for kinship studies: an investigation of people who subscribe to ideologies of kinship, provided that the investigation maintain a resolutely critical stance toward the substantiveness of the families and relatives entailed in those ideologies.

In institutional terms, the main impact of the critique of kinship appeared to be prohibitive: Don't come to the curriculum committee with a new course on kinship. Don't locate your dissertation in a dying field. After all, there's hardly any "there" there to study. The decline in interest could be charted by many measures, including conferences organized, courses listed, publication and dissertation topics, probably even specializations listed in the American Anthropological Association's faculty guide.[1]

But what if scholars were to approach the critique of kinship as something more than the dismantling of a hallowed analytic concept and a nay-saying to further study? What if they took a Foucauldian turn to notice, just around the corner, the productive effects of that injunction to repress further study in the name of liberation from naturalism and structural-functionalist compartmentalization? In this case the narrative changes. The story of kinship within anthropology no longer reproduces itself as the tale of a subfield that has lost (and in more recent tellings, reinvented) its object. Instead, the Foucauldian reading allows interest to shift to what the critique of kinship has produced by and through its very "no." How do the productive effects of this legacy continue to shape kinship studies, even in its newly resurrected form? Without such an understanding, it becomes difficult to move the new kinship studies in directions that do not unreflectively retrace the old. Like colonists at their most myopic, "new" versions of "old" fields have a tendency to settle where others have lived, mistakenly celebrating the conquest of a wilderness that is anything but unexplored space.

One productive effect of the critique of kinship is easy enough to make out: the subsumption of topics that used to be studied under the rubric of kinship into other areas of study. Gender, race, nationalism, transnationalism, and identity politics have taken up much of the slack. Essays on gender incorporate lively discussions of relations within marriage; treatises on politics are only too happy to point out the uses of genealogy in an era of nation-states. But precisely because the kinship terminology embedded in these accounts enters obliquely, it tends to remain unexamined. The analyst subtly reasserts the doctrine of know-one-when-you-see-one: Everybody knows what genealogy means, and after all, my topic is nationalism, so let's just move on. Missing are the kinds of fine distinctions provided by a critique that sets its sights directly on kinship. The corresponding loss of an institutional base for kinship within departments of anthropology left anthropologists badly positioned to comment on, much less meaningfully contribute to, the social debates that brought so-called family issues to the center of public attention during the 1990s.

When a somnambulant kinship studies finally *did* awaken, it was to the sounds of public controversy. In the "new" kinship studies, surrogate motherhood, genetic engineering, in vitro fertilization, and lesbian parenthood have displaced charts, rules, and heavily normative accounts of how the so-and-so's practice kinship. This orientation toward controversy can also be considered a lingering, and extremely productive, effect of the critique of kinship. A few scholars, such as Carol Delaney, Rayna Rapp, Marilyn Strathern, and Sylvia Yanagisako, persisted in turning out important work during what might retrospectively be characterized as a hiatus in kinship studies. But most who now see themselves engaged in the study of kinship (at least in the United States) responded at a later date to calls from outside the discipline to attend to bitterly fought social struggles that, as Judith Stacey (1996) would have it, stake their claims in the name of the family: international adoption, "traditional values," same-sex marriage, parenting on the run. The call of controversy echoed loudly in the institutional space cleared out by the critique of kinship's "no." Yolanda Moses and Carol Mukhopadhyay have argued that something similar could and should happen to "race," a concept like kinship that was handily dispatched by theoreticians of a previous generation, yet remains so intimately bound up in contemporary power relations that analysts ignore it at everyone's peril (Moses 1997; Moses and Mukhopadhyay 1997).

And what of the legacy of the critique of kinship in this new era of kinship studies? I have whimsically termed the history of the critique of kinship short because, at a crucial moment of disciplinary reinvention, it celebrated the end of a history. To the extent that the critique proposed to fracture the notion of kinship once and for all, it represented a break with the past that might have foreclosed the possibility of further ethnography under kinship's standard. It is with no small sense of irony, then, that I would argue that the new kinship studies remains bound to the past in the form of at least two additional long-term effects of the critique of kinship. While both effects can be considered productive in the Foucauldian sense, one I see as problematic in the extreme; the other, a matter of great potential.

The first, highly problematic consequence derives from the nature of the tools used to disassemble kinship in the original critique. Schneider's work relied heavily on symbolic analysis, to the detriment of any investigation of the ties that bound kinship ideologies to political and economic developments. This bad debt, as it were, to the symbolic anthropology of the 1970s leaves the new kinship studies both in and out of history. In, because the controversies at the center of the new kinship studies are eminently historical, always located quite specifically with respect to the sociopolitical tensions that prevail in a particular time and place. Out, because the symbolic approach that characterized the critique of kinship scarcely bothered itself with power inequities, much less historical change.[2] Such a legacy makes it all the more important for scholars to treat historical developments as part of the phenomena in need of explanation, rather than just historical background to whatever kinship controversies may have caught the analytic eye.

On the positive side, the critique of kinship has provided a tonic for the fetish. If, as the critique would have it, kinship is basically the reification and naturalization of certain forms of belonging, then the critique of kinship opens the way to descry forms of relatedness and linkages that have been cut up and fetishized as kinship versus, well, something else. Here again, the critique turns loquacious with its ostensibly prohibitive "no." A "no" to reification solicits inquiries into the processes that create the sorts of naturalized ties that people take as given (see Yanagisako and Delaney 1995). The proclamation "not kinship" also doubles as an invitation to a new way of seeing, a way of looking relationally at the betwixt and between and beforehand of received social categories.

Before beginning to sketch out the kind of analysis that could illustrate my point, I want to underscore the importance of any legacy that can work as an antidote to fetishization. When scholars today search for new forms of kinship, they walk a fine line between the investigation of relatedness in "indigenous" terms and a return to the voyages of discovery that did so much to naturalize the landscape of social science. The new kinship studies remains suspiciously enamored of biology, even in the critique.[3] With history pushed into the background, there is a tendency to ally science with technology and take up each instance of technology as an artifact of some bold new supermodern moment.[4] Artificial insemination then signifies a high-tech innovation, regardless of its historical subordination to the goals of the eugenics movement and the rather pedestrian apparatus (medicine dropper, turkey baster) required for its implementation.

Recent years have witnessed a concomitant gravitation back toward European and U.S. constructions of relatedness (as evidenced, for example, in the attention given to procreation and parent-child ties). None of these scholarly preoccupations are, in and of themselves, wrong. All bear investigation. Yet it is worth sounding a cautionary note when "family resemblances" — the old baby making and the new baby making, so to speak — emerge in the midst of an avowed period of intellectual innovation. A cumulative focus on interrogations of biology and science, in the absence of an equivalent interest in connecting some different and less familiar dots, suggests that the new kinship studies is still indentured to kinship in the time-honored sense of the term.

These trends may only indicate a tendency to go where ideology leads, but I wonder. It's tempting to approach kinship studies as though the referent were there, waiting for analysis, albeit not in the same unexamined sense as before the critique. Paradoxically, however, kinship studies — even in its new, improved, repackaged, vitamin-fortified form — cannot afford to reconstitute itself. The new kinship studies may be many things, but it can no longer legitimately concern itself with the study of a freestanding thing called kinship. If kinship studies has an organizing question in the aftermath of the critique, it would ask how to take the traffic in kinship ideologies into account, how to attend closely to matters of relatedness, without reifying kinship as an object of study.

What it means to pursue this line of inquiry remains to be worked out, as research, controversy, and social developments continue apace. My own inclination is to attempt to use the perspective afforded by the critique of kinship to move discussion back toward big-picture questions about power and social struggle without necessarily moving toward totalizing answers. What happens, for instance, when investigation shifts from the issue of what makes a relative to the question of what relatedness makes? When political economy begins to organize topics broached as well as observations made?[5]

What sort of a twist can be given to current debates by setting the reified categories of kinship (younger daughter, nuclear family, mother's brother) and identity politics (race, nation, religion, gender) side by side, bracketing the lot, then thinking "relation" instead of "thing"? The result should not be another study of cultural differences in the ways that people "do family," distinctive ways of conceptualizing kinship ties, or even contests over what it all means. Demystifying kinship entails an examination of the production and reification of the very demarcations, enmities, and solidarities that produce family ties as something apart from, though implicated in, identity-based bonds.

Still, an analyst needs a way in. In the remainder of this essay, I take up just one example of relations that are not necessarily (or not yet) congealed into relationship: the sharing of substance as a historically contextualized, material practice. A critical examination of the concept of shared substance, especially as it figures in kinship theory in the United States, is long overdue. Yet my purpose here is not to approach the concept simply as a metaphor awaiting excavation. I intend to waylay the concept for my own theoretical purposes by using it to take a closer look at historical controversies that have clustered around literal transfers of bodily fluids.

If kinship can ideologically entail shared substance, can transfers of bodily substance create—or threaten to create—kinship? Can they create—or threaten to create—other forms of social responsibility? What investment do people have in depicting the transfer of blood, organs, and sperm as sharing, giving, or donation? What investment do they have in resisting such transfers (or the vehicles of transfer)? Alternatively, how do people work to construe transfers as "signifying nothing" with respect to race, sexual contact, religious identity, and so on (Thompson, this volume; Kahn 2000)?

Not all transfers of bodily substance, for instance, lend themselves easily to being characterized as a donation. Once saliva takes the form of spit (almost by definition an unwanted offering), it's hard to construe as a gift. Insult or weapon of the weak, yes; donation, no. Lawsuits have sought to portray blood and saliva as deadly weapons when wielded by HIV-positive men (even though the concentrations of HIV in saliva are not high enough to transmit the virus). Jehovah's Witnesses have fought court battles to limit the power of the state to force blood transfusions that their religious beliefs proscribe. Even mythical transfers, such as the movement of blood from victim to vampire, don't rate highly in the gifting and altruism department. Likewise with sponsored research studies associated with the Human Genome Diversity Project, which not only involves attempts to patent bodily substances but has also been dubbed by opponents "the vampire project" in recognition of its reliance on blood sampling for DNA analysis (Rifkin 1998b, 14; see also Coombe 1998; Rifkin 1998a; Marks, this volume).

Under what historical circumstances does something like a blood transfusion, or the implantation of sperm-manufacturing cells in a "host" body, arouse fear and opposition? How are social classifications of bodies and belonging built into the institutions that mediate transfers of bodily substance: the medevac flight, the blank for authorizing organ donation on state-issued driver's licenses, the establishment of "banks" to process and distribute blood and sperm? What can a historically informed consideration of blood transfusions, specifically, teach about the site-specific meanings that have allowed transfusions to substantiate "brotherhood" in one instance, illicit sexuality in another, altruism in another, and in yet another, an incitement to racial invective and homicide? Connection replaces kinship and transfers replace technology at the heart of the analysis.

BLOOD TYPES, EMBODIMENT, AND THE TIE YOU CAN'T BANK ON

In one of his early novels, *Youngblood,* John Oliver Killens portrays race and class relations in prewar Georgia from the vantage point of 1954. Hindsight can be a source of insight as well as regret. By tracing elements of controversies from the 1940s and 1950s regarding the transfer of blood back into the earlier period in which the novel is set, Killens allowed his own location in history to show, usually to good effect.

During the 1930s, the setting for the latter part of the novel, the National Association for the Advancement of Colored People (NAACP) was on the move not only in the fictionalized town of Crossroads, Georgia, but across the United States. Chapter by chapter, town by town, it had assumed a key role in the mobilization of a movement for what would retrospectively be termed civil rights. The attempt to organize a labor union across racial lines recorded in the novel also had its "real-life" counterparts in depression North America. Joe Louis, the Scottsboro Boys, and other historical figures make an appearance on the same pages that chronicle the struggle of *Youngblood*'s African American characters to maintain a faith in progress and racial uplift. Progress? Why, there hasn't been a lynching in Crossroads for over a year!

Little more than a decade after the events described in *Youngblood,* blood transfusion would become a matter for increased regulation and public debate in the United States. World War II provided an impetus for the development of newly industrialized techniques for collecting, handling, and preserving blood (Starr 1998). The establishment of "colored" battalions in the newly integrated armed forces brought with it the possibility of field hospitals in which blood would be moved from body to body across racial lines, making blood transfusion a locus for controversy and the renegotiation of racial boundaries. Following the war, President Truman issued his 1948 Executive Order prohibiting racial discrimination in the armed forces, supplying a tool and a spur to an emerging civil rights movement.[6]

Away from the exigencies of battle, the practice of direct transfusion began to give way (for those who could afford it) to the mediated administration of blood via so-called banks. Blood transfer had become an industry, with its share of bureaucracy and rules. When regulations in the new blood banks did not prohibit African Americans outright from making donations, administrators established a system of racial coding for blood samples and discrete facilities for storing "Negro blood." Blood tests designed to identify sickle-cell anemia began to be used to "detect" miscegenation and bolster fallacious arguments for the existence of bounded racial groups (Wailoo 1997, 145 passim).[7] In the warehousing and processing of this bodily fluid, as in so many institutionalized practices of the day, the rationale of separate but equal carried, with an emphasis on the separate.

The racial tension in *Youngblood* builds steadily, giving way to a beating here, a moment of studied disrespect there, incidents of mistrust and want-to-trust, humiliations calculated to turn son against mother and father against son, until in the final chapters, a white boss shoots Joe Youngblood down. Youngblood has made the "mistake" of asking the white man who distributes money to the "colored" pay line to stop shortchanging him on his pay. When the boss pulls out a gun from beneath the counter, Joe decks him and runs for what he knows to be his life, only to be shot twice in the back at close range by another white supervisor.

Coworkers in the "colored line" gather Youngblood up and take him to the city hospital, where he is refused admission even to the Colored Ward. Word travels in a small town, and the word passed from white mouth to ear is that a "Big Black Burly Negro Has Run Amuck" (Killens 1954, 443). After the police come looking to arrest Youngblood, friends carry his unconscious body to the part of town known as The Quarters. There, the exclusively African American residents organize patrols to ward off an expected—and duly materialized—attack by the Ku Klux Klan. Meanwhile, Dr. Jamison, the town's black doctor, goes in search of a portable X-ray machine (which white doctors repeatedly refuse to lend), returning in a car with the headlights off to set up blood transfusions and operate as best he can.

After testing, Joe Youngblood turns out to be Type O, a blood group shared by none of his "blood kin" and only three of the next twenty volunteers who come forward. The first to give blood is Richard Myles, a young schoolteacher from New York who "felt like a blood relation" to Youngblood's wife, Laurie Lee (443). But he is only the first.

Over in Peckerwood Town, Oscar Jefferson can't sleep. Uneducated, poor, and white, he has spent much of his life hauling barrels in the same turpentine factory as Youngblood. Jefferson has come as close to befriending Youngblood as is possible across the lines of "cracker" and "colored," which is to say, they haven't managed a friendship at all. But Oscar has been seen walking out of the factory with Joe, grumbling about ill treatment at the hands of their mutual boss. He is the first white person to sign a union card down at the hotel where Youngblood's son, Rob, is trying to organize the workers. When the word "nigger" comes to Jefferson's mind unbidden, he quickly substitutes "Negro." When African Americans "sass" him, he's quick to anger with a white man's rage. In childhood he listened to his friend, Little Jim Kilgrow: "You poor white trash and I'm a Negro—so what goddammit have you got to be so glad about?" (232). Then he fought Little Jim anyway. His brother-in-law down at the hotel calls Oscar "nigger lover" like it was his middle name. "A funny cracker," the Youngbloods call him: "A pretty nice old cracker." Oscar Jefferson is too poor and too independent minded to be a classic liberal, but he walks the line.

On the night of the shooting, Jefferson calls two of his sons back to prevent them from joining the lynch mob going after Youngblood. Then he sets out for The Quarters with a third son, Junior, the one he can talk to, the one who added another signature to those union cards. Oscar Jefferson has come to help, but the kind of help that's really needed, he's not quite prepared to give.

The men on patrol at the edge of The Quarters have already turned back the Klan once. When they see Jefferson and his son coming down the road, they come close to shooting the two white men, then present Oscar with a choice. If he really wants to help, he can donate blood. Joe Youngblood needs more, and those who can give already have.

Oscar Jefferson wavers with a vacillation that is excruciating in its predictability. He is not the only one who hesitates. Two of the African American men guarding the road into The Quarters also exchange words. "'Is white blood any different from colored?' Elwood asked uneasily. 'Man, blood is blood,' Ray said. 'I'm surprised at you.'" Oscar echoes Elwood's concern once he and his son enter the house where doctors, family, and friends have hidden Joe

Youngblood away. Jefferson directs his questions to the liberal white doctor whom Myles, the schoolteacher, has browbeaten into assisting. "'Is it all right, doc?' Oscar asked. 'Do white blood mix with colored?' . . . 'There's no white blood and there's no black blood,' Dr. Riley said. 'All blood is red-blood. The only difference is in the different types'" (460).

In the event, Oscar Jefferson's fears refuse to submit to the reassurance of science. He experiences "shame-faced relief" when his type does not match Joe's. But that relief is short-lived, because his son Junior turns out to have "the right kind of blood." He watches Junior's face grow "whiter and whiter" as his son struggles with the decision. Finally, Junior moves to lie down next to Joe and the transfusion begins.

What makes father and son so apprehensive? They do not couch their fears in a rhetoric of health and disease; they are not even candidates to receive blood. A clue resides in the cover art for the mass paperback edition of the book (see figure 5.1). On the cover, an alert Junior lies on a makeshift pallet next to Youngblood, who has his eyes closed in an attitude that suggests sleep. Their heads incline toward one another, their hands remain upturned and outstretched, as a bright red fluid courses through a tube that snakes its way from arm to arm. The inferred movement of Junior's blood is the only touch. This scene, which stands in for the book as a whole, renders visible the transfer of substance from body to body through the device of a clear length of tubing.

There is an intimacy to this act. A slash of red joins length to length, body to body, man to man. In this sense, it is significant that the person with the "right" blood turns out to be not Oscar Jefferson but his son Junior. Direct transfusion introduces a homoerotic counterpoint into an already deadly score. Miscegenation has long supplied the pretext for a call to action; lynching, the white response to perceived intimacies between white women and black men. Liberal views on sex and marriage are well known to crumble when the subject turns to your daughter or mine. It is not incidental that characters in *Youngblood* discuss blood transfusion in terms of "mixing."[8]

"Oscar could feel his entire body running hot and cold. . . . [The thought of] giving his blood, a white man's blood, and letting it mix with a black man's blood was more than he had counted on" (459). Mixing threatens the color-coded boundary that marks a racialized hierarchy. It is a hierarchy from which Jefferson benefits, though not in the same way as the white factory owner who runs the town. Even when Jefferson doesn't benefit, the notion that he *should* provides him guilty solace. After the transfusion merges black and white into

FIG. 5.1 The cover of the 1955 Cardinal Giant paperback edition of John Oliver
Killens's novel, *Youngblood.* Reprinted by permission.

red, dissolving hierarchy into an impossible chromatography, it places all the participants at odds with entrenched ways of doing relationship. And where does that leave Oscar or his son in terms of belonging?

The transfer of blood between *these* particular bodies sweeps the Jeffersons, the Youngbloods, and other African Americans who have found shelter in The Quarters into a new and tenuous sort of connection. In and of itself, the transfusion does not create a bond of kinship between Junior and Joe, any more than it does between Joe and the black men and women who had previously contributed blood. What does change is alliance, in ways that draw on ideologies of kinship yet do not tarry there.

In the aftermath of the transfusion, the Jeffersons seem to have proven themselves. "With a serious smile on his face," Fat Gus, the friend of Youngblood's son, Rob, announces, "'Far as I'm concerned, Oscar, you and Junior all right with me. Y'all members of the club.'" His figurative embrace evokes notions of the club as a voluntary association of like-minded folks, an association whose very inclusiveness rests on an exclusion practiced by gatekeepers who regulate the flow of members in and members out.

But Fat Gus's declaration also resonates with another old saying, "Welcome to the club": an expression used to address someone who has previously and unwittingly benefited from privilege, at a moment when that privilege is lost and the person finds him- or herself, even momentarily, in the company of others who have been getting short shrift all along. This latter sense of membership is not entirely welcoming, for it carries elements of irony, censure, and chastisement. You thought you were so central, so smart. You thought you knew, but now you know.

Up to this point, events have given readers no reason to disagree with the assessment voiced by Ellis, Rob's coworker at the hotel: "'[Oscar Jefferson] was a cracker before he was a worker. . . . You can't trust a white man no shape, form or fashion, especially down here in Georgia'" (404). Every tentative step across the color line has ended in a betrayal of black folks by white folks and by the circumstances that hedge them in. With the transfusion comes the first real possibility of trust, albeit a trust more easily accomplished for African Americans with one wary hand on the barrel of a gun. Jefferson himself has taken to carrying a pistol, knowing that he and Junior could easily become subject to the "justice" of the lynch mobs monitoring traffic in and out of The Quarters.[9]

Notice how these shifting alignments are mediated not only by the transfer of blood between "black" and "white" bodies but also by Oscar Jefferson's relationship as father to the son. The only drop of blood that Oscar contributes is for testing. Following the transfusion, his "kinship" relation to Junior both facilitates trust and lends force to the iconography of miscegenation. The shift in relations of belonging—"Y'all members of the club"—cannot be understood apart from ideologies of kinship, yet ideologies of kinship are insufficient to explain it.

In the novel, kinship is not readily achieved across racial lines, even when it brushes aside the formalities of biogenetic connection, sex, or marriage. After being beaten by his father as a child, Oscar Jefferson had to run for shelter to the house of a black friend, Little Jim Kilgrow. Oscar tells Little Jim:

> "Your folks sure wuz nice to me—" And Little Jim told him it wasn't anything. His folks were nice to everybody. "Taking me in like this and treating me, a whi—, treating me like I was they own son—I ain't never gon forget it—" His voice choked off. He could hear the toughness leaving Jim's voice. "Look, Ossie Jefferson, it really ain't nothing. My folks are Christian folks. I tell you how my Daddy feels about it, and I reckin my mother. He don't trust a white man living or dead, but if one of them is ready to take one step forward, Pa'll meet him halfway. . . . But even if Pa ever trusted a cracker, he would always keep his gun cocked and ready." (237)

What signifies kinship to one may signify something quite different to a person on the other side, especially the "down" side, of a racialized divide.

Long before the Jeffersons arrive in The Quarters, the novel has complicated the relationship of kinship to belonging. Killens describes Rob Youngblood in the hours when the doctors are running out of blood:

> And Rob watched the big man losing ground and the man was his father, but it was more than that, the man was his friend and more than that, the man was a man, the man was Joe Youngblood, and what made it especially painful to Rob was the helpless feeling, because Rob and Mama and Jenny Lee couldn't even give blood to Daddy. (452)

This passage features a complex interplay among the meanings attached to race, gender, and manhood, with family moving over into friendship, friendship into adulthood, adulthood into humanity, and humanity back again into kinship with the naming of Mama, Daddy, and Rob's sister, Jenny Lee.[10] Together they have confronted limitations—unforeseeable and heartbreaking limitations—to what Schneider (1968) would call code for conduct. All Rob can do is literally stand by his father, immobilized by the irony of blood kin who can contribute everything they have to a loved one's survival but blood.

So direct transfusion of blood, despite its characterization by lay science as a mixing of red with red (that is to say, hardly a mixing at all), tacks back and forth from black to white, black to black, and white to white. The school-teacher and the son of the funny cracker link themselves to Joe Youngblood, to the friends and relatives gathered around Youngblood's bed, and to social struggle, through a medium that blood relations, backed by all the symbolic force of biology and love, cannot utilize. Kinship turns transient in the process, diffusing through a wider set of shifting alliances of friendship, neighborliness, opposition, and race politics. Paradoxically enough, kinship ideologies mediate the whole thing.

Youngblood is above all a novel about solidarities, about the ways that people try and often fail to stick together. These are not solidarities that endure but solidarities that allow people to endure. Early in the book, two white men bribe, shame, and cajole Rob Youngblood into boxing with his best friend, Fat Gus, for their pleasure. "Come on, boys," they say, "Les mix it up. Quit that waltzing around. Git rough with each other. Y'all ain' no kin" (71). Rob can't figure out how to keep an already untenable situation from getting worse until his furious mother comes along, takes his arm, and drags him away. A few chapters later, a group of African American children surround two grade-schoolers. Both combatants are black, but they have turned against one another in part because of words exchanged about their different shades of skin color. "Go ahead and fight," the circle of kids shouts. "Y'all ain' no kin" (104). Kinship here constitutes the principal bar to conflict between those who have every reason to join together to fight a bigger fight. The body-to-body transfers of blood that usher the novel toward its conclusion suggest another way.

AWAY FROM THE BODY, BACK TO THE BOND

Just a few decades ago, people came to blows and created structures of exclusion in response to the prospect of blood transfers that threatened to link bodies already drafted into the signification of racial difference. More recently, these border skirmishes have shifted to the line imagined to differentiate homosexual from heterosexual. With the onset of AIDS and the early identification of AIDS with homosexuality, many blood banks prevented (or strongly discouraged) gay men from donating blood. Lesbians, never collectively designated "at risk" by public health organizations, nevertheless experienced similar treatment.[11] The designation of risk groups itself encouraged the misunderstanding that HIV transmission followed identity rather than behavior. Men who had unprotected sex with men but did not identify as gay sometimes wrongly understood themselves to run no risk of HIV infection. Heterosexually married people who received blood from banks that did not screen for sexual identity (whether or not they screened blood samples for HIV) sometimes wrongly understood themselves to run an increased risk of HIV infection.[12]

From the beginning, HIV was a virus constructed through social identity. Gay-related immune deficiency, or GRID, supplied the mnemonic precursor to AIDS. Even with improved documentation of modes of transmission and the scope of the epidemic, phrases that invoke identity such as "IV drug users" (rather than "sharing needles" or "IV drug use") continue to dominate news coverage. Contrast the treatment historically accorded anemias, which although increasingly the focus of professional concern, were not taken up into identity politics until the codification of a disease entity called sickle-cell anemia. With the development of clinical testing, sickled cells were quickly tagged as a marker of "Negro blood," allowing the test to be used to sustain the fiction of bounded and separable races.[13]

The politicization of gay identity is as much at stake in recent controversies about blood transfers as any etiology of disease. Blood-to-blood contact undoubtedly constitutes one vector for the transmission of HIV, but "gay blood" is a very different social entity than blood that tests HIV-positive. Fears of "mixing" as well as disease have left donors and recipients — very much like Junior and Jefferson — trembling at the thought. The issue is not so much giving versus receiving: the Red Cross had to stage a publicity campaign to reassure potential donors that they could not contract HIV from giving blood. Fears of disease mark the site of connection, serving as a reminder that behind the impersonality of those plastic-wrapped red sacks distributed from a bank lie differently colored, desiring, and all-too-mortal bodies.

Youngblood provides historical context for the fear that transfers of specific bodily substances such as blood will create unanticipated, even unwanted, forms of connection. Class and race figure centrally in the narrative, much as they did in Georgia back in the day. In Killens's dramatization, a politics and economics of division set the terms of the encounter, allocating hospital access to some, makeshift surgery or death without medication to others. In certain contexts, however, transfers of blood can symbolize hope rather than fear. By the 1990s, the very "mixing" promised by blood-to-blood contact had come to signify (especially for white audiences?) the transcendence of violence and race/class conflict.

By way of contrast, I want to juxtapose the controversial blood transfusion from the 1930s described in *Youngblood* with media coverage of the 1997 blood drive for Betty Shabazz. Shabazz, a scholar in her own right but more widely known as the widow of Malcolm X, was severely burned in a fire set by her grandson, Malcolm's namesake. According to the *New York Times,* the blood drive in Harlem "drew donors of all complexions and convictions, whose contact would usually be limited to street corner bump-and-run but who yesterday spent hours in intimate conversation while they waited to give a pint of blood" (Gross 1997). Positioned here as (self-)sacrificing grandmother — the adult African American figure least threatening to a white audience and the one most easily assimilated to "mammy" imagery — Shabazz "naturally" appears to elicit support across fractures of race and class.[14]

The *New York Times* article goes on to picture "Ted Yanow, an elderly doctoral student in sociology," sitting down together with a bank president, "Bahia Lee, a home health aide, Ruth W. Messinger, a candidate for Mayor, and Bruce Thornton, a cook in a Harlem church. . . . For Mr. Thornton, it was a pleasing contrast to the time years ago when, unemployed, he sold his blood for money." Readers also learn of the donor who writes on a card for "the Shabazz family": "I gave blood to you because of the blood your husband lost when he was alive" (Gross 1997). The *Amsterdam News,* which cosponsored the drive, did not pitch the same "rainbow" angle on the story to its predominantly African American and Afro-Caribbean readership.

The present status of AIDS as an incurable and deadly condition prevents sexual identity from working as a signifier of transcendence in quite the same way as race or class when the topic concerns bodily fluids. A story about "people of all sexualities coming together to donate blood" would be more likely to generate panic than to support the dangerous (but popular) fiction that racism and homophobia are matters of ancient history. Take a closer look at the spin put on the blood drive for Shabazz in the *Times* story. What, besides sexuality, is missing from this ode to race/class harmony? Blood type, for one, and blood banks, for another.

There is, of course, no connection between phenotype and blood type, between the appearance of two bodies and their compatibility for the purposes of transfusion, any more than there is a correlation between skin color and the color of blood. At one time investigators attempted to bend the concept of blood types to racist ends, but in general, blood groups have not become a site for identification or mobilization.[15] Many people do not know whether they "belong" to Type O, A, B, or AB, much less feel a sense of affiliation with others in "their" groups. This is a significant absence for a society in which blood carries a heavy symbolic freight, inside and outside ideologies of kinship.[16]

The mere mention of blood types in a newspaper story dedicated to "getting along" would raise the nasty issue of incompatibility. When types do not match, blood transmutes from a gift into a poison capable of sending the recipient into shock. There is no room for such alchemy if blood donation is to signify the possibility of overcoming any and every social divide, at least in the "paper of record" for the powers that be.

At first glance, the division of humanity into four blood groups seems to crosscut both kinship and race, providing an alternative (though underutilized) basis for affiliation. At the same time, there is an interesting symmetry between the classification of four blood "types" or "groups" (with Rh thrown in almost as an afterthought) and the color coding of race typologies in the United States. Red-Yellow-Black-White: an assemblage so inadequate to describe the range of hues and identities in North America that people sometimes jokingly refer to it as "the four food groups." Although the notion of blood type minimizes references to race through a crosscutting move, its exhaustive fourfold structure reconstitutes the idea of biologically bounded entities. A person "is" either A, B, AB, or O. Yet and still, medical exigencies do not demand the concept of group or type. Blood transfers could just as well be conceptualized, like organ donation or arranged marriage, as an occasion to check a series of compatibility factors in search of a match.[17] Even as the notion of blood type appears to challenge racial hierarchy (as it does in *Youngblood*), it can carry a raced subtext.

In the United States, the marketing of type appears to be increasingly pervasive. From the "only in America" files comes a photograph of a billboard that reads, "Who's the father? 1-800-DNA-TYPE." Smaller letters at the bottom of the billboard reveal the ad's sponsor: *Identi*gene Precise Paternity Testing (Belluck 1997). Other advertisements target the apparatus for transfer. A billboard glimpsed a few years ago on a major truck route through Kansas promoted surgical services to men who were having second thoughts about their vasectomies. Fertility restored by picking up your phone and dialing "1-800-REVERSE."

The Shabazz story, in contrast, bypasses discussion of type in favor of an individualized discourse of donation. In 1990s' Harlem, blood donation across racial lines, which in a Killens novel would have turned black folks "ashen" and Anglos whiter than white, remains a peaceable affair. Unlike the characters in *Youngblood,* the donors who gather in Harlem are portrayed as comfortable, talkative, at ease sitting down with one another as they traffic in bodily fluids. No controversy here! The whole bloody business comes to symbolize a triumph of the human spirit, with an emphasis on the human. Altruism brings together people of every color and occupation (and what else, the story implies, could get a white person to Harlem, except perhaps political opportunism in the case of a candidate for mayor?). This is an altruism that takes hierarchy, hostility, difference, even a ride on the A-Train in stride.

The *New York Times*'s coverage treats bodies as interchangeable under circumstances when blood type says they are anything but. How is this possible? By overlooking factors of type and compatibility, each donor can speak as though her or his blood were going directly to Shabazz. That fantasy lends a curiously disembodied quality to an act (transfusion) that requires access to bodies at their most material. Conspicuously absent in this celebratory reading of donation are the institutions that screen, sort, process, regulate, and recruit bodies for their blood.[18] Since the beginning of the twentieth century, the dominant mode of blood transfer has shifted from direct transfusion to one mediated by blood banks. It is this warehousing of blood in an intermediate stop between bodies that allows blood transfers to be resignified to represent a timeless, depoliticized, *universal* solidarity.[19] Once every individual becomes the potential secret sharer, there is no impetus to come to terms with damage or differences organized through class/color hierarchies. This sort of solidarity — one without allies, context, or contingencies — would have been a stranger to both Joe Youngblood and Junior Jefferson.

At the blood drive for Shabazz, tubing does not join mahogany to cinnamon or white arm to black. However red the blood may flow, it runs from body to vial and body to pouch. A particular set of technologies and institutions establishes itself before transfers of blood override type in order to conjure up a naturalized "brotherhood of man" [*sic*].

There is an irony here, of course. Blood transfusion in *Youngblood* works to create an alliance precisely because the bodies are visible, the connection is visible, and the bodies (and their histories) are known. A blood drive works quite differently. While donors may have imagined making a direct contribution to Shabazz's recovery, the blood separated from their bodies quickly passed over into the measured anonymity of units, factors, and types. Spokespeople for area blood banks rejoiced in this windfall at a time of "low blood supply." Yet the supply to which they referred existed in banks, not bodies. No one in that room in Harlem had to negotiate the tensions or possibilities that accompany a direct transfusion. The disembodiment of the blood and the invisibility of the process of transfer allowed them to picture a connection (to humanity, to Shabazz) that transcends even differences as concrete as the incompatibility that can turn a pint of the "wrong" blood into a vector of death.[20]

Throughout, institutions tend to downplay their participation in the classification and alteration of the "natural" substances they collect. In the era of blood screening and blood banking, even using one's own blood for surgery carries potential hazards, since processing can change that blood enough to cause the body to reject it as other. So a bodily substance is not quite the same substance once mediated by the medical industry, just as units of blood administered during a hospital stay signify as something more than sharing once a patient receives the bill.

With the intervention of banks, bodies as donors and bodies as recipients cease to occupy the same social space. Transfusions become subject to measurement and standardization; blood comes packaged in plastic sacks instead of persons. Blood "products" replace a corporeal flow; hepatitis, HIV, and other forms of blood-borne disease are reconfigured in the context of donation as a kind of willful, even criminal, product tampering. This institutionally enforced segregation gives concrete form to what Rosi Braidotti (1994) has termed the production of organs (and fluids) without bodies. Science renders blood more and more like money: a universal instrument of exchange supposed to make all bodies commensurable. In consumer America, the folk adage "Everybody bleeds red" supplements the sales motto "Everybody's money is green." In a society without racism, no one would need to make such a statement.

While there are pragmatic reasons for blood banking (ready access, screening for disease), the ultimate effect has been not connection but disembodiment. Disembodiment is dangerous precisely because it takes no account of the color of the hand that pays over the money and the color of the hand that collects, the condition of the body that solicits blood and the condition of the body that yields.[21] Any perspective on inequality is lost, and with it, the opportunity to think relationally about the bond.

What happens after the blood drive, when the bank president goes back to his job and the home health aide to hers? Suppose their paths were to cross again in site-specific fashion the day she walks through the doors of his bank to cash her meager paycheck in the very same building where he sits secluded, occupied with "higher" things. Meeting schedules, office walls, the briefest of lunch breaks intervene. As they move through common space in their still-common humanity, each is unlikely to recognize the other on this occasion, when the exchange involves not blood but that more classic instance of universal commodification, money. What will it take this time around to make mute substance speak? There's not a whole lot of donation going on down at the bank.

In the meantime, the blood banking structure continues to keep accounts. It remains engaged in social classification at the very moment that its standardized procedures proclaim the universalism of its enterprise. Types ("Type B," "right blood," "wrong blood") and identities ("HIV-," "Negro blood") have historically been produced through the very operations designed to accomplish the material sharing of substance, or its refusal. First appeals for blood when the "supply" runs low often go out to "blood family" in the narrowest genealogical sense.

What results is not the sharing of substance Schneider described in *American Kinship* (1968), where couples imaginatively create a biogenetic tie through heterosexual intercourse. The blood ties created through the use of sperm banks and blood banks abjure full-body contact, sexual desire, even casual touch. If industry cannot chemically synthesize all the bodily substances in which it trades, it can certainly regulate their transfer, and with that transfer, social relations.[22]

It is in the modes of transfer and analysis of bodily substances that power shows its hand. Colored caps now mark the vials of semen at many sperm banks in the United States. In one clinic, clients who require more than popular culture to decipher the code receive a list: white indicates "Caucasian," yellow means "Asian" (but apparently only East Asian), black codes "African/African American," and red serves as residual category that stretches all the way from "American Indian" to "East Indian" (South Asian). And what of donors whose forebears have nibbled away at more than one of the four food groups? Semen from a man who claimed both African American and Native American heritage ended up with a red stopper.[23] The caps are there to offer reassurance, just like the story on the blood drive for Shabazz. But to whom?

"Racial mixing," according to Elizabeth Noble, remains "one of the very common fears of DI [donor insemination] couples" (1987, 129). In her guide for prospective parents, she quotes from one "personal account" of insemination: "I had nightmares all through my pregnancy. The child looked different each time. Last night he was Chinese and cross-eyed" (71). Noble's book includes an index entry for "Genetic Contamination" that reads, "See also racism." Color-coded vials of semen attempt to *reembody* the anonymous source of a visually homogeneous substance, as parents worry about what children might look like as well as inherit. If those parents happen to be seeking sperm that fall into the red category, I suppose there's little reassurance to be had.

AND FROM HERE?

At its best, the critique of kinship addressed a field in bondage to certain modes of thinking relationship. At its most productive, it continues to entice scholars to think not just in terms of connection but connecting; not just relatives but racialization; not just technologies but modes of transfer; not just substance but the history of social struggle. This is an approach that asks whether we should be studying the colored caps used in fertility clinics in conjunction with the funds invested in the development of bloodless surgery (see Langone 1997). This is an approach that links the organization of blood banks to prospects for union organizing; the push by eugenics proponents to inseminate working-class women with "high-IQ" sperm to the creation of HIV-positive as a disease identity; the controversy over adding a biracial category to the U.S. census form to custody decisions that privilege so-called blood ties; the training of militias to the denigration of friendship; the institution of the blood drive to corporate ad campaigns that picture a techno-global village as a fait accompli. Viewed through the lens of political economy, kinship appears not as a coherent ideology or core concept but rather as something congealed. As it sets, kinship leaves unnamed and unrecognized those shifting affiliations that refuse the claims to ideological stability of even a radically contested term like "chosen family." The question for study then becomes: Congealed how, for whose benefit, and from what?

If you go on to ask how things have changed (or not) from rural Georgia in the 1930s to Harlem in the 1990s, you won't come up with a narrative of progress or even redemption. All the blood in the world cannot bring Betty Shabazz and Joe Youngblood back. But you might gain new insight into the possibilities and limitations of speaking substance to power before seeking analytic comfort in more standardized grids of belonging.

What's at stake in this reformulation of kinship studies? An understanding of what gives force to the incantation threaded through John Oliver Killens's narrative indictment of inequality in the United States: "Go ahead and fight — y'all ain' no kin." An understanding of alliances that can and shall overcome. An understanding of the part that relation continues to play in the everyday drama of bonds broken and solidarities ventured, whatever kin y'all is, are, or ain't.

NOTES

1 This despite Schneider's lifelong commitment to teaching kinship courses, supervising dissertations on kinship, and so forth. Of interest to me here is one popular narration of the presumed long-term effects of the critique of kinship, a narration that achieved its widest circulation within the United States, where biology (however conceived) continues to occupy a central position in discussions of relatedness. The degree to which kinship studies actually fell into abeyance in various locales is another matter entirely.

2 Although it could be argued that history shadows Schneider's every analytic step, in the sense that the symbolic prominence of "blood" in the reckoning of kinship in the United States cannot be separated from the bloody history of the colonization of a continent. Throughout the nineteenth and twentieth centuries, the government appealed to racialized conceptions of "Indian," "white," "Oriental," and "Negro" blood in order to justify decisions to appropriate land, redefine treaty obligations, establish property rights, reserve voting rights, restrict immigration, deny sovereignty, and allocate citizenship (see, for example, Dominguez 1986; Vizenor 1990).

3 On the relation of reproductive technologies to reckonings of kinship, see Franklin 1997; Franklin and Ragoné 1998; Hartouni 1997; Kahn 2000; Rapp, Heath, and Taussig, this volume. On the impoverished understandings of biology that often inform this area of scholarship, see also Franklin, this volume.

4 On supermodernity in relation to the comeback of the individual (faced here with an excess of reproductive "choices"), see Auge 1995.

5 As occurs in the contributions by Gillian Feeley-Harnik and Susan McKinnon to this volume.

6 The injustices facing African American men in the military is a topic central to another of Killens's novels, *And Then We Heard the Thunder* (1962).

7 Compare Melbourne Tapper's chapter (this volume), which links testing for sickle-cell anemia to the drawing of borders in colonial Africa, where officials used such testing to classify subaltern populations into allegedly discrete ethnic groups.

8 See also Siobhan Somerville (2000), who suggestively ties the policing of a black/white boundary in the United States to the historical division of bodies into two new categories: homosexual and heterosexual.

9 "For Southern white workers to openly express solidarity with African Americans," writes the historian Robin D. G. Kelley, "was a direct challenge to the public transcript of racial difference and domination. . . . [W]hen white workers were exposed as 'nigger lovers' or when they took public stands on behalf of African Americans, the consequences could be fatal" (1994, 32).

10 On the politics of asserting manhood in the face of the emasculation associated with legacies of slavery and colonization, see Carby 1998; Johnson 1994; Nandy 1983; Nelson 1998; Sinha 1995; Stecopoulos and Uebel 1997.

11 A reaction fueled by what Eve Kosofsky Sedgwick (1990) has termed a minoritizing approach to the construction of lesbian/gay (and to some extent bisexual) identity.

12 Cindy Patton (1990, 144–45) briefly discussed the administration of risk-assessment checklists by blood banks in the years before an HIV antibody test was developed.

13 Keith Wailoo (1997, 5) attaches particular significance to the fact that many anemias did not readily become a locus for panic or social identity, in contrast to smallpox, tuberculosis, yellow fever, and scarlet fever. This, despite anemias' apparently deadly potential. For a historical perspective on the scapegoating of various groups for infectious diseases, including HIV, see Rushing 1995.

14 On the enduring legacy of the racist imagery associated with "the mammy," see Collins 1991; Goings 1994; Turner 1994. I am grateful to Christine Gailey for underscoring this point.

15 For a brief account of Nazi attempts to justify genocide and imperial expansion by citing research on the geographic distribution of blood types, see Starr 1998, 72–76.

16 An exception that appears to bolster the rule concerns the popular diet book, *Eat Right for Your Type,* which makes nutrition contingent on blood group (D'Adamo 1996). Although the book uses "type" as its organizing principle, on matters of affiliation the author tends to equivocate. Peter D'Adamo encourages readers to identify with membership in a blood group primarily in order to arrive at the "*individualized* diet solution" (emphasis added) promised in the subtitle. I am grateful to Jennifer Hyndman for drawing this source to my attention.

17 Compare the personalization of the relationship—and body part—that joined Karen Anderson to Sue Tschirhart. Already related through union membership and employment by the state of Michigan, the two came to "share Bud, a kidney that Anderson gave to Tschirhart" after learning about Tschirhart's deteriorating condition due to a genetic kidney disease (A Few Things 1998).

18 For a discussion of the coding of transfers of eggs and sperm as donation, a concept that (like banking) dovetails neatly with consumerism and tethers action to individual inclination, see Strathern 1992; Thompson, this volume. A discourse of donation also underplays the importance of institutions such as schools, labor unions, and prisons in securing substances for transfer. According to Jerry Lewis, coordinator of National Donor Day for the United Auto Workers, "Labor has long been in the vanguard of blood collection. . . . Sixty percent of all blood collected is done so at the workplace" (UAW 1998). On the political economy of organ donation, including the coercive aspects that poverty introduces into transplantation, as well

as controversies surrounding donations mandated by the state, see Missouri 1998; Hogle 1999; Rothman 1998; Scheper-Hughes 1996; Youngner, Fox, and O'Connell 1996.

19 The metaphor of banking has since, of course, been extended to the processing and storage of other bodily substances such as eggs and sperm. On the tensions between the selling and gifting of blood in different cultural and economic contexts, see Eckholm 1998; Titmuss 1971. Banking veils these tensions, just as the terminology of sharing and donation can obscure elements of obligation or coercion. Sharing is no more or no less politicized than the conditions under which transfers of substances occur. In Germany, there have been attempts to get away from the twofold association of banking with commerce and Holocaust imagery of "stockpiled" body parts by, for example, substituting "laboratory" for "bank" in the titles of tissue procurement agencies (see Hogle 1999, 120).

20 Compare the kind of perspectivalism that Marilyn Strathern explores (1992), which elevates the significance of knowing (for example, the identity of one's parents). In contrast, the disembodied reading of connection in the coverage of the blood drive for Shabazz requires a kind of not knowing (blood group, compatibility, the actual destination of the blood) in order to work its humanist alchemy.

21 Compare the decision by the Court of the Fifth Circuit in *Hopwood v. Texas,* which struck down the implementation of affirmative action in admissions decisions at the University of Texas Law School. "In *Hopwood* the appeals court reached the remarkable conclusion that a student's race is no more relevant to diversity of life experiences on campus than 'choices based upon the physical size or *blood type* of applicants'" (Hair 1996; emphasis added). At issue here is something more than an absence of collective identification on the basis of blood type. In *Hopwood,* blood type becomes emblematic of a color-blind approach to addressing inequity and social conflict.

22 Although industry continues to work toward such a synthesis. "Artificial blood" has already been produced in forms with limited applicability (Wang 2001).

23 Interview with a client of the clinic, which uses a private company as its supplier. The clinic does not allow copies of the code list to leave the premises.

REFERENCES

Auge, Marc. 1995. *Non-Places: Introduction to an Anthropology of Supermodernity.* Translated by John Howe. New York: Verso.

Belluck, Pam. 1997. Everybody's Doing It: Paternity Testing for Fun and Profit. *New York Times,* 3 August.

Braidotti, Rosi. 1994. *Nomadic Subjects: Embodiment and Sexual Difference in Contemporary Feminist Theory.* New York: Columbia University Press.

Carby, Hazel V. 1998. *Race Men.* Cambridge: Harvard University Press.

Collins, Patricia Hill. 1991. *Black Feminist Thought: Knowledge, Consciousness, and the Politics of Empowerment.* New York: Routledge.

Coombe, Rosemary J. 1998. *The Cultural Life of Intellectual Properties: Authorship, Appropriation, and the Law.* Durham, N.C.: Duke University Press.

D'Adamo, Peter J., with Catherine Whitney. 1996. *Eat Right for Your Type: The Individualized Diet Solution to Staying Healthy, Living Longer, and Achieving Your Ideal Weight.* New York: G. P. Putnam's Sons.

Dominguez, Virginia. 1986. *White by Definition: Social Classification in Creole Louisiana.* New Brunswick, N.J.: Rutgers University Press.

Eckholm, Erik. 1998. Hoping to Control Spread of AIDS, China Bans the Sale of Blood. *New York Times,* 1 October.

A Few Things in Common. 1998. *Solidarity,* October, 15.

Franklin, Sarah. 1997. *Embodied Progress: A Cultural Account of Assisted Conception.* New York: Routledge.

Franklin, Sarah, and Helena Ragoné, eds. 1998. *Reproducing Reproduction: Kinship, Power, and Technological Innovation.* Philadelphia: University of Pennsylvania Press.

Goings, Kenneth W. 1994. *Mammy and Uncle Mose: Black Collectibles and American Stereotyping.* Bloomington: Indiana University Press.

Gross, Jane. 1997. Compelled by Shabazz's Situation, Hundreds Give Blood. *New York Times,* 10 June.

Hair, Penda D. 1996. Color-Blind—or Just Blind? *Nation,* 14 October, 12–14.

Hartouni, Valerie. 1997. *Cultural Conceptions: On Reproductive Technologies and the Remaking of Life.* Minneapolis: University of Minnesota Press.

Hogle, Linda F. 1999. *Recovering the Nation's Body: Cultural Memory, Medicine, and the Politics of Redemption.* New Brunswick, N.J.: Rutgers University Press.

Johnson, Charles. 1994. A Phenomenology of the Black Body. In *The Male Body: Features, Destinies, Exposures,* edited by Laurence Goldstein. Ann Arbor: University of Michigan Press.

Kahn, Susan Martha. 2000. *Reproducing Jews: A Cultural Account of Assisted Conception in Israel.* Durham, N.C.: Duke University Press.

Kelley, Robin D. G. 1994. *Race Rebels: Culture, Politics, and the Black Working Class.* New York: Free Press.

Killens, John Oliver. 1954. *Youngblood.* Athens: University of Georgia Press.

———. 1962. *And Then We Heard the Thunder.* New York: Alfred A. Knopf.

Langone, John. 1997. Fear of AIDS Is Only One Reason Doctors Are Calling for Bloodless Surgery. *Time,* special issue on heroes of medicine, fall, 74–76.

Missouri May Spare Inmate Organ Donors. 1998. *New York Times,* 23 March.

Moses, Yolanda T. 1997. An Idea Whose Time Has Come Again: Anthropology Reclaims "Race." *Anthropology Newsletter* 38, no. 7: 1, 4.

Moses, Yolanda T., and Carol Mukhopadhyay. 1997. Is It "Race"?: Anthropology on Human Diversity. *American Anthropologist:* 517 passim.

Nandy, Ashis. 1983. *The Intimate Enemy: Loss and Recovery of Self under Colonialism.* Delhi: Oxford University Press.

Nelson, Dana D. 1998. *National Manhood: Capitalist Citizenship and the Imagined Fraternity of White Men.* Durham, N.C.: Duke University Press.

Noble, Elizabeth. 1987. *Having Your Baby by Donor Insemination: A Complete Resource Guide*. Boston: Houghton Mifflin.

Patton, Cindy. 1990. *Inventing AIDS*. New York: Routledge.

Rifkin, Jeremy. 1998a. *The Biotech Century: Harnessing the Gene and Remaking the World*. New York: Jeremy P. Tarcher.

———. 1998b. The Biotech Century: Human Life as Intellectual Property. *The Nation*, 13 April, 11–20.

Rothman, David J. 1998. The International Organ Traffic. *New York Review of Books*, 26 March, 14–18.

Rushing, William A. 1995. *The AIDS Epidemic: Social Dimensions of an Infectious Disease*. Boulder, Colo.: Westview Press.

Scheper-Hughes, Nancy. 1996. Theft of Life: The Globalization of Organ Stealing Rumours. *Anthropology Today* 12:3–11.

Schneider, David M. 1968. *American Kinship: A Cultural Account*. Englewood Cliffs, N.J.: Prentice-Hall.

———. 1984. *A Critique of the Study of Kinship*. Ann Arbor: University of Michigan Press.

Sedgwick, Eve Kosofsky. 1990. *Epistemology of the Closet*. Berkeley: University of California Press.

Sinha, Mrinalini. 1995. *Colonial Masculinity: The "Manly Englishman" and the "Effeminate Bengali" in the Late Nineteenth Century*. New York: Manchester University Press.

Somerville, Siobhan. 2000. *Queering the Color Line: Race and the Invention of Homosexuality in American Culture*. Durham, N.C.: Duke University Press.

Stacey, Judith. 1996. *In the Name of the Family: Rethinking Family Values in the Postmodern Age*. Boston: Beacon.

Starr, Douglas. 1998. *Blood: An Epic History of Medicine and Commerce*. New York: Alfred A. Knopf.

Stecopoulos, Harry, and Michael Uebel, eds. 1997. *Race and the Subject of Masculinities*. Durham, N.C.: Duke University Press.

Strathern, Marilyn. 1992. *Reproducing the Future: Anthropology, Kinship and the New Reproductive Technologies*. New York: Routledge.

Titmuss, Richard M. 1971. *The Gift Relationship: From Human Blood to Social Policy*. New York: Pantheon.

Turner, Patricia A. 1994. *Ceramic Uncles and Celluloid Mammies: Black Images and Their Influence on Culture*. New York: Anchor Books.

UAW and Saturn Team up on National Blood Donations. 1998. *Solidarity*, March–April.

Vizenor, Gerald. 1990. *Crossbloods: Bone Courts, Bingo, and Other Reports*. Minneapolis: University of Minnesota Press.

Wailoo, Keith. 1997. *Drawing Blood: Technology and Disease Identity in Twentieth-Century America*. Baltimore, Md.: Johns Hopkins University Press.

Wang, Linda. 2001. Blood Relatives: First-Generation Artificial Blood Is about to Hit the Market. *Science News* 159:206–207.

Weston, Kath. 1997. *Families We Choose: Lesbians, Gays, Kinship.* 2d ed. New York: Columbia University Press.

Yanagisako, Sylvia J., and Carol Delaney, eds. 1995. *Naturalizing Power: Essays in Feminist Cultural Analysis.* New York: Routledge.

Youngner, Stuart J., Renee C. Fox, and Laurence J. O'Connell, eds. 1996. *Organ Transplantation: Meanings and Realities.* Madison: University of Wisconsin Press.

CHAPTER 6

Strategic Naturalizing: Kinship in an Infertility Clinic
Charis Thompson

What might California infertility clinics in the 1990s reveal about contemporary kinship? This essay raises that question by going inside clinics and analyzing the work done during gestational surrogacy and egg donation to establish and disambiguate kin relations. Patients, practitioners, and third-party reproducers (egg and sperm donors and surrogates), with the help of medical techniques, lab standards, body parts, psychological screening, and rapidly evolving laws, all take on part of this work. The examples below show that the clinic is a site where certain bases of kin differentiation are foregrounded and recrafted while others are minimized to make the couples who seek and pay for infertility treatment — the intended parents — come out through legitimate and intact chains of descent as the real parents. All other parties to the reproduction, human and nonhuman, are rendered sufficiently prosthetic in the reproduction as to prevent (if all goes well) contest over who the child's parents are. The alignment of procreative intent and biological kinship is achieved over time through a mixed bag of surprisingly everyday strategies for naturalizing and socializing particular traits, substances, precedents, and behaviors. The dynamics of this are described below.

This essay is inspired by the writings of Marilyn Strathern (1992), Sarah Franklin (1997), and their colleagues on the role of reproductive technologies in complicating naturalized linear cognatic descent, and in reinvigorating the study of Western kinship (Edwards et al. 1999; Franklin and Ragoné 1998; Ragoné 1994). The cases analyzed here elaborate Strathern's and Franklin's counterintuitive discovery of the underdeterminacy of biogenetic ways of determining kinship. I attempt to show that biology can nonetheless be mobilized to differentiate ambiguous kinship. In the process, the meaning of biological motherhood is somewhat transformed; in particular, biological motherhood is becoming something that can be partial. This work is thus about "doing" kinship, as opposed to simply "being" a particular and fixed kind of kin. I also draw on the literature in science and technology studies on the interconnections between, or coproduction of, politics and ontology, nature and culture. Rather than simply observing the dissolution of the boundary between nature and culture, I specify the means by which the facts and practices of biomedicine and the social meanings of kinship are used to generate and substantiate each other in specific cases. The analytic stress on naturalization is indebted to scholars who have pointed out the ubiquitous and multiple means by which identities get naturalized (Yanagisako and Delaney 1995). The emphasis on the strategies for enforcing procreative intent resonates with studies indicating that reproduction is always already stratified (Ginsburg and Rapp 1995; Rapp 1999). Again, I attempt to contribute to these exciting areas of analysis by providing an account of some of the processes whereby the ontology of naturalization and politics of stratification occur.

THE ARGUMENT

Human reproduction is routinely "assisted" in infertility clinics, using many of the same techniques of modern biology that inform dominant systems of Western kinship reckoning, such as genetics and evolutionary biology. Paradoxically, in reproductive technology clinics there is both more explicit biological definitions of relatedness, on the one hand, and more precise social definitions of parenthood, on the other, but these are not always complementary. One might expect to find the connections enhanced between relatedness as determined by biological practice and socially meaningful answers to questions about who is related to whom. The science would help to hone or perfect an understanding of such terms as "mother," "father," and "child." Tracking biomedical interventions in infertility medicine from the perspective of kinship theory reveals something altogether different, however. Rather than finding the natural ground to social categories exposed at its most concrete level, one discovers a number of disruptions of the categories of relatedness (especially parent and child, but also sibling, aunt, uncle, and grandparent). In particular, one sees that the connections between the biological facts taken to be relevant to kinship and socially meaningful kinship categories are highly indeterminate. Keeping biological and social accounts aligned, and utilizing biology as a resource for understanding the latter, takes work. Norms governing the family; laws regulating reproductive technologies, custody, and descent;

the medical technologies themselves; and the financial dynamics of third-party, medically assisted reproduction are the feedstocks and products of this kinship work.[1] Infertility patients, third parties, and practitioners routinely, and largely informally, do this kinship work; they are practical metaphysicians. In documenting kinship negotiations in infertility clinics, this essay is therefore an empirical argument about metaphysics.

The cases discussed below involve two technically identical procedures that lead to different kinds of kinship configurations — gestational surrogacy and in vitro fertilization (IVF) with ovum donation — as they arose in contemporary California infertility clinics. The two procedures draw on substance and genes as natural resources for making parents and children, but they distribute the elements of identity and personhood differently. It is possible to map out what is rendered relevant to establishing parenthood (what I call a "relational" stage in the process of conceiving and bearing a child because it can support claims of parenthood) and what is rendered irrelevant (what I label "custodial" because it is a stage of the procedure that involves caring for the gametes or embryos as ends, not means, yet it cannot sustain parental claims). From this mapping exercise, one can suggest some elements that underlie the various uses of biology to configure kinship. The examples chosen are all complicated cases, involving friendship egg donation, intergenerational though intrafamilial egg donation, and family member surrogates. Of the six cases, only one involves an egg donor or surrogate who is commercially contracted because I wanted to focus on instances where there is the greatest need to disambiguate kinship — namely, cases with close friends or family members as donors or surrogates. Here, the need to rule out the possibility of incest and adultery meant that the parties to the reproduction were very explicit about how the correct kinship relations were being created and maintained.

In attempting to show the choreography and innovativeness of processes of naturalization, I make three claims, which are taken up again in the conclusion. First, drawing on the different ways in which these gestational surrogacies and egg donations distribute what is natural, I argue against a fixed or unique natural base for the relevant categories of kinship.[2] I also contend that high-tech interventions in reproduction are not necessarily dehumanizing or antithetical to the production of kinship and identity, as some critics of the procedures — including, for example, mainstream Catholic theologians and some feminists — have maintained.[3] Indeed, in the clinical setting, gestational surrogacy and donor egg IVF are means through which patients exercise agency, and claim or disown bonds of ancestry and descent, blood and genes, nation and ethnicity.[4] Third, and for reasons that will turn out to be intricately related to the first two assertions, I maintain that the innovations offered by these technologies do not intrinsically provide only new ways of drawing these fundamental distinctions, nor do they simply reinforce old ways of claiming identity (see Farquhar 1996). The technologies contain both elements.

SUBSTANCE VS. GENES

Most people are used to thinking of there being just two biological parents who both donate genetic material: what is termed a bilateral or cognatic kinship pattern is inscribed in the understanding of biogenetics. A baby is the product of the fusion of the mother's and father's genetic material. Kin are divided into blood relations and non-blood-relations, and it is usually assumed that blood relations share biological substance with one another in a manner that simply reflects the genetic relationship. By the end of the 1990s, however, it was already a commonplace that a woman can share bodily substance with a fetus to whom she is not genetically related. As a result of donor egg IVF and gestational surrogacy, the overlapping biological idioms of shared bodily substance and genes come apart.[5] The maternal genetic material, including the determinants of the blood type and characteristics of the fetus, is contributed by the egg, which is derived from the ovaries of one woman. Nonetheless, the embryo grows in and out of the substance of another woman's body; the fetus is fed by and takes form from the gestational woman's blood, oxygen, and placenta. It is not unreasonable to accord the gestating mother a biological claim to motherhood. Indeed, some have suggested that shared substance is a much more intimate biological connection than shared genetics, and more uniquely characteristic of motherhood, as genes are shared between many different kinds of relations.[6] Where gestational motherhood arises from egg donation rather than surrogacy, and is thus backed up by procreative intent, financial transaction, laws sympathetic to a birth mother's claim to be a child's legal mother, and so on, the case for considering the woman who gestated the fetus as the "natural" mother can become almost unassailable. The examples from the field recounted below illustrate the in situ constructions of a case for natural motherhood as it arose in infertility clinics where I worked.

Gestational surrogacy means that eggs from one woman are fertilized with her partner's sperm in vitro (occasionally, donor eggs or sperm are used in place of the gametes of one partner from the paying patient couple) and then transferred to the uterus of a different woman who gestates the pregnancy. The woman who gestates the pregnancy is known as a gestational surrogate (see Ragoné 1994). In some states, the woman from whom the eggs were derived, and her partner, have custody of the child and are the parents at the child's birth. In other states, although the laws are rapidly changing, the genetic mother and her husband have to adopt the baby at birth, and the surrogate's name goes on the birth certificate. If donor eggs from a third woman were used, the woman from the paying couple is still the mother and she adopts the baby at birth, as in conventional surrogacy. A combination of intent, financial transaction, and genetics trace maternity through the various bodies producing the baby in commercial gestational surrogacy. In noncommercial gestational surrogacy, an emotional or familial commitment takes the place of a financial transaction.

Gestational surrogacy is procedurally identical to donor egg IVF: eggs from one woman are fertilized in vitro and then gestated in the uterus of another woman. Two things make donor egg IVF and gestational surrogacy different from each other. In the case of donor egg IVF, the sperm with which the eggs are fertilized comes from the gestational woman's partner (or a donor standing in for him and picked by that couple), whereas in gestational surrogacy, sperm comes from the partner of the provider of the eggs (or a donor standing in for him). From a lab perspective, there is no difference—sperm collected by masturbation is prepared and added to retrieved eggs, and the embryos are incubated and transferred identically in both cases. The sperm comes from the person standing in the right sociolegal relationship to whichever of the women is designated as the mother-to-be. The identity of the intended mother depends on who came into the clinic for treatment for infertility, the various parties' reproductive history, and in the case of private clinics, who is paying. Where additional donors are used, or where the egg donor or gestational surrogate is being contracted on a commercial basis, the importance of who is paying for the treatment in deciding who the designated parents are is reinforced.[7] In cases where motherhood is contested, one or more of these aspects breaks down or falls out of alignment with the others. Both gestational surrogacy and donor egg IVF separate shared bodily substance and genes, but whereas donor egg IVF traces motherhood through the substance half of this separation, gestational surrogacy traces it through the genetic half.[8]

CASES FROM THE FIELD

IVF with Donor Egg

CASE 1: GIOVANNA *Summary: Giovanna will gestate embryos made from donor eggs from an Italian American friend and sperm from Giovanna's husband. Giovanna and her husband will be the parents if pregnancy ensues.*

One afternoon, I was in an examination room getting ready for the next patient's ultrasound scan in preparation for a cycle of IVF. The patient, Giovanna, was already in the room, changed, and ready for her scan, so we talked as we awaited the physician's arrival. Giovanna described herself as an Italian American approaching forty years of age. She explained that she had tried but "failed" IVF before, using her own eggs and her husband's sperm. Her response to the superovulatory drugs and doctor's recommendation had persuaded Giovanna to try to get pregnant using donor eggs from a younger woman. Almost all clinics report better implantation rates in IVF using donor eggs, which are retrieved from women under thirty-five years old, than those obtained using an older patient's eggs.

Giovanna said that she had decided to use a donor who was a good friend, rather than an anonymous donor. Choosing a friend for a donor seemed to be an important part of reconfiguring the experience of pregnancy: if conception was not to occur inside her body or with her eggs, then it was preferable that she had emotional attachments of friendship to, and could make the corresponding demands on, the woman who was to be her donor. Giovanna described her friend as also Italian American, and said that she was excited and ready to help. She depicted the shared ethnic classification as being "enough genetic similarity." Further, Giovanna accorded her gestational role a rich biological significance: she said that the baby would grow inside her, nourished by her blood and made out of the very stuff of her body all the way from a four-celled embryo to a fully formed baby.

There is currently a gradual de-privatizing trend creeping further and further back in pregnancy, socializing gestation and opening the pregnant woman up to medical scrutiny as well as state regulation and intervention. Examples of the trend include fetal monitoring and surgery, right-to-life political movements, the improved survival rates of significantly premature infants, and a predominantly child-based perspective for discussing the social and ethical dimensions of human reproduction. In these arenas, gestation is increasingly assimilated to the care one provides to a child once it is born. When gestational surrogacy is uncontested (see below), everything except for fertilization is de-privatized and equated to child care, despite its biological nature. This makes genetics into the essential natural component that confers kinship and minimizes the role of gestation. In Giovanna's case, however, she cast her gestation as conferring kinship because of its biological nature, despite the absence of genetic connection. Against the de-privatizing and genetic essentialist cultural trend, she renaturalized gestation.

Giovanna pried apart the natural, biological basis for specifying mother/child relations into separable components. In addition, she complicated the natural status of the genetic component that would be derived from her friend by socializing genetics. She said that what mattered to her in genetic inheritance was that the donor share a similar history to her own. She said that because her friend was also Italian American, they both came from the same kind of home, and because they both had Italian mothers, they had grown up with the same cultural influences. So genes were coding for ethnicity, which Giovanna was expressing as a national/natural category of Italian Americanness. As in so many instances of contemporary biomedicine, it turns out, then, that genes have social categories built into them, without which they would not make sense or be relevant. This is a reversal of what is often presumed to be the unidirectionality of genealogy. Genes figure in Giovanna's kinship reckoning because there is a chain of transactions between the natural and cultural that not only grounds the cultural in the natural but gives the natural its explanatory power by its links to culturally relevant categories.

Giovanna's separation of biology into shared bodily substance and genetics, and her formulation of what matters to her about genetics in the context of her procedure, resists the scientistic impulse to assume that biology underwrites sociocultural potential and not the other way around, and that biology is sufficient to account for sociocultural reality. For her, the reduction to genes is only meaningful because it codes back to sociocultural aspects of being Italian American (it is not unidirectional). Likewise, the ethnic category does not just perform a transitional function between nature and culture but is an elision, collecting disparate elements and linking them without any assumption that every one of the sociocultural aspects of having an Italian American mother, for example, needs to map back onto biology.

CASE 2: PAULA *Summary: Paula will gestate embryos made from donor eggs from either her sister or an African American friend and sperm from Paula's husband. Paula and her husband will be the parents if pregnancy ensues.*

In a related case, an African American patient, Paula, who I met at the clinic only once, spontaneously offered commentary on the kinship implications of her upcoming procedure. Paula had undergone "premature ovarian failure" and entered menopause in her early thirties before she had had any children. She and her husband had decided to try donor egg I V F, and she was hoping to be able to carry a pregnancy. They had not yet chosen an egg donor, and Paula said that she would first ask her sister and a friend, to see if either of them would be willing to be her egg donor. Paula expressed a strong preference for using a donor "from my community."[9] She said that using a donor was not as strange as it might at first seem, as it was like something "we've been doing all along." When I asked her what she meant, she explained that in African American communities, it was not unusual for women to "mother" or "second mother" their sister's or daughter's or friend's child(ren).

Paula's explanation suggests the possibility of legitimizing the natural "deviance" of her procedure by pointing to its social basis: it was OK to give birth to a child made with another woman's eggs, as sharing child raising was already a common social phenomenon. This is the reverse of the familiar strategy where naturalization can normalize social deviance, as for example, when behavior is explained by genetics or an underlying mental or medical problem. If using a donor to get pregnant is just one more way of doing something that is already a prevalent social phenomenon—dividing different aspects of mothering across generations, between friends and sisters—then it is not a radical departure from existing social practice. In presenting it like this, Paula was normalizing her reproductive options. Rather than being exploitative, using a donor is assimilated to other ways in which women help each other to lead livable lives.

Gestational Surrogacy Where the Surrogate Is a Family Member

CASE 3: RACHEL, KAY, AND MICHAEL *Summary: Rachel will gestate embryos made from Kay's eggs and sperm from Kay's husband, Michael. Rachel will give birth, but Kay and Michael will be the parents. In addition, Rachel is Michael's sister.*

Michael and Kay had a history of long-term infertility, including two unsuccessful attempts to get pregnant with I V F. They decided to maximize their chances on one last attempt at I V F by using a gestational surrogate, Michael's sister, Rachel. Rachel was referred to approvingly as an ideal surrogate by several staff members during the weeks of treatment. Her own family of three children was already complete. She was actively compliant, making explicit references to how she would organize her life so as to do whatever was in the treatment's best interests. She was good-humored about the long waits during appointments at the clinic. Her husband's job was lucrative enough that she could assume the risks associated with taking a leave of absence from work, and Rachel said she was glad of a break from work and a chance to spend more time at home with her children. The generic role of the "good patient," then, was masterfully deployed by Rachel to emphasize the fact that her part in this was subordinate to those whose procreative intent they were all working to realize. I followed Rachel's treatment as a case study of gestational surrogacy.

An important activity during their treatment involved ruling out Rachel as a parent and counting in Kay, because of the incest with her brother Michael that would be implied if Rachel were the mother. Such conventional strategies as distinguishing between medium and information, and between nature and nurture, were used by the parties involved in the pregnancy to rule out incest, and negotiate descent and heredity. During one appointment Rachel, the surrogate, turned to Kay, the mother-to-be, and said that it was lucky that she, Rachel, had had her tubes tied after her last child. Kay raised her eyebrows, seeming not to understand, and Rachel elaborated by saying that otherwise there might be a danger of one of her eggs being in her tubes or uterus and some spare sperm out of the petri dish from her brother fertilizing her egg. Kay understood, laughed, and agreed. I was struck at the time that this would be incest, but that gestating her brother's baby was obviously not, despite the fact that her brother's baby would grow inside her. If the procedure had utilized a donor egg, the gestating woman, that is, Rachel, would have been the mother; then this same medical procedure would have been incest, because Rachel would have been the mother and her brother the father.

Five embryos resulted from the egg retrieval from Kay and subsequent fertilization with Michael's sperm. On the day of the embryo transfer, the doctor tried to persuade Kay and Rachel to let him transfer three embryos into Rachel and two into Kay. The doctor was being quite insistent, reiterating "Are you sure you don't want to split the embryos?" several times, but Kay and Rachel stood firm. Later on in the staff room, the doctor expressed disappointment that Kay and Rachel would not both have an embryo transfer, thereby enabling him to "make history" as he called it. If they had both become pregnant, it would have been the first time that a single set of twins would have been born from different mothers.

Rachel's husband, referred to by the staff as an "awkward attorney," was not present for the embryo transfer and was conspicuously absent throughout the whole treatment cycle. Kay's husband (and Rachel's brother), Michael, was in the room, though, as the father-to-be. Rachel's prosthetic role was heightened during the embryo transfer by the presence of her brother while she was lying with her legs in stirrups. After the embryo transfer, Rachel had to remain in a prone position for two hours. Michael left soon after the embryo transfer, but Rachel and Kay were "in this together," as Kay expressed it, and so Kay stayed by Rachel's side.

During the two-hour wait, Kay and Rachel discussed what the baby would look like if Rachel became pregnant. Rachel began by flattering Kay, saying that if the baby looked like a combination of her brother, Michael, and Kay, it would be good-looking. This fit the normal genetic reckoning of half the characteristics coming from the egg (Kay's) and half from the sperm (Michael's). Kay responded, however, by saying that it might look more like Rachel, and that if it came out looking like her nephews and niece (Rachel's children), she would be happy. Perhaps Kay was just returning the compliment. But if the baby could look like Rachel, then Rachel was not merely as custodial in this pregnancy as the logic of gestational surrogacy seems to need her to be so as not to be incestuous. Rachel took up the thread, asking rhetorically whether the baby could get anything of her from growing inside her. They joked about dogs looking like their owners and mentioned that identical twins can have different birth weights depending on how they fare during pregnancy, both classic cases of the effect of "nurture" on "nature." They resolved the question by accepting that if Rachel had an effect on what the baby looked like, it would be because she had provided a certain environment for the baby to grow in, not because she was part of the baby's "nature." Rachel's role in the pregnancy was thus returned safely to the realm of caregiver and provider of a nurturing environment. Their narrow geneticization of incest prevented biological embodiment of her brother's child from being incest; the genetic discourse of naturalization worked in opposition to the discourse of biological kinship through embodiment by denaturalizing the latter. The threat of incest was again avoided, leaving the logic of the procedure and both compliments intact.

Ten days later, Rachel's pregnancy test was positive. The embryologist recounted the story that she had just been told by Rachel: Rachel didn't phone Kay straightaway but instead went out and bought a little teddy bear, to which she attached a note saying, "Your child(ren) are doing fine with Auntie Rachel—can't wait to meet you in eight and a half months." She took the teddy around to Kay's house, left it on the doorstep, rang the doorbell, and hid herself. Apparently Kay opened the door, found the bear, and burst into tears. It was not until Rachel came in for her final infertility clinic scan that her husband, the awkward attorney, was mentioned in connection with the pregnancy. Rachel told the doctor that her husband was happy about the twins that she was carrying. Apparently he had suggested naming the twins after the doctor—calling one by the doctor's first name and one by his last name. In choosing names and the male doctor for eponymy, Rachel's husband was able to contribute to the babies' lineage. In building in quasi-patrilineal kinship through naming practices, Rachel's husband also illustrated the manner in which people in this site routinely used tropes (including conservative ones like male eponymy) with which they were familiar from other contexts, extending them to cover and disambiguate kinship in this novel setting.

CASE 4: JANE *Summary: Jane will gestate embryos made from an infertile patient's eggs and sperm from that patient's husband. Jane will give birth, but the patient and her husband will be the parents. Jane is married to the infertile patient's brother, so she is the patient's sister-in-law by marriage.*

While Rachel's treatment cycle was in progress, another noncommercial surrogacy treatment was ongoing at the same clinic. In this case the surrogate, Jane, was related, but only by marriage, to the intended infertile couple. The surrogate was married to the brother of a woman and her husband who were providing the gametes and hoping to be parents. Staff members compared Jane unfavorably with Rachel from the beginning, complaining that her heart was not in it, and that Jane and her husband's sister (the mother-to-be) were "passive aggressive" toward each other. When Jane failed to get pregnant after two attempts, the clinic's psychologist went so far as to suggest at the weekly staff meeting that Jane's "unresolved feelings," deemed evident from her psychological evaluation, were getting in the way of implantation of the embryos. The psychologist felt, or at least presented a narrative constructed thus, that the demands of the emotional contract necessary to undertake a pregnancy on someone else's behalf could not be sustained unless the two had a very close relationship. She voiced a strong preference for close girlfriends or sisters over relations by marriage when a noncommercial surrogate was needed. In Jane's case, then, reproductive failure was blamed on a relationship that was insufficiently biologically or socially grounded to sustain the biological demands of this particular form of custodial care.

Intergenerational Donor Egg IVF

CASE 5: FLORA *Summary: Flora will gestate embryos made from her daughter's eggs and sperm from Flora's second husband. Flora will give birth, and her second husband will be the father. Flora's daughter will be the baby's half sister, not its mother.*

A fifty-one-year-old woman, Flora, came in for treatment. She was perimenopausal and had five grown-up children from a previous marriage. She didn't fit the typical patient profile of the elite, white, postponed-childbearing woman. Flora was Mexican and crossed the border from an affluent suburb of Tijuana, where she lived, to southern California for her treatment. With five children, she already had what many would probably consider "too many" offspring. She had recently been remarried to a man many years her junior who had not yet had children. Flora was quite explicit about the gender, age, and financial relations between herself and her new younger husband, and her desire to, as she put it, "give him a child."

Because of her age, it was suggested that if Flora wanted any significant chance of getting pregnant, she should find an egg donor. The donor eggs would be inseminated by Flora's husband's sperm, and the resulting embryos would either be transferred to Flora's uterus or frozen for use in subsequent cycles. Flora read widely in the medical and popular literature, and frequently made suggestions about or fine-tuned her own protocol. She also picked her own egg donor: one of her daughters in her early twenties, who herself already had children.[10] The mother's and daughter's cycles were synchronized, and the daughter was given superovulatory drugs to stimulate the simultaneous maturation of several preovulatory follicles. The daughter responded dramatically to the drugs, and at the time of egg recovery, the physician and embryologist removed sixty-five eggs from her ovaries (ten, plus or minus five, is "normal"). The eggs were inseminated with Flora's husband's sperm, forty-five fertilized, and five fresh embryos were transferred to Flora's uterus that cycle. Flora did not get pregnant in the fresh cycle or in the first two frozen cycles, but did in the third.

Flora did not seem overly perturbed by the intergenerational confusion of a mother giving birth to her own "grandchildren" and to her daughter's "daughter/sister." Neither did I ever hear her mention the fact that her resulting child would be genetically related to her ex-husband as well as her current one. Instead, she discussed her daughter's genetic similarity to her. Like Paula, the African American woman mentioned earlier, Flora also assimilated her case to existing social practice, in this instance to the prevalence of generation-skipping parenting (where a grandparent parents a child socially and legally) in the communities with which she was familiar. Flora nonetheless signaled some ambivalence on the part of her daughter. When asked who her donor was, she replied, "My daughter," adding that her daughter was "not exactly excited but she doesn't mind doing it." The daughter herself said, when the mother was out of the room, that she didn't mind helping them have a single baby but that the huge number of embryos stored away was unsettling. After all, she added, her mother already had a family: "She doesn't need to start a whole new family—one baby is one thing, but . . . !"

The daughter's reluctance to see her mother having "a whole new family" might have been due in part to a distrust or disapproval of her mother's relation to her new husband, or with a reluctance to have the grandmother (Flora) of her children back being a mother of babies again. The daughter's anxiety about the stock of embryos that were frozen, however, seemed to be at least partly an anxiety about the existence of unaccounted for embryos using her eggs and her stepfather's sperm. Using one of her eggs to help initiate a pregnancy that was clearly tied into a trajectory on which it was Flora's and her husband's child was all right. It placed Flora between the daughter and her stepfather. The embryos in the freezer, though, were in limbo. If they were not used to initiate a pregnancy in Flora, then they existed as the conjoined gametes of the daughter and stepfather. As in all the cases recounted here, the trajectory of treatment, as a proxy for procreative intent, was of paramount importance. Where one step of that trajectory led clearly to the next, keeping biologized notions of descent in line with that intent, and keeping incest and adultery at bay, was obviously possible in the world of the clinic, structured as it is around treatment trajectories. The status of the embryos in the freezer—even though technically owned by Flora and her husband—were off that trajectory, and provoked Flora's daughter to express anxiety about inappropriate kinship.

Intergenerational Gestational Surrogacy

CASE 6: VANESSA AND UTE *Summary: Vanessa will be a surrogate for Ute and her husband, using donor eggs from Ute's daughter.*

A final case concerns Vanessa, who started up her own surrogacy agency shortly after herself being a commercial gestational surrogate and giving birth to a baby for another couple. Vanessa had seen a program on television in which she noticed the "joy in the mother's eyes" when the baby was handed over by the surrogate. Vanessa's family was in some financial difficulty at the time as their small-scale manufacturing operation had just closed, and the approximately twelve thousand dollars she might make as a successful surrogate was attractive. She expressed the decision to try surrogacy in a religious idiom, as a chance offered by God simultaneously to do good and make a fresh start. Vanessa was introduced to "her" couple, a "German woman of about forty" (Ute) and an "Asian man."

On the first treatment cycle, Ute ovulated before the physician took her to surgery for ovum pickup and they only got one egg at surgery. The one egg was successfully fertilized with Ute's husband's sperm and transferred to Vanessa, but Vanessa did not get pregnant. For the second treatment cycle, Ute and her husband decided to combine gestational surrogacy with donor egg IVF. Ute had an adult daughter from a previous marriage who agreed (as Flora's daughter had) to be her mother and stepfather's donor. It was decided that the use of the daughter as a donor would be kept secret by the daughter as well as Ute and her husband from everyone outside the clinic setting. Ute explained that using her daughter's eggs was the next best thing to using her own eggs because of their genetic similarity. The daughter was safeguarded from being considered the biological mother in the pregnancy by making the relevant fact be the genetic relation of her eggs to Ute. This reduction to the genetics of the eggs and protection it afforded the daughter were both reinforced by removing the daughter herself by keeping her role secret. The logic of gestational surrogacy, essentializing the genetic aspect of biological kin, and making the blood and shared bodily substance of gestation custodial rather than relational, was also maintained. Ute was providing the essential genetic component, even though that genetic material had traveled a circuitous route from her down a generation to her daughter and back up again. This required reversing the usual temporal direction of genealogy, but naturalizing kinship to genetics to a large extent removed the need to mark kinship by descent, and so removed the temporal direction from the kinship reckoning.

Vanessa did not get pregnant on the fresh IVF cycle using the daughter's eggs, but there had been sufficient embryos to freeze some for a subsequent attempt. On the frozen cycle, Ute's daughter and husband's remaining embryos were thawed, transferred to Vanessa's uterus, and Vanessa became pregnant with a singleton. The pregnancy, unlike her four previous ones, was not easy for Vanessa. Under her surrogacy contract, she was not allowed to make her own medical decisions while pregnant, and she had to consult with the recipient couple and the doctor before taking any medications or changing her agreed-on routine in any way. The recipient couple and the physicians took over jurisdiction of Vanessa's body for the twelve months of treatment and pregnancy, disciplining her body across class lines. Nonetheless,

Vanessa described the pregnancy almost wistfully, explaining how exhilarating the intimacy with the couple was and how spoiled she had been. During the pregnancy, Ute and her husband took Vanessa out, bought her fancy maternity clothes, and temporarily conferred on her their privileged social status. Vanessa underlined the ambivalence of the "kin-or-not" relationship between the surrogate and recipient couple in commercial surrogacy arrangements with the oxymoronic observation that they are "the couple you're going to be a relative with for a year and a half."

Vanessa seemed surprised by the severing of the ties of relationship between herself and the recipient couple after the baby was born and handed over. She said that the couple stopped contacting her, and that when she called them to find out how they and the baby were, the couple made excuses and hung up quickly. Other commercial gestational surrogates have recounted similar experiences. Vanessa's relationship to the couple for the year and a half was enacted because she was prosthetically embodying their germ plasm and growing their child, but she was at no point related to the recipient couple or the baby in her own right. Unlike the cases described above, Vanessa was commercially contracted, and her reproduction was classically "alienated" labor. The commissioning couple honored the capitalist contract; they paid her and appropriated the surplus value of her reproductive labor—namely, the baby. The genius of capitalism is sometimes said to be that the fruits of one's labor can be exchanged for money, without setting up a chain of reciprocal obligation. Thus, once the baby was born, Vanessa was in many ways just like any other instrumental intermediary in establishing the pregnancy, such as the embryologist or even the petri dish. The fact that she cared for and had good reasons for continuing to feel connected to the couple and baby, and so did things like make phone calls, meant perhaps that she needed some postnatal management to be kept in the background. But because she had been commercially contracted, the logic of disconnection was the same as for other intermediaries in the recipient couples' reproduction. The irony was that this particular naturalization was heightened by the deeply entrenched conventions of capitalism.

MAKING KINSHIP: RELATIONAL AND CUSTODIAL

I try here hypothetically to isolate some of the strategies that were used in the clinical setting in each case for delineating who the mother was for each child (or the children). These strategies are not exhaustive and cannot be expected to be invariant in different arenas of the patients' lives either. For example, legal and familial constraints bring their own sources of plasticity and relative invariance that are quite powerful in determining kin. But the clinic is one significant site of negotiation of kinship, and it is of particular interest because it articulates between the public and private, and because it illustrates flexibility in biological and scientific practice. I emphasize the mothers' relatedness because in the cases I have chosen, it is into motherhood in particular that the procedures raise a challenge to biological essentialism through the separability of egg, gestation, and biological mother. The cases also challenge biologically essentialist understandings of daughter, husband, father, grandmother, aunt, and child, however. For each case, I distinguish different key intermediaries in establishing the pregnancy. I then sort the intermediaries as to whether they are relational or custodial in the determination of who counts as the mother. I also ask where and under what conditions the ways of designating the mother are liable to breakdown or contestation.

In infertility clinics, clinicians, patients, family members, surrogates, and others together embody the intent and effort that is crucial to reproduction in these settings. Yet procreative intent only inscribes some of these parties (usually a paying patient couple) as kin of the anticipated child(ren). As noted earlier, I call any stage in the establishment of a pregnancy *relational* if it implicates kinship. I am primarily interested here in working out who the mother is, so a relational stage in this determination would be one that implicates a (or more than one) mother. As the cases showed, there are many resources for making a stage relational that are not necessarily well differentiated. Biology and nature are resources; so are a wide range of legal, socioeconomic, and familial factors that make up procreative intent, such as who is paying for treatment, who owns the gametes and embryos, who is providing the sperm, and who is projected to have future financial and "nuclear family" responsibility for the child. Depending on the kind of parenting in question, different kinds of coordination are appropriate. By contrast, I call a stage *custodial* if it enables relatedness, but does not itself thereby get configured in the web of kinship relations.[11] A women is custodial in conceiving and bearing a child if she is biologically involved in bringing the child into the world and yet is not (or not primarily) implicated as its mother. A custodial stage is somewhat like an instrumental intermediary, then, and yet custody is not merely instrumental. Both the custodial woman and the child(ren)-to-be are ends in themselves, not mere means.[12] There are degrees of custodianship, ranging from those that are strictly limited to those implying long-term commitment even if they don't confer parenthood. The cases described above exhibited different strategies for achieving kinship implication of some people and not others. Breakdown (from the point of view of clinics or designated recipient couples), contestation, and prohibition usually occur when an attempt by at least some of the actors to render one or more stage as custodial rather than relational is contested or fails.

DESIGNATING MOTHERHOOD

In the first case, that of Giovanna, the Italian American woman who was planning to undergo a donor egg procedure with the eggs of an Italian American friend of hers, the two potential candidates for motherhood were the donor friend and Giovanna herself. The friend was made appropriately custodial using three strategies. First, the friend's contribution of the eggs was biologically minimized by stressing the small percentage of the pregnancy that would be spent at the gamete and embryo stage versus the length of time that the fetus would grow inside Giovanna. In addition, genetics were redeployed, so that the friend's genes were figured as deriving from a common ethnic gene pool (Italian American) of which Giovanna was a member and so also represented. Then, too, the friend was secured as a custodial intermediary in the pregnancy by emphasizing her other bonds to Giovanna of friendship and mutual obligation. Despite her custodial role in donating the eggs destined to make Giovanna's baby, her relation to the baby could be reregistered as enhancing her already significant cultural and personal connections to Giovanna. To further disambiguate who should be considered the mother, Giovanna put forward strategies through which she could assert her own relationality. Giovanna's claim to motherhood was to come from her gestation of the baby as well as the provision of the bodily substance and functioning out of which the baby would grow and be given life. Giovanna stressed the significance of the gestational component of reproduction along with the importance of the experiential aspects of being pregnant and giving birth in designating motherhood. Further, Giovanna was married to, and would parent with, the provider of the sperm.

In Paula's case (the African American woman who was going to use an African American friend or one of her sisters as her donor), the strategies of separating relationality and custodianship were similar to those employed by Giovanna, but there were also interesting differences. The most striking difference was that Paula drew the line between who was a kin relation and who a custodian more tenuously, being content to leave more ambiguity in the designation of motherhood. She took legitimacy for the procedure from the fact that shared parenting was commonplace among people she identified with racially, and she also commented on the natural, biological confirmation of these social patterns that her upcoming procedure would provide. Socially and biologically, her motherhood — including its ambiguity — would be recognizable and legitimate. Her motherhood would be sufficiently relational and her donor sufficiently custodial, without either needing to be wholly so. Like Giovanna, then, Paula gave an ethnic or racial interpretation to the genes such that, by getting genetic African Americanness from her donor, the baby would share genetic racial sameness with Paula. The familiar trope (underlying, for example, the Human Genome Diversity Project) that genes code for racial distinctions, group inclusion and exclusion, and ethnic purity, seemed to be readily available to patients like Giovanna, Paula, and Flora, where group racial or ethno-national identity was culturally significant. The equally prevalent trope (exemplified in the Human Genome Project) that genes provide the definitive mark of individuality, "the DNA fingerprint," that is passed down cognatically from a mother's and father's individual contributions was the template used by the patients of unmarked or hegemonic racial and ethnic origin. Depending on whether genetics was socialized or individualized, different naturalization strategies were available. The African American Paula seemed to be the most comfortable of the patients whose cases are discussed in this chapter with de-individualizing genetics. Giovanna, Flora, and Ute all also mobilized the idea of genetic ethnic or individual (depending on the case) similarity with their gamete donors to assert genetic connection to their offspring, but unlike Paula, they were all reasonably strongly invested in making their claims to motherhood individual and exclusive.

Michael, Kay, and Rachel (the gestational surrogacy between a brother, his wife, and his sister, respectively) deployed yet other familiar resources for assuring the custodial role of Rachel and the relationality of Kay. Because of the need to protect Michael and Rachel from incest, the negotiations over custody versus relationality were explicit and repeated at different phases of the treatment. Although the opportunities for ambiguity were legion, there was a "zero-tolerance" standard for ambiguity in the designation of Kay, not Rachel, as the mother. Kay was the infertile paying patient, receiving treatment and hoping/intending to parent. She also provided the eggs containing the genetic information, and was married to and intending to parent with the provider of the sperm. These elements of her claim to motherhood were stabilized by emphasizing the unidirectional individualized genetic basis of heredity along with the mirroring of biological kinship and this understanding of heredity. When a threat arose as to the uniqueness of this basis of heredity (when Kay said to Rachel that she wouldn't mind if the children looked like Rachel and the ensuing conversation), it was removed by assimilating that kind of acquisition of characteristics to environmental custodial factors. The provision by Rachel of the bodily substance and site for fetal development was made custodial, rather than parental or incestuous, through two strategies. First, Rachel was assimilated at all points by her active compliance and the kinds of boundary discussions she initiated, such as how lucky it was that her tubes were tied, to a model on which pregnancy and birth were instrumental phases of Kay and Michael's reproduction, with which she was helping. Second, Rachel's relatedness to Kay and Michael as well as the children she was carrying was used to make her custodial assistance exactly what would be expected of her social role. As Rachel put it, the children were fine with their auntie (whose social role would be expected to be custodial), but couldn't wait to be reunited with their parents. The natural relation of aunt underwrote a social role of custodianship, which in turn, helped denaturalize Rachel as a potential mother to the children.

In Flora's case (the perimenopausal woman from Mexico whose daughter was the donor, and from whom sixty-five eggs were retrieved), a significant strategy in making her daughter custodial was to see the daughter as custodian rather than origin of the genetic material. The eggs used were not the daughter's per se but were retraced to Flora by "rewinding" genealogical time, such that they contained genetic material sourced from Flora. The daughter's gamete contribution was expressed as a detour to her mother's genetic material, which could no longer be accessed directly from Flora. Flora, perhaps more closely than any of the other donor egg patients whose cases are described here, attempted to recapture in her own claims to motherhood the genetic idiom of linear descent. Flora's case was complicated by the intergenerational element, however, and her daughter's custodianship was threatened from at least two sources. Flora and her daughter discussed the similarity of what they were doing to other intergenerational parenting in which a grandparent can be the social and legal parent. Drawing an analogy with prevalent social practices, as Paula had done, Flora strengthened the legitimacy of the procedure and so stabilized her claim to being the mother of the child. In making this analogy, though, the daughter's role was in danger of being compromised, because grandparenting often allows for the "real" parent to reclaim his or her parental jurisdiction. Unlike for Paula, this analogy to social practices did not loosen the designation of who was to count as mother but was meant to disambiguate it even beyond the norm for the social practices with which she was drawing the analogy. Both Flora and her daughter were adamant that there was to be no ambiguity in who was to be the mother — Flora. Flora's marriage to the provider of the sperm and the incestuous implications of reckoning it otherwise reinforced the lack of an analogy with social grandparent parenting. The other threat to Flora's daughter's custodial role came from the unintended stockpiling of embryos formed from the daughter's eggs fertilized with her stepfather's sperm. The frozen embryos in the lab were only tenuously tied to the trajectory of Flora's reproduction and its social, legal, economic, and emotional umbrella of procreative intent. The embryo's quasi-independence left room for them to seem like the products of incest or agents of additional unintended pregnancies, both of which were troubling to the daughter.

In Vanessa's pregnancy (which she carried as a commercial surrogate for Ute and her husband, from an embryo formed with eggs donated by Ute's daughter), there were three potential candidates as to who should be designated as the mother. There was Vanessa herself, the commercial gestational surrogate; there was Ute, the intended mother, who was the wife in the paying patient couple; and there was Ute's daughter, the egg donor. As for Rachel and Jane, Vanessa was made custodial by assimilating her role in gestating the fetus to the provision of a temporary caring environment. Unlike Rachel's and Jane's cases of gestational surrogacy, however, Vanessa's custodial role was not elicited by the obligations of a prior relationship to the recipient couple. Her services were instead contracted commercially, and Vanessa had no further claim on the child after the birth. This disconnection was underwritten by the assumption of contractual arrangements that both parties agree that recompense is satisfactory despite possible incommensurability of the things being exchanged. Furthermore, contracts assume that the transaction itself is limiting and does not set up any subsequent relationship or further obligation. Vanessa's custodial role was threatened when she experienced the sudden severing of relations after the birth of the baby as baffling and troubling. Like Flora's and Ute's daughters, Vanessa was "de-kinned," but whereas the former two desired this, Vanessa did not (or at least mourned the relationship). The contractual relation assured the temporary relation of shared bodily substance with the recipient couple, but insofar as it was uncontested, it sustained no further relationality.

Ute's daughter, who was acting as the egg donor, was excluded from being the baby's mother in two ways. First, the genetic contribution contained in her eggs was described as being closely similar to her mother's genetic material. This is not quite the same argument as that made by Flora and her daughter, where the daughter became a vehicle or detour through which genetic material originally from Flora had passed; in this case, the mother and daughter simply alluded to the similarity of the mother's and daughter's genes. The daughter was further spared from being implicated in parenthood by the recipient couple's commitment to keeping her role a secret. Ute sustained her claim as the intended mother not by wholly capturing either of the predominant biological idioms (genetics as represented by providing the egg, or blood and shared bodily substance as represented by gestation). Instead, the genetic component from the daughter was deemed similar enough to stand in for her genetic contribution, and the blood component was made custodial in the contracting out of the gestation. Neither natural base was sufficiently strong to overwhelm her claim to be the mother, which she asserted through being married to the person who supplied the sperm, through her daughter's compliance with her desires, and through having the buying power to contract Vanessa.

PROGNOSIS

The genetic essentialism of gestational surrogacy in procedures such as Rachel's and Jane's seems to be faring very well, even as it extends and reconfigures preexisting ontologies. There have been gestational surrogates who have contested custody, but decisions have gone against them more often than for conventional surrogates who are genetically related to the child in question. Several of the patients coded genetics back to socioeconomic factors and thereby in some sense de-essentialized genetics in this setting just as they no doubt did in other areas of their lives. Eliding ethno-national, racial, and class-based categories with natural grounds for designating kinship is a strategy fundamental to bilateral, blood-based kinship systems. Nonetheless, developments in other contemporary U.S. sites over the same period as this fieldwork, such as decisions in legal custody disputes, have tended to favor genetic essentialism in determining motherhood, although this has not been universal. On the other hand, they have often followed procreative intent in determining legal custody, regardless of the decision on motherhood (see Seibel and Crockin 1996, 111–216).

The donor egg procedures seem to offer the potential somewhat to transform biological kinship in the directions indicated, for example, by Giovanna when she draws on the trope of blood connection and shared bodily substance without genetics. If an overwhelming predominance of nonclinical cultural contexts come down on the side of genetic essentialism, donor egg procedures might well become assimilated to adoption or artificial insemination with donor sperm. The bid to make gestation in donor egg procedures a means of conferring biological kinship would have failed. A newer procedure, reports of which began to appear in journals and the press in 1997, uses the eggs of older patients, but "revivifies" them by injecting cytoplasmic material derived from the eggs of younger women into the older eggs before fertilization; this donor procedure preserves the genetic connection between the recipient mother and fetus, and so brings the genetic and blood idioms back into line. It thereby tightens up again the flexible ontological space for designating biological motherhood that had been opened up by donor egg procedures. The meritocratizing and commercializing of the donor egg market (much like the sperm market, only much more expensive) of the late 1990s has emphasized the extent to which egg donation is beginning to match the paternity template. On the one hand, motherhood, like fatherhood, is determined by the genes; on the other hand, if a proxy is used for the intended mother, the gametes should encode socioeconomic mobility in the way the sperm market does.

Paula used a more mixed ontology for motherhood than the other cases recorded here. For her, it was satisfactory if there was not an exclusive answer to who the mother was, and she was happy to accept that in some ways there might be more than one mother. Likewise, because she raised the possibility of biologically enacting what she described as already prevalent social practices (shared mothering), there was less at stake in having gestation without genetics confer motherhood biologically. Shared mothering was not presented as necessarily involving a natural kinship rift; indeed, it was presented as a practice that preserves racial identity and integrity. Conventional adoption has historically predominantly gone in one direction, with African American children being adopted into Caucasian families, arguably disrupting racial identification without disrupting racism. For Paula, having her procedure assimilated to some kinds of social parenting would still entitle her to make appeal to notions of biological sameness because of the group understanding of genetics offered paternalistically to, and taken up defensively by, minority groups. The option to individualize or personalize genetic generative agency is only differentially available.

The likely stability of Flora's and Ute's claims to motherhood is hard to gauge. Ute's claim could have been challenged by Vanessa's desire for contact with the child after its birth, set against the purchasing power of the contracting couple. Flora is likely to encounter social censure, just as she did in the clinic, for her desire to bear a child "for" her younger husband. If either Ute or Flora confess to using, or are found to have used, their daughters as donors, they may be condemned for coercion and putting their daughters through medical interventions so as to regain their own youth. If either daughter contests the circumstances of her role at a later date, the settlement of who is the designated mother might break down. Likewise, the relations of the daughters' own children to the ones born from their eggs may become complicated. But it is also possible that parenting with donor eggs for perimenopausal and postmenopausal women will play a part in dismantling some of the more oppressive aspects for women of the "biological clock." If Flora and Ute can maintain their claims to motherhood, they will be cases to hold against the elision of women's identities, femininity, youth, and ovulation. If Flora is buying into the cult of youth to keep her husband, as she claims, she may yet be subverting the wider essentialist identification of women's identities with their youthful biologies, as she also maintains.

PRACTICAL METAPHYSICS AND THE DYNAMICS OF NATURALIZING

It has become commonplace to talk of the implosion or collapse of nature and culture; to claim that all concepts of nature, including scientific ones, are always already shaped, marked, and interpenetrated with the imprimatur of culture, and (somewhat less frequently) that all concepts of culture invoke legitimizing natural grounds for their systems of classification. Critics of these postmodern sensibilities rightly distrust the looseness or voluntarism that this seems to imply. Ontologically, they decry the violation of common sense: of course there is a real material world subject to more or less regular laws, and of course there is a distinction between truth and falsehood, science and myth. Politically, they disparage the loss of an Enlightenment platform, and the neglect of persistent stratification among people implied by the moral and ontological relativism of a nature/culture implosion. Talking about a nature/culture collapse in vague and programmatic terms is almost always counterproductive. And yet there is something extraordinarily important about the insight that nature and culture are coproduced, and that the explanatory relations between them are eminently revisable.

In an attempt to rescue and further this insight, I have tried to avoid hand-waving statements about the collapse or dissolution of nature and culture. I instead discussed small and detailed examples of productive (not deconstructive) negotiations of the boundaries and explanatory relations between cultural and natural concepts in one specific arena: the contemporary U.S. biomedical infertility clinic. The advantage of this, if it has been successful, is that it should make it clear that the coproductive thesis about nature and culture is no more a "culturalist" position than it is a "naturalist" one. It doesn't dismiss the reality of the realm of biology any more than it dismisses the realm of culture. Indeed, studying the strategies used to bring order to new reproductive and kinship situations convinced me that making distinctions between social and natural roles and facts, and then using natural roles and facts to ground cultural categories, is absolutely fundamental to meaning making in contemporary U.S. society. At the same time, however, the cases made a compelling argument for the absence of a unique biological ground for answering the question, "Who is the mother?" There was more than one possible answer here, and cultural dynamics—most predominantly the bundle of "factors" that make up procreative intent—propelled the sorting and classifying of some things and not others as the biological facts of relevance. The narratives of the trajectories of reproductive intent were choreographed between cultural and natural constraints at all points, and were neither biologically nor culturally voluntaristic. The ambivalence evident in feminist theory, for example, about the relative virtues of naturalism and social constructivism is entirely appropriate: sometimes important political and ontological work is done by denaturalizing what has previously been taken to be natural and deterministic; sometimes the reverse is necessary. What cases like these drawn from infertility medicine reveal is that it is not necessary for the theorist to champion one strategy rather than another. Modern medicine offers many cases where the choreography between the natural and cultural is managed flexibly by ordinary people (the practitioners and patients using the technologies in question).

In focusing on the dynamics of naturalization in the clinics, as just discussed, some aspects of the process of cultural change in the midst of technological innovation became evident. First, the cases suggested that high-tech interventions are not necessarily antithetical to the production of affiliation and identity, the claims of antimodern Luddites that technology is intrinsically dehumanizing notwithstanding. In this clinical setting, gestational surrogacy and donor egg IVF were means through which racial, ethno-national, familial, and individual desires and biologies were all promulgated. In the kinship innovation described here, the various naturalization strategies drew on deeply rooted and familiar ways of forming and claiming kin as well as simultaneously extending the reference of the kinship terms being disambiguated through the strategies. Given this slightly counterintuitive aspect of these high-tech sites that technological innovation and cultural history implicate each other so strongly, it is no wonder that progressive cultural critics cannot decide whether the new reproductive technologies are best judged as innovative ways of breaking free of bondage to old cultural categories of affiliation, or whether they are best denounced as part of a hegemonic reification of the same old stultifying ways of classifying and valuing human beings. The technologies are fundamentally both. Technological change and cultural conservatism go hand in hand; the famous lag between technological innovation and cultural reaction is nothing of the sort. The lag simply refers to the "catch-up" requirements in social, legal, and ethical spheres to organize and calibrate the coemergence of entities and relations produced in these extended cultural and natural biologies.

NOTES

I substantially rewrote this essay twice from its earlier published form (Cussins 1998; reproduced in part with the kind permission of Robbie Davis-Floyd and Joe Dumit). The second rewriting was in response to a generous and perceptive set of critical comments from this volume's editors, to whom I would like to express my gratitude.

1 For discussions of the question of procreative intent relevant to this kinship work, see Dolgin 1995. For a discussion of the only sometimes kin-conferring qualities of the transmission of substance, see Weston, this volume.

2 I take this not as antirealism but as attentiveness to the contingent realities of complex phenomena. See Latour 1999.

3 See Catholic Church 1987.

4 Bruno Latour expressed it as showing that "high-tech processes can be reemployed to provide powerful fetishes — in the good sense of the word — to produce affiliation and identity" (1999).

5 IVF involves the fertilization of an egg (or eggs) with sperm outside the body, usually in a petri dish in a lab. The egg (or eggs) is surgically removed from the ovaries of a woman who has (usually) taken hormones to induce the maturation of multiple follicles, and then the egg is inseminated in vitro with a partner's or donor's sperm.

Any embryos that result are transferred back to the same woman's or a different woman's uterus, or else they are made available for research or donation. Anonymous eggs can either be purchased commercially or gifted as leftovers from other women's treatments. It is rare for eggs to be gifted during IVF, however, as it is standard practice to attempt to fertilize all the eggs retrieved, even for women with many eggs, so that they have some embryos in reserve for future attempts.

6 This lies behind the feminist claim that egg donors should be thought of as second fathers, while the gestating woman should be considered the mother.

7 At the start of the twenty-first century, demand for eggs far outstrips supply, as human eggs are a scarce commodity par excellence. There are several differences between the meritocratization of commercial eggs and that of commercial sperm. Sperm does not vary widely in its price, but eggs do; the man is rewarded for his act of donation, not the quality of offspring he is promising the clients. Sperm banks handle the storage, marketing, and meritocratizing. Eggs, on the other hand, are stored in the body in immature form and are not routinely expelled, so they are difficult to harvest. Immature eggs are also hard to mature in vitro, and no human eggs freeze and thaw well yet. This means that the woman embodying the eggs becomes the market interface, and must be attracted according to the market value of her standardized and hierarchized qualities. The hunt for ideal egg donors with particular characteristics, the high prices (up to fifty thousand dollars at the time of this writing) being offered as recompense to chosen egg donors, and the competition among, for example, elite college students to be selected, have become something of a cultural phenomenon in the United States. There is an unspoken etiquette that one seek roughly to match the qualities and phenotype of the infertile partner in both donor egg and sperm, but it is nonetheless expected that this will be interpreted leniently enough to permit upward mobility or "maximization" in certain areas such as height or IQ.

8 As well as raising the specter of eugenics, commercial egg donation or surrogacy introduces other kinship prerogatives based in particular on class, as explored in-depth for commercial conventional surrogacy in Ragoné 1994. When biological relationship is crosscut by class, the donor's or surrogate's reproduction can be temporarily purchased (see case 6, Vanessa, below). Ownership of the child and the donor's or surrogate's reproduction is a means of trumping biology and forging kinship in reproductive technologies. In slavery, rape, and so on, ownership of another's reproduction and offspring can be a means of the exact opposite: denying kinship.

9 This woman was what I would call upper-middle-class and living in an affluent neighborhood (like most—but by no means all—infertility patients); I think the relevant notion of community, given how she elaborated it in explaining to me the alternative kinds of mothering, was primarily one based on a shared African American identity.

10 In Britain, daughters are not allowed to be donors for their own mothers because the relationship is seen as necessarily involving a coercive element. Frances Price (Edwards et al. 1999, 36–37) recounts the British test case at the end of 1986 that re-

sulted in what was then the Voluntary Licensing Authority declaring mother/daughter egg donations out of bounds.

11 Here, I am following the common usage of the word custody to mean "a guarding or keeping safe; care; protection, guardianship."

12 According to the Catholic Church, no part of human reproduction can be made instrumental and alienated. Every part of the process must be relational, tracing a trajectory of ownership and presence at all points. It is my contention that the difference between being custodial and instrumental is underappreciated, and that the former does not imply treating any person or potential person as a means rather than an end. In commercial surrogacy, the mother comes close to being merely instrumental at the moment of handover (see text on this point), but typically even if the surrogacy contract was entered into for economic gain, the infant is not treated as a means, for a moral discourse intervenes between the transaction and the gift of life.

REFERENCES

Catholic Church, Congregation for the Doctrine of the Faith. 1987. Instruction on Respect for Human Life in Its Origin and on the Dignity of Procreation. In *Gift of Life: Catholic Scholars Respond to the Vatican Instruction,* edited by Edmund Pellegrino, John Collins Harvey, and John Langan. Washington, D.C.: Georgetown University Press.

Cussins, Charis. 1998. "Quit Snivelling Cryo-Baby. We'll Work Out Which One's Your Mama!" In *Cyborg Babies: From Techno-Sex to Techno-Tots,* edited by Robbie Davis-Floyd and Joseph Dumit. New York: Routledge.

Dolgin, Janet L. 1995. Family Law and the Facts of Family. In *Naturalizing Power: Essays in Feminist Cultural Analysis,* edited by Sylvia J. Yanagisako and Carol Delaney. New York: Routledge.

Edwards, Jeanette, Sarah Franklin, Eric Hirsch, Frances Price, and Marilyn Strathern. 1999. *Technologies of Procreation: Kinship in the Age of Assisted Conception.* 2d ed. London: Routledge.

Farquhar, Dion. 1996. *The Other Machine: Discourse and Reproductive Technologies (Thinking Gender).* London: Routledge.

Franklin, Sarah. 1997. *Embodied Progress: A Cultural Account of Assisted Conception.* London: Routledge.

Franklin, Sarah, and Helena Ragoné, eds. 1998. *Reproducing Reproduction: Kinship, Power, and Technological Innovation.* Philadelphia: University of Pennsylvania Press.

Ginsburg, Faye D., and Rayna Rapp, eds. 1995. *Conceiving the New World Order: The Global Politics of Reproduction.* Berkeley: University of California Press.

Latour, Bruno. 1999. Personal correspondence with the author.

Ragoné, Helena. 1994. *Surrogate Motherhood: Conception in the Heart.* Boulder, Colo.: Westview Press.

Rapp, Rayna. 1999. *Testing Women, Testing the Fetus: The Social Impact of Amniocentesis in America.* New York: Routledge.

Seibel, Machelle, and Susan Crockin, eds. 1996. *Family Building through Egg and Sperm Donation: Medical, Legal, and Ethical Issues.* Sudbury, Mass.: Jones and Bartlett.

Strathern, Marilyn. 1992. *Reproducing the Future: Anthropology, Kinship and the New Reproductive Technologies.* New York: Routledge.

Yanagisako, Sylvia J., and Carol Delaney, eds. 1995. *Naturalizing Power: Essays in Feminist Cultural Analysis.* New York: Routledge.

CHAPTER 7

Self-Conscious Kinship: Some Contested Values in
Norwegian Transnational Adoption

Signe Howell

We felt that our daughter was born at Fornebu [Oslo international airport] on the
day that she arrived home. — Norwegian adoptive mother of a Korean girl

When I first started to work on adoption cases more than twenty years ago, we
thought that identity and personality development was a matter of 30 percent nature
and 70 percent nurture [*arv og miljø*]. Today research has shown that it is correct
to turn these figures around. — Norwegian social worker

Some of the implications of the above two statements will be the topic of
this essay. Concepts that will be considered are "our daughter," "born," and
"home" in the first quote, and the relationship between "nature" and "nurture" in the second. In these concepts lie, I suggest, much to be untangled
about the complex cultural values concerning the meaning and emotionality
of kinship, parenthood, family life, and procreation in contemporary Norway.
The statements belie any seemingly straightforward perception about transnational adoption; not least because there is, at times, a tension between personal desires (of adoptive parents) and public values and norms (of agencies
and public administrators).

Unlike the new reproductive technology, adoption — whether transnational or not — has received little anthropological attention (major exceptions
are Modell 1994; Fine 1998). I believe that the study of adoption has several
important contributions to make to the study of kinship precisely because,
as a process of procreation, it is nonbiological. Yet, the semantics and the
choreographic value of biology lurk in the background. Thus, transnational
adoption highlights several key issues in novel ways, not only about the relationship between nature and culture in the construction of significant soci-

ality but also about the significance of origins, reproduction, and place. Most adoptive parents (like the infertility patients discussed by Thompson in this volume) struggle with their handling of the biological basis conventionally taken for granted as being relevant to kinship. An expression like "blood is thicker than water" exists in most European languages, and Norwegian adoptive parents and adopted children know it, and use it, but promote different interpretations of it according to the particular context. Moreover, *transnational* adoptions provoke issues of race and radically different cultural backgrounds in a kinship domain already vulnerable in its handling of relatedness.

Using ethnographic material obtained from a number of different Norwegian social arenas centered on transnational adoption, this essay will concentrate on two main issues. First, by examining aspects of the sociocultural background of the practice in contemporary Norway, I shall argue that the dominant motivation for infertile adults to adopt is not to fulfill some biological desire to give birth and/or reproduce themselves but a wish for significant sociality within a conventional model of the so-called normal family. I shall also explore how relations are created and maintained by oscillating appeals to biological and cultural codes of relation by the various actors involved. What might be described as a quintessentially social form of kinship, ends up being alternatively naturalized and denaturalized, or biologized and de-biologized.

Methodologically, a consequence of this realization is that analytic allowances have to be made for multiple discursive practices. In Bruno Latour's terms, we are in a world of hybridity: "we moderns" believe that we divide society from technology, culture from nature, human from nonhuman in a modernist attempt to create distinctions, and yet, at the same time, we do not deploy these divides in the way we interact in and with the world (1993, 10–13; Strathern 1996, 522). Implicit and explicit values and practices in connection with transnational adoption demonstrate the ambivalences that are at large in contemporary Norway. Nevertheless, people's abilities to handle these without losing their grip on their own realities confirm, I suggest, their tolerance toward both multiple and hybrid discourses. In order to maintain such tolerance, adoptive parents create cognitive boundaries between different contexts in which diverse elements of discourses are constitutive. This enables them to engage in seemingly contradictory understandings of the process. They negotiate a fine balancing act between biological and social accounts in which they underdetermine the paradoxes (see Thompson, this volume). Whereas paradoxes exist in the mind of the anthropologist and can become highly problematic, the same paradoxes need not bother one's informants. For analytic purposes, however, this in itself raises questions about the sociological employment of boundaries and categories that, arguably, raise inappropriate expectations for social analysis (see Strathern 1996, 520).

Norway, with a population of four and a half million people, is a wealthy, well-developed country where the ideals of social democracy to a large extent have been realized. It is a country where the women's movement has born real socioeconomic fruits. It is also a country where family values are high on the agenda. Moreover, in Norway, the percentage of women who give birth (94 percent) is among the highest in the world (Sundby 1999). Family life is not only culturally elaborated, it is also politically endorsed, and increasingly so. Many factors support such a suggestion. I can only briefly indicate some here. Today, state provisions for birth leave are extremely generous (twelve months), and fathers are strongly encouraged to share the "birth leave" with the mother.[1] Last year, my department was missing its male head, its male senior administrator, and its male student adviser because they were all spending up to six months at home looking after their babies while the mothers had returned to work.[2] These provisions are intimately connected to values already at large. Cultural expectations, across socioeconomic categories, hold that women, and increasingly men, cannot fulfill themselves without embracing motherhood, or respectively fatherhood. Implicitly, these roles are understood to be grounded in the nuclear family, not in individuals. This puts enormous pressure on those couples who find themselves unable to have their own children.[3]

A SHORT HISTORY OF TRANSNATIONAL ADOPTION IN NORWAY

Adoption of children from Asia began in an organized manner in Norway in the late 1960s. The first children came from South Vietnam and South Korea (Dalen and Sætersdal 1992). Children today come from several other Asian countries, from most of the Latin American countries, and from Ethiopia. Since the collapse of the Soviet Union, children are being adopted from Russia, Bulgaria, and Romania as well. There are about fifteen thousand foreign adopted children living in Norway at present, and about six hundred arrive each year. In terms of adoption per capita, Norway ranks top in the world, closely followed by Sweden and Denmark. More than 1 percent of the annual "birthrate" is made up of children adopted transnationally (Botvar 1994). By comparison, Great Britain and Germany adopt less than one-tenth of the Norwegian figure in terms of relative population, while in France, the number is about half.

A major reason for the rise in transnational adoption is the sharp decline in Norwegian-born babies available for adoption. This is assumed to be due to the availability of modern contraceptive devices, the legalization of abortion on demand, the disappearance of a social stigma attached to single mothers and the accompanying economic support such mothers receive from the state, and the effects of the feminist movement in raising women's social status. Added to this, surrogacy and egg donation are not allowed, and the practice of new reproductive technologies is tightly controlled. Given the cultural and political endorsement of children in families, it is perhaps not so surprising that Norway has embraced transnational adoption so enthusiastically as a method of reproduction and procreation.

Interestingly, unlike in Britain (see *Independent,* 28 August 1998) and the United States (see Chimezie 1975) where issues of race play a dominant part in debates about transnational adoption, Norwegian discourse hardly touches the issue. This may partly be accounted for by the remarkably homogeneous makeup of Norwegian society. Non-European immigration is of recent origin and a still-small percentage of the population consists of nonindigenous Norwegians. Racism has only lately become a topic of serious concern in the country, but this does not seem to effect the demand to adopt transnationally (Howell in press a). To the contrary, the demand increases every year.[4]

SIGNIFICANT RELATEDNESS AS A DOMINANT VALUE

Many contradictory ideas may be observed in public and private attitudes to the process of transnational adoption. These raise existential and ontological questions pertaining to indigenous meanings of nature and culture, biology and sociality, and the significance of procreation and children. My contention is that in some contexts (and I will be examining a few here), biological explanatory models are foregrounded at the expense of sociocultural ones, and in other contexts, sociocultural models are foregrounded while those of biology are ignored.

When all is said and done, though, it is kinship as an idiom of significant relatedness that emerges as dominant in the various discourses and practices that surround transnational adoption (Howell unpublished ms.). In the popular Norwegian view, kinship (*slektskap*) is about descent and blood relatedness. The idiom of kinship encloses the family within biologically grounded relations. Adoption clearly challenges such notions. Yet in particular circumstances, the kin network may be opened to incorporate nonbiologically related persons into existing categories that are predicated on biology. Hence, the boundaries of relatedness within the conventional kinship classification may be expanded as well as restricted, and socioemotional characteristics of actual people will be emphasized rather than biological ones. Legal provisions recognize this, and the 1986 Adoption Act in Norway made adopted children kin on par with biological children. Children adopted transnationally are thus incorporated into existing kin categories, such as son/daughter, grandchild, cousin, and niece/nephew. In addition, family origin narratives are frequently created that bring the adopted children into meaningful connectedness with their adoptive parents and their kin. Despite no shared substance (see Carsten, this volume) between adopted children and their adoptive parents, they nevertheless are transformed into kinfolk through what I have called elsewhere a process of "kinning" (Howell in press b; unpublished ms.). This is achieved by the parents through the emotional loadings that constitute their understanding of the category parent/child and that are brought to bear on the relationship from the moment of the child's "birth" (see below). These are children who are powerfully desired (Weigel 1998) and were "conceived in the heart" (Ragoné 1994).

More surprisingly, inside informal adoption networks particular nonbiologically related adoptive families may be transformed into "as-if kin" due to the positive quality of their social and emotional connectedness with each other. They relate to each other as uncles and aunts, nieces and nephews, and cousins, as will be discussed below. At the same time, particular biological uncles and aunts may virtually disappear from the kin network due to negative social and emotional connectedness. Thus, emotions dictate to some extent code of conduct.

Although the incorporation of adopted children into standard kin structures may, at first glance, seem relatively straightforward, adoptive parents work extremely hard at making themselves and their adopted children conform to their notion of a normal family. Through the various stages that the adoptive parents pass, by creating symbolic pregnancy and birth events for themselves, they normalize their own experience and make "as-if blood" bonds with their child. Like David Schneider's "Americans" (1968), blood is the defining metaphor of Norwegian discourse on descent and kin relatedness. Adopting a child and making it part of a family may, in effect, be regarded as a process whereby the child's blood is symbolically transformed into that of his/her parents. Adoption thus confirms, but also changes, the parameters of the biological basis for family and kin. This finding both confirms and expands Schneider's assertion that "without the biological relationship . . . adoption makes absolutely no sense" (1972, 36). Conversely, it could be argued that adoption makes sense of the biological relationship, that the "made" relationship delineates the "natural" one. The Norwegian material indicates that adoptive families re-create the ideals embedded in cultural values about biological relatedness, but that they do so self-consciously and adaptively to accommodate their particular needs. Adoption both challenges and confirms received ideas at the same time. Discussing the related phenomenon of assisted conception, Sarah Franklin and Helena Ragoné make the point, "At stake are not only traditional definitions of family, disability, parenting, kin connection, and inheritance, but the conventional understandings of nature, life, humanity, morality and the future" (1998, 9). Such situations make for what I call self-conscious kinship. One may describe the process as one of "kinning." By this I mean that the child is being incorporated into its adoptive parents' kin network.

THE SOCIALLY EMBEDDED INDIVIDUAL

Despite an increasing emphasis on the individual and individual rights as a dominant value (Dumont 1986) in Norwegian social and cultural life generally, people nonetheless seem to orient themselves on a personal, emotional level in relation to significant others within a set of references consistent with traditional family and kin ideology. Meaningful sociality becomes inseparable from individual satisfaction. Most couples who choose to adopt are involuntary infertile. According to my findings, the overriding incentive for most couples is precisely a desire for substantive sociality — to be a family interacting with other families. Social life predicated on child-related activities and preoccupations is a crucial part of the adult life of Norwegians between the ages of twenty-five and forty. Participating in this becomes highly valued; failure to achieve it is seen as highly problematic. On the personal level, infertile couples feel that without children, they are deprived of the chance to use and develop important potential qualities of themselves — that of being a father or mother. On the social level, they wish to negate their exclusion from the social life around them. There is thus a shift in emphasis from the individual within networks of other individuals to parents within networks of other parents.

In adoptive circles, notions of what constitutes a family are conventional.

Despite appearances to the contrary, Norwegian adoptive parents—much as Norwegian homosexuals—are not iconoclasts when it comes to family life.[5] The longed-for institution of family is made up of mum, dad, two (increasingly three) children, a house with a garden, and a cabin in the mountains or by the sea. The family expresses itself through family outings and activities of various kinds, spending time with grandparents, uncles, aunts, and cousins on the conventional occasions, and with other families with children of the same age at child-related events.

This observation is confirmed by my own inquiries as well as from interviewing social workers and adoption agency personnel. "Why do you want a child?" is one of the first questions prospective adoptive parents are asked. In order to save your marriage? To create a family? To save an unfortunate child in a poor country? Or to fulfill yourself? Of these, creating a family is the most frequently chosen reason. It is also the one looked on with most favor by the authorities, and this, of course, reinforces it.[6]

THE OSCILLATION BETWEEN BIOLOGY AND CULTURE

Four main stages may be discerned in the process of creating a family through transnational adoption in Norway. I have chosen to describe the stages using the standard vocabulary of prepregnancy, pregnancy, birth, and family life. With the exception of prepregnancy, these terms are used by parents and adoption agencies alike—a fact that in itself demonstrates the hybridity of the adoption discourse. On the one hand, adoption is presented as a social event: the bringing together of adults and children who are total strangers with radically different sociocultural backgrounds. On the other hand, the vocabulary employed indicates that the whole purpose of the exercise is to create a relationship of parents and children, and make them into a normal family. My argument highlights one dimension of this process: how people's construction of each stage is made up of a process of biologizing and de-biologizing the family relationship, with an oscillation between nature and culture as constituting reference.

Prepregnancy
The prepregnancy stage begins when a couple decides that they want to have a child. The persistent failure to conceive leads to a round of medical checkups, which may or may not include assisted conception. It ends in the decision to adopt a child from a foreign country, born by unknown biological parents

and looking quite different from themselves. My research has shown that of those who have adopted in the last five years, approximately two-thirds have tried some form of assisted conception. During this period, women more than men stress their "biological desire" to be pregnant and give birth, and express the grief provoked by their inability to achieve this. "To want, but not to have, biological children is a crisis, albeit a drawn-out and unpredictable one. In my opinion, it does not resemble any other crisis. How can you grieve over something that never existed? When should one start to grieve a pregnancy which still might occur?" asks a Swedish woman who wrote a book about her own infertility, numerous unsuccessful in vitro fertilization attempts, and subsequent adoption of a Vietnamese child (Weigel 1998, 32).

The process that leads to a decision to adopt can be a long and painful one for many couples. Once they have decided on this course of action, however, most couples put the grief of infertility behind them and want the event to happen fast. They experience a profound sense of frustration when they realize that they have to go through a lengthy investigative process by various social services in order to be approved. The criteria are restrictive and normative. The heterosexual married couple with a stable economy and conventional life-style is, in practice, the only acceptable category. Couples register with one of the three adoption agencies through which children are allocated and choose a country. Once the go-ahead is given by the national adoption bureau, formal application is sent to the country in question. This is a time when couples are adjusting their expectations from that of having their own "homemade" child, as the jargon runs in adoptive circles, to adopting a stranger.

For many, this is a period characterized by a fair amount of self-examination. Starting from an unreflected focus on biology through infertility treatment, during which most experience the grief of failure expressed by the Swedish author cited above, they end up with a fairly assertive culturalist approach favoring adoption. This process moves from one extreme to another, during which the means and ends correspondingly shift. The new reproductive technologies can be said to be a biological means to a biological and social end, whereas adoption is a social means to a social end dressed in biological jargon.

Pregnancy
Once the couple has received the stamp of approval as suitable parents from the public authorities, the pregnancy may be said to start. Unlike biological

pregnancy, however, pregnant adoptive parents do not know how long it will last, and they are completely at the mercy of a number of institutions and individuals with whom they have an impersonal relationship. They must wait until a child is made available to them in the country concerned. Depending on the donor country, this takes from half a year to three years. In the intervening time, the agencies take care to prepare them for the event. While this used to be rather casual and haphazard in the early days, now the agencies have developed a fairly organized approach. There have also been several changes in their attitudes. One may discern a certain difference in approach between agencies and prospective parents during this period. The agencies increasingly see their role as disabusing any "false notions of relatedness" between adoptive parents and children. The parents, while more or less accepting this, at the same time emphasize the pregnancy and birthing idiom of the process.

In recent years, the agencies have jointly published several pamphlets and edited volumes with titles such as *The Adoption Family: Information and Guidance for Adoptive Parents* (Carli and Dalen 1997), *Adoption of Foreign Children* (1994), and *Who Am I? A Brochure Written by and for Those Adopted from Different Countries* (1997). These are written and compiled by people with research or practical experience of the subject (mainly from a psychological standpoint), and deal with many different issues pertaining to transnational adoption. One clear message running through these publications is that adopting children from different cultural backgrounds is not a trivial matter. Earlier assumptions that adopted children would effortlessly become Norwegian have now been replaced by a stress on the importance of biological relationships and the child's "original culture" (Howell in press b). Today, parents are admonished to instill in their children a sense of pride in their original cultures. They are warned against letting the child forget its different "roots." In contrast to previous advice, parents are now advised to retain one of the child's original names — as a reminder of origins and an aid in the formation of identity (I return to this below).

The agencies also publish newsletters for their members. Apart from providing information regarding changes in regulations and practices related to transnational adoption, they carry articles on topics thought to be of common interest, such as education, language acquisition, puberty and problems of identity, and racism. They announce activities organized by the various local or thematic subgroups and publish letters from members raising issues for discussion, as well as photographs of new children arrived "home" to member families. The agencies are thus a major force in shaping attitudes. At the same time, it is likely that their own attitudes are being influenced by public discourses in society at large.

The local branches of the agencies organize courses for the expecting parents in which the couples are prepared for their role as parents of an adopted child from a different culture. In addition, mutual support groups are established; books about transnational adoption are read and discussed; lectures are attended; and parents, siblings, and friends are prepared for the event. The activities arranged for couples at this stage have increased in recent years.

The pregnancy period is a time characterized by hybrid discourses and rapid shifts between constituting reference points.

Birth

The social birth of a transnationally adopted child may be said to extend beyond the moment of the child's arrival. Just as in many African and Asian understandings, in which a child is not a person until various rituals have been performed before and after the actual moment of birth, so also the person-making and kinning of the transnationally adopted child. When a particular child is allocated for a particular couple, I maintain that the birth may be said to have started. It may still take several months before they may collect the child and bring it "home" (see below).

Formally, the child arriving in Norway is treated as a tabula rasa. The main actors are the parents and judiciary, both of whom are concerned with the incorporation of the child. It is given a new name, new citizenship, new home, new kin, new social and cultural expectations, and new relationships beyond the family. This is a time marked by an extreme effort to de-biologize origins and create kin relations. Several important processes are carried out during the birthing of the transnationally adopted child. The statement quoted at the outset of this essay by the expectant adoptive mother receiving her child at the airport bears this out. In their different ways, they all normalize the relationships, incorporating the adopted child into its parents' reference points and networks.

MAKING PLACE, MAKING KIN The symbolic umbilical cord is not cut until the parents have fulfilled their obligations to the donor country. This includes sending regular reports on the child's progress, along with snapshots, to the donor orphanage. The image that is created through these reports is one of happy families and is their own recapitulation of these ideals. The child is presented together with his/her parents and grandparents in stereotypical settings well-known from media and advertising: at home having a nice time on the sofa around the coffee table with candles, coffee, and cakes; in the child's own specially fitted-out bedroom; in front of the open fire at the cabin in the mountains; at Christmas, on national day, and on birthdays dressed in national costume; being engaged in healthy outdoor activities — skiing or skating in the winter, boating and bathing in the summer — with mum and dad, or cousins of the same age. I have not seen any urban settings in these chosen photos, or the child engaged in any activity outside the immediate family or kin-grounded places. What the photos in the reports state, again and again, is, "Look, the child is a Norwegian child. We are a typical Norwegian family. We have kin and are connected to places embedded in kin relations."

This placing of the child in familiar localities can be traced to the importance in Norwegian personal discourse given to identifying a place of origin: a district, valley, fjord, or farm from which one's ancestors came. Place of origin, and belonging to a place, plays an integral part in personal narratives that are constituent in the makeup of Norwegian identity. Through photographing the adopted child in places of parental descent or belonging, the child is being symbolically planted in them. During this process, not a single reference is made to the place of origin of the child.[7]

From the point of view of adoptive parents, their new child has come home. This is the jargon employed by all the agencies. In their annual reports, they provide figures for how many children have supposedly come home from the various countries with which they have an arrangement. By coming home, they all seem to be saying, the child finally arrives where it was meant to be all the time, thus backgrounding biological processes. Through a linguistic sleight of hand, the biological parents in the country of origin are transformed into temporary caretakers. There are thus many inherent paradoxes in the agencies' own attitudes.

CREATING ORIGIN NARRATIVES In different contexts, the special origin of the adopted child is foregrounded, while at the same time, the idiom of Norwegian-grounded kinship and belonging is maintained. A narrative of as-if blood relations emerges out of relationships that were forged with other prospective adoptive parents during the pregnancy stage. Couples with whom prospective adoptive parents interacted while they were waiting for their children, mainly through participating together in parenthood preparatory courses, or with whom they traveled to receive their children,[8] often become closely attached to each other and talk of being like kinfolk (*i slekt*).

These relationships are interesting from several perspectives. First, the shared experience of being uncertainly pregnant together has, in itself, created bonds between these couples. No matter how sympathetic biological kin and friends are to infertile couples, they will argue that only those who have gone through the same experience can appreciate the strain and stress of it. As well, the special makeup of adoptive families creates emotional bonds. The parents look like each other (white, blondish, tallish); whereas most of the children, regardless of their country of origin, look more like each other than they do their parents (darker skinned, dark haired, brown eyed, shortish). Only when they come together are the families "normal," provoking no surprised looks or comments by outsiders. Third, to those who traveled and lived together when receiving their children, the shared experience along with a shared sense of place are important. The strange town, hotel, and orphanage become places of common origins. Adopted children have no shared place of origin with their parents except the place where they first met. Others who have "given birth" at the same place thus become participants in the same origin narratives. Whereas maternity clinics do not usually take on heavy symbolic loading for most biological parents, the orphanage, and the town where it was located, often do so for adoptive parents. Employees at the orphanage, the judge at the local court, the manager of the hotel, all become key characters in the birth drama. So when parents meet each other after the children have come home, conversations return again and again to those days and weeks when their child was being born to them.

Adoptive families gather at annual social get-togethers of the Korea Association, Columbia Association, and so on, where they seek out those parents from other parts of Norway whom they know. They visit each other during holidays, send Christmas and birthday cards to each other's children. All the time, the reason for these meetings is expressed the same way: "It is so good for the children to maintain relationships with children from the same place." My argument, however, is that it is good for the parents to maintain relationships with other parents who have the same experience about the place of origin and main actors connected to it. Parents need to maintain the relationships, not the children; and parents seek a resolution to the paradox of their special situation by engaging in Norwegian sociality in the name of Korean (or whichever country's) culture.

By and large, the adopted children soon lose interest in these reunions, but are dragged along by their parents until they become old enough to resist effectively. At these meetings, the parents retell for each other again and again incidents from their time in Seoul, Bogota, Addis Ababa, and so forth. They thereby anchor the birth to a common social place—a place from which their children are as-if descended, making them as-if kin. To produce shared narratives of origin linked to a place of origin is an important aspect of the formation of the new family and its relations with other families. Thus, kin status can be extended to those outside the blood kin network. Everyone knows that they are not real kin—blood is the determining factor—but they interact in ways that are recognizably kinlike. Unlike the parents of Down's syndrome children or children suffering from other genetic diseases (discussed by Rapp, Heath, and Taussig, this volume), who join in mutual support groups, the get-togethers of adoptive parents can be interpreted more along the lines of family reunions.

MATCHING "US AND OUR CHILD" Another part of the origin narrative concerns the matching of a particular child with a particular set of parents.[9] Many are convinced, wrongly according to my information, that the orphanage director puts a great deal of effort into choosing a child that would be most compatible with the parents—if not in looks, then in personality traits or interests. Parents rarely feel that it is a matter of chance which child comes to them. Somehow they are "meant for each other." Once, at a gathering of parents who had traveled together to collect their children from China, there were two mothers whose children were born one week apart. The conversation turned in the direction just indicated, when one of the mothers exclaimed, half-jokingly, "How would it have been if I had been given your child and you mine!" The other woman immediately insisted, "But that would have been impossible. My child is so right for us, but would have been completely unsuited to you. It would not have worked out at all!" In other words, a psychological bonding occurs on the part of the parents at the moment when they receive details about the child allocated for them.

The Family in Daily Life

Once the birth process is complete, once both parents return to work and the child has settled into kindergarten and then school, the family has to function in daily life. At this point, parents begin to foreground the fact that the child has a biological and ethnic origin that they do not share, but which they have been told by all the experts during the pregnancy stage that they must not allow themselves—or the child—to forget. Indeed, in certain contexts, culture is biologized. There is much talk of "original culture," "cultural background," and "search for roots" even when the child arrives as a small baby. To some extent, this may be a euphemism for race, but my material indicates that it is more complicated.

FOLKLORIZATION OF CULTURE Coupled with the growing focus on biological relations in society, it is noticeable that the agencies increasingly encourage adoptive parents to learn about the donor country and familiarize their children with it. The conceptualization of "culture," however, is both reified and superficial, confined to certain cultural markers such as food, dress, and artifacts that are easily consumed without having to confront real sociocultural differences. Virtually no serious information is provided about the social, economic, or political institutions and conditions of the donor countries, and few of the parents interviewed expressed much interest in these aspects of their child's country of origin.

The subgroups of adoptive families that are organized by the agencies may be based on different assumed commonalities. The fact of having adopted a child transnationally may be regarded as sufficient to warrant special needs for social interaction. In such cases, the country of origin is of little or no interest. Alternatively, the groups may be based on a common country of origin. Whether the assumed bond is created through an event (adoption) or place/culture (country of origin), intriguing questions arise about the assumed commonality of backgrounds, be these based on national/ethnic/cultural criteria or just on personal historical trajectories. Are these children Norwegian or are they Columbian? According to which standards one should judge such an issue is an important question that is rarely addressed directly.

The ambivalence is nevertheless repeatedly expressed. At organized social gatherings, members are asked to bring a dish from the country from which their child comes. Children arrive dressed in either clothing from their country of origin, a Norwegian *bunad* (national costume), or some currently fashionable attire worn by most children of their age. However one wishes to interpret the choices made by the parents, it is clear that this is not a neutral domain. Rather, statements are necessarily being made at these gatherings about identity and belonging, all of which necessarily express ambivalence and ambiguity (for a discussion of the significance of ambivalence in social discourse, see also Peletz, this volume).

SEARCHING FOR ROOTS Further ambivalence about identity is manifest in debates about roots and the search for roots, which is high on the agenda these days. Changes in attitudes over time can be observed on the part of the agencies regarding this. Now, they are at pains to explode the myth that the adopted child was born at the moment he or she was united with his or her adopted parents. Not only was the child born in a foreign country, they stress, he or she was born by a flesh-and-blood mother, into a foreign and exotic culture. Unlike legal attitudes, the child obtained is not a tabula rasa but a human being with a personal history. These facts will affect the child throughout his or her life, and may lead to problems of identity and adjustment as he or she grows up (Howell in press b). The child's "natural desire" to seek his or her roots must be accommodated by the adoptive parents.

Again and again, the messages transmitted by the adoption agencies can be seen as ambiguous. On the one hand, parents are taken through a pregnancy that will lead to a birth. "We have never failed to deliver a child to a waiting couple," states one agency in its information material. The agencies bring home, as it were, a certain number of children each year to the "expectant" couples. On the other hand, the children are not of their parents' making, either biologically or culturally; they will always demonstrate their different origins in their looks. Interestingly, the fact of their different looks may be the reason that their cultural background is so emphasized. There should be a fit between appearance and culture, seems to be the underlying assumption. Statements by adopted children to the effect that they "have a Norwegian soul in a Korean/Indian/Columbian body" are frequently cited to demonstrate an identity problem, but also as an incentive to the parents to enable the children to reunite with their alleged roots. And yet, as the story told below of the girl adopted from Bangladesh shows, when people actually go to their countries of origin, they often find that despite a physical resemblance, they do not share cultural understandings with the local population. They are, indeed, happy to come home to Norway. So the situation today is more complex than it might at first sight imply.[10]

WHO AM I THEN? "I am really a typical Bærum girl," said a twenty-two year old adopted from Bangladesh when six months old in a recent television reportage of her first visit to Bangladesh. She felt no rapport with the culture she encountered, nor with her biological mother, father, and sisters, all of whom she met. "OK, so I have seen the country and them, but I will never want to go back or have anything more to do with them. From now on I'll stick to package holidays," she concludes back home in her room in her parents' house in affluent suburban Bærum.

Several people I have spoken to about this program felt that she was acting unnaturally. "She must be suppressing something," was the general verdict. In fact, when compared to similar stories being published and broadcast, her reaction was unusual. A popular Norwegian television series, *Tore on the Trail*, helps people track down some lost relative or friend. These are usually Norwegian-born people who were adopted or fostered as children, or who for some other reason were separated from their biological relatives. As adults, they wish to be reunited with their biological kin. Tore, the show's host, sets about tracing them. The quest is in keeping with a large popular literature, and folklore, on precisely this topic. Recently, Tore was approached by a young woman adopted as a two year old from Ecuador. Tore found her biological grandmother and some sisters of her deceased mother.

The resultant program was an intense buildup to the dramatic and exultant meeting between the girl and her biological grandmother. It was skillfully captured by the Norwegian film crew, with Tore's excited commentary running throughout. Unlike the Bangladeshi girl's story, this was a tale that conformed to most peoples' expectations. I watched it while attending a workshop arranged by one of the adoption agencies for course leaders for a new class called Adoption and Puberty. There was not a dry eye among those who watched, all of whom were adoptive mothers.[11] The discussion afterward was tense. What struck me about the comments was their concern for the adoptive parents. Everyone had noted their anxious faces when they saw their daughter off at the airport, and their relief when she returned home and told them that although she was happy to have "seen for herself," she nevertheless belonged with them in Norway. The young woman's wish to seek her biological origins was taken for granted, and the material for the preparatory course in fact is built around such an unquestioned need. At the same time, the adoptive parents are highly sensitive to any hint that the child is not their real child.

The public focus on roots has led to a sharp increase in organized family "return" visits to the adopted child's country of origin. Invariably, these include a visit to the orphanage where, ideally, children can meet the person(s) who looked after them, and in some countries, they are allowed to see all the papers that relate to their own history and even try to locate biological relatives. In such contexts, the adoptive children are conceptually relinked with their biological parents, but never to such an extent that the social kin relations with their adoptive parents are seriously challenged. From interviewing some families who have participated in these return visits, and reading the programs and background information issued by the organizing adoption agency, my impression is that the overall image being presented is that of a tourist trip, albeit one with a major difference. The sights to be seen are emphasized, as are the exotic differences between Norway and the country in question. The mixed narratives that arise in connection with such trips appear, nevertheless, to be handled by the participants without producing undue worry.[12]

There are thus interesting shifts in Norwegian transnational adoption practices. Initially, the posed analytic — and empirical — opposition between pater/genitor and mater/genitrix did not raise much of a problem. From one perspective, the reality of the separation was obvious for all to see because the adopted children could rarely be passed off as biological. They simply did not look like their parents. Yet in the early days of Norwegian transnational adoption, the parents wished to minimize this, and many played down the fact of adoption, so much so that I have been told by young adult adoptees that the issue was never brought up — something that produced anxieties in them. There used to be little or no concern with the country of origin, and the agencies saw their role exclusively as providers of children. Uncertainties and ambivalences most likely existed for the families concerned, however. Indeed, the Adoption Act of 1986 demonstrates the ambivalences without addressing them. While adopted children are made legally and morally equal to those born biologically, the law also states that at age eighteen, all children have the right to be told who their biological parents are (provided the information exists). So, within the pages of the same law, one finds contradictory messages being transmitted about the adopted child as regards his or her status as a biological and social being.

THE EMOTIONALITY OF RELATEDNESS

As this essay asserts, the fact of getting and having children is not primarily about individuals but about relatedness — about mutuality, responsibility, belonging, and affection. A sense of their own unrelatedness to others seems to drive many couples toward adopting children. While the meaning of kinship in Norway generally may have been transformed in some of its institutional aspects in the postwar period, significant personal relationships are still expressed in a kin idiom. Research on adoption can throw into relief some past and present values about the meaning and operationality of kinship in Norway. Indications are that adoptive families may be closer to realizing the so-called ideals of family life than biological families in the rest of the population. There are fewer divorces among adoptive parents than is the national norm, and since single-parent adoption is not allowed, a nuclear family structure is ensured at the outset. Moreover, a study conducted on the conditions of life of transnationally adopted children in Norway shows that the children see their grandparents on average once a week—a phenomenon far above the national average (Botvar 1994). Although the vast majority of adoptive parents interviewed started their path toward parenthood on an unquestioned assumption that their own bodies would do the work, my material reveals that once the decision to adopt was taken, procreation took on a totally new meaning. The Warnock report of 1984 in Britain, on the legal and ethical implications of the new reproductive technologies, states that having children is "for many, a powerful urge to perpetuate their genes through a new generation. This desire cannot be assuaged by adoption" (Warnock 1984, 8–9). This is not borne out by the Norwegian material. Once engaged in, adoption is not experienced as second best.

Transnational adoption is so common in Norway that most people have some personal knowledge of it. With an increased public focus on genetics and reproductive technology, which leads to an increasing biologization of discourses about personhood, the public gaze on adoption is correspondingly being biologized. Yet this is a contested domain, and an uneasy set of paradoxes and ambivalences are noticeable in the discourse and practice surrounding transnational adoption. This is largely resolved by the parents through creating a cognitive boundary between contexts. Sometimes biological and sometimes cultural models are foregrounded. Overall, a refocusing from biological to nonbiological children, from their own bodies to social relations can be observed. The shadow of biology, however, always looms in the background, making most discursive practices hybrid.

The material from Norway indicates that adoptive families re-create the ideals embedded in notions about biological relatedness. So I would agree with Judith Modell's conclusion that "adoption upholds the biological basis for parenthood . . . [and] inscribes the natural relationship" (1994, 238). But I am dubious about describing this, as Modell does, as "artificial kinship" (238) because whether we focus on how adoptive parents work at symbolically transforming the blood of their children to their own or on how they encourage them in a quest for roots, the notion that they are related in an artificial way does not seem to be relevant. Rather, as an approach that allows adoptive parents to expand the categories of kin according to the particular quality of relatedness with others, it might be more appropriate to call it self-conscious kinship.

NOTES

My research on transnational adoption in Norway began in 1997. I wish to express my gratitude to Monica Dalen and Barbro Sætersdal for their encouragement, and Ånund Brottveit and Pål Ketil Botvar for their interested cooperation. The staff of Adopsjonsforum, Verdens Barn, and Inoradopt gave generously of their time, as did the members of the Association of Adoptive Parents. Without the resourceful assistance of Esben Leifsen and the many creative interchanges with Marit Melhuus, this research would not have advanced as much as it has. I wish to thank the two editors of this volume for the valuable comments they made on my original conference paper. I hope to take account of more of them in future publications. Finally, I want to express my appreciation to the numerous adoptive parents who invited me into their homes and answered my many questions.

1 Birth leave consists of a full year of leave, nine months of which is at full salary and the remaining three at 70 percent. Fathers must take four weeks immediately following the birth.

2 The current conservative Christian People's Party government has built on these provisions and values to instigate a highly controversial financial grant system that keeps the mother (the father is left out of the debate) at home with her one-year-old child at the end of the birth leave for up to two years.

3 Only married heterosexual couples may adopt. There is currently a debate raging in the media about allowing single and homosexual people to adopt, but it is unresolved. It looks as if an opening may be made for singles, but not for homosexuals. Were this to be passed, all the indications are that restrictions on single applicants will be severe.

4 The most dramatic expression came when the extreme right-wing party, the White Alliance, specified in its 1997 political program an intention to sterilize all foreign (that is, nonwhite) adopted children. The party leader was taken to court and sentenced to prison on the grounds of inciting racist conflict. There has been no noticeable change in public attitudes to transnational adoption as a result of this, although parents are perhaps more alert to manifestations of racism.

5 Many homosexual couples seek to gain public acceptance for their union. They regularize their relationship through a legally binding partnership contract. Currently, homosexuals are fighting for the right to adopt, arguing that they may provide just as stable an environment for the growth of a child as a heterosexual couple. Lesbian couples who give birth while in a partnership are eager to live as a normal family, and many begin to engage actively in various family events once the child is born (Riksaasen 2001). On a national basis, 17 percent of all children, and closer to 40 percent in the southeast region, are brought up in single-parent families. Nevertheless, the two-parent family ideal has the status of a norm.

6 There has been a change in the motivations of both the parents and authorities. Earlier, a wish to help poor and deprived children in the so-called Third World was a common argument from both sides. Today, the parents are more focused on

their own desires, and the agencies are suspicious of idealistic motives. In Norwegian adoption thinking, the relative importance of adults and children has shifted from the original "in the best interests of the adults" to "in the best interests of the child." There is a move in some circles (primarily among singles and homosexuals) to make it a right to have a child, regardless of personal or social status, thereby returning to the notion of in the best interests of the adult.

7 The exercise is directed exclusively at the donors, but no consideration seems to be given to the possible divergence in cultural values and expectations of what constitutes the good life.

8 Many choose to pick up their children themselves. They will have to spend anywhere from ten days to six weeks in the donor country before they return home with their child.

9 Prospective parents have to send the orphanage a dossier about themselves with photos. In turn, they are sent pictures and a brief description of a child, and are given a few days to decide whether they want to accept him or her. I have not yet met a couple who refused. One look at the picture and report was enough to find some quality that somehow resonated within them. As-if blood relations are created and consolidated in different contexts during pregnancy and birth, and through recapturing the moment of the so-called birth.

10 It will be interesting to observe how these arguments are applied, and adopted, in relation to children who come from Russia and Eastern Europe. In looks, many of these children could have been born by Norwegian parents.

11 Including myself. The fact of having adopted my daughter from Nepal while still living in Britain alerted me to the potential for anthropological research on the topic after having moved to Norway, where the notions and procedures about transnational adoption are dramatically different from those in Britain.

12 Since writing this paper, I have participated in one such "motherland tour" to South Korea. On the whole this confirmed my previous assumptions about its significance (for details, see Howell unpublished manuscript).

REFERENCES

Botvar, Pål Ketil. 1994. *Ny sjanse i Norge: Utenlandsadoptertes oppvekst og levekår.* Oslo: Diaforsk.

Carli, Amalaia, and Monica Dalen. 1997. *Adopsjonsfamilien: Informasjon og veiledning til adoptivforeldre.* Oslo: Pedagogisk Forum.

Chimezie, Anita. 1975. Transracial Adoption of Black Children. *Social Work* 70, 296–301.

Dalen, Monica, and Barbro Sætersdal. 1992. *Utenlandsadopterte barn i Norge: tilpasning—opplæring—identitetsutvikling.* Ph.D. diss., University of Oslo.

Dumont, Louis. 1986. *Essays on Individualism: Modern Ideology in an Anthropological Perspective.* Chicago: University of Chicago Press.

Fine, Agnés, ed. 1998. *Adoptions: Ethnologie des Parentés Choisies.* Paris: Editions de la Maisons des sciences de-l'homme.

Franklin, Sarah, and Helena Ragoné. 1998. *Reproducing Reproduction: Kinship, Power, and Technological Innovation.* Philadelphia: University of Pennsylvania Press.

Howell, Signe. In press a. The Backpackers That Come to Stay: New Challenges to Norwegian Transnational Adoptive Families. In *The Anthropology of Adoption,* edited by Fiona Bowie. London: Routledge.

———. In press b. Community Beyond Place: Adoptive Families in Norway. In *Rethinking Communities,* ed. Vered Amit-Talia. London: Routledge.

———. Unpublished ms. The Kinning of Selves: Creating Life Trajectories in Adoptive Families. Paper presented to the Workshop on Kinship and Temporality, Goldsmiths College, London University, 17 December.

Latour, Bruno. 1993. *We Have Never Been Modern.* New York: Harvester.

Modell, Judith S. 1994. *Kinship with Strangers: Adoption and Interpretations of Kinship in American Culture.* Berkeley: University of California Press.

Ragoné, Helena. 1994. *Surrogate Motherhood: Conception in the Heart.* Boulder, Colo.: Westview Press.

Riksaasen, Guri. 2001. To mammaer, går det an? En annerledes familieplanlegging. In *Blod—Tykkere een Vann? Betydninger av slektskap i Norge,* edited by Signe Howell and Marit Melhuus. Bergen: Fagbokforlaget.

Schneider, David M. 1968. *American Kinship: A Cultural Account.* Englewood Cliffs, N.J.: Prentice-Hall.

———. 1972. What Is Kinship All About? In *Kinship Studies in the Morgan Centennial Year,* edited by Priscilla Reining. Washington, D.C.: Anthropological Society of Washington.

Strathern, Marilyn. 1996. Cutting the Network. *Journal of the Royal Anthropological Institute* 2, 517–36.

Sundby, Johanne. 1999. Conversation with author. Oslo, Norway, 7 May.

Warnock, Mary. 1984. *The Warnock Report: Report of the Committee of Inquiry into Human Fertilization and Embryology.* London: Her Majesty's Stationary Office.

Weigel, Kerstin. 1998. *Langtansbarnen: Adoptivföreldrar Berettar.* Stockholm: Norstedts.

CHAPTER 8

Practicing Kinship in Rural North China

Yunxiang Yan

In August 1966, my father was wrongly accused of having been a capitalist prior to the 1949 revolution (he actually had been a small shop owner), and as a result of the Red Guards' efforts to make Beijing politically pure and clean during the Cultural Revolution, our family, like many other families in similar situations, was forced to leave the capital city and relocate in my father's natal village in northern China. This village is a patrilineal community where all the male members share the same surname, Yan. At that time, "class struggle" was the primary concern of the Communist Party leaders; so it became national practice in everyday life. Chinese people were divided into various good-class categories (those who had been exploited and oppressed before the revolution) and bad ones (those who had been exploiters and oppressors); the former were mobilized by the state to monitor and struggle against the latter. Hence, in our village there were the members of the good class, the supposedly revolutionary Yans, and the members of the bad class, the allegedly antirevolutionary Yans. Because my father was labeled a capitalist, he and, by virtue of our kin relationship, our entire family were considered politically polluted and thus we were all excluded from many social activities in which only good-class people were allowed to participate.

An odd thing occurred in the first autumn (1967) following our relocation to the countryside. My father's aunt (the mother of his patrilineal cousin, who, based on complicated kinship terminology, I called "sixth grandmother") died at the age of seventy-seven. She was survived by a large number of children, grandchildren, and great-grandchildren. Because of her age and because she had so many descendants, an elaborate funeral, based on local customs, was called for. Unfortunately, she died during the peak of the Cultural Revolution when the young Red Guards were sweeping through the whole nation to attack traditional culture and customs, including life-cycle rituals. After intensive discussions among themselves, as well as negotiations with the village authority, the family members of the deceased finally decided to provide the deceased woman with an appropriate funeral, which she so much deserved. To show their willingness to go along with the new customs proposed by the Communist leaders, the family members agreed to reduce the length of the ritual to two days (instead of the three or seven days that it should have been) and observe only the most important ceremonial procedures, while omitting many others, including the traditional white mourning dress and musical band.

Much to the surprise of our family, my father was also called on to participate in the funeral and play his role in all the major rites as a close nephew of the deceased, despite the fact that he was a political outcast. During this public event, my father became kin to those good-class villagers, some of whom were village cadres, political activists, or even Red Guards. Because his generational rank was quite senior, he was addressed by all but a few individuals by such terms as "uncle" or "grandfather"—terms that definitely should not have been used to address a class enemy. He later recalled that initially he had felt uncomfortable with such a sudden change of position in public life, and the other villagers had also felt the same way. But as the ritual proceeded, most people seemed to forget the political boundaries between the good- and bad-class categories.

During the second night, a final farewell ceremony was performed in front of the deceased, who had been placed inside her coffin. Members of the entire sublineage assembled in the courtyard, with the males on one side and females on the other. The participants were lined up in rows based on their generational rank. Although I had successfully avoided the major part of the funeral (I was thirteen years old at the time and quite afraid of the ceremony), an older cousin took me from my home and literally threw me into the crowd of mourners, who were kneeling in rows and kowtowing when the ritual specialist gave the order. I remember being completely terrified by the performance and forgetting to do what I had been told. Then someone lifted me by the ear and carried me past several rows to place me in the second row in the front. Then he kicked the back of my knees. I next found myself kneeling on the ground along with more than a dozen men in the row, all of whom I was used to addressing as "cousin" in everyday life, regardless of their age. Following their example, I proceeded to do what they did during the rest of the ritual.

Even after I grew up, I always had a feeling of fear whenever I recalled my experience during that night. As time passes, however, I no longer fear the ghosts or my older cousins; what I still fear is perhaps the mystic power of the funeral itself, as well as the strange feeling that I am one of the Yans and thus bound to all the other Yans regardless of whether I like them or not.

Now looking at the event in retrospect, I realize that it actually reveals a complex situation of kinship practice in that particular historical moment. On the surface, it shows once again the tremendous power of patrilineal ideology and kinship norms, as villagers felt compelled to recognize their kinship position in public and perform the funeral in accordance with traditionally defined kinship norms, despite the state-sponsored, antitradition radicalism during the Cultural Revolution. As a result, the political boundaries between the good and bad classes were blurred publicly by the kinship ties during the ritual—perhaps a small victory for the villagers' passive resistance to the penetration of state power.[1]

Nevertheless, a closer look reveals interesting changes, which occurred during the funeral. First, the state had obviously reshaped the practice of kinship to such an extent that the villagers had to consider many factors when deciding whether or not to perform a proper funeral. During my 1991 fieldwork in the village, interestingly enough, I was told by a couple of villagers that my seventh uncle (the son of the deceased lady) had indeed encountered some trouble after the funeral, even though he had confessed his guilt for practicing a traditional ritual in front of a portrait of Chairman Mao Tse-tung right after the event. Second, the villagers had to make modifications to their ritual practice, such as shortening the duration of the funeral and simplifying the ritual procedures. Finally (and perhaps more important), despite the fact that the mourners acted as a collective during the funeral, each individual had to make a decision before and during the process whether to respond to the event socially, politically, and emotionally (admittedly a child's decision did not count much, as illustrated by my own case). For instance, although most members of the sublineage participated in the funeral, several young and radical villagers refused to attend the ritual so as to demonstrate their firm revolutionary standpoint.

These changes reveal the other side of kinship relations: that is, in practice, kinship relations are actually a set of rather flexible interpersonal relations negotiated by individual agents in response to social changes that occur in the larger setting. Here, individual agency is as significant as external factors, such as state policies and social changes. A newer kind of theoretical eye is also critical for a better understanding of the current patterns of kinship practice in China. The fluid and flexible nature of kinship as well as the negotiated, processual features of kinship practice, which are recently discussed at length by anthropologists working on non-Western societies (see, for example, Astuti 1995; Carsten 1995), have been by and large ignored in existing studies of Chinese kinship. As Charles Stafford (2000) correctly points out, a formalist approach, which emphasizes the centrality of patriliny, has obscured in anthropological accounts the lived experience of Chinese kinship.

It is, therefore, necessary and important to study kinship in the context of practice, or to borrow one of Pierre Bourdieu's terms, to reexamine kin relations as practical kinship. It should be noted that in this essay, the phrase "practical kinship" is used differently from Bourdieu's original definition (1977, 33–38; 1990, 166–87). Bourdieu's dichotomy of official and practical kinship is rather problematic because it merely continues the long-existing division between public kinship organization and the domestic family established by E. E. Evans-Pritchard and Meyer Fortes.[2] Still, Bourdieu's emphasis on practice and individual agency is noteworthy, and practical kinship also seems to be an appropriate appellation. Hereafter I will borrow the term, but I will use it in my own way—namely, to refer to the fluid and flexible nature of kinship in practice, not in opposition to official kinship.

In the following, I introduce the kinship organization of the village where I conducted fieldwork and locate practical kinship in terms of the local category of guanxi networks. I argue that both community and kinship relations tend to be incorporated into person-centered guanxi networks. I then examine some features of current kinship practices, including the elasticity of kinship distance, the uncertainty of kinship alliance, the active role played by women, and the shift in emphasis from cross-generation links to same-generation connections. I conclude the essay by discussing three major factors that contribute to an understanding of the kinship system in rural China— that is, social change, scholarly models, and the changing practice of kinship itself.

KINSHIP ORGANIZATION AND GUANXI NETWORKS IN XIAJIA VILLAGE

The present study is based on data collected during a series of field studies in Xiajia village, Heilongjiang Province, in 1991, 1993, 1994, and 1997. According to the household register of 1991, Xiajia had a population of 1,564 in 365 households, and it remains today a farming community, growing mainly maize and soybeans. As a result of constant immigration throughout its history, the village currently consists of more than thirty agnatic groups. The largest one is the Xia, which has 104 households, a fact well reflected in the name of the village, which literally translates as "Xia's home." Besides the Xia, there are seven sizable agnatic groups, such as the Xu and the Wang, each with more than 15 households.

Prior to the 1949 Communist revolution, the significance of patriliny and agnatic solidarity was ritually demonstrated and reinforced during the *Qingming* festival (grave sweeping). The Xia lineage collectively owned land and trees near the ancestral tombs. During the Qingming festival, Xia males gathered to visit their ancestors' tombs, located six kilometers away from the village. After the visit, a banquet was provided at the home of the lineage head. Similar gatherings were held on the eve of Chinese New Year when the year-end, grand-ancestor worship ritual was performed at the homes of the senior males of each sublineage. Other major agnatic groups in Xiajia village had similar practices, but their scale was smaller compared to that of the Xia. These agnatic groups were also the major organizational form of social and economic activities for most ordinary villagers. The overall power of lineage organization in Xiajia village, however, was never as strong as that along the southeast coast (see Freedman 1966; J. Watson 1975; R. Watson 1985).

The Communists took the southern region of Heilongjiang Province during 1946–1947, so Xiajia villagers witnessed the dramatic social changes three years prior to the founding of the People's Republic of China. In Xiajia and the surrounding area, land reform was launched in late 1946 and collectivization, another radical social engineering project sponsored by the state, began during the mid-1950s. When the collectives in Xiajia were dismantled as part of the economic reform program at the end of 1983, once again the order of social life in the village was altered to a great extent (see Yan 1992). The average per capita net income in Xiajia village was 616 yuan in 1990, which when compared to a national average of 623 yuan, places it at the midpoint economically among Chinese farming communities.

During the postrevolution era, especially after the high tide of radical collectivization—aimed at destroying traditional patterns of social organization—the power of the patrilineage in Xiajia was considerably diminished. The ancestral land and trees were redistributed among villagers during the land reform, and a public cemetery was established outside the southeastern gate of Xiajia. The Xia and other groups whose ancestral tombs were far away from Xiajia began to bury their dead in the public graveyard. The Qingming visits to the ancestral tombs and associated banquets no longer took place. Domestic ancestor worship during the spring festival continued until the Cultural Revolution (1966), and it was resumed in the early 1980s. Nevertheless, it was performed within the lineage subbranch (*fang*) at the home of a senior agnate, and there were no organized, lineage-wide activities in public settings. A major reason for the decline of ancestor worship was the state-sponsored attack on lineage organization along with the ideological campaign against feudal values and superstition. Some core notions of lineage ideology, such as filial piety, male preference, and generational superiority, were also attacked during repeated political campaigns. Despite all these efforts and the state's hostility toward large-scale kinship organizations, the importance of kinship per se has not declined. Instead, the practice of kinship has been moved onto a new stage in which kinship ties have been absorbed into the more general and open-ended structure of guanxi networks.

The Chinese notion guanxi, which may be translated roughly as social networks, contains multilayered meanings and has been a central concern among China scholars in recent decades. Existing scholarly accounts tend to regard guanxi as an element in a uniquely Chinese normative social order (see, for example, King 1991; Kipnis 1997; Hwang 1987) or treat it as a practical means for advancing specific personal interests (Walder 1986; Yang 1994). My study in Xiajia shows, however, that villagers perceive their guanxi networks as the very foundation of society — the local moral world in which villagers live their lives. As such, guanxi constitutes a total social phenomenon in the Maussian sense because it provides one with a social space that at once incorporates economic, political, social, and recreational activities (see also Kipnis 1997). In a given guanxi network, the immediate family and closest agnates and affines make up a "core zone" of social connections; good friends and less close relatives who can always be counted on for help form a larger "reliable zone"; and finally, an "effective zone" embraces a large number of distant relatives and friends in a broader sense (see Yan 1996, 98–102).

A careful analysis of patterns of gift exchange, the most central means of building up and maintaining guanxi in everyday life, shows that the overall structure of the guanxi networks in Xiajia is characterized by a heavy reliance on friendship ties, as opposed to (official) kinship relations, the involvement of a large number of fellow villagers, and the active role of affines.[3] For instance, kinship ties make up 37 percent of the donors in villagers' gifting networks; by contrast, nonkin relationships, which include fellow villagers, friends, and colleagues, occupy a total of 62 percent of the donors. Within the system of kinship ties, affines occupy 21 percent, outnumbering the agnates (9 percent) more than twofold. More important, Xiajia villagers have gone beyond the boundary of the kinship system to build networks through all kinds of personal relations based on friendship: friends, colleagues, and fellow villagers (locally called *tunqin,* which literally means relatives by coresidence). In other words, most relationships in guanxi networks, such as affines, friends, and colleagues, are not inherited from their parents or ancestors but are made or cultivated by villagers themselves, who want to do something with these connections for their practical concerns (Yan 1996, 105–21). It is this stress on extended relatedness, as opposed to inherited or blood-based relatedness, that draws my attention because the former has to be made and maintained, and therefore, heavily depends on individual choice and agency. The increasing significance of extended relatedness, or nonkinship relations, in guanxi networks has in turn affected both the practice of kinship and villagers' perception as well as our view toward it.

THE FLOW OF PRACTICAL KINSHIP

Looking at kinship practice from the perspective of guanxi networks, it becomes clear that kinship relations are fluid and transformative. It is true that close kin tend to form the core of an individual's network; but in many cases, close kin can also be transformed into a more marginal status in guanxi and, as a replacement, best friends can be brought into the core zone of guanxi. Below are some recent findings from Xiajia village.

The Elasticity of Kinship Distance
It should be noted that the patrilineal ideology remains influential in some crucial areas of contemporary village life, such as in the reckoning of descent and inheritance of family properties. Thus, agnatic ties are still considered more essential and closer in distance than any other kin relations. In practice, however, villagers must frequently evaluate and reevaluate kinship distance in accordance with their ongoing interactions with relatives, and when they do this, agnatic ties may not necessarily be at the top of their list. For instance, I repeatedly asked my informants a simple question: "Who is closer to you — your brother or your wife's brother?" Many informants regarded this as a difficult question, and most responded that they were closer to their brothers yet had a better relationship with their wives' brothers, which was reflected in more frequent mutual help and the exchange of more generous gifts. Here, the

difference between a closer and better relationship exemplifies the differences between kinship ideology and practice.

Such a difference became more obvious when the practice of socialism basically destroyed the organizational infrastructure of the patrilineage as well as its ideology, thereby offering more room and flexibility for villagers to choose with whom they would ally themselves. Under this new circumstance, affines, as opposed to agnates, tend to be more desirable. As reflected by the gift lists, there are twice the number of affines involved in gift exchange as there are agnates (except among the Xia families); in addition, affines present the more valuable gifts. Even for families of the Xia lineage, the dominant patrilineal group in the village, affines still constitute the main body of donors within the kinship relations (for more details, see Yan 1996, 112–14).

It should also be noted that while emphasizing the importance of affines, Xiajia villagers seem to have a narrower definition of patrilineal kinsmen. When asked to identify the donors on their gift lists, they were reluctant to include all lineage men in their inner cycle of guanxi networks, which was quite different from their positive attitudes toward affines. According to Mr. Xia, a knowledgeable informant who has been the host of ancestor worship rituals in his sublineage for many years, his significant agnates include only those who are the descendants of his great-great-great-grandfather (which is a local understanding of the five mourning grade system in official Chinese kinship). Those beyond the boundaries of this five-generation circle are similar to fellow villagers (tunqin), even though they share the same surname, Xia. When I pointed out that they were the descendants of his remote ancestors, he laughed and said: "Close neighbors are better than remote relatives" (*yuanqin bu ru jinlin*).

The Uncertainty of Kinship Alliances

As kinship distance is increasingly redefined in accordance with individual discretion, the making of kinship alliances has become a less predictable business in contemporary village society. The old rule that one should always stand with one's own brothers against outsiders as well as against less-close relatives sometimes no longer holds. Under certain circumstances, friendship has proven to be more reliable and valuable than close kinship.

A good example of this connection is the case of a political battle that was reaching its peak when I revisited Xiajia village in the summer of 1997. Basically, a group of villagers led by the former village party secretary were trying to remove the current party secretary from office, and they had made various efforts toward this end (including direct confrontation, sending reports to upper-level party organizations, and filing suit against the current party secretary for embezzlement and adultery). This political battle had split a number of villagers who otherwise were closely related by either agnatic or affinal ties, such as the five siblings of the Xu family. Among them, the eldest brother was one of the firmest opponents to challenge the current party secretary, the third brother remained neutral, the second and fourth brothers were the closest allies of the current party secretary, and their younger sister allegedly was having an extramarital affair with the current party secretary.

During my interviews with the Xu brothers, they defended their various positions in accordance with their different perceptions of their relations with the two party secretaries. The eldest brother decided to side with the former party secretary for two reasons: they were cross-cousins; and the extramarital affair between the current party secretary and his younger sister had damaged the reputation of the Xu family. The second brother had been the best friend of the current party secretary for a long time and had been promoted to village head by the latter prior to the outbreak of the political battle. So he decided to help his best friend against the former party secretary—his own cross-cousin. The youngest brother simply followed in his second elder brother's footsteps because, as he put it, they had been on good terms ever since he was a child. By the time I left Xiajia village, however, it was said that the youngest brother had been won over by the eldest brother and had joined the ranks against the current party secretary.

In another case, which occurred during 1996 and 1997, a man had to shift his loyalty toward close kin several times. Through family connections, this man had obtained a well-paid and lucrative position to supervise the local milk collection station for a dairy factory jointly owned by the Nestle company and a Chinese partner. When more hands were needed, not surprisingly, this man hired his elder brother and his brother's son. He soon discovered that they were taking the favor for granted and did not work hard. Later, when he was under tremendous pressure from some local bullies and did not get the expected help from his brother and nephew, he fired both of them and hired his wife's brother, who was a young and militant discharged soldier. Within a few months, he found himself in trouble again—his wife's brother was more ambitious than he had thought and actually started to take over the station. So he had to get rid of him, too. When the latter refused to leave, he asked his best friend, a nonrelative, to help. When I left Xiajia village in the late summer of 1997, the struggle between this man and his wife's brother was still at its peak, and both had invited their respective friends to join the fight. The involvement of outsiders (friends) was considered by some older villagers as scandalous. They commented that it was all due to the influence of money; without so much money at stake, the relatives would have remained on good terms.

Although not always as dramatic as the above two cases, there are many other examples of alliance making that do not follow the recognized rules of kinship: that is, villagers do not always ally with their closest relatives within the pool of their networks. For instance, a number of villagers chose not to let their own close kinsmen (father, brothers, or uncles) farm their land when they departed to the cities for industrial work. Instead, they offered the land to their friends or less-close relatives with whom they had maintained better relationships. (Farmland still belongs to the state, yet in practice, individual villagers have exclusive users' rights, which are granted by the state for thirty-five years. Such land transactions are thus possible.)

The Flattenization of Kinship
Another feature of current kinship practice is the slow process of the flattenization of kin relations. By "flattenization," I mean a shift in emphasis from cross-generation links to same-generation connections—a process that parallels the increasing importance of affines and friends in villagers' networks as well as the shifting balance of power from the senior generation to the junior one within individual families.

It is widely agreed among scholars that the fundamental kin relationship in Chinese society is that of patrilineal descent. Individuals from different generations are bound closely by the everlasting link of patriliny, which expresses itself in terms of both consanguinity and reciprocity. As Hugh Baker notes, in traditional Chinese society, the living individual is "the personification of all his [*sic*] forebears and of all his descendants yet unborn. He exists by virtue of his ancestors, and his descendants exist only through him" (1979, 26–27). Thus, "all the living are in the shadow of their ancestors" (Hsu [1948] 1967, 243). Consequently, the link between the living and dead has received the most scholarly attention, and cross-generation kin relations, such as parent-child ties, have always been regarded as more significant than same-generation relations, such as that between siblings.

In contemporary Xiajia village, though, it is the connections among individuals of the same generation that constitute the core of the guanxi network within which kinship is practiced. Elsewhere I examine the shift of power from the senior to the junior generation, and along with it, the replacement of the vertical, parent-son relationship by the horizontal, conjugal tie as the central axis of family relations and the foundation of the family ideal shared by most villagers (see Yan 1997). As more and more young couples leave their husbands' parents to establish their own conjugal family soon after their marriage, they have to start building their own social networks from scratch. In this aspect of family life, many young women prove to be more successful than their husbands because they have a ready resource to turn to — their natal families. As a result, noninherited, same-generation connections — such as affines, friends, and colleagues — constitute a major part of individual villagers' guanxi networks, particularly those of young villagers. A common feature shared by affines, friends, colleagues, and fellow villagers in these guanxi networks is that they are all lateral (or horizontal) connections between families rather than vertical filiation within families, such as agnatic ties. These relations represent alliances that are created by individual villagers and maintained through mutual indebtedness in social exchange.

Moreover, because these same-generation connections are maintained by and revolve around a couple in a given family (as opposed to a group of ancestors), the notion of kinship authority also has been redefined. Generational rank and age seniority, the very basis of authority in the Chinese kinship system, have become less important in comparison to individual capabilities for getting things done. It is common that in everyday cooperation among relatives and friends, the leaders are younger and better educated, while the senior people have to play a secondary role. And these young villagers are much more interested in indulging their own children than in worshiping their ancestors. The previous kinship authority structure based on generational seniority and age rank has weakened, as vividly demonstrated by the waning of ancestors.

Women and the Changing Kinship Practice
As indicated by the flattenization of kinship connections, women take an active part in maintaining family networks in everyday life, which is itself a new development of the Chinese kinship system. As I demonstrate elsewhere, women not only participate in gift exchange activities as household representatives but have also created several new rituals revolving around human reproduction — childbirth, abortion, and female sterilization (see Yan 1996, 53–55). Through these rituals, which are by and for women, village women can build up their own social connections and thus successfully go beyond the traditional boundaries of the male-centered kinship web.

In terms of kinship distance, understandably, women's criterion of closeness does not always fit that of their husbands', nor that of the patrilineal kinship ideology. Because of the crucial role played by wives, one's relationship with one's wife's sister's husband is considered quite significant in local practice. The closeness of this kind of relationship is reflected in its local term, *lianqiao,* which literally means men who are linked by a bridge — namely, the bridge of the sororal relationship between their wives. Unlike the relationship between brothers, men linked by their wives' sororal relationship have no inherited conflicts of interest, and mutual assistance and cooperation can be easily supported and facilitated by their wives (see Judd 1989). The analysis of the gift lists shows that the most generous gifts can be expected from one's wife's sisters' husbands, and in daily life, they are also among the first to offer help. For instance, the most lucrative crop in the area is watermelon, but it requires larger capital investments and depends on unpredictable market demands. Therefore, villagers prefer to plant watermelon together, working with one or two partners, in order to share the risks. In 1991, seven out of the nine watermelon farmers in the village cooperated with their wives' sisters' husbands in various forms, while no one worked with their own brothers. When asked why, they told me that it was easier to work with one's wife's sisters' husbands because they were more reasonable and trustworthy.

In addition, it is at least inaccurate to portray women's kinship activities only within the domestic or private domain. Ethnographic evidence from Xiajia village reveals that women are critical in many aspects of the public domain. In the above-mentioned case of political struggle between the former and current party secretary, a key figure is the younger sister of the Xu family. As explained earlier, by kinship ties she is close to the former party secretary, but she also is emotionally involved with the current party secretary. Because of her intimate relationship with the latter, she was assigned several important jobs at various times, such as supervising the village election in 1996 and managing a small village enterprise. Because of the Xu sister's deep involvement in the activities of the village office, her eldest brother and his friends tried hard to win her over from the opposite camp. Nevertheless, she chose to stand firmly with her lover — the current party secretary — despite public opinion and tremendous pressure from her kin. In this highly publicized case of village politics, the kinship alliance was defeated by the individual bonds between the two lovers.

It is true that village women usually do not fill as dramatic a role as the Xu sister did; instead, they transform kinship practice in a more subtle yet equally effective way, as shown in the case of the ghost festival ceremony. Local custom traditionally forbade women to participate in the visit to the ancestor tombs of their natal families during the ghost festival (on the fifteenth day of the seventh month in the lunar calendar). This taboo, however, was broken by a woman single-handedly. In 1995, a young daughter-in-law thought it was unreasonable that she should be prevented from visiting her deceased grand-father, whom she loved very much. So she went to the graveyard of her natal family and burned paper money in front of her grandfather's tomb, just like a man would do. She seemed to be a perfect candidate to break the traditional taboo since she was well-known for being an independent, capable, and some-times ill-tempered young woman in the village; as well, she was considered to be responsible for encouraging her husband to leave his parents and set up his own conjugal family shortly after his wedding. No one dared to stop or blame her. And the following year, more women took her lead. When I visited Xiajia village in 1998, I saw as many women as men burning paper money in the graveyard during the ghost festival. It was also interesting to find that married women prefer to visit the ancestor tombs of their natal families before they attend to their husband's families' ancestral tombs. When I learned that the daughter-in-law of my landlord had visited her late father's tomb first, I was told by my landlord that this was nothing new. "This is why nowadays girls are better than boys [to their parents]," commented my landlord.

THE EMOTIONAL DIMENSION OF KINSHIP PRACTICE

In my earlier study of gift-giving networks (see Yan 1996, 139–45; see also Stafford 2000), I examined how Xiajia villagers were emotionally attached to some close relatives and good friends for a very long time. They described these attachments in terms of the expression of *ganqinghao,* which means having good feelings toward one another. They maintain that interactions in daily life (*wanglai* in local terms) do not necessarily imply the existence of good feelings between two parties because in many cases, people are obligated to interact with kin they do not like. This is particularly true in cases of gift exchange at such ritual situations as weddings or funerals. For those who do have good feelings toward one another, though, their interactions are greatly intensified. In addition to routinized gift exchange, people with good feelings visit one another quite often, spend spare time together, and emotionally de-pend on one another, too. In local terms, this type of intimate interaction is called *zoudong,* literally meaning "walking and moving," a metaphor for mutual visits.

The local distinction between wanglai and zoudong reveals an interesting relationship between kinship norms and practices. On the one hand, the morality and principle of kinship require the maintenance of certain kinds of formal relations along with the completion of the institutionalized and prescribed task of interacting with one's kin (wanglai). On the other hand, one can also find room to develop emotional ties with select people in terms of more intimate, informal, and nonritualized interactions in daily life (zoudong), which is often the case with practical kinship.

In 1991, one informant told me that he had not visited his father's youngest sister for more than ten years, even though she was married to a Xiajia man and lived in the same village. The reason, according to him, was due to a personality conflict: he could not stand his father's sister's bad temper, and she had not treated him well when he was a small boy. "We did not have good feelings toward each other from the very beginning," the informant concluded. Nevertheless, he had to fulfill his obligation of ritualized gift giving and the prescribed visits during the Chinese Spring Festival, which could not be affected by individuals' emotional concerns. As a compromise, he sent his wife to represent him on these occasions and increased the value of his gifts in an effort to show his respect (this is a common strategy frequently used by many villagers). In this case, the emotional quality of kinship practice works in a negative way—whenever the informant can make his own choice, he avoids interacting with his father's sister, who has been excluded from the core zone of this man's guanxi network.

As a result of the recent changes in kinship and the larger social settings, the emotional dimension of kinship practice has now become more important because with less-constraining forces of official ideology and institutional principles, the personalities and emotional ups and downs of individual agents are more easily reflected in their interactions with one another. A simple example is the case of the above-mentioned political struggle in Xiajia village where the youngest Xu brother decided to support his second-oldest brother merely based on his good feelings toward the latter, and the Xu sister firmly sided with her illicit lover regardless of her own brothers' attempts to win her over to the other camp.

One of the reasons that I have found Bourdieu's notion of practical kinship unsatisfactory is that he completely ignores the role of emotionality in kinship practice. In his discussions of the "usefulness" or "utility" of practical kinship, he rarely explores the possibility that people may also need to build up (which in fact they do) kinship networks for moral/emotional support, in addition to a number of more practical purposes. This is best illustrated by Bourdieu's analysis of the working of practical kinship in marriage negotiations (1977, 34–35; 1990, 168–86), in which his notion of practical kinship turns out to be nothing more than pragmatic kinship. The Xiajia case shows that once individuals can make their own choices, personal and emotional elements indeed play a central part in kinship practices. Without taking into consideration the emotionality of individual agents, one runs the risk of reducing people in the real world to abstract rational actors who are driven merely by the desire to maximize utility of whatever resources they hold.

SCHOLARLY MODELS, SOCIAL CHANGE, AND KINSHIP PRACTICE

How should the current patterns of kinship practice in rural north China be understood? Are they recent developments resulting from the Communist revolution or merely new to scholarly eyes that have now been liberated from the constraints of the previously dominant structural-functional model of kinship study? The answer is not a simple yes or no; both the kinship practice of Chinese villagers and our scholarly practice of kinship study are changing within the context of the ever changing society at large. It follows that all three elements have to be considered: the scholarly models, social change, and the dynamics of kinship practice itself.

Some of the above-mentioned kinship practices may have existed for a long time, but they were neglected by scholarly scrutiny because students of Chinese kinship did not look for them. In my opinion, most studies of Chinese kinship fall into one of two lines of inquiry. The first might be loosely called the Confucian model, whereby scholars stress the pervasive influence of Confucian ideas and values—such as filial piety, chastity, and ancestor worship—on Chinese kinship. A well-known example is Francis Hsu's *Under the Ancestors' Shadow* ([1948] 1967; for a recent and sophisticated analysis of the role of Confucian values in Chinese kinship, see Chun 1996).

The second approach was established by Maurice Freedman, who creatively applied the African model of lineage organizations in social anthropology to China and developed a "lineage paradigm" of Chinese society (1958, 1966). This paradigm "assumes a fundamental model of Chinese society in which the ideology of patrilineal descent takes precedence over all other principles of social organization" (J. Watson 1986, 274). Shifting away from the previous emphasis on Confucian values, Freedman and his followers focused on the working mechanisms of lineage property and organization. Since the 1960s, this paradigm has been applied to all major studies of powerful patrilineal organizations in south China (see, for example, Potter 1968; J. Watson 1975; R. Watson 1985).

The limitations of the lineage paradigm were noticed by those who worked in regions outside the patrilineal belt of south China, notably in Taiwan. They challenged the universality of the lineage model in Chinese societies by demonstrating that matrilateral and affinal relationships are as essential as agnatic ties, and that kinship is not the only working system that binds people together in Taiwan (see, for instance, Diamond 1969; Gallin and Gallin 1985; Harrell 1982; Pasternak 1972; Sangren 1984).

Recognition that other kin relations are equally as significant as agnatic ties, however, does not take one far beyond the lineage paradigm. The key issue here is that both the Confucian model and lineage paradigm tend to focus on the fixed norms, rules, and moral expectations of kin groups defined by demonstrated genealogy; thereby, they stress the centrality of a kinship collectivity represented by powerful ancestors and tend to study only those social facts that reflect durable structural principles. Missing is the role played by individual agents in their everyday cooperation, negotiation, and competition with one another over issues such as emotional attachment, moral obligation, power and influence, and economic resources—the specific processes that are not necessarily reflected in the genealogical composition of a kin group (see Yanagisako 1979, 184–89). In other words, an emphasis on how kinship functions to sustain the social structure may have precluded scholarly inquiries into how villagers in everyday life make their kinship system work for them.

As indicated above, when asked, Xiajia villagers would say one's own brothers are closer than one's wife's brothers. This fits well with the patrilineal ideology, which has been underscored in most studies of Chinese kinship. Still, in practice many villagers do the opposite—in some cases they prefer to cooperate with their brothers-in-law (one's wife's brother or one's wife's sister's husband) in economic activities and to maintain closer ties with them in social activities; in other instances they shift back and forth between different categories of kin. Moreover, women may have had a different standard of kinship distance long before the Communist revolution, as manifested in the long-existing doubts of a daughter-in-law's loyalty toward her husband's family. This can be, nevertheless, easily dismissed by the structural-functional model as insignificant because it belongs to individual acts taking place within the domestic sphere and thus has no effect on social structure.

The obstacle of previous scholarly models, however, should not be over-stated because kinship practice itself also changes over time in response to the changes in society at large. It is therefore also possible that some previously insignificant or probably latent social actions have now become more impor-tant and salient, such as, again, the active role played by women and youth in village life. As far as the Xiajia case is concerned, two major social changes are particularly noteworthy: the practice of socialism after 1949 and the impact of the market-oriented reforms in the recent two decades.

As explained in the first section, the socialist state was especially hostile to traditional lineage organization and kinship ideology. Through adminis-trative means and political campaigns, the state was generally successful in eliminating organized lineage activities for nearly three decades, greatly shak-ing the foundation of traditional kinship ideology. The state also made efforts to transform the organization of social life in rural China—such as reforming life-cycle rituals. Villagers had strategized their acts accordingly in order to cope with a powerful and revolutionary political authority, as shown in the anecdote at the beginning of this chapter. Furthermore, through collectiviza-tion and other political campaigns, the state successfully mobilized women and youth to become a major force in the socialist transformation of rural society. As a result, a clear shift in the balance of power from the senior to the junior generation has been identified throughout rural China (see White 1995; Yan 1997), a distinguishable youth subculture has emerged (see Yan 1999), and women, particularly young women, have become a major social force chal-lenging patriarchal traditions in the sphere of private life (see Yan 1998). The rise of these previously marginalized players in the Chinese kinship system certainly has had a profound influence on the current practice of kinship. A good example in this connection is the political struggle between the current party secretary, who was supported by a group of youth, and his predecessor, who was supported mostly by middle-aged males. According to older vil-lagers, fifty years ago the active and public involvement of the young woman (the Xu sister) in this political conflict would have been impossible from the very beginning.

Second, the introduction of both commodity production and a market-oriented economy during the past two decades has created new life aspira-tions for villagers, especially for rural youth, to pursue their individual needs, sometimes at the expense of the interests of larger kin groups. This is evidenced by the dramatic rise in the centrality of the conjugal relationship and the decline of parental power in family life that I have documented elsewhere (see Yan 1997). The ongoing process of commercialization has created more latitude and instrumentality for individual maneuvering in dealing with interpersonal relations as well. A directly related development is the increasing importance of friendship in an individual's social network (that is, guanxi network). Commodity production and market-related activities require connections beyond conventional kinship ties and village boundaries; the number of one's outside connections and friendship ties thus has become an obvious sign of social capital in village society (see Yan 1996). In many cases, these newer ties can be absorbed into the core zone of existing guanxi networks without causing any conflicts, but in other instances, they may also prove to be hostile to kinship ties, such as in the above-mentioned fight between the brothers and relatives over control of a milk station in Xiajia village. In these new forms of kinship alliances, individual economic power has replaced generational seniority and age rank as the new basis for social hierarchy. And due to the unpredictable changes in business interests and expansion of individual guanxi networks, some of the old kinship obligations and behavioral norms have been undermined, too. All of these may partially contribute to the new developments noted above.

It is incorrect and unnecessary, therefore, to single out either the shift in the scholarly model or consequences of social change as the major factor contributing to the current changes in descriptions of kinship practice in rural north China. Some developments are due to social changes (as discussed above) and others to the rediscovery of some old social practices as a result of our shift to a new theoretical emphasis. It is more likely that, in practice, there are consistent interactions of all these factors, thus leading to the ever changing practice of kinship study itself.

The real challenge now is to determine how to go beyond the old scholarly models and develop new ones that can conceptualize or theorize current patterns of kinship practice. As indicated at the start of this essay, fluidity and flexibility are definitely the most important features of current kinship practice, which seems to revolve more around strategic individuals than a representational collectivity. In other words, kinship ties are better viewed as a set of differentially valued relations, which may mean different things relative to one another in different contexts.[4] The relativity of kinship relations may be a key to understanding the nature of an ever changing kinship system. In this connection, two Chinese notions—*chaxu geju* and guanxi—are particularly noteworthy.

The term "chaxu geju" was first coined by the famous Chinese sociologist Xiaotong Fei more than half a century ago. To describe the different structural principles in Chinese society, he wrote: "In Chinese society, the most important relationship—kinship—is similar to the concentric circles formed when a stone is thrown into a lake" ([1947] 1992, 63). In such a network of concentric circles, "everyone stands at the center of the circles produced by his or her own social influence. Everyone's circles are interrelated. One touches different circles at different times and places" (62–63). Fei refers to such a mode of social origination as chaxu geju, translated as the "differential mode of association." Through this concept, Fei argues that Chinese society is not group oriented but egocentric—a view quite different from that of mainstream China studies. The most intriguing point of the notion chaxu geju is that the relational links—namely, the concentric circles—are valued differently by the person in the center, and accordingly, the norms of social interactions and moral judgments also vary when they are applied to discrete categories of people in these circles. Unfortunately, Fei's 1947 book remained unnoticed in the West until the late 1980s, and during this period, the study of Chinese kinship was dominated first by the Confucian model and then the lineage paradigm. The relativity of kinship relations, as well as other relations in Chinese society, has thus also been overlooked until recently.

Unlike Fei's chaxu geju (differential mode of association), guanxi was first a term used by ordinary people in their everyday lives; in recent years, guanxi also has become a key category in scholarly analyses of Chinese society and culture. My study of the Xiajia case shows that at least during the past two decades or so, there has been a tendency for both kinship and community relations to be absorbed into person-centered guanxi networks. In everyday social practices, guanxi networks provide the moral world as well as channels of opportunity for individual agents. And to a great extent, it is the individual agents who determine which strings—kinship and nonkinship alike—in a given network are pulled in dealing with various issues in social and personal lives. More important, a fundamental feature of guanxi is that it exists only in the process of practice, and as such, can counterbalance the previous emphasis on the normative/structural aspects of the kinship system in Chinese society.

NOTES

The present study is based on fieldwork supported by the Research Council of the Academic Senate, University of California, Los Angeles, and the Chiang Ching-Kuo Foundation for International Scholarly Exchange. I am grateful to Carol Delaney, Gillian Feeley-Harnik, Kath Weston, and other participants at the Mallorca conference for their comments on the early draft. Special thanks are due to Susan McKinnon and Sarah Franklin for their insightful and detailed suggestions for the revisions of this essay.

1   I should add that the funeral improved my father's status in public life for only two days; afterward, he was back in the outcast position and later humiliated at a public meeting by several young villagers who regretted what they had had to do during the funeral.

2   To surmount the shortcomings of both objectivist and subjectivist tendencies in kinship studies, Bourdieu proposes a distinction between official and practical kinship: the former refers to the abstraction of norms, rules, and regulations of kin groups, while the latter refers to the transformation of such an abstraction into strategies of practice by active agents in everyday life. Although the function of official kinship is to order the social world and legitimate that order, it is practical kinship that is used by individual agents to achieve social goals in everyday life (Bourdieu 1977, 33–38; 1990, 166–87). Despite the fact that Bourdieu always stresses the centrality of individual agency in practice, such an arbitrary division between official and practical kinship actually precludes the importance of individual agency in political, public life. Moreover, since practical kinship—as defined by Bourdieu—is confined to the domestic sphere, which does not have much political significance, it also tends to ignore women's active role in gender politics in particular and kinship practice in general (see Yanagisako and Collier 1987).

3   My inquiry into guanxi networks began with a collection of villagers' gift lists. In Xiajia village, as in most rural communities in China and some other East Asian societies as well, villagers always write a gift list for each major family ceremony they host—a document that records the names of the gift givers as well as a description of all gifts received. Families carefully keep these gift lists and use them for future reference when reciprocal gifts need to be offered. From a researcher's point of view, a gift list may serve as a repository of data on the changing nature of interpersonal relations and a social map that vividly displays guanxi networks. In my 1991 fieldwork, I collected 43 gift lists based on a stratified selection of households and put them into a computer database, containing a total of 5,286 individual gift transactions. For more details about gift lists, see Yan 1996, 49–52.

4   Here I am particularly in debt to Susan McKinnon for probing me to think along these lines.

REFERENCES

Astuti, Rita. 1995. *People of the Sea: Identity and Descent among the Vezo of Madagascar.* Cambridge: Cambridge University Press.

Baker, Hugh. 1979. *Chinese Family and Kinship.* New York: Columbia University Press.

Bourdieu, Pierre. 1977. *Outline of a Theory of Practice.* Translated by Richard Nice. Cambridge: Cambridge University Press.

———. 1990. *The Logic of Practice.* Translated by Richard Nice. Stanford, Calif.: Stanford University Press.

Carsten, Janet. 1995. The Substance of Kinship and the Heat of the Hearth: Feeding, Personhood, and Relatedness among Malays in Pulau Langkawi. *American Ethnologist* 22, no. 2:223–41.

Chun, Allen. 1996. The Lineage-Village Complex in Southeastern China: A Long Footnote in the Anthropology of Kinship. *Current Anthropology* 37, no. 3:429–40.

Diamond, Norma. 1969. *K'un Shen: A Taiwanese Village.* New York: Holt, Rinehart and Winston.

Fei, Xiaotong. [1947] 1992. *From the Soil: The Foundations of Chinese Society.* Translated by Gary Hamilton and Wang Zheng. Reprint, Berkeley: University of California Press.

Freedman, Maurice. 1958. *Lineage Organization in Southeastern China.* London: Athlone.

———. 1966. *Chinese Lineage and Society: Fukien and Kwangtung.* London: Athlone.

Gallin, Bernard, and Rita Gallin. 1985. Matrilateral and Affinal Relationships in Changing Chinese Society. In *The Chinese Family and Its Ritual Behavior,* edited by Hsieh Jih-chang and Chuang Ying-chang. Taiwan: Institute of Ethnology, Academia Sinica.

Harrell, Steven. 1982. *Ploughshare Village: Culture and Context in Taiwan.* Seattle: University of Washington Press.

Hsu, Francis L. K. [1948] 1967. *Under the Ancestors' Shadow: Chinese Culture and Personality.* Reprint, New York: Doubleday and Company.

Hwang, Kwang-kuo. 1987. Face and Favor: The Chinese Power Game. *American Journal of Sociology* 92, no. 4:944–74.

Judd, Ellen. 1989. Niangjia: Chinese Women and Their Natal Families. *Journal of Asian Studies* 48, no. 3:525–44.

King, Ambrose. 1991. Kuan-hsi and Network Building: A Sociological Interpretation. *Daedalus* 120, no. 2:63–84.

Kipnis, Andrew. 1997. *Producing Guanxi: Sentiment, Self, and Subculture in a North China Village.* Durham, N.C.: Duke University Press.

Pasternak, Burton. 1972. *Kinship and Community in Two Chinese Villages.* Stanford, Calif.: Stanford University Press.

Potter, Jack M. 1968. *Capitalism and the Chinese Peasant.* Berkeley: University of California Press.

Sangren, Steven. 1984. Traditional Chinese Corporations: Beyond Kinship. *Journal of Asian Studies* 43, no. 3:391–415.

Stafford, Charles. 2000. Chinese Patriliny and the Cycles of *Yang* and *Laiwang.* In *Cul-*

tures of Relatedness: New Approaches to the Study of Kinship, edited by Janet Carsten. Cambridge: Cambridge University Press.

Walder, Andrew. 1986. *Communist Neo-Traditionalism: Work and Authority in Chinese Industry.* Berkeley: University of California Press.

Watson, James L. 1975. *Emigration and the Chinese Lineage: The Mans in Hong Kong and London.* Berkeley: University of California Press.

———. 1986. Anthropological Overview: The Development of Chinese Descent Groups. In *Kinship Organization in Late Imperial China, 1000–1940,* edited by Patricia B. Ebrey and James L. Watson. Berkeley: University of California Press.

Watson, Rubie S. 1985. *Inequality among Brothers: Class and Kinship in South China.* Cambridge: Cambridge University Press.

White, Martin. 1995. The Social Roots of China's Economic Development. *China Quarterly* 144:999–1019.

Yan, Yunxiang. 1992. The Impact of Rural Reform on Economic and Social Stratification in a Chinese Village. *Australian Journal of Chinese Affairs* 27:1–23.

———. 1996. *The Flow of Gifts: Reciprocity and Social Networks in a Chinese Village.* Stanford, Calif.: Stanford University Press.

———. 1997. The Triumph of Conjugality: Structural Transformation of Family Relations in a Chinese Village. *Ethnology* 36, no. 3:191–212.

———. 1998. Girl Power: Young Women and Family Change in Rural North China. Paper presented at the workshop, Women and Modernity in Twentieth-Century China, 6 March, University of California, Santa Barbara.

———. 1999. Rural Youth and Youth Culture in North China. *Culture, Medicine, and Psychiatry* 23, no. 1:75–97.

Yang, Mayfair Mei-hui. 1994. *Gifts, Favors, Banquets: The Art of Social Relationships in China.* Ithaca, N.Y.: Cornell University Press.

Yanagisako, Sylvia J. 1979. Family and Household: The Analysis of Domestic Groups. *Annual Review of Anthropology* 8:161–205.

Yanagisako, Sylvia J., and Jane F. Collier. 1987. Toward a Unified Analysis of Gender and Kinship. In *Gender and Kinship: Essays toward a Unified Analysis,* edited by Jane F. Collier and Sylvia J. Yanagisako. Stanford, Calif.: Stanford University Press.

CHAPTER 9

The Shift in Kinship Studies in France:
The Case of Grandparenting
Martine Segalen

As elsewhere in the Western world, France has witnessed significant changes in both kinship and the family as well as in kinship studies, which are no longer restricted to exotic or peasant societies but also aim at understanding contemporary ones. These transformations are embedded in consequent economic and cultural changes that have led to important transformations in the legal system.

Grandparenting is an especially good arena to examine some of these issues because: it relates to the specific history of kinship research in France over the past fifty years, during which time social anthropology shifted its focus from non-European to peasant societies along with modern urban ones, where it is presently meeting sociology; it highlights one of the specificities of the French position regarding kinship—an ambivalence between biological and social definitions; and more generally, in the Western context, it is only a matter of status without norms attached to it, and therefore, it helps us consider the practical uses of kinship in everyday rounds, on an emotional and social basis. The research presented here testifies to the centrality of kinship in contemporary society. Nevertheless, if much attention has been devoted to divorce or recomposed families, it is commonplace to say that grandparents have been the invisible kin in the anthropology of modern European families.[1] The acknowledgment of their role is suddenly rendered clearer because of the tremendous changes observed in family relationships over the past thirty years. The fragility of the conjugal couple and the development of recomposed families have been accompanied by crucial demographic changes: four-generation families are now numerous, and a new figure has emerged—that of the "new grandparents."

The aim of this essay is thus twofold: to present a quick survey of the history of French kinship studies, which is set in a relatively different context from that of England or the United States; and to use some of my data on grand-parenting to illuminate a few of the recent changes in paradigms and meth-ods. The scrutinization of contemporary grandparenting brings to the fore the central question of the nature of filiation bonds and their stubborn impor-tance in a society that has cherished for many decades the volatility of love and ephemeral conjugality.[2] To address the nature of this link is to go back to fun-damental questions discussed by anthropologists in the decades between the 1930s and 1960s. But on the French scene, the structural-functionalist theories of kinship have enjoyed a quite specific fate, which is linked to the history of the circulation of ideas between different university traditions, and between countries, notably including the problem of long delays in the translation of works.

A FRENCH HISTORY OF KINSHIP THEORIES

From Durkheim to Lévi-Strauss

One can attribute to Émile Durkheim the birth of both the sociology of the family and anthropology of kinship—domains that the scholar himself did not separate. The first chair of sociology in France was created for him, and the first course he taught in 1888 was titled Introduction à la sociologie de la famille. In this course, he related his analysis of changes in the family to the question of the reconciliation between individualism and social solidarity—topics he addressed in his subsequent writings that dealt with religion and ritual. His position was definitely evolutionist, though not quite along the same lines as those developed by Lewis Henry Morgan (see Feeley-Harnik, this volume; McKinnon, this volume), and his sources were mainly consti-tuted by the anthropological literature to which he compared the contem-porary situation in France. Under the heading *Organisation familiale*, he re-viewed for *l'Année sociologique* historical and anthropological works, mainly articles and books dealing with kinship and family in past times and other cultures.[3] Durkheim's interests in the topic of the sociology of the family con-cerned the significance of family and kinship as core units of social cohesion, and his research was both textually based and comparative. But in his later years, he moved toward the question of the sociology of religion.

His works have enjoyed a different fate in Great Britain. It is common nowadays to state that the British structural-functionalist school found its in-spiration in the work of Durkheim. As Adam Kuper writes, A. R. Radcliffe-

Brown was much influenced by "the scientific method, the conviction that social life was orderly and susceptible to rigorous analysis" (1983, 39). From the complex Durkheimian heritage, Radcliffe-Brown picked the study of social relations. Yet the work of Radcliffe-Brown, E. E. Evans-Pritchard and Meyer Fortes, which considered descent as part of the politico-jural domain, had less impact on the French Africanist school that developed than it did in England, in the wake of the colonization of the 1920s and 1930s. Although Marcel Mauss was also a follower of his master and uncle, he placed more stress on the study of religion, ritual, and indigenous cosmogonies than on kinship, and so did the professional anthropologists trained by Mauss at the Institut d'ethnologie du Musée du Trocadéro.

Bronislaw Malinowski's ethnography inspired Mauss's theory of the gift, which in turn inspired Claude Lévi-Strauss's thinking on kinship and marriage. Although Lévi-Strauss acknowledged the influence of Durkheim in his work, notably titling his book *Les structures élémentaires de la parenté* as a tribute to *Les formes élémentaires de la religion,* he rejected the evolutionist approach and stressed the premises of what was to become a structural analysis. The preeminence of Lévi-Strauss's works as well as the intellectual and institutional position he held explains the specific course of research on kinship in France in the 1970s. While Anglo-Saxon social anthropologists were discovering the limitations of the structural-functionalist theory, French social anthropologists were dedicated to illustrating some aspect or other of Lévi-Strauss's works in their respective fields. The exchange of women so as to implement the universal prohibition of incest along with the distinction between elementary and complex systems became the breviary of French social anthropologists.

In the 1970s, the tremendous impact of Lévi-Strauss's theoretical agenda instigated research on kinship in peasant societies, definitely established the ethnology of France as an endeavor distinct from its previous folkloric positions, and severed links with anthropological museums. To become an acknowledged social anthropologist at home, one had to hold a passport stamped with an "interest in kinship."[4] The idea was to pick up where Lévi-Strauss had stopped. Could any regularities be found in complex marriage systems of European societies, where only a few kin were prohibited in marriage? Was kinship of any consequence in the formation of alliances? A team of social anthropologists in the research group headed by Lévi-Strauss produced a pioneer work on these topics based on research in a Burgundy village (see Jolas et al. [1968–1982] 1990). They showed the primary importance of kin in social relationships and were the first to uncover, beyond the "permanent turbulences," a pattern of regularities in these nonprescriptive systems of alliance—that of "relinking of marriages"—which was to be further studied later in a Breton village with computerized data (see Segalen and Richard 1986). Assessing the impact of *Les structures élémentaires* since its publication—already a half century ago—Françoise Héritier stresses that if "we cannot yet elaborate the general theory to which Lévi-Strauss referred . . . with the help of new tools and new hypothesis, research has considerably progressed" (1999, 83).

In the 1960s, anthropological debates about endogamous and exogamous marriages were also taken up by geneticists who, investigating the genetic causes of hereditary diseases, used the concept of "isolate," which was defined as an area of closed marriage.

The encounter with the historical dimension was doubly inevitable: first, to understand inheritance rules and practices, one needs to observe a long span of generations; second, historical demography and social history were buoyed by the development of *l'Ecole des Annales,* in the 1970s, and its interest in people's mentalities and attitudes intersected with the question of family and kinship at many levels.

When Anthropology Meets History and Historical Demography

While French historical demography at the Institut National d'Etudes démographiques (INED) focused on the nuclear family and fertility trends, the English school led by Peter Laslett, Roger Schofield, and Tony Wrigley of the Cambridge Group for the History of Population and Social Structure oriented the debates around the historical forms of domestic groups. For once, the dialogue was both truly international between the French and their English counterparts and truly interdisciplinary, since social anthropologists brought into the discussion their knowledge about households, underlined their connections with the wider kinship systems, and made use of the concept of family life cycle that Fortes and subsequently Jack Goody had developed.

The publication in 1972 of a paper by the historian Emmanuel Le Roy Ladurie was extremely influential in that it showed the diversity of inheritance systems that had prevailed throughout France before the Napoleonic Code, which led him to oppose the northern conjugal family to the southern linear one.

To discuss the variety of inheritance patterns in peasant societies, social anthropologists and historians used the same set of theoretical questions and collected a similar stock of material: genealogical and marriage data, inventories, and notarial archives. Historians remained in the archives; anthropologists visited the field, talked to peasants, and tried to understand the relevant rules, strategies, and practices, which did not always cohere. It was clear that filiation and kinship were key questions, but they were detached from the structural-functionalist approach for two main reasons. On the one hand, their role in the political cohesion of the social group was not as prominent as it was in societies devoid of central organizations such as the state, church, judicial courts, etc. The idea was rather to show the importance of kinship in articulation with these other social levels—what Lévi-Strauss has called the *feuilletage* of complex societies. On the other hand, the possession of land and goods is individual and very rarely collective in the European peasant context.

Thus, Goody's comparative work (1976) on the modes of reproduction was extremely influential as it described the cultural variety of inheritance patterns throughout peasant societies in France (and also Europe). Southern areas and especially the mountainous southern ones are characterized by a unilineal pattern of inheritance, with only one heir, generally the eldest son, leaving the younger children disinherited or living at home as bachelors and spinsters. The patrimony is transmitted without fragmentation. This impartible type is generally associated with a principle of stem family, a domestic group with three coresiding generations, where authority is passed down along the family line from male ancestor to male descendant. This type bears the generic name of *système à maison,* or according to the local terms, *ostal, oustaou,* or *ousta.* There people belong to one or another ostal, through which a social status is assigned to them. The discovery that this system of unilineal descent, linked to impartible rules of transmission, lasted long after the Napoleonic Code had imposed an egalitarian rule of inheritance, gave a new actuality to the works of Frédéric Le Play, a social scientist of the 1850s whose work had been shunned by generations of scholars because it was markedly inspired by conservatist thought.

Social anthropologists and historians were fascinated by the coherence of the stem family model, which reconciles the necessity of transmitting goods among generations and that of maintaining the stability of production units so as to ensure their viability. At the time when Radcliffe-Brown's positions were rejected in England, French scholars were proud enough to discover a form of corporation in southern family lines. The adoption of concepts of lineages and family lines also helped to bring together into a common discussion anthropologists and historians. Among the latter, medievalists unearthed better examples of patrilineality and descent groups than anthropologists of "exotic" tribes.

Lévi-Strauss, himself, in a paper called "Histoire et ethnologie," bridges both disciplines and various Western and non-Western areas in the definition he gave of the concept of "house" (1983, 1224). The concept of "la maison"—whether discussed in relation to European peasant families or aristocracy—has proved in its turn to be a powerful tool of analysis of Southeast Asian or even Amazonian societies (see MacDonald 1986; Carsten and Hugh-Jones 1995).

In contrast to the southern type of inheritance, another pattern was found in the northern and western areas of France, where peasants generally were not the owners of their lands. The diverging principle is active there, inasmuch as there are only movable goods to transmit. Domestic groups, which are much more often of complex form than nuclear, move from one farmstead to another throughout their life cycle. Hence, there is no strong attachment to the land as is the case in the Pyrenees or southern Alps. Filiation is predominantly bilateral, and the operative family unit is the bilateral kindred, which works on the same principles as those described for the Iban of Borneo: ad hoc groups that are not corporate.

An effort was also made to link residence and inheritance patterns to marriage systems in order to investigate the questions put forth by Lévi-Strauss. This meant accumulating large bodies of demographic data; still, no clear model emerged. Consanguineous marriages were not more numerous in partible areas (as it had been thought that cousin marriages would join together lands that the inheritance pattern had divided during the previous generation), nor were the double marriages of brothers and sisters or cousins more frequent in impartible areas.

A flurry of research was thus produced on these themes in the 1980s and contributed a rich body of knowledge on the various reproductive patterns of peasant societies. Some authors were looking for structural principles (Augustins 1990), while others tried to link norms and rules to practices, mainly by enlarging the context of study of the community and examining the impact of migrations, the presence of cottage industry, or the changing agrarian and/or demographic patterns, and so forth (Albera 1994).

This rather schematic survey shows the double specificity of French kinship studies—distant both from the English position toward pedigree and the U.S. obsession with biology. There exists a striking contrast between Britain, where there are no restrictions on testations, and France, where one of the goals of the Napoleonic Code was to impose such restrictions. This is connected with national differences in social structures: England was a class-based nation in the nineteenth century with a rich and landed aristocracy whereas France was a nation of small peasant landowners and newly landed bourgeoisie who had emerged after the revolution. In nineteenth-century France, the basic question of kinship, so well related in literature from Guy de Maupassant to Émile Zola, was how to transmit wealth to the next generation. Kinship and pedigree, in Britain, are the concern of aristocrats and the upper class; in France, except for the working classes slowly emerging at the end of the nineteenth century, everybody shares a concern with pedigree, since genealogy is linked to succession (to the farmstead or workshop) and inheritance. Besides, in British kinship, although pedigree means property, it also means blood, and this accounts for the typical interest in animal breeding. As Mary Bouquet states, quoting W. R. H. Rivers, the inventor of the genealogical method who makes the rapprochement himself: "The practical importance of the subject of genealogy is well recognized. Our own pedigrees are collected and preserved as the means whereby to show property and rank, and those of animals have long been an indispensable instrument to guide the breeder and the fancier" (1993, 39).[5]

In France, the attention paid to biology has not been as great as it has been for British or U.S. anthropology (see Franklin, this volume) because there is a common assertion running from Durkheim to Héritier that kinship is first and foremost social. As David Schneider notes:

> And so, argues Durkheim, the earliest forms of kinship group or family were almost totally independent of consanguineal ties, these having only more recently been assigned social significance. . . . to be a member of a family or kinship group, it is sufficient to have something of the totemic being, of the sacred quality that serves as the group's collective emblem. This can result from birth, but it can be gained in many other ways: by tattooing, by all the forms of food prohibitions, blood communion, and so forth. Even birth alone is not adequate to make the child an integral member of the group; religious ceremonies or some kind of social formality must be added. (1984, 100)[6]

If Héritier, for her part, stresses the existence of three irreducible biological facts—"two anatomically distinct sexes that have to unite to procreate offspring of either sex; an irreversible order of generations; a succession in the order of births within sibling groups and thus the existence of collateral lines" (1996, 23) — it is to emphasize the cultural inventions of the variety of kinship systems, owing to a fourth characteristic — the "differential valence of sexes" (1996, 24) — that explains the different symbolic constructions of the kinship universes (see Delaney, this volume).

From Anthropology to Sociology

French social anthropologists studying kinship in France and Europe, then, revealed the importance and diversity of the filiation patterns without being stirred by the radical revisions that were at the same time developing in Anglo-Saxon countries with the feminist critique of Fortes's positions (see Collier and Yanagisako 1987) or the doubts vehemently put forth by Edmund Leach (1961) or Schneider (1984). While social anthropologists at home were dealing with the various facets of peasant family systems, the "modern," "contemporary" family changes were left to the sociologists and demographers scrutinizing the causes and consequences of the fall in the rates of marriages and births, as well as the increase in the number of unmarried couples and divorces. In the 1970s and 1980s, this sociological work was mostly severed from the anthropological thought on kinship, which as a matter of fact, seemed of little help in explaining contemporary rapid changes. Never was the divide stigmatized by Goody so evident:

> In books covering the whole field, kinship is usually assigned to anthropologists and family to sociologists, with their contributions touching at only a few points. This situation results from the general trend of many nineteenth-century studies which assumed that there was no family in early societies. Though these assumptions have now been discarded, they continue to influence the topics studied by different sets of specialists. (1996, 1)

A sociology of the contemporary family amounted to a sociology of divorce and youth cohabitation. Marilyn Strathern also has observed that the study of kinship in modern society was largely peripheral. The Parsonian thesis was partly accountable for this neglect, as it stressed that the family has been deeply transformed by the Industrial Revolution, cutting down the number of those included in the family and highlighting the model of the "conjugal family" as the specific kinship model of Western society. Moreover, the welfare state had deprived the family of its former roles, such as socializing children and taking care of the sick, disabled, and old. Such was the common scientific wisdom.

The institutional organization of research on the family in France also explains this neglect of kinship ties, as INED's research was predominantly (though not totally) absorbed in explaining the baby boom of the 1950s and 1960s and the ensuing *babykrach*.[7] In the 1970s, there had been some research by INED members showing the importance of family links between generations, but its orientation was rather psychosociological, and always set in the context of the welfare state and its consequences for the loss of functions of the family.

By the end of the 1980s, a renewed interest in filiation emerged in conjunction with new developments related to the family, such as the lengthening of life, the multiplication of recomposed families, and the development of *Procréations médicalement assistées* (PMA).[8] The body of scientists who took up the discussion of kinship and filiation included sociologists, jurists, and psychoanalysts, and they often ignored most of the debates that had occupied this anthropological arena for many decades.

The reason why kinship seemed irrelevant to the analysis of Western societies is because such societies are described as being grounded in the cult of autonomy, individualism, and an ethic of self-valorization, rendering family ties superfluous. Except for the socialization of babies and young children, which cannot be accomplished outside the nuclear family, whatever was obtained in "primitive societies" by belonging to one descent line or another was now furnished by other social mechanisms. Salaries, housing, education, and health care, among other things, were all provided for outside the family.

Yet the lengthening of life, copresence of three and four generations, and invention of a new "third age" are now commonplace evidence in Western societies at the start of the twenty-first century. This third age is an invention of modernity. A cohort of people aged fifty-five to seventy-five, in good health, have enjoyed the benefits of the postwar economic boom, and are thus in a position to help both the younger generation and that of their own parents—now experiencing the difficulties of the "fourth age," that of decrepitude, as a national survey representative of the French population has shown (Attias-Donfut 1995).

Unquestionably there are fashions for scientific topics, and that of intergenerational relationships is à la mode these years among Western sociological researchers, notably French-speaking sociologists—Belgian, Swiss, or

Quebecois—but also English ones.[9] As Michael Peletz (this volume) notes, in the United States, greater interdisciplinarity has played a seminal role in the reconfiguration of the field of kinship due to the "repatriation of anthropology"; in France, through a different history of the discipline, the results are identical, and both social anthropologists and sociologists are working on the same topics. If social anthropology converges nowadays with sociology, it is because sociology has shifted its emphasis from the "agent" to the "actor"; as well, men's and women's actions are not only seen to be dictated by their position in a social class, and it is also admitted that they retain an autonomy of choice.

Areas of Contemporary Kinship Studies
Inheritance and property, sociability, and assistance seem to be the main domains related to family structure and dynamics that form current topics of research. Whether these relationships are material or immaterial, they frequently overlap and are all symbolically constituted.

Inheritance is no longer linked solely to death but follows the family life cycle: parents help children when they settle down in a relationship (married or not) and when grandchildren are born. Inheritance, too, is acknowledged as a significant factor for family cohesion. Due to the grip of marxism on sociology until the 1980s, the topic of inheritance was taboo because it was associated with the means of production and reproduction of the dominant upper classes. Today, 70 percent of the French population have received an inheritance, and 50 percent of all households own a home or an apartment that will be passed along to the next generation (see Gotman 1988). These postmortem goods help members of the young, or not so young, generation buy a house, an apartment, or a secondary home.

Besides their value on the market, these goods carry a family history where memory and consciousness of the past are grounded. The "gift of death" implies that it should be accepted and passed along in its turn: this helps create the idea of a line because the items received through death, rather than transmitted, should be *re*transmitted. The family houses are both items of capital and symbolic value, and also offer a setting for the development of family links, mainly during holidays shared together.

The second domain of contemporary research on family ties, under the general heading of "sociability," covers the various forms of exchange and assistance that seem to be on the increase because of the relative affluence of the third age, and conversely, because this daily and relatively trivial assistance is crucial to the members of the younger generation, who have difficulty finding jobs and child care. The intergenerational link is thus grounded in material and concrete transfers from the older to the younger generation. The third domain of the contemporary family is the assistance to dependent parents; such aid only runs upward and is extremely active in connection to the various funds provided by the welfare state agencies.

The intergenerational link, embedded in both material and immaterial exchanges, is symbolically constituted. A good example is revealed by the genealogy craze, which has taken off in large social groups. In research on French postal workers who are amateur genealogists, I found a number of persons who had no family roots or memories, but who endeavored, after months and years of archival research, to construct a genealogical tree that served their own longing. They emphasized the line with which they wanted to be associated and hence choose to nestle their identity. One of the informants said the exercise helped him hear "the rumors of family memories" (see Segalen and Michelat 1991) and that he was constantly living with his dead ancestors. Genealogy, then, appears as mental structures whose versatility helps carry varied social functions and imaginary representations. This symbolic dimension of family, which was long denied to modern societies, is now acknowledged. Although there are no clans associated with a specific totem, the common origin of large family groups is often celebrated after lengthy and patient genealogical research, which is used to bring together all the descendants of a common ancestor in large family gatherings.

Sociologists who discover the importance of kinship ties in modern societies are rather ill at ease with this phenomenon. This discipline has always denounced and criticized the prevailing social order, and marxist theories have been influential longer in French sociology than in French social anthropology. Therefore, analyzing family, inheritance, and exchange patterns has long been left aside because it stunk of conservatism and right-wing positions. Either out of ignorance or to show a distance from anthropology, sociologists use a specific vocabulary relating to other concepts: networks, exchange, transmission, and more often than not, "solidarity," which sets family links in the realm of charity, on the side of nature and affective links, and outside the world of production. It is often used in connection with the announced crisis of the welfare state and social protection. Some other researchers have had recourse to anthropological concepts in investigating the nature of these family exchanges. If neither the alliance theory of Lévi-Strauss nor the British descent theory are applicable because there are no descent groups, the Maussian concept of the gift seems topical. Families build themselves along the life dimension of individuals as well as the generational dimension. This is why the word "exchange" is rather improper because it does not account for temporal dimensions. Goods, services, and assistance circulating among kin are neither of the same nature nor of equal amount. Parents at some point in their lives give to their children, who later on will help aging parents while giving to their own children. Exchange suggests reciprocity. But all that circulates within families is neither identical nor immediately reciprocated; a debt is not canceled within one generation but rather over the course of several generations. This position in turn leads one to consider, as Fortes asserts, the moral aspect of family obligations: "Kinship is binding; it creates inescapable moral claims and obligations" (1969, 242). Yet these obligations are not fixed; they offer a supple framework within which the normative rules are negotiated in each instance (see Finch 1989; Segalen 2000).

This short history of the recent trends in kinship studies in France forms the background of the research that will be presented in the next section, where I will scrutinize the many consequences of new family forms that have resulted from recent demographic and cultural changes.

THE ROLE OF THE NEW GRANDPARENT:
A FRENCH SOCIOANTHROPOLOGICAL INVESTIGATION

Grandparenting is an interesting area to explore because it doubly puts filiation back into the family frame. On the macrolevel, it deals with some of the social consequences of the copresence of four or five generations in the Western world; on the microlevel, it investigates the various effects of longitudinal relationships on the identity of individuals as the life cycle, with its various crises, develops.

The research presented here on grandparenting has been conducted with Claudine Attias-Donfut in France.[10] It rests on socioanthropological material with two characteristics: a quantitative survey of three-generation families — a representative sample of the French population — that investigates exchanges of all kinds between the three generations; and a qualitative survey of a subsample of these three-generation families that addresses, through open interviews, questions of transmission, memory, ancestry, quality of family links as well as areas of conflict (Attias-Donfut and Segalen 1998).[11]

Our research is an example of this encounter between various disciplines around a topic that has been dealt with at length by social anthropology.[12]

Africanists have shown the importance of old age and the alternate relation-ship between generations; the circulation of children as well as fosterage and adoption practices have been described in African, Oceanian, and Asian soci-eties. Our first concern was to understand why there had been so little re-search on grandparenting in Western countries. Among other reasons, it is linked to the much-despised image of old age and decrepitude in Christian civilization. As such, the emergence of a new phase in the aging process of contemporary society brings to the fore the image of new grandparents, who have been innovators in their youth (since they are now in their mid-fifties), and notably, include women who have enjoyed the benefits of birth control and entered into the job market in large numbers. These aging families will enjoy good pensions in retirement. For the first time in history, the old will not be a burden to the younger generations, but quite the reverse: they are ready and willing to help their children and grandchildren, who are becoming a rarer item because of the new fertility trends.

The "New" Grandparents

Our study shows the incredible investment by grandparents in the young adult generation that mainly takes the form of caring for grandchildren on a regular basis and during holidays. This is observed among families where both grand-parents are still employed and yet manage to invest themselves in a social relation that they cherish and that the younger generation, struggling with difficult working conditions, enjoys. Of course, this typically depends on the spatial propinquity of families, which enables this kind of frequent relation. Young couples develop strategies to be at once residentially independent, yet relatively close to their families, so that these crucial family ties can be main-tained.

This model of grandparenting is different from that prevailing up to the previous generation.[13] When they were young, our grandparents experienced two contrasting types of relationships: either they were entirely brought up by grandparents, with their parents being only occasional visitors and over-seers from afar, or they had only distant contacts marked by respect and bore-dom. Nowadays (save for specific cases), grandchildren are not brought up by grandparents but the relation is frequent, close, and affectionate.

Our research deals also with the second age of the grandparenting life cycle, when grandchildren become older and entertain different though still inten-sive relationships with their aging grandparents. Grandparenting thus appears to be a key part of social networks in present-day France, in spite of and in collaboration with the assistance of a still-generous welfare system. Contrary to contemporary China (see Yan, this volume), lineal assistance is clearly more important than same-generational aid. This relates to the contemporary dilemmas concerning filiation of which the grandparents are part and parcel.

The Crisis of Filiation in France

In France today, over 30 percent of children are born out of wedlock; one in three marriages ends in divorce. Single fathers and mothers form new households, and in 90 percent of the cases, it is a man who enters a household headed by a single or divorced mother. What kind of relationships prevail within these "recomposed families"? Toward which children do grandparents have obligations when their offspring bring over for Christmas both biological children and their half and stepsiblings?

Over the past twenty years, the formation of the couple has appeared as a private matter concerning only the two individuals and their mutual relationship, based on love. It is not considered necessary to implicate society and the state in such a relationship. Individuals consider themselves as free to join in their union as they feel free to break from it if sentiments have vanished. The difficulty is that even if one considers a union a private affair, not necessitating papers, the birth of a child is always a public event. It is quite acceptable that a couple might separate — because it is the choice of adults, supposedly in full power of their decisions. But the relation between parents and children survives since children and parents are not in an equal bargaining position.

Changes in laws regarding family have followed the dramatic changes witnessed in family formation. The French juridical construction dating to the Napoleonic Code was remarkably coherent, if manifestly machist. It held together the strings of marriage and descent since a child was his or her father's as long as this man was legally married to the woman who gave birth to the child. In their haste to adopt new legal dispositions reflecting the new attitudes toward marriage, and also echoing the development of biotechnologies since the 1970s, jurists have disarticulated marriage and filiation. More and more children are raised and enjoy the benefits of a paternal presence, though the father is not *quem nuptiae demonstrant* (to whom the wedding points). The father, according to the Napoleonic Code, was the man who gave his genes, gave his name, and daily raised the child in his home. These three components of filiation have been disassociated in recomposed families. In such families, a father is not the biological father, but a man who lives with the mother — married or not — and helps to raise and nurture the child. In the present state of the French law, he cannot transmit any property to these nonbiological offspring. Private and public spheres, conjugal and social ties, were initially articulated in French law. This is not the case anymore: thus, one can refer to a crisis of filiation since it is no longer governed by a single body of law but more and more by the will of individuals and the choices of judges who are left without any point of reference other than their own sense of morality.

In place of the clear norms of the law, the social management by judges of each specific case has been substituted. A French law of 1993 provides for joint custody. But in actuality, in cases of divorce or the separation of cohabiting couples, each judge decides the future of the child in the secret of his or her soul and under the vague heading of the "interest of the child." Because society and the law have given full strength to the individual and individual desire, then, people find themselves face-to-face with themselves and feeling very much insecure.

Recent debates (see Théry 1987; Meulders-Klein and Théry 1993) consider the possibility of establishing a legal status for the stepfather, the man who is not the biological father. A large number of children are currently raised by men who take care of them on a daily basis, often more so than their biological fathers. Research has developed in France, under the influence of U.S. scholars (see Cherlin 1978), that reveals the existence of two types of models: either family recomposition tends to erase the former union and place of the biological father; or it adds to the preexisting family network, and the biological father and his line are not forgotten (see Le Gall and Martin 1993). The first situation is more often encountered among working classes where the "traditional" idea of family — one marriage partner for life — prevails. Therefore, the new couple will endeavor to cut the ties with the biological father and his kin, and this goes as far as having the child adopted by the new husband of the mother, so that the child should have the same family name. This is frequently done with the agreement of the biological father, who given economic difficulties, will not pay alimony and will maintain very little contact with his children. The adoptive father will replace the biological one. The second solution is employed by more affluent couples who try to negotiate a new modus vivendi between the various partners and their children, who are consequently not detached from their biological line. The biological father retains an important role and is not replaced by the stepfather, who has to find a role for himself and, notably, a name. The younger the children and the better the quality of relationships between the ex-spouses, the better the chance for the new partner to find a role for himself near his social children. Between these two extremes, however, many different situations are encountered, and these are linked to various sociological traits: the nature of the divorce, the age and number of children, the fact that the new father also comes from a recomposed family, the fact that the new couple subsequently bears children of their own, and so forth. These fascinating data should encourage social anthropologists to scrutinize the diversity of these situations—since sociologists are more interested in discussing these topics in relation to economic vulnerability, the nature of state assistance for single parents, and the breakdown of social relationships.

This is decidedly a place to explore the "moral power of blood ties" versus the power of social ties, for which no legal link is at present recognized. This means, for instance, that the social father cannot transmit his wealth to the social children he helped raise. Moreover, the grandparents do not know whether they are or are not grandparents. Quite paradoxically, given the fact of the vast number of recomposed families, French law is now on the side of the blood tie—a consequence of the new reproductive techniques and the possibility of establishing, through genetic-print techniques, the paternity of individuals.[14] Kinship in contemporary France is about inclusions and exclusions: in some cases, people do not know whether they are or are not legally linked to somebody.[15] On the anthropological side, the blood tie is suddenly made explicit, thus bridging the former gap with Anglo-American positions.

Grandparenting and the Filiation Crisis

In past peasant societies, given demographic patterns, grandparents generally held a symbolic position. This is made obvious by the practices of godparenting. Grandparents were commonly the godparents, and thus bestowed their first name on their grandchildren: it was a way to affiliate them to the family line and also to mark their rights to the family patrimony. This pattern of godparenting/grandparenting has disappeared, and there are now many signs of the grandparents' fragile position. The legal hesitations regarding adoption exemplify the crisis in filiation. The French laws were revised in 1966, 1976, 1993, and 1996. Originally, French law accepted only complete adoption, which meant total severance of links between the child and its line of origin. It meant that if a widow, widower, or divorced person should remarry and wanted to adopt the child of his or her new spouse in order to reinforce the new union, the child would lose its name and all that was associated with its line of origin. In the case of the death of their son/daughter, grandparents would have lost a child and also grandchildren. As such, the new dispositions have provided for "simple" adoption where the child is affiliated to his or her new line without losing his or her affiliation with the original one.

As regards grandparenting, our survey clearly shows that divorce diminishes in every case the relations between generations, save for young women who divorce after the birth of a child and return home. Opposite trends are created by divorce and remarriage or family recomposition: a line can either be added or subtracted. In some instances, children may have many sets of active grandparents, and in others, only one set. One has to distinguish between grandparents' and parents' divorce. Until twenty years ago, in France, only younger parents were divorcing. But these parents have now aged and are also divorced grandparents. Several sociological characteristics emerge in this situation: the grandparental link is elective; if there is a familial recomposition, grandparents and grandchildren can create a nurturing bond only if the child is under five years of age; after that age, their consciences will be loaded with a family past that has already crystallized their identities; they will be able to address their grandparents with a familial name such as "Papi" and "Mamie." Even in the case of nonconflictive recompositions, as mentioned above, ties can be created only if they are frequent and active. In what follows, I examine some specific situations that exemplify that grandparents are part of the filiation crisis, too.

As seen in figure 9.1, a white-collar and liberal family from Lyon has been, over three generations, repeatedly recomposed and subject to a series of family misfortunes including fatal diseases and violent deaths. Over five generations, one son is always named Henri. Henri, born in 1922, is the son of a first marriage that ended in divorce. His first wife, Madeleine, was already the daughter of divorced parents (during a time when divorce was uncommon, especially among bourgeois families). Henri's first wife died after the birth of their two children, Christiane and Jean-Pierre, and he remarried a divorced woman who had a son, Pierre. This son has now divorced and remarried. Henri's children have known rather different fates. Christiane, born in 1941, has married a much older divorced man, who already had a daughter. A son, Laurent, was born to Christiane and her husband in 1966. But Christiane's husband died accidentally. Jean-Pierre, Henri's son, married and fathered two daughters, who both died of a genetic disease, and adopted a third one, Audrey.

The generational relationships are complex. Christiane never got on with her mother's mother, Benedicte, who disliked her equally (so she says). Chris-

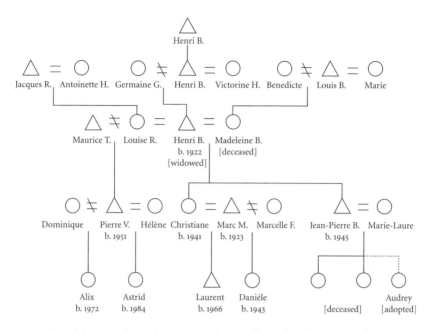

FIG. 9.1 Multiple generations of recomposed families descending from Henri of Lyon.

tiane thus called her maternal grandfather's second wife, Marie, "grand-mère," while the biological grandmother cherished her grandson, Jean-Pierre. In his turn, Henri is much closer to Laurent than to his granddaughters. Henri has helped finance Laurent's costly managerial studies. By contrast, he learned of the death of his granddaughters, as a consequence of their genetic disease, in a newspaper. As far as the son of Henri's wife is concerned, the boy came into the family rather young and could call Henri's parents (his social grand-parents) "Pépé" and "Mémé." Henri considers himself close to his stepson's daughters, viewing them as grandchildren "through assimilation."

Clearly, this case illustrates a process of rupture of kin ties, caused by re-peated family divorces over the generations. Not only are patrimonial inter-ests contested each time a death occurs in the family but when considering the apical ancestor, one can point to the differences in the degrees of closeness and integration into the family lines. Laurent's affiliation is primary to his ma-ternal grandfather, having lost the connections on his father's side, whereas it was the reverse for the little girls before their deaths. Pierre's daughters, Alix and Astrid, will consider Henri their grandfather, but they know that on his death none of his patrimonial assets can be transmitted to them.

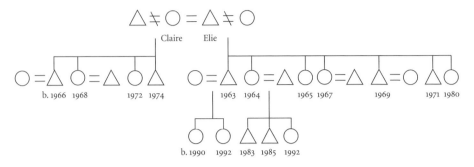

FIG. 9.2 The recomposed families of Elie and Claire.

Some cases are described as nonconflictual, as grandparents are more engaged in social activities with their age group than dedicated to grandchildren's care. This is often the result of adults remarrying late, waiting for their children to grow up before separating from their spouse. In such instances, the aging newly remarried couple wants to have a life of their own and does not want to put their relationship in jeopardy with intergenerational family problems. A way to minimize the difficulties is to involve oneself as little as possible.

Figure 9.2 shows Elie, fifty-eight, and Claire, fifty-seven. Both belong to the upper Parisian bourgeoisie and have divorced after having raised their respective children — Elie, seven children, and Claire, four. Family relationships take place mainly in their vast Brittany house, where they can accommodate their children and grandchildren. The new couple is far from being troubled by the burdens of grandparenthood; they devote a large amount of time to partying with friends and playing bridge or golf. To Elie and Claire, the situation is problem free since "grandchildren share themselves between three instead of two."

Although this is a sort of superficial statement given to the interviewer, remoteness nevertheless does seem to characterize the relationships, all the more because the grandchildren are Elie's and Claire is not close to her adult stepchildren.

Turning to the parents' divorce, a sociological pattern has been observed where daughters are closer to their family than sons, which means that a matrilineal trend is clearly emerging. The grandchild will thus have a privileged relationship with maternal kin and this branch will play the role of "watchdog," described by U.S. sociologists (see Troll 1983) — the grandparent being the keeper of the family continuity. By contrast, a grandchild will lose

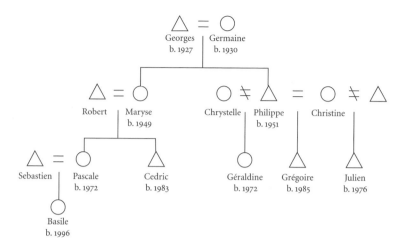

FIG. 9.3 The recomposed families of Georges and Germaine's son.

contact or have much looser ties with the paternal line. The degree of contact
is correlated with the degree of consensus or conflict in the divorce.

Georges, seventy, and Germaine, sixty-seven, have retired from their jobs
(figure 9.3). He was working as a team manager at Peugeot, while she was a
salesclerk in a department store. Their son, Philippe, left his wife when his
daughter, Géraldine, was only two in order to marry another woman who
already had a son, Julien. Georges and Germaine disapproved of their son's
actions, and remained on the side of their former daughter-in-law, Chrys-
telle, who went back to live close to her parents, who in turn helped her raise
her daughter. With the new daughter-in-law, relations have always been sour,
and this makes it difficult for them to accept even the new biological grandson, Grégoire, who was born subsequently. These grandparents refused to give
to the woman's first son, Julien, the benefits of a social line, even when they
learned that their son had decided to give his family name to this boy who he
had not fathered. Hence, the relationship was minimal with the two boys, both
the social and biological grandsons, until the latter reached the age of five.
Georges and Germaine decided to activate the relation so as "not to lose" their
grandson. But somehow it was too late; the relation remains quite formal. The
grandparents cannot offer personalized gifts inasmuch as they are unaware of
the boy's tastes; instead, they put money in a bank account for him. For his
part, Grégoire refuses to call them papi and mamie.

Many grandparents intervene actively, at the request of their children, in times of family crisis linked to divorce, not only on behalf of younger children—who will find with grandparents the stability they could not find at home—but also often for adolescents as well. This gives a new sense of usefulness to life when old age is looming. A sixty-eight-year-old woman who takes her retarded grandson to both a tennis class and motor therapy session on Wednesdays sighs: "This does not give you any eagerness to die, or to play bridge."

The uncertainties of filiation are part of grandparenting as well, and they bring about both anxiety and guilt. This is far from the idyllic portrait of grandparenting offered by magazines, which paint this social role in rosy colors. Contrary to conventional images, grandparents are not always the menders of family breakups. They can both provide and deny an identity for their grandchildren.

Terms of Address

As exemplified above, the terms of address are quite revealing of the nature of the filial situation and intragenerational tensions: here, the power of some anthropological tools to analyze modern society are rediscovered.[16]

The figure of the new grandparent inserted between the older great-grandparent and parents obliges people to devise new names. In past generations, grandparents would succeed one another, the older generation dying at the point when the younger one was entering this stage, thereby taking over the kin terms held by the ancestors. Now, because of the coexistence of four generations, new kin terms have to be devised. These terms reveal the degree to which grandparents engage in their role and control the naming process. In this way, they have recuperated some of the control over the descent line they have lost when the custom of giving their first name to grandchildren collapsed.

The age at grandparenting is an important parameter in the choice of the term. Feeling too young to be a grandmother is often expressed by women in their mid-forties who have just finished bringing up their children and are uncomfortable when they are associated with a role they do not want to endorse. They thus refuse the classical kin terms Papi and Mamie, which are most commonly used nowadays in France, and prefer to be called by their first names or some transformation of them that conveys an idea of closeness and keeps it specific for this particular relationship. Psychoanalysts show, in effect, that when a woman becomes a grandmother, it is as though she was deprived of her reproductive capacity and had transmitted it to her daughter.

On the man's side, it is well-known that although parenting is always a plus and helps achieve the full status of adulthood and manhood in the eyes of society, becoming a grandfather indicates the road to retirement and aging, and some men are reluctant to accept this prospect. I have a case in my material of a prospective grandfather, who when he learned of his forthcoming situation, declared he did not want to be called papi but rather something like tonton (a familiar French term used to address uncles). Refusing the grandparental kin term, the grandfather refused symbolically to accept the child in his line and consequently deprived him of the benefits of lineal identification. On account of this, a break occurred between his daughter and himself. This example shows clearly—and the contrary would be quite surprising—that the flexible aspect of filiation is not only associated with the breakdown of marriages and development of unstable cohabitation but connects with the rise of individual choices even among the older generation. In former times, there existed a grandiloquent disavowal of a child who had betrayed familial expectations: by disinheriting him or her, the ancestor was precisely watching over the integrity of his or her line and chasing out whoever was reluctant to comply with its norms. Today, this process is attributable to individual choices.

The use of the first name generally marks a feeble engagement in the grandparental role, which might be accentuated by the fact that grandchildren have been produced by sons, and daughters-in-law remain remote. By contrast, when grandparenting is accepted and even eagerly anticipated, and when a pregnancy is announced, the grandparents-to-be's first reaction is to discuss the terms by which they will be addressed. Once the baby is born, they generally accept a designation that is more than often bestowed by the eldest child giving birth, and this is all the more so if this child is a daughter. The process is well portrayed by the following case:

> Roger, a former artisan in a Parisian suburb, born in 1928, and his wife, Micheline, born in 1932, have two children and four grandchildren.
> *Roger:* For all our grandchildren, we are papi and mamie.
> *Interviewer:* Why?
> *Micheline:* In fact, it is Dominique, our eldest daughter, who made this choice. When the first was born, she chose mamie because my mother was still alive and was called mémère. Thus to differentiate us, she took over the name I used to call my own grandmother. And the name remained. That's how it was done.

Such continuity is often linked with a positive relationship between the generations. For instance, papi might become papou, while mamie might become nanou as deformations coming from the babbling of the grandchild. Terms are therefore loaded with a large dose of affect and reinforce the inter-generational link. But more often than not, younger grandparents shun the classical papi-mamie and embark on inventing terms either formed from their first names—for example, Bernard and Martine becoming Pabé and Maty—or incorporating some Anglo-Saxon influences—as when Danièle becomes Dany and her husband Daddy. This linguistic creativity has to comply with the following variables. The name and kin terms must: bear some connection with the specific activity of the grandfather/mother—for instance, "Papi-velo" to refer to somebody who is a cycling addict; retain some semantic connotation that helps classify them in the category of names that will be used within the intimate, private circle and only for that purpose; form a duet with the other grandparental term, reinforcing the "couple" aspect of the grandparents, which is particularly significant in the case of divorced parents; be capable of being babbled by the child; and distinguish the maternal and paternal lines, so that each family has its particular set of names.

This naming pattern, then, reveals the potential for intergenerational conflicts either to decrease or increase over time. It also shows a flexibility in kinship and usages that would make Morgan and all the other analysts of kinship terminology turn over in their graves. Lastly, it is a reminder of the power of naming as a way to "make" kinship links. Hence the common concern of grandparents-to-be to help generate new names that will be meaningful for their new identity.

KINSHIP BETWEEN THE INDIVIDUAL AND THE STATE

If grandparenting can appear in some respects as an antidote to the breakdown of family lines, it nevertheless is also part of the trend. Grandparents have the choice to endorse or reject the role associated with their status. Divorce, more often than not, tends to sever the links with one line, thereby depriving children of a source of identification, which is all the more regrettable given that, nowadays, social milieus are much less homogeneous than they were formerly. On family recomposition, many different patterns prevail, depending on the age, the number of children, and the circumstances of the formation of the new marital pair. More research should be conducted to evaluate the differential roles of grandparents vis-à-vis biological grandchildren as opposed to stepgrandchildren. For grandparents, as for parents, filiation is optional to some extent, and this seems to be a new development in Western cultures.

If the meaning of filiation has deeply changed, this is also a result of the new status of children. In non-Western societies (and in rural societies until recently), children are valued future producers; sterility is always seen as a curse and fertility is particularly esteemed. After a few years of nurturance, children can be producers, and without the central agency of the welfare state, they are the only security against illness and death for aging parents. The descendants will take care of all the symbolic aspects of death and the fate of the soul as well. Children belong more to a line than to their individual parents and circulate between kin because their labor force belongs to all the members of the descent line. In some African societies, children are placed with the kin with whom they can be most useful and often with their grandparents, who socialize them while having them cultivate their lands or perform domestic chores.

By contrast, the Western urban conception of kinship has been totally transformed by the fact that the individual is valued first and foremost. I do not use the term individualism, which carries a good dose of moral value, but consider the implications of filiation contextualized by the emergence of the individual and the accomplishment of his or her desires. Children are produced, in limited quantities, for totally different reasons; they embody the continuation of the love of the couple. They are educated at a great cost and, at present, depend on their parents' resources for longer periods than ever; these children are not expected to take care of their elders (even though they might reciprocate much later in life).

The study of grandparenting highlights Marilyn Strathern's statement that kinship is important, provided that "in kinship, one is talking about the formation of intimate relationships, one is not talking about institutional or social forms of groupings or units as such" (1997, 8). In historical and traditional societies, being a member of a household afforded individuals access to local political power. This is not the case anymore, and citizenship is acquired through different processes. In this sense, it can be admitted that filiation is not associated with institutional forms. Yet kinship cannot be sent back to the private domain—not only because of the many connections it maintains with wider social processes but also because filiation appears to be a kind of backbone for both individuals and societies. In former times, this used to go without saying; in modern times, it is constantly claimed.

This essay exemplifies also the new directions in kinship research presently developed in France together with the new social trends. It testifies to a shift in the questions around filiation, which in the French tradition and national collective representations, were more often debated in reference to patrimony than blood. A new equilibrium, balancing between the line and the individual, between blood and social links, is at this moment being sought. Grandparenting is itself a social innovation emerging out of flexibility and choice that can promote either affiliation or disaffiliation, and it thus manifests the contrasting forces present in contemporary society.

NOTES

1 Contrary to the United States, where there is an abundant literature on this subject. See, among others, Neugarten and Weinstein 1964; Bengtson and Robertson 1985; Cherlin and Furstenberg 1992; Kornhaber 1996. There is also a vast literature on grandparents raising their grandchildren.

2 In this text, filiation refers to the blood or social ties of an individual to the lines he or she is descended from, whether on the paternal or maternal side. It does not refer to an institutionalized descent group. Line again refers to either patriline or matriline — the French literature on contemporary kinship mentions the *lignée paternelle* or *maternelle* — without any mention of a unilineal system, since we are in the domain of cognatism. Of course, this line can be rather short and mixes across the other line at points in time.

3 For example, *La Cité Antique* by Numa Denis Fustel de Coulanges (1864), *Studies in Ancient Society* by John Ferguson McLennan (1866), *Das Mutterrecht* by Johann Jakob Bachofen (1861), and *Ancient Society* by Lewis Henry Morgan (1867).

4 Adam Kuper notes: "Kinship is the central discipline of anthropology" (1988, 241). Robin Fox has remarked: "It is to anthropology what the nude is to art. It is the technical core of social anthropology, the insider's special field, the least accessible, the most jargon-ridden, the most susceptible to abstract, quasi-mathematical models" (1967, 10).

5 Quoted from W. H. R. Rivers's 1914 "Notes on the Heron pedigree collected by the Rev. George Hall."

6 Schneider is here referencing Émile Durkheim's 1898 "Zur Urgeschichte der Ehe, Prof. J. Kohler," *Année sociologique* 1:306–19.

7 If the baby boom refers to the sharp rise in fertility, babykrach points to its steep fall. These terms were coined as reflections of the traditional French concern with the national fertility decline.

8 Although it refers to the same medical processes, PMA is not the equivalent of the new reproductive technologies, which stress the demand on the part of sterile parents as opposed to the offer of new techniques.

9 Louis Roussel produced a pioneering work in 1976; for recent publications, see

Segalen and Michelat 1991; Segalen 2000; Gullestad and Segalen 1997. On the nature of kinship networks, see Bonvalet et al. 1993; Héran 1988. On kinship networks in Belgium, see Bawin-Legros and Kellerhals 1994; in Switzerland, see Coenen-Huther, Kellerhals, and Von Allmen 1994; in Quebec, see Dandurand and Ouellette 1992; and in England, see Finch 1989. These works demonstrate that kinship is relevant in many social domains, including housing and work.

10 Research director at the Caisse nationale d'assurance vieillesse, Paris.

11 The survey focuses on a representative sample of French families with three generations: 1,958 individuals aged forty-eight to fifty-two, 1,217 parents of these individuals, and 1,493 of their children who have left home. The quantitative surveys cover about thirty three-generation families, and includes one hundred interviews conducted in Paris and the Parisian suburbs, Aquitaine, Bretagne, Lorraine, Lyonnais, and Sud-Ouest toulousain.

12 Besides sociology and anthropology, we are dwelling on demographic and historical data, and on texts written by psychoanalysts as well as novel writers.

13 One of the virtues of our data is that we are able to contrast the experience of grandparenting over three generations, both from the point of view of grandparents and grandchildren.

14 The goal of this 1972 law is to let "the truth triumph"—in other words, to open the possibility for fathers to establish through biological tests the "true filiation" with all the results attached to it. For a study of the consequences of this law, see Laborde-Barbanègre 1998.

15 A rather appalling example of these debates is the case of French singer Yves Montand, whose corpse was exhumed from his grave for a genetic marker sampling following a suit by a woman who claimed he had fathered her daughter. The case was entrancing from the perspective of a social anthropologist since it stirred such controversial debates, though rather sad from a human point of view. Eventually, Aurore Drossart was found not to be Montand's daughter.

16 Some material on terms of address has been collected by students of Paris X-Nanterre, maîtrise de sociologie, in 1996.

REFERENCES

Albera, Dionigi. 1994. Familles, Destins, Destinations: Entre portrait-robot et mosaïque. *Le monde alpin et rhodanien* 3:7–26.

Attias-Donfut, Claudine. 1995. Le double circuit des transmissions. In *Les solidarités entre générations. Vieillesse, famille, Etat,* edited by Claudine Attias-Donfut. Paris: Nathan.

Attias-Donfut, Claudine, and Martine Segalen. 1998. *Grands-parents: La famille à travers les générations.* Paris: Odile Jacob.

Augustins, Georges. 1990. *Comment se perpétuer? Devenir des lignées et destins des patrimoines dans les paysanneries européennes.* Paris: Société d'ethnologie.

Bawin-Legros, Bernadette, and Jean Kellerhals, eds. 1994. *Relations intergénérationnelles:*

Parentés, transmission, mémoire. Proceedings of the Liège Symposium, 17–18 May 1990. International Association of French Speaking Sociologists and Association of French Speaking Belgian Sociologists.

Bengtson, Vern L., and Joan F. Robertson, eds. 1985. *Grandparenthood.* Beverly Hills, Calif.: Sage.

Bonvalet, Catherine, Dominique Maison, Hervé Le Bras, and Lionel Charles. 1993. Proches et parents. *Population* 1:83–110.

Bouquet, Mary. 1993. *Reclaiming English Kinship.* Manchester: Manchester University Press.

Carsten, Janet, and Stephen Hugh-Jones, eds. 1995. *About the House: Lévi-Strauss and Beyond.* Cambridge: Cambridge University Press.

Cherlin, Andrew. 1978. Remarriage as an Incomplete Institution. *American Journal of Sociology* 84, no. 3:634–50.

Cherlin, Andrew, and Frank Furstenberg. 1992. *The New American Grandparent: A Place in the Family, a Life Apart.* Cambridge: Harvard University Press.

Coenen-Huther, Josette, Jean Kellerhals, and Malik Von Allmen. 1994. *Les réseaux de solidarité dans la famille.* Lausanne: Réalités sociales.

Collier, Jane F., and Sylvia J. Yanagisako, eds. 1987. *Gender and Kinship: Essays toward a Unified Analysis.* Stanford, Calif.: Stanford University Press.

Dandurand, Renée B., and Françoise R. Ouellette. 1992. *Entre autonomie et solidarité: Parenté et soutien dans la vie de jeunes familles montréalaises.* Quebec: Institut québécois de recherche sur la culture.

Durkheim, Émile. 1898. Zur Urgeschichte der Ehe, Prof. J. Kohler. *Année sociologique* 1:306–19.

Finch, Janet. 1989. *Family Obligations and Social Change.* Cambridge, U.K.: Polity Press.

Fortes, Meyer. 1969. *Kinship and the Social Order: The Legacy of Lewis Henry Morgan.* Chicago: Aldine.

Fox, Robin. 1967. *Kinship and Marriage.* Harmondsworth: Penguin.

Goody, Jack. 1976. *Production and Reproduction: A Comparative Study of the Domestic Domain.* Cambridge: Cambridge University Press.

———. 1996. Introduction to *A History of the Family,* edited by André Burguière, Christiane Klapisch, Martine Segalen, and Françoise Zonabend. Vol. 2. Cambridge, U.K.: Polity Press.

Gotman, Anne. 1988. *Hériter.* Paris: Presses Universitaires de France.

Gullestad, Marianne, and Martine Segalen, eds. 1997. *Family and Kinship in Europe.* London: Pinter.

Héran, François. 1988. La sociabilité, une pratique culturelle. *Economie et statisique* 216:3–22.

Héritier, Françoise. 1996. *Masculin/Féminin: La pensée de la différence.* Paris: Odile Jacob.

———. 1999. La citadelle imprenable. *Critique: Claude Lévi-Strauss* 55, nos. 620–21 (January–February): 61–83.

Jolas, Tina, Marie-Claude Pingaud, Yvonne Verdier, and Françoise Zonabend. [1968–

1982] 1990. *Une campagne voisine, Minot, un village bourguignon.* Reprint, Paris: Editions de la Maison des Sciences de l'Homme.

Kornhaber, Arthur. 1996. *Contemporary Grandparenting.* Thousand Oaks, Calif.: Sage.

Kuper, Adam. 1983. *Anthropology and Anthropologists: The Modern British School.* London: Routledge.

————. 1988. *The Invention of Primitive Society: Transformations of an Illusion.* London: Routledge.

Laborde-Barbanègre, Michelle. 1998. La filiation en question: De la loi du 3 janvier 1972 aux lois sur la bioéthique. In *Adoptions: Ethnologie des parentés choisies,* edited by Agnès Fine. Paris: Éditions de la Maison des Sciences de l'Homme.

Leach, Edmund. 1961. *Rethinking Anthropology.* London: Athlone Press.

Le Gall, Didier, and Claude Martin. 1993. Transitions familiales, logiques de recompositions et modes de régulation conjugale. In *Les recompositions familiales,* edited by Marie-Thérèse Meulders-Klein and Irène Théry. Paris: Nathan.

Le Roy Ladurie, Emmanuel. 1972. Système de la coutume: Structures familiales et coutumes d'héritage en France au XVIe siècle. *Annales Economie, Sociétés, Civilisations,* nos. 4–5 (July–October): 825–46.

Lévi-Strauss, Claude. 1983. Histoire et ethnologie. *Annales Economie, Sociétés, Civilisations,* no. 6 (November–December): 1217–31.

MacDonald, Charles, ed. 1986. *De la hutte au palais: Sociétés "à maison" en Asie du Sud-Est insulaire.* Paris: Éditions du Centre National de la Recherche Scientifique.

Meulders-Klein, Marie-Thérèse, and Irène Théry, eds. 1993. *Les recompositions familiales.* Paris: Nathan.

Neugarten, Bernice, and Karol Weinstein. 1964. The Changing American Grandparent. *Journal of Marriage and the Family* 26:199–204.

Roussel, Louis. 1976. *La famille après le mariage des enfants.* Paris: Institut National d'Etudes Démographiques–Presses Universitaires de France.

Schneider, David M. 1984. *A Critique of the Study of Kinship.* Ann Arbor: University of Michigan Press.

Segalen, Martine. 2000. *Sociologie de la famille.* 5th ed. Paris: Armand Colin.

Segalen, Martine, and Claude Michelat. 1991. L'amour de la généalogie. In *Jeux de familles,* edited by Martine Segalen. Paris: Presses du Centre National de la Recherche Scientifique.

Segalen, Martine, and Philippe Richard. 1986. Marrying Kinsmen in Pays Bigouden Sud. *Journal of Family History* 11, no. 2:109–30.

Strathern, Marilyn. 1997. On Kinship. *European Association of Social Anthropologists Newsletter* 19 (March).

Théry, Irène. 1987. Remariages et familles recomposées: Des évidences aux incertitudes. *L'Année sociologique* 37:119–52.

Troll, Lillian. 1983. Grandparents: The Family Watchdogs. In *Family Relationships in Later Life,* edited by Timothy H. Brubaker. Beverly Hills, Calif.: Sage.

PART III

Nature, Culture, and the

Properties of Kinship

CHAPTER 10

The Economies in Kinship and the Paternity of Culture:
Origin Stories in Kinship Theory
Susan McKinnon

The opening illustration of Robert Wright's article (1994) in *Time* magazine on evolutionary psychology depicts two men sowing a deeply furrowed field with little sperm/seeds that are alternately portrayed as dollar bills. The woman accompanying the first man looks over her shoulder toward the second to assess the relative value of the two men in this "spermatic economy" (Barker-Benfield 1974) of evolutionary origins. What interests me here is not the remarkable recurrence of the seed and soil metaphor of pro/creation (Delaney 1991) but rather the association between paternity, kinship, economy, and the evolutionary forces that are thought to bring about culture in such social scientific origin stories. In this essay, I explore this set of associations in two origin stories that are key to kinship theory in anthropology: Lewis Henry Morgan's *Ancient Society* and Claude Lévi-Strauss's *The Elementary Structures of Kinship*.

I examine *these two* origin stories because, taken together, they are figure and ground to one another: while they share a core developmental narrative, one struggles long and hard to bring into focus what the other presupposes. I examine these two *origin stories* because, projecting a reflection on the screen of the unknowable, they comprise a rich treasury of images of a "society's notion of itself" (Yanagisako and Delaney 1995, 2) — its subliminal desires as well as its dominant distinctions, values, and ideas of development (see also Conkey and Williams 1991). Indeed, these two texts together provide the organizing framework for a great deal of anthropological kinship theory over the past century.

Much of what might be called the "new" kinship studies has sought to explore how kinship is being reconfigured as it is "enterprised-up" (Strathern 1992b, 38) within the global marketplaces of the new genetic and reproductive biotechnologies (see also Edwards et al. 1993; Ragoné 1994; Franklin 1997; Franklin and Ragoné 1998; Haraway 1997). In reading these new kinship studies, I have found myself looking backward to the "old" kinship studies and seeing even more clearly just how central "enterprise" has always been to anthropological conceptions of kinship. I am concerned not simply with the assertion that Euro-American cultural and theoretical ideas about kinship (as well as culture itself) posit the social transformation of the "natural facts of life" (Strathern 1980, 1988, 1992a, 1992b; Yanagisako and Delaney 1995; Franklin 1997; Franklin and Ragoné 1998) or that this social transformation is often imagined as the province of the pro/creative forces of paternity (Delaney 1986). Rather, I wish to study more specifically how the paternity of culture is configured in relation to property and in terms of enterprise—the enterprising up of more "natural" (female) re/productive resources—what, in reference to recent developments, Donna Haraway has called the transformation of "kind" into "brand" (1997, 49–87; see also Franklin, this volume).

Furthermore, at least with regard to Morgan and Lévi-Strauss, the enterprising of kinship into the paternal economies of culture takes two narrative forms. Using analogies of labor, property, and inheritance, Morgan's account moves from a state of diffuse, unbounded relationality in primitive promiscuity through a gradual series of matrimonial and patrimonial "exclusions," which mark increasing states of distinction that culminate in monogamous marriage and a discrete line of inheritance. Using analogies of scarcity, risk, market speculation and exchange, Lévi-Strauss's narrative moves from the initial isolation of natural, bounded consanguineal groups through an all-or-nothing transformation to establish relations of reciprocity, and then increasing states of inclusiveness and integration.[1] In another place, it would be worth contemplating the historical and social factors that precipitate the appearance of a model of capital accumulation and restricted inheritance as opposed to that of market speculation and exchange. Here, however, I wish to scrutinize the relation between the two models, and think about the possibility that both remain integral to the landscape of kinship and kinship theory in a capitalist society.

PATERNITY, PROPERTY, AND INHERITANCE IN MORGAN'S *ANCIENT SOCIETY*

Morgan's evolutionary trajectory begins from an initial state of indistinction and diffuse relatedness, and then moves gradually through states of increasing distinction and exclusion as the boundaries of relatedness are drawn more and more tightly around what comes to be the monogamous nuclear family and the male line of inheritance. The prime movers in this process of increasing restriction are the logic of natural selection articulated by a sequence of matrimonial "exclusions" in the first half of the evolutionary sequence and, in the second half, the logic of labor and property articulated by a sequence of patrimonial "exclusions." Throughout the sequence, there is a parallel development between ideas of kinship and marriage and those of labor and property. Moreover, the image of kinship that is the sign of civilization is one in which the "natural" relationality derived from maternity in the first half of the sequence is encompassed by and enterprised into a form of paternal relatedness that is configured through and nearly indistinguishable from relations of property. This is not simply a "social recognition" of the "natural facts" of biology. Rather, the supposedly natural maternal base of relatedness is transformed by labor to create a patent, as it were, on kinship relatedness as paternal property and propriety (see Rose 1993, 5, 114; Haraway 1997, 82, 90). Paternity, property, propriety, and civilization are all but simultaneous and indistinguishable (see Coward 1983, 63–66).

Primitive Promiscuity and the Spontaneous Fruits of the Earth

Below even his first stage of evolution, Morgan presupposes an antecedent period of primitive promiscuity. "Man in this condition could scarcely be distinguished from the mute animals by whom he was surrounded" (Morgan [1877] 1974, 507). Morgan imagines that humans in this original state lived "in groves, in caves and in forests, for the possession of which they disputed with wild beasts — while they sustained themselves with the spontaneous fruits of the earth" (20). Living "in a state of promiscuous intercourse like the gregarious animals" (508), humans were "ignorant of marriage" (507) and presumably mated just as spontaneously as they ate the fruit from the trees. Here is an image of complete negative definition and relational merging: humans are indistinguishable from animals; generations lack separation one from another; lineal relations are merged with collateral; consanguinity remains undifferentiated from affinity; and promiscuity is the same as incest. This negative definition and relational merging is associated with a lack of labor expended in both subsistence and mating: both are spontaneous and indiscriminate.

Savagery and the Progress of Matrimonial Exclusions

Morgan's three stages of savagery are characterized by the "natural" kinship of maternity and matrilineality, which Morgan considers to be the only kind of kinship knowable outside of monogamous marriage (402, 442), and by group marriage, which he depicts as promiscuity "with the addition of a method" (52). Although Morgan sees this era as one that remains encompassed within the more natural forms of maternal kinship and promiscuity, he traces the development of three crucial distinctions — or what he calls exclusions — in the system of marriage: first between parents and children; then between "own" sisters and brothers; and finally between collaterals.

Out of the diffuse relational merging and indiscriminate promiscuity of the antecedent age, the consanguine family of the lower status of savagery was marked by the implicit exclusion of parent-child (or intergenerational) marriage at the same time that it sanctioned group marriage between brothers and sisters, both "own and collateral" (48, 417, 422, 509). Generations emerge as distinct through the exclusion of marriage relations between them. Within a generation, however, there is only an indistinguishable mass of sisters and brothers who are simultaneously wives and husbands to each other. Thus, not only do lineal and collateral relations remain indistinguishable but so too do relations of consanguinity and affinity since one's wife is one's sister and one's husband is one's brother (see also 418).

The next step out of the promiscuous blur was taken, in middle savagery, when the punaluan family was made possible by distinguishing "own" sisters and brothers from all others within the same generation, including collaterals (48, 433–35, 437, 509). "Given the consanguine family, which involved own brothers and sisters and also collateral brothers and sisters in the marriage relation, . . . it was only necessary to exclude the former from the group, and retain the latter, to change the consanguine into the punaluan family" (433). Indeed, the distinction between "own" and "collateral" emerges from the exclusion of one set of siblings as possible marriage partners. The final step in this sequence was taken with the inception of the gens — which Morgan saw as the most crucial achievement of the era — and involved the extension of the exclusion from marriage to collateral siblings within the same gens.

> It is evident that the punaluan family was formed out of the consanguine. Brothers ceased to marry their own sisters; and after the gentile organization had worked upon society its complete results, their collateral sisters as well. But in the interval they shared their remaining wives in common. In like manner, sisters ceased marrying their own brothers, and after a long period of time their collateral brothers; but they shared their remaining husbands in common. (437)

The exclusion from marriage of collaterals within the gens brought into being the categorical distinction between consanguines and affines (466, 509–10).

In the three eras of savagery, then, Morgan imagines a series of exclusions or marriage prohibitions that gradually establish the distinctions central to his understanding of kinship: those between generations, between lineal and collateral, and between consanguinity and affinity. It is significant that Morgan calls these marriage prohibitions exclusions rather than incest taboos. With the use of the term exclusion, Morgan places an emphasis on a prior undifferentiated mass of relations, out of which these exclusions gradually carve a set of distinguishable categories. He does not envision a taboo being applied to a set of preexisting kinship categories.

The logic that drives this succession of exclusions is one of "natural selection," which involves the gradual recognition of the "evils" that result from the failure to distinguish certain relations and prohibit their intermarriage (47, 58–60, 433–34, 466–69, 509). The transition from the consanguine into the punaluan family, Morgan argues, "was produced by the gradual exclusion of own brothers and sisters from the marriage relation, the evils of which could not forever escape human observation" (433). The sequence of exclusions also involved a gradual recognition of the "beneficial influence" (509) that was the consequence of excluding certain relations from marriage, and resulted in "superior men" (74) and "more vigorous stock" (468).

> To effect the exclusion of the one class and the retention of the other was a difficult process, because it involved a radical change in the composition of the family, not to say in the ancient plan of domestic life. It also required the surrender of a privilege which savages would be slow to make. Commencing, it may be supposed, in isolated cases, and with a slow recognition of its advantages, it remained an experiment through immense expanses of time; introduced partially at first, then becoming general, and finally universal among the advancing tribes, still in savagery, among whom the movement originated. It affords a good illustration of the operation of the principle of natural selection. (433–34)

Morgan will contrast the logic of this natural selection, which works through exclusions relating to marriage and drives the first half of the evolutionary trajectory, with the logic of labor and property, which works through exclusions relating to inheritance and drives the second half. In the epoch of savagery, one is far from the "spontaneous" and indiscriminate mating and subsistence of the previous promiscuous era. Yet the advances, in Morgan's view, were driven by natural selection and remained submerged within the overall framework of natural maternal kinship and the residual promiscuity of group marriage.

Like the advances made in kinship relations, those made in economics and subsistence were crucial, but not yet sufficient to remove humans from their encompassment by nature. The stages of savagery begin with the gathering of fruits and nuts, and proceed to fishing and the discovery of fire, and finally to hunting with bows and arrows. While the effort to subsist is no longer spontaneous, still this labor did not yet involve the transformation of re/productive resources that would generate wealth and result in substantial property. Just as plants and animals remain embedded within their natural habitat, so too land, houses, and all other resources remain embedded within what Morgan understood to be the more natural matrilineal gens. "With the institution of the gens came the first great rule of inheritance, which distributed the effects of a deceased person among his gentiles" (538). The nascent logic of labor and property is here encompassed by the natural kinship relations of maternity and the matrilineal gens, which are characterized by community and communal sharing. These will be posed against the final "individuality" of paternity, private property, and lineal inheritance that heralds civilization (see Coward 1983, 63–67).

Barbarism and the Progress of Patrimonial Exclusions

As an antithesis to the thesis of savagery, the growing logic of labor, property, and paternity comes into conflict with the "natural" communalism of maternal kinship as Morgan's evolutionary trajectory unfolds. In terms of kinship, the epoch of barbarism begins with the matrilineal gens, the unit of kinship that Morgan sees as the most basic form in the absence of knowledge of paternity ([1877] 1974, 402, 442). Following on the sequence of matrimonial exclusions that had generated distinctions in kind (generational, lineal, collateral, consanguineal, affinal) in the period of savagery, barbarism added only a quantitative exclusion, or distinction in number, with the gradual reduction in the number of spouses allowed in a matrimonial union. But this quantitative exclusion is seen as a crucial one since it is linked to the emergence of paternity as a category.

> The custom which led the more advanced savage to recognize one among a number of wives as his principal wife, ripened in time into the prac-

tice of pairing, and in making this wife a companion and associate in the maintenance of a family. With the growth of the propensity to pair came an increased certainty of the paternity of children. (510)

The possibility of paternity is here tied to the marriage of pairs. Yet in the age of barbarians, the exclusivity of pairing marriage was not yet firmly achieved — because either husband or wife could "seek a new mate at pleasure," and neither had rights to expect exclusive cohabitation (510–11).

> The old conjugal system [that is, group marriage], now reduced to narrower limits by the gradual disappearance of the punaluan groups, still environed the advancing family, which it was to follow to the verge of civilization. Its reduction to zero was a condition precedent to the introduction of monogamy. (511)

Out of the diffuse promiscuous relatedness and natural maternal kinship of the savage epoch, Morgan charts a course of development that is marked by progressive exclusions that carve out smaller and smaller marital units (400). By the early stages of barbarism, that unit has come close to the "zero point" of monogamous marriage. Still, to the extent that monogamy is not yet assured, any nascent recognition of paternity remains encompassed by the "natural kinship" of maternity and the matrilineal gens.

This liminal situation might have been maintained indefinitely had property not taken the place of natural selection as the prime mover of the evolutionary sequence (see Sahlins 1976, 60). The impulse to develop the idea of property derived from the domestication of animals in the Eastern hemisphere and the beginnings of agriculture in the Western hemisphere. In contrast to labor in the epoch of savagery—which was productive of tools though not sufficient to wrest the re/productive potential of land and animals from the encompassing grasp of nature—in barbarism this is precisely what was achieved. It was not the simple gathering of the fruits of the earth that gave rise to property but rather the cultivation and transformation of land through labor (540, 542, 553). Likewise, it was not the simple hunting of game that gave rise to property but rather the domestication and "husbandry" of animals through labor (542, 553). Several assumptions are made here: that those who labored should own the fruits of their labor (see Locke [1690] 1988); that those who labored in the cultivation of land and the domestication of animals were men; and that men therefore owned the productive resources of land and domesticated animals (see Coward 1983, 67).

The state of affairs created by the multiplication of property due to the rise of agriculture and the domestication of animals engendered what Morgan saw as an intolerable contradiction. Under the laws of inheritance within the matrilineal gens, a man could not pass on property earned by his labor to those whom he was beginning to see as his own children because they belonged to the gens of their mother.

> The natural remedy was a change of descent from the female line to the male. All that was needed to effect the change was an adequate motive. After domestic animals began to be reared in flocks and herds, becoming thereby a source of subsistence as well as objects of individual property, and after tillage had led to the ownership of houses and lands in severalty, an antagonism would be certain to arise against the prevailing form of gentile inheritance, because it excluded the owner's children, whose paternity was becoming more assured, and gave his property to his gentile kindred. A contest for a new rule of inheritance, shared in by fathers and their children, would furnish a motive sufficiently powerful to effect the change. With property accumulating in masses and assuming permanent forms, and with an increased proportion of it held by individual ownership, descent in the female line was certain of overthrow, and the substitution of the male line equally assured. (Morgan [1877] 1974, 355)

What is significant here is that although, by the barbarian epoch, paternity had been suspected or recognized (if not yet fully assured by monogamous marriage), there was no motive to effect any social consequences of paternity until the institution of property provided such motivation (67, 354–55; see also Coward 1983, 63–66). In contrast to the maternal relation, which was thought to generate a natural form of social relation in the matrilineal gens (but one whose maternal communalism was inherently antithetical to ideas of individual property), the paternal relation was seen as incapable of generating any social form *until property was added to it*. It was only by "enterprising up" paternity that there was cause to bring into being the patrilineal gens.

Yet even after the invention of the patrilineal gens, two further steps needed to be taken. From the undifferentiated blur of the patrilineal gens, the scope of inheritance had to be narrowed through a further set of exclusions. From among the entire membership of the gens, the agnatic kindred had to be distinguished, and from the agnatic kindred, a man's "own" children had to be distinguished. Continuing on from the passage just cited, Morgan notes:

For a time, in all probability, they [a man's children] would share in the distribution of the estate with the remaining agnates; but an extension of the principle by which the agnates cut off the remaining gentiles, would in time result in the exclusion of the agnates beyond the children and an exclusive inheritance in the children. Farther than this, the son would now be brought in the line of succession to the office of his father. ([1877] 1974, 355–56)

Again, Morgan's trajectory proceeds by a logic of progressive exclusions from a larger undifferentiated mass through which ever smaller units are delineated: the gens, then the agnatic kindred, and finally a man's "own" line (75). Indeed, here the restrictive categories of father and son along with the line relating them emerge only after numerous epochs, tremendous effort, and as the end point of a long series of exclusions.

As Morgan outlines this progression, it is clear that it is the addition of labor that establishes rights over property (land and domestic animals). Moreover, it is evident that this labor-added value, which results in property, is what motivates the shift in inheritance from the maternal to the paternal gens and the subsequent distinctions between the agnatic kindred and the entire gens (in the "second great rule of inheritance" [541–48]) and between one's "own" children and the agnatic kindred or collateral lines (in the "third great rule of inheritance," [553]). Speaking of the Latin, Greek, and Hebrew tribes, Morgan first notes their appreciation of domestic animals, which given their ability to multiply, "revealed to the human mind its first conception of wealth" (553). He then goes on to comment on the significance of labor on the land in shifting the mode of inheritance.

Following upon this [the domestication of animals], in [the] course of time, was the systematical cultivation of the earth, which tended to identify the family with the soil, and render it a property-making organization. It soon found expression, in the Latin, Grecian and Hebrew tribes, in the family under paternal power, involving slaves and servants. Since the labor of the father and his children became incorporated more and more with the land, with the production of domestic animals, and with the creation of merchandise, it would not only tend to individualize the family, now monogamian, but also to suggest the superior claims of children to the inheritance of the property they had assisted in creating. Before lands were cultivated, flocks and herds would naturally fall under the joint ownership of persons united in a group, on the basis of kin, for subsistence. Agnatic inheritance would be apt to assert itself in this condition of things. But when lands had become the subject of property, and allotments to individuals had resulted in individual ownership, the third great rule of inheritance, which gave the property to the children of the deceased owner, was certain to supervene upon agnatic inheritance. (553)

It is not surprising that the paternal line is thought to be demarcated by relation to labor in the domestication of animals (see Franklin n.d.) and cultivation of land (see Delaney 1991). Indeed, in this extraordinary passage, Morgan implicitly draws a parallel between the control over reproductive resources in monogamous marriage and the control over productive resources in livestock "husbandry" and agriculture. He visualizes the achievement of both monogamous marriage and landed property as an enclosure of re/productive resources, and both are achieved in tandem during the last stage of barbarism. When Morgan is making a case for the Greek's recognition of private landed property, he observes:

> Mention is made in the Iliad of *fences* around the cultivated fields, of an *enclosure of fifty acres,* half of which was fit for vines and the remainder for tillage; and it is said of Tydeus that he lived in a mansion rich in resources, and had corn-producing fields in abundance. There is no reason to doubt that lands were then fenced and measured, and held by individual ownership. It indicates a large degree of progress in the knowledge of property and its uses. ([1877] 1974, 552)

This passage immediately recalls another kind of enclosure: that of women in the form of monogamous marriage in the late barbarian epoch. When Morgan traces the development of monogamous marriage, he notes that Tacitus, in writing about the German tribes, "mentions the two material facts in which the substance of monogamy is found: firstly, that each man was contented with a single wife . . . and, secondly, that the women lived *fenced around* with chastity" (479; emphasis added). As Morgan goes on to survey the development of monogamy among the Greeks, he comments on the "studied selfishness at work among the males" that "reveals itself in their plan of domestic life, which in the higher ranks secluded the wife to enforce an exclusive cohabitation, without admitting the reciprocal obligation on the part of her husband" (482). In a footnote that continues for a page and a half, he details, with some dismay, the extent of the seclusion of women under the Grecian patriarchal family (483–84). Morgan actually appears to find the patriarchal family—with its overbearing paternal power, seclusion of women, and absolute servitude of women, children, and slaves—to be something of an embarrassment, a phase with "limited" influence on the overall evolutionary trajectory (28, 511). Nevertheless, he values it for the "individuality" it produces. What concerns Morgan is the individuality of the restricted line of patrilineal inheritance that is produced in a family with "a single male head and an exclusive cohabitation" (511; see also 474–75, 477). The individuality of patrilineal inheritance of property in the later stages of evolution is explicitly contrasted with the absence of property rights and the communalism of matrilineality, in which the individual is encompassed within the group. As Rosalind Coward remarks, paternal rights, individuality, and individual property rights are conflated (1983, 63).

Two points may be made at this juncture. First, it is important to stress that, for Morgan, property rather than paternity is the prime mover:

> The growth of property and the desire for its transmission to children was, in reality, the moving power which brought in monogamy to insure legitimate heirs, and to limit their number to the actual progeny of the married pair. . . . It explains the new usage which made its appearance in the Upper Status of barbarism; namely, the seclusion of wives. An implication to this effect arises from the circumstance that a necessity for the seclusion of the wife must have existed at the time, and which seems to have been so formidable that the plan of domestic life among the civilized Greeks was, in reality, a system of female confinement and restraint. ([1877] 1974, 485)

It is thus property that motivates the delimitation of paternity; paternity does not motivate property. Second, there is a double enterprise here: property enterprises up paternity; and the economies of paternity encompass and enterprise up a henceforth subordinated as well as more "natural" maternal re/productivity. The economies of kinship and the paternity of culture proceed through parallel enclosures of land and women.[2]

Civilization and the Fine Lines of the Spermatic Economy

For Morgan, the status of civilization is achieved with the advent of exclusive monogamous marriage and the consequent certainty of the restriction of the male line of inheritance to the closest degree of relatedness. The exclusions of the previous epochs culminate here in the epitome of what counts as civilization: a line of inheritance of accumulated male capital (where spermatic and economic resources are now nearly indistinguishable) narrowed into the thinnest channel of transmission.

The progression Morgan envisions is striking: from that diffuse, undifferentiated mass of relatedness defined by primitive promiscuity, natural maternity, and communal sharing, the epochs unfold through a series of exclusions—first matrimonial and then patrimonial—out of which gradually emerge a set of differentiated categories and the distinct qualities of their relation. At the beginning of the progression, the "germ" of property was encompassed by the natural indistinction of maternal relation and community. By the end, its full flowering in paternity has encompassed, in turn, its natural maternal and communal origins, and in a terrible passion of accumulation, engendered hierarchy where equality once reigned (560). Morgan shudders at what his evolutionary trajectory has wrought, and he looks forward to the next step in the progression by harking back to the egalitarian values of earlier epochs and forecasting "a revival, in a higher form, of the liberty, equality, and fraternity of the ancient gentes" (562).

PATERNITY AND THE REGULATION OF THE "SCARCE PRODUCT" IN LÉVI-STRAUSS'S *THE ELEMENTARY STRUCTURES OF KINSHIP*

It is no wonder that Lévi-Strauss dedicated *The Elementary Structures of Kinship* to Morgan, for his 1949 volume is virtually the mirror image of *Ancient Society*. The problem that motivates Morgan's origin story is how to generate a precisely demarcated line of inheritance and capital accumulation out of a primal state of diffuse relationality, indistinction, and promiscuity. This is solved by tracing the imagined development of this demarcation through a series of matrimonial and patrimonial exclusions. Lévi-Strauss's origin story takes up where Morgan's leaves off—with the isolated nuclear family—and it is motivated by the problem of how to generate the structures of sociality from this initial state in which they are entirely lacking. As is well known, he accomplishes this through the institution of reciprocal exchange, which follows on the incest taboo. In the remainder of *The Elementary Structures,* he analyzes a series of forms of marital alliance that are more and more "inclusive" in their integrative force. Like Morgan, Lévi-Strauss links his understanding of sexuality and marriage closely to ideas about economics, although the analogies he uses focus on scarcity, risk, speculation, and market exchange in contrast to Morgan's analogies of labor, inheritance, and accumulation of property. And like Morgan, Lévi-Strauss's image of culture depends on the enterprising up of a natural base—but here, consanguinity and female sexuality are "marketed" into a cultural form of alliance and exchange managed by fathers and brothers. In transforming female sexuality by regulating its distribution and consumption, and by taking speculative risks in the exchange of "scarce products," men claim a patent on kinship as paternal (and fraternal) property and propriety. Paternity, proprietary rights in the exchange of women, and culture are all but simultaneous and indistinguishable.

Natural Distinctions and Cultural Relations

Perhaps nowhere is Lévi-Strauss's image of the state of nature more clearly articulated than in his article modestly titled "The Family."

> As [Edward Burnett] Tylor has shown almost a century ago . . . in order to free itself from a wild struggle for existence, [the family] was confronted with the very simple choice of "either marrying-out or being killed-out." The alternative was between biological families living in juxtaposition and endeavoring to remain closed, self-perpetuating units, over-ridden by their fears, hatreds, and ignorances, and the systematic establishment, through the incest prohibition, of links of intermarriage between them, thus succeeding to build, out of the artificial bonds of affinity, a true human society despite, and even in contradiction with, the isolating influence of consanguinity. (1956, 278)

Here, the isolated nuclear family is given as an inherent fact of nature and biology. It is not the end point of a long evolutionary sequence of exclusions but a precultural condition for human existence in the state of nature. The particular form that Lévi-Strauss envisions for the transition from nature to culture depends on this understanding of what belongs to nature and what is the province of culture.

Interestingly, Lévi-Strauss sees the "double rhythm of receiving and giving" as central to *both* nature and culture. But "the two moments of this rhythm, as produced by nature, are not viewed indifferently by culture" (Lévi-Strauss [1949] 1969, 30), and this difference creates an opening for the transition from nature to culture. In the first moment of this rhythm, nature's "receiving" beat of biological kinship renders "culture powerless, for a child's heredity is integrally inscribed in the genes transmitted by the parents; whatever they are, such will be the child" (30). Indeed, Lévi-Strauss views descent and heredity as "stable," "repetitive," and "doubly determined": "firstly as a law—there is no spontaneous generation—and secondly as a specification of the law, for nature not only says that one must have parents, but that one will be like them" (30–31). In the second moment of this rhythm, nature's "giving" beat of marriage leaves an opening for culture. "Nature is satisfied with affirming the law, but is indifferent to its contents. . . . Thus, mutations aside, nature contains one solitary principle of indetermination, revealed in the arbitrariness of marriage" (31). Finishing the narrative sequence with one of his rhetorical flourishes, Lévi-Strauss proclaims the distinction and the transition:

> Culture yields to the inevitability of biological heredity. . . . But culture, although it is powerless before descent, becomes aware of its rights, and of itself, with the completely different phenomenon of marriage, in which nature for once has not already had the last word. There only, but there finally culture can and must, under pain of not existing, firmly declare "Me first," and tell nature, "You go no further." (31)

What might appear as a similarity between Morgan's exclusions and Lévi-Strauss's incest taboo is belied by the fact that the latter's taboo is less an exclusion than an injunction to relate—to establish affinal relationships outside the group. Whereas Morgan's exclusions carve ever smaller and more distinct units out of a previously undifferentiated mass of matrimonial and patrimonial relations, Lévi-Strauss's taboo enjoins integration and ever-more-inclusive relations between units that begin already as small and distinct as possible.

The overarching developmental frameworks that Morgan and Lévi-Strauss construct in their origin stories contrast in a number of ways. Unlike Morgan, for whom the isolated nuclear family and a clearly demarcated line of heredity/inheritance were the ultimate cultural productions, Lévi-Strauss positions biological heredity, descent (lines), gender distinctions, and the family firmly in a precultural nature. Kinship categories and lines of descent do not emerge as the result of exclusions, as they do in Morgan's narrative; rather, their distinctions are already given in the nature of things. The problem of culture, for Lévi-Strauss, was *not to create but rather to relate* these discrete, bounded units into a scheme of sociality (see Wagner 1967, 1975, 1977; Strathern 1988, 1992a, 1992b).

"The System of the Scarce Product"

Both Morgan and Lévi-Strauss generate kinship in the state of civilization/culture by enterprising up a base of kinship relatedness that is presumed to be natural. We have already seen how Morgan does this through a movement that adds property to paternity and subsequently encompasses maternal re/productive resources. Although Lévi-Strauss accomplishes the same end through a more abstract articulation of nature, culture, and the incest taboo, beside this structural logic there lies another line of argumentation that resorts to "the system of the scarce product" (that is, women), and imagines the enterprising spirit of fathers and brothers, who control and regulate the distribution and consumption of this scarce product. In the process, Lévi-Strauss tilts the axis of articulation from the transmission of accumulated capital within a family and across generations, to the regulation of scarce resources within a generation and across family lines.

At one level, Lévi-Strauss's depiction of the incest taboo is the simple working out of a structural logic of opposition and mediation. The power of the incest taboo to provoke the transition from nature to culture resides in its mediation of the opposition: for the taboo is simultaneously both nature (universal) and culture (a rule) (Lévi-Strauss [1949] 1969, 12).[3] Yet the abstract (and seemingly neutral) structural articulation of the relation between nature and culture, between human sexuality and the rule of marital exchange, quickly takes on twin narrative entanglements relating to gendered and economic forces. Although this is a volume that inaugurates structural analysis—and accordingly Lévi-Strauss explicitly rejects any account that relies on biology, innate tendencies, historical contingencies, or reconstructions (12–15)—he nevertheless paradoxically constructs an account of the incest taboo and the origin of reciprocity that relies on all of these. Moreover, although this is a volume that, following Marcel Mauss's *The Gift* ([1950] 1990), investigates the explicitly noncapitalist forms of the "elementary structures" of exchange and reciprocity, he paradoxically characterizes both their origin and nature in decidedly capitalist terms. While not denying either the structuralist nature of *The Elementary Structures,* or its singular focus on the forms of noncapitalist exchange, I am nonetheless interested in exploring the ways in which both of these intentions are controverted in specific ways by other cultural narratives of gendered economies.

Slipping into his functionalist disguise, Lévi-Strauss asserts that the "prime rôle of culture is to ensure the group's existence as a group," and thus the cultural intervention into nature—in the form of a rule—"is raised, and resolved in the affirmative, every time the group is faced with the insufficiency or the risky distribution of a valuable of fundamental importance" ([1949] 1969, 32). He argues that the rationing of commodities during times of crisis is not a recent invention but a basic requirement of social order.

> "The system of the scarce product" constitutes an extremely general model. . . . a state of affairs regarded as virtually normal in primitive society. Thus, "the system of the scarce product," as expressed in collective measures of control [of distribution and consumption], is much less an innovation, due to modern conditions of warfare and the worldwide nature of our economy, than the resurgence of a set of procedures which are familiar to primitive societies and necessary to the group if its coherence is not to be continually compromised. (32)

One might wonder why Lévi-Strauss gives himself this initial scarcity with regard to sexuality and marriage since even he recognizes that simple demographics argue to the contrary (37). According to Lévi-Strauss, this scarcity naturally arises for two reasons: men are inherently polygamous and women are inherently unequally desirable. "Social and biological observation combine to suggest that, in man, these [polygamous] tendencies are natural and universal, and that only limitations born of the environment and culture are responsible for their suppression" (37). As a consequence, this "deep polygamous tendency, which exists among all men, always makes the number of available women seem insufficient" (38). Yet the problem is not simply that there never seems to be enough women but also that all women are not "equally desirable." "Hence, the demand for women is in actual fact, or to all intents and purposes, always in a state of disequilibrium and tension" (38). In a remarkable combination of appeals to biology, innate tendencies, and historical reconstruction, Lévi-Strauss fabricates "the system of the scarce woman" in order to motivate the institution of the incest taboo. In the process, the abstract logic of nature and culture takes on a gendered economy of power, desire, and unequal attraction and accumulation.[4]

These hierarchical asymmetries of gender and power are part of the "nature" that Lévi-Strauss gives himself as an initial condition.

> It might be expected that privileges would arise in that natural aggregation called the family, by reason of the greater intimacy of its interindividual contacts, and by the lack of any social rule tending to limit this family and to establish equilibrium in it. We are not suggesting that

every family would automatically maintain a monopoly of its women. This would be to assert the institutional priority of the family over the group, a supposition far from our mind. We merely postulate, without posing the question of the historical precedence of the one over the other, that the specific viscosity of the family aggregation would act in this direction, and that the combined results would confirm this action. As has been shown, such an eventuality is incompatible with the vital demands not only of primitive society but of society in general. (41)

The "specific viscosity" of the family's distinctions of power and desire are such that paternal and fraternal (but presumably not maternal) incest — the power to "keep to oneself" (where "one" is always male) — is the definition of the precultural state of nature. The incest taboo is then the mechanism put in place to counter these inherent tendencies toward hierarchy (between men) and the inequitable accumulation of scarce products. The incest taboo

> refuses to sanction the natural inequality of the distribution of the sexes within the family, and on the only possible basis it institutes freedom of access for every individual [*sic*] to the women of the group. This basis is, in short, that neither fraternity nor paternity can be put forward as claims to a wife, but that the sole validity of these claims lies in the fact that all men are in equal competition for all women, their respective relationships being defined in terms of the group, and not the family. (42)

The incest taboo effects the transition from nature (constituted by the paternal and fraternal rights to unequal accumulation of the scarce products in women) to culture (framed as the paternal and fraternal rights to regulate the market of scarce products to ensure the equal distribution and consumption of women). As Gayle Rubin pointed out long ago,

> "Exchange of women" is a shorthand for expressing that the social relations of a kinship system specify that men have certain rights in their female kin, and that women do not have the same rights either to themselves or to their male kin. In this sense, the exchange of women is a profound perception of a system in which women do not have full rights to themselves. (1975, 177)

But in Lévi-Strauss's imagination (unlike that of Morgan, Engels, or Rubin), women *never* had full rights in themselves, even in his wildest vision of the precultural state. The transition from nature to culture does not precipitate the "world historical defeat" of women, as it does for Friedrich Engels ([1942] 1972, 120) and even Morgan ([1877] 1974, 481–82). For Lévi-Strauss, the world historical defeat of women was a natural fact. In this calculus of the scarce product, all that changes in the transition from nature to culture is that the system shifts from one of unregulated accumulation ("keeping to one-self") with its hierarchical implications to one of regulated market exchange with its egalitarian consequences (for men, but not for women).

If Morgan's evolutionary narrative concludes with the enclosure and re-striction of wives within the bounds of the monogamous nuclear family, Lévi-Strauss's narrative commences with the release of daughters and sisters from the incestuous bounds of the nuclear family. If Morgan's account ends with the cultural accumulation of re/productive resources and their transmission from father to son, Lévi-Strauss's begins with the suppression of such "natu-ral" accumulative tendencies among both fathers and sons, and an injunction to circulate the scarce product among "all men." And if the enterprising logic of kinship in culture is, for Morgan, one of property and the accumulation of capital, for Lévi-Strauss, it is one of regulatory mechanisms that control the distribution and consumption of the scarce product.

The Speculative Risks of the Exchange

To the extent that Lévi-Strauss's analogy for kinship in the state of culture in-volves the regulation of the distribution and consumption of scarce women, then different regulatory systems are distinguished by reference to their rela-tive inclusiveness — their relative ability to risk longer and longer cycles of ex-change in order to integrate more and more groups into a system of exchange. The increasing exclusiveness of Morgan's three great rules of inheritance is mirrored by the increasing inclusiveness of Lévi-Strauss's three elementary structures of alliance: sister exchange, patrilateral cross-cousin marriage, and matrilateral cross-cousin marriage.

Lévi-Strauss's insistence on an initial equality of men, which is consequent on the incest taboo and regulation of the exchange, has further consequences for his analysis of systems of marriage. It means that he begins from the propo-sition that marital alliances involve the exchange of a woman for a woman, not a woman for goods — a provision that is meant to guarantee the equality of "all men."[5] The simplest way to fulfill this requirement is the symmetrical and immediate exchange of sisters between two exogamous groups. The ad-vantage of this strategy is that the exchange is immediate and there is little risk; its limitation is that it is capable of integrating only two groups. With the symmetrical but delayed exchange of patrilateral cross-cousin marriage (group A gives a woman in one generation to group B, which returns the woman's daughter to group A in the second generation), the risk increases since both the number of groups and the time involved to complete the exchange increase. But so, too, does the level of integration increase. It is, however, only with the asymmetrical and delayed exchange found in matrilateral cross-cousin marriage (group A gives a woman to group B, which gives a woman to group C, . . . which gives a woman to group N, which gives a woman back to group A), that the full integrative potential of the elementary structures is achieved.

> A human group need only proclaim the law of marriage with the mother's brother's daughter for a vast cycle of reciprocity between all generations and lineages to be organized, as harmonious and ineluctable as any physical or biological law, whereas marriage with the father's sister's daughter forces the interruption and reversal of collaborations from generation to generation and from lineage to lineage. In one case, the overall cycle of reciprocity is co-extensive with the group itself both in time and in space, subsisting and developing with it. In the other case, the multiple cycles which are continually created fracture and distort the unity of the group. They fracture this unity because there are as many cycles as there are lineages, and they distort it because the direction of the cycles must be reversed with each generation. (Lévi-Strauss [1949] 1969, 450)

Nevertheless, Lévi-Strauss suggests that, as the integrative potential of matrilateral cross-cousin marriage increases both the number of groups and amount of time involved in the exchange, the risks involved increase dramatically. Because Lévi-Strauss's egalitarian presuppositions require an exchange of a woman for a woman (not a woman for valuables), the matrilateral cycle is not completed until the initial woman given by group A is reciprocated by a woman returned by group N. He therefore sees the "risk" as increasing substantially as the cycle lengthens.

Lévi-Strauss's discussion of cross-cousin marriage often engages in an abstract and almost mathematical accounting of the balance between "credits" and "debts." At various points, though, his accounting becomes entangled with further economic analogies to the point where one might confuse this primer on marriage alliance with a textbook on the workings of capitalism and the stock exchange. Referring to the symmetrical yet delayed exchange of patrilateral cross-cousin marriage, he notes:

It can be said that marriage with the father's sister's daughter contrasts with other forms of cross-cousin marriage as an economy based on exchange for cash contrasts with economies practising [*sic*] operations on deferred terms. . . . Marriage with the patrilateral cousin is indeed a form of marriage by exchange, but such an elementary form that the exchange can only be described as an exchange in kind, since the substantial identity of the thing claimed and the thing ceded is pursued, through the sister, in her own daughter. It represents the Cheap-Jack in the scale of marriage transactions. (449)

If patrilateral cross-cousin marriage is the "Cheap-Jack," matrilateral cross-cousin marriage rivals Wall Street in its speculative character.

Generalized exchange establishes a system of operations conducted "on *credit*." . . . There must be the *confidence* that the cycle will close again, and that after a period of time a woman will eventually be received in compensation for the woman initially surrendered. The belief is the basis of trust, and *confidence opens up credit*. In the final analysis, the whole system exists only because the group adopting it is prepared, in the broadest meaning of the term, *to speculate*. But the broad sense also implies the narrow sense: the *speculation* brings in a *profit*, in the sense that with generalized exchange the group can live as richly and as complexly as its size, structure and density allow. . . .

[G]eneralized exchange *gains* "at every turn," provided, of course, it takes the initial *risk*. But the element of chance is to be seen in it in more ways than one. Born as it is out of collective *speculation*, generalized exchange, by the multiplicity of the combinations which it sanctions, and the desire for safeguards which it arouses, invites the particular and private *speculations* of the partners. Generalized exchange not only results from chance but invites it, for one can guard oneself doubly against the *risk:* qualitatively, by *multiplying the cycles* of exchange in which one participates, and quantitatively, by *accumulating securities*, i.e., by seeking to corner as many women as possible from the wife-giving lineage. The widening of the circle of affines and polygamy are thus corollaries of generalized exchange (although not exclusive to it). (266; emphasis added)

Here, the cautious regulation of the "system of the scarce product" has given way to a vast speculative market in credits and debts — a market whose profits stand in direct relation to its risks. While fathers and brothers have, in Lévi-

Strauss's scheme, always had rights over women, what changes is their willingness to risk their capital in a market that is ever expanding—from the precultural state of the isolated family, where fathers and brothers "kept to themselves," to the cautious immediacy of sister exchange, to the Cheap-Jack of patrilateral cross-cousin marriage, to the Wall Street speculations of matrilateral cross-cousin marriage. I suggest that the analogy that focuses on the power of paternity (and fraternity) to mobilize more "natural" female resources through the enterprising spirit of the market is not "just" a metaphor but an analogy central to anthropological understandings of what kinship and the creation of culture are all about.

Whereas Morgan's restrictive economy of inheritance ends up with the breakdown of the original equality (of men and women) in the gens, Lévi-Strauss's expansive economy of marriage exchange ends with the breakdown of the equality among men that was instituted through the regulated exchange of women. In Lévi-Strauss's scenario, the speculative character of matrilateral cross-cousin marriage encourages strategies to guard against the risk involved in the delayed exchange. These strategies—the multiplication of cycles and the accumulation of women in polygamy—have the effect of generating hierarchy, thus contravening the initial fundamental egalitarian conditions of exchange (226). Indeed, for Lévi-Strauss, the contradictions involved in the hierarchical implications of generalized exchange lead to the transition between the elementary and complex structures of kinship.[6]

Thus, the suppression of equality in favor of hierarchy marks Lévi-Strauss's understanding of the transition from elementary to complex structures of kinship as much as it does Morgan's conceptualization of the transition from savagery to civilization. Both men mourn what has been lost in the course of the developments they have traced. Yet while Morgan ends *Ancient Society* with a hopeful vision of a future "revival, in a higher form, of the liberty, equality [for both men and women], and fraternity of the ancient gentes" ([1877] 1974, 562), Lévi-Strauss concludes *The Elementary Structures* with wistful nostalgia for the "joys" of a world "eternally denied to social man, . . . in which one might *keep [women] to oneself*" ([1949] 1969, 497).

THE ECONOMIES OF KINSHIP THEORY

In their imaginings of the origin of culture, Lévi-Strauss and Morgan have, between them, managed to generate almost the entire range of capitalist economic utilities. For Lévi-Strauss, the fullest realization of the integrative potential of the elementary structures of kinship is achieved by an expansion of the enterprising spirit of the market — by the willingness to risk one's capital (in women) in exchange for future return. In Morgan's account, by contrast, the fullest realization of kinship is achieved by the discriminating potential of property to contract and demarcate a restricted line of patrilineal inheritance and capital accumulation. They begin from mirror-image premises about the state of nature (Morgan's diffuse relationality; Lévi-Strauss's predefined distinctions) and proceed to establish the origins of culture in mirror-image achievements (Morgan's restricted lines of inheritance and capital accumulation; Lévi-Strauss's suppression of natural accumulative tendencies in increasingly speculative risk and integrative exchange). Either way, however, the "progress" of kinship and origins of culture are marked by the relative control and encompassment of more natural (female) re/productive resources by the enterprising spirit that constitutes the paternity of culture.

NOTES

I wish to thank the participants of the Wenner-Gren conference, New Directions in Kinship Study, for a lively discussion of this paper, and more specifically, James Boon, Carol Delaney, Sarah Franklin, and Dan Segal for their thoughtful comments on earlier drafts of this essay.

1 Roy Wagner (1967, 230–40; 1975) developed this contrast between the creation of distinctions out of a prior undifferentiated state, on the one hand, and the creation of relation between a priori defined and bounded units, on the other, in his analysis of the difference between Daribi understandings of kinship and marriage and those of Lévi-Strauss. He generalized this contrast as a framework for comparing what different cultures presuppose as given and what they suppose must be created by culture (Wagner 1975). Marilyn Strathern developed these ideas further, using them to explore the cultural differences between Euro-American and Melanesian ideas of gender and kinship (1980, 1988) as well as to analyze English kinship (1992a) and the new reproductive technologies (1992b). The material in this essay would suggest that to imagine each of these processes as characteristic of a different type of society obscures the complexities of countervailing configurations within a single society, and that they should not be used to imagine a generalized contrast between Euro-American and other cultures.

2 Similarly, literary commons had to be "enclosed," like landed estates, in order for the concepts of the individual author, intellectual property, and copyright to come into being (see Rose 1993; Haraway 1997, 71–72).

3 Eleanor Leacock and June Nash (1981) effectively critique Lévi-Strauss's assumption of the universality of the nature-culture opposition (and its correlation with the

opposition between female and male) as well as his idea that the exchange of women mediates between nature and culture.

4 Eleanor Leacock (1981) also critiques these points in Lévi-Strauss's argument and goes on to make a much broader critique of his assumption that the exchange of women by men is a general characteristic of systems of marriage exchange.

5 Edmund Leach (1951, [1954] 1965) begins from the opposite set of assumptions: that matrilateral cross-cousin marriage fundamentally implies both hierarchy and the exchange of women for goods. For an analysis of the contrast between Leach and Lévi-Strauss on hierarchy and equality in systems of matrilateral cross-cousin marriage, see McKinnon 1991.

6 Some years later, Lévi-Strauss interposed an intermediate form—that of "house societies"—in between the elementary and complex structures of kinship. For a critique of the evolutionary implications of this sequence of structures, see Carsten and Hugh-Jones 1995, 6–21; McKinnon 1991, 30–31; 1995, 172–74.

REFERENCES

Barker-Benfield, Ben. 1974. The Spermatic Economy: A Nineteenth-Century View of Sexuality. *Feminist Studies* 1:45–74.

Carsten, Janet, and Stephen Hugh-Jones, eds. 1995. *About the House: Lévi-Strauss and Beyond.* Cambridge: Cambridge University Press.

Conkey, Margaret W., and Sarah H. Williams. 1991. Original Narratives: The Political Economy of Gender in Archaeology. In *Gender at the Crossroads of Knowledge: Feminist Anthropology in the Postmodern Era,* edited by Micaela di Leonardo. Berkeley: University of California Press.

Coward, Rosalind. 1983. *Patriarchal Precedents: Sexuality and Social Relations.* London: Routledge and Kegan Paul.

Delaney, Carol. 1986. The Meaning of Paternity and the Virgin Birth Debate. *Man,* no. 21:494–513.

———. 1991. *The Seed and the Soil: Gender and Cosmology in Turkish Society.* Berkeley: University of California Press.

Edwards, Jeanette, Sarah Franklin, Eric Hirsch, Frances Price, and Marilyn Strathern. 1993. *Technologies of Procreation: Kinship in the Age of Assisted Conception.* Manchester, U.K.: Manchester University Press.

Engels, Friedrich. [1942] 1972. *The Origin of the Family, Private Property, and the State: In the Light of the Researches of Lewis H. Morgan.* Reprint, New York: International Publishers.

Franklin, Sarah. 1997. *Embodied Progress: A Cultural Account of Assisted Conception.* New York: Routledge.

———. n.d. The Erasure of Culture from Science: An Anthropologist Considers Dolly. Paper presented at the British Association for the Advancement of Science, 9 September 1997, Leeds University.

Franklin, Sarah, and Helena Ragoné. 1998. Introduction to *Reproducing Reproduction:*

Kinship, Power, and Technological Innovation, edited by Sarah Franklin and Helena Ragoné. Philadelphia: University of Pennsylvania Press.

Haraway, Donna J. 1997. *Modest_Witness@Second_Millennium.FemaleMan©_Meets_ OncoMouse™.* New York: Routledge.

Leach, Edmund R. 1951. The Structural Implications of Matrilateral Cross-Cousin Marriage. *Journal of the Royal Anthropological Institute* 83:23–55.

———. [1954] 1965. *Political Systems of Highland Burma.* Reprint, Boston: Beacon Press.

Leacock, Eleanor. 1981. The Changing Family and Lévi-Strauss, or Whatever Happened to Fathers? In *Myths of Male Dominance: Collected Articles on Women Cross-Culturally,* edited by Eleanor Leacock. New York: Monthly Review Press.

Leacock, Eleanor, and June Nash. 1981. Ideologies of Sex: Archetypes and Stereotypes. In *Myths of Male Dominance: Collected Articles on Women Cross-Culturally,* edited by Eleanor Leacock. New York: Monthly Review Press.

Lévi-Strauss, Claude. [1949] 1969. *The Elementary Structures of Kinship.* Translated by James Harle Bell, John Richard von Steumer, and Rodney Needham. Reprint, Boston: Beacon Press.

———. 1956. The Family. In *Man, Culture, and Society,* edited by Harry L. Shapiro. New York: Oxford University Press.

Locke, John. [1690] 1988. *Two Treatises of Government.* Edited by Peter Laslett. Reprint, Cambridge: Cambridge University Press.

Mauss, Marcel. [1950] 1990. *The Gift: The Form and Reason for Exchange in Archaic Societies.* Translated by W. D. Halls. Reprint, New York: W. W. Norton.

McKinnon, Susan. 1991. *From a Shattered Sun: Hierarchy, Gender, and Alliance in the Tanimbar Islands.* Madison: University of Wisconsin Press.

———. 1995. Houses and Hierarchy: The View from a South Moluccan Society. In *About the House: Lévi-Strauss and Beyond,* edited by Janet Carsten and Stephen Hugh-Jones. Cambridge: Cambridge University Press.

Morgan, Lewis Henry. [1877] 1974. *Ancient Society, or Researches in the Lines of Human Progress from Savagery through Barbarism to Civilization.* Reprint, Gloucester, Mass.: Peter Smith.

Ragoné, Helena. 1994. *Surrogate Motherhood: Conception in the Heart.* Boulder, Colo.: Westview Press.

Rose, Mark. 1993. *Authors and Owners: The Invention of Copyright.* Cambridge: Harvard University Press.

Rubin, Gayle. 1975. The Traffic in Women: Notes on the "Political Economy" of Sex. In *Toward an Anthropology of Women,* edited by Rayna R. Reiter. New York: Monthly Review Press.

Sahlins, Marshall. 1976. *Culture and Practical Reason.* Chicago: University of Chicago Press.

Strathern, Marilyn. 1980. No Nature, No Culture: The Hagen Case. In *Nature, Culture, and Gender,* edited by Carol P. MacCormack and Marilyn Strathern. Cambridge: Cambridge University Press.

———. 1988. *The Gender of the Gift: Problems with Women and Problems with Society in Melanesia.* Berkeley: University of California Press.

————. 1992a. *After Nature: English Kinship in the Late Twentieth Century.* Cambridge: Cambridge University Press.

————. 1992b. *Reproducing the Future: Anthropology, Kinship, and the New Reproductive Technologies.* New York: Routledge.

Wagner, Roy. 1967. *The Curse of Souw: Principles of Daribi Clan Definition and Alliance.* Chicago: University of Chicago Press.

————. 1975. *The Invention of Culture.* Englewood Cliffs, N.J.: Prentice-Hall.

————. 1977. Analogic Kinship: A Daribi Example. *American Ethnologist* 4, no. 4:623–42.

Wright, Robert. 1994. Our Cheating Hearts: Devotion and Betrayal, Marriage and Divorce; How Evolution Shaped Human Love. *Time* 33 (August 15): 36–44.

Yanagisako, Sylvia J., and Carol Delaney. 1995. Naturalizing Power. In *Naturalizing Power: Essays in Feminist Cultural Analysis,* edited by Sylvia J. Yanagisako and Carol Delaney. New York: Routledge.

CHAPTER 11

Biologization Revisited: Kinship Theory
in the Context of the New Biologies
Sarah Franklin

Perhaps it was . . . around 1860 or so, when the cultivation of nature was replaced by
its own grounding naturalism, that is, by apprehension of nature as a natural system. Given a concern with reproduction ("inheritance") of organisms, one might
suggest that evolutionary thinking also facilitated the equation of procreation and
biology. The "natural facts" of life were natural in the sense of belonging to the
biology of the species. — Marilyn Strathern, *After Nature*

Amid the many transformations that have reshaped the study of kinship over
time, the question of the significance of biological facts has remained a persistent quagmire — as easy to fall into as it is difficult to leave behind. This
sticky controversy is historically more profound and seemingly intractable in
British and U.S. anthropology than in other, especially continental European,
traditions, but it nonetheless continues to be central to the debate about kinship. This controversy has taken on additional dimensions as biology has become more visibly and globally dominant as a science in the second half of the
twentieth century — a transformation that has seen the biology of plants, animals, humans, and microorganisms become more technologically mediated
and amenable to reconstruction. Superficially, it can be said that the domain
of the biological is today more visibly "constructed" than ever before. This has
consequences not only for how we think about biology, biotechnology, and
our relations to them but also for how we figure what counts as a biological
tie. Exploring in more detail some of the issues laid out in the introduction
to this volume, this essay revisits the question of what biology is "all about"
both within and beyond kinship studies.

In a manner similar to Janet Carsten's piece (this volume) on substance,
which revisits that term with an eye to both its breadth of meanings and their

consequent ambiguities, the aim here is to interrogate meanings of biology, biologization, and biological facts, arguing that they have meant quite different things to different commentators, both in relation to kinship and more generally. Unlike the term "substance," however, "biology" refers both to a body of authoritative knowledge (as in the science of reproductive biology) and a set of phenomena (as in the biology of human reproduction). In referring, therefore, to "human reproductive biology" it is arguable that a conflation of a system of knowledge with its objects occurs, whereby the study of biology becomes coterminous with the existence of an ontological reality that exists independently "out there" in the "real world" as a set of actual "facts." This is one of several ways in which the very word biology can become complicated, and in ways that are revealing of the specificity of the relations between knowing, being, and doing characteristic of post-Enlightenment secular culture in the West, or what could also be described as the discursive conditions of modernity.[1]

Paul Rabinow has introduced the term "biosociality" to portray a set of shifts whereby the biological and, in particular, the new genetics are no longer modeled on nature, but have become more visibly "modeled on culture understood as practice," thus becoming more "artificial" (1996, 99). Marilyn Strathern similarly describes "the vanishing of taken-for-granted assumptions about natural process" (1992, 180) and the "enterprising up" of life itself characteristic of the late twentieth century, in which, as Donna Haraway (1992) has claimed, nature and culture have "imploded." This view of nature having become artifice — itself a hallmark of postmodernism[2] — sets up an interesting ricochet for the analysis of both kinship and gender as well as their relation to "the facts of life." It is as if the long struggle to "denaturalize" kinship and gender, by disembedding them from the biological, has come to be accompanied by a denaturalization of biology itself from within, as it were. Not only within biological science but also within biological bodies, it has become more difficult to determine what it means to speak in "strictly biological" terms. What I am describing here as both the "new biologies" (by which I mean the material-semiotic practices of the contemporary biological sciences) and "new biologicals" (by which I refer to new entities such as cryopreserved human embryos, cloned transgenic animals, genetically modified seeds, and patented gene sequences) can be said to defamiliarize the very nature of what it is to do biology or be biological. This process of defamiliarization casts a historically distinctive kind of uncertainty onto the question of the status of "biological facts." I argue this contemporary uncertainty thus presents an opportunity to reconsider the question of the role of so-called biological facts, "biological determinism," and "biologization" in relation to kinship theory.

In asserting that biology has, in a sense, itself been denaturalized, I need to make clear at the outset that the opportunities for reanalysis of the role of biological facts in relation to gender and kinship I am describing are not offered to applaud some new, more flexible, recombinant biology that is less constraining than in the past or is to be welcomed as liberatory. The contention here is neither celebratory nor utopian. I am making a more preliminary argument suggesting that biological facts continue to matter very much to how both "kinship" and "gender" are understood, but that they do so in ways that require careful attention, and are not as self-evident as they might appear. Inevitably, I therefore use a comparison with past anthropological models of biological facts, as I also consider the new biologies as an opportunity to reflect on their histories.

Enhancing these openings is the powerful interrogation of the biological that has emerged from feminist scholarship and science studies over the past three decades. Hardly a new area of critical study, but arguably a rapidly widening area of theoretical concern, the impetus to ask what difference biology makes, as both a material and semiotic condition, has gained momentum. Amid the constant remolding of the biological that has become, among other things, a major component of new capital markets and technological innovation worldwide, both the uncertainties and authority of the life sciences have become the subject of increasing public and scholarly attention. In particular, the rapid development of new genetic technologies has placed a premium on familiar anthropological questions, such as the meaning of genealogy, parenthood, or a so-called blood tie. Similarly, within many fields of inquiry, from sociology to science studies, an emergent corpus of work on "cultures of nature" has produced suggestive connections to issues of long-standing anthropological concern.[3] These debates are usefully brought into dialogue with the new kinship studies explored in this volume, as they are not only relevant to ongoing debates about kinship within anthropology but demonstrate how anthropological models of kinship are traveling into other areas of study as well.

BIOLOGY AS A CULTURAL SYSTEM

As noted in the introduction, the kinship concept in anthropology has been criticized as ethnocentric on numerous grounds and has been depicted as a paradigmatic example of how anthropologists have conflated their own conceptual apparatus with the underlying "realities" of social life elsewhere — as if everyone "has" kinship in the same sense that everyone "is" biological. Indeed, these two claims have had a closely related history, and kinship has often been defended by traditionalists as a universal attribute of human societies precisely because it is seen to be "based on" the biological facts of human sexual dimorphism and heterosexual reproduction. In contrast to this claim, and as discussed in the introduction, other more reflexive accounts of kinship have alleged it is a projection of Eurocentric assumptions about certain universal features of the human condition, which rests on a tautological biologism that presumes as self-evident the very aspects of social life that need to be explained. As David Schneider famously maintained in his short correspondence in *Man* as part of the "virgin birth" debates in the mid–twentieth century, not everyone assumes people reproduce like animals (1968; and see further 1984). To the contrary, he argued, the importance of modern biological science in shaping understandings of kin relatedness is culturally specific, of recent origin, and uniquely dominant in the Anglo-American context.[4]

Schneider was primarily concerned with the question of how biological models operate as a cultural "system" shaping American kinship beliefs. He described two main effects of biology as a cultural system. First, he contended that biological facts have *symbolic qualities.* He saw these qualities as "additional" to their scientific meaning. Biological facts, he wrote in *American Kinship,* "have *as one of their aspects* a symbolic quality, which means that they represent something other than what they are, over and above and *in addition to* their existence as biological facts" (1980, 116; emphasis added). Schneider clearly believed that this additional symbolic dimension did nothing to diminish the scientific truth of biological facts. As he put it unequivocally, "The biological requirements of human existence . . . exist and remain. The child . . . does not come into being except by the fertilized egg. . . . These are the biological facts. They are the facts of life and the facts of nature" (116). Schneider was not concerned, as later generations of anthropologists have been, with the cultural dimensions of scientific facts as scientific facts.[5] He did not address the question, so central to feminist anthropology and the critique of the concept of race, of how the biological sciences construct truth claims in relation to supposedly natural facts. Schneider said nothing about how biology is used as a means of naturalizing inequalities, nor indeed about the distinctive power of ideas about the natural in U.S., or British, culture — topics that have both received more elaborate treatment elsewhere (see Haraway 1989, 1991, 1992; Yanagisako and Delaney 1995).

These absences become more significant in relation to the other key effect of biological facts on the definition of American kinship described by Schneider, which is his claim that because of their symbolic importance, biological facts also had constitutive power to create kinship *in and of themselves.* As Schneider claimed, "In American cultural conception, kinship is defined as biogenetic. This definition says that kinship is whatever the biogenetic relationship is. If science discovers new facts about biogenetic relationship, then that is what kinship is and was all along" (1980, 23). Schneider's observation — that biological facts are seen to constitute kinship in and of themselves — points directly to the conflation discussed earlier in relation to "biology," whereby the process of naming, studying, or classifying something is conflated with that entity itself. "Kinship" has similarly been criticized for being used to portray a preexisting reality, presumed to be universally and biologically present, whether anyone was aware of it or not. According to this definition of kinship, for example, a kinship tie not known to exist can be discovered. The acquisition of certain kinds of knowledge can produce a kinship tie where none existed before, *because knowledge itself can make kinship appear.* This is the second effect of biology "as a cultural system" articulated by Schneider: biology is both symbolic and constitutive of what kinship is seen to be in U.S. culture.

In relation to Schneider's claim that science not only symbolizes but in a sense can create kinship by discovery, as it were, Marilyn Strathern has cogently asked what this also says about Euro-American models of knowledge, property, and identity. Noting that "the quest for facts about the way the world works is also part of the Euro-American quest for self-hood," Strathern suggests that biological knowledge has constitutive consequences for identity because it can reveal facts, such as genetic information, about ancestry (1998, 3). People can acquire an identity by discovery because, according to Strathern, "knowledge creates relationships: relationships come into being when the knowledge does" (4). Paradoxically, then, it is because scientific knowledge is seen to be objective and universal that it can have such intimate and personal effects. Strathern's argument thus foregrounds Euro-American assumptions about knowing as being: she is intrigued by the fact that what science says exists "out there" can tell us who and what we are "in here." We are seen to embody scientific knowledges. They describe the very nature of our being.

As Strathern points out, the model of knowledge necessary for the discovery of scientific facts to tell us who we really are also depends on specific, codependent concepts of individuality, property, and possession. The isomorphism between the way we are seen to possess identities and knowledge of them can be generalized to reveal the way possession of knowledge about the world is so deeply ingrained in Western assumptions about individual agency, identity, and subjectivity. These rely on a very specific model of knowledge: as possessive, constitutive, and irrevocable. Put the other way around, it is arguably by examining how knowledge is conceived that one can see more clearly how modern Western subjects imagine selves, identities, and actions in the world. What is significant in Strathern's account is how kinship connects these domains.

The sequential perspectives of Strathern and Schneider on the question of how biological facts matter to kinship reckoning thus provide two divergent models of their relation. Schneider divides biology as a cultural system into its symbolic and constitutive dimensions, and offers a model of culture as a form of practice, which he separates from questions about biology as a science. Strathern reconfigures the question of biological facts as one that indexes the specificity of Euro-American knowledge systems: her recontextualization reveals the ways in which bodies, identities, connections, and knowledges are linked through forms of possessive individualism. In contrast to Schneider, it is implicit in Strathern's argument that all Euro-American knowledge claims are contingent, including biological ones. It is the consequences of how Western knowledge practices figure possession as a feature of knowledge itself that are explored in Strathern's more recent work on intellectual property disputes (1999) — a set of linkages that bring kinship issues to the heart of science studies, as I discuss further in relation to the work of Haraway below.

THE GENDER OF BIOLOGY

Before turning to science studies, however, it is also useful to consider briefly the connections linking the new kinship studies to recent developments in gender theory — a suggestion first explored by Sylvia Yanagisako and Jane Collier (1987), but as yet lacking a more detailed exegesis, which this chapter can only gesture toward. Whereas the strategy proposed by Yanagisako and Collier emphasized the unity of gender and kinship as fields of anthropological inquiry, as both "start from what are construed as the same biological facts of sexual reproduction" (34), these linkages have remained largely unexamined in recent works addressing gender and kinship (Maynes et al. 1996; Stone 1997; compare Weston 1996).

Writing in 1974, Sherry Ortner famously reiterated the claim of Simone de Beauvoir that "it is simply a fact that proportionately more of a woman's body space is taken up with the natural processes surrounding the reproduction of the species" (74–75). By the end of that decade, however, such assertions had become almost taboo among feminists. Far from self-evident, biological explanations of sex and gender came increasingly to be viewed within feminist anthropology as culturally and historically specific, ideologically reactionary, and male defined. Through publications such as Carol MacCormack and Marilyn Strathern's *Nature, Culture, and Gender* (1980), attention began to shift away from the notion of biological facts and toward an examination of the knowledge practices through which such claims acquired legitimacy, authority, and "obviousness." Moving away from a notion of "biological differences," the focus of feminist thought shifted to address ideas of the natural and their relation to gender categories more broadly.

Addressing the historical processes through which pregnancy became the object of an intense clinical surveillance and fascination in the eighteenth century, for example, Ludmilla Jordanova (1980) described a gendered epistemology of the maternal body in which the penetrating gaze of the physician/anatomist recapitulated a form of sexual conquest and masculine heroism. Jordanova's work, alongside that of other feminist historians such as Carolyn Merchant (1982), began to revise the historical question of how gender has been shaped by the emergence of modern science into one that asked precisely the reverse—that is, how the emergence of modern science has been shaped by gender. Addressed as much to the "making of the modern body" as to the emergence of modern anatomy, biology, and medicine, studies by social historians Catherine Gallagher and Thomas Laqueur (1987; see also Laqueur 1990), Londa Schiebinger (1989), and Barbara Duden (1991) have argued that the so-called biological facts of sexual reproduction are produced to confirm the rigid binarism of sex categories by encoding them as pre-existing "natural" differences.

Since the 1980s, feminist scholarship on science and sexuality has become one of the most significant forces shaping theories of gender, and tying questions of embodiment, identity, and power to those of knowledge formation, or what Michel Foucault describes as "power-knowledge" (1970). The critique of biological facts has been central to this effort for numerous reasons, from the direct consequences of how biology is used to restrict women's roles in society, to the difficulties faced by women scientists (see Hubbard 1990; Schiebinger 1989), to the gendered assumptions that shape cell biology (see Fausto-Sterling 1985) and the new genetics (see Keller 1992). Holding together a wide range of feminist approaches to scientific discourse has been a concern with what Haraway calls its "world-building consequences" (1991)— what Schneider might have labeled as the constitutive effects of biology as a cultural system or what Strathern identified as the cultural effects built into certain forms of knowledge production. In sum, the feminist critique of biology, and science more generally, corresponds to what Evelyn Fox Keller has dubbed a "double shift in perception" characterizing contemporary feminist theory: "First, from sex to gender, and second, from the force of gender in shaping the development of men and women to its force in delineating the cultural maps of the social and natural worlds these adults inhabit" (1992, 17).

"FEMALE" TROUBLE

This "double shift" is strongly evident in the work of numerous feminist biologists—including Ruth Hubbard (1990), Lynda Birke (1986), and Anne Fausto-Sterling (1985)—who have recast the question of the biology of gender into one that addresses the gender of biology. Their efforts are aided by wider shifts in gender theory, whereby a radical critique of the category "woman" has been succeeded by an equally thorough deconstruction of the biological category "female." This shift in gender theory derives from a reconceptualization of gender as a technology for producing meaning and, in particular, organizing the production of difference, which has its roots in poststructuralism and psychoanalysis (see De Lauretis 1984, 1987).

In *Gender Trouble* (1990), Judith Butler took direct inspiration from feminist anthropology to recast the relation of sex to gender, or biology to embodiment, in what remains one of the most influential "denaturalizations" of biological facts to emerge from within feminist scholarship in the 1990s. Disputing the seemingly commonsense view that "being female constitute[s] a 'natural fact,'" and arguing instead that such "foundational categories of identity . . . can be shown as productions that create the effect of the natural, the original and the inevitable" (x), Butler proposes a model that radically repositions allegedly natural facts *as an effect of gender categories,* rather than the reverse. She describes the purpose of *Gender Trouble* as an effort "to trace the way in which gender fables establish and circulate the misnomer of natural facts" (xiii), and as a project designed to expose the circularity of "that felicitous self-naturalization" (33). For Butler, sex categories (male and female) comprise "a discursive formation that acts as a naturalized foundation" (37), and gender is defined as "the repeated stylization of the body . . . within a highly rigid regulatory frame that congeal[s] over time to produce the appearance of substance, of a natural sort of being" (33).

In emphasizing that gender is an effect — an embodied performance or stylized repetition of enactments — Butler seeks to disrupt the assumption that a binary difference between male and female simply exists as a presocial fact. In this effort, Butler follows a similar path to that set out by Collier and Yanagisako in their assertion that "the next phase in the feminist reanalysis of gender and kinship should be to question the assumption that 'male' and 'female' are two natural categories of human beings whose relations are everywhere structured by their biological difference" (1987, 7). Arguing for an approach that locates the production of difference within a broader social whole, Collier and Yanagisako suggest that "instead of asking how the categories of 'male' and 'female' are endowed with culturally specific characters, thus taking the difference between them for granted, we need to ask how particular societies define difference" (35).

Butler's contention, though pointing in a different direction toward contemporary identity politics, likewise interrogates the presumption that "there is a natural or biological female who is subsequently transformed into a socially subordinate 'woman,' with the consequence that 'sex' is to nature or 'the raw' as gender is to culture or 'the cooked'" (1990, 37). In a direct reprise of MacCormack and Strathern's arguments in *Nature, Culture, and Gender* (1980), Butler claims that "the analysis that assumes nature to be singular and prediscursive cannot ask, what qualifies as 'nature' within a given cultural context, and for what purposes?" (1990, 37). In addition, Butler presses forward Yanagisako's prediction that "having recognized our model of biological difference as a particular cultural mode of thinking about relations between people, we should be able to question the 'biological facts' of sex themselves" (1987, 42). In a revealing analysis of scientific claims to have discovered the "master switch" of sex determination, Butler demonstrates the ways in which a presumption of binary sex is imposed even within studies based on "ambiguously" sexed persons, whose chromosomal and morphological sex diverge. The repeated imposition of a binary order on these "incoherent" sexes, even when they clearly demonstrate its nonbinary existence "in nature," proves, according to Butler, "that cultural assumptions regarding the relative status of men and women and the binary relation of gender itself frame and focus the research into sex determination" (1990, 109). In other words, it is the assumption of gender binarism that produces the mandate for the discovery of biologically binary sex categories, not the reverse. In a critique of this circularity that directly parallels Schneider's impatience with kinship theorists who have a genealogical grid in mind even when they say they don't, Butler concludes, "The task of distinguishing sex from gender becomes all the more difficult once we understand that gendered meanings frame the hypothesis and the reasoning of those biomedical inquiries that seek to establish 'sex' for us as prior to the cultural meanings that it acquires" (109). It is, in fact, the discursive expectation of sex binarism that is revealed as prior in this scientific "explanation" demonstrating the extent to which biomedicine not only contributes to but mandates "the repeated stylization of the body . . . within a highly rigid regulatory frame that congeal[s] over time to produce the appearance of substance, of a natural sort of being" (33). Thus echoing Collier and Yanagisako's complaint that "the standard units of our genealogies, after all, are circles and triangles about which we assume a number of things" (1987, 32), Butler maintains that it is "only from a self-consciously denaturalized position [that] we can see how the appearance of naturalness is itself constituted" (1990, 110).

The implications of Butler's argument for kinship theory have begun to be sketched not only in terms of her critique of biology but also in terms of the new ways in which kinship idioms are being used in the context of lesbian and gay "cultures of relatedness," such as those discussed by Kath Weston (1991, 1998), Ellen Lewin (1993), Corinne Hayden (1995), and Jacquelyne Luce (1998). In such ethnographic accounts of lesbian and gay kinship, the meanings of the biological are interwoven within the language of kin formation in complex ways that both aspire to and also self-consciously mimic the authenticity and enduring permanence symbolized by so-called biological ties. Although not explicitly parodic or deliberately subversive, as in Butler's accounts of gender performativity, such means of "blending" kinship closely resemble Butler's notions of "bending" gender. The same can equally be said of kinship in the context of new reproductive technologies, as Charis Thompson (in this volume, Cussins 1998), as well as others have shown (see also Franklin 1997, 1998, 1999a, 1999b; Franklin and Ragoné 1998; Ragoné 1994; Edwards et al. 1999). The result is both categorical reinforcement (for example, of kinship as a distinct category of relationships) and destabilization (for instance, of who counts as kin and how). In turning back to science studies and, in particular, the recent work of Haraway, the question of biological facts takes yet another turn.

ALL OUR KIN

From a somewhat different direction from those discussed so far, Haraway explains the power of biological knowledge in *Modest_Witness@Second_ Millennium.FemaleMan©_Meets_OncoMouse™*. As Haraway states,

> Biology discursively establishes and performs what will count as human in powerful domains of knowledge and technique. . . .
>
> Biology is not the body itself but a discourse on the body. . . . Biology is not everyone's discourse about human, animal, and vegetable flesh, life, and nature; indeed, *flesh, life,* and *nature* are no less rooted in specific histories, practices, languages and peoples than *biology* itself. . . . It is, rather, a complex web of semiotic-material practices that emerged over the past 200 years or so, beginning in "the West" and travelling globally. (1997, 217)

According to this list, biology is primarily discursive "in powerful domains of knowledge and technique." It is historically and culturally specific, but has become increasingly powerful and transnational in the past two centuries. Haraway challenges the idea that biology tells us who we really are at an ontological level, distinguishing between "the body itself" and "a discourse on the body." Haraway's distinction between knowledges and bodies is both philosophical and political. It is also enabling for Haraway as a theorist, in that she is free to rewrite what kinship can be, which is one of the major tropes she uses for her arguments in *Modest_Witness*.

As "the body" is separate from biology, so too is kinship. Haraway claims that kinship is similar to gender, both of which she has depicted by analogy to the grammatical function of producing kinds and types (of words) (1991). She describes kinship "in short" as "the question of taxonomy, category, and the natural status of artificial entities," adding that "kinship is a technology for producing the material and semiotic effect of natural relationship, of shared kind" (1997, 53). Haraway writes that "establishing identities is kinship work in action" (67), and that kinship is about both "kinds of membership and kinds of liveliness" (284 n. 23).

She uses kinship models to perform a variety of functions in *Modest_ Witness,* to which the concept of kinship is central. On the one hand, kinship is used as an analogy or metaphor for a naturalized system of interconnection, so that Haraway portrays "the kinship exchange system in which gender, race, and species — animal and machine — are all at stake" (217). She also uses kinship to link the three key "figures" or "guides" in the book — Modest_Witness, FemaleMan©, and OncoMouse™ — who she describes as "kin" to one another and to herself as narrator: "I need my sibling species to get me through this life story; our bodies share substance; we are kin" (1997, 120). In a more complex analogy, Haraway compares the ordering of elements in the periodic table to a kinship chart, or what she calls "a potent taxonomic device for what my people understand as nature" (54). She continues:

> Uranium is the naturally occurring earthly element with the highest atomic number, 92. Uranium is where the evolution of elements that make up the solar system stopped. In that sense, uranium represents a kind of "natural limit" to the family of terran elements as well. (54)

Pointing out that plutonium, a transuranic synthetic element, has an atomic value of ninety-four (making it an unnatural kind), and that the explosive bomb-grade Pu238 was manufactured in a breeder reactor in 1942 (making it an unnatural offspring), Haraway develops an analogy to transgenic animals, such as OncoMouse™, similarly created by humans, after nature, and existing in out-of-evolutionary time. Her collective term for such entities, chemical and zoological, is "trans." As Haraway observes:

> The techniques of genetic engineering developed since the early 1970s are like the reactors and particle accelerators of nuclear physics: Their products are "trans." . . . Like the transuranic elements, transgenic creatures, which carry the genes from "unrelated" organisms, simultaneously fit into well-established taxonomic and evolutionary discourses and also blast widely understood senses of natural limit. What was distant and unrelated becomes intimate. By the 1990s, genes are us; and we seem to include some curious new family members. (56)

Haraway is describing here the kind of kinship evident in the context of new reproductive technologies, in which "unnatural kinds" become familiars (Franklin 1997, 1998, 1999a). The sense that a cryopreserved embryo suspended in a liquid nitrogen tank is a biological relative is a commonplace experience for couples undergoing in vitro fertilization (IVF), for example. This is kinship shorn of a sense of natural limit, but it is surely a sense of relatedness based on shared bodily substance and genetic ties. The uncertainty surrounding this form of "kinship" is most often occasioned by straightforward denial: IVF couples have been repeatedly documented to insist that having a baby via assisted conception is "just like" having a normal, natural pregnancy (see Sandelowski 1993; Franklin 1997). Haraway is not interested in these forms of denial or displacement: she wishes to embrace fully the promise of "unnatural" minglings, while she remains ever astute to their dangers. Kinship also serves an important function in her argument here, for as transuranics share a kinship with transgenics, so too does she position herself as kin to these unnatural kinds: "Like it or not," Haraway says, "I was born kin to Pu239" (1997, 62).

Here, then, is the perfect postmodern parody of Schneider's account of kinship discussed earlier, in a form of "kinship trouble" that mocks the naturalness of genealogy, by showing its artifice. According to Schneider, "Kinship is whatever the biological relationship is. If science discovers new facts about biogenetic relationship, then that is what kinship is and was all along" (1980, 23). But what if "science discovers new facts about biogenetic relationship" that enable a fish to be crossed with a tomato? In Haraway's view, people may be kin to transgenic animals, such as OncoMouse™, who carry human genes, but such relations also "blast widely understood senses of natural limit" (1997, 56). In other words, the ways in which humans are today connected and related through biology *undoes the very fixity that the biological tie used to represent.* To note the irony that this transmogrification of the biological has come from within biology itself is only once again to encounter the expectation that biology perform itself otherwise — that is, that biology authenticate and secure a "nature" in line with expectations, whether or not they are there.

Haraway complicates her account of kinship in the context of the new biologies (and biologicals) still further by introducing a process of contemporary cultural change that she labels as *a shift from kind to brand.* In relation to both kinship and gender, as systems for producing kind and type, she suggests that the commercialization of life itself is epitomized in the moment when "type becomes brand," when the very genome of OncoMouse™ is patented, as a form of intellectual property. Haraway notes that

> in the process of materialized refiguration of the kinship between different orders of life, the generative splicing of synthetic DNA and money produces promising genetic fruit. Specifically, natural kind becomes brand

or trademark, a sign protecting intellectual property claims in business transactions. (1997, 65–66)

Haraway makes explicit reference to the similarity she is depicting between branding and gendering by stating in her introduction that she is "riveted by 'brand names' as 'genders'" (7–8). Like genders, brands are "generic marks that are directional signals on maps of power and knowledge" (8). In other words, the kind of type, or typing, once secured by gender or kinship systems is now analogously performed by branding. What was once secured by nature is now supplied by capital accumulation strategies and by genetic signatures on higher mammals reproduced under corporate-owned trademarks as a form of brand equity.

Like kinship, branding produces particular descent lines or "species" of products, linked in multigenerational lineages and by family resemblance. As in the maintenance of kinship or gender systems, the marketing of these lines, species, and families of products involves the constant performance of boundary work, to include certain products or traits and exclude others (see Coombe 1998).

But why is kinship a useful idiom to understand such relations? What kind of connection does kinship enable Haraway to draw, and why call it kinship at all? I interpret the move Haraway is making in her adoption of the kinship concept to examine new forms of capital accumulation as both a local and situated reading, which is also an attempt both to take literally and mock the power still inherent in the ability to naturalize connections — even when they are clearly as artificial as are those linking commodities to their "parent" company or one another. Haraway's reading is local and situated in its understanding of kinship as a means of "naturalizing power" — a meaning of kinship arguably specific to the Euro-American context in which it emerged. Her reading takes literally this power, and she demonstrates how it can be put to use to secure the relation of a product to its parent company, under the sign of its brand name or trademark, without which its reproduction is both illegitimate and nonviable (or "fruitless").[6] At the same time, Haraway's promiscuous claims to relatedness undo the propriety of such orderly lineages, making use of hyperbole to claim she is related to a mouse.

Kinship for Haraway describes the kind of commercial propriety a brand confers, in its function as a form of intellectual property protection. As has frequently been pointed out, the origin of intellectual property law is in copyright, which was established in seventeenth-century British law by analogy to paternity (see Rose 1993). The kind of propriety conferred to authorship through copyright was explicitly argued on the basis of a father's inherent rights in and to his offspring. This reliance on authorship is also institutionalized in the classification systems of botany and zoology, whereby the type specimen establishing a species is named for its author. Copyright is naturalized by analogy to paternity, through the idiom of authorship, in which discovery and creation are linked to the ability to create new kinds and originary types, such as the type specimen of a species. In a manner that is directly reminiscent of Susan McKinnon's discussion of paternity and enterprise in the preceding chapter, the authorial paternity that signifies both direct descent and creation is already defined as propriety. In both Haraway's and McKinnon's analyses, as in much of Strathern's work, "naturalization," like paternity, thus appears less as a sequitor to nature than a product of enterprise.

There is a tension in Haraway's invocation of kinship that is further revealing of her ambivalent position within it. She uses kinship both to signify the perils of a puritanical insistence on continuity of the germplasm and to invite explosive unions that rupture supposedly natural limits. In an irritated postscript, Haraway denounces kinship ties:

> I am sick to death of bonding through kinship and "the family," and I long for models of solidarity and human unity and difference rooted in friendship, work, partially shared purposes, intractable collective pain, inescapable mortality, and persistent hope. It is time to theorize an "unfamiliar" unconscious, a different primal scene, where everything does not stem from the dramas of identity and reproduction. Ties through blood — including blood recast in the coin of genes and information — have been bloody enough already. I believe there will be no racial or sexual peace, no livable nature, until we learn to produce humanity through something more and less than kinship. (1997, 265)

In this passage, it is clear that Haraway is referring to kinship-as-it-has-been, to what might be dubbed "bloody kinship" (listening also to the British inflection of this rendering). In proposing she is kin to OncoMouse™, Female Man©, and Modest_Witness, as well as Pu239 and its transgenic cousins, Haraway foregrounds a hyperbolic, promiscuous, and transgressive kinship — a kinship that is after nature, out of the bounds and bonds of blood, postracial hygiene, presexual binarisms, meta- to species, trans- to elements, and hyper- to organic kinds and types. As in her earlier publications in which hybrid unions figure provocatively, *Modest_Witness* contains many unsettling primal scenes, in which Haraway explores kinship through the figures of the monster, vampire, cyborg, simian, and extraterrestrial. Although it is perfectly obvious why she is "sick to death" of "kinship," "the family," and "ties through blood," it is also evident that these are idioms she is reluctant to ignore.

Haraway's model of kinship as a means to transform definitions of naturalized kind parallels Strathern's (1998) concern with kinship as a template for knowledge production linked to the establishment of ownership of new forms of biowealth. Both accounts demonstrate not only the emergence of important links between kinship theory and science studies but also the continuing influence of the debate about biological facts for kinship theory, much as that may seem not only outdated but complicit with unhelpful traditions from the past as well.

Clearly, there are significant reasons to be wary of continuing to analyze kinship in relation to biology, much as biology may have shape-shifted into something now more visibly associated with innovation and change than fixity, stability, or continuity. To begin with, it is essential to widen the possibilities of what can count as kinship out from under the long shadow that genealogy and biology still cast over this field of study — an association that is arguably furthered by the assumption that new forms of biological reproduction are places to look for new kinds of kinship. As some have claimed, such an expectation can both obscure the ways in which emergent forms of kinship are not new at all, and appear to be merely contributing to the hype and controversy surrounding such techniques generally. A related danger is the tendency to overestimate not only the novelty but the determinism of new forms of technological innovation, such as cloning, the patenting of transgenic animals, or new reproductive technologies. Without careful contextualization, studies of such developments can easily fall into a pattern of attributing to technology an agency and power that it does not have. A final qualification must be the simple question of for whom biological innovation represents such an important discourse concerning the future of the human, for it is plainly not of interest to everyone, or in the same way, as recent studies of organ transplantation (see Hogle 1999) and sperm donation (see Kahn 2000) amply demonstrate.

At the same time, and as Haraway's use of kinship in spite of her reluctant loathings indicates, it is equally a mistake to overlook the profound ways in which a redefinition of the biological comprises a distinctive site of cultural change. From emerging capital markets to genetic screening to public debate over genetically modified soybeans and cloned sheep, the new biologies and biologicals have unfolded as a defining feature of turn-of-the-millennium culture, at both the local and global levels, and with far-reaching as well as often intimate consequences.

KINSHIP IN THE CONTEXT OF THE NEW BIOLOGIES

Despite the enormity of such changes, anthropology has to date underestimated the significance of work on kinship in the context of the new biologies, and the linkages connecting kinship study to gender theory, science studies, and other fields of critical inquiry. One reason for this has been an overemphasis on the qualifications I raised above, about overvaluing novelty or being overly celebratory about technology. Another is the familiar narrative about postmodernism, poststructuralism, and deconstruction having "gone too far" at the expense of the discipline's core concepts. For example, in his recent volume *Kinship: An Introduction to Basic Concepts,* anthropologist Robert Parkin complains:

> In the last ten to fifteen years, anthropology has undergone a definite shift away from traditional approaches to the study of kinship, formerly one of its central concerns. Initially, this was occasioned by statements that there is really no such thing as kinship, at least comparatively speaking, and that only by giving our attention almost exclusively to indigenous categories can anything worthwhile be said on the matter. Later, kinship came to be subsumed more and more under studies into gender, personhood, the body, ritual, etc. — something reflecting this very same anti-formalist tendency. . . . Now, however, a feeling has arisen in some quarters that things have gone a little too far down the road towards this sort of deconstruction, and that to neglect kinship is to disregard a good deal of what any society explicitly recognizes. (1997, ix)

According to Parkin, whose views are not exceptional, no one who is trying to do anything with kinship other than indigenize it, subsume it under other formal categories, or deconstruct it figures in his account of kinship theory, which tenaciously seeks to preserve the biological versus social facts distinction throughout. But neither is the question of kinship and new biomedical technologies absent from Parkin's analysis — indeed, an entire section is devoted to this topic in his chapter 10. Following the rote recital of what current techniques involve, and the dismissive disclaimer that the fragmentation of parenthood occasioned by these techniques is "nothing new," Parkin incorrectly claims that at present the dilemmas produced by IVF and similar technologies only emerge as "a 'problem' for the essentially Western societies that have developed them rather than for other societies in the world" (126). Since IVF was reportedly developed in Bombay—before the birth of Louise Brown—and is now widely used in India, Singapore, China, Taiwan, Japan, and many parts of Africa, not to mention Israel, Kuwait, Saudi Arabia, and many other parts of the world, it is clear this assertion itself betrays certain unhelpful assumptions. It is unclear why Parkin feels it necessary to insist that anthropology provides many examples of "dilemmas concerning succession and inheritance" demonstrating that it is society, law, and public opinion that determine "which definitions of kinship are acceptable" (127), since to do so is in no way incompatible with also recognizing how the dilemmas associated with such techniques are also dissimilar from those encountered in the past. This vein of plus ça change argument, inaugurated by Peter Rivière in 1985, may well serve as an important counterweight to the overreaction that may occasion developments such as cloning.[7] The oversight of this account, however, is its inability to appreciate the ways in which kinship in the context of new reproductive technologies does not concern merely "new ways of making babies" but a much wider set of issues, such as how knowledge is produced, how capital is accumulated, and how identity categories are transformed. As Hayden writes in her prescient analysis of how the human is refigured in the context of the struggle to secure new forms of biowealth:

> These different arenas [of biotechnology] form part of a rich narrative field in which ideas about kinship, nature, and culture are woven together in complex and historically dense ways. That these discursive ricochets continue to be elaborated is not a matter of epistemological self-replication, but a result of concrete instances of cross-pollination through which biologized constructions of "our" reproductive pasts and futures are powerfully articulated and refigured. (1998, 197–98)

The important anthropological work being done at present on kinship in the context of the new biologies is not complacent about some celebrated "implosion" of nature and culture, or transgressively postmodern breach of genealogical time and space, but is instead attentive to the how and why of explaining forms of cultural change and social organization emergent in the context of an altered grid of relationality. Both the elements and structural relations of kinship are continually transformed in terms of how they are imagined and practiced in a cultural context, such as contemporary Britain, where biology signifies both nature and the ability to transcend natural limits. If culture is nothing if not paradoxical, such a set of phenomena are nothing if not cultural.

In chastising the biologism of Anglo-American kinship theory, Schneider both anticipated and overlooked key components of biologization. To him, as to many, biology was seen as a rigid and constraining gridwork, within which kinship became a matter of natural fact at the expense of expanding an appreciation of what can count as a cultural certainty. He was right to draw attention to biology as a cultural system and describe its unique symbolic authority. Nevertheless, he ignored the extent to which biology, even in its traditional form, is about change. Biotechnology is today the matrix of unprecedented life-forms that have as little to do with the nature biology once depicted as they do with the biology portrayed by Schneider.

Feminist approaches to biology captured a great deal more of this ambiguity within the biological, if for no other reason than the sheer volume of critical studies devoted to biology as a discourse from both outside and within its professional and epistemological parameters. One of the most significant benchmarks set by the work of Haraway has been her ability to understand so profoundly the importance of the ways in which biology can make itself strange as quickly as any of its critics. This is largely because Haraway has never abandoned the delights of the biological:

> I still use biology, animated by heterodox organisms burrowing into the nooks and crannies of the New World Order's digestive systems, to persuade my readers and students about ways of life that I believe might be more sustainable and just. I have no intention of stopping and no expectation that this rich resource will or should be abandoned by others. Biology is a political discourse, one in which we should engage at every level of the practice — technically, semiotically, morally, economically, institutionally. And besides all that, biology is a source of intense intellectual, emotional, social and physical pleasure. Nothing like that should be given up lightly — or approached only in a scolding mode. (1997, 104–5)

Like the biblical, the biological is diminished by literalism. This is not to deny the worrisome and disturbing signs of a renewed genetic essentialism in the age of Genes 'R' Us. Nor is it to underestimate the many dangers evident in the global treasure hunt to find, patent, and bank new forms of bio-wealth. Rather, in the interests of producing better accounts of exactly why such developments matter in ways to do with forms of identity and related-ness seemingly far distant from the corporate biotechnology laboratory, there is a loss involved in inattention to the increasing complexity of the biologi-cal as it is dramatically reshaped. In particular, for all of the reasons so much emphasis has been placed on the importance of biological models to U.S. and British kinship systems, as well as the ethnocentric tracings of the biologi-cal in how kinship has been recognized elsewhere, there is utility in asking whether the biological facts are doing the same kind of cultural signification today as they were when many of the most well-known arguments describing kinship's cultural functions were articulated to begin with.

NOTES

I would like to thank the Wenner-Gren Foundation for Anthropological Research for funding the conference for which this essay was originally prepared. In addition, I would particularly like to thank Jackie Stacey and Susie McKinnon for their helpful suggestions and comments.

1 A similar assertion can be made about the ways in which "biology" is conflated with "nature" and also with technology.

2 Fredric Jameson (1998), for example, makes a similar argument that "culture" has replaced "nature" in the context of both late capitalism and postmodernism.

3 See, for example, Dickens 1996; Macnaghten and Urry 1998; Robertson et al. 1996; and Wilson 1992.

4 Similar assertions have been made by numerous social historians, including Michel Foucault (1970), Thomas Laqueur (1990), Londa Schiebinger (1989), and Ludmilla Jordanova (1980, 1989)—that contemporary models of life, sex, procreation, and species are of recent vintage, and directly linked to the rise of modern biology and, more generally, Western science.

5 Analyses of gendered and discursive dimensions of biological facts in the context of conception can be found in the work of Emily Martin (1991) and Sarah Franklin (1995).

6 Significantly, violations of brand propriety, whereby a product is marketed under a falsified or inauthentic trademark, such as "bootleg" videos of feature films or "imi-tation" designer goods, are referred to as "cloned" products.

7 Oddly, Parkin claims that new reproductive technologies raise the possibility of "a society in which relationships need no longer be defined at all in ways that make ex-plicit reference to kinship" (1997, 128), which he concludes would indicate that they deserve no further discussion since such a development "would mean leaving the world of kinship behind us completely" (129).

REFERENCES

Birke, Lynda. 1986. *Women, Feminism, and the New Biology: The Feminist Challenge.* Brighton, U.K.: Wheatsheaf.

Butler, Judith. 1990. *Gender Trouble: Feminism and the Subversion of Identity.* New York: Routledge.

Collier, Jane F., and Sylvia J. Yanagisako, eds. 1987. *Gender and Kinship: Essays toward a Unified Analysis.* Stanford, Calif.: Stanford University Press.

Coombe, Rosemary J. 1998. *The Cultural Life of Intellectual Properties.* Durham, N.C.: Duke University Press.

Cussins, Charis. 1998. Producing Reproduction: Techniques of Normalization and Naturalization in Infertility Clinics. In *Reproducing Reproduction: Kinship, Power, and Technological Innovation,* edited by Sarah Franklin and Helena Ragoné. Philadelphia: University of Pennsylvania Press.

De Lauretis, Teresa. 1984. *Alice Doesn't: Feminism, Semiotics, Cinema.* Bloomington: Indiana University Press.

―――. 1987. *Technologies of Gender: Essays on Theory, Film, and Fiction.* Bloomington: Indiana University Press.

Dickens, Peter. 1996. *Reconstructing Nature.* London: Routledge.

Duden, Barbara. 1991. *The Woman beneath the Skin.* Cambridge: Harvard University Press.

Edwards, Jeanette, Sarah Franklin, Eric Hirsch, Frances Price, and Marilyn Strathern. 1999. *Technologies of Procreation: Kinship in the Age of Assisted Conception.* 2d ed. London: Routledge.

Fausto-Sterling, Anne. 1985. *Myths of Gender: Biological Theories about Women and Men.* New York: Basic Books.

Foucault, Michel. 1970. *The Order of Things: A History of the Human Sciences.* New York: Vintage.

Franklin, Sarah. 1995. Postmodern Procreation: A Cultural Account of Assisted Reproduction. In *Conceiving the New World Order: The Global Politics of Reproduction,* edited by Faye D. Ginsburg and Rayna Rapp. Berkeley: University of California Press.

―――. 1997. *Embodied Progress: A Cultural Account of Assisted Conception.* London: Routledge.

―――. 1998. Making Miracles: Scientific Progress and the Facts of Life. In *Reproducing Reproduction: Kinship, Power, and Technological Innovation,* edited by Sarah Franklin and Helena Ragoné. Philadelphia: University of Pennsylvania Press.

―――. 1999a. Making Representations: Parliamentary Debate of the Human Fertilization and Embryology Bill. In *Technologies of Procreation: Kinship in the Age of Assisted Conception,* edited by Jeanette Edwards, Sarah Franklin, Eric Hirsch, Frances Price, and Marilyn Strathern. 2d ed. London: Routledge.

―――. 1999b. Dead Embryos: Feminism in Suspension. In *Fetal Subjects, Feminist Positions,* edited by Lynn M. Morgan and Meredith W. Michaels. Philadelphia: University of Pennsylvania Press.

Franklin, Sarah, and Helena Ragoné, eds. 1998. *Reproducing Reproduction: Kinship, Power, and Technological Innovation.* Philadelphia: University of Pennsylvania Press.

Gallagher, Catherine, and Thomas Laqueur, eds. 1987. *The Making of the Modern Body: Sexuality and Society in the Nineteenth Century.* Berkeley: University of California Press.

Haraway, Donna J. 1989. *Primate Visions: Gender, Race, and Nature in the World of Modern Science.* New York: Routledge.

———. 1991. *Simians, Cyborgs, and Women: The Reinvention of Nature.* New York: Routledge.

———. 1992. The Promises of Monsters: A Regenerative Politics for Inappropriate/d Others. In *Cultural Studies,* edited by Lawrence Grossberg, Cary Nelson, and Paula Treichler. New York: Routledge.

———. 1997. *Modest_Witness@Second_Millennium.FemaleMan©_Meets_Onco Mouse™.* New York: Routledge.

Hayden, Corinne P. 1995. Gender, Genetics, and Generation: Reformulating Biology in Lesbian Kinship. *Cultural Anthropology* 10, no. 1:41–63.

———. 1998. A Biodiversity Sampler for the Millennium. In *Reproducing Reproduction: Kinship, Power, and Technological Innovation,* edited by Sarah Franklin and Helena Ragoné. Philadelphia: University of Pennsylvania Press.

Hogle, Linda F. 1999. *Recovering the Nation's Body: Cultural Memory, Medicine, and the Politics of Redemption.* New Brunswick, N.J.: Rutgers University Press.

Hubbard, Ruth. 1990. *The Politics of Women's Biology.* New Brunswick, N.J.: Rutgers University Press.

Jameson, Fredric. 1998. *The Cultural Turn: Selected Writings on the Postmodern, 1983–1998.* London: Verso.

Jordanova, Ludmilla. 1980. Natural Facts: A Historical Perspective on Science and Sexuality. In *Nature, Culture, and Gender,* edited by Carol MacCormack and Marilyn Strathern. Cambridge: Cambridge University Press.

———. 1989. *Sexual Visions: Images of Gender in Science and Medicine between the Eighteenth and Twentieth Centuries.* Minneapolis: University of Minnesota Press.

Kahn, Susan. 2000. *Reproducing Jews: A Cultural Account of Assisted Conception in Israel.* Durham, N.C.: Duke University Press.

Keller, Evelyn Fox. 1992. *Secrets of Life, Secrets of Death: Essays on Language, Gender, and Science.* New York: Routledge.

Laqueur, Thomas. 1990. *Making Sex: Body and Gender from the Greeks to Freud.* Cambridge: Harvard University Press.

Lewin, Ellen. 1993. *Lesbian Mothers: Accounts of Gender in American Culture.* Ithaca, N.Y.: Cornell University Press.

Luce, Jacquelyne M. 1998. Negotiated Relations: Dykes, Reproductive Technologies, and the Politics of Conception. Paper presented at the ninety-seventh annual meeting of the American Anthropological Association, Philadelphia, Pennsylvania, 5 December.

MacCormack, Carol, and Marilyn Strathern, eds. 1980. *Nature, Culture, and Gender.* Cambridge: Cambridge University Press.

Macnaghten, Phil, and John Urry. 1998. *Contested Natures*. London: Sage.

Martin, Emily. 1991. The Egg and the Sperm: How Science Has Constructed a Romance Based on Stereotypical Male-Female Roles. *Signs* 16, no. 3:485–501.

Maynes, Mary Jo, Ann Waltner, Brigitte Soland, and Ulrike Strasser, eds. 1996. *Gender, Kinship, Power: A Comparative and Interdisciplinary History*. New York: Routledge.

Merchant, Carolyn. 1982. *The Death of Nature: Women, Ecology, and the Scientific Revolution*. London: Wildwood House.

Ortner, Sherry. 1974. Is Female to Male as Nature Is to Culture? In *Woman, Culture, and Society*, edited by Michelle Zimbalist Rosaldo and Louise Lamphere. Stanford, Calif.: Stanford University Press.

Parkin, Robert. 1997. *Kinship: An Introduction to Basic Concepts*. Oxford: Blackwell.

Rabinow, Paul. 1996. *Essays on the Anthropology of Reason*. Princeton, N.J.: Princeton University Press.

Ragoné, Helena. 1994. *Surrogate Motherhood: Conception in the Heart*. Boulder, Colo.: Westview Press.

Rivière, Peter. 1985. Unscrambling Parenthood: The Warnock Report. *Anthropology Today* 1, no. 4:2–6.

Robertson, George, Melinda Mash, Lisa Tickner, Jon Bird, Barry Curtis, and Tim Putnam, eds. 1996. *Future Natural: Nature, Science, Culture*. London: Routledge.

Rose, Mark. 1993. *Authors and Owners: The Invention of Copyright*. Cambridge: Harvard University Press.

Sandelowski, Margarete. 1993. *With Child in Mind: Studies of the Personal Encounter with Infertility*. Philadelphia: University of Pennsylvania Press.

Schiebinger, Londa. 1989. *The Mind Has No Sex? Women in the Origins of Modern Science*. Cambridge: Harvard University Press.

Schneider, David M. 1968. Virgin Birth. *Man* 3, no. 1:126–29.

———. 1980. *American Kinship: A Cultural Account*. 2d ed. Chicago: University of Chicago Press.

———. 1984. *A Critique of the Study of Kinship*. Ann Arbor: University of Michigan Press.

Stone, Linda. 1997. *Kinship and Gender: An Introduction*. Boulder, Colo.: Westview Press.

Strathern, Marilyn. 1992. *Reproducing the Future: Anthropology, Kinship, and the New Reproductive Technologies*. Manchester, U.K.: Manchester University Press.

———. 1998. Thought Experiments. Paper prepared at the Wenner-Gren conference, New Directions in Kinship Study: A Core Concept Revisited, Mallorca, Spain, 27 March–4 April.

———. 1999. *Property, Substance, and Effect: Anthropological Essays on Persons and Things*. London: Athlone Press.

Weston, Kath. 1991. *Families We Choose: Lesbians, Gays, Kinship*. New York: Columbia University Press.

———. 1996. *Render Me, Gender Me: Lesbians Talk Sex, Class, Color, Nation*. New York: Columbia University Press.

———. 1998. *Long Slow Burn: Sexuality and Social Science*. New York: Routledge.

Wilson, Alexander. 1992. *The Culture of Nature: North American Landscape from Disney to the Exxon Valdez.* Cambridge, U.K.: Blackwell.

Yanagisako, Sylvia J., and Jane F. Collier. 1987. Toward a Unified Analysis of Gender and Kinship. In *Gender and Kinship: Essays toward a Unified Analysis,* edited by Jane F. Collier and Sylvia J. Yanagisako. Stanford, Calif.: Stanford University Press.

Yanagisako, Sylvia J., and Carol Delaney, eds. 1995. *Naturalizing Power: Essays in Feminist Cultural Analysis.* New York: Routledge.

PART IV

'R' Genes Us? The Uses of Gene/alogies

CHAPTER 12

Blood/Kinship, Governmentality, and
Cultures of Order in Colonial Africa
Melbourne Tapper

The task [facing a district officer and an anthropologist working together as a team]
is twofold, and may be summarized in two questions: (1) is the local government
based on tribal loyalties and traditional authority, deriving from the past, acceptable in the present, and, as far as can be judged, capable of appropriate development
to meet future conditions? and (2) are the people well governed and content? The
first step might be to obtain a general historical account of the tribe, its origins, traditions, and organization, to be followed by a description on the broadest lines of
the political, economic, and social conditions in which it finds itself to-day, and the
administrative structure, British and native, set over it. A comparison might follow of the old tribal hierarchy with the existing administrative and judicial organs,
showing differences and if possible accounting for them. — Philip Mitchell, cited in
Anthropology in Action

The blood relation long remained an important element in the mechanisms of
power, its manifestations, and its rituals. For a society in which the systems of alliance, the political form of the sovereign, the differentiation into orders and castes,
and the value of descent lines were predominant; for a society in which famine,
epidemics, and violence made death imminent, blood constituted one of the fundamental values. It owed its high value at the same time to its instrumental role . . .
to the way it functioned in the order of signs (to have a certain blood, to be of the
same blood . . .), and also to its precariousness (easily spilled . . . too readily mixed,
capable of being quickly corrupted). — Michel Foucault, *The History of Sexuality*

The above remarks on the symbolics of tribes and on blood by Mitchell and
Foucault, respectively, mark out the problem to which the provisional notes
assembled in this essay respond. I wish to inquire about a problem in the

now considerably advanced discussion about kinship that responded to David Schneider's *A Critique of the Study of Kinship*. The problem circulates around the *Critique*'s undoing of the notion underlying traditional anthropologies of kinship, not so much as in the famous and irresistible statement that "blood is thicker than water" as in the suggestion that "kinship might then become a special custom distinctive of European culture, an interesting oddity, like the Toda bow ceremony," and that "such a way of dealing with kinship would teach us a great deal" (Schneider 1984, 175, 201). Just what is it that this fact of kinship would teach us? Schneider tells us that he prefers to leave this for another book. But does he?

Throughout the *Critique,* Schneider returns again and again to that haunting fact that anthropologists have come home to find that their discoveries — other peoples' kinship — have turned out, in the end, to be nothing more than their own shadows. That is, anthropologists have been chasing their own tails (see Buchler 1994, 242). As Schneider insists:

> So much of what passes for science in the social sciences, including anthropology, derives directly and recognizably from the commonsense notions, the everyday premises of the culture in which and by which the scientist lives. These postulates of European culture are simply taken over and put in a form that is customary for rational scientific discourse, appropriately qualified and made slightly more explicit in places and served up as something special. . . . That is, the study of kinship derives directly and practically unaltered from the ethnoepistemology of European culture. (1984, 175)

Schneider is clearly critical of the commonsense rationality underlying the study of kinship experience — a methodology he describes as "ethnoepistemology." But he may not have carried his critique far enough — beyond the critique of the teleology of universality (given his seeming willingness to deliver the rendered object into yet another reductionism), known in its most banal specification as "seeing is believing." As Schneider writes:

> The one ground on which [anthropologists] might proceed is to take kinship as an empirical question, not as a universal fact. . . . The immediate and salient questions are: Given this definition of kinship, do these particular people have it or do they not? If so, detailed ethnographic evidence must be presented to substantiate that position; if not, specific ethnographic evidence should be presented showing wherein they differ. (200)

And so another teleology was set in motion (or, was it a restatement of what anthropologists have been doing all along? After all, is this not the age-old question—that is, which ideas and representations of the plethora of occurring forms are most appropriate to the way the world is? Which ideas are right, correct, and which are wrong, false?). Schneider's polite solution to the problems, as Ira Buchler (1994, 241) observed, was to leave intact precisely what was problematic and in need of explanation in the first place—the sense of reality, the way of knowing that sustains the construct of Euro-American kinship.

It is not my intention here to take on Schneider. I simply wish to make explicit a question that his critique of the study of kinship merely implies: namely, whether kinship—and the constructions and presuppositions inscribed within it—is implicated in colonial governance. Ultimately, it matters little whether anthropologists have provided an "objective" rendering of the local customs of "genuine Africa." Kinship might be more appropriately addressed from a wholly different base than that of epistemology with its correspondence theory of knowledge—that other base being political rationalities and, in the case at hand, the political rationalities of colonial power (see Rorty 1979). Baldly stated, I am interested in promoting an understanding of "kinship"—specifically in its representational form of the "tribe"—in terms of governmentality. Rather than seeking to delineate whether tribes existed prior to the imposition of colonial rule or were an effect brought on by such rule (compare Vail 1989; Lentz 1994), this essay begins by accepting the materiality of the rendered object while showing how it circulates between the symbolics of blood (with its specific instrumentality of power) and the biogenetic representations of blood (with its wholly new instrumentality of power), thus creating a surface structure for making possible certain tactical interventions, surveillances, and withdrawals of government. But more still, I argue here that a paradigmatic construct of tribes was discursively constituted at the intersection of anthropology and medicine during the colonial period. Medicine provided the sanction and intellectual justification for the epistemic production of the tribe beyond that situated in terms of the pre-existing, nonmedical symbolics of blood. Hence, Mitchell's comments regarding the anthropologist and district officer consequently indicate a "project" with both discursive and practical import. As he notes:

> there would be valuable experience to be gained from a practical attempt to solve the difficulty [of combining taxing administrative duties with academic study] by linking specialist research [anthropological] to

the day-to-day business of administration, in a manner which might be compared to the relation between laboratory worker and practising doctor, and that an attempt of this nature would have to be confined in the first place to a limited field and to proceed experimentally towards the discovery of methods capable of general application. (Mitchell, cited in Brown and Hutt 1935, xiii)

There is a congruence here between the attitudes of the provincial government and those of anthropology toward African peoples. They agreed not only on the desirability of an orderly, affectionate, and loyal population but also on what was meant by order and the means of its achievement and enforcement.

Michel Foucault (1991) has summed up these tactical concerns under the labels *pastoral power* and *governmentality*. On the one hand, both the provincial (or local) colonial government and the anthropologist (and, as we will see, the colonial physicians) had turned their attention to the management of the population—a project that highlights the way in which pastoral power crisscrossed governmentality. On the other hand, as colonial projects are never uniformly constituted (never nondiscursive), there is competition and at times contradiction between pastoral power and governmentality. But contradiction here can be read as a positive position of power. This is what I take Mitchell to have meant when he noted the formation of a mutual space for the anthropologist working with the government (see also Asad 1985).

In his writing on politics and governmentality, Foucault reasoned that a pastoral modality of power came to be inscribed in a form of government that took the management of the entire population as its object: "To govern a state will therefore mean to apply economy . . . at the level of the entire state, which means exercising towards all its inhabitants, and the wealth and behavior of each and all, a form of surveillance and control as attentive as that of the head of a family over his [*sic*] household and goods" (1991, 92). Here, Foucault notes a significant shift from the early modern period when the family or household was seen as an assemblage of the state or community (and thus supplying a model for government) to that of an autonomous rationality of government that requires families and households to be seen as components of the population that is to be governed (88). In colonial Africa, however, the cultural geographies of these various modalities of power crystallize in different, local ways. It might be more appropriate to think of the tribe (rather than the family) as the unit that is transformed from a model of good government to an instrument of government.

This observation leads me to a consideration of a group of colonial physicians active in the 1950s in East Africa, where the local geographies of pastoral power and governmentality crystallized in specific ways. In trying to understand the occurrence of a disease termed sickling among "native" people residing in what was then the Balovale region of East Africa, colonial physicians articulated the concept of tribe with particular clarity. There could be no making sense of this disease and no understanding of its epidemiological picture free of an understanding of tribal histories and social relations. Medical history and examination (not unlike confession and expiation) thereby came to incorporate a myriad of questions about migration, family history, consanguinity, polygamy, and so on; in the cognition of colonial medics, all these inquiries spun around purity and tribe. As a device for mapping tribe that gradually took hold after the Second World War (see Worby 1994), sickling was an imperial space that lay at the crossroads of tribe and geography. It constituted a wholly new understanding of the relationship between tribal identities and sociogeographic space at a time when named tribes fixed by other means were shifting identities in ways that eluded the mapping imperative and thereby put certain individuals, groups, and places outside the gaze of government (see Blake 1999, 79–83; Comaroff and Comaroff 1992, 215–33; Gilman 1985; Miller 1985; Mudimbe 1988; Packard 1989, 77–93; Vaughan 1991). Colonial physicians' understanding of sickling was bound up with African peoples' tribal heritage, which was itself bound up in the calculations made regarding migration, sexuality, place, and physiognomy. This would not have been new to these physicians, since their understanding of disease was already bound up with British notions of class, gender, geography, and race. Yet, it was a local form of imperialism that relied on a tribal model of community and on individual (life history) examination. For the colonial physicians, to have sickling meant to be from certain tribes, located in a determined cartographic space, having a particular purity index, and so on.

BY WAY OF A DETOUR

In the mid-1920s, Thomas B. Cooley and Pearl Lee, two U.S. pediatricians from Detroit who were also well-known for their work on sickle cell anemia, proposed a project for medical practitioners in Africa: "Might not men [*sic*] working in Africa, where the negro strains are still well separated, perhaps find a tribe in which sicklemia is the rule . . . ?" (1926, 340). Much can be gleaned from this question, which is emblematic of its time in many ways.

First, it is obviously informed by the discourse of "racial" distinctiveness and purity that dominated medico-anthropological thinking in the late nineteenth and early twentieth centuries. Second, it echoes the idea, predominant in ethnological circles as well as in the popular imagination at the turn of the nineteenth century and beyond, that Africa constituted a kind of primordial reality[1]; that is, in this context, a place where, as opposed to the Americas (the New World), at least some native "races" or "negro strains" had remained uncontaminated by "admixture." An important implication of this conceptualization of Africa as an instance of the past (characterized by "racial purity") in the present (where "miscegenation" reigns) is that the African body was deemed likely to hold the key to the true "racial" and biological nature of its derivative, the "Negro" body (that is, the diasporic African body). Sickling among "Negroes" in the United States could not be fully understood, it was implied, until an account of sickling among Africans had been made.

Third, it resonates with the colonial administrative discourse on the African social that early in the twentieth century, in conjunction with ethnology, systematically elaborated and promoted the category of the "tribe" as a means of "governing"—or rendering "governable"—the African people. For Cooley and Lee, writing in the 1920s, tribe was a transparent term that one could use, without qualification, when referring to the individual units making up the African social. Current historians and anthropologists have pointed out, however, that the tribe, far from being the original (precolonial) African social form, was an *effect* of colonialism, more specifically of the discourse and practice of indirect rule, a form of colonial administration elaborated by the British in equatorial Africa at the beginning of the twentieth century.[2] As historian John Iliffe aptly puts it: "The British wrongly believed that Tanganyikans [and other Africans] belonged to tribes; Tanganyikans created tribes to function within the colonial framework" (1979, 38).

Lastly, Cooley and Lee's question is instructive because of the linkage it establishes between tribes and blood. In the 1920s, when talking about sicklemia, sickling researchers were referring to the presence of sickle-shaped cells in the blood. They were not, in other words, necessarily making reference to a medical condition (clinical symptoms) but rather to a particular status of the blood that could be documented through laboratory tests. By suggesting that "men working in Africa" search for "a tribe in which sicklemia is the rule," Cooley and Lee made a case for the use of blood as a valid marker of supposed tribal identity. Thus, they joined ranks with those who would naturalize ethnological entities (such as tribes) by defining them in biological terms. More pointedly, by linking sicklemia (a certain blood picture) to a specific form of tribal identity, they followed the lead of the serologists of their day who used blood types to divide populations into racial groups (Hirszfeld and Hirszfeld 1919, 675–79). Sicklemia, in the view of Cooley and Lee, was yet another particular type of blood that could be used to establish racial distinctions between people. Their statement exemplifies, then, the extent to which medicine and ethnology were intertwined, epistemologically and sociopolitically, during the first two decades of the twentieth century.

In 1926, the date of Cooley and Lee's statement, there was one reported case of sickle cell anemia in Africa. It involved an Arab boy from the Sudan (see Archibald 1925–1926, 389–93). No surveys of sickling in African populations had yet been carried out. So what was it that allowed them to envision the existence of an entire African tribe in which sicklemia was the rule? Since sickling is found among African Americans and presumably constitutes a racial trait, so their reasoning went, and since the African American population originates in Africa, sickling must exist in Africa and among Africans. It is clear, then, that their rendering of sickling as a likely problem for Africa and Africans owed nothing to concrete clinical evidence and everything to ethnological speculation.

The colonial medics who eventually came to study sickling in Africa seem to have taken Cooley and Lee's challenge strictly to the letter. That is to say, they pursued the phenomenon primarily as an ethnological matter, their main concern being what sickling (blood) could reveal about tribal histories, differences, and identities as well as about the very origin and true biracial nature of the so-called African.

PRYING A FRAME

In 1945, the *East African Medical Journal* carried an editorial titled "Sickle Cell Anaemia," introducing a paper of the same title by H. C. Trowell (1945), a physician and lecturer at the Uganda Medical School in Kampala. The significance of Trowell's essay, according to the editorial, was that it was the first to document in a systematic way that sickle cell *anemia* did indeed constitute a considerable medical problem in Africa. The editorial began as follows:

> Dr. Trowell's paper . . . brings out the importance of a comparatively new form of chronic haemolytic anaemia in Africans, that must often have

passed unrecognized, because unknown, in many an African hospital and for many a long year. (Sickle Cell 1945, 33)

In the article introduced by the editorial, Trowell reported finding thirty-five cases of the anemia distributed among seven East African tribes. Earlier researchers such as R. Winston Evans had documented the existence of sickling among "West African Natives," but did not distinguish between sickling as a clinical phenomenon (sickle cell anemia) and the mere appearance of sickle-shaped cells in the blood (which does not necessarily produce any clinical symptoms and whose exact status was therefore highly contested) (Evans 1944, 281–86; see also Findlay, Robertson, and Zacharias 1946, 83–86). Up until Trowell's report, the significance of sickle cell anemia in Africa had been subject to intense debate, many medics leaning toward the belief that the phenomenon did not present a problem there insofar as only a handful of sporadic cases had ever been documented. But now that Trowell had shown that sickling did indeed exist in Africa, the editorial seemed to be saying, it must be assumed that if sickling appeared to have been absent from that continent, it was because no one had been looking for it. In other words, the editorial viewed the perceived absence of sickling in Africa as a result of the inadequacy of the diagnostic criteria available to—and the ignorance of—the medical researchers working there. (Even after Trowell published his findings, some researchers remained skeptical, claiming that in spite of their heightened awareness of sickling and protracted efforts to identify new instances, they had been unable to document more than a few sporadic cases.)

If the editorial is worth mentioning here, however, it is because it is, in a general way, paradigmatic of the colonial medical discourse on sickling in Africa. Let me cite another passage:

> [Sickling] was first recognised no more than twenty-five years ago in African negroes in America; but as the x-ray examination of the skulls of Mayan Indians from Mexico, dating back to hundreds of years ago, has shown evidences like those found in the skulls of sickle cell patients today, one may assume that this form of the anaemia has really a history reaching far back into the past. And sickling has been observed recently in Mexicans; the vast majority of the cases reported so far have been found in America, and it is of interest to note that a very similar condition of the blood has been discovered in deer. (Sickle Cell 1945, 33)

Although the editor does acknowledge the clinical importance of sickle cell anemia in contemporary Africa, s/he is just as intrigued by the fact that Trowell's findings allow for further refinement of the disease map of Africa past and present. In general, what characterized colonial medical discourse and practice was the emphasis put on the identification and classification (as opposed to treatment) of diseases, and on the usefulness of disease in identifying and classifying people.[3] The editorial, typically, moves from the clinical via the ethnological and historical to the zoological. This suggests that the colonial medical discourse on phenomena specific to elsewhere and others did not restrict itself to the realm of clinical medicine. That is, colonial medical researchers, in discussing Africa (as opposed to the West), did not extricate the clinical realm from other realms of knowledge, particularly not those of ethnology and ethnohistory. As a consequence, their clinical investigations were also always ethnological enterprises.

Trowell, in one of the first epidemiological investigations of sickling to be carried out in Africa, drew a map showing the migratory movements of Africa's populations from south to north into "Arab countries" and from North Africa further north into "southern European countries." This map, Trowell claimed, quite easily explained the occurrence of sickling in places outside of Africa:

> Since Bantu slaves were freely taken into Arab countries, the Sudan and also Egypt, and since the sickle cell trait is probably a Mendelian dominant, it follows that some cases of this disease should be found in these countries. Indeed, since African slaves travelled freely to the southern European countries, where they became absorbed into the general population, it is not surprising that six out of the seven cases in Europeans have been in Greeks, Italians and Sicilians. (1945, 34)

If Trowell saw the occurrence of sickling—a supposedly Negro disease—in Arab and southern European countries as posing few or no problems in that it was a direct result of an easily identifiable ethnohistorical factor—namely (ironically), the "freedom to travel" of African slaves—he had no such simple answer when it came to accounting for the differential distribution of sickling among so-called Negroes within the African continent. In his view, sickling within Africa represented a higher level of obfuscation. This was so because the notion of "the freely travelling African slave," which obviously translated as "infusion of Negro blood into Caucasian populations" or "miscegenation," and as such explained sickling in the Americas and southern Europe (Tapper 1995, 76–93), seemed to have no pertinence in the context of Africa and Africans. How could there be miscegenation if there were no distinct ("black" and "white") races to be mixed?

As I have shown elsewhere (Tapper 1997, 263–89), the term Negro when occurring in a U.S. context, always designates a nonwhite (as opposed to black) individual. It implies, in short, an order of things based on the distinction between whites and others. In a context that is seen as exclusively black African, the term thus defined has no relevance. It seems that there can be no African equivalent of the U.S. Negro—the "hybrid." Not so. The colonial medical researchers who eventually made sense of sickling in Africa did so with reference to the so-called Hamitic thesis, according to which physical variations among African peoples reflected true racial differences, more precisely the extent to which various groups had been "infused" with the blood of the "pastoral Caucasians" known as the Hamites—that is, with white blood. They thus operated within a discursive space in which some Africans were defined as more white than others and where the term Negro came to designate the "true Negro"—that is, the African free of Hamitic or white blood (Seligman 1939, 55). In such a context, the admixture thesis would once again have currency.

To be sure, Trowell remained uncertain about the adequacy of the term Negro for the description of the ethnological realities of Africa. This became obvious when Trowell stated that "the term Negro does not correspond closely to any ethnographic unit [in Africa], [even though] it connotes the descendants of the Bantu tribes of West Africa" (1945, 34). The problem, as Trowell saw it, was primarily whether or not the anemia existed in Africa; but it was also a problem of visualization, by which he ultimately meant a problem of establishing a relation between the phenomenon and a particular racial body. While he explicitly contended that "the slow recognition of the anaemia in Africa is . . . due to the fact that the clinical picture is not clearly visualized, and that it is extremely easy to confuse the disease with malaria" (34), it is apparent that he saw Africa's social and racial diversity—the myriad of tribes, the complex dynamics of inter- and intratribal relationships, the multiple physical variations—as complicating the picture of sickling. Implicit in his writings, then, is the idea that no clear picture of sickling in Africa could be drawn until an adequate account of the "confusing" African social fabric and racial makeup had been made.

PRODUCING TRUTH EFFECTS

If Trowell and others (for example, Evans 1944; Findlay, Robertson, and Zacharias 1946) acknowledged that the complexity of the internal ethnological divisions of Africa would problematize any attempt at accounting for sickling on that continent, it was E. A. Beet, a medical officer and specialist in tropical medicine and hygiene working at the Colonial Medical Service of Northern Rhodesia (Zambia), who came to place sickling at the center of a whole new medico-ethnological semiotics of "blood." This was a discursive event with considerable implications for colonial administrative practice. By mapping the differential distribution of the phenomenon among various African peoples, Beet's work would make possible not only the redrawing of heretofore commonly accepted tribal lines but also the rewriting of well-established tribal histories, thus rendering governable heretofore "wild" and "unruly" populations.[4]

While both Trowell and Beet considered the systematic screening of Africans attending colonial hospitals to be the appropriate way of getting a handle on the extent of sickling in Africa, Trowell did not, to the same extent as Beet, situate the practice of screening within a broader ethnohistorical context. Even though he meticulously remarked the tribal affiliation of the patients he screened, this information remained a mere notation, his main objective being to show simply that sickling did indeed exist in Africans. Beet, on the other hand, while similarly screening the blood of people seeking medical treatment at the hospital where he was working, was concerned with more than merely documenting the presence of sickling in his African patients. As a matter of fact, one might say that his work began where Trowell's left off. Thus, from its very inception, his study engaged the predominant ethnological discourse on the physical and social environment that constituted the "natural setting" of his patients. That is, he took into consideration from the outset the social space in which sickling existed outside the hospital (and the individual body), thus linking the phenomenon not only to certain geographic locations but to certain tribes.[5]

Beet was credited in 1949 (with James V. Neel) for having worked out the genetics of sickling. In 1946, he had published the results of a major survey on sickling from the Balovale district in northern Rhodesia. Beyond the fact that it further documented the existence of sickle cell anemia in Africa, this report is interesting because it raised many of the questions that were to define the debate on sickling in Africa in the 1940s and 1950s, and even up until today—

questions regarding, for example, the "origin" of the phenomenon, its differential distribution among tribal (and more recently, "ethnic") groups, its relations to phenomena such as malaria and other kinds of anemia, and its relevance for defining a "norm" for the African body.[6]

Beet presented his project as "an investigation . . . into the incidence of the sickle cell trait among the local Bantu population," asserting that "no work on this subject has previously been carried out in this District" (1946, 76). Characteristically, he began his report by describing the geography of the area in which his investigation took place—the Balovale district of northern Rhodesia:

> The Balovale District of Northern Rhodesia is in the Kaonde Lunda Province of that Territory. The Province occupies the northwest corner of Northern Rhodesia, and Balovale is the most westerly of its three Districts. . . . To the north and west of Balovale is Angola, the boundary to the north running parallel to latitude 13° south and that to the west parallel to longitude 22° east; running approximately through the centre of the District from north to south is the Zambesi River. The southern boundary is formed by the rivers Lungwevungu and Kabompo, which flow into the Zambesi from the west, and east respectively; to the south is the Barotse Province of Northern Rhodesia. The eastern boundary is formed by the Manyinga River, which flows into the Kabompo, the latter continuing in a southerly direction and then turning sharply to the west. (75)

He then offered a short portrait of the people who inhabited the district, insisting on their almost complete isolation from Europeans ("civilization"):

> The African population of the District is about 60,000 men, women, and children; the European population is very small. . . . Balovale must be one of the most rural areas remaining in east Africa, the people coming into contact with Europeans only through one of the three missions and the Government Boma staff (which consists of two Administrative Officers and one Medical Officer). The nearest point on the line of rail in Northern Rhodesia is at Chingola, 480 miles away from the Boma over very bad roads, and there is only a sporadic lorry service which connects the two; the railway in Angola is much nearer being only 300 miles distant, however, there are no roads going from Balovale into Portuguese Territory. An area such as this presents ideal conditions for the study of any disease, particularly one, like sicklemia, known to be of a familial nature. (75)

From the outset, then, Beet, the physician, situated his project at the intersection of geography, ethnology, and medicine. A geographically well-defined "rural" (read "primitive") region, the Balovale district, whose inhabitants had little contact, if any, with the outside world (were uncontaminated by "civilization" and "miscegenation"), would be a site of choice for any classic ethnological investigation. For Beet, this controlled environment with its isolated and therefore, it is implied, authentically indigenous inhabitants was akin to an ethno-medical laboratory. If it "present[ed] ideal conditions for the study of any disease, particularly [those] . . . known to be of a familial nature," as he stated, it was because it offered the medical researcher the opportunity to observe a given disease process in a significant yet finite number of persons who were situated in a social and physical space that could be known in its entirety because of its circumscription. Because they were other, persons could be dealt with through the specification of the features of the group, as the medical historian Megan Vaughan (1991, 81) explains, rather than through the detailed specification of individual features. Persons could be treated as human specimens. As a "field laboratory," the Balovale district made possible the visualization of disease in geographic and ethnological (tribal and kinship) terms as well as in medical ones—all forms of visualization that Beet deemed crucial for the understanding of a "familial" disease such as sickling.

Examining blood from 815 consecutive inpatients attending the Government Hospital at Balovale, Beet was able to calculate a sickling incidence of 12.9 percent, which "represent[ed] the District as a whole" ["as cases were drawn from all areas"] (Beet 1946, 82). These figures, he pointed out, compared well with those found elsewhere in Africa.[7] Still, Beet continued, only one case of classic sickle cell anemia was seen. Beet next divided the Balovale district into seven areas, which he called A, B, C, D, E, F, and G. He claimed that these areas were marked out "on a geographical basis, rather than on a scheme based on tribal distribution, as the population is concentrated along the banks of rivers and streams" (1946, 82). Interestingly, in spite of his contention that his map was drawn solely on the basis of geography, Beet had already demonstrated his engagement with ethnology. Thus, in a previous sentence, he described the people resident in the areas in question as "being of adjacent chiefs" (82). Although the stated principal task of his account was to show the distribution of sickling among specific geographic areas, it is clear, then, that Beet used geography, in a strategic appropriation, as a metaphor for the social. In other words, ethnology, in particular its concern with tribes, remained, even when he explicitly denied it, the organizing principle of Beet's research. This is, of course, what makes his way of seeing paradigmatic of the colonial medical enterprise.

The fusion of geography, ethnology, and medicine did more than produce knowledge that might be helpful in treating or curing disease. It generated information about so-called African society, including its tribes and the origin of the African. Thus, Beet's general account of the distribution of sickling within the district reads as follows:

> Most of the cases came from area A, as this is a heavily populated part of the District (of about 13,000 to 14,000 persons) and the Government Boma of Balovale is situated in the middle of it. By far the greater part of the population resides to the east of the Zambesi River (45,000 out of a total of 60,000) and this accounts for the greater number of patients examined from areas A–E inclusive. (82)

In this passage, Beet seems to be saying that the distribution of sickling in the Balovale district can be explained with reference to the law of frequency: the more people, the more cases. He notes elsewhere, however, that "area F which occupies the west bank of the River throughout its length has a very low incidence, compared to all the others and is obviously in a class by itself" (83).

In order to make sense of the discrepancy between the sickling rates identified for the east and west sides of the river, respectively, Beet turned to ethnohistory:

> This interesting distribution of the sickle cell trait among the people of the District can be explained by studying tribal history; area F is occupied by the Lovale tribe but to the east of the river are resident the Lunda and other tribes, the Lunda being predominant. In 1890, there was the Lunda-Lovale war and up to this time, and for some time afterwards, there was not much mixing of the two tribes. In 1907, the Government Boma station was opened at Balovale and from that time onwards there was a tendency for the Lovale to move across the river and to mix with the Lunda, either as individuals or as family groups, but no similar migration took place by the Lunda into Lovale territory. All this is confirmed by the distribution of sicklaemia. Originally the sickle cell trait must have arisen, in this District, in the people living to the east of the Zambesi. As time passed the incidence of this condition must have arisen gradually to its present figure; but, owing to the lack of movement from east to west, sicklaemia never became established to any extent in the Lovale tribe, with the re-

sult that today two Bantu tribes are living adjacent to each other with a marked difference in their sickling rates. Apart from the Lovale living in Northern Rhodesia there are members of this tribe living across the border in Angola, from this group. It is at once apparent that there cannot have been much mixing of these two sections of the same tribes, in the near past, as there is a considerable difference in their sickling rates (3.5 percent and 11.4 percent). It is known that, apart from the Lovale emigration to the east already referred to, the Portuguese Lovale have also been moving into the areas A–E, with the result that now there are considerable numbers of the Lovale living there. (83)

Extricating an ethno-statistical profile of sickling from his examinations of the inhabitants of the Balovale district, Beet rendered the latter as a population consisting of subgroups that were internally differentiated in terms of their respective sickling rates. Or to rephrase it, using the parameters of the physical and social environment, he made of the Balovalese well-defined units of analysis (populations), and as we shall see, (more easily) manageable and manipulable objects of colonial administration (tribes).

To further illustrate this point, let me cite the remainder of Beet's argument:

> It was decided to use the figures obtained for the distribution of sickle cell trait in the District to determine the composition of the Lovale people who have emigrated into the land adjacent to the east bank of the river; the knowledge thus obtained would be useful as it would enable one to get an idea of the amount of alien emigration that has taken place, in recent years, into the east-central portion of the Balovale District. To do this the natives examined from areas E, A, and West B were classified by tribes, it was found that the Lunda and Lovale were the most numerous and so attention was devoted to these two only. Of the 220 Lunda from here 34 were sicklers giving an incidence of 15.5 percent, of the 120 Lovale 20 were sicklers giving an incidence of 16.7 percent. The rate for these Lovale is considerably greater than that for their fellows across the river in Northern Rhodesia (3.5 percent) but is similar to that found among the Portuguese Lovale (11.4 percent). This shows that the emigration of Portuguese natives into the area concerned has been considerably greater than any movement of the Northern Rhodesia Lovale into the same area. Therefore, it can be concluded that there is now a considerable alien population resident within the boundaries of the Balovale District. (84)

Why would it be "useful," as Beet claims, to know "the amount of alien emigration that has taken place, in recent years, into the east-central portion of the Balovale District"? Answering this question amounts to determining the discursive location of the term "useful." It is important here that this apparently transparent term be problematized, situating it within the rationality of governance, or more specifically, within the context of colonial administrative discourse and practice. In order to do so, it is necessary to take a closer look at the ethnohistorical rendering of the Balovale district and its people relied on by the colonial administrators of the 1940s.

Most ethnohistorical accounts of the Luvale and Lunda peoples in the upper Zambesi depict them as remarkably similar in material culture, sharing a common historical tradition, with enough linguistic similarities to make communication relatively easy and intermarriage commonplace. Despite the many features perceived by ethnologists as commonalities linking the two groups, the Zambesi district of the 1940s and 1950s was a place of continuous strife as witnessed by the numerous states of emergency that the authorities declared (see Papstein 1989, 372–94).

To explain the tension between the groups, ethnohistorians usually refer to the tribal history of the district. Robert Papstein, a historian who has done extensive work on the Luvale-speaking peoples of the upper Zambesi, for example, observes that in 1907, when the Balovale Boma was opened, the Luvale and Lunda found themselves under the administration of the Lozi "chief" Lewanika. The latter had struck a deal with the British South Africa Company (BSAC), which had the right to administer all of Bulozi and its dependents. The BSAC had placed Balovale, as it was then called, under the auspices of Lewanika, who had convinced BSAC that the upper Zambesi was part of the Lozi domain. The Luvale and Lunda joined forces to fight Lozi encroachments, presenting their case to the local authorities. At the same time as the Luvale and Lunda were appealing their cases, however, the British, Portuguese, and Belgian colonial governments drew up the colonial borders between their respective principalities. The agreement between these three colonial governments effectively distributed the Luvale and Lunda groups among northern Rhodesia, Angola, and the Congo Free State (see Papstein 1989, 378).

Although the Luvale and Lunda cooperated in resisting Lozi sovereignty, their relationship continued to be marred by tension, a situation that made it difficult for the colonial administration to effectively "govern" them. Therefore, in 1923, District Commissioner Bruce-Miller, in an attempt to end the strife between the two groups and bring about administrative "order," requested that the Zambesi River be used as a dividing line between the Luvale and Lunda. According to Papstein, "The use of the river as a tribal boundary would have resulted in the bulk of the best arable land in Chavuma [the area straddling the Zambesi where it flows from Angola into northern Rhodesia] falling under Lunda authority when, by all accounts . . . Chavuma was a predominantly Luvale area" (378). This, of course, had the support of the Lunda, their alliance with the Luvale against the Lozi notwithstanding. But it also meant that the Luvale residing in the Chavuma — an ethnically heterogeneous area since the late eighteenth century — had to be relocated. All attempts at relocating the Luvale engendered resistance, and eventually led to violent strife between the Luvale and Lunda groups, thereby resulting in the abolition of the policy. Nevertheless, as Papstein notes,

> the use of the Zambesi as an administrative border . . . was so compulsively appealing that virtually all District Commissioners attempted to employ it. . . . [I]t became an article of faith among subsequent District Commissioners that the Luvale belonged "properly" on the Zambesi's west bank and the Lunda on its east bank. . . . Commitment to this point of view, reflected in the formulation of subsequent policies, has been the single most important stimulus to tribal strife between Lunda and Luvale. Every local political decision was — and still is — evaluated in terms of whether it would further or diminish each side's claim to the Chavuma, the area's best agricultural land. (378)

REDRAWING MAPS, RESTORING AUTHORITY

Beet concluded his report by letting it be known that "an investigation of sickle cell disease in an area may confirm beliefs about recent tribal movements, and thus assist investigators interested in tribal history" (1946, 85). In other words, he read the results of his research as pointing to the potential of sickling (genetics) to resolve, once and for all, the tribal conflicts outlined above. Hence his reference to the usefulness of his findings. It is most significant to notice in this context that he actually invited Charles M. N. White, the district officer of Balovale, to comment on his findings and conclusions. White, himself a fledgling ethnohistorian who authored two publications on the Balovale district (1949, 1950), remarked:

> The final conclusion — that very few of the Lovale now living east of the Zambesi came from west of the river, but in actuality came from Angola

for the most part—is the most unexpected result of this study. It had always been assumed that the Lovale on the east of the river had come from the west of the Zambesi, and political tension between the Lunda and Lovale has been frequently centred around this assumption. No detailed investigation of the origin of the Lovale now residing east of the Zambesi has ever been made, however, and in view of Dr. Beet's finding, an investigation of this nature should be undertaken when opportunity offers since definite information upon this point would have administrative value. (cited in Beet 1946, 85)

White obviously shares Beet's view that sickling research can be used to rewrite the history of peoples (tribes) under colonial administration. More specifically, he is saying here that the relationship between the Lunda and Luvale is marked by "political tension" caused, among other things, by the "assumption" that the Luvale is an alien population originating in the area west of the Zambesi. Yet, he continues, the results of Beet's investigation indicate that the Luvale living on the east side of the river do not originate on the west bank but rather in Angola. According to White, then, the implication of Beet's findings is that the political tension between the two tribes is based on a false assumption about the past—more precisely, about the origin of the Luvale. In other words, White considers tribal politics in the Balovale district to be based on an incorrect version of the area's tribal history. If White welcomes Beet's findings, then, it is because they provide his administration with an opportunity to correct, on a biomedical basis, the version of history informing the intertribal conflicts of the day—a correction, it is implied, that will definitively settle these conflicts and render governable the unruly Lunda and Luvale. Hence, the "administrative value" of the findings.

Let me reiterate here that in the colonial Africa of the 1940s, there was nothing new about using ethnological knowledge for administrative ends (see Asad 1985; for an attempt at a fascinating though unnecessarily underdeveloped project, see Scott 1995, 191–220). In 1935, for example, G. Gordon Brown, an anthropologist, and Bruce Hutt, the district officer of the Iringa district (Tanganyika territory), published *Anthropology in Action,* a book examining, in the authors' words, "to what extent anthropological knowledge can be made applicable to problems surrounding the administration of an African tribe" (1). In the foreword he was asked to write for the book with which he was involved from its very inception, Sir Philip Mitchell, the chief secretary of Tanganyika territory, specifies that it is in fact an account of an actual "practical experiment in co-operation between a District Officer administering his District and an anthropologist" (cited in Brown and Hutt 1935, xi). What makes Mitchell relevant in this context is not only his belief that the results of anthropological research can be fruitfully put to administrative use. More important, notice his juxtaposition of, on the one hand, the anthropologist and the district officer, and on the other, the "laboratory worker" and the "practising doctor." For this defines a discourse field in which ethnology, colonial administration, and medicine interlock to the point where they can no longer be extricated from one another; and this is the same discursive field within which Beet situates his work and from which it derives its significance.

When sickling became implicated in the colonial enterprise of rendering governable the social environment of Africa, a space was opened up for addressing tribes in biomedical terms. Sickling research as it unfolded in the work of Beet brought together discourses on disease, early African tribal history, ethnology, and linguistics. But the categories of ethnohistory, ethnology, and linguistics that identified past vestiges of tribes and current tribal groups had been problematized by the emergence, in their midst, of the biomedical technologies of blood. To the external criteria of similarity and difference had been added a criterion from the archives of the body—the blood picture (sickling status) of individual tribespeople. The tribe, in short, had been naturalized.

We have seen that Beet regarded his medico-statistical findings as being of immediate relevance to the colonial administration of the Lunda and Luvale. More precisely, he perceived the truth about the origins and the right to land of these groups to be speaking through their blood (as objectified by biomedicine), rather than through their own rendering of the past. Sickling, in his view, was a most reliable means of identifying tribes, "when the other stigmata of [their] descent ha[d] disappeared" (Beet 1947–1949, 279–84); that is, of maintaining the notion of tribal difference even where no difference could be established in ethnological or political terms.

Beet would ask why high rates of sickling were identified for some groups of Africans while significantly lower rates were found for others residing between them. Such a question could not be answered, of course, by the naked data produced through the screening of blood in the laboratory. Instead, a concurrent study of the contacts and relationships defining African social space (see Armstrong 1983, 11) seemed to be called for. This is why Beet eventually shifted his focus from the laboratory of the clinic to that of the field.

In 1949, taking advantage of a health survey of Lala schoolchildren in the Serenje district of northern Rhodesia during which all the children were tested for the sickle cell trait, Beet sought to demonstrate "how the trait be-have[d] in a pure stock Bantu tribe" (1947–1949, 280).[8] Having determined the incidence of the condition among this group,[9] he went on to investigate the families of certain of the children:

> Family trees were drawn up and every individual who could be contacted was tested for the trait; this entailed visits to many villages and in a few cases medical officers elsewhere were requested to trace and test certain persons who had moved to their areas. (280)

Based on his analysis of four family trees, Beet showed that of the offspring produced by the mating of a sickle-celled subject with an allegedly normal one, about 50 percent would be heterozygous; and that of the offspring pro-duced by the mating of a sickle-celled subject with another sickle-celled sub-ject, at least 75 percent would be homozygous. He concluded that the sickle cell trait behaves as a Mendelian dominant, and suggested that sickle cell ane-mia occurs in homozygotes only.

I have already noted above that following the publication of these find-ings, Beet was credited, independently of Neel, with having worked out the genetics of sickling. If I cite his work here, however, it is because of the par-ticular discursive location of his study. At first glance, Beet's analysis seems to fall squarely within the realm of Mendelian genetics. Insofar as it is about a population and its specific characteristics, such as its state of health in general and its sickling rate in particular, it can also be viewed as an instantiation of the analytics of sexuality in the manner of Foucault. Indeed, by the time Beet got around to examining them, the Lala schoolchildren had been visualized as a population in that they had already been the object of a "health survey"; more specifically, in that their bodily attributes and deficiencies had already been inscribed through the quantifying techniques of the survey. Beet con-tinued the project of visualization initiated by the survey by registering the details of the genealogies of a select group of the children—those who were found to possess the sickle cell trait and whose families "were reasonably ac-cessible" (Beet 1947–1949, 280). Based on the family trees thus produced, he carried out the analysis of sickling and mating that eventually led him to the "discovery" of the genetics of the phenomenon.

Although a comparison of Neel and Beet would lead well beyond the bounds of this immediate project, I would like to point to some revealing dif-ferences between the discourses they drew on to arrive at their similar conclusions. Neel's approach was defined by the emerging clinical and population genetics. He proceeded by moving from the clinic into specified populations and then immediately returning to the clinic. Sickling, to him, was an object of analysis *as well as* a target of clinical intervention (that is, of diagnosis, counseling, and treatment). A closer look at Beet's study reveals that, unlike Neel's, it was not concerned with the clinical implications of the findings it presented. Rather, the centrality it afforded to concepts such as "purity," "stock," and "tribes" betrays its engagement with Galtonian (eugenic) genetics (see Rose 1979, 20). More precisely, Beet had not extricated himself from the particular way of seeing that Foucault labeled the symbolics of blood. In his work, the concern with purity, stock, and tribes remained instrumental in the production of knowledge. Sickling thus ultimately emerged less as an individual or collective health issue, and more as a powerful (biogenetic) tool in the ethnological enterprise of writing identity and difference.

It is crucial to note here that Beet was working within the African social whose "opacity," in the eye of the colonial outsider, never ceased to "inspire" and then complicate attempts at making sense of it. Neel, on the other hand, carried out his work in Detroit, among African and Italian Americans who were seen as well-defined populations; that is, he was operating within a social realm that was perceived as "transparent," as posing no problems of categorization to be resolved. My point is that, in general, Beet's work, like that of most other colonial physicians, was ultimately determined by the aforementioned broader colonial discourse on the African social according to which the latter was of an essentially "obscure" nature, and as such, invariably challenged and complicated attempts at shedding light on its internal organization. This, in turn, meant that his work, like most colonial medical work, had to be primarily a project of visualization. The main problem facing Beet, in other words, was to make sickling visible, to make it emerge, as it were, from the obscure (social) environment that was Africa. Through his work on the Balovale district with its limited and isolated population, for instance, Beet visualized sickling by first accounting for the phenomenon in ethnological terms (along tribal lines) and then using it to problematize the very ethnological categories (tribal demarcations) underpinning his initial analysis. Beet's work, then, while making sickling visible, also illuminated a segment of the opaque African social—more specifically, some of its organizing principles (migration and tribal expansionism). This simultaneous investment in medicine and ethnology is what makes it emblematic of the colonial medical enterprise in Africa.

By situating the logic of colonial medicine in anthropological practice and examining the discursive parallels, I have argued here that the study of sickling by colonial physicians in Africa existed in certain specifics only in concert with anthropology. By pursuing the vexing problem of tribe across the shifting political landscape of colonial medicine, anthropology, and government, we gain insight into the mechanisms through which kinship and social identity are fashioned—in particular, the use of blood/disease to represent relations of political power over bodies and geographical spaces. As Eric Worby (1994, 392) has also noted, it is paradoxical that, at a time when the colonial state policy discouraged tribal identities in favor of modern ones such as class, a renewed interest in tribal cartographies arose.

Consider these possibilities by way of a conclusion: Sickling and the constructions inscribed within it naturalized the relic of "tribe," remotivated it symbolically, and reconstituted its eminence; and that sickling had become, by the colonial period, a mechanism for a new strategy of intervention and withdrawal by the state. The strategy was to construct and naturalize social identities, and to constitute itself as a new instrumentality of power—blood/governmentality. Making tribes (kinship) was, in the view here, a positively positioned product of power that made possible certain tactical interventions of surveillance and control. As such, it was far from a simple matter of affirming what was already in place.

NOTES

This essay is a revised version of "Medical Problems with Ethnological Solutions: The Colonial Construction of Sickling in Africa," which is chapter 3 of my book, *In the Blood: Sickle Cell Anemia and the Politics of Race* (University of Pennsylvania Press, 1999). I thank University of Pennsylvania Press for granting me the rights to publish this version.

1 Johannes Fabian (1983) offers an excellent discussion of this discursive project, showing how anthropology constructs its others by placing them in a different time. But his thesis is equally applicable, it seems, to medico-genetic discourses on Africa.

2 The systematically elaborated category of the tribe was central to colonial administration in Africa, in particular to the discourse and practice known as indirect rule (see, for example, Willis 1993, 53–68; Mafeje 1971, 253–61; Mamdani 1996, 145–51). In 1925, on assuming the governorship of Tanganyika (Tanzania), Sir Donald Cameron, one of the first colonial administrators to implement that particular form of governance in East Africa, defined it as the practice of "administer[ing] the people through the instrument of their own indigenous institutions"—that is, their own "tribal" institutions (cited in Graham 1976, 3). But as it turned out, indirect rule was not easily

implemented. If tribal units were to be the primary means for governing Africa, tribes had to be rendered knowable, countable, and manipulable. The problem, however, as historian James D. Graham points out (1976, 5), was that the inhabitants of any given African territory did not necessarily constitute tribes so much as infiltrations and migrations of sections of ethnic groups. In other words, what colonial administrators delineated as tribes did not necessarily correspond to any preexisting social organization. Africans may eventually have come to see themselves as belonging to the distinct tribes defined by the colonial administration, yet this sense of belonging should be seen as the effect rather than the cause of tribalism.

3   For the role of science in this regard, see Haraway 1989. A number of medical historians have now pointed out how early tropical medicine was characterized by a concern with vectors and pathogens, rather than people and politics. Just when this division of early and presumably late tropical medicine came about is not clear. My argument, however, is that in the 1940s, colonial medicine was very much concerned with populations, politics, and history (see Vaughan 1991; MacKenzie 1990, 187–212; L. White 1995, 219–45).

4   These terms were used by colonial administrators in northern Rhodesia to describe the Lunda and Lovale people, who were also the object of Beet's investigations (see Papstein 1989, 378).

5   Megan Vaughan, a medical historian working in Uganda, argues that colonial medicine favored the tribe over the individual as its primary unit of analysis. More specifically, Vaughan shows how "culture and race took over, not simply as mediators of disease, but sometimes as sources of disease in themselves" (1994, 289; see also Vaughan 1991, 82).

6   On the distinction between tribal and ethnic groups, Aidan W. Southall puts it this way: "However much it wounds our romantic souls . . . the term 'tribe' should usually be applied only to the small-scale societies of the past which retained their political autonomy, and . . . the new associations derived from them in the contemporary context should be referred to as ethnic groups" (1970, 48).

7   Beet compares his findings with those of R. Winston Evans (1944), who had examined the blood of 561 West African ("Askari") soldiers coming from the races (as he called them) of Nigeria, the Cameroons, the Gold Coast and Gambia, and found a sickling rate of 19.9 percent, as well as those of Findlay, Robertson, and Zacharias (1946), who found the "incidence" among 300 Gold Coast Askari to be 15.5 percent.

8   One of the issues confronting colonial medical researchers attempting to make sense of disease in Africa was the fact that a "norm" for the African body had not been established. One thing seemed obvious to them, however: the standards that applied to the African body were not the same as those defining the European one. Among Africans, for instance, parasitic infestations and anemia appeared to be the norm—the "normal" African body, then, being malarial and anemic. Further complicating the establishment of a bodily norm for the African was the fact that African bodies, in the discourse of colonial medical practitioners, were always already, as we have seen, categorized in terms of their perceived tribal affiliation. Once the tribe

was established as defining African social reality (just as race is defining the social in today's United States), the notion of a generally valid norm for the African body became difficult to maintain. If, for example, the members of two or more tribes inhabiting the same geographic area could be found to differ in terms of sickling rates, how could one uphold the notion of a bodily norm that transcended tribal boundaries? Blood, in general, and the sickle cell trait, in particular, played crucial roles in the making of the normal African body. In 1945, Trowell had proclaimed that "no blood-count on an African can be considered complete unless a sealed drop preparation is made and examined for sickle cells" (1945, 42). Beet echoed this view when stating, a year later, that "no routine laboratory examination on an African is complete unless the simple test for sickling in vitro is carried out" (1946, 80). Three years after Beet, Alan B. Raper, a physician working in Uganda, would warn that "it deserves emphasis that in Africa a test for sickling forms part of the basic examination of African patients without which his [*sic*] reaction to adverse conditions cannot be gauged" (1949, 14).

9 Of 308 Lala schoolchildren tested, Beet (1947–1949, 281) found 42 to possess the trait—an incidence of 13.6 percent.

REFERENCES

Archibald, R. G. 1925–1926. A Case of Sickle Cell Anemia in the Sudan. *Transactions of the Royal Society of Tropical Medicine and Hygiene* 19:389–93.

Armstrong, David. 1983. *A Political Anatomy of the Body: Medical Knowledge in Britain in the Twentieth Century.* Cambridge: Cambridge University Press.

Asad, Talal, ed. 1985. *Anthropology and the Colonial Encounter.* London: Ithaca Press.

Beet, E. A. 1946. Sickle Cell Disease in the Balovale District. *East African Medical Journal* 23:75–86.

———. 1947–1949. Genetics of the Sickle-Cell Trait in a Bantu Tribe. *Annals of Human Genetics* 14:279–84.

Blake, Lynn A. 1999. Pastoral Power, Governmentality and Cultures of Order in Nineteenth-Century British Columbia. *Transactions of the Institute of British Geographers* 24:79–93.

Brown, G. Gordon, and A. McD. Bruce Hutt. 1935. *Anthropology in Action: An Experiment in the Iringa District of the Iringa Province, Tanganyika Territory.* London: Oxford University Press.

Buchler, Ira. 1994. Making Kinship: Framed Constructions and Their Margins. *Semiotics* 101, no. 3–4:241–321.

Comaroff, John, and Jean Comaroff. 1992. *Ethnography and the Historical Imagination.* Boulder, Colo.: Westview Press.

Cooley, Thomas B., and Pearl Lee. 1926. The Sickle Cell Phenomenon. *American Journal of Diseases of Children* 32:334–40.

Evans, R. Winston. 1944. The Sickling Phenomenon in the Blood of West African Natives. *Transactions of the Royal Society of Tropical Medicine and Hygiene* 37:281–86.

Fabian, Johannes. 1983. *Time and the Other: How Anthropology Makes Its Object.* New York: Columbia University Press.

Findlay, G. M., W. Muir Robertson, and F. J. Zacharias. 1946. The Incidence of Sicklaemia in West Africa. *Transactions of the Royal Society of Tropical Medicine and Hygiene* 40:83–86.

Foucault, Michel. 1991. Governmentality. In *The Foucault Effect: Studies in Governmentality,* edited by Graham Burchell, Colin Gordon, and Peter Miller. Chicago: University of Chicago Press.

Gilman, Sander L. 1985. *Difference and Pathology: Stereotypes of Sexuality, Race, and Madness.* Ithaca, N.Y.: Cornell University Press.

Graham, James D. 1976. Indirect Rule: The Establishment of "Chiefs" and "Tribes" in Cameron's Tanganyika. *Tanzania Notes and Records* 77–78:1–9.

Haraway, Donna. 1989. *Primate Visions: Gender, Race, and Nation in the World of Modern Science.* New York: Routledge.

Hindess, Barry. 1997. Politics and Governmentality. *Economy and Society* 26, no. 2:257–72.

Hirszfeld, L., and H. Hirszfeld. 1919. Serological Differences between the Blood of Different Races: The Results of Researches on the Macedonian Front. *Lancet* 2:675–79.

Iliffe, John. 1979. *A Modern History of Tanganyika.* Cambridge: Cambridge University Press.

Lentz, Carola. 1994. "They Must Be Dagaba First and Any Other Thing Second . . .": The Colonial and Post-Colonial Creation of Ethnic Identities in North-Western Ghana. *African Studies* 53, no. 2:57–91.

MacKenzie, S. M. 1990. Experts and Amateurs: Tsetse, Nagana, and Sleeping Sickness in East and Central Africa. In *Imperialism and the Natural World,* edited by John M. MacKenzie. Manchester: Manchester University Press.

Mafeje, Archie. 1971. The Ideology of Tribalism. *Journal of Modern African Studies* 9:253–61.

Mamdani, Mahmood. 1996. Indirect Rule, Civil Society, and Ethnicity: The Africa Dilemma. *Social Justice* 23:145–51.

Miller, Christopher L. 1985. *Blank Darkness: Africanist Discourse in French.* Chicago: University of Chicago Press.

Mudimbe, V. Y. 1988. *The Invention of Africa: Gnosis, Philosophy, and the Order of Knowledge.* Bloomington: Indiana University Press.

Packard, Randall M. 1989. "Healthy Reserve" and the "Dressed Native": Discourses on Black Health and the Language of Legitimation in South Africa. *American Ethnologist* 16, no. 4:686–703.

Papstein, Robert. 1989. From Ethnic Identity to Tribalism: The Upper Zambesi Region of Zambia, 1830–1931. In *The Creation of Tribalism in Southern Africa,* edited by Leroy Vail. Berkeley: University of California Press.

Raper, Alan B. 1949. Sudden Death in Sickle-Cell Disease. *East African Medical Journal* 26:14–22.

Rorty, Richard. 1979. *Philosophy and the Mirror of Nature.* Princeton, N.J.: Princeton University Press.

Rose, Nikolas. 1979. The Psychological Complex: Mental Measurement and Social Administration. *Ideology and Consciousness* 5:5–68.

Schneider, David M. 1984. *A Critique of the Study of Kinship.* Ann Arbor: University of Michigan Press.

Scott, David. 1995. Colonial Governmentality. *Social Text* 43:191–220.

Seligman, Charles G. 1939. *Races of Africa.* London: Oxford University Press.

Sickle Cell Anaemia. 1945. *East African Medical Journal* 22:33.

Southall, Aidan W. 1970. The Illusion of Tribe. In *The Passing of Tribal Man in Africa,* edited by Peter C. W. Gutkind. Leiden, Netherlands: Brill.

Tapper, Melbourne. 1995. Interrogating Bodies: Medico-Racial Knowledge, Politics, and the Study of a Disease. *Comparative Studies in Society and History* 37, no. 1:76–93.

———. 1997. An "Anthropathology" of the "American Negro": Anthropology, Genetics, and the New Racial Science, 1940–1952. *Social History of Medicine* 10:263–89.

Trowell, H. C. 1945. Sickle Cell Anaemia. *East African Medical Journal* 22:34–45.

Vail, Leroy, ed. 1989. *The Creation of Tribalism in Southern Africa.* Berkeley, Calif.: University of California Press.

Vaughan, Megan. 1991. *Curing Their Ills: Colonialism, Power, and African Illness.* Stanford, Calif.: Stanford University Press.

———. 1994. Healing and Curing: Issues in the Social History and Anthropology of Medicine in Africa. *Social History of Medicine* 7:283–95.

White, Luise. 1995. Tsetse Visions: Narratives of Blood and Bugs in Colonial Northern Rhodesia, 1931–1939. *Journal of African History* 36, no. 2:219–45.

White, Charles M. N. 1949. The Balovale Peoples and Their Historical Background. *The Rhodes-Livingstone Journal* 8:26–41.

———. 1950. Notes on the Political Organization of the Kabompo District and Its Inhabitants. *African Studies* 9:185–93.

Willis, Justin. 1993. The Administration of Bonde, 1920–1960: A Study of the Implementation of Indirect Rule in Tanganyika. *African Affairs* 92:53–68.

Worby, Eric. 1994. Maps, Names, and Ethnic Games: The Epistemology and Iconography of Colonial Power in Northeastern Zimbabwe. *Journal of Southern African Studies* 20, no. 3:371–92.

CHAPTER 13

"We're Going to Tell These People Who They Really Are":
Science and Relatedness

Jonathan Marks

The title of this essay is derived from the justification given for the Human Genome Diversity Project (HGDP) by a spokesman, to an audience of bioethicists, in an unsuccessful attempt to drum up support for the project at the International Congress of Bioethics in 1996. A Native American activist responded from the audience: "I know who I really am. Shall I tell you who *you* really are?"

Identity and descent — the constructions of *who* and *what* you are — are traditional foci of anthropological studies of kinship. David Schneider presented as a cultural fact that American beliefs about kinship are strongly rooted in folk-hereditary ideologies, expressed as the proportional sharing of "biogenetic substance" (1968, 23–25). It is not surprising, then, that the development of genetics in the twentieth century would be accompanied by a strong claim of authority by the science of genetics in precisely those contested cultural arenas of identity and descent.

Here, I look at one such claim — that of population genetics — expressed recently in the controversial proposal for the founding of the HGDP, a consortium of population geneticists attempting to establish itself as "big science," with the goal of retrieving and storing genetic samples from indigenous peoples. The justification for the HGDP resides in the promise of an ultimate microphylogeny of the human species, a goal that is both intractable and anthropologically problematic. Nevertheless, the HGDP successfully managed to represent itself as the locus of authority in population-level studies of relatedness. There are any number of precedents in the last hundred years for bio-genetic studies to cast themselves in opposition to anthropology. Presently situated on the cutting edge of modern ideologies of identity, relatedness, and history, as well as on the cutting edge of modern bioethics, the HGDP may necessitate rethinking the place of anthropology in the larger academic community.

GENETICS AND ANTHROPOLOGY IN THE EARLY PART OF THIS CENTURY

In 1911, the same year that Franz Boas published *The Mind of Primitive Man* and established the case for the conceptual divorce of biology (i.e., race) and culture (i.e., history), geneticist Charles Davenport published *Heredity in Relation to Eugenics*. Equally paradigmatic, Davenport approached similar questions in different ways, arguing that culture was a direct outcome of the newly discovered Mendelian genes, and that there was a direct translation between superior genes and superior cultures.

Davenport, however, had an advantage. He presented his ideas with the well-financed and well-respected cachet of modern biological science. As the American eugenics movement emerged in the next two decades, it would consciously cast itself as the modern, scientific antidote to the newly emerging field of anthropology. On one level, it was an idealistic expression of the desire to impose some form of rationality on the capricious acts of marriage and reproduction; on another, it carried a racist and elitist appeal to restrict the immigration of populations with bad "germ-plasm," and to sterilize the poor, involuntarily if need be.

It is thus easy to find unsettling appeals in unlikely places. For example, the first edition of a popular genetics textbook by E. W. Sinnott (later the dean of Yale's graduate school) and L. C. Dunn (later an outspoken critic of racist biology) exhorts students to sterilize their neighbors (or worse?) on the basis of their social position:

> Even under the most favorable surroundings there would still be a great many individuals who are always on the border line of self-supporting existence and whose contribution to society is so small that the elimination of their stock would be beneficial. (1925, 406)

To oppose eugenics was to oppose modernity, science, and evolution. Although critiques were available—for example, by Boas (1916), Alfred L. Kroeber (1916), and Clarence Darrow (1926)—no biologist published a serious challenge to the ideology and methodology of eugenics until Raymond Pearl's article, "The Biology of Superiority" (1927), which became newsworthy for that very reason.

The eugenics movement ultimately failed not so much because of new data or the persuasive merits of alternative ideologies but because the Great Depression graphically illustrated the lack of fit between genes and social standing; and its embrace by the Nazis touched off a reciprocal concern for individual rights in the United States that had been lacking a generation before (see Paul and Spencer 1995). For a while, however, the eugenics movement was eminently successful in popularizing its cause as well as influencing public opinion and legislation, largely by virtue of representing itself as a modern, scientific analysis of cultural phenomena — in other words, as an improved alternative to anthropology.

HUMAN GENETICS AS RACIAL HISTORY

It is not terribly difficult to find the same scenario repeated in slightly different contexts throughout the twentieth century. The discernment of the fundamental divisions of the human species, for example, was taken to be the basic task of physical anthropology in the first half of that century. The earliest blood group data, inherited as simple Mendelian factors, were immediately taken to supersede the old-fashioned, anatomically based anthropological data. The fact that these new data created random artificial associations between the Poles and Chinese, and among the peoples of New Guinea, West Africa, and Southeast Asia, did not seem to diminish the geneticists' zeal in the 1920s (see Snyder 1926), nor again a generation later (see Boyd 1947).

These studies incorporated the ABO blood group, the earliest genetic "marker" — that is, a trait passed on perfectly intact, without adulteration either by the circumstances of life or by gross convergence due to common environmental adaptation. It simply marked a bit of heredity. But what good was a genetic marker unless it could reveal the deep aspects of ancestry?

Harvard's Earnest Hooton, the dean of U.S. physical anthropology, had graphically represented the complex ancestry of human populations literally as blood relations, evoking the anastemoses and capillaries of the circulatory system (see figure 13.1). Daunting and value-laden as the depiction of these historical relations seems to be (with Keltic and Nordic representing the top of the main trunk of the species, and an obvious subtext of purity, for example), it nevertheless served to illustrate the ostensible affinities of these groups as subject to the dual forces of growing apart and together.

The exercise proved too daunting for most other physical anthropological treatises. Racial anthropology generally limited itself to maps and classifications, not to branching diagrams representing ancestry. Indeed, Hooton's

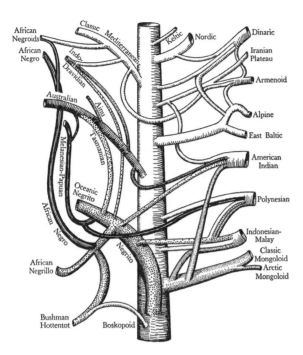

FIG. 13.1 Blood streams of the human races from Earnest A. Hooton, *Up from the Ape,* 2d ed. (New York: Macmillan, 1946).

"blood streams of the human races" (1946) was not based on genetic markers at all—he was skeptical of the genetic data for the very reason that it tended to give strange results.

Neither the critical book on race by the geneticist William Boyd (1950) nor the notoriously anachronistic and politicized work of Carleton Coon (1962) represented human microevolution in such a fashion. Neither did it appear in the 1950 Cold Spring Harbor Symposium volume, *Origin and Evolution of Homo Sapiens,* nor in the 1963 Wenner-Gren conference volume, *Classification and Human Evolution.* Physical anthropologist Frederick Hulse posed the question directly: "Perhaps the standard design of the ancestral tree, so useful in representing the descent of different species [which are always diverging], has misled us. Is such a design appropriate as a representation of sub-specific diversification?" (1962, 931). And he answered in the negative, proposing instead a "grid or trellis." This way, the pervasive fact of intermixing would be rendered neither invisible nor intractable in representations of human history, and the constructed nature of human groups might be rendered more evident.

The study by geneticists L. Luca Cavalli-Sforza and A. W. F. Edwards (1965),

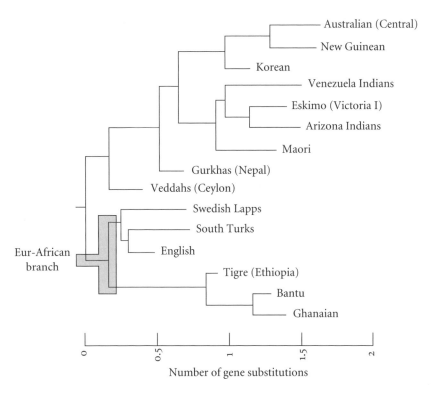

FIG. 13.2 Dendrogram of human genetic relationships, redrawn after L. Luca Cavalli-Sforza and A. W. F. Edwards, "Analysis of Human Evolution," in *Genetics Today: Proceedings of the XI International Congress of Genetics,* ed. S. J. Geerts (Oxford, U.K.: Pergamon, 1965).

then, came as something of a novelty. They adopted the fledgling philosophy of "numerical taxonomy" (Sneath and Sokal 1962) and generated branching trees to depict the similarity among fifteen (quickly expanded to thirty-five) populations, based on their frequencies of five blood-group alleles (see figure 13.2). Numerical taxonomy was controversial within biological systematics for it focused specifically on similarity at the expense of phylogeny or relatedness, and was quickly supplanted by cladistics (which reversed the emphasis; see below). Nevertheless, Cavalli-Sforza and Edwards believed they had generated a "phylogenetic tree" (1965, 927) that represented "ancestries" (923) and "the evolutionary pathway" (927).

Cavalli-Sforza and Edwards had in fact generated a phenetic tree, one representing *similarity,* and speciously interpreted it as depicting *phylogeny.* (These would be isomorphic only if evolutionary rates are constant and equal over all lineages. Otherwise, one particular rapidly evolving lineage might be closely related to another, but quite dissimilar from it, and therefore the fact of relatedness would be masked.) The most interesting aspect of the tree was that it appeared to juxtapose Oceanic and Asian populations against Eur-African populations, indicating that a fundamental biological division existed in our species, along an east-west axis (see figure 13.2). They noted "a remarkable similarity between the blood group map thus obtained, and the geographical map; this fact is not too surprising, as physical proximity implies, on average, higher rates of gene diffusion" (929–30). In other words, there are two reasons why peoples might be genetically similar: either recent divergence or coming back together, but they only graphically illustrated and considered *divergence*. This point is crucial because the analysis is predicated on taking cultural or political entities as natural units, and inferring historical bifurcations from the patterns of similarity of these units. Neither of these assumptions is valid since the structure of the tree is sensitive to the composition of the populations, their demographic expansions and contractions, the statistical algorithm applied, and the gene systems analyzed (Harpending 1994) — in addition to any ethnohistorical genetic contact among them that may make them inseparable as natural categories. In other words, the inflexibility of the tree metaphor led to the reification and naturalization of units that were not genetically stable, and as we shall see, probably illusory.

But the geneticists went a step further. Extracting data from a classic compendium (Rudolf Martin's *Lehrbuch der Anthropologie in Systematischer Darstellung*), they proceeded to generate a tree from twenty-six anthropometric traits for fifteen matching populations — subsuming classic gross measurements such as stature, chest girth, prognathism, nose height, skin color, and ear length. The tree generated from these characteristics had a fundamentally different branching structure: it appeared to link Europeans and Asians in juxtaposition against Africans — a north-south division (with Oceanics split between them). While critical of their naive selection of anthropological data, William Howells (1973, 1976) generated a concordant tree of his own based on craniometric data for sixteen worldwide populations.

Cavalli-Sforza and Edwards used the dichotomy between their genetic and anthropometric trees to argue for the superiority of the genetic tree as a representation of the ancestry of the human species. The scientific rhetoric quickly recalled an earlier era. For instance, in a popular 1974 article in *Scientific American*, Cavalli-Sforza again juxtaposed the anthropometric tree against his genetic one, explicitly labeled the "evolutionary" tree. Thus, anthropology was old-fashioned and creationist; genetics would be modern and scientific. "The study of single genes is probably more useful for reconstructing a common ancestry than the study of superficial traits" (1974, 89), Cavalli-Sforza concluded, somewhat self-servingly. (So had, it should be noted, J. B. S. Haldane a generation earlier: "The blood-groups on the other hand, give information of a more fundamental nature on racial structure, just as do the palaeozoic rocks on geological structure" [1940, 477; see also Marks 1996].)

And yet, there were irreconcilable tensions within the genetic analysis itself, which were rendered invisible in the presentation. A different computer algorithm applied to the same class of genetic data by a different group of population geneticists would yield a tree more harmonious with the anthropometric tree than with the original Cavalli-Sforza genetic tree (see Nei and Roychoudhury 1974, 1981). In this genetic tree, the deepest node distinctly separated the African populations from Europeans and Asians (and Oceanics), suggesting a fundamental north-south division in human ancestry — similar to what the anthropometric trees had appeared to yield — if read literally as biohistory (see figure 13.3). Even though these population geneticists were somewhat skeptical of reading the details of such a tree literally, they nonetheless proceeded freely to do so, calculating that "the divergence between the Negroid group and the Caucasoid-Mongoloid group seems to have occurred about 110,000 years ago" (Nei and Roychoudhury 1981, 13). This, it is important to remark, was in considerable contrast to Cavalli-Sforza's calculation for "the oldest separation in the tree [that is, Eur-Africans versus Asians] . . . as being approximately 35,000 to 40,000 years ago" (1974, 89).

While claiming authority for the biological microevolutionary history of our species, the analytic techniques utilized in human population genetics in fact made unrealistic assumptions about human population histories, and rendered those assumptions largely invisible through the representational medium of the evolutionary tree. The evolutionary results were more unstable and more context dependent than was readily apparent, but they nevertheless seemed to generate quantitative, genetic, scientific answers to archaic anthropological questions.

SYSTEMATICS AND THE RACES

The assumptions of numerical taxonomy or "phenetics" (and its subsequent rejection in the 1980s) are worth a digression. The construction of relationships among groups of organisms was an arcane specialty through the 1950s,

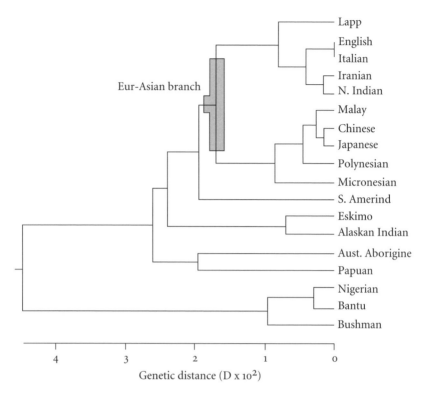

FIG. 13.3 Dendrogram of human genetic relationships, redrawn after Masatoshi Nei, "Human Evolution at the Molecular Level," in *Population Genetics and Molecular Evolution,* ed. Tomoko Ohta and Kenichi Aoki. Berlin: Springer-Verlag, 1985, page 54.

the product of long careers spent in museum basements. A new philosophy arose concurrently with the development of computers and rooted itself in inductive logic. It challenged the pedagogical bias that the best way to classify organisms was to study and become intimately familiar with them, and then to reason out their phylogenetic relationships and devise a suitable taxonomic scheme to describe them (see Gregory 1910; Simpson 1945, 1961). This was insufficiently rigorous for a modern science, argued the advocates of numerical taxonomy (see Sneath and Sokal 1962).

The advocates of numerical taxonomy began by conceptually divorcing classification from phylogeny. Phylogeny (that is, the genealogical history of species), they contended, could never be known accurately, and therefore was not worthy of study except as a byproduct. One could, however, compare and classify things. The goal, therefore, would be a correct classification. The clas-

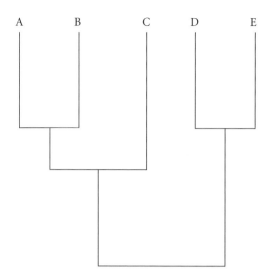

FIG. 13.4 A dendrogram, representing similarity among operational taxonomic units, labeled A, B, C, D, E.

sification would be generated by measuring many characteristics and allowing a computer to sort the organisms ("operational taxonomic units" or OTUs) into groups based simply on their similarity. The product was thus a branching diagram, a dendrogram, which established nested patterns of similarity — resembling a convention of football goalposts — with the vertical axis as an empirical scale of similarity (see figure 13.4). Classifications would be read simply by taking clusters of organisms at particular arbitrary degrees of similarity. Once the proper classificatory tree had been generated, the phylogeny might be read from it.

Phylogeny, however, is crucial to post-Darwinian biology, and patterns of similarity sometime conceal it. A species that has evolved extensively in a short period of time may be closely related to a species to which it is not very similar. (A classic example, of course, is chimpanzees being closely related to humans, yet physically similar to orangutans — a result of the rapid evolution of the human form over the last few million years.) Thus, two taxa may be different either because of distant common ancestry or because one of them diverged from the other rapidly. Numerical taxonomy was not equipped to differentiate between these alternatives, and consequently, focused only on similarity, rather than ancestry (see Hull 1970).

Further, the phenetic method ignored key aspects of modern biology. Species, for example, are conventionally seen as natural units unified by reproductive criteria, not by general similarities; to ignore that fact seemed unbiological. The problems were even greater operationally. One could not get males and females of sexually dimorphic species to cluster together in a dendrogram without introducing a priori knowledge that they were indeed the same species (see Boyce 1964), which defeated the inductive philosophical assumptions of the method. The goal was ostensibly to feed data to the computer and then let the computer mindlessly decide the relationships of the species; but if one had to introduce decisions about placing males and females together in spite of their appearance, the "objectivity" of the method vanished.

As a result, the 1970s saw the development of a rival systematic philosophy, phylogenetic systematics or "cladistics" (see Hennig 1965; Eldredge and Cracraft 1980). The goal of cladism was quite explicitly the reconstruction of patterns of descent, and it began by discriminating among the kinds of similarity that exist and establishing a lexicon to accommodate them. Similarity due to remote ancestry would be "plesiomorphy"; such similarity could be independently retained in many different lineages and were thus not useful in phylogenetic reconstruction, so they would be ignored in that context. (Imagine the futility of sorting primate relations on the basis of quadrupedalism, a trait possessed by the vast majority of species.) Only shared evolutionary novelty or "synapomorphy" was indicative of common ancestry. (Bipedalism would be a synapomorphy, and all primate species habitually doing it are considered close relatives, hominids. All primates sharing the feature of quadrupedal locomotion, by contrast, are a diverse lot, not necessarily very close relatives.) Hence, a chimpanzee and orangutan are similar to one another, both looking "apish," with long arms, hairy bodies, and large canine teeth; but details of the chimpanzee's upper palate place it as a close relative of the human, not of the orangutan. The new emphasis, then, would be on key particular features rather than on overall similarities. Cladistics thereby reversed the relationship between classification and phylogeny established by numerical phenetics: phylogeny was now the goal, and classification would be derived from it. Cladists redefined the criteria of "difference" and altered the representation of their analytic results.

Importantly, the new innovations in taxonomic philosophy altered the significance of temporality in depictions of relationships. The cladists represented their work with "cladograms," branching diagrams representing patterns of common ancestry, but without a temporal dimension (see figure 13.5). Animals living at different times would be placed together along the top, among their closest relatives. Only afterward would the time dimension be

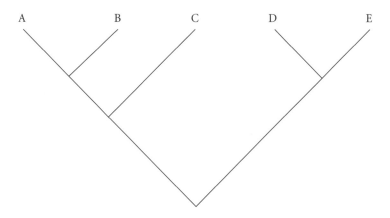

FIG. 13.5 A cladogram, representing shared common ancestry among species, labeled A, B, C, D, E.

added to help infer ancestor-descendant relationships and produce a "phylogenetic tree." Here, the vertical axis represents the relative recency of shared ancestry. Cladism thus focuses on establishing "close relatives" at the expense of literal lineal ancestors, and as such, has been criticized for downplaying biological descent.

Both schools of thought—cladists and phenetics—focused on specific aspects of biological evolution and represent their results with characteristic diagrams as emblems (both classically utilizing right angles, but differently oriented). Both "work" to some extent *above* the species level, where lineages always diverge. On the other hand, neither of these affords an accurate depiction of the processes of evolution *below* the species level, particularly of human microevolution, where blood lines diverge and remerge. Numerical taxonomy omitted rates of change, indeed it omitted evolution altogether— for the products of evolution are not more or less similar groups of things but more or less recently descended taxa.

The intervening decades since Cavalli-Sforza and Edwards's work have seen the populations and genetic markers increase, but the rise of DNA technology in the 1980s made possible the direct comparison of the hereditary material, rather than merely their weak surrogates, the blood proteins. The breakthrough study of the DNA relationships within the human species was the famous "mitochondrial Eve" analysis of Rebecca Cann, Mark Stoneking, and Allan Wilson (1987). Genetic similarities were sampled across the mitochondrial genome, which has the properties of being small (16,500 bases in-

365

stead of 3.2 billion in the nucleus), readily isolated, and inherited clonally through the maternal lineage (and thus not subject to the vagaries of Mendelian assortment and recombination). The compactness, simplicity, and unilinearity of mtDNA permitted the possibility of inferring genetic linkages more directly. This newer generation of molecular systematics produced a tree that was neither strictly phenetic (based on similarity) nor cladistic (based on evolutionary novelties) but parsimonious—constructed by minimizing the number of evolutionary events or mutations that must be invoked to link all the taxa into a network. This method entails assumptions about the modes of mutational change and its rarity, which are themselves contested. But for the present purposes, the crucial feature of this work is that the tree was constructed specifically from the 140-odd individuals studied, not from any a priori groupings (see figure 13.6). The computer (a program called PAUP—Phylogenetic Analysis Using Parsimony) generated a tree linking all the mtDNA sequences into the shortest network. Only subsequently was the geographic origin of the samples imposed on the result.

Most aspects of the mtEve study, and the evolutionary model that accompanied it, have been effectively criticized in the last decade, but the basic findings have stood up well: that Africans are more genetically diverse than Europeans and Asians; that they indeed subsume the genetic diversity found in the rest of the world; and that racial clusters are not inherent in genetic comparisons of humans but must be imposed by the investigator.

These conclusions, however, trickled down into the genetics community in curious ways, for they were not readily translated into methodological revisions. Cavalli-Sforza quickly identified in genetic data the African–EurAsian split he had denied decades earlier (Cavalli-Sforza et al. 1988). This new analysis comprised frequencies of 120 nuclear alleles across 42 populations, among which the division between Africans and non-Africans would now be dated to 92,000 years ago, but from essentially the same analysis. (The headline, though, involved the isomorphism between the tree obtained genetically and a classification of world languages, itself anthropologically problematic.)

It must nevertheless be observed that the most direct implication of the Eve work was not the appearance of a deep division between Africans and Eur-Asians but a deep division *within Africans,* of which one branch included Eur-Asians. In other words, the Cann, Stoneking, and Wilson (1987) genetic study found Africans to be paraphyletic—incorporating the genetic diversity of non-Africans, and thus not a single separate branch (see figure 13.7a) —while the Cavalli-Sforza genetic study took Africans as monophyletic—a

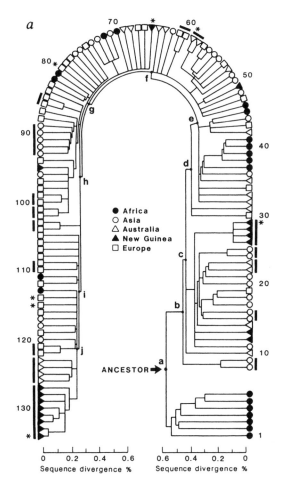

FIG. 13.6 Parsimony tree, the shortest network (that is, the one ostensibly invoking the smallest number of mutational events) linking all the mtDNA sequences, from Rebecca L. Cann, Mark Stoneking, and Allan C. Wilson, "Mitochondrial DNA and Human Evolution," *Nature* 325: 33.

single branch—and still calculated the divergence of that group from others (see figure 13.7b). These two studies, in short, encoded extremely different biohistorical narratives.

Yet with the optimism that more populations and genetic markers could resolve what an earlier generation had called "the racial history of man" (in spite of the history of the research, the unresolved methodological flaws, and epistemological difficulties), and further bolstered by the success of the Human Genome Project and the public interest generated by mitochondrial Eve, population geneticists put a new project before the American public: the Human Genome Diversity Project.

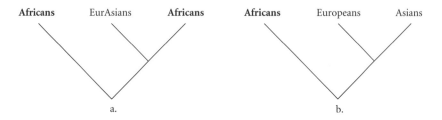

FIGS. 13.7A–B Alternative genetic relationships of the "races": a. Africans subsume Europeans and Asians, as per Cann, Stoneking, and Wilson 1987; and b. Africans contrast with Europeans and Asians, as per Cavalli-Sforza et al. 1988.

GENETICS AND IDENTITY POLITICS

I first heard about the HGDP from Leslie Roberts, a journalist for *Science* magazine who was researching a story about it. A few months earlier in 1991, a small group of geneticists, led by Cavalli-Sforza, had formally proposed the large-scale collection of DNA from indigenous populations in the journal *Genomics*. Now, an argument had erupted over the strategy such a project should adopt. Cavalli-Sforza expected that samples would be collected according to ethnic grouping: Yanomamo, Hopi, Chukchi, and so forth—which of course would be ideal for the kinds of studies he had been doing since the 1960s. Allan Wilson, senior author of the Eve study, maintained that since named groups did not map onto genetic diversity particularly well, a more objective sampling strategy should be sought—namely, simple geography. Lay a grid over the world, asserted Wilson, and sample our species by transect. I sympathized with Wilson's approach over the phone (but I ended up on the cutting room floor when the article appeared) and then ran out to read the *Genomics* proposal.

What the HGDP represented was the culmination of the previous three decades in neo-racial history studies: it held out the extraordinary promise of revealing the ultimate biological history of our species, very much in line with similar attempts over the course of the twentieth century, although this time on a grander scale and with the highest level of genetic resolution. At the same time, however, its own rhetoric was decidedly antiquated. As if the lessons of racial anthropology had never been learned, its Web site presently highlights the collection of these data specifically "to see if, for example, the Irish are more closely related to the Spaniards or to the Swedes." Answers to such odd questions would become available through the collection of DNA samples, which would be retrieved and stored for the use of geneticists. The Irish, Spanish, and Swedish, however, were not their principal targets; their targets were remote, exotic peoples, presumably on the verge of disappearance.

> The populations that can tell us the most about our evolutionary past are those which have been isolated for some time, are likely to be linguistically and culturally distinct, and are often surrounded by geographical barriers. . . . Isolated human populations contain much more informative genetic records than more recent, urban ones. Such human populations are being rapidly merged with their neighbors, however, destroying irrevocably the information needed to reconstruct our evolutionary history. (Cavalli-Sforza et al. 1991, 490)

The appeal to "salvage" research was a familiar one to anthropologists (see Gruber 1970), but less so to geneticists. But even though it was addressed to geneticists, the proposal was notably lacking in epistemological detail. For example, it glaringly failed to make clear exactly whose evolutionary past was to be illuminated by the study of, say, the !Kung San's genes, or how one could reliably extract any evolutionary history from these data given the failures of the science to do so thus far.

Nonetheless, the implication was clearly that "our evolutionary past" was that of the "recent, urban" populations reading the article, and it was to be illuminated by other people's genes. Contemporary bioanthropological knowledge, of course, holds it to be exceedingly unlikely that the genes of any specific socially constructed group of people are going to shed any light onto anybody's evolutionary history but their own. The idea that the genes of indigenous peoples are somehow more representatively primitive than those of "recent, urban" peoples is a holdover from an earlier era, which anthropologists remember with regret. Yet according to its first major publicity in *Science,* the San, Pygmies, Basques, and Yanomamo offer (quoting one of the HGDP's principal spokesmen) "a window into the past," and even more explicitly, "a unique glimpse into the gene pool of our ancestors who lived thousands of years ago" (Roberts 1991a, 1614).

As the proposal came out, research on the genetic history of human populations was still proceeding, as it had been for thirty years. Cavalli-Sforza's research group published a paper the same year in the prestigious *Proceedings of the National Academy of Sciences,* for example, that examined the DNA of two groups of African pygmies, native-born Chinese living in San Francisco, and a heterogeneous European sample, and concluded that "ancestral Europeans are estimated to be an admixture of 65 percent ancestral Chinese and 35 percent ancestral Africans" (Bowcock et al. 1991, 840). And these findings were eagerly consumed by the popular science press: as *Time* magazine duly reported in promoting the research and the project, "All Europeans are thought to be a hybrid population, with 65 percent Asian and 35 percent African genes" (Subramanian 1995, 55).

The paradox that became the signature theme of the HGDP was the celebration of modern techno-science applied within the framework of archaic racialist language and thought, clearly loaded with astonishingly archaic assumptions of primordial division and purity of certain large segments of the human species—assumptions that were not being acknowledged. Particularly noteworthy was its acceptance as authoritative information in the derivative literature—capitalizing, as the genetics of earlier eras did, on the combination of technology and modernity associated with the field, and engendering little, if any, criticism.

One striking example of the broad insensitivity of human population genetic studies to the complexities of identity construction and of ethnohistory, and of the general absence of effective critique, involved a recent study of two sites on the Y chromosome, passed on from father to son (the opposite of mtDNA). Here, 54 percent of self-designated Hebrew priests (Cohanim), many of whom have the surname Cohen, had the same configuration of two genes on the Y chromosome, as opposed to only 33 percent of Jews who did not think they were priests (Skorecki et al. 1997). The authors inferred that this particular configuration was the bona fide genetic constitution of the Jewish priestly line, inherited directly from biblical Aaron and, by implication, reflecting the genetic makeup of his brother, the lawgiver himself.

Of course, men with the same last names are going to be more closely related than those with different last names, reflecting recent common shared ancestry. Anthropologists call this "isonymy" and have used it effectively as a crude measure of local inbreeding (see Lasker 1985). In the absence of information on the distribution of Y chromosome haplotypes of a sample of Horowitzes or Steinbergs, however, the inference that the one simply represented at 54 percent rather than 33 percent must be authentic and primordial for the ancient lineage of "Cohanim" is highly dubious. (Not to mention the fact that it assumes that the origin myth recorded in the book of Exodus is literally true.)

More important, the authors of that report quickly found themselves in the middle of an identity controversy, as people wanted to know authoritatively if they were "really" Hebrew priests or not (see Grady 1997). Since there is no Temple or priesthood, nobody's a Hebrew priest, although apparently a lot of people would like to be.

But the Jewish priest study was not a central focus of the HGDP, which was to be principally directed at exotic, "isolated" peoples. Scholars interested in, say, the gene pool of African Americans were not greeted warmly by the HGDP—as a "hybrid" population it was of little interest, given the HGDP's assumptions about the genetic purity of indigenous peoples. For example, this purity was argued to be manifested in the !Kung San, who were featured in most of the early write-ups of the HGDP, in strong counterpoint to their ethnohistory.

> What these populations have in common is that each has been isolated and has only rarely—if ever—intermixed with its neighbors. (Roberts 1991a, 1614)

> Such populations, isolated for hundreds or thousands of years, contain in their genes clues to human evolution, migration, and diversity. (Roberts 1991b, 517)

This assumption of isolation is what permits the reticulating evolutionary tree drawn by Hooton (see figure 13.1) to be simplified into the bifurcating evolutionary tree of Cavalli-Sforza and Edwards (see figure 13.2), which is now firmly planted in the soil of modern genetic essentialism. The underlying genetic fallacy is not new, and was pointed out explicitly a generation earlier to geneticists studying the blood groups of the Navajo and identifying them as pure, when Clyde Kluckhohn could readily produce ethnohistoric evidence that they were not such at all (Kluckhohn and Griffith 1950).

It should be noted that the new generation of geneticists working in "racial history" comes with a liberal political bent, acknowledging the equality of the so-called races, while even at the same time often reifying them. The HGDP, for example, alleges that the results of the project are expected to undermine the popular belief that there are clearly defined races, to contribute to the elimination of racism as well as to make a major contribution to the understanding of the nature of differences between individuals and between human populations. Yet their flagship literature presented color-coded maps of the world in which "four major ethnic regions are shown. Africans are yellow, Australians red, [Mongoloids blue], and Caucasoids green" (Cavalli-Sforza, Menozzi, and Piazza 1995, unnumbered page, color plate 1; see also Subramanian 1995; Piazza 1997).

It was precisely this inability to reconcile folk ideologies, liberal politics, and science that has led the HGDP into its greatest difficulties, and to its ultimate failure. At the bioethics conference that produced the exchange at the beginning of this essay, a German bioethicist, Benno Müller-Hill, posed a question to the HGDP's spokesman, Marcus Feldman. Expressing his discomfiture with what he had heard from anthropologists and representatives of indigenous groups about the HGDP, the bioethicist posed a simple problem. "Someday," he said, "we will find some gene that influences some aspect of intelligence. Further, we're going to find that it's not perfectly equally distributed among all populations. As custodian and spokesperson for the genetic diversity of our species, how will you handle that?"

The HGDP geneticist stammered through an answer that simply denied the premise of the question—he didn't think there would be any gene that might influence intelligence, so the scenario would never arise. The bioethicists resoundingly found it unsatisfactory, simply another example of the project's inability to think through its political and ethical implications, while simultaneously asserting scientific hegemony over the study of human population history.

PRESENT STATUS OF THE HGDP

The HGDP's decline began with an issue that was not actually its fault. On 14 March 1995, a patent was awarded to the National Institutes of Health to cover a cell line derived from a man from a Papua New Guinean population known as the Hagahai. Although in this case a deal had actually been negotiated in the Hagahai's interests by a medical anthropologist, whereby the tribe would receive a significant proportion of any profits, there was nothing compelling the scientific interests to do so, and it could just as easily not have been the case. This was troubling to some.

The Hagahai problem for the HGDP was twofold. First, its elder sibling, the Human Genome Project, had successfully used a campaign of purple prose to drum up public support for its multi-billion-dollar cause. The human genome was routinely represented as "the holy grail," "book of life," "essence of humanity," or something along those lines. Suddenly, that rhetoric of its elder sibling could be flung in the face of the HGDP, for if DNA was the essence of life, then the Hagahai man no longer owned his own essence— it was now the legal possession of a branch of the U.S. government. This, of course, conjured an image of the West economically exploiting the very bodies and cells of indigenes on the scale promoted by the HGDP. The second problem was more directly related to the HGDP: the project had steadfastly maintained the economic neutrality, and financial disinterest, of the HGDP program. Anyone who raised that concern, or more broadly the possibility of classic economic exploitation of indigenous people, was dismissed as overly suspicious and unrealistic. A catechism from its Web site, dated 6 October 1994, acknowledged the need to protect indigenous peoples from financial exploitation by genetics, but emphasized that the HGDP "does not intend to patent the samples or any products made from them. The Project is not a commercial enterprise. It seeks knowledge, not profit." After all, "it is not clear whether any commercial products are likely to emerge from its samples or data" (http://www.stanford.edu/group/morrinst/hgdp/faq.html). As the HGDP's bioethicist, Hank Greely, stated in *Discover* magazine in November 1994, "There's no commercial money in the project. No pharmaceutical-industry backing. This is pure science" (cited in Gutin 1994, 75).

Clearly, however, there was indeed a great deal of financial interest; the purity of the science was as illusory as the purity of the people the researchers wanted to study. Although the HGDP was not itself involved in the Hagahai case, the case showed in high relief that as official custodians of the human gene pool, either the HGDP spokesmen were lying, or they were extraordinarily naive and not sufficiently attuned to the implications of their proposed research to be entrusted with it. Presented with an opportunity to take a strong ethical stand, the HGDP demurred. It took a beating from a nongovernmental organization called RAFI (Rural Advancement Foundation International, see Christie 1996).

On 21 October 1997, a panel convened by the National Research Council (NRC) on behalf of the National Academy of Sciences released its summary report evaluating the merits of the HGDP. In an extraordinary gesture, the panel found the project too nebulous even to evaluate. As the committee's fact-finding progressed, it became apparent that the precise nature of the proposed HGDP was elusive; different participants in the formation of the "consensus" document had quite different perceptions of the intent of the project and even its organizational structure. Accordingly, because there was no sharply defined proposal that the committee could evaluate, it chose to examine the scientific merit and value of research on human genetic variation as well as the organizational, policy, and ethical issues that such research poses in a more general context.

Agreeing that the study of diversity in the human gene pool was a valid scientific goal, the report went on to describe how the panel felt it ought to be done, in effect jettisoning the work of the HGDP itself over the last eight years. Part of the reason they had such difficulty was that the goals of the project had begun to change when it quickly became clear that human microphylogeny — or the clumsy representations of it adduced by the HGDP — did not resonate with the public. So they had begun to emphasize other goals, especially bio-medical (see Kidd, Kidd, and Weiss 1993; Weiss, Kidd, and Kidd 1992). But since the project was planning to collect genotypes, and not medical histo-ries to associate with the genotypes, there was actually relatively little chance of deriving biomedical benefits (see Marks 1995b). Thus, as the press release issued in October of 1997 summarized: "Following an exhaustive examina-tion, the committee found the proposal does not clearly explain the purpose of the project or provide the necessary safeguards for protecting participants" (compare National Research Council 1997).

It may be difficult to imagine the leading population geneticists in the United States, after seven years of brainstorming, half-a-million dollars of National Science Foundation money, publicly and privately funded seed money and meetings, unable even to explain *the purpose of the project* ade-quately to a review panel. Nevertheless, that was the panel's judgment. A brief attempt at "spinning" the NRC report (see Cavalli-Sforza, Bodmer, and Dausset 1997; Merriwether 1997) was aided by conflicting accounts in the leading journals. *Nature* stated that the report recommended dumping the HGDP (MacIlwain 1997), while *Science* noted that the project had been given a thumbs-up (Pennisi 1997). Ultimately, NRC committee members themselves were obliged to clarify the record: "Nowhere in the report does our committee endorse the HGDP," wrote Virginia Dominguez (1998; see also Schull 1998).

At the time of this writing (mid-1999), the HGDP still has money allotted, but is undergoing a major reorganization. Desperately trying to salvage an image, it has gone so far as to claim credit for discovering the absence of bio-logical races in our species (see Marshall 1998) — despite decades of anthro-pological research and teaching of that very point (see Marks 1995a). The American Anthropological Association's statement on race not only makes that point, but details the long-standing institutional commitment of anthro-pology to the position that biological races, equivalent to zoological subspe-cies, do not exist in *Homo sapiens.*

BIOLOGICAL ANTHROPOLOGY AS A FORUM FOR THE
UNIFICATION OF GENETICS AND ANTHROPOLOGY

Perhaps the most tragic aspect of the Human Genome Diversity Project lay in its relationship to biological anthropology. In principle, the project might have benefited immensely from this field, in areas such as the critique of the relationship between named populations and natural categories, or from the collection of anthropological and medical data to correlate with the genotypes in order to expand the questions the project could address. In practice, however, the HGDP managed to attract a tragically sycophantic biological anthropology: the geneticists organizing it saw no need for anthropological input until the major decisions had already been made, and the biological anthropologists were grateful to be included in such a big project. Its major anthropologists have now dropped out.

The role of anthropology in the HGDP is best encapsulated in an exchange from the *Anthropology Newsletter*, in which HGDP insider Ken Kidd (1996), of Yale's genetics department, wrote an indignant letter contesting the point that anthropologists were not involved in the planning of the project. According to Kidd, "By any objective criteria — publications, academic appointments, training of students, society memberships — most people would agree that Luca Cavalli-Sforza, Mary[-]Clair[e] King and I are anthropologists" (2). Actually, they probably wouldn't. But more important, to this geneticist, there is no body of scholarship or expertise that might differentiate a geneticist interested in humans from an anthropologist interested in human genetics. This may sound like a trivial bit of turf patrolling, but it reflects a serious issue in biological anthropology that stretches back to the modern origins of the field.

When the science of human genetics was the science of eugenics, few anthropologists could be counted among its advocates (a notable exception was Yale's Clark Wissler). But the two leading American *physical* anthropologists, Earnest Hooton and Aleš Hrdlička, were both members of the advisory council of the American Eugenics Society (along with many American geneticists and other intellectuals). As the representatives of the biological/scientific arm of anthropology, they chose to follow the "real" scientists in claiming to approach anthropological issues scientifically, rather than lead the nonanthropologists to a better grasp of the relevant anthropology. A similar phenomenon was at work with respect to the HGDP, as some prominent biological anthropologists chose to follow the intellectual course charted by the geneticists, as if human population genetics itself could exist in a timeless bubble of cultural purity and isolation.

And as in the 1920s, contemporary genetics successfully managed to portray itself as a modern alternative to anthropology. *Nature,* the leading science journal in the world, editorialized that

> with physical anthropology under a cloud for its habit of using measurable skeletal indices as proxies for less tangible attributes (cranial capacity as a measure of intelligence, for example), it would be better to invest what goodwill there is in some quite different field. The Human Genome Diversity Project is already battling to win the consent of distinctive racial groups to schemes for collecting and analysing DNA. (Bias-Free 1995, 184)

Where *Nature* could have gotten such an archaic view of anthropology is a good question, for it is precisely the juxtaposition of scientific and humanistic issues that is the greatest intellectual strength of contemporary anthropology. As the HGDP succeeded in representing itself as a scientific program, but foundered humanistically, it would seem to have been an ideal forum for the establishment of a *truly* biological anthropology—a program that acknowledges the cultural dimensions of all human activities, including science; that casts an analytic humanistic eye on the construction of genetic facts; and that mediates the genetic and anthropological realms, "biogenetic substance," and notions of identity and descent.

Budding geneticists learn to think technologically. It is the current generation that is being forced to think about responsibilities and obligations to their subjects as well as accountability. A significant shift can be seen in contemporary science—from "designing a research project" to "designing a research project so that you don't harm, victimize, or stigmatize anybody, because you will be held accountable if you do."

That is, of course, a central problem with the HGDP. Should there be a research museum or warehouse of genetic material on the diversity of the human species? The question is *how* it should be established; and the problem is quite simply that technology was considered to be the central issue and responsibility to be something that would be dealt with at some vague time in the future. It is not simply that, as Alan Swedlund said at a 1993 Wenner-Gren conference on the HGDP, it is twenty-first-century technology put to the service of nineteenth-century ideas (compare Lewin 1993). These well-intentioned geneticists went to bed with the idea of a genetic repository of the human species—a nice idea, and one that has been proceeding on a small scale for decades—and they woke up on the cutting edge of anthropological ethics and bioethics—having to account publicly for the apparent exploitation of the bodies of indigenous peoples in an ostensibly postcolonial world—and were unfortunately entirely unprepared for it.

As they attempt to construct an authoritative (possibly accurate, but *decidedly* authoritative) approach to social/historical identity based on DNA, the HGDP replays some of the major themes of contemporary issues in kinship study: Who owns the body? On what criteria is racial membership based? How are social groups constructed and constituted through time? What is the role of heredity in establishing self-identity, both in the organic and social realms? Of what significance is genealogy to cultural understandings of "who we really are"?

MRS. BURNHAM'S BABY

I will end this essay, as I began it, with a flashback to the 1920s. In January 1928 eugenics was a household word and the educated classes took it for granted that good germ-plasm was the secret to a healthy nation. Long before Dan Quayle and Murphy Brown, long before Dolly the cloned ewe, there was Mrs. Burnham. Grace Mailhouse Burnham was a wealthy thirty-seven- (or forty-one-) year-old social worker and widow who decided she wanted a child more than another husband. So she selected a consort, one with good genes, and on 10 January 1928, had a baby, whom she named Vera. For the father's name in the birth registry, she signed "Karl Graham," the last name as a contraction of her own, and the first name after a well-known social theorist she admired. Then she told friends that she had borne the first "eugenic baby."

Immediately, Mrs. Burnham became a cause célèbre in New York and, indeed, around the nation. Newspapers presented readers with the opinions of Clarence Darrow ("Mrs. Burnham's venture is her own personal business"); Valentino's widow, Natacha Rambova ("If she's poor, it's all quite different"); Nan Britton, who claimed to have borne Warren Harding's child ("How is it possible for a woman to want the child of a man she does not love?"); actress Olga Petrova ("Woman has the right to conceive children any way she pleases"); as well as judges, writers, ministers, and advice columnists. A photo of the understandably reclusive Mrs. Burnham was finally obtained from the passport office to adorn the stories (see figure 13.8), and her baby became the focal point for a public referendum on the American family, "companionate

FIG. 13.8 Mrs. Burnham, halftone originally published in the *New York Mirror,* 25 January 1928; taken from a photo on file at the United States Passport Bureau.

marriage," sex, marriage, illegitimacy, and reproduction. More than that, the public clamored to know, "Who is the baby's father?"

When a photographer from the *New York Mirror* actually managed to get a shot of baby Vera, it was front-page news on 6 February. Indeed, the story was widely enough known that when Eugene O'Neill's play *Strange Interlude* opened a week later, nearly every review related the motherhood of O'Neill's character Nina (whose husband comes from a line of mentally ill folk, so she secretly has his best friend sire their child) to that of Mrs. Burnham. Walter Winchell's review punned on O'Neill's name, calling the play (which would go on to win the Pulitzer Prize for drama) "Another Eugenic O'Neill Baby."

"Eugenic" had subtly become a euphemism for "illegitimate, wealthy" — bastardy legitimized by science. Spokespeople for the American Eugenics Society quickly assured the public that they were really in favor of traditional family values — home, hearth, and two parents of different sexes — although their writings had previously only mentioned good genes. And in April of that year, England received its own eugenic baby, suffragette Sylvia Pankhurst's son Richard — greeted with international headlines.

It is obviously no coincidence that a similar class of questions about reproduction and kinship is being raised in public in the era of the Human Genome Project as in the era of eugenics. If, as David Schneider observed of American culture, new facts of biology are new facts of kinship (1968:23), it is hardly surprising that the genetic discoveries occurring on a nearly weekly basis must be seen to produce new cultural forms, too. I would venture to guess that these social questions were not resolved in the 1920s because of the depression and world war, and the subsequent disfavor into which human genetics fell as a result of the Nazis' enthusiasm for it.

The importance of heredity in cultural and biological life is the heart of the matter. As folk notions of "who you are and what you are" are reinforced by extravagant scientific claims, a prior scientific generation's mistakes loom larger. While the HGDP is free of the taint of genetic determinism, it is not free of the folk ideology—the cultural meanings—of heredity. Neither is it immune from the ethical questions produced by global inequalities of wealth and status. Consequently, even as they were promoting the study of "declining human populations" (Diamond 1991) and "ethnic groups on the verge of extinction" (Lewin 1993), the HGDP scientists were obliged to endure criticism for their apparent insensitivity to the real problems faced by the indigenous peoples they were targeting. The project was represented in a Dutch magazine by a photo of a geneticist visiting a presumably isolated people, sarcastically captioned, "Hooray, we've come to save your DNA!" (Rozendaal 1995). Was their DNA indeed the most important thing to preserve?

The HGDP promised to study the closest molecular facsimile of the folk "biogenetic substance" all over the world—a promise that resonated in crucial ways with modern contested sites of descent and identity. Are the descendants of Sally Hemings, for example, also those of Thomas Jefferson? Perhaps their DNA would tell. And indeed, some of her descendants "really are" Jeffersons, and others "really aren't"—although those conclusions do not alter the material conditions of American slavery and its legacy, which were certainly more prominent in determining the life courses of the intervening generations.

Is "Kennewick Man" an ancestral Native American or an ancient Caucasoid? Perhaps its DNA would tell. Literally, of course, he was very possibly ancestral to no one—there is no reason to think he was a *genitor;* so his role as ancestor would be in all cases symbolic, the relationship of "his" people to modern people. But having situated these remains in the midst of a highly racialized discourse makes it very difficult to imagine that there might exist a "pure," "isolated" scientific value of such a find (see Marks 1998).

More tragically, these human remains have been invoked to challenge the identity of Native American "scientifically," an ignominious political role for science at best, although not without precedent. Obviously Kennewick Man is "native" (he is the earliest known inhabitant of the continent) and equally obviously he is "American" (that is, indeed, the landmass on which he was found). His relationship to contemporary populations might be a valid scientific issue, but perhaps not at the cost of cavalierly humiliating and disorienting the indigenous groups that claim him.

It's not that the Indians don't know who they really are and the geneticists do, or vice versa. It's that people's own notions of who and what they are, are important to them and cannot be taken lightly; and that scientific notions are themselves cultural products. When the science is loaded with specious and archaic assumptions about the composition of populations, the ontology of races, and the relationships of ancient and modern peoples, it is of no great benefit either to science or to society. A truly biological anthropology, at once biological and anthropological, might assume a central place in public discourse over these issues. Situated on the boundary between the classically juxtaposed culture and nature, fictive and blood relations, science and humanities—such a field would seem ideally suited for such work. The structure of the discipline is such, however, that we are unlikely to see that— until modern biological anthropology becomes more self-consciously aware of its anthropology.

NOTES

This essay was originally prepared for the Wenner-Gren conference, New Directions in Kinship Study: A Core Concept Revisited, held 27 March–4 April 1998 in Illetas, Mallorca. My deepest appreciation goes to Susie McKinnon and Sarah Franklin for the invitation to participate in the symposium, their incisive comments on this essay, and their brilliant editing; and as well to the other participants for their helpful input. Thanks also to Dr. George Whitney for access to archival material about the American Eugenics Society, including clippings about Mrs. Burnham.

REFERENCES

Bias-Free Interracial Comparisons. 1995. *Nature* 377:183–84.
Boas, Franz. 1916. Eugenics. *Scientific Monthly* 3:471–79.
Bowcock, Anne M., Judith R. Kidd, Joanna L. Mountain, Joan M. Herbert, Luciano Carotenuto, Kenneth K. Kidd, and L. Luca Cavalli-Sforza. 1991. Drift, Admixture,

and Selection in Human Evolution: A Study with DNA Polymorphisms. *Proceedings of the National Academy of Sciences* 88:839–43.

Boyce, A. J. 1964. The Value of Some Methods of Numerical Taxonomy with Reference to Hominoid Classification. In *Phenetic and Phylogenetic Classification,* edited by V. H. Heywood and J. McNeill. London: Systematics Association.

Boyd, William C. 1947. The Use of Genetically Determined Characters, Especially Serological Factors Such as Rh, in Physical Anthropology. *Southwestern Journal of Anthropology* 3:32–49.

———. 1950. *Genetics and the Races of Man.* Boston: Little, Brown.

Cann, Rebecca L., Mark Stoneking, and Allan C. Wilson. 1987. Mitochondrial DNA and Human Evolution. *Nature* 325:31–36.

Cavalli-Sforza, L. Luca. 1974. The Genetics of Human Populations. *Scientific American* 231, no. 3:81–89.

Cavalli-Sforza, L. Luca, Walter Bodmer, and Jean Dausset. 1997. Support for Genetic Diversity Project. *Nature* 390:221.

Cavalli-Sforza, L. Luca, and A. W. F. Edwards. 1965. Analysis of Human Evolution. In *Genetics Today: Proceedings of the XI International Congress of Genetics,* edited by S. J. Geerts. Oxford, U.K.: Pergamon.

Cavalli-Sforza, L. Luca, P. Menozzi, and A. Piazza. 1995. *The History and Geography of Human Genes.* Princeton, N.J.: Princeton University Press.

Cavalli-Sforza, L. Luca, A. Piazza, P. Menozzi, and J. Mountain. 1988. Reconstruction of Human Evolution: Bringing Together Genetic, Archaeological, and Linguistic Data. *Proceedings of the National Academy of Sciences* 85:6002–6.

Cavalli-Sforza, L. Luca, Allan C. Wilson, Charles R. Cantor, Robert M. Cook-Deegan, and Mary-Claire King. 1991. Call for a Worldwide Survey of Human Genetic Diversity: A Vanishing Opportunity for the Human Genome Project. *Genomics* 11:490–91.

Christie, Jean. 1996. Whose Property, Whose Rights? *Cultural Survival Quarterly* 20, no. 2:35–41.

Coon, Carleton S. 1962. *The Origin of Races.* New York: Alfred A. Knopf.

Darrow, Clarence. 1926. The Eugenics Cult. *American Mercury* 8, no. 30:129–37.

Diamond, Jared M. 1991. A Way to World Knowledge. *Nature* 352:567.

Dominguez, Virginia. 1998. Misleading News Coverage Concerning HGDP. *Anthropology Newsletter* (January): 18.

Eldredge, Niles, and Joel Cracraft. 1980. *Phylogenetic Pattern and the Evolutionary Process.* New York: Columbia University Press.

Grady, Denise. 1997. Who Is Aaron's Heir? Father Doesn't Always Know Best. *New York Times,* 19 January, 1.

Gregory, William King. 1910. The Orders of Mammals. *Bulletin of the American Museum of Natural History* 27.

Gruber, Jacob W. 1970. Ethnographic Salvage and the Shaping of Anthropology. *American Anthropologist* 72:1289–99.

Gutin, Joann. 1994. End of the Rainbow. *Discover,* November, 70–75.

Haldane, John B. S. 1940. The Blood-Group Frequencies of European Peoples, and Racial Origins. *Human Biology* 12:457–80.

Harpending, Harry. 1994. Gene Frequencies, DNA Frequencies, and Human Origins. *Perspectives in Biology and Medicine* 37, no. 3:384–94.

Hennig, Willi. 1965. Phylogenetic Systematics. *Annual Review of Entomology* 10:97–116.

Hooton, Earnest A. 1946. *Up from the Ape*. 2d ed. New York: Macmillan.

Howells, William W. 1973. Cranial Variation in Man. *Papers of the Peabody Museum of Archaeology and Ethnology,* Harvard University, no. 67.

———. 1976. Explaining Modern Man: Evolutionists versus Migrationists. *Journal of Human Evolution* 5:477–95.

Hull, David L. 1970. Contemporary Systematic Philosophies. *Annual Review of Ecology and Systematics* 1:19–54.

Hulse, Frederick S. 1962. Race as an Evolutionary Episode. *American Anthropologist* 64:929–45.

Kidd, Kenneth K. 1996. Anthropology's Role in the HGDP. *Anthropology Newsletter* (March): 2.

Kidd, Judith R., Kenneth K. Kidd, and Kenneth M. Weiss. 1993. Forum: Human Genome Diversity Initiative. *Human Biology* 65:1–6.

Kluckhohn, Clyde, and Charles Griffith. 1950. Population Genetics and Social Anthropology. *Cold Spring Harbor Symposium on Quantitative Biology* 15:401–8.

Kroeber, Alfred L. 1916. Inheritance by Magic. *American Anthropologist* 18:19–40.

Lasker, Gabriel. 1985. *Surnames and Genetic Structure*. New York: Cambridge University Press.

Lewin, Roger. 1993. Genes from a Disappearing World. *New Scientist,* 29 May, 25–29.

MacIlwain, Colin. 1997. Diversity Project "Does Not Merit Federal Funding." *Nature* 389:774.

Marks, Jonathan. 1995a. *Human Biodiversity: Genes, Race, and History*. Hawthorne, N.Y.: Aldine de Gruyter.

———. 1995b. The Human Genome Diversity Project: Good *for* If Not Good *as* Anthropology? *Anthropology Newsletter* 36, no. 4:72.

———. 1996. The Legacy of Serological Studies in American Physical Anthropology. *History and Philosophy of the Life Sciences* 18:345–62.

———. 1998. Replaying the Race Card. *Anthropology Newsletter* 39, no. 5:1, 4–5.

Marshall, Eliot. 1998. DNA Studies Challenge the Meaning of Race. *Science* 282:654–55.

Merriwether, D. Andrew. 1997. National Research Council Report on Evaluating Human Diversity. *Anthropology Newsletter* (December): 38–39.

National Research Council. 1997. *Evaluating Human Genetic Diversity*. Washington, D.C.: National Academy Press.

Nei, Masatoshi. 1985. Human Evolution at the Molecular Level. In *Population Genetics and Molecular Evolution,* edited by Tomoko Ohta and Kenichi Aoki. Berlin: Springer-Verlag.

Nei, Masatoshi, and Arun K. Roychoudhury. 1974. Genic Variation within and between the Three Major Races of Man, Caucasoids, Negroids, and Mongoloids. *American Journal of Human Genetics* 26:421–43.

———. 1981. Genetic Relationship and Evolution of Human Races. Vol. 14 of *Evolutionary Biology*. New York: Plenum.

Paul, Diane B., and Hamish G. Spencer. 1995. The Hidden Science of Eugenics. *Nature* 374:302–4.

Pearl, Raymond. 1927. The Biology of Superiority. *American Mercury* 12, no. 47:257–66.

Pennisi, Elizabeth. 1997. NRC OKs Long-Delayed Survey of Human Genome Diversity. *Science* 278:568.

Piazza, Alberto. 1997. Un concept sans fondement biologique. *La Recherche* (Paris) 302:64–68.

Roberts, Leslie. 1991a. A Genetic Survey of Vanishing Peoples. *Science* 252:1614–17.

———. 1991b. Genetic Survey Gains Momentum. *Science* 254:517.

Rozendaal, Simon. 1995. Hoera, we komen uw DNA redden. *Elsevier* (Amsterdam), 11 November, 112–16.

Schneider, David M. 1968. *American Kinship: A Cultural Account.* Englewood Cliffs, N.J.: Prentice-Hall.

Schull, William J. 1998. Genetic Diversity Survey. *Science* 279:14.

Simpson, George G. 1945. The Principles of Classification and a Classification of Mammals. *Bulletin of the American Museum of Natural History* 85.

———. 1961. *Principles of Animal Taxonomy.* New York: Columbia University Press.

Sinnott, Edmund W., and Leslie C. Dunn. 1925. *Principles of Genetics.* New York: McGraw-Hill.

Skorecki, K., S. Selig, S. Blazer, R. Bradman, N. Bradman, P. J. Warburton, M. Ismjlowicz, and M. F. Hammer. 1997. Y Chromosomes of Jewish Priests. *Nature* 385:32.

Sneath, Peter H. A., and Robert R. Sokal. 1962. Numerical Taxonomy. *Nature* 193:855–60.

Snyder, Laurence. 1926. Human Blood Groups: Their Inheritance and Racial Significance. *American Journal of Physical Anthropology* 9:233–63.

Subramanian, Srivala. 1995. The Story in Our Genes. *Time,* 16 January, 54–55.

Weiss, Kenneth M., Kenneth K. Kidd, and Judith R. Kidd. 1992. The Human Genome Diversity Project. *Evolutionary Anthropology* 1:79–81.

CHAPTER 14

Genealogical Dis-Ease: Where Hereditary Abnormality,
Biomedical Explanation, and Family Responsibility Meet
Rayna Rapp, Deborah Heath, and Karen-Sue Taussig

While core anthropological concepts in kinship studies offer more than a century of experience with the social construction and variability of "what makes a relative," current international genomic practices in molecular biology provide a powerful counterpoint: relatedness consists in the transmission of biological substance at the level of DNA, gene, protein product, and chromosome. Committed to what David Schneider and those anthropologists influenced by him understand to be a substance model of kinship (compare Schneider 1968; Strathern 1992a; Yanagisako and Delaney 1995; Franklin 1997), contemporary biomedical researchers study transmission, mutation, and expressions of genetic matter within families, and increasingly use taxonomic models based on metaphors of family resemblances to describe molecular genetic relations. These practices are especially important for researchers in tracking pathological entities and processes.

Yet when viewed historically and cross-culturally, kin-based groups have always coped with phenotypical diversity and atypical, indeed problematic births. A wide range of practices — from infanticide to apotheosis, from extreme social segregation and community stigma to religious and cosmological discourses on nature's mysteries and God's special angels — developed to represent, explain, and intervene in relations within kin groups responsible for atypical members. Now, those who fall under the expanding shadow of genomic mapping and clinical genetics (in those countries where such practices are both culturally influential and socially available) are being offered a powerful schema of explanation out of which to make meaning of misfortune.

Here, we report on how some of those affected by some genetically defined syndromes and conditions and their familial intimates construe genealogical relationships under the shadow of genomic thinking. We attempt to put what we have learned about genetic dis-ease from affected families and their support organizations into conversation with what research scientists and clinicians understand when they use concepts of family and kinship. Our goal is to examine the mutuality, disjuncture, and transformations of biomedical and familial forms of knowledge as they intersect in discourses and practices of kin relations in the United States.

We are concerned in this essay to explore "what makes a relative" in the context of rapidly expanding biotechnical knowledge. In tracking the traffic in languages of kinship in light of an explosion of new knowledge about biology, we keep in mind Schneider's (1972) point that American notions of kinship are based on popular ideas about "biological facts" and that if new "facts" are discovered by scientists, then that is what kinship will be described as always having been. Yet new scientific ideas about biological relatedness are themselves highly cultural. As Gillian Beer (1983), Sarah Franklin (1997), and Marilyn Strathern (1992a, 1992b) have all usefully remarked, Darwin himself borrowed popular and prescientific concepts such as "degrees of kinship and affinity" (Strathern 1992b, 15) to elaborate his theory of natural selection. These concepts were then and are now read back as inhering in nature. As Strathern observes, "We make fresh concepts by borrowing from one domain of life the imagery by which to structure other areas" (15). In elaborating the contemporary traffic in languages of kinship among researchers, clinicians, and people affected by genetic syndromes, we aim to illustrate the ways in which ideas about kinship travel and are transformed as people seek to understand what makes a relative.

As both admirers and critics have consistently maintained, the Human Genome Project is rapidly changing the face of biomedicine (see Annas and Elias 1992; Keller 1992a, 1992b; Kevles and Hood 1992; Murray, Rothstein, and Murray 1996; Suzuki and Knudtson 1989). The biotechnical interventions enabled by these developments are controversial to different constituencies for various reasons that are beyond the scope of this essay (but see Hubbard 1990; Hubbard and Wald 1993; Rapp 1999; Rothman 1986, 1989, 1998). It is nevertheless important to note that all imply an increasing reliance on biomedical intervention to screen the quality of acceptable and unacceptable offspring. Biomedicine as currently understood and practiced is, of course, already deeply enmeshed in a thoroughly social world. In this essay, we attempt to apprehend the ways in which notions of kinship weave themselves into this world. We argue that ideas about kinship are woven not only through the affected families but also through the scientific and clinical practices we have been observing, helping to shape a worldview that complicates any simple interpretation of genomic practices. Here, we hope to index the ways in which human genetics is a powerful ethnoscience to which kinship reckoning speaks a related and alternative language of possibility and truth. What might the traffic among these languages of kinship reveal?

GENEALOGIES OF AFFLICTION

So I went up there [to my first Little People of America meeting in 1965] to Gloucester City, New Jersey. I'm sitting on the floor with new people and they introduce the speaker, they say, you know, Dr. Victor McKusick, . . . and he got up there and . . . spoke about their interest in the Amish and what they inherited.[1] . . . And Dr. McKusick, he looks out into the audience with maybe a hundred people in the room and all of a sudden his mind started working, he was thinking, "Look how different they are," you know, "Look at all these people and they're all different," so he's looking . . . and he's starting to classify, he's putting all these people like that in his mind. . . . All those people are tall and have shorter bodies and longer legs over there. So that was the beginning of his real focus and . . . what they asked for in that meeting was, "If you would like to donate your time and volunteer . . . because we're doing a study at Hopkins." — Dee Miller, Clinic Coordinator, Greenberg Center for Skeletal Dysplasia, Johns Hopkins Medical School

The complex history of research into heredity is beyond the scope of the present essay and, indeed, of our collective research project. But notes toward its production would surely index an interest from the Greek materialists forward in theories of generation as well as long-standing debates on the relative contributions of nature and nurture to the formation of the physical, mental, and moral characteristics of people. By the later nineteenth century, Sir Francis Galton had transformed the interest in inheritance (with its dual notions of property transmission and bases for structural formation) into the study of heredity: he developed tools for the statistical description of population characteristics across generations. Not uncoincidentally, Galton also coined the word "eugenics" in 1883 to encourage interventions alleged to improve the quality over generations of human populations. But Galton's "hereditary" features ranged wildly from measurements of stature and health to those of depravity and nomadism. It was only with the rediscovery of Gregor Mendel's pea plant experiments at the turn of the twentieth century that "unit characters" could begin to be studied through the emergent laboratory-based methods of cytology as well as the older uses of hybrid pedigrees. In the contemporary controversies that swirled around Mendelianism, the stage was set for William Bateson's invention of the term "genetics," Wilhelm Johanssen's distinction between genotype and phenotype, and Thomas Hunt Morgan's focus on the study of chromosomes. While Anglo-American scientists tended to concentrate on chromosomes in the cell nucleus (still the major focus of the Human Genome Project's vast undertaking), their German colleagues remained much more interested in extranuclear cytoplasm (see Keller 1995, 2000). With emergent work on sex chromosomes in the 1930s, specific human characteristics like color blindness and hemophilia were linked to chromosomal positions. And the normal human chromosome count was only reliably ascertained in contrast to the chromosome count for people with Down's syndrome in 1958 (see Lejeune et al. 1959). Yet long before biomedical researchers were able to associate specific pathologies with chromosomal locations, their clinical peers had developed expertise in reading the pathological human body through multiple clues.

Biological scientists are no strangers to familial analyses: from at least Carolus Linnaeus forward, scientific thinkers have used what they understood to be family resemblances to classify, assign taxa, and experiment with the building blocks of life. While the study of inheritance in the classic era mainly involved plant and animal hybrids, modern medical genetics has always depended on the pedigree within individual families and the "family resemblances" across pathological instances to advance diagnoses and interventions.

Close observation and classification of abnormalities is, of course, a central strategy in the development of clinical medicine. Normality, as the work of George Canguilhem (1978) and others asserts, is defined in a contrastive system with abnormality. Tracing family pedigrees and imagining the various routes by which affliction was transmitted among those with recognizable pathologies are two classic methodological strategies for accumulating knowledge about diseases and disorders. In the nineteenth century, these closely reasoned characterizations of abnormal people were conventionally assigned the name of their medical surveyors, who often drew quite philosophical lessons from their patient populations—for example, Dr. John Down's famous syndrome was based on his humanist insistence that the "racial regression" involved in "Mongolism" proved the unity of the human species since the parents of the affected were almost always English people of normal intelligence, rather than individuals from a "lower" race (Down

1866, 1877; compare Gould 1980). In such clinical/populational intersections, theories of degeneration, racial slippage, and devolution and other cultural morality tales involving kinship connection are always categorical possibilities: yesterday's science quickly becomes today's prejudice, as older labels of the mentally retarded as "degenerative" or "animalistic," and newer controversies around genetic versus maternal pathology theories of autism or homosexuality, should remind one.

Since World War II, medical genetics has reinvented itself as a field of research and treatment, thanks largely, in the United States, to the work of McKusick. Arguably the most significant figure in the development of the modern field in the United States, and still highly productive in his retirement, McKusick is quite legendary; he has written his own story of the relation between caring for patients and their families and solving the genetic mysteries of their disorders (McKusick 1975, 1992, 1997). He labored to classify and treat medical pathologies as diverse as intestinal polyps, aortic weakness, and dramatically short stature, all the while searching for their genetic origins at the Johns Hopkins School of Medicine, with which he has had a lifelong association (McKusick 1997). He launched two of the most influential textbooks in post–World War II medical education, *Mendelian Inheritance in Man* (1968–present, nine editions, prior to becoming on-line-MIM in 1993), and *Heritable Disorders of Connective Tissue* (1956–present). And he trained an extraordinary line of geneticists, many of whom have inherited not only his taxonomic and clinical skills, moving them into the realm of molecular biology and gene mapping, but his commitment to patients both as individuals and repositories of research. McKusick's first encounter with the Little People of America (LPA) in 1965 — described above by Dee Miller, who now administers the Johns Hopkins clinic where large numbers of short-statured patients are seen — led to a long-standing involvement with the organization. Soon after McKusick's taxonomic epiphany in New Jersey, he invited the LPA to hold its meeting at Johns Hopkins. As Miller continues,

> Dr. McKusick footed the bill for this huge lawn party for the little people and they came from all over . . . [to] Evergreen House, which is part of the Johns Hopkins University. . . . He had this long catered afternoon Sunday lawn party and it was the real beginning of how the little people identified Victor McKusick. And the same week before the national convention, he opened up to the little people and he brought in all these people for a week of free full physicals or whatever. . . . We have pictures where the

[hospital] floor was turned over to all these short-statured families and patients, and Billy Barty [founder of LPA] was one of those families, . . . and they were getting in with him a little bit more . . . and all those people had such a great time being in this hospital ward, you know with all these other families, and they were really the very beginnings of how Johns Hopkins was identified [with the LPA].

From these interactions, an extraordinary research-and-treatment collaboration developed: the Medical Advisory Board was founded in 1981, and Charles Scott (one of McKusick's former genetics fellows) became its chair. Indeed, the McKusick lineage is particularly apparent at the LPA, where many of the physicians who serve on the Medical Advisory Board are closely "related" to McKusick through their professional training. The board advises the membership of the LPA of new treatment options with potential benefits and provides intensive clinics for families attending the national convention gratis. To be seen by a world-renown expert in your (or more likely, your child's) condition is a gift of inestimable value, especially for those bearing a rare diagnosis, living without a diagnosis, or living far from medical research centers where a specialist in the relatively rare chondrodysplasias (skeletal anomalies) might be located. At the same time, LPA members were recruited as research subjects: members make savvy jokes about "spotted dwarfs," referring to the badges left on their bodies from the multiple skin biopsies through which they have donated tissue. Many new orthopedic interventions that have been tried on the short statured have been evaluated through studies that recruited members of the LPA. A recent survey of the membership concerning the fraught topic of prenatal diagnosis was conducted by LPA-affiliated biomedical researchers. The first longitudinal health survey of U.S. dwarfs was carried out among members. Without the tissue samples, skeletal measurements, pen-and-paper survey responses, and life stories of several generations of LPA members, research on dwarfing conditions would be immeasurably impoverished. At the same time, the Medical Advisory Board, heavily weighted with Johns Hopkins University–affiliated clinicians and researchers, provides considerable services to this population. Thus, a first contention of this essay resides in the simple observation that it is the marriage of biomedical researchers, clinicians, and carriers of genetic conditions that enables the social reproduction of their united and divided interests in an atypical phenotype to move forward.

Like any "old" marriage, this one is not without its tensions. As Clair

Francomano, chief of the Medical Genetics Branch of the National Center for Human Genome Research/National Institutes of Health and longtime researcher in skeletal anomalies, put it,

> The first thing I saw when I came to this convention last year [after the discovery of the gene for achondroplasia was publicized] was one of the people wearing that "Endangered Species" T-shirt. It really made a very big impact on me. And I really worry about it. I worry about what we're doing and about how it's going to be used and what it means to the people here.

Francomano's ethical concerns were overtly discussed at a workshop she ran at the 1997 LPA national convention; observing such a workshop, we heard some of her patients professing both great love and respect for her, and also contesting sharply the value of geneticists' discoveries of the genes responsible for dwarfing conditions. Her willingness to put herself into continuous conversation with those who have the most to both gain and lose through her research is notable, as is the general attitude of respect and concern expressed by many LPA-affiliated clinician/researchers.

The LPA is among the oldest voluntary health organizations for a genetic condition in the United States.[2] Founded in 1956 by Barty, a Hollywood actor, the organization has served as an enormous social support system at both local and national levels. When viewed by a team of genetics-obsessed anthropologists, its Medical Advisory Board looms large, but from the vantage point of most members, the real action is social: the Dwarf Athletic Association of America games held in conjunction with the LPA along with the fashion shows, dinner dances, pool parties, and workshops on family life are the reasons most people articulate for their desire to attend convention week. Moreover, for people with achondroplasia (the most common form of dwarfism), medical problems may seem minor or only preoccupy certain moments in the life cycle. This is a relatively "nonmedicalized" population, able to live a normal life span in a biological sense; given the bias and prejudice dwarfs regularly confront, their concerns focus on living a normal life in the social sense (compare Ablon 1984, 1988). These issues animate much of the organization's agenda, and inform many activities that help integrate dwarf children and, in some cases, their average-statured parents into a familial milieu that is increasingly delineated by genetics. The researchers and clinicians who serve on the Medical Advisory Board and offer their services at convention clinics are also drawn into this milieu. When we attended convention activities such as the talent shows, we saw many of the researchers and physicians in the audience, cheering on their patients, and we also saw them kicking up their heels at the dances. In comparing the LPA, with its predominantly social focus, with other genetic support groups, there are notable contrasts in the ways in which biomedical and social concerns are brought together. These differences draw attention to contrasting experiences with both medical intervention and daily life for those living with different heritable conditions. The case of Marfan's syndrome, for example, which Deborah Heath has been tracking since 1992, highlights some of these distinctions. While dwarfs live with their often socially stigmatized identities from birth, many people with Marfan's syndrome are diagnosed only later in life, frequently on the occasion of a life-threatening aortic aneurysm. While misdiagnosis is still a problem, advances in surgical and pharmaceutical intervention in the past two decades have significantly improved longevity for people with Marfan's.

Mitigated social stigma and successful medical intervention have contributed to the ways in which meetings of the National Marfan Foundation (NMF) differ from those of the LPA. The NMF was founded in 1981 on the premise that better public and medical awareness about this condition would lead to better life-saving medical diagnosis. NMF national conventions give a more prominent place to biomedical workshops than do LPA conventions, dividing time evenly between biomedical "days" and "consumer days." During the biomedical sessions, researchers and clinicians report on advances in diagnosis and case management; during psychosocially oriented sessions on the consumer days, patient-activist concerns dominate, and the medical personnel are less likely to be in attendance in the hotel convention rooms where members gather. The relative prominence of the clinical workshops at NMF conventions may be linked to the crucial and, for many, successful role that medical treatment has had in increasing the life span of affected individuals. The NMF, like the LPA, addresses a range of social issues that aim to normalize difference: discussing the challenges that face teens with Marfan's, since they are likely to be the tallest among their peers; offering comfort and support to unaffected siblings; and using humor to cope with chronic pain. Unlike the LPA, NMF meetings lack the intense focus on providing opportunities for dating. For people with Marfan's syndrome, though many mention the discomforts that come with being singled out as taller than average, the work of finding a mate seems less fraught than has been the case for many little people.

A final example of hybrid medical/social organization is offered by the proliferation of Down's syndrome support groups. The National Down Syndrome Society was formed in 1981; its primary mission involves fund-raising for research on chromosome 21. The older National Down Syndrome Congress is more support-group oriented: its workshops, athletic events, and toll-free information services are intended to integrate people with Down's syndrome and their families into a social world of acceptance, achievement, and satisfying relationships. At the local level (which is where Rayna Rapp participated in Down's syndrome support-group work), the biomedical/social functions are fused: public workshops drawing anywhere from ten to fifty people cover rotating topics as diverse as cutting-edge genetic research, coaching for special education public school evaluations, and reports from Down's syndrome teenagers about their aspirations and adjustments toward independent living.

By noting the contrasts among different lay organizations, we are better able to attend to the specific embodied experiences of those with different heritable conditions. This, in turn, provides us with a way to articulate the diverse types of rapidly emergent social forms in the age of genetics. The LPA attributes the enormous increase in registration numbers at the national convention (from 1,000 in 1996 to over 1,500 in 1998) to the use of the Internet: more families with short-statured members now use cyber-services, and the posting of the meeting's agenda brought a vast increase in e-mail inquiries and registration. Many rare disorders have on-line chat groups. In the case of Familial Dysautonomia (a classic Ashkenazi recessive disorder involving atypical development of the autonomic nervous system), families in Australia, Latin America, Western Europe, Canada, and the United States regularly "check in" with one another, comparing survival strategies, and venting their anguish and anger at the medical attention (or inattention) their children receive. Parenthetically, folk theories of genetic transmission and pathogenesis abound on the Internet. Our research has tracked the ways in which some geneticists collaborate with lay advocates to organize cyberspace chat groups that bring clinicians, patients, and researchers together on-line to compare notes on "their" conditions (see Heath et al. 1999). Thus, the recent invention and expansion of cyberspace as a widespread public tool has created hybrid genetic organizations for those with the resources to plug in.

There are also marriages, mergers, and traffic among these organizations. The Coalition of Heritable Connective Tissue Disorders was formed by the heads of seven voluntary health groups: its goal is to lobby nationally for policies of collective concern, including federal research funding, and to cosponsor scientific workshops. The Coalition of Patient Support Groups for Skin

Disease Research concerns itself with public awareness and research funding for a wide range of skin diseases. The National Organization of Rare Diseases puts families with arcane diagnoses in touch with one another; its main issue is the problem of "orphan drugs" (pharmaceuticals that are essential to small numbers of people, but are not profitable under the current market conditions, and hence, face the constant threat of being discontinued). The Alliance of Genetic Support Groups, founded in 1986 and renamed the Genetic Alliance in 2000, brings together the full range of associations concerned with genetic policy and support. It serves as a clearinghouse for information and mobilization, connecting new members to "their" relevant disease group and forging coalitions among over 250 groups. As these brief sketches suggest, these groups are diverse in goals, methods, and memberships; their success depends on carving out a specific mission relevant to the constituency they both define and serve (see Weiss and Mackta 1996).

Yet across that diversity, such groups share certain properties: despite the highly variable meld of biomedical-informational and social support functions, they are all based on the mobilization of an identity anchored in a genetically marked category. Their proliferation since the 1960s and 1970s indexes a growth in biosociality: the forging of collective identities under emergent categories of biomedicine and allied sciences (see Rabinow 1992). For Paul Rabinow, biosociality involves increasing enrollment into biomedical categories that people come to identify as central to their social lives. These categories of emergent "identity politics" are powerfully described through the science of genetics.[3] As Rabinow argues, then, contemporary social life is being rescripted in terms of molecular biology. Sculpting a collective identity through a hereditary disorder provides a way to both cope with difference and normalize it. This strategy for empowerment also here entails the construction of an imagined kindred. Those who "share a gene" (or chromosome) for a disorder are felt to be related. But on what is their "diffuse solidarity" based?

In some cases, it is premised on a "reading of the body" widely and popularly shared: many people believe, for example, that those with Down's syndrome have "more in common" with one another than they do with members of their family of origin. There is an active network for fostering and adopting other children with this condition among families who have already borne one Down's syndrome child. Several said that they wanted a "look-alike" child who they imagined would share a basic personality with their already-affected son or daughter (see Rapp 1999, 2000). The LPA also sponsors a successful adoption service for placing little people children. In these cases, the grim history of childhood neglect, abuse, and institutionalization is part of the collective memory: families with affected members band together to offer a safety net for other affected children they imagine as "their own."

At the 1993 annual convention of the NMF, a choral group called the Melodic Marfettes sang a satirical composition that captured the sense of familial connection among those living with Marfan's, here captured in the last two lines of the song: "I looked at these Marfans and what did I see? A whole brand-new family that looks just like me" (Heath 1997a). This sentiment is echoed regularly in hallways and workshops at NMF meetings. At the 1997 NMF conference, a husband of a woman with Marfan's attending his first meeting looked around the dining hall with affection and bemusement, declaring,

> I used to think those deep-set eyes belonged just to Mary, but now I see them everywhere. It's like a family reunion.

In other instances, the "imagined community" has deep and deeply historical ethnic-racial referents. Where autosomal recessive conditions run at relatively elevated risks among ethnically defined populations, group identity is multistranded. For example, a mother whose child had recently died of Familial Dysautonomia — as mentioned earlier, an Ashkenazi recessive disorder — continued to participate in the Internet chat group for that condition, saying,

> I'm still the proud carrier of that stubborn gene. . . . I'll continue to say "we" — Rebecca and I will always be connected to you all. Her memory is a blessing. After all, we will always share that common ancestor way back when in some shtetl.[4]

And sickle cell anemia, most prevalent in those of African descent, has been the object of political activism and mobilizations for respectful community screening programs (see Duster 1990).

Might there be important social differences that run along the trajectories of heritable transmission? To take one case, autosomal recessive conditions are classically "revealed" only when a mating of two (unaffected) carriers produces an affected child, say, in Tay-Sachs disease, Familial Dysautonomia, sickle cell anemia, or cystic fibrosis. How might familial experiences compare with those of parents whose child is diagnosed with a de novo autosomal dominant condition (for instance, a new mutation for dwarfism)? And surely, they may express a different sense of connection than those parents who both themselves experience and pass along a genetic difference — for example, when dwarfs marry and reproduce (see Taussig, Rapp, and Heath 2002). When such diverse "genealogies of affliction" are mobilized for support and empowerment, what role does kinship play?[5]

THE WORK OF KINSHIP

You could say we're one large family, united by 250 kinds of dwarfism. So welcome to the LPA. — First Lady's "New Members" orientation workshop, national LPA convention, 1997

What's the matter with you? Was your father a giant? — third grader taunting a classmate who has Marfan's syndrome

The language of kinship runs through genetic support groups in multiple directions and projects: the NMF's "Adopt a Hospital" program uses a metaphor drawn from extended kinship to imbue its project with positive reference. Its goal is the education of local emergency room staff in the diagnosis of Marfan's syndrome; NMFers hope that young people complaining of chest pain will not be sent home with a misdiagnosis of "the flu" when a rare yet life-threatening condition may be lurking. In local Down's syndrome parent support groups, activists refer to "our children." Explains one mother of a six year old with Down's syndrome:

> You also feel a sense of parenthood for everyone's child, there's a sense they're all my children, you know. Which I don't think you feel with your normal children.

Another mother, with a five-year-old Down's syndrome child, adds:

> Our kids need special classrooms in caring schools. Our kids need speech therapists and physical therapists who know their special needs. But most of all, our kids need respect. As a mother, it's my job to get those things for our kids.

And the First Lady of the LPA's welcoming speech cited above refers to short-statured people across all their genetic variety as a "family." This language of kinship provides a powerful rhetoric of social inclusion; it invokes the positive sense of collective responsibility that kinship is alleged to demarcate. We will return to the mobilizing power of this rhetoric of inclusion in the final section of this essay. But first, note that the lines of kinship may also rank and exclude as well as include: Members of the LPA told us compelling stories about the history of their organization.

In the 1950s and 1960s, before the widespread availability of growth hormone (first in "natural" and then synthetic form), LPAers described an organizational hierarchy based on proportion. Pituitary dwarfs (whose short stature was caused by a growth hormone deficiency) were widely viewed as the elite of the organization. Normally proportioned, they dominated social functions and held all the important offices, at least in the memory of several older activists. Achondroplasts ("achons"), with their alternative proportions (longer trunks, shorter limbs, and larger heads), were considered the plebes of the population. Now, virtually all children with medical insurance who see pediatricians are referred for evaluation and treatment if they consistently fall below the fifth percentile of growth curves, and are often treated with growth hormone.[6] While the ultimate addition to height induced by growth hormone (and associated) treatment may not be enormous, it is enough to have eradicated a recognizable pituitary dwarf population. And according to doctors knowledgeable in endocrinology, short-statured children and adults whose height is not dependent on a genetic condition are hesitant to join organizations based on a stature "problem."[7] Yet the LPA does not define itself as a "genetic" support group. Its membership requirements are based exclusively on height, whatever the cause of shortness: anyone whose adult stature falls at four feet, ten inches or less is considered a little person according to the criteria of the organization. Thus, evolving medical classifications and interventions carve out categories of identity that marked constituencies may adapt, contest, or transform to their own ends.

Marfan's syndrome has a nosology based on clinical manifestations, not genetic diagnosis: the gene for the condition is a long one, and each family seems to have its own mutation. Long before (and now after) the gene was located and characterized in molecular terms, checklists of skeletal, cardiovascular, and ophthalmologic symptoms were used to assign suspected cases to this diagnosis. Moreover, international diagnostic criteria have changed several times in the last decade: some people originally classified as "Marfan" are now "marfoid," or thought to be the bearers of "shadow syndromes." Yet, as one father of an undiagnosed teenage daughter put it at a family workshop at the NMF meetings,

> If it looks like a duck and quacks like a duck, it's a duck. I'm diagnosed and she's not diagnosed but we've both got it.

So the question of who "belongs" to the family categorically invoked (and often well served) by genetic support groups is historically variable in part as medical understandings and interventions change.

Then, too, participation in genetic support groups may vary over the individual and domestic cycle. As one mother of a seven year old with Down's syndrome said of her now-rare appearance at monthly support group meetings,

> It's mainly for new families, with new babies and toddlers. I know all that stuff already. It makes me feel good to be in a room with them, to see how many of us there are, but I'm not goin' to learn much from attending.

Down's syndrome support groups revisit important topics like how to get the most from the special education bureaucracy in the public schools because they appeal to a cohort of relatively new members. These kinds of topics are also covered each year at the LPA national convention in a series of workshops organized to support parents of young children with dwarfing conditions. Support is especially valuable as disabled children "age out" of specific services (like early intervention, primary school special education, or public education) and families scramble to inform themselves about the next set of services that may accommodate their children's needs. Because activism is often punctuated by life-cycle phases, organizations need to recruit "new blood" from the recently diagnosed and their intimate supporters. Of course, not "everybody" who fits the diagnostic criteria (and who might benefit from group services) joins such organizations: as Rapp has tried to show elsewhere, the class-inflected etiquette of voluntary organizations may feel more comfortable for middle-class families who are used to assuming "new" professional identities and seeking help from specialized sources. Working-class, and especially racial-ethnically marked populations, particularly if they are well anchored in local religious institutions, may find alternative sources of support that do not focus on health problems or genetic identity categories (see Rapp 1995, 1999, 2000).

In most genetic support groups, the kinship activists are disproportionately wives and mothers. Historically, self-help voluntary organizations focused around health problems grew from three sources: turn-of-the-twentieth-century immigrant societies, veterans' associations following major international wars, and the model provided by Alcoholics Anonymous in the 1930s (see Rapp 1999; Weiss and Mackta 1996; Young 1996). All were initially masculinist in leadership and constituency. But over the course of the twentieth century, a substitution effect occurred: health activism became increasingly marked as the domain of female volunteerism, especially as the sweethearts, wives, and mothers of veterans came to represent the importance of nursing and chronic care. It is thus not surprising that many of the local and national groups that we have been observing were founded by women, usually mothers, staking public claims on the turf of family health. We might want to speculate that "family health," conventionally imagined as a "women's issue," is doubly marked in this case: when a health problem can be laid at the door of reproductive anomaly, it is conventionally characterized as a "female" domain. And as historian Susan Lindee pointed out to us in 1998, it is mothers who are likely to have the greatest working "emotional knowledge" of the differently abled bodies of their small children. Hence, the concern with the impact of "special needs" members on family life, building medical management into domestic routines, practical matters associated with education and social life, and attention to "psychosocial issues" of difference predominate in many of the sessions and workshops we have attended. This is not to say that men do not take active roles in such events: many workshops at national meetings are facilitated by male presenters, and fathers spoke up with great commitment and concern at all the national conventions we attended. But the majority of officers we have encountered are women; many speak a maternalist language when describing their aspirations, strategies, and orientations.

A signal exception to this pattern is the national LPA. Founded under the leadership of Barty, the Hollywood actor mentioned earlier who initially recruited his professional peers, the organization has a decidedly masculinist feel: key offices are held by men, and the influence of athletic prowess is considerable, as the Dwarf Athletic Association of America games are held in conjunction with the national convention. Traveling directly from the LPA to the NMF during the summer of 1997 (that is, from a stay among the very short to a visit among the very tall), our research team was struck by a difference in gendered aesthetics between the two meetings. The first appeared quite masculine; the second more feminine. Might the difference reflect a gendered dilemma attached to diagnosis? It is surely less culturally acceptable to be a short man than a short woman; and conversely, being a very tall man is not culturally coded as a problem, although being a very tall woman well may be. It has in the past been the case that young women with Marfan's syndrome have been offered hormonal treatment to arrest growth far more frequently than are young men with the same condition.

But masculinist or feminine, genetic support groups are highly focused on the issues of social and biological reproduction: the LPA has a well-deserved reputation as a dating service. Many little people report that they met long-term partners and spouses at the national convention or through dates arranged locally by other LPA members. Some LPA parents described flying in a friend their teenager had met at a national convention to serve as a prom date. A key theme running through the national convention concerns teen activities and the relative merits of supervision or freedom. There are teen and singles pages attached to the LPA Web site where "dates" get organized. When we visited the local holiday party in Brooklyn, the young ticket taker joked that she had the best job in the house: she was determined to snag any attractive men as they walked through the door.

This interest in dating and mating is quite understandable. Although numbers can only be approximate, Joan Ablon (1984) reports that a high percentage of marriages among LPA members are stature endogamous. And because achondroplasia is by far the dominant form of dwarfism, and it is genetically an autosomal dominant disorder, there is a long-standing concern about reproductive options among those with this condition. One-fourth of the fetuses conceived by two people with achondroplasia will be of average stature; half will replicate their parents' condition; and one-fourth will receive a "double dominant" gene dose, which is lethal. This Mendelian grid has been understood since at least the 1950s, when McKusick and his associates conducted extensive pedigree studies. Anecdotally, collective knowledge of the odds involved in dwarf reproduction probably has a much longer history. But the risks involved — most obviously, of bearing a child destined for stillbirth or neonatal death; less obviously, of bearing and raising an average-statured child — influenced many little people couples not to reproduce or to adopt dwarf babies when available. Likewise, many parents of young adults with Down's syndrome worry about their children's sexuality and potential fertility.[8] According to hospital-based social workers, ultra–Orthodox Jews send their anomalous babies and children to live with distant relatives or to be placed in institutions in other countries: they know that the existence of a problematic family member reduces the desirability of arranged marriages in their direct lineage. When transmission of an abnormality is known to be hereditary, then the social niche of dating, mating, and reproduction is highly fraught.

Increasingly, medical intervention is available and implicated in reproductive decision making: kinship "by choice" arises in contexts where the risks of atypical hereditary conditions is known to be relatively high. It is a truism of prenatal diagnostic ethics in general that the availability of testing not only allows for the abortion of affected fetuses but also increases the options for those who carry genetic disorders and would not choose to reproduce without assurance that they will not pass their conditions along. In this case, little people do not consider that the diagnosis of achondroplasia justifies abortion; but double dominance surely does for many. Experiments in preimplantation embryo diagnosis are ongoing for families carrying the Marfan and EB genes.[9]

The most widespread use of prenatal diagnosis is, of course, predicated on the desire of many people to eliminate potential offspring with Down's syndrome and other rarer chromosome abnormalities. A standard amniocentesis is offered to pregnant women of "advanced maternal age"; anyone with a near relative with Down's will also be offered the test. Although these interventions are controversial to different constituencies for various reasons that are beyond the scope of the present essay, our purpose is to point out that all imply an increasing reliance on biomedical intervention to screen the quality of acceptable and unacceptable offspring.[10] Surely, this growing presence of prenatal intervention into the limits of "what makes a relative" is the most obvious site where the utopian and dystopian elements of genealogical disease meet.

Affected families are not, of course, the only interested parties in interventions involving hereditary transmission. Dedicated researchers at the National Human Genome Research Institute of the National Institutes of Health (NIH) have connective tissue and skeletal dysplasia protocols through which they gather information in search of the many genes (some autosomal dominant, some recessive) that cause specific anomalies and disorders. In addition to the successful search for the achondroplasia gene, genes for the less common SED and Morchio dwarfing syndromes have recently been found, and a new protocol involving families that carry Sticklers syndrome (involving early severe arthritis, profound myopia, and skeletal anomalies) has of late been launched (compare McKusick et al. 1996). Each of these studies involves "collecting families" who volunteer pedigrees, medical and life histories, and tissue samples. Such families are often recruited through support-group newsletter announcements. NIH researchers are acutely aware of the importance of family participation; some expressed concern about what families included or excluded from specific studies might "get" about the research, and what happens when extended family members previously unknown to one another meet through tissue and pedigree collection.

The idea that genetic disorders are familial not only through pedigree studies but also at the level of DNA mutation, protein molecule, clinical symptom, and grouping of symptoms is increasingly implicated in genomic thinking. In 1996, a special issue of the *American Journal of Medical Genetics* was devoted to "the evolution of the bone dysplasia family"; in 1997, *Science* focused its special genome issue on "gene families." In such cases, "family knowledge" is at once clinical, molecular, and sociocultural: as our observations and Susan Lindee's historical research both suggest, it is the intersection of these multiple knowledges that is key to the transformation of how genetic connections are characterized.

These new knowledge coalitions involving "emotional knowledge" and "technical knowledge" (Lindee's distinction) are emergent; they sometimes bring biomedical researchers onto terrain that may be unfamiliar and even unsettling. NIH researchers described the intensity of their feelings as they sat in on intake interviews with Ehlers-Danlos syndrome families whose members bore phenotypes for whose causes they were on a molecular search. (People with E-D have a variety of disorders involving skin, connective tissue, joints, and blood vessels.) Such "modest interventions" link researchers and the prevailing experience of "their" molecules (Heath 1997a) in "real time." These interactions overlap the concept of "habitus" as used to portray lived abnormalities in biomedicine with the sociocultural "habitus" that Pierre Bourdieu–inflected anthropologists immediately recognize (see Heath 1997a, 1997b): multiple divisions of labor—professional, familial, gendered, age divided—enable communication and intervention into "the normal and the pathological" (Canguilhem 1978).

Such emergent and coalitional knowledge production is fraught with discursive tensions. A contemporary debate, for example, concerning the name of a syndrome, speaks to transitional knowledge and its multiple interested parties. Two eminent geneticists disagreed about how to refer to the condition widely known in the literature as "thanatophoric dysplasia": the Greek root of the name indexes its severe, indeed fatal, characteristics. Yet one of the geneticists, who had several young patients living with the condition, was distressed on behalf of "her" families: constant reminders of their child's likely fate, she argued, were unnecessarily cruel. The second researcher voiced concerns about the importance of continuity in the literature for researchers. Recently, the two agreed to refer to the condition as SADDAN, which captures the severe achondroplasia and developmental delays involved in the condition, minus the lethal label. One geneticist described efforts to say "altered" or "changed" rather than "mutant" when depicting atypical genes. "Midget" became unacceptable to little people many decades ago; now, the LPA is debating whether to change its name. It has also, of course, become a sign of insufficient education to refer to "mongolism" rather than Down's syndrome, although the former term was in use well into the 1970s in the medical literature (compare Lippman and Brunger 1991; Rapp 1999). Dee Miller pointed out how derogatory a name like "birdhead dwarfism" is to its bearers. In 1975, McKusick suggested that genetic syndromes ought to be named descriptively for attributes that would inspire additional medical inquiry; the Doctor Riley for whom Riley-Day syndrome was initially named, himself renamed it Familial Dysautonomia a few years after he was cocredited with its discovery. This cascade of language battles and shifts sounds deeply familiar to (participant) observers of contemporary U.S. cultural life. In these cases, claims and counterclaims are encoded about whose standing "in relation" to a hereditary condition holds most weight. When the multiple truths of clinicians, biomedical researchers, and affected individuals and families collide, whose shall prevail?

One response to the problem of multiple truths is indicated by the following narrative, developed through an ongoing dialogue beginning in the 1990s between Heath and Lynn Sakai, the biochemist who discovered fibrillin. Sakai asserts,

> Now I think it is pretty clear that the secret of life is really the secret of gene expression . . . not only what happens on the inside of the cell but what happens on the outside over time.

Quoting University of Wisconsin researcher Judith Kimball, Sakai describes orientations toward genetics and developmental biology that differ between European and North American researchers. Europeans often value pedigree and family as their central metaphors: a cell becomes what its pedigree decrees. But U.S. researchers are less concerned with lineage, and more interested in what Sakai and Kimball depict as neighborhood: cells may be functionally pluripotent, able to differentiate into a range of tissues, organs, or systems depending on the extracellular environment. Sakai's use of this transformatory metaphor arose through an exchange that signaled a shared interest on the part of an anthropologist and a biochemist in relational perspectives. For us, the metaphor points to wider cultural questions: How might metaphors of family and environment coexist or transform one another in the production of new forms of knowledge about both biology and biosociality?

PEOPLE WITH GENES

We know that every human being inherits at least four or five (maybe more) marginally functional or nonfunctional genes that predispose them to various conditions or diseases. This is not to say that human disease is written into our genes as a preordained fact of life. Rather, these irregular genes may convey an increased risk to those who inherit them. It is the life-long interplay of genes, environment, and life-style that will determine if, when, and how these predispositions manifest themselves. — Francis Collins, afterword to *Toward the Twenty-First Century*

Thirty-five years after co-discovering the structure of the DNA molecule, Dr. James Watson launched an unprecedented experiment in American science policy. In response to a reporter's question at a press conference, he unilaterally set aside 3 to 5 percent of the budget of the newly launched Human Genome Project to support studies of the ethical, legal, and social implications of new advances in human genetics. . . . "I still don't understand," one senior official said after hearing Watson describe his plans at a 1990 briefing for the assembled directors of the NIH institutes, "why you want to spend all this money subsidizing the vacuous pronunciamentos of self-styled 'ethicists'!?" When Watson responded that, for better or worse, "the cat was out of the bag" with respect to the public's concern over the ethical issues, the official retorted: "But why inflate the cat? Why put the cat on TV?" — Eric Juengst, "Self-Critical Federal Science?"

Watson's experiment in self-consciously tracking the policy issues inherent to scientific advances in genome mapping quickly became known as ELSI (as the felicitous acronym for ethical, legal, and social implications arranged itself). It had a dual organizational structure: the ELSI program manages grant making and contract competitions to fund reconnaissance papers on emergent issues, descriptive studies, policy analyses, policy conferences, educational projects, and training grants. Using well-established peer-review NIH mechanisms, ELSI has spent more than twenty-five million dollars since its inception in 1990 funding a robust mix of science, social science, and humanities research and publications, including ours.

ELSI's second more highly original structure was its Working Group. Comprised of a rotating pack of basic scientific researchers in genetics, physicians representing relevant fields and specialties, social scientists, philosophers, lawyers, and public advocates, the ELSI Working Group's mission was to identify key issues on which policy-related research, debate, and action would be needed. A freewheeling and controversial entity that never quite fit the shape of the commissions, hearings, and task forces for which Washington already had models, the Working Group addressed a range of problems. It subsidized a task force on insurance and genetic discrimination along with one on the quality of genetic tests. It cooperated with the Institute of Medicine to produce a pamphlet on genetic risk assessment for the public, and with the Equal Employment Opportunity Commission to issue guidelines for the then-new Americans with Disabilities Act to cover genetic predispositions. It helped to debate new Institutional Review Board standards for informed consent. Denounced by its critics as "window dressing" or "policy impotent," the ELSI Working Group might be abstractly viewed as a public forum for antieugenics concerns at the heart of genomic science itself. After a five-year review in 1996, the Working Group was disbanded by Francis Collins, director of the National Human Genome Research Institute/National Institutes of Health in 1997, its functions dispersed into the Presidential Bioethics Commission, an advisory council to report to the secretary of health and human services, and an ELSI committee to be housed in the National Human Genome Research Institute that Collins directs. This new arrangement infused ELSI concerns throughout the relevant institutional structure; it also made ELSI projects directly accountable to Collins, who was troubled by the unwieldy and time-consuming efforts that placed experts and advocates from so many fields into consequential and open-ended policy discussions.

While it might best be viewed as a bureaucratic victim of its own hybrid successes, the short-lived ELSI Working Group undertook many creative initiatives (see Juengst 1996). Among its many sorties into public policy, it made one failed foray to the Hill to argue the case for the importance of genetic privacy legislation in the early Clinton hearings on the pending Health Care Security Act of 1993. In the shadow of the looming HMO revolution — a revolution in health care reform from the marketplace whose consequences are highly debatable — Working Group members were quite concerned about the potential for insurance discrimination that increasing knowledge of genetic predispositions in families and individuals portended. Unable to take partisan legislative stands as a government-commissioned entity, some Working Group members joined together as individuals with public interest health lobbyists and organizations to form a coalition called People with Genes (Juengst 1996, 81). It was on behalf of People with Genes — that is to say, everybody — that the effort to influence legislators and legislation was launched.

We return to this 1993 effort at biosociality by genomic intellectuals at the risk of belaboring the obvious: we all "have genes," and with them, we have disease predispositions. That these "run in families" is increasingly clear at the levels of DNA, gene, proteins, tissues, and organ systems, as well as in the more overtly cultural meanings attached to family life. As we noted at the beginning of this essay, the Human Genome Project is rapidly changing the face of biomedicine. But biomedicine as we currently apprehend and practice it is deeply enmeshed in the world of multinational pharmaceuticals, national and international venture capital, and insurance-directed health care services. As our essay helps illustrate, it is already thoroughly social. The proclivity to reduce models of and interventions into phenotypic variability to basic genetic elements that can be profitably mined or cost accounted is thus overdetermined, and strong. Yet at the same time, the methods attendant on pedigree research and kinship reckoning everywhere infiltrate and construct genomic thinking, offering many possibilities for new knowledge production. Some of this new production is occurring at the crossroads where hereditary abnormality, biomedical explanation, and family responsibility meet. (How) might the biosociality whose emergence this essay maps contribute to the establishment of new discursive environments in which enculturation to genomic thinking occurs? While there is a long and problematic eugenic legacy that separates those with hereditary disabilities from those viewed as "normal," current genomic practices also muddy the waters: phenotypic variation is multiply produced and complex. It expresses genotypic vulnerabilities in which everyone is implicated. Dystopian and eugenic fears rightly haunt any simple notion of progress in genomic theory and practice. Yet to the extent that we recognize ourselves, in all our diversity, as "people with genes," we have a collective stake in imagining both genetic kinship and "neighborhoods" in which the full range of humanly expressed variability may dwell.

NOTES

The field research on which this essay draws was supported by NIH/NHGRI/ELSI Grant #1RO1 HG01582, for which we are deeply grateful. We also want to acknowledge Joan Albon for the help, in print and person, she provided us. Her long-term work with the Little People of America was very much appreciated by its membership, which eased our entry into this field site.

1 See McKusick 1997.
2 Susan Lindee's current research on the history of post–World War II human genetics in the United States credits the Familial Dysautonomia Foundation, established in 1951, as the earliest family-based genetic support group.

3 Karen Sue Taussig's work on genetics in the Netherlands (1997a, 1997b), where support groups work toward a goal of providing normalcy rather than a distinctive identity, is a reminder that this is a particularly U.S. phenomenon. See also Rabinow's analysis of genetics in France (1999), which stresses the French preoccupation with the national character of lineage.

4 See Mittman et al. 1999. Troy Duster, Diane Beeson, and their students at the Institute for Social Change at the University of California, Berkeley, have been following African American families with sickle cell affected members to ascertain how they understand genetic risk.

5 Faye Ginsburg should be thanked for continual discussion on this topic.

6 David Sandberg with the Division of Endocrinology at the Children's Hospital of Buffalo notes that our knowledge of treatment and its impact among short-statured children is based on those with insurance, for the treatments are continuous and costly. We therefore know relatively little about short stature among the poor—in this country, disproportionately of racial-ethnic minority backgrounds.

7 We thank David Sandberg for an illuminating research exchange with Rapp on 6 February 1998. See also Sandberg, Brook and Campos 1994; Sandberg et al. 1999.

8 People with Down's syndrome have a highly reduced fertility rate.

9 Epidermolysis Bullosa (EB) is a family of rare blistering skin diseases. While the milder forms may affect the quality of life but not shorten or end it, severe forms are lethal, either for small babies or for those who survive to young adulthood. Families in DEBRA, the national support organization, have supported the development of voluntary prenatal testing for these devastating forms of the disease.

10 For various sides of the controversy, see Berube 1996; Finger 1990; Rapp 1999; Rothman 1986; Saxton 1984; any publication of the right-to-life movement.

REFERENCES

Ablon, Joan. 1984. *Little People in America: The Social Dimensions of Dwarfism*. New York: Praeger.

———. 1988. *Living with Difference: Families with Dwarf Children*. New York: Praeger.

Annas, George, and Sherman Elias, eds. 1992. *Gene Mapping: Using Law and Ethics as Guides*. New York: Oxford University Press.

Beer, Gillian. 1983. *Darwin's Plots: Evolutionary Narrative in Darwin, George Eliot, and Nineteenth-Century Fiction*. London: Routledge and Kegan Paul.

Berube, Michael. 1996. *Life as We Know It: A Father, a Family, and an Exceptional Child*. New York: Pantheon.

Canguilhem, Georges. 1978. *On the Normal and the Pathological*. Dordrecht, Netherlands: Reidel.

Down, John Langdon. 1866. *Observations on an Ethnic Classification of Idiots*. London: London Hospital Reports.

———. 1877. *Mental Affections of Childhood and Youth*. London: Churchill.

Duster, Troy. 1990. *Backdoor to Eugenics*. New York: Routledge.

Finger, Anne. 1990. *Past Due: A Story of Disability, Pregnancy, and Birth.* Seattle, Wash.: Seal Press.

Franklin, Sarah. 1997. *Embodied Progress: A Cultural Account of Assisted Conception.* New York: Routledge.

Gould, Stephen Jay. 1980. Dr. Down's Syndrome. In *The Panda's Thumb: More Reflections in Natural History,* edited by Stephen Jay Gould. New York: W. W. Norton.

Heath, Deborah. 1997a. Bodies, Antibodies, and Modest Interventions. In *Cyborgs and Citadels: Anthropological Interventions in Emerging Sciences and Technologies,* edited by Gary L. Downey and Joseph Dumit. Santa Fe, N.Mex.: School of American Research Press.

———. 1997b. Locating Genetic Knowledge: Picturing Marfan Syndrome and Its Traveling Constituencies. *Science, Technology, and Human Values* 23, no. 1:71–97.

Heath, Deborah, Erin Koch, Barbara Ley, and Michael Montoya. 1999. Nodes and Queries: Linking Locations in Networked Fields of Inquiry. *American Behavioral Scientist* 43:450–63.

Hubbard, Ruth. 1990. *The Politics of Women's Biology.* New Brunswick, N.J.: Rutgers University Press.

Hubbard, Ruth, and Elijah Wald. 1993. *Exploding the Gene Myth.* Boston: Beacon.

Juengst, Eric T. 1996. Self-Critical Federal Science? The Ethics Experiments within the U.S. Human Genome Project. *Social Philosophy and Policy* 13, no. 2:63–95.

Keller, Evelyn Fox. 1992a. Nature, Nurture, and the Human Genome Project. In *The Code of Codes: Scientific and Social Issues in the Human Genome Project,* edited by Daniel J. Kevles and Leroy Hood. Cambridge: Harvard University Press.

———. 1992b. *Secrets of Life, Secrets of Death: Essays on Language, Gender, and Science.* New York: Routledge.

———. 1995. *Refiguring Life: Metaphors of Twentieth-Century Biology.* New York: Columbia University Press.

———. 2000. Decoding the Genetic Program. In *The Concept of the Gene in Evolution and Development: Historical and Epistemological Perspectives,* edited by Raphael Falk, Peter Beurton, and Hans Jorg Reinberger. Cambridge: Cambridge University Press.

Kevles, Daniel J., and Leroy Hood, eds. 1992. *The Code of Codes: Scientific and Social Issues in the Human Genome Project.* Cambridge: Harvard University Press.

Lejeune, Jerome, Marthe Gauthier, and Raymond Turpin. 1959. Etudes des chromosomes somatiques de neuf enfants mongoliens. *Comptes Rendus de l'Academie des Sciences* 248:1721–22.

Lippman, Abby, and Fern Brunger. 1991. Constructing Down Syndrome: Texts as Informants. *Santé Culture Health* 8, nos. 1–2:109–31.

McKusick, Victor. 1975. The Growth and Development of Human Genetics as a Clinical Discipline. *American Journal of Human Genetics* 27:261–73.

———. 1992. Human Genetics, the Last 35 Years, the Present, and the Future. Presidential address, Eighth International Congress of Human Genetics. *American Journal of Human Genetics* 50:663–70.

————. 1997. Observations over Fifty Years concerning Intestinal Polyposis, Marfan Syndrome, and Achondroplasia. *Nature Medicine* 3, no. 10:1065–68.

McKusick, Victor, Joanna Amberger, et al. 1996. Progress in Medical Genetics: Map-Based Gene Discovery and the Molecular Pathology of Skeletal Dysplasias. *American Journal of Medical Genetics* 63, no. 1:98–105.

Mittman, Ilana S., Victor B. Pechaszadeh, and M. G. Secundy, eds. 1999. The National Dialogue on Genetics. *Community Genetics* 1, no. 3 (Special issue).

Murray, Thomas H., Mark A. Rothstein, and Robert F. Murray Jr., eds. 1996. *The Human Genome Project and the Future of Health Care.* Bloomington: Indiana University Press.

Rabinow, Paul. 1992. Artificiality and Enlightenment: From Sociobiology to Biosociality. In *Incorporations,* edited by Jonathan Crary and Sanford Kwinter. New York: Zone.

————. 1999. *French DNA: Trouble in Purgatory.* Chicago: University of Chicago Press.

Rapp, Rayna. 1995. Risky Business: Genetic Counseling in a Shifting World. In *Articulating Hidden Histories: Essays Exploring the Influence of Eric R. Wolf,* edited by Jane Schneider and Rayna Rapp. Berkeley: University of California Press.

————. 1999. *Testing Women, Testing the Fetus: The Social Impact of Amniocentesis in America.* New York: Routledge.

————. 2000. Blue Tulips and Extra Chromosomes: Medico-Familial Interpretations. In *Intersections: Living and Working with the New Medical Technologies,* edited by Margaret Lock, Alberto Cambrosio, and Allan Young. Cambridge: Cambridge University Press.

Rothman, Barbara Katz. 1986. *The Tentative Pregnancy, Prenatal Diagnosis, and the Future of Motherhood.* New York: W. W. Norton.

————. 1989. *Recreating Motherhood: Ideology and Technology in a Patriarchal Society.* New York: W. W. Norton.

————. 1998. *Genetic Maps and Human Imaginations: The Limits of Science in Understanding Who We Are.* New York: W. W. Norton.

Sandberg, David E., Amy E. Brook, and Susana P. Campos. 1994. Short Stature: A Psychosocial Burden Requiring Growth Hormone Therapy? *Pediatrics* 94, no. 6: 832–40.

Sandberg, David E., et al. 1999. Quality of Life (QOL) among Formerly Treated Child-Onset Growth Hormone–Deficient (GHD) Adults: A Comparison with Unaffected Siblings. *Journal of Clinical Endocrinology and Metabolism* 83:1134–42.

Saxton, Marsha. 1984. Born and Unborn: The Implications of Reproductive Technologies for People with Disabilities. In *Test-Tube Woman,* edited by Rita Arditti, Renate Duelli Klein, and Shelley Minden. Boston: Pandora Press.

Schneider, David M. 1968. *American Kinship: A Cultural Account.* Chicago: University of Chicago Press.

————. 1972. What Is Kinship All About? In *Kinship Studies in the Morgan Centennial Year,* edited by Priscilla Reining. Washington, D.C.: Anthropological Society of Washington.

Strathern, Marilyn. 1992a. *After Nature: English Kinship in the Late Twentieth Century.* Cambridge: Cambridge University Press.

———. 1992b. *Reproducing the Future: Anthropology, Kinship, and the New Reproductive Technologies.* Manchester: Manchester University Press.

Suzuki, David, and Peter Knudtson. 1989. *Genethics.* Cambridge: Harvard University Press.

Taussig, Karen Sue. 1997a. Calvinism and Chromosomes: Religion, the Geographical Imaginary, and Medical Genetics in the Netherlands. *Science as Culture* 6, no. 4:495–524.

———. 1997b. Normal and Ordinary: Human Genetics and the Production of Dutch Identities. Ph.D. diss., Johns Hopkins University.

Taussig, Karen-Sue, Rayna Rapp, and Deborah Heath. 2002. Flexible Eugenics: Discourses of Perfectibility in Late Twentieth-Century America. In *Anthropology in the Age of Genetics,* edited by Alan Goodman, Deborah Heath, and Susan Lindee. Berkeley: University of California Press.

Weiss, Joan O., and Jayne Mackta. 1996. *How to Start and Sustain Genetic Support Groups.* Baltimore, Md.: Johns Hopkins University Press.

Yanagisako, Sylvia J., and Carol Delaney, eds. 1995. *Naturalizing Power: Essays in Feminist Cultural Analysis.* New York: Routledge.

Young, Allan. 1996. *The Harmony of Illusions.* Princeton, N.J.: Princeton University Press.

PART V

Ambivalence and Violence

at the Heart of Kinship

CHAPTER 15

Ambivalence in Kinship since the 1940s
Michael G. Peletz

I believe that more unhappiness comes from this source than any other—I mean from the attempt to prolong family connection unduly and to make people hang together artificially who would never naturally do so. The mischief among the lower classes is not so great, but among the middle and upper classes it is killing a large number daily. And old people do not really like it much better than the young. —Samuel Butler, *The Note Books of Samuel Butler*

I am sick to death of bonding through kinship and "the family," and I long for models of solidarity and human unity and difference rooted in friendship, work, partially shared purposes, intractable collective pain, inescapable mortality, and persistent hope. . . . Ties through blood—including blood recast in the coin of genes and information—have been bloody enough already. I believe that there will be no racial or sexual peace, no livable nature, until we learn to produce humanity through something more and less than kinship.—Donna J. Haraway, *Modest_ Witness@Second_Millennium.FemaleMan©_Meets_OncoMouse™*

One afternoon some years ago, I was talking with an elderly Malay man and the conversation turned to the local system of kinship. He summed up his disillusionment with the system by remarking "*kasih bunga, balas tahi,*" which means "you give flowers, but get shit in return." This type of sentiment is widely shared among Malays (see Peletz 1996; Carsten 1997), the majority of whom are nonetheless deeply committed to the moral ideals enshrined in local kinship. Such a paradox is one reason why I attempt to make sense of ambivalence (the simultaneous experience of powerful, contradictory emotions or attitudes toward a single phenomenon). A second reason is the prominence of ambivalence in much of the work carried out in the reconstituted field of kinship—hereafter referred to as the "new kinship studies" (see, for example, Weiner 1976, 1992; Rapp 1982; Trawick 1990; Weston 1991; Strathern 1992a, 1992b). A third has to do with the fact that in anthropology as a whole, there have been few if any efforts to chart out why such themes have become salient in recent years. More broadly, anthropologists have devoted scant attention not only to the myriad sources of ambivalence but also to their implications for an understanding of structure and agency as well as critically important processes of sociality, domination, and resistance. One consequence of this relative neglect is that many treatments of these latter processes are, to borrow Sherry Ortner's (1995) term, "culturally thin"; another, more general consequence is the limited ability to address effectively the Janus-faced dimensions of the human experience, which as John Comaroff (1994) has noted, are central to a good deal of contemporary scholarship.

The present essay represents a modest exploratory effort to help rectify this situation. My main objectives are to highlight the treatment of ambivalence in various sites in the study of kinship since the 1940s, to explain why the theme has become especially salient in the past two decades, and to emphasize its significance for future studies of kinship and social relations. The discussion takes the form of a historically oriented survey that begins with selected examples of the "old kinship studies" and proceeds to various sites in the new kinship studies. I argue that in dealing with kinship, early anthropologists' concerns with structure, function, and homeostatic systems left little room for analytic discussions of *ambivalence as such*. Many adherents of the new kinship studies, in contrast, devote considerable analytic attention to the theme of ambivalence. This is partly because the new kinship studies are heavily gendered, and display a pronounced concern with power, practice, agency, and sociality, all of which are thoroughly suffused with—or inevitably raise issues having to do with—mixed emotions, and are thus highly conducive to discussions of them. I also assert that notwithstanding recent advances in our understanding of the latter issues, ambivalence remains relatively undertheorized in contemporary work on kinship, and that in this particular respect, there is a frequently overlooked continuity between the old and new kinship studies.

One final set of introductory comments relates to terminology and conceptual orientation. Following the *Oxford English Dictionary* (*OED*), I use the term "ambivalence" to refer to the simultaneous "coexistence . . . [of two or more powerful] contradictory emotions or attitudes (as love and hatred) towards a person or thing," which may entail emotional or attitudinal "oscillation, fluctuation, variability," and so on. (Some of the *OED*'s literary references to ambivalence are instructive: "Christianity has always had an ambivalent attitude toward the family"; "the story of ambivalent love is . . . characteristic . . . of the 19th century"; and "Auden's attitude in his poetry is ambivalent; he cannot help disapproving [and] . . . praising.") Ambivalence may be relatively "bivalent" or "binary," involving a "back and forth" between two (or two sets of) powerful, conflicting emotions or attitudes toward a single phenomenon; or it may be more "multi-" or "polyvalent," as in one technical meaning of the Latin root *ambi-* ("around" or "about"), thereby suggesting perambulatory emotions or attitudes.[1] It may, in any case, derive from divergent interests, each calculated with respect to different values, aims, or constraints. Ambivalence is distinguished from "diffidence" — modesty, bashfulness, or reluctance to express one's emotions, attitudes, or self — which is sometimes (mis)taken as shallowness or absence of affect (as in the celebrated protagonist of Albert Camus' *L'Etranger*). Ambivalence also differs from "ambiguity," which refers to phenomena of a more cognitive — as distinct from emotional — sort. More specifically, the term ambiguity is used here to index uncertainty, in the sense that some expressions, gestures, and so forth are capable of being understood in two or more ways, and so have double, multiple, or indeterminate signification. Something that is ambiguous is therefore indistinct, equivocal, not clearly defined, and in some instances, obscure. The terms ambivalence, diffidence, and ambiguity are thus analytically distinct, although there is semantic and experiential overlap for a variety of reasons: emotions and attitudes have cognitive entailments; cognitive phenomena may be colored by "feeling-tones"; ambivalence may foster ambiguity, and vice versa; and both may follow from the internalization of multiple frameworks of evaluation.

AMBIVALENCE IN KINSHIP FROM THE 1940S THROUGH THE 1970S

In his first monograph on the Nuer, E. E. Evans-Pritchard (1940) recognized that kinship as a moral system necessarily cuts both ways, and that the double-edged nature of kinship stems partly from the fact that kinship is heavily freighted with moral entailments in the form of expectations and obligations that are often burdensome or impossible to fulfill.[2] Evans-Pritchard also made clear that honoring such expectations and obligations brings little guarantee of the diffuse (or other) reciprocity or solidarity that is so frequently inscribed in kinship as a whole, and that is in any case typically enjoined on those who benefit most directly from honoring the expectations and obligations in question.

Additional points to bear in mind about Evans-Pritchard's treatment of mixed emotions in kinship are that many of his observations on the subject pertain to Nuer ambivalence toward fellow clansmen, were disparate and scattered, and were not worked into his heavily idealized analysis of Nuer social relations. These features of Evans-Pritchard's work are in keeping with the precedent set by his mentor, A. R. Radcliffe-Brown, especially in the latter's celebrated exposition ([1924] 1952, [1940] 1952) of joking relationships. They are evident in the following passages:

> If you wish to live among the Nuer you must do so on their terms, which means that you must treat them as a kind of kinsman and they will then treat you as a kind of kinsman. Rights, privileges, and obligations are determined by kinship. Either a man is a kinsman, actually or by fiction, or he is a person to whom you have no reciprocal obligations and whom you treat as a potential enemy. Every one in a man's village and district counts in one way or another as a kinsman, if only by linguistic assimilation, so that, except for an occasional homeless and despised wanderer, a Nuer only associates with people whose behaviour to him is on a kinship pattern. (Evans-Pritchard 1940, 183)

So far, so good: kinship—and patrilineal descent specifically—provides an orienting framework for the content and ideology of Nuer social relations as well as the hegemonic idioms in terms of which such all-encompassing relations are cast. But Evans-Pritchard proceeds to observe that these relations also make explicit certain imperatives: "Nuer must assist one another, and if one has a surplus of a good thing he must share it with his neighbors. Consequently no Nuer ever has a surplus" (183). Evans-Pritchard is unequivocal on this point:

> Nuer are most tenacious of their rights and possessions. They take easily but give with difficulty. This selfishness arises from their education and from the nature of kinship obligations. A child . . . learns that to maintain his equality with his peers he must stand up for himself against any encroachment on his person and property. . . . [H]e must always be prepared to fight, and his willingness and ability to do so are the only protection of his integrity as a free and independent person against the avarice and bullying of his kinsmen. They protect him against outsiders, but he

must resist their demands on himself. The demands made on a man in the name of kinship are incessant and imperious and he resists them to the utmost. (184)

The contention that Nuer resist demands of kinship may strike readers as hyperbole, especially in light of Evans-Pritchard's claims that ideologies of kinship reorder and contain all "ground-level noise." More important is that the implications of these and other statements bearing on contradictory imperatives, divergent interests, and the internalization of multiple frameworks of evaluation were not integrated into Evans-Pritchard's overarching model of Nuer society. (Such generalizations also apply to Radcliffe-Brown, as indicated earlier.) Nor, I should add, were the implications of the ambivalences documented in his second volume on the Nuer (Evans-Pritchard 1951), which dealt more directly with marriage, family, and household relations. In other words, while Evans-Pritchard and Radcliffe-Brown alike drew attention to ambivalence in a dramatic and explicit fashion, the theme does not inform the central theoretical concepts of their writing. This is because the (structural-functional) concept of structure that undergirds Evans-Pritchard's and Radcliffe-Brown's work led them to focus primarily on the formal interrelations and reproduction of corporate groups, and the extent to which they could be seen as "hav[ing] a high degree of consistency and constancy" (Evans-Pritchard 1940, 262). Such a stress involved the relative analytic neglect of the sociality of everyday life—in which context one is quite likely to encounter mixed emotions—even though in Evans-Pritchard's case, it was his firsthand observations and experiences of this very sociality that provided him with both his entrée into Nuer society—including the politico-jural domain—and much of the raw data for his understanding of it.

Evans-Pritchard's comments about Nuer resisting the demands of kinship resonate with observations made in subsequent years by Meyer Fortes, who was both a student and colleague of Evans-Pritchard. Since Fortes, unlike Evans-Pritchard, went to some length to develop an understanding of the morality of kinship, it is useful to first turn to some of his ideas on the latter subject.

Many of Fortes's ideas on the morality of kinship are summed up in his discussions of "the axiom of amity" (1969), a concept that is more complex than is often recognized and one that does make provision for some measure of ambivalence.[3] On the one hand, Fortes talks of "kinship morality that is rooted in the familial domain and is assumed everywhere to be axiomatically binding. This is the rule of prescriptive altruism which I . . . refer to as the principle of kinship amity and which . . . [some have called] the ethic of generosity" (232). On the other hand, Fortes explicitly draws attention to the ambivalence built into "the ideal that kinsfolk should love one another" by saying that "many ties of close kinship (notoriously, siblingship) . . . subsume rivalries and latent hostilities that are as intrinsically built into the relationships as are the externally oriented amity and solidarity they present" (237–38; compare Kelly 1977; Marshall 1981; Smith 1983; Peletz 1988). Unfortunately, however, like Radcliffe-Brown ([1924] 1952, [1940] 1952) and Claude Lévi-Strauss (1949, 1963) who, in different ways, make partial provision for similar dynamics, Fortes never explains *why* rivalries and latent hostilities are intrinsically built into relationships of close kinship. Fortes provides some hints, though, in his comments that "the rule posits . . . that 'kinsfolk' have irresistible claims on one another's support and consideration in contradistinction to 'non-kinsmen,' simply by reason of the fact that they are kin. Kinsfolk must, ideally, share . . . and they must, ideally, do so without putting a price on what they give" (1969, 238). In any event, there is a bottom line ("fiduciary element") in all this: "We do not have to love our kinsfolk, but we expect to be able to trust them in ways that are not automatically possible with non-kinsfolk" (249).

Fortes's views concerning the sources of ambivalence—and no less significant, his sense of the universal validity of his observations—can also be seen in his commentary on the following passage from Michael Young and Peter Willmott's classic study of family and kinship in East London:

> Parents do not choose their children, nor children their parents; the relationship exists whether or not either has the qualities which might arouse affection. Both are usually accepted despite their faults . . . and what applies to parents and children applies in some measure to other relatives as well. . . . Affection . . . becomes as reciprocal as duty. Affection, for its part, helps to make duty not so much the nicely balanced correlative of rights as a more or less unlimited liability beyond the bounds of self interest and rational calculation. ([1957] 1962, 194; cited in Fortes 1969, 242)

Fortes remarks that he has "recorded sentiments that are exactly the same among the Tallensi and the Ashanti, and their parallels can be found in any of the classical monographs on kinship in tribal society" (242).

I will return to some of the latter themes in due course. In the meantime, it bears noting that Fortes qualifies his position on the scope and force of pre-scriptive amity by acknowledging that "no society . . . expects the general and diffuse moral prescriptions to be invariably adhered to" (238). To illustrate his point, he invokes Tallensi references to "criminal characters . . . sinners . . . selfish, foolish, dishonest, hypocritical people, and others of weak character" (238–39) who, as the Tallensi emphasize, do not adhere to the moral prescriptions at issue. What is interesting about this reference is the way its deploy-ment bifurcates and purifies the social universe, thus more or less ruling out the existence of mixed—specifically, negative—emotions among the morally upright (those who are not criminals, sinners, fools, and so on), and simul-taneously denying the existence of positive emotions among those who are not virtuous. This bifurcating and purifying move occurs even though Fortes has just made clear his view that rivalries and latent hostilities are intrinsically built into relationships of close kin. This move is even more curious in light of the fact that Fortes goes on to speak of jealousy and competitiveness in such relations (241) and presents observations such as: the recovery of money is said to be "doubtful" if lent to someone of one's own lineage; salaried employ-ees among Ashanti in the 1940s "constantly complained of the demands made upon them by kinsfolk"; and "teachers and clerks preferred to be posted far from their natal communities to escape these irresistible demands" (246).

Questions thus arise as to whether the bifurcation and purification under consideration occurs because the Tallensi prefer not to elaborate on the nega-tive sentiments and dynamics, and the divergent interests, at issue, or because Fortes does not want to sully his account or model, either of Tallensi kinship or of Kinship—with a capital *K*—in general. Whatever the answer, similar types of bifurcating moves amounting to what Marilyn Strathern (1988, 1992a, 1992b) refers to as "domaining" occur in the ways Fortes sharply distinguishes kin and affines, kinship and locality (or polity), and of course kinship ("pri-vate") and political ("public") domains. Analogous domaining is evident in Fortes's tendency to treat data on witchcraft, sorcery, and the like as largely irrelevant to kinship and the social order.

Fortes's views as to the sources of ambivalence in kinship are clear enough: irresistible moral claims on one's autonomy and resources that are lodged in the name of kinship; the lack of choice available to those on whom such claims are lodged; and the fact that affection must be harnessed to duty and does indeed become duty, which is but one way of talking about the pre-scribed performance of emotion. But many questions are still left unanswered. Of broader concern is that in the case of Radcliffe-Brown, Evans-Pritchard,

Fortes, and a good many other British social anthropologists (for instance, Firth [1951] 1963; Leach 1954, 1961a, 1961b), ethnographic evidence of mixed emotions exists alongside a marked reluctance or inability to incorporate such data into the larger analytic framework. This is partly because the authors' overdetermined Durkheimian concerns with structure and function, coupled with their particular (structural-functional) perspectives on structure, order, solidarity, coherence, and homeostasis (or equilibrium) within the politico-jural domain, tended to preclude detailed analyses of sociality, as well as intentionality and agency (gendered or otherwise), power, and social trans-formation, all of which inevitably raise issues having to do with mixed emo-tions.[4] Also relevant to the failure to incorporate evidence of ambivalence into models is that by the mid–twentieth century, anthropology's links with psy-chology, which had flourished earlier in the century, had been pared down; especially in British social anthropology, psychology was to a significant de-gree purged after W. H. R. Rivers and Bronislaw Malinowski.

A different and more recent version of this attention to, yet theoretical ne-glect of the pervasiveness of ambivalence can be seen in Carol Stack's pioneer-ing treatise (1974) on African American kinship networks in an area around Chicago referred to as "The Flats." Stack's marxist-feminist orientation an-ticipates various aspects of the new kinship studies inasmuch as she situates her analysis of local kinship within a framework of gender and political econ-omy, paying particular attention to the effects of joblessness, poverty, racism, and state welfare policies on gender relations, patterns of residence, infor-mal adoption, and the durability and stability of conjugal bonds.[5] Kinship, for Stack, becomes a strategic site of social action and resistance to the disen-franchisements of a racist society. But like Evans-Pritchard and Fortes, Stack's descriptions and interpretations play up the safety net as well as other utili-tarian and Rousseauean features of local kinship, and are, in these and other ways, both idealized and romanticized.

Stack makes no analytic provision either for the potentially exploitative dimensions of local kinship or the profoundly mixed emotions expressed in some of the vignettes and other data she presents, such as those pertaining to Ethel, who helped raise a young woman, Georgia, and her children, con-siders Georgia's children as her own grandchildren, and "feel[s] intense love, obligation, and bitterness" toward them (1974, 75). This despite Stack's recog-nition that "close kin who have relied upon one another over the years often complain about the sacrifices they have made and the deprivation they have endured for one another" (36). As another woman remarked to Stack of the imperatives underlying her relationship with her mother: "I'm all worn out from running from my house to her house like a pinball machine. . . . I'm doing it 'cause she's my mother and 'cause I don't want to hurt her. Yet, she's killing me" (36).

Some of Stack's data are strikingly reminiscent of passages of the sort cited above from the works of Evans-Pritchard and Fortes. Others speak to the frustrated longing and disillusionment associated with Rayna Rapp's (1982) observation that while many women in the United States marry for love, they often find themselves quickly overwhelmed with babies and bills. Most germane for present purposes is that Stack makes no comment on the fact that if the residents of The Flats are financially able to do so, they commonly endeavor to move far away and completely sever ties with kin who have remained behind. Thus, one woman (Ruby) quipped of the possibility of marriage, which could potentially provide the financial security to safely withdraw from local kin networks: "If I ever get married, I'm leaving town!" (Stack 1974, 115). Stack goes on to note, without comment: "While this study was in progress, Ruby did get married, and she left the state with her husband and her youngest child that very evening" (115).

Limitations of space preclude further discussion of the analytic marginalization of ambivalence in Stack's scholarship and in other classics typifying the theoretical approaches that dominated the study of kinship from the 1940s through the 1970s, such as those of Claude Lévi-Strauss (1949, 1963), P. E. de Josselin de Jong (1951), Rodney Needham (1958a, 1958b), George Murdock (1949), Ward Goodenough (1951), Harold Scheffler and Floyd Lounsbury (1971), David Schneider (1968), and Hildred Geertz and Clifford Geertz (1975). The foregoing will hopefully suffice to illustrate the fact that significant data bearing on ambivalence are certainly included in some of the classic studies representing the hegemonic paradigms in the field, but tend not to be theorized or otherwise worked into the analytic models of those who helped develop or refine the paradigms in question.

These generalizations do, of course, allow for certain (arguably partial) exceptions, such as the work of Victor Turner (1957), Melford Spiro (1977), and James Boon (1977). Each of the latter scholars was in important (albeit different) ways writing against the prevailing culture(s) of kinship studies, the more general contention being that hegemonies are never total or absolute, or as we shall see in the next section, eternal.[6] Turner, for instance, took as his point of departure Max Gluckman's view of "social system[s] as . . . field[s] of tension, full of ambivalence, of co-operation and contrasting struggle" (Turner

1957, xxii). It is noteworthy that Turner's ideas on social dramas and rituals as mechanisms of redress that resolve or ameliorate ambivalence and discharge tensions in fields of social relations were initially worked out in the context of a volume on kinship, *Schism and Continuity in an African Society* (1957). Equally worth mentioning is that while Turner (along with Clifford Geertz) was a key figure in the formulation of interpretive anthropology and also anticipated the subsequent emergence of practice theory and many other domains of contemporary inquiry, his initial interest in rituals of kinship led him, ultimately, to develop an anthropology of ritual—and to lay crucial groundwork for an anthropology of emotion and experience—rather than of kinship per se (see Turner 1967, 1969; Turner and Bruner 1986). Had Turner set his analytic sights in the years after 1957 on kinship as such, we would no doubt be in a stronger position at present with respect to the theorization of ambivalence in kinship and of kinship generally.

Most relevant here, however, is that scholars such as Turner constitute the exceptions that prove the rule: In the approaches dominating the study of kinship from the 1940s through the 1970s, data bearing on ambivalence tend to be dealt with as one or another caveat tempering a general model, or as little more than an afterthought—as in the justly famous final paragraphs of Lévi-Strauss's 497-page *The Elementary Structures of Kinship*. It is precisely on grounds such as these that I maintain that from the 1940s through the 1970s, the topic of ambivalence was relegated to the analytic periphery of kinship studies.

AMBIVALENCE IN KINSHIP IN THE 1980S AND 1990S

This section combines a review of changes in kinship studies with several summaries of recent approaches and issues that arise in them, with the aim of highlighting the relevance of these theoretical and empirical shifts for an understanding of ambivalence in kinship and social relations.[7] Ambivalence has come to assume greater analytic centrality in kinship studies as ethnographers have begun to take more seriously the need to better account for and contextualize the heterogeneous data bearing on mixed emotions encountered in the field. Ambivalence is still somewhat undertheorized, although as a consequence of the trends noted here, we are now in a better position to develop a richer and more nuanced sense of how kinship and social relations of other varieties are practiced, experienced, understood, and represented in specific societies and the myriad contexts that comprise them.

Significant changes in the study of kinship since the 1970s have included the rethinking of basic assumptions informing earlier work in the field (concerning the basic "building blocks" of kinship, for example), the waning of structural-functionalism as a guiding paradigm, and the fact that traditionally defined studies of kinship (like studies of other domains conceptualized in functionally defined institutional terms) experienced a precipitous decline in status within the discipline of anthropology as a whole. The nature of these transformations and the reasons for them have been discussed elsewhere (see Schneider 1984; Collier and Yanagisako 1987; Peletz 1995), and so need not detain us. Of more immediate concern here is that since the 1980s, the field of kinship studies has been reconfigured and revived due in large part to the increased centrality within anthropology and other human sciences of marxist perspectives—including practice theory as developed by Pierre Bourdieu (1977), Marshall Sahlins (1981, 1985), and Sherry Ortner (1984, 1989, 1996)—as well as numerous variants of feminism, poststructuralism, and postmodernism (for example, Ortner and Whitehead 1981; Rapp 1982, 1990; Goody 1983, 1990; Gailey 1987; Collier and Yanagisako 1987; Collier 1988; Strathern 1988, 1992b; Bloch 1989; Trawick 1990; Weiner 1992; Kelly 1985, 1993).

One of the more fruitful features of the reconstituted field of kinship studies is the scholarly energy devoted to understanding concrete social actors along with the specific contexts in which they organize themselves and their resources as well as create meaning and order in their lives. Inspired by the interpretive anthropology developed by Victor Turner and Clifford Geertz, and by the writings of Antonio Gramsci, Pierre Bourdieu, and Michel Foucault, much recent research has focused on the quotidian rounds and practices of variably situated, embodied social actors and the emotional tenor (feeling-tones) of their daily experiences of intimacy and subordination (see, for example, di Leonardo 1984; Yanagisako 1985; Weston 1991). A good deal of this research has dealt with the politics of reproduction (for example, Ginsburg 1989; Ginsburg and Rapp 1995), and, not surprisingly, has frequently grappled with themes of ambivalence. Ann Anagnost's work on post-Mao China, for instance, reveals deeply mixed emotions concerning the state's birth control policies—"the center of party activism . . . in the 1980s and early 1990s" (1995, 32). Given the prevalence in China of public discourses relating, according to Anagnost, "bodily quality to national strength," and the "sense of being caught between fears of social disorder and cultural stasis" (28), Chinese express "tremendous ambivalence" about those aspects of national policies aimed at "downsizing the population to allow for the disciplined ordering of bodies subject to a central educating authority" (28, 31). The case of Romania under the Nicolae Ceauşescu regime reveals other types of ambivalences as rigid pronatalist policies aimed at building the labor force and, by extension, a triumphant socialism entailed the banning of birth control, compulsory pregnancy tests for women, and the keying of promotion and wage increases to fertility (see Kligman 1995). The resulting horrors of such policies included massive numbers of children abandoned by their mothers and warehoused in understaffed institutions where they often died of illness or neglect, or were exported via international adoption.

Related themes addressed by proponents of the new kinship studies include incest and domestic violence (see McKinnon 1995; Delaney, this volume) as well as abduction and rape in warfare as instruments of military strategy. Some of the most chilling narratives in this literature are from women taken as hostages following the partitioning of India and Pakistan. Hindu and Sikh women abducted by Muslim men, along with Muslim women abducted by Hindu or Sikh men, were in many cases forced into sexual relations and marriage by their captors. Testifying to a common scenario, one woman, when "rescued" and offered her "freedom," responded: "You have come to save us . . . [and] take us back to our relatives. You tell us that our relatives are eagerly waiting to receive us. You do not know our society. It is hell. They will kill us" (Das 1995, 224). Many of these women chose violent death for themselves rather than return to live among kin whose codes of honor and purity would have rendered their lives extremely difficult at best.

Different kinds of violence, and different kinds of "exclusions, denials, and betrayals" (Delaney, this volume), are taken up by scholars who have documented the "coming out" narratives linking lesbians and gays involved in the creation of "chosen families" with their "straight" kin (Weston 1991). These narratives stress the performative dimensions of kinship both within chosen families ("love makes a family, nothing more, nothing less") and the straight families forced to confront their lesbian and gay kin. Many of these encounters result in painful censure and a renunciation of theoretically binding kinship, further heightening their emotional intensity (see also Weston, this volume; Lewin 1993).

Textual emphases on narrative, voice, practice, personhood, sex, and violence have played a seminal role in the reconfiguration of kinship studies. So, too, has the repatriation of (sociocultural) anthropology. In the case of kinship studies, this repatriation has involved a focus on the dynamics and reproduction of families and households among diverse groups of Europeans and Americans. Particular analytic attention has been devoted not only to lesbian and gay kinship but also to new reproductive technologies as well as the variegated ways in which symbols, idioms, and practices of kinship are implicated in identity politics and different types of racial, class, nationalist, and transnationalist discourses (see, for example, Rapp 1982, 1991; Yanagisako 1985; Yanagisako and Delaney 1995; Martin 1987; Strathern 1992a, 1992b; Borneman 1992; Bouquet 1993; Ragoné 1994; Franklin 1997).

Two sets of issues addressed by ethnographers involved in the repatriation of kinship studies merit special note. The first concerns the exclusions, denials, betrayals, and disappointments associated with discontinuities and crises in filiation. As discussed by Charis Thompson (this volume), some of these discontinuities and crises are engendered by the disruptions in experiences, understandings, and representations of relatedness that occur in infertility clinics. These are exacerbated by the profound emotional labor that is necessary both to keep biological and social accounts of relatedness aligned in culturally meaningful ways, and to manage the anxiety associated with the failures of masculinity and femininity that are often experienced by the infertile. Other crises in filiation documented in recent years are linked to the intergenerational tensions, uncertainties, and discontinuities arising from widespread cohabitation and divorce, the ambivalence attendant on becoming a grandparent, and the fact that grandparents can both provide identity and deny it. Denials of the latter sort aggravate the crises in filiation besetting France (see Segalen, this volume) and perhaps all other societies where kinship remains central to "the formation of intimate relationships . . . [though not necessarily to] institutional or social forms of groupings or units as such" (Strathern 1997; cited in Segalen, this volume).

A second (and related) set of topics addressed by those involved in the repatriation of kinship studies has to do with transnational and domestic transracial adoption. This literature is redolent with data bearing on ambivalence, partly because the types of adoption at issue are often seen, like adoption generally, as an "inferior" way of forming or adding to a family (see Gailey 1998). Other factors that figure into the frequently wrought emotional terrain include adoptive parents' deep apprehensions that birth parents may change their minds about relinquishing their child(ren), and anxious concerns about birth parents' class, ethnic, racial, and national backgrounds. These issues are all the more fraught in the case of "extra-tribal" adoptions of Native American children, which have been key components of coercive assimilationist policies that have resulted in holding Native American children captive to families and an entire society that seeks to transform them into their kin (see Strong, this volume).

In general, the repatriation of kinship studies has also involved greater interdisciplinarity as anthropologists working in Western milieus have realized the value of engaging sociology, social history, feminism, and sexuality studies in order to make sense of their data. The increasingly fruitful dialogue and blurring of boundaries between anthropology and sociology is particularly significant in light of the ethnographic turn taken by certain sociologists (discussed below), coupled with the long-standing centrality of conflict theory in the sociological tool kit, which is partly responsible for sociologists' acute analytic sensitivity to European and especially American families and households as contested sites of highly politicized debate and experience. Recent work on the sociology of the family, in other words, has focused squarely on themes that entail consideration of or invoke ambivalence (as well as alienation and tragedy) and has helped situate such topics at the heart of anthropological studies of kinship in Western settings and beyond.

Consider, for one, Nazli Kibria's (1993) ethnography of Vietnamese American families in Philadelphia, which reveals the complex and often contradictory reworking of Vietnamese traditions bearing on kinship and gender in a late-twentieth-century diasporic context. Taking issue with accounts that depict Vietnamese in the United States as yet another example of an Asian immigrant "success story," Kibria shows how Vietnamese cope with life in the States and how "modernization" is a highly uneven, ambivalence-laden process. Vietnamese American women experience what the author terms "triple oppression" and "multiple jeopardy" (19–20), but their households as well as kinship and gender roles are not simply arenas of subjugation. They are also sites of resistance and vehicles through which these women and their families struggle to survive. Equally important, while the ideology of family unity is frequently pressed into service to mask — thereby unwittingly symbolizing — discordant interests, conflict, and resistance among household members, it is simultaneously a highly valorized component of the cultural identities of Vietnamese Americans, which like those of Cambodian Americans (Smith-Hefner 1999), Japanese Americans (Yanagisako 1985), Italian Americans (di Leonardo 1984), and many others, are hybrid, protean, and thoroughly suffused with ambivalence.

The prevalence of ambivalence and turbulence in gender-based struggles to control familial and other resources and institutions is powerfully foregrounded in Judith Stacey's (1991) ethnography of domestic upheaval among the "brave new families" of Silicon Valley. This study of families both literally and figuratively "on the faultline(s)" is one of many recent ethnographies documenting domestic comforts, crises, and contradictions in California, which according to Stacey, is "in the vanguard of post-industrial social transformations" (20), much as Karl Marx predicted in 1880 when he remarked of the Golden State that "nowhere else has the upheaval most shamelessly caused by capitalist centralization taken place with such speed" (cited in Soja 1989, 190). Stacey investigates the frontiers of contemporary morality through a focus on "divorce-extended" and other "recombinant" families among working-class whites buffeted about by cycles of economic expansion and "downsizing" along with other aspects of contemporary global capitalism. Underscoring that "traditions" are not given or fixed but continuously reworked in ironic and unintended ways, Stacey emphasizes themes of contradiction, paradox, and mixed emotion in the lives of the women she studied, much as Carol Stack had done for a previous era. Some of these women are heavily involved in local variants of patriarchal (yet also feminist-inspired) evangelical Christianity as a strategy to achieve emotionally sustaining and empowering intimacy in their marriages. Religiously sanctioned domestic submission thus emerges as one of the prices these women pay for new ways of belonging to variously imagined and frequently crosscutting class, ethnic, and moral communities. Not surprisingly, their domestic lives are heavily freighted with ambivalence (compare Ong 1995).

Other recent sociological research has more deeply probed some of the underlying causes of ambivalence in kinship, and has also dealt more analytically with the political and economic contexts that both frame and engender the ambivalences at issue. Arlie Hochschild (1983, 1990, 1997), for example, has elucidated the underside of certain classic themes (such as "the axiom of amity") highlighted by Fortes and noted to a lesser extent by Evans-Pritchard. In her early scholarship on the commercialization of human feeling in the workplace, Hochschild developed the concepts of "emotion work" and "feeling rules." To paraphrase, emotion work refers to the typically time-consuming and arduous emotional labor involved in forging, deepening, and repairing relationships, presupposing the (also) typically time-consuming and arduous tasks of noticing, acknowledging, and empathizing with the feelings of others, resolving quarrels, and soothing hurt feelings associated with the experience of real or imagined indignities (1997, 210). Feeling rules, for their part, pertain to the cultural guidelines specifying the mixes of feeling that are acceptable in particular contexts. Utilizing these concepts, Hochschild makes a number of critical points relevant to the mythology of the family as a "haven in a heartless world": "The family is often considered a 'relief zone' away from the pressures of work, a place where one is free to be oneself. It may indeed be a refuge from the emotion work required on the job, but it quietly imposes emotional obligations of its own" (1983, 69). Hochschild elaborates by emphasizing that "in reality, . . . the subterranean work of placing an acceptable inner face on ambivalence is actually all the more crucial [in the family]" (68), where for instance, "parental love . . . is so important to security and sometimes so difficult to sustain" (69). "In fact, the deeper the bond, the more emotion work and the more unconscious we are of it. In the most personal bonds, then, emotion work is likely to be the strongest" (68).

Hochschild's more recent scholarship (1997) develops some of these themes in the course of documenting the unchecked expansion and speed-up of "work culture" at the expense of "family culture," and illustrating how the resultant Taylorization and temporal constriction of home life wreaks havoc on the increasingly devalued and neglected emotional lives of family members. The problem is not simply that the "emotional magnets beneath home and workplace are in the process of being reversed" as "tired parents flee a world of unresolved quarrels and unwashed laundry for the reliable orderliness, harmony, and managed cheer of work" (Hochschild 1997, 44). There is also "a new emotional economy at home," characterized in part by a climate of "emotional deregulation" in which "caring now seems to move around like financial capital to new investment opportunities whenever they appear" (162). The emotional liquidity at issue can make life frightening and traumatic for those on the receiving end of "emotional downsizing" or flight (162), though in such a climate everyone pays a psychic price, realized in part in (further) alienation and disinclination to trust.

What is not clear in the larger scheme of things, however, is Hochschild's view as to where all this ambivalence is coming from. It is implicit in her work that capitalism inflames or drives a wedge in most if not all types of kinship ties. But it is not at all obvious whether the main locus of ambivalence in the terrain of kinship that Hochschild surveys is the potentially arduous and unrequited emotion work involved in intimate kinship, the potentially jarring and traumatic disjunction between heavily idealized expectation and oftentimes painful experience, or some combination of these or related factors.

Despite these lacunae, Hochschild's influential sociology has productively informed the reconfiguration of kinship studies in anthropology. Her early writing (1983) provides theoretical inspiration for Unni Wikan's (1990) work on the management of "turbulent hearts" in Bali that stands as an exemplar of a certain type of practice theory, sometimes called the "anthropology of experience." Wikan's main objective is to "de-exoticize" and "de-essentialize" Bali by fleshing out the contours of Balinese interpersonal relations and social experience that have been given short shrift by Western observers captivated by cockfights, temple festivals, and irrigation societies. Wikan situates the long neglected topic of friendship squarely within the anthropological gaze, avoids the artificial separation of kinship from friendship and other social ties, and offers a most nuanced and sophisticated treatment of ambivalence and alienation, though strictly speaking, neither ambivalence nor alienation are among her primary concerns.

Wikan concentrates on the commonplace, the "concepts with which . . . [Balinese] feel and think about, and handle, the tasks and tribulations of their individual existences" (1990, xvi), including their "feeling-thoughts" about the seamier side(s) of human nature and social relations. This emphasis stems from her conviction that the more encompassing institutions and structures of Balinese society have already been well described, and that while the famed commitments of Balinese to graceful performances are partly about "beauty for beauty's sake," they are also motivated by anxious concerns to avoid offending and provoking the ire of intimate others. This is, after all, a society where roughly half of all deaths are attributed to black magic or poisoning (43) — the significance of which, one might add, was largely lost on earlier investigators (for example, Geertz and Geertz 1975) due to analytic domaining that led them to exclude black magic and poisoning from their considerations of kinship.

Somewhat similar terrain is covered by Margaret Trawick's treatise on love in Tamil families, which underscores that "'meaning' cannot be pinned down, is always sought but never apprehended, . . . [and] is always inherently elusive and always inherently ambiguous" (1990, xix). Like Wikan's work on Bali, this study deals in a rather unsatisfactory manner with the actual structure and operation of the economy, caste, gender relations, and kinship as a system of signs that organizes "production and reproduction . . . [as well as] the transfer of surplus from one category of person to another" (Bloch 1989, 137). It does, moreover, elide the distinction between ambiguity and ambivalence — an analytic oversight that also detracts from the otherwise sophisticated and incisive work of Maurice Bloch (1989) and Zygmunt Bauman (1991). It nonetheless reveals in deeply interesting ways that ambiguity permeates "Hindu concepts of the sacred . . . and pervades [everything] . . . from speech to sexuality, from dreaming to blood" (Trawick 1990, 41); that "love" (*anpu*) is, without question, the most ambiguous — and ambivalent — of all; and that Tamil kinship "creates longings that can *never* be fulfilled" and is most appropriately understood "as a web maintained by unrelieved tensions, an architecture of conflicting desires" (152; compare Boon 1977).

Much more could be said about the theoretical treatment of ambivalence in Trawick's work as well as in that of Wikan and others discussed earlier in this section so as to further underscore the analytic centrality of ambivalence in the new kinship studies as compared with its relative marginalization in the approaches dominating the study of kinship from the 1940s through the 1970s. The foregoing should suffice, however, to provide an indicative sense of the increased salience of ambivalence in the study of kinship in the 1980s and 1990s. It should also help in identifying some of the variables that have brought about this change: the wane of long dominant (especially structural-functional) paradigms; the emergence of new approaches involving the blurring of disciplinary lines; the repatriation of kinship studies; the gendering of the field; the heightened attention devoted to issues of personhood, agency, voice, power, reproduction, denials, and exclusions; and last but not least, the absolute increase in the sum total of uncertainty, alienation, and ambivalence that exists in the world.[8] It remains to offer some exploratory comments concerning what general insights and lessons can be gleaned from this recent work, and where one might go from here.

THE PRODUCTION OF AMBIVALENCE IN KINSHIP AND BEYOND

Balinese, and perhaps Tamils, are forever anxious about "liv[ing] always exposed and vulnerable" (Wikan 1990, 81) to the threats of others, and in this respect have much in common with Malays (see Peletz 1996; Stivens 1996; Carsten 1997). Particularly relevant here are Balinese and Malay perceptions that they live in panopticons in which all kinship and social relations are ultimately power laden and hierarchical, and all social activities are scrutinized and evaluated by intimate and not-so-intimate others. This is not the panopticon of Foucault (1977), where Big Brother or his agents, with their unrelenting gazes and disciplinary mechanisms, penetrate the most intimate recesses of personal space and consciousness. Indeed, the feelings of vulnerability experienced by Balinese and Malays differ markedly from those experienced by the inhabitants of Foucault's panopticons inasmuch as they are only minimally related to their positions in class or other relatively fixed status hierarchies, and are only minimally keyed to the presence of Big Brother or his agents. These feelings stem instead from the hundreds if not thousands of big *and* little brothers and sisters peopling their kinship and social universe(s) — good numbers of whom are assumed to be deploying the social and cultural resources at their disposal in order to enhance (or at least maintain) their own status and prestige while simultaneously undercutting the status and prestige claims of others.

Balinese and Malay feelings of vulnerability serve as powerful moral constraints and thus need to be given their full analytic due. This is especially so when exploring themes of central import in contemporary social theory, such as structure and agency, domination and resistance. I make the point partly because moral variables tend to be given insufficient attention in studies of domination and resistance that speak to issues of structure and agency unless they "muddy the 'class waters'" or otherwise impinge on relations of power and domination between major status groups (landlords and tenants, "rich" and "poor," and so on).

The underlying issue is that while many scholars of resistance (for instance, Taussig 1980; Scott 1985) frequently distance themselves from marxist theories of exploitation and class, they often preserve one of marxism's hidden premises: the tendency to regard class as somehow the most "essential," natural, or unfetishized of all social groupings, and therefore to see class interests as the most important or rational of all social interests. Data from Bali, Malaysia, and elsewhere indicate that if one is to understand kinship or social relations of any variety, one needs to take more seriously culturally specific (as well as generalized) forms of personal submission, humiliation, degradation, and "coercive incorporation" (Carsten 1997) that are not tied to class-based (or feudal) hierarchies, or to systems of caste, apartheid, slavery, and the like (see Peletz 1997; Ortner 1995). Put differently, just as kinship is as much about institutionalized power relations as class, the focus on class has obscured many power-laden and other significant dimensions of kinship and social relations of other varieties.

As anthropologists, we need to deploy a more critical gaze in order to understand the symbols, meanings, emotional economies, and social actions implicated in prescriptive amity, "diffuse, enduring solidarity," and attendant imperatives embedded in normative cultural statements such as "Home is the place they have to let you in." At the least, we need to ponder more deeply the analytic implications of three (related) sets of issues bearing on the key point that people everywhere internalize — and operate in the world in accordance with — multiple evaluative frameworks and structures of feeling. First, the sentiments and moral obligations encoded in normative statements of the sort cited above may well be reassuring to those knocking on the door of a close or long-lost relative, but may also entail a profound degree of anxiety concerning the authenticity of prescribed emotion. Furthermore, for reasons that were noted long ago by Evans-Pritchard and have since been explored more thoroughly by others, the sentiments and moral obligations at issue are not necessarily all that comforting, and may indeed be rather disconcerting, to those who feel that they must (or should) answer the door. The last set of issues concerns certain insights developed in different ways by Sigmund Freud, Georg Simmel, Erving Goffman, and others: *all* emotional attachments are conducive to the realization of ambivalence; intense attachments are *thoroughly* suffused with mixed emotions; and as Turner remarked some time ago of the Ndembu and would most likely generalize far beyond, "the closer the tie, the greater the ambivalence of feeling" (1957, 249; compare Weiner 1992; Beidelman 1993).

These insights lead me to suggest that (among other things) more consideration be devoted to certain psychological perspectives that have the potential to shed additional light on the mechanisms and loci implicated in the production of various types of mixed emotions. Highly germane are views bearing on some of the psychological dynamics entailed in the construction of difference, the pervasive tendency to convert difference into hierarchy, and the ways identity is produced through negation. As Peter Stallybrass and Allen White observe, in all systems of hierarchy the dependence of the "top" on the "bottom," the "high" on the "low," produces a "mobile, conflictual fusion of power, fear, and desire in the construction of subjectivity" (1986, 5), and thus necessarily involves profound ambivalence. This is especially relevant to the themes of this essay in that symbols and idioms of kinship and gender are invariably "about" differentiation and exclusion, as well as commonality and inclusion, and are, more broadly, key components of systems of morality and virtue that encode hierarchically phrased and heavily value-laden difference. Among Malays and other Muslims such as Acehnese, Minangkabau, Javanese, and Bedouin who I compare to Malays elsewhere (see Peletz 1996), part of the dynamic at issue has to do with the fact that masculinity is cast in strongly relational terms (colored, at least in the instance of Malays from Negeri Sembilan, by the disjunction between the idealized role of the older brother that informs the husband/father role, on the one hand, and the actual, economistically defined performance of the husband/father role, on the other). Men are troubled by the fact that on some levels, they define themselves in complementary opposition to females (also cast in heavily relational terms), yet simultaneously see and fear in themselves the constellations of features that index femininity as well as the inferior moral status of children and ethnic others. For their part, women are often stigmatized and sometimes deeply troubled by the same ideological framework that they commonly turn on men to assert their own moral superiority. These patterns are inflected by class and have a decidedly Islamic hue, yet the underlying dynamics are broadly distributed cross-culturally (see Gregor 1985; Chodorow 1989).

> A recurrent pattern emerges: the "top" attempts to reject and eliminate the bottom for reasons of prestige and status, only to discover . . . that it is in some ways frequently dependent upon that low-Other (in the classic way that Hegel describes in the master-slave section of the *Phenomenology*), . . . and that the top *includes* that low symbolically, as a primary eroticized constituent of its own fantasy life. The result is a mobile, conflictual fusion of power, fear, and desire in the construction of subjectivity: a psychological dependence upon precisely those Others which are . . . opposed . . . at the social level. (Stallybrass and White 1986, 5–6)

Many other sites in the production of ambivalence merit serious analytic consideration in the context of the themes discussed in this essay, but unfortunately cannot be explored at length here. Some of these sites, I should note, are not universally deeply intertwined with, or in the very nature of, kinship, while others are. These (at times overlapping) sites include: the tragedies of humankind's self-consciousness, elements of which sometimes take the form of nagging and potentially debilitating awareness of existential "absurdities" (of the sort variously celebrated by Albert Camus, Jean-Paul Sartre, Vladimir Nabakov, and Woody Allen—to mention only a few not so strange bedfellows); the antinomies of religious experience; the interrelationship and emotional power of sex, birth, death, and aging; the sundered selves and countless double binds and paradoxes of modernity; and the role of kinship in providing conceptual linkages between—indeed, key features of the very definitions of—human society and culture, on the one hand, and the domain of "nature," on the other, especially in contexts where nature is increasingly seen as full of "contradictions, tensions, and ambiguities" that necessarily suffuse and "infect" kinship (Jordanova 1986, 39 [cited in Strathern 1992a, 209 n. 23]; see also Bauman 1991; Weigert 1991; Appadurai 1996).

In most societies, moreover, regardless of whether people are heavily exploited subjects without codified rights or modern, rights-bearing citizens, the forces of market and state constrict and devalue private lives. This is all the more true when elites and others pursue projects of ethnic cleansing, racial purification, modernity, or civil society. The intentional and unrelenting destruction of households, families, and virtually all private domains and personal spaces in Cambodia under the Pol Pot regime (1975–1979), which "probably exerted more power over its citizens than any state in world history" (Kiernan 1996, 464), is but one extreme case of what is surely a universal phenomenon: a polity (in this instance a modern state) posited on compliance that transcends feeling. Even when projects of modernity and/or civil society do not involve ethnic cleansing or racial purification, their achievement usually engenders profound ambivalence since they typically presuppose foregrounding or appropriating certain sentiments and discourses of kinship while simultaneously delegitimizing or deforming other modalities of relatedness (for example, "extended kinship") in which people still feel morally or materially invested.

FINAL THOUGHTS

In light of the myriad sites in the production of ambivalence that have been enumerated here, it seems reasonable to suggest that ambivalence is a feature of virtually all kinship systems, and that this is so not only because of the contradictory structural imperatives inherent in such systems (and all other institutions) but also because something like prescriptive amity or "diffuse, enduring solidarity" seems to be a feature of virtually all such systems. This necessarily involves a number of "things": webs of deep-seated longing; potentially time-consuming, arduous, and/or alienating (if only because frustrating and/or unrequited) emotional labor associated with the invariably precarious transformation of duty into authentic emotional motivation; the possibility of profoundly disheartening disjunction between yearning or expectation, on the one hand, and actual experience, on the other; and of course, morally compelling demands to share, give up, or exchange, which frequently have very real material consequences with respect to the pursuit of individual and collective interests.

To advance this general argument about the ubiquity of mixed emotions — particularly after citing the psychoanalytic formulations of Stallybrass and White — is not to claim that ambivalence is equally (socially or culturally) elaborated in all systems, or that its elaboration is experienced or enacted to the same degree, or in similar ways or domains, in all systems. There is tremendous cross-cultural and historical variation in the social expression and cultural elaboration of ambivalence. And there are a plethora of gendered, racialized, and class-specific sites in the production of ambivalence in any given society at any particular moment in time, and for any individual over his or her life course — as well as multitudes of combinations of variably inflected mixed emotions, many of which may be keyed to different sets of interests and imbued with potentially disparate constellations of values, significance, and meaning. One formidable challenge facing ethnographers is thus to do a better job engaging, accounting for, historicizing, and otherwise contextualizing and distinguishing the heterogeneous data bearing on ambivalence encountered in the field and archives. This may well require developing a more sophisticated vocabulary and theoretical apparatus bearing on feeling-tone and experience (or becoming more familiar with the tool kits of disciplines that already have them). It will in any case necessitate keeping sight of the value of theorizing not only the phenomena about which one is generalizing but also the ways such phenomena are reproduced and transformed by the encompassing structures — of markets, states, and nationalist discourses, for example — that inform individual and collective interests, and otherwise impinge on the everyday practices, experiences, and meanings of people's lives.

The highly complex and heterogeneous nature of the feeling-tones at issue is one of the reasons why, despite important advances in recent years, ambivalence remains relatively undertheorized in the literature (but see Weigert 1991; Bauman 1991; Wolfe 1989), especially the ethnographic literature, although other variables figure in as well. The latter include various instances of domaining: for example, the tendency, which is pronounced in structural-functionalist texts and certain treatises of a more symbolic/interpretive nature, to treat sorcery and witchcraft in discussions and analyses that are separate(d) from those bearing on kinship and the social order; and the contemporary proclivity, when focusing on private and intimate experience, to give relatively short shrift to large-scale structures and theory alike. Other variables include the long-standing disinclination of anthropologists to deal critically with the "negative" dimensions of the societies they study; this derives partly from the "myth of primitive harmony" (Edgerton 1992) underlying much of twentieth-century anthropology — the more encompassing dynamic being the romantic motives and sensibilities informing the anthropological enterprise since its inception. A somewhat related variable that has come into play in recent decades is the reluctance of many American feminists and others to fully engage the psychoanalytic literature on dependency, anxiety, and identity.[9]

Regardless of what constraints have inhibited the theorization of ambivalence, it is clear that our analytic gaze needs to be focused not simply on official structures, ideologies, exegetic idioms, and public contexts but also on suppressed, submerged, and other alternative discourses that bear on the seamier side(s) of human nature and social relations, and that are in many cases articulated primarily in relatively private contexts or with reference to personal experience. Such a focus may yield data and perspectives whose airing strikes some observers as impolitic with respect to the sensitivities of those among whom they work. But it seems to me that a far greater disservice is done to them by producing heavily idealized and one-dimensional (ethnographically thin) accounts of their social worlds and their lived relations to them. To put this in more positive terms, I would argue that the most important contributions to the various communities with which anthropologists are involved are contextually sensitive and otherwise ethnographically thick descriptions and interpretations of the diverse structural arrangements, modalities, and representations of human sociality in all their fascinating richness and complexity, warts and all.

I believe that if such accounts are undertaken, anthropologists will be better positioned to develop a richer and more nuanced sense of how kinship and social relations of other varieties are ordered, practiced, experienced, understood, and represented in specific societies and the multiple contexts that comprise them. Such accounts will also facilitate a better understanding of phenomena that are central to a good deal of contemporary scholarship in the human sciences, including structure and agency, power and resistance (as mentioned earlier), as well as ideology. As regards ideology, four sets of issues merit brief remark. First, ideologies must be psychologically compelling if they are to be effective; as well, the psychologically compelling nature of ideologies has both cognitive *and* emotional dimensions (see Althusser 1969); and as such, both of these dimensions must be dealt with analytically. Second, subversive discourses are often fueled by the disjunctive relationship between hegemonic ideological formations, on the one hand, and sentiments and dispositions engendered in everyday, practical experiences or "lived relations to the world," on the other (see Bourdieu 1977, Abu-Lughod 1986). The third point, which follows from the others, is that failure to attend to such sentiments and dispositions—and more generally, to the "structures of feeling" (see Williams 1977) that may entail "the stirring of 'emergent' forms of consciousness" (Eagleton 1991, 49) — hinders our understanding of key sources of subversive discourses, and likewise leaves us with an overly "muscular" sense of culture's formative or constituting capacities. The fourth and most fundamental point in all of this is that by attending more carefully to the interplay of culture, political economy, and emotion, and to the politics of ambivalence in particular, we will be able to engage and account for more of our data, and will be able to produce descriptions and analyses that are more comprehensive and elegant as well as better theorized. We will, in short, be better able to appreciate the Janus-faced nature of the human condition.

I return, finally, to the *OED*, whose entries on ambivalence were cited at the outset of this essay. The *OED*'s examples of usage of the term in the early twentieth century includes entries in psychiatry textbooks to the effect that ambivalence is a debilitating disease: "It is chiefly ambivalent complexes that influence pathology"; "ambivalence is . . . one aspect of the not yet fully understood disorder of association which [is] . . . suppose[d] to be the fundamental defect in schizophrenic thinking." In the present context, such views seem quite antiquated. We are, I think, on firmer ground if we conceptualize ambivalence as "an underappreciated but responsible moral stance, and one well suited for democratic citizenship" (Stacey 1991, 270–71). To put this in Alan Wolfe's terms: "Given the paradoxes of modernity, there is little wrong, and perhaps a great deal right, with being ambivalent — especially when there is so much to be ambivalent about" (1989, 211).

NOTES

I am grateful to Sarah Franklin and Susan McKinnon for incisive comments on drafts of this essay, portions of which are adapted from earlier publications (see Peletz 1995, 1996). Robert Dentan, Gillian Feeley-Harnick, James Hagen, Raymond Kelly, Jennifer Krier, Michael Lambek, Peter Schweitzer, and Dan Segal also provided insightful feedback, as did anonymous reviewers and Sherry Ortner, whose work (1984) helped inspire the title. Special thanks to Adrienne Ruffle for invaluable research assistance and enlightening discussions of themes addressed in the text.

1　Both meanings are suggested by the term "Janus-faced." Janus, the Roman deity who served as the doorkeeper of heaven and the patron of beginnings and endings, is typically represented as having two faces, one in front and the other at the back of his head. The two faces lead some to think of the bivalent aspect(s) of ambivalence; but with two faces, Janus could see *all around* him, thus pointing to the multi- or polyvalent aspect(s) of ambivalence.

2　The decision to begin the discussion with works of the 1940s is based chiefly on limitations of space. I am not suggesting that kinship studies did not exist before 1940, or that contributions to the field published prior to 1940 were necessarily similar to those produced in the 1940s. That said, the relative analytic neglect of ambivalence is also characteristic of most kinship studies before 1940.

3 "The axiom of amity" resonates deeply with the notion of "diffuse, enduring solidarity" that David Schneider (1968) identified as a key symbol of American kinship (Schneider and Smith 1973, 14). Nevertheless, Schneider (1980, 120–21) has rejected the claims of Fortes and others that something like prescriptive amity or "diffuse, enduring solidarity" is a feature of *all* kinship systems.

4 Edmund Leach (1954) constitutes a partial exception to some of my generalizations concerning British social anthropologists; see also the brief discussion of Victor Turner (1957) below.

5 Stack's attention to political economy brings to mind major French figures in kinship studies who are excluded here for reasons of space—for example, Emmanuel Terray, Claude Meillassoux, and Maurice Godelier.

6 I should emphasize that since my universe in this section of the essay consists of anthropologists who helped define the field of kinship studies from the 1940s through the 1970s, the work of Margaret Mead, Ruth Benedict, and Edward Sapir is only indirectly relevant, as is true for the later period of the contributions of Clifford Geertz, Michelle Rosaldo, and others who have dealt explicitly with experience and emotion—including ambivalence—but are not generally regarded as central to the field of kinship. A lengthier treatment of the themes addressed here would confirm my arguments, yet would also be more nuanced: for example, by discussing the period since the 1940s in terms of more subtle temporal distinctions; by elaborating on differences (and similarities) in dominant and alternative theoretical approaches; and by analyzing the works of Bronislaw Malinowski, Margaret Mead, Gregory Bateson, and others.

7 This section focuses on the 1980s and 1990s, but includes discussion of work in this volume (2001).

8 Concerning this increase, see Weigert 1991; Bauman 1991; Wolfe 1989.

9 For a discussion of this point, see Hollway and Featherstone 1997; exceptions to the generalization include Spiro 1977; Chodorow 1978, 1989; and Gregor 1985.

REFERENCES

Abu-Lughod, Lila. 1986. *Veiled Sentiments: Honor and Poetry in a Bedouin Society.* Berkeley: University of California Press.

Althusser, Louis. 1969. *For Marx.* London: New Left Books.

Anagnost, Ann. 1995. A Surfeit of Bodies: Population and the Rationality of the State in Post-Mao China. In *Conceiving the New World Order: The Global Politics of Reproduction,* edited by Faye D. Ginsburg and Rayna Rapp. Berkeley: University of California Press.

Appadurai, Arjun. 1996. *Modernity at Large: Cultural Dimensions of Globalization.* Minneapolis: University of Minnesota Press.

Bauman, Zygmunt. 1991. *Modernity and Ambivalence.* Ithaca, N.Y.: Cornell University Press.

Beidelman, Thomas O. 1993. *Moral Imagination in Kaguru Modes of Thought.* Washington, D.C.: Smithsonian Institution Press.

Bloch, Maurice. 1989. *Ritual, History and Power: Selected Papers in Anthropology.* London: Athlone Press.

Boon, James. 1977. *The Anthropological Romance of Bali, 1597–1792: Dynamic Perspectives in Marriage and Caste, Politics and Religion.* Princeton, N.J.: Princeton University Press.

Borneman, John. 1992. *Belonging in the Two Berlins: Kin, State, Nation.* Cambridge: Cambridge University Press.

Bouquet, Mary. 1993. *Reclaiming English Kinship: Portuguese Refractions of British Kinship Theory.* Manchester, England: Manchester University Press.

Bourdieu, Pierre. 1977. *Outline of a Theory of Practice.* Cambridge: Cambridge University Press.

Carsten, Janet. 1997. *The Heat of the Hearth: The Process of Kinship in a Malay Fishing Community.* Oxford, U.K.: Clarendon Press.

Chodorow, Nancy. 1978. *The Reproduction of Mothering: Psychoanalysis and the Sociology of Gender.* Berkeley: University of California Press.

———. 1989. *Feminism and Psychoanalytic Theory.* New Haven, Conn.: Yale University Press.

Collier, Jane F. 1988. *Marriage and Inequality in Classless Societies.* Stanford, Calif.: Stanford University Press.

Collier, Jane F., and Sylvia J. Yanagisako, eds. 1987. *Gender and Kinship: Essays toward a Unified Analysis.* Stanford, Calif.: Stanford University Press.

Comaroff, John. 1994. Foreword to *Contested States: Law, Hegemony, and Resistance,* edited by Mindie Lazarus-Black and Susan F. Hirsch. New York: Routledge.

Das, Veena. 1995. National Honor and Practical Kinship: Unwanted Women and Children. In *Conceiving the New World Order: The Global Politics of Reproduction,* edited by Faye D. Ginsburg and Rayna Rapp. Berkeley: University of California Press.

di Leonardo, Micaela. 1984. *The Varieties of Ethnic Experience: Kinship, Class, and Gender among California Italian-Americans.* Ithaca, N.Y.: Cornell University Press.

Eagleton, Terry. 1991. *Ideology: An Introduction.* London: Verso.

Edgerton, Robert. 1992. *Sick Societies: Challenging the Myth of Primitive Harmony.* New York: Free Press.

Evans-Pritchard, Edward Evans. 1940. *The Nuer: A Description of the Modes of Livelihood and Political Institutions of a Nilotic People.* New York: Oxford University Press.

———. 1951. *Kinship and Marriage among the Nuer.* New York: Oxford University Press.

Firth, Raymond. [1951] 1963. *Elements of Social Organization.* Reprint, Boston: Beacon Press.

Fortes, Meyer. 1969. *Kinship and the Social Order: The Legacy of Lewis Henry Morgan.* Chicago: Aldine Publishing Company.

Foucault, Michel. 1977. *Discipline and Punish: The Birth of the Prison.* Translated by Alan Sheridan. New York: Vintage.

Franklin, Sarah. 1997. *Embodied Progress: A Cultural Account of Assisted Conception.* London: Routledge.

Gailey, Christine. 1987. *Kinship to Kingship: Gender Hierarchy and State Formation in the Tongan Islands.* Austin: University of Texas Press.

———. 1998. The Search for Baby Right: Race, Class, and Gender in U.S. International Adoptive Kinship. Paper presented at the Wenner-Gren International Symposium, New Directions in Kinship Study: A Core Concept Revisited, Mallorca, Spain, 27 March–4 April.

Geertz, Hildred, and Clifford Geertz. 1975. *Kinship in Bali.* Chicago: University of Chicago Press.

Ginsburg, Faye D. 1989. *Contested Lives: The Abortion Debate in an American Community.* Berkeley: University of California Press.

Ginsburg, Faye D., and Rayna Rapp, eds. 1995. *Conceiving the New World Order: The Global Politics of Reproduction.* Berkeley: University of California Press.

Goodenough, Ward. 1951. *Property, Kin, and Community on Truk.* Yale University Publications in Anthropology. Vol. 46. New Haven, Conn.: Yale University Press.

Goody, Jack. 1983. *The Development of the Family and Marriage in Europe.* New York: Cambridge University Press.

———. 1990. *The Oriental, the Ancient, and the Primitive: Systems of Marriage and the Family in the Pre-Industrial Societies of Eurasia.* New York: Cambridge University Press.

Gregor, Thomas. 1985. *Anxious Pleasures: The Sexual Lives of an Amazonian People.* Chicago: University of Chicago Press.

Hochschild, Arlie Russell. 1983. *The Managed Heart: Commercialization of Human Feeling.* Berkeley: University of California Press.

———. 1990. *The Second Shift.* New York: Avon.

———. 1997. *The Time Bind: When Work Becomes Home and Home Becomes Work.* New York: Metropolitan.

Hollway, Wendy, and Brid Featherstone, eds. 1997. *Mothering and Ambivalence.* London: Routledge.

Jordanova, Ludmilla. 1986. Introduction to *Languages of Nature,* edited by Ludmilla Jordanova. New Brunswick, N.J.: Rutgers University Press.

Josselin de Jong, Patrick Edward de. 1951. *Minangkabau and Negri Sembilan: Socio-Political Structure in Indonesia.* Leiden, Netherlands: Ijdo.

Kelly, Raymond. 1977. *Etoro Social Structure: A Study in Structural Contradiction.* Ann Arbor: University of Michigan Press.

———. 1985. *The Nuer Conquest: The Structure and Development of an Expansionist System.* Ann Arbor: University of Michigan Press.

———. 1993. *Constructing Inequality: The Fabrication of a Hierarchy of Virtue among the Etoro.* Ann Arbor: University of Michigan Press.

Kibria, Nazli. 1993. *Family Tightrope: The Changing Lives of Vietnamese Americans.* Princeton, N.J.: Princeton University Press.

Kiernan, Ben. 1996. *The Pol Pot Regime: Race, Power, and Genocide in Cambodia under the Khmer Rouge, 1975–1979.* New Haven, Conn.: Yale University Press.

Kligman, Gail. 1995. Political Demography: The Banning of Abortion in Ceausescu's Romania. In *Conceiving the New World Order: The Global Politics of Reproduction,* edited by Faye D. Ginsburg and Rayna Rapp. Berkeley: University of California Press.

Leach, Edmund. 1954. *Political Systems of Highland Burma: A Study of Kachin Social Structure.* Boston: Beacon Press.

———. 1961a. *Pul Eliya, A Village in Ceylon: A Study of Land Tenure and Kinship.* Cambridge: Cambridge University Press.

———. 1961b. *Rethinking Anthropology.* London: Athlone Press.

Lévi-Strauss, Claude. 1949. *The Elementary Structures of Kinship.* Boston: Beacon Press.

———. 1963. *Structural Anthropology.* New York: Basic Books.

Lewin, Ellen. 1993. *Lesbian Mothers: Accounts of Gender in American Culture.* Ithaca, N.Y.: Cornell University Press.

Marshall, Mac, ed. 1981. *Siblings in Oceania: Studies in the Meaning of Kin Relations.* Ann Arbor: University of Michigan Press.

Martin, Emily. 1987. *The Woman in the Body: A Cultural Analysis of Reproduction.* Boston: Beacon Press.

McKinnon, Susan. 1995. American Kinship/American Incest: Asymmetries in a Scientific Discourse. In *Naturalizing Power: Essays in Feminist Cultural Analysis,* edited by Sylvia J. Yanagisako and Carol Delaney. New York: Routledge.

Murdock, George. 1949. *Social Structure.* New York: Free Press.

Needham, Rodney. 1958a. The Formal Analysis of Prescriptive Patrilateral Cross-Cousin Marriage. *Southwestern Journal of Anthropology* 14:236–53.

———. 1958b. A Structural Analysis of Purum Society. *American Anthropologist* 60:75–101.

Ong, Aihwa. 1995. State versus Islam: Malay Families, Women's Bodies, and the Body Politic in Malaysia. In *Bewitching Women, Pious Men: Gender and Body Politics in Southeast Asia,* edited by Aihwa Ong and Michael G. Peletz. Berkeley: University of California Press.

Ortner, Sherry. 1984. Theory in Anthropology since the Sixties. *Comparative Studies in Society and History* 26, no. 1:126–66.

———. 1989. *High Religion: A Cultural and Political History of Sherpa Buddhism.* Princeton, N.J.: Princeton University Press.

———. 1995. Resistance and the Problem of Ethnographic Refusal. *Comparative Studies in Society and History* 37, no. 1:173–93.

———. 1996. Making Gender: Toward a Feminist, Minority, Postcolonial, Subaltern, etc., Theory of Practice. In *Making Gender: The Politics and Erotics of Culture.* New York: Beacon Press.

Ortner, Sherry, and Harriet Whitehead, eds. 1981. *Sexual Meanings: The Cultural Construction of Gender and Sexuality.* Cambridge: Cambridge University Press.

Peletz, Michael G. 1988. *A Share of the Harvest: Kinship, Property, and Social History among the Malays of Rembau.* Berkeley: University of California Press.

———. 1995. Kinship Studies in Late Twentieth-Century Anthropology. *Annual Review of Anthropology* 24:343–72.

———. 1996. *Reason and Passion: Representations of Gender in a Malay Society.* Berkeley: University of California Press.

———. 1997. "Ordinary Muslims" and Muslim Resurgents in Contemporary Malaysia: Notes on an Ambivalent Relationship. In *Islam in an Era of Nation-States: Politics and Religious Renewal in Muslim Southeast Asia,* edited by Robert Hefner and Patricia Horvatich. Honolulu: University of Hawaii Press.

Radcliffe-Brown, Alfred Reginald. [1924] 1952. "The Mother's Brother in South Africa." In *Structure and Function in Primitive Society.* Reprint, New York: Free Press.

———. [1940] 1952. On Joking Relationships. In *Structure and Function in Primitive Society.* Reprint, New York: Free Press.

Ragoné, Helena. 1994. *Surrogate Motherhood: Conception in the Heart.* Boulder, Colo.: Westview Press.

Rapp, Rayna. 1982. Family and Class in Contemporary America: Notes Toward an Understanding of Ideology. In *Rethinking the Family: Some Feminist Questions,* edited by Barrie Thorne and Marilyn Yalom. New York: Longman.

———. 1990. Constructing Amniocentesis: Maternal and Medical Discourses. In *Uncertain Terms: Negotiating Gender in American Culture,* edited by Faye D. Ginsburg and Anna Tsing. Boston: Beacon Press.

———. 1991. Moral Pioneers: Women, Men, and Fetuses on a Frontier of Reproductive Technology. In *Gender at the Crossroads of Knowledge: Feminist Anthropology in the Postmodern Era,* edited by Micaela di Leonardo. Berkeley: University of California Press.

Sahlins, Marshall. 1981. *Historical Metaphors and Mythical Realities: Structure in the Early History of the Sandwich Islands Kingdom.* Ann Arbor: University of Michigan Press.

———. 1985. *Islands of History.* Chicago: University of Chicago Press.

Schneider, David M. 1968. *American Kinship: A Cultural Account.* Englewood Cliffs, N.J.: Prentice-Hall.

———. 1980. Twelve Years Later. In *American Kinship: A Cultural Account.* 2d ed. Chicago: University of Chicago Press.

———. 1984. *A Critique of the Study of Kinship.* Ann Arbor: University of Michigan Press.

Schneider, David M., and Raymond T. Smith. 1973. *Class Differences and Sex Roles in American Kinship and Family Structure.* Englewood Cliffs, N.J.: Prentice-Hall.

Scheffler, Harold, and Floyd Lounsbury. 1971. *A Study of Structural Semantics: The Siriono Kinship System.* Englewood Cliffs, N.J.: Prentice-Hall.

Scott, James. 1985. *Weapons of the Weak: Everyday Forms of Peasant Resistance.* New Haven, Conn.: Yale University Press.

Smith, DeVerne. 1983. *Palauan Social Structure.* New Brunswick, N.J.: Rutgers University Press.

Smith-Hefner, Nancy. 1999. *Khmer American: Identity and Moral Education in a Diasporic Community.* Berkeley: University of California Press.

Soja, Edward W. 1989. *Postmodern Geographies: The Reassertion of Space in Critical Social Theory.* London: Verso.

Spiro, Melford. 1977. *Kinship and Marriage in Burma: A Cultural and Psychodynamic Analysis*. Berkeley: University of California Press.

Stacey, Judith. 1991. *Brave New Families: Stories of Domestic Upheaval in Late Twentieth Century America*. New York: Basic Books.

Stack, Carol. 1974. *All Our Kin: Strategies for Survival in a Black Community*. New York: Harper and Row.

Stallybrass, Peter, and Allen White. 1986. *The Politics and Poetics of Transgression*. Ithaca, N.Y.: Cornell University Press.

Stivens, Maila. 1996. *Matriliny and Modernity: Sexual Politics and Social Change in Rural Malaysia*. Clayton, Victoria: Allen and Unwin.

Strathern, Marilyn. 1988. *The Gender of the Gift: Problems with Women and Problems with Society in Melanesia*. Berkeley: University of California Press.

———. 1992a. *After Nature: English Kinship in the Late Twentieth Century*. Cambridge: Cambridge University Press.

———. 1992b. *Reproducing the Future: Anthropology, Kinship, and the New Reproductive Technologies*. New York: Routledge.

———. 1997. Marilyn Strathern on Kinship. *EASA Newsletter,* 19 March, 6–9.

Taussig, Michael. 1980. *The Devil and Commodity Fetishism in South America*. Chapel Hill: University of North Carolina Press.

Trawick, Margaret. 1990. *Notes on Love in a Tamil Family*. Berkeley: University of California Press.

Turner, Victor. 1957. *Schism and Continuity in an African Society*. Manchester: Manchester University Press.

———. 1967. *The Forest of Symbols*. Ithaca, N.Y.: Cornell University Press.

———. 1969. *The Ritual Process: Structure and Anti-Structure*. Chicago: Aldine Publishing Company.

Turner, Victor, and Edward Bruner. 1986. *The Anthropology of Experience*. Urbana: University of Illinois Press.

Weigert, Andrew. 1991. *Mixed Emotions: Certain Steps toward Understanding Ambivalence*. Albany: State University of New York Press.

Weiner, Annette. 1976. *Women of Value, Men of Renown: New Perspectives in Trobriand Exchange*. Austin: University of Texas Press.

———. 1992. *Inalienable Possessions: The Paradox of Keeping While Giving*. Berkeley: University of California Press.

Weston, Kath. 1991. *Families We Choose: Lesbians, Gays, Kinship*. New York: Columbia University Press.

Wikan, Unni. 1990. *Managing Turbulent Hearts: A Balinese Formula for Living*. Chicago: University of Chicago Press.

Williams, Raymond. 1977. *Marxism and Literature*. Oxford: Oxford University Press.

Wolfe, Alan. 1989. *Whose Keeper? Social Science and Moral Obligation*. Berkeley: University of California Press.

Yanagisako, Sylvia J. 1985. *Transforming the Past: Tradition and Kinship among Japanese Americans*. Stanford, Calif.: Stanford University Press.

Yanagisako, Sylvia J., and Carol Delaney, eds. 1995. *Naturalizing Power: Essays in Feminist Cultural Analysis.* New York: Routledge.

Young, Michael, and Peter Willmott. [1957] 1962. *Family and Kinship in East London.* Reprint, Baltimore, Md.: Penguin.

CHAPTER 16

Cutting the Ties That Bind: The Sacrifice
of Abraham and Patriarchal Kinship
Carol Delaney

It may seem odd at the beginning of the twenty-first century to return to the Bible, specifically to Genesis, for insight into kinship theory and inspiration for its reconceptualization. Yet kinship theory developed in the nineteenth century in cultures heavily influenced by the Bible in which notions of kinship and family appear simultaneously natural and divinely ordained.

During the nineteenth century, the biblical worldview was shaken by discoveries and theoretical advances in geology and archaeology, and by contact with "primitives." Not only did the bottom drop out of the cozy time frame of human habitation on the planet but also Europeans and North Americans suddenly became aware of the myriad peoples and cultures that had existed prior to and during biblical times, yet are never mentioned.[1] In addition, the Victorian worldview was challenged by biblical criticism that alleged that the Bible, at least the Torah or Pentateuch, had been constructed from numerous strands from different times and places rather than being communicated in toto from God to Moses. This opened the door to speculation about the human authorship of the Bible, and thus the possibility that the social forms and norms were not God given, natural, or obligatory.

Social thinkers such as Lewis Henry Morgan, Johan Jakob Bachofen, Henry Maine, and Charles Darwin staked their theories of human origins on scientific ground, but in the process, they nevertheless incorporated assumptions about kinship from the Bible, however unwittingly. Primary was the unexamined notion that kinship was a *natural* phenomenon created by the seemingly self-evident and natural process of procreation. Furthermore, as natural phenomena, both kinship and procreation were obviously universal.

When peoples were discovered who had kinship systems different from the Euro-American one with which scholars were familiar, the scholars assumed that such people were ignorant of the real, true facts of procreation (and therefore correct kinship).[2] Because kinship systems were generally imagined as the expression of biological relationships, "as known or knowable," the different systems could be used as evidence of the lack of knowledge of the biological facts, and societies could then be ranked on an evolutionary scale according to the type of kinship system. In this way, kinship was theorized as a separate domain that could be abstracted from and studied across cultures and religious traditions. And with a few exceptions, that is the way it has been studied up until now. Such an approach precluded a consideration of the ways in which various peoples have imagined the process of procreation and how these imaginings linked up with their notions of "coming-into-being" more generally. That is, anthropologists have ignored the ways in which notions of procreation and kinship might be linked with origin stories. Turned around, this opens the way for considering how Western notions of kinship might also be rooted in the predominant origin story of the West, namely Genesis.

GENESIS

When anthropologists study other cultures, they often look at origin myths as a clue to a people's notion of who they are and how they came to be. The reason is not necessarily or even primarily to ascertain historical origins but to elicit key concepts and values. Rarely, though, have Western anthropologists turned to Genesis, the predominant origin story of their own culture, to explore the notions of gender, procreation, family, and kinship embedded in it.[3]

Although Genesis begins with the creation of the world and the first humans, the story of Abraham is arguably the pivotal story. All of the narratively earlier stories—such as Adam and Eve, Cain and Abel, Noah and the Flood, and the Tower of Babel—have parallels in the Sumerian, Akkadian, and Babylonian literature, whereas the Abraham story is unique. Like many scholars of the Bible today, I believe that the biblical authors/editors borrowed the narratively earlier stories from their Near Eastern neighbors and reworked them according to their beliefs about the one God. It is Abraham, however, not Adam, Cain, or Noah, who is symbolically the one through whom the concept of the one God entered human history.[4] Although that conception entered history at a particular time, it was projected back to the beginning—a vision not just of the way things are but of the way things had always been. The early, reworked stories in Genesis were then attached as a frame for what biblical scholars aptly call the "patriarchal narratives" that begin with Abraham. The story of Abraham is thus important not only because of the supposed revelation of the one God but also because it incorporates notions of gender and generativity, family, kinship, and nation that have been with us ever since.[5]

The Significance of the Story of Abraham

Abraham is culturally the first patriarch; as Abram, his name means something like "exalted father," and as Abraham, the "father of many nations"; regardless, he is considered the "father of faith" in the three monotheistic religious traditions: Judaism, Christianity, and Islam. Despite the distinct revelations given to Moses, Jesus, and Muhammad, all three traditions trace their descent from Abraham, which is why they are called the "Abrahamic religions." There are many episodes in the Abraham story, and I shall touch on some of them shortly; however, the story that is foundational and makes him the father of faith is the one that occurs in Genesis 22 — the story in which he is willing to sacrifice his son because God asks him to do so. That is, he becomes the father of faith, and the quintessential father, *not* for protecting his son but for his very *willingness* to sacrifice him when God commanded:

> Take now thy son, thine only son Isaac, whom thou lovest, and get thee into the land of Moriah; and offer him there for a burnt offering upon one of the mountains which I will tell thee of. (Gen. 22:2)

How could he imagine doing such a thing? This is the son he waited so long to have, this was the son God promised. Yet, he is ready to cut the ties that bind them together as he takes the knife to slit his son's throat. While seeming to eschew or deny a bond of kinship, I contend that it establishes a particular view of it even more strongly.

This story, told in Genesis 22 of the Hebrew Bible and, with a few differences, in Sura 37 of the Qur'an, is the pivotal story at the foundation of faith in these traditions; none of them would make sense without it. It is not merely one story among others. "It is," according to Jewish scholar Judah Goldin, "central to the nervous system of Judaism and Christianity" (cited in Spiegel 1969, backcover). I would also add Islam. The sacrifice story is ritually and theologically at the core of the three monotheistic religions: Jews recite the story at the annual services of Rosh Hashanah; Hasidic Jews recite it daily. Some scholars also link it to Passover (see Davies 1979; Levenson 1991; Sandmel 1956; Segal 1987). Christians believe it prefigures the defining event in Christianity—when God the Father sacrificed his only begotten Son; Genesis 22 is traditionally recited during Easter Week. Muslims mimetically reenact it at the culmination of the rituals of the Hajj. At that time, each male head of the household (whether in Mecca or at home) sacrifices a sheep (or suitable substitute) in commemoration of Abraham's faith, and each Muslim child can imagine that there, but for the grace of God, go I.

In addition, the story is performative, for Abraham's act of obedience established his faith as well as the faith traditions it set in motion; his act also gave shape and substantive reality to the God to whom the action was directed—the action and concept are inseparable. But the focus on faith, and the enormity of what God demanded of him, deflects attention away from considering that the foundational story revolves around a male-imaged God, a father and a son, an indication, perhaps, that it is not only about faith, power, and authority but also about gender and generativity, especially paternity. Abraham's position as apical *ancestor,* as father of many nations, was constituted by a series of ruptures, referred to in biblical commentary as his "trials," in which he cuts the ties that bind—to his father, his kin, other peoples, his wife, his concubine—and, ultimately, the closest tie of all, to his sons.[6] I will briefly describe the episodes in which he severs the bonds of kinship before turning to a discussion of the way these acts work, paradoxically, to establish patriarchal kinship.[7]

A Series of Cuts

The first cut occurs when he receives the command, "Get thee out of thy country and from thy kindred and from thy father's house" (Gen. 12:1). There are stories in both Jewish midrash (medieval commentaries on Hebrew scriptures) and Muslim legend about the superstitions and false gods of his father that appear to rationalize and legitimate Abraham's departure. Setting out from Haran, he cuts the bonds that tie him to his father and brothers; there is no mention in the text of his mother or sisters. Indeed, the entire lineage in Genesis 11:10–27 that begins with Shem and ends with Abraham is an account only of the men who *begat;* there is no mention of any women involved. It is as if they procreated parthenogenetically. If Abraham leaves his father's house, God promises to make of him a great nation and to reward him with territory: "Unto thy seed will I give this land" (Gen. 12:7). This promise is repeated several times with increasing specificity: "For all the land which thou seest, to thee will I give it, and to thy seed for ever" (Gen. 13:15), and "Unto thy seed have I given this land, from the river of Egypt unto the great river, the river Euphrates" (Gen. 15:18).

Another more literal "cutting" occurs in Genesis 17:10–11:

> This is my covenant, which ye shall keep, between me and you and thy seed after thee: Every man child among you shall be circumcised. And ye shall circumcise the flesh of your foreskin; and it shall be a token of the covenant betwixt me and you.[8]

The sign of the covenant, engraved on male flesh, works to exclude women from an intimate I-Thou relationship with God. Since there is not another covenant made with women, one is left to assume that women are included only as they are related to men—their fathers or husbands. The focus on the penis also serves to establish the priority of the male in the process of procreation. This "cut on the male sexual organ . . . [is] a partial castration analogous to an offering, which in return will bring God's blessing upon the organ that ensures the transmission of life and thereby the survival of the Hebrew people" (Soler 1977, 25). Whether circumcision is imagined as a symbolic castration, a sacrifice (see Levenson 1993), or a "pruning" in order to make the organ more fruitful (see Eilberg-Schwartz 1990), the penis is the focus of the covenant precisely because it is imagined as *the* organ of procreation.[9] Not only are women excluded from the covenant; they are not imagined as those who "transmit life." Indeed, that may be the underlying reason they are excluded. They are the ones who, like Eve, shall *bear* children (in sorrow) but not *beget* them. The contemporary scholars cited, not to mention the general public, perpetuate antiquated notions of procreation and gender when they do not use modern knowledge—namely, that both men and women are *agents* of procreation since both supply half of the genetic elements to the embryo. By ignoring the substantive contributions of women, such scholars reinforce rather than critically examine the gendered assumptions and implications of statements like the one quoted above.

In addition to the gender exclusions in the genealogies and the covenant of circumcision there are national exclusions as well. Circumcision functions not just to exclude women but also to cut Abraham off from other peoples. It carves out one lineage—the line beginning with Abraham—to be a sacred line. Abraham, his sons, and their sons "throughout the generations forever," are singled out from among all others.[10] God promises Abraham: "And I will give unto thee, and to thy seed after thee, the land wherein thou art a stranger, all the land of Canaan, for an everlasting possession" (Gen. 17:7–8). With this pronouncement, kinship, nationhood, territory, and religion are intertwined, as Conor Cruise O'Brien, among others, recognized.

> Nationalism, as a collective emotional force in our culture, makes its first appearance, with explosive impact, in the Hebrew Bible. And nationalism, at this stage, is altogether indistinguishable from religion; the two are one and the same thing. God chose a particular people and promised them a particular land. (1988, 2–3; see also Kohn 1960)

What O'Brien downplays, anthropologist David Schneider foregrounds. O'Brien focuses on the interrelations between nationalism and religion; he mentions "a particular people," but does not examine the kinship element. Schneider suggests that strong connections between kinship, nationalism, and religion exist because the bonds that tie people together — what he calls "diffuse, enduring, solidarity" (1977:67) — are the same, at least symbolically, in each of these domains. Furthermore, he notes that people become members of these three seemingly separate domains in the same ways: either by being born into them or by being "naturalized." Nevertheless, neither he nor O'Brien noticed the gendered component — that all are organized patriarchally. That is, the head of the family is the father; the head of the nation is, normatively and often literally, a man, as father of the state; and the head of the religion is a male-imaged God, often referred to as Father.[11]

The covenant of circumcision also involved a change of name. "Neither shall thy name any more be called Abram, but thy name shall be Abraham; for a father of many nations have I made thee" (Gen. 17:5). No longer merely "exalted father," but now "father of many nations" — nations, however, that flow only from him. Yet even though God continually promises Abraham land and "seed" through which he will become the father of many nations, the promises never seem to materialize. Not only does Abraham have no land; he has no children. Paradoxically, however, and on two occasions, he cuts himself off from the very means of obtaining sons; he passes his wife, Sarah, off as his sister and relinquishes her to other men (to Pharoah in Genesis 12 and to Abimelech, king of Gerar, in Genesis 20) in order to save himself.[12] When his deception is realized, the men release Sarah, sending her and Abraham on their way. God punishes Pharoah and Abimelech, but not Abraham, who is instead again rewarded with the promise of land and seed.

Abraham was getting old and the many promises of "seed" began to seem hollow; he gets more and more obsessed. "What wilt thou give me, seeing I go childless?" (Gen. 15:2) he beseeched. The lack of an heir consumed him until finally Sarah gave him her Egyptian handmaid, Hagar, as a concubine (Gen. 16) so that he might get a son with her.[13] Although it is Abraham all along who is desperate for a son, at this point the text shifts the desire onto Sarah, making her complicit: "I pray thee, go in unto my maid; it may be that *I* may obtain children by her" (Gen. 16:2). Abraham's wish is finally granted when Ishmael is born. Then, sometime later, Sarah miraculously conceived in her old age and gave birth to Isaac. Soon thereafter, Abraham cut the ties that bind him to his firstborn son. When God told him, "In Isaac shall thy seed be called" (Gen. 21:12), Abraham banished Ishmael (and Hagar) to the desert (Gen. 21:14). It is as if he no longer exists, for in the next chapter Isaac is called his *only* son: "Take now thy son, thine only *son* Isaac, whom thou lovest" (Gen. 22:2).

Genesis 22 is the most dramatic and poignant episode in the Abraham cycle. Abraham does not hesitate or argue with God as he does over the fate of the few good men left in Sodom and Gomorrah (Gen. 19) but is willing and ready to sacrifice his son Isaac when God commands. Abraham's desire for a son motivates so much of his story, yet he is ready to cut the tie of kinship as he simultaneously binds the boy in preparation for the sacrifice — to prove his love of God. He could not know that God would intervene in time, for that would eviscerate the power of the story. Indeed, his faith depends on his *willingness* to go through with it. By being willing to sacrifice his son, and thus his future, Abraham shows that he loves God more than his son. But if the whole story is about fatherhood and establishing patriarchal kinship, as I claim, how can this be? The power to bestow life comes from God — Abraham's deed acknowledges this — but at the same time, at the human level, (pro)creative power flows through Abraham. The power of generation, of generativity, of paternity, is allied with divine power.

> Because thou hast done this thing, and hast not withheld thy son, thine only son. . . . I will bless thee, and in multiplying I will multiply thy seed as the stars of the heaven, and as the sand which is upon the seashore; and thy seed shall possess the gate of his enemies; And in thy seed shall all the nations of the earth be blessed; because thou hast obeyed my voice. (Gen. 22:16–18)

Because of his obedience, Abraham gains back the son through whom he will finally become the father of nations, the apical ancestor. Established is both a hierarchy of authority and a flow of it: patriarchal authority is rooted in the divine, and this divine blessing (this chosenness) flows from God to Abraham and on through Abraham's seed. The multiple exclusions have functioned to establish one sacred line — only those who can trace their descent from Abraham can partake of the divine blessing. As we shall see, however, *who* is the true seed of Abraham becomes a contentious and continuing issue.

A QUESTION OF KINSHIP

Much of what motivates the Abraham story is his desire to have a son; only a son will fulfill God's promise that Abraham would be a father of nations. But why a son and not a daughter? Why is the father exalted above the mother? Furthermore, what allowed Abraham, or more accurately, what allowed the biblical writers to assume the child was *his* to sacrifice — and without consulting Sarah, the child's mother? In centuries of commentary, these questions do not arise. Commentators begin with the story; they do not ask why it was constructed that way or what the assumptions are without which it would not make sense. They take it for granted that the child belonged to Abraham in a way that he did not belong to Sarah, but they do not articulate the rationale. Today, people typically respond that a child belonged to the father *because* of patriarchy. Yet such a response assumes what needs to be explained; it implies that patriarchy is natural, self-explanatory, and presumably universal. Since "patriarchy" means "power of the fathers," though, at the very least one needs to ask, What is it about fatherhood that conveys such power?

The focus on fatherhood pervades Genesis. One need only think of all the "begats" and the stress on patrilineage to realize this is the case. A number of the books in Genesis are merely recitations of lineage: "This is the book of the *generations* of Adam," "And Adam lived a hundred and thirty years and *begat* a son in his own likeness . . . and called his name Seth," and "Seth *begat* Enos, and Enos *begat* Cainan" (Gen. 5). Throughout, it is fatherhood that is emphasized, not motherhood. In the biblical tradition, Abraham is not referred to as a king, as is David, nor a teacher, as is Moses, nor a savior, as is Jesus, nor a messenger, as is Muhammad (in Islamic tradition); instead, he is referred to as a father. The issue of gender and generativity emerge as central elements in the story. Could Genesis have encoded not just a new notion of God and creation but of human procreation, too? The terms often taken for granted as natural and self-evident facts, namely, "father" and "mother," are perhaps not so transparent. Perhaps they are not merely labels that can be attached to male and female custodians of specific children but are instead meaningful terms whose meaning derives from the way procreation is (or was) imagined.

If father and mother are meaningful terms integral to a particular *theory* of procreation, rather than natural roles, one needs to know something about the theory of procreation, as well as the culturally perceived roles of male and female that are embodied in the Abraham story, and perhaps in Genesis as a whole. While it may never be possible to know exactly, there are clues scattered throughout the text. The "begats" is surely one of them. So, too, is the seemingly simple word "seed."

One must read the Hebrew, Greek, Latin, or King James English version of Genesis to read "seed," because the Revised Standard Version (RSV), under pressure to make the language more gender neutral, has translated the word as "progeny" or "children." This is an important instance in which the attempt to use more inclusive language obscures the extremely patriarchal nature of the text. Progeny may have been the intended meaning, but they were imagined as the product of seed, and only men were thought to produce it. The word seed occurs more times in Genesis than anywhere else in the entire Bible. And Sarah is the first woman who is characterized as "barren" (Gen. 11:30) — an analogy that symbolically associates her with the soil, with the earth. The story exemplifies a particular theory of procreation, gender, and kinship.

Identity, whether of plant or person, was imagined as a matter of seed. "Let the earth bring forth grass, the herb yielding seed, and the fruit tree yielding fruit whose seed was in itself after his kind" (Gen. 1:11). In human terms, seed (and identity) came from the father.

The seemingly simple word seed is anything but simple or neutral. By evoking associations with agriculture and the natural world, the image naturalizes a structure of power relations as it also conceals it (see Yanagisako and Delaney 1995). Represented as seed and soil, respectively, male and female roles were differentially valued and hierarchically ordered.

Paternity has not meant merely the idea of a physiological relationship between a specific man and specific child, as so many people assume, nor the social role built on that recognition. Paternity has meant the *primary, creative, engendering* role. The uncertainty about or difficulty of proving paternity in any particular case does nothing to undermine the concept. Obviously, babies come out of the bodies of women; that is a natural fact. But notions of how they got there, of what they are composed, and how the process is conceived vary considerably across cultures. Rather than merely different concepts of "maternity," I am claiming that just as paternity is a concept specific to a particular theory of procreation, so too is maternity. It is not a natural fact but a concept constructed simultaneously with paternity within the seed-soil

theory of procreation. Maternity has meant giving nurture and birth as opposed to cocreator; men beget, women bear. The mother is the one in whom
the seed is planted; she nurtures and brings it forth, but is not herself the
source of the seed. The meaning of maternity is, therefore, simultaneously
constructed within the same theory of procreation; it is not something separate and prior to the so-called discovery of paternity, as numerous theorists
have assumed. This way of thinking also stressed that the discovery of paternity marked a tremendous advance in the evolution of human culture (see, for
example, Bachofen [1861] 1973; Morgan [1877] 1974; Engels [1884] 1972; Freud
1909; Bakan 1974, 1979. For critical perspectives, see Coward 1983; Delaney
1986, 1991; McKinnon, this volume; Pomata 1996).

Today, of course, it is acknowledged that women provide half the genetic
makeup to a child in addition to the nurture, giving birth, and caring that
have traditionally been the sole definitions of motherhood. These concepts
of paternity and maternity were constructed long ago, long before biogenetic
theory. But because they are linked to a much wider cosmological/theological
system, they do not change in relation to changes in knowledge about procreation. The seed imagery of procreation in nonmedical contexts persists
and perpetuates these ancient notions and sentiments, even in such common words as "inseminate" (literally, to put the seed in) or "impregnate"
(to make pregnant, to inseminate), which again gives the impression that the
male is the agent of procreation. Moreover, the relatively recent knowledge
of women's creative, substantive contribution is being quickly obscured and
eroded by the new reproductive technologies in which the various aspects
of motherhood have become fragmented—egg donor, gestational or birth
mother, social mother (Cussins, this volume).

In the Bible, the power to beget, to generate life, comes only from one
source; for that reason, I have called it a "monogenetic" theory of procreation
(Delaney 1986), and it is, I believe, correlative with the concept of monotheism
—attributed, symbolically at least, to Abraham. While there is a difference of
scale (micro versus macro), both have to do with origins, or with notions of
coming-into-being more generally. Men became symbolically allied with God
the Creator, while women became symbolically associated with what was created—namely, the earth. The very notion of paternity, therefore, already embodied *authori*ty and power. Creative power *is* divinity. Human (pro)creative
power was bestowed by God to Adam, the first man. It is Adam, not Eve, who
begat; all men have the power, and it is through men that the divine spark
of life flows. But it is the story of Abraham that symbolizes this knowledge—

the symbolic interrelation between monogenesis and monotheism—which I believe, was used as the guiding thread in reframing the narratively earlier stories as they were borrowed from Near Eastern neighbors.

In other words, the terms father and mother do not primarily denote natural or, as we would say today, biological roles; they are concepts—meaningful terms—that are relative to a specific theory of procreation. That there were different theories of procreation around the world was something social theorists and anthropologists were aware of, especially after the publication of Malinowski's works on the Trobriand Islanders. His works sparked a protracted debate among anthropologists that is too complicated to enter into here except briefly.[14] Among the Trobrianders, Malinowski asserted, there was no concept of father, even though there was a role for the male in relation to the children of his wife. Instead, they had a theory of procreation in which a child was imagined as the incarnation of a maternal ancestor. Like Westerners, they admitted that sex was a necessary though insufficient element of procreation, but unlike Westerners, they did not go on to make the further assumption that the male is therefore physiologically related to the child. The male role was to open the pathway for the "spirit-child" to enter the womb of the woman; semen was lubricant for sex and food for the child. The Trobriand theory of procreation was intimately integrated with their cosmological theory.

The knowledge of the Trobriand kinship and cosmological system might have alerted Western anthropologists to investigate the deep interrelations between their own notions of kinship and cosmology, especially when Malinowski himself pointed the way. He recognized the intimate connection between paternity and Christianity: "The whole Christian morality . . . is strongly associated with the institution of a patrilineal and patriarchal family, with the father as progenitor and master of the household" ([1929] 1982, 159). Such a religious system, he alleges, must attempt to show that the paternal relation has a *natural* foundation (159). Furthermore, Malinowski maintained that Trobriand beliefs about coming-into-being at both the human and cosmological levels were "to the savage what, to a fully believing Christian, is the Biblical story of Creation, of the Fall, of the Redemption by Christ's sacrifice on the Cross" ([1948] 1954, 100).

For all of Malinowski's insight into the Trobriand system, however, he was unable to dispense with the term father. "The term 'father' as I use it here, must be taken not as having the various legal, moral and biological implications that it holds for us, but in a sense entirely specific to the society with which we are dealing" (Malinowski [1929] 1982, 4). Rather than rethinking the notion of father by means of Trobriand kinship terms, he reified it as a kind of Platonic idea that could be filled with native meanings.

What has bedeviled kinship study is not just the assumption that kinship is natural and based, always and everywhere, on sex and biology but the prior, and generally unexamined, assumption that *procreation* is quintessentially a natural and thus universal process, and as such, can be considered separately from particular cultures and religious traditions. Yet anthropologists are aware that not all people have the same ideas about nature and what is natural — for that is very much intertwined with a cosmological (or metaphysical/theological) system. Still, anthropologists rarely use this awareness to criticize their own system.

The theory of procreation embedded in Genesis is a monogenetic one — there is only one principle of creation, whether on the divine or human plane; only men can transmit life and the patriline. Genesis encodes a patrilineal descent system. Women are the means through which the line is established, but are not themselves the ones who perpetuate it.[15] The line passes from father to son down the generations, for only sons have the ability to produce seed and thus transmit it. Because of the importance of sons in this system, a man must be able to know that his son is from his own seed. This desire is translated into practices related to the seclusion of, and restrictions on, women.

> The ultimate purpose of biblical genealogies was to establish the superior strain of the line through which the biblical way of life was transmitted from generation to generation. In other words, the integrity of the mission was to be safeguarded in transmission, the purity of the content protected by the quality of the container. (Speiser 1964, 93–94)

Within this theory of procreation, the relation of father and son is the closest one imaginable. The son is, quite literally, the essence of the father because he is his father's seed, he *belongs* to the father through the power bestowed by God. No wonder the foundational story revolves around a male-imaged God, a father and a son. It is through producing sons that a patrilineage is established; and it is through his sons that Abraham would become the father of nations.

Yet Abraham cuts the very ties that bind him to his sons and them to him. He banishes one son into the desert and is prepared to sacrifice the other. It is difficult to imagine how this is related to the establishment of patriarchal kinship. The hints are there, however; the point is not to be blinded by the paradoxical nature of it. The power to procreate, imagined as a divine power, transforms a merely patrilineal system into a patriarchal one. The story is clearly about establishing a hierarchy of power and authority; as Abraham is obedient to God, so too is Isaac to his father. By relinquishing some of his power to God, Abraham receives it back a hundred-thousand-fold. Divine power flows through him; he is the means through which it enters human intercourse—in both senses of the term—even though this conception appears to be there from the beginning. It was the means through which to rework and reorganize the framing narratives. Paternity comes to partake of divine creativity, which in all three monotheisms, is imagined as masculine in character.

The concept of God established by the story is, I would suggest, a denaturalized and reified paternity, while the human father is a naturalized divinity. As one theologian notes: "There is something fatherly in God, and something divine in the Father" (Quell 1967, 807–8). Similarly, Seyyed Hossein Nasr, a prominent Muslim scholar, asserts that "the Muslim family is the miniature of the whole of Muslim society. . . . The father's authority symbolizes that of God in the World" ([1966] 1985, 110).

Although the power to procreate was a male prerogative, only one line in the Bible was singled out—that begun by Abraham. But who does it denote? Does Abraham's seed refer only to Isaac or more widely to all Jews? Does it include Ishmael and thus all Muslims? Does it also include Christians or does it refer primarily to Jesus Christ? There is a long Christian tradition that argues that the true referent of Abraham's seed is Christ, and the first sentence of the New Testament traces Jesus' lineage back to Abraham. These sibling faiths have been fighting over who is the true seed of Abraham, and thus, who can claim the patrimony. Scholars have noticed the significance of seed, but their focus was on *who*, not *what*. That is, their concern was the objective referent of seed rather than its meaning (see, for instance, Swetnam 1981). They have not seen, let alone criticized, the meanings of the words as well as their gendered implications for the construction of family and kinship.

The symbolic representation of the family exemplified in the Abraham story creates a hierarchical and value-laden distinction between men and women, between women (concubine versus wife—Hagar versus Sarah), between sons and daughters, and between sons (legitimate and illegitimate—Ishmael and Isaac). Women are set against each other competing for men; brothers are set against each other competing for the patrimony; sisters are not even in the picture.[16]

THE VIOLENCE OF KINSHIP

Monotheism, especially as it is expressed in the Abraham story, has a violent legacy (see also Schwartz 1997). Regardless of what Abraham's story might convey about faith, it also conveys notions of family and kinship, authority, and obedience. Because this has formed the backdrop of Western notions of gender, family, and kinship, it has a taken-for-granted quality that few have challenged.

The price of establishing the notion of paternity was violence, exclusion, denial, and betrayal—of Hagar, Sarah, Ishmael, Isaac, and ultimately Abraham's own humanity. Further betrayals have been perpetrated by theologians—for assuming the spiritual message could be treated separately from the social relations embodied in the story—and by anthropologists—for assuming the reverse, or that kinship is a separate domain unconnected with religious or cosmological categories. Both have been guilty of assuming that the Western, biblically based notions of kinship, procreation, and gender are the standards against which all others are compared.

When I speak of violence, I include not just physical but also emotional or psychological violence. Betrayal, for example, does violence to a person's trust. The theory of procreation helps to expose the violence of patriarchal kinship that parallels, yet does not exactly coincide with the series of cuts and trials that Abraham experienced. Abraham was forging his own destiny, in an I-Thou relationship with the all-powerful God; what happens to the others is the carnage left in his wake.

The first violence occurs when Abraham severs his ties with his own father (and presumably his mother, who is not mentioned); only in this way can he establish himself as the apical ancestor, the founder of a new line and faith. The second violence is directed at Sarah. Abraham was so obsessed with having a son that his wife, Sarah, who had been unable to provide him with one, finally suggested he try with her handmaiden, Hagar. When Hagar produced a son, Sarah began to feel excluded and belittled. Caught by the patriarchal logic, she could not win. No wonder the story blames her for the banishment of Hagar. Yet none of this would have happened without Abraham's obsession. That is integral to the system. The system creates a hierarchy of women, the wife and mistress, creating tension between them and assigning different value. Perhaps the son through Sarah is considered the purer carrier of the line since Abraham and Sarah are siblings— "she is the daughter of my father, but not the daughter of my mother; and she became my wife" (Gen. 20:12)—and thus, the seed and field come from the same source, while Hagar is foreign.[17] Only certain mothers are honored; others are banished beyond the pale of patriarchal society. The banishment of Hagar is the third exclusion, the third violent act.

The fourth is the exclusion and denial of his firstborn son, Ishmael. Not only is Ishmael banished into the wilderness but he is also excluded from any inheritance. Then, when God said to Abraham, "Take your son, your *only* son," Abraham did not contradict him and say, "But I have two sons." When God added, "whom you love," Abraham didn't proclaim, "But I love both." Out of sight, out of mind, Ishmael has vanished.

The story precludes any consideration of daughters—but why is it only a son that would satisfy Abraham? Or the biblical writers? Why is the firstborn always assumed to be a son? Why didn't girls count? The fifth and virtually invisible exclusion is, therefore, of daughters.

The sixth act of violence is the deception and betrayal of Sarah—when Abraham takes Isaac to sacrifice without consulting her. She is Abraham's wife and she is the boy's mother. How could he presume to take the boy unilaterally without telling her? She, too, had been surprised that she would bear a child in her old age—a child that would finally bring her the honor and prestige bestowed on women who produce sons. We do not know how she reacted when she learned what Abraham was prepared to do. We never hear from her again. In the next chapter (Gen. 23), she is dead. That has led to speculations, at least in Jewish midrash, that the shock must have killed her.

In Genesis 23, we also learn that Sarah was buried "in a cave of the field of Machpelah, before Mamre: the same *is* Hebron in the land of Canaan" (Gen. 23:19). This is Abraham's first purchase of land in Canaan, and hence, his first foothold to claims on that land; Sarah becomes, literally, identified with the land. The significance of this deed lives on today in the violent fights over Abraham's patrimony. It is perhaps worth pointing out that this place was the site of a terrible massacre in February 1994 when an ultra–Orthodox Jew killed, with a spray of gunfire, a number of Muslims praying there, ignoring, of course, that they too claim descent from Abraham.

The most poignant betrayal in the Abraham cycle occurs in the text itself. Isaac asks: "Father, behold the fire and the wood. But where is the lamb for the burnt offering?" (Gen. 22:7). Abraham does not tell him the truth. He shifts the responsibility to God and betrays Isaac's trusting innocence. "My son, God, himself will provide the lamb for the burnt offering" (Gen. 22:8).

In the Muslim version, it must be noted, Abraham does tell his son (who is not named) that he is to be sacrificed.[18] And the son responds: "Do what you must, you will find me among the steadfast" (Qur'an 37:102). The son has become the willing victim, the perfect sacrifice. So, too, is Isaac imagined in biblical tradition—the willing victim, perfectly obedient to his father as Abraham is to God. This idea is elaborated theologically in both Judaism and Christianity, and is central to the theology of the Crucifixion. To be the perfect victim demands that the son be obedient to his father, that his will be at one with that of his father. At-one-ment, Atonement.

The story also betrays Abraham's humanity. By doing the bidding of a higher authority, he relinquishes his own responsibility—his ability to respond humanly to his son. What happens is out of his hands, yet those hands are the instrument of the intended sacrifice. He has cut the ties that bind parents to children, husbands to wives, and more generally, people to people. The quintessential lesson of the story is that the tie to God should supersede all human ones. This idea is continued, perhaps even more prominently, in Christianity in statements such as the following: "He that loveth father or mother more than me is not worthy of me: and he that loveth son or daughter more than me is not worthy of me (Matt. 10:35–37; see parallels in the other Gospels). While pronouncements like this appear to loosen kinship ties, they also strengthen them by attaching them to something beyond the earthly and human. They do not discount the gendered hierarchy but ground it in divine precepts. Patriarchal kinship is backed up by the power of God, but on earth obedience is hierarchically ordered.

Theologians collude in the betrayal by ignoring what Abraham sacrificed in the process of being willing to sacrifice his son. They make a virtue out of Abraham's obedience and focus on the spiritual message to the exclusion of the implications for human relationships. The love of God must come before love of one's child or fellows; as Abraham submits to God, so too must the son submit to the father.[19] At the same time, divine power, the power to bestow life, flows through them.

Anthropologists made the opposite mistake when they assumed that kinship was only about sex, gender, and reproduction—that is, about what is supposedly natural. They seem to have forgotten that concepts of the natural exist within a cosmological system, as Marilyn Strathern eloquently reminds us in her article, "No Nature, No Culture" (1980). Had they remembered, they might have returned to Genesis, which established the view that nature is that which was created by God. Early modern scientists assumed they could discover the order in the natural world precisely because it had been ordered by

God; and the notion of order remained even when God began to drop out of the picture as occurred with increasing force in the nineteenth century. Also what remained was the notion that kinship was a natural phenomenon produced by the natural processes of procreation in which paternity was, and still is to a great extent, imagined as *the* generative role.[20]

Secularized versions of biblical kinship underlie anthropological theories of kinship from Lewis Henry Morgan to Claude Lévi-Strauss. Morgan, who is often credited with originating the study of kinship, was well aware of the enormous variety of kinship systems; nevertheless, he grounded them in the bloody lines created through sexual reproduction. Not only that, he assumed that the "descriptive" system (in which there is a specific term to denote each relative constituted by the natural process of reproduction), a modified version of which was in use by Europeans and North Americans, was the pinnacle of civilization toward which the barbaric peoples were slowly but inevitably advancing.

> As a system it is based upon a true and logical appreciation of the natural outflow of the streams of blood, of the distinctiveness and perpetual divergence of these several streams, and of the difference in degree, numerically, and by lines of descent, of the relationship of each and every person to the central *Ego*. (Morgan 1871, 468–69)

Morgan and his followers, including Lévi-Strauss, "take it as a matter of definition that the invariant points of reference provided by the facts of sexual intercourse, conception, pregnancy and parturition constitute the domain of kinship" (Schneider 1972, 37). But while motherhood was assumed to be obvious, it was paternity that drove the system since only by knowing who the real, true father was, could the genealogical lines be accurately drawn. In addition, knowledge of paternity propelled the anthropologists' theories.

The emphasis on paternity is also evident in sociobiology, especially its notion of paternal investment whereby the purpose of the male is to *disseminate* his genes widely. The etymology of the word is instructive: to scatter widely as in sowing seeds. Transferred unwittingly to the nonhuman, animal world, the patriarchal model of kinship seems natural and really real, as the studies of pedigrees, lineages, and male dominance in the higher apes abundantly shows. Patriarchal kinship, symbolized by the notion of seed, is often assumed to be substantive — that is, assumed to involve the transmission of substance. It has always been my argument, however, that substance, conceptualized as matter or material, has been what the female contributes. The male contribution, whether conceptualized as seed or a highly concocted form of blood, as Aristotle imagined, is merely the organic vehicle for transmitting the form, *life,* and soul. Thus, to me, there has not been much of a conceptual leap when the biological essence of kinship is reduced to genetics (see, for example, Franklin 1995; Strathern 1992; Franklin, this volume; Helmreich, this volume), which can and is being interpreted in terms of information. Once again, it is merely abstracting the information from its organic substrate. If genetics is thought of primarily as information, then it is not so surprising to see how it is incorporated in notions of "artificial life." Computer-generated life is virtual rather than biological, yet rather than imagining new or different structures of life, the program designers have not only taken on the role of God in relation to their creations, particularly obvious in Thomas Ray's creation of *Tierra,* as Stefan Helmreich describes (this volume, 1998); they have also unthinkingly, perhaps, encoded patriarchal forms of kinship as the "real" and only way to do it. The thread that binds these proliferating contexts together has become so transparent that we fail to see it, and thus, also fail to see that they are "webs of significance that we ourselves have spun" (Geertz 1973, 5; paraphrasing Max Weber).

Because biblical notions of kinship are embedded in secular scientific theory, it is difficult to move beyond them. Kinship may be about procreation, but procreation is not just about biology, however conceived. From the beginning, it has incorporated aspects of the divine. Hence, in reconceptualizing kinship, we should not fool ourselves that we are dealing only with what is construed as natural; we are also engaged in something akin to theology — constructing notions of coming-into-being, or in other words, new notions of genesis. Or are we simply recycling the same old ones in a new (dis)guise?

NOTES

1 Geology provided evidence of earthly origin far earlier than the 4004 B.C.E. date of Creation Archbishop James Ussher (see Trautman 1987), archaeology discovered remains of sophisticated civilizations reminiscent of, but predating, the biblical stories (see Sarna 1966; Ceram 1951; Pritchard 1950). Contacts with contemporary so-called primitives challenged the belief in descent from Adam and Eve — in human origins and unilinear progress (see Stocking 1987).

2 One exception was John Ferguson McLennan (1896), who thought that the kinship terminology systems were merely those of address; however, even McLennan held that kinship itself was a matter of blood and procreation.

3 Edmund Leach (1969) and Alan Dundes (1988) are exceptions. A few others — Mary

Douglas (1966), Gillian Feeley-Harnik (1981), and Robert Paul (1996) — have trained their anthropological attention on the Bible, if not on Genesis.

4   Regardless of whether this is historically true, it is rhetorically, religiously, and symbolically so.

5   I have dealt with this at great length in my book, *Abraham on Trial: The Social Legacy of Biblical Myth* (1998).

6   His trials are sometimes believed to be ten in number. See, especially, Shalom Spiegel's *The Last Trial* (1969), which is a reference to the last trial — the Akedah — the Jewish name of the story of the sacrifice.

7   Søren Kierkegaard also dealt with the seeming paradox of faith in *Fear and Trembling* ([1843] 1941), but in a way very different from my analysis.

8   Although God commands that every male child be circumcised on the eighth day, Ishmael was thirteen at the time. Muslims, who trace their descent from Abraham via Ishmael, follow his precedent and perform the operation on boys around the age of thirteen.

9   It is my belief that because the penis is imagined as the organ of procreation par excellence, it becomes the "phallus," the signifier of law and power in Lacanian theory. Yet theorists of that persuasion deny any necessary relation between the penis and phallus.

10   This biblical phrase became the title of Nancy Jay's (1992) book on sacrifice.

11   I have critiqued the neglect of the patriarchal nature of the structure of kinship, nationalism, and religion in Delaney 1995.

12   As we shall see, there is reason to believe that Abraham and Sarah are half siblings — sharing the same father, but different mothers (Gen. 20:12) — and there has been a fair amount of scholarly attention to this (see, for example, Speiser 1963; Firestone 1990).

13   In some translations, the word "concubine" is rendered as "wife." Yet it is also clear from the text that Hagar is a slave woman so that even if she was a second wife, her status could never be the same as Sarah's. Therefore, concubine or mistress seems more appropriate.

14   For those interested in this debate, consult Malinowski [1929] 1982; Leach 1967; Ashley-Montagu 1937; Spiro 1968; Jones 1924; Schneider 1968; and my critique of it, Delaney 1986.

15   Although "religion" in the sense of Jewishness is passed through women, many Jews are not aware that it was a relatively late introduction and had nothing whatever to do with Genesis. It had more to do with women who married non-Jews. For a discussion of this issue, see Cohen 1985. Moreover, even if Jewishness is passed through women, Judaism is hardly a matrilineal, even less a matriarchal, society. The personal-status laws controlling marriage, divorce, and custody of children are still extremely patriarchal.

16   Regina Schwartz's recent book, *The Curse of Cain* (1997), discusses the violence of sibling rivalry in the Bible, and its relation to the creation of boundaries and nationhood.

17   I found a similar logic operating with regard to patrilateral parallel cousin marriage

in my research in a Muslim village in Turkey; although people do not marry siblings, they do marry the children of siblings.

18 Many contemporary Muslims assume the son was Ishmael, but the first name mentioned later in the same text is Isaac. Reuven Firestone observes that Muslim traditions and commentaries on the story are almost equally divided: "One hundred thirty authoritative statements consider Isaac to be the intended victim; one hundred thirty-three consider it to have been Ishmael" (1990, 135).

19 This structure of authority and obedience is also promulgated in the military, where following the orders of a higher authority allows soldiers to kill other people with impunity. The film *A Few Good Men* is an excellent example of this. The story of Abraham has traditionally been invoked in times of war — both to justify and fortify fathers who send off their sons to fight *their* battles, and to dignify their decision and their son's deaths with honor.

20 For the ways in which the primacy of the male continues in contemporary, even medical, imagination, see Martin 1991.

REFERENCES

Ashley-Montagu, Montague Francis. 1937. *Coming into Being among the Australian Aborigines.* London: George Routledge and Sons.

Bachofen, Johan Jakob. [1861] 1973. *Myth, Religion, and Mother Right.* Translated by Ralph Manheim. Reprint, Princeton, N.J.: Princeton University Press.

Bakan, David. 1974. Paternity in the Judeo-Christian Tradition. In *Changing Perspectives in the Scientific Study of Religion,* edited by Allen W. Eister. New York: John Wiley.

———. 1979. *And They Took Themselves Wives: The Emergence of Patriarchy in Western Civilization.* San Francisco: Harper and Row.

Ceram, C. W. 1951. *Gods, Graves, and Scholars: The Story of Archaeology.* New York: Alfred A. Knopf.

Cohen, Shaye J. D. 1985. The Origins of the Matrilineal Principle in Rabbinic Law. *Journal of the Association for Jewish Studies* 10, no. 1:19–53.

Coward, Rosalind. 1983. *Patriarchal Precedents.* London: Routledge and Kegan Paul.

Davies, Paul. 1979. Passover and the Dating of the Aqedah. *Journal of Jewish Studies* 30:59–67.

Delaney, Carol. 1986. The Meaning of Paternity and the Virgin Birth Debate. *Man* 21, no. 3:494–513.

———. 1991. *The Seed and the Soil: Gender and Cosmology in Turkish Village Society.* Berkeley: University of California Press.

———. 1995. Father-State, Motherland, and the Birth of Modern Turkey. In *Naturalizing Power: Essays in Feminist Cultural Analysis,* edited by Sylvia J. Yanagisako and Carol Delaney. New York: Routledge.

———. 1998. *Abraham on Trial: The Social Legacy of Biblical Myth.* Princeton, N.J.: Princeton University Press.

Douglas, Mary. 1966. *Purity and Danger.* London: Routledge and Kegan Paul.

Dundes, Alan. 1988. *The Flood Myth.* Berkeley: University of California Press.

Eilberg-Schwartz, Howard. 1990. *The Savage in Judaism.* Bloomington: Indiana University Press.

Engels, Friedrich. [1884] 1972. *The Origin of the Family, Private Property, and the State.* New York: International Publishers.

Feeley-Harnik, Gillian. 1981. *The Lord's Table: Eucharist and Passover in Early Christianity.* Philadelphia: University of Pennsylvania Press.

Firestone, Reuven. 1990. *Journeys in Holy Lands: The Evolution of the Abraham-Ishmael Legends in Islamic Exegesis.* Albany: State University of New York Press.

Franklin, Sarah. 1995. Romancing the Helix: Nature and Scientific Discovery. In *Romance Revisited,* edited by Lynne Pearce and Jackie Stacey. London: Falmer Press.

Freud, Sigmund. 1909. Notes upon a Case of Obsessive Neurosis. In *The Standard Edition of the Complete Psychological Works of Sigmund Freud,* edited by James Strachey. Vol. 10. London: Hogarth Press.

Geertz, Clifford. 1973. *Interpretation of Cultures.* New York: Basic Books.

Helmreich, Stefan. 1998. *Silicon Second Nature: Culturing Artificial Life in a Digital World.* Berkeley: University of California Press.

Jay, Nancy. 1992. *Throughout Your Generations Forever: Sacrifice, Religion, and Paternity.* Chicago: University of Chicago Press.

Jones, Ernest. 1924. *Essays in Applied Psychoanalysis.* London: Hogarth Press.

Kierkegaard, Søren. [1843] 1941. *Fear and Trembling.* Reprint, Princeton, N.J.: Princeton University Press.

Kohn, Hans. 1960. Hebrew and Greek Roots of Modern Nationalism. In *Conflict and Cooperation among Nations,* edited by Ivo Duchacek. New York: Holt, Rinehart and Winston.

Leach, Edmund. 1967. Virgin Birth. *Proceedings of the Royal Anthropological Institute, 1966–1967,* 39–48.

———. 1969. *Genesis as Myth.* London: Jonathan Cape.

Levenson, Jon. 1991. "The Good Friday-Passover Connection." *New York Times,* 3 March.

———. 1993. *The Death and Resurrection of the Beloved Son.* New Haven, Conn.: Yale University Press.

Malinowski, Bronislaw. [1929] 1982. *The Sexual Life of Savages in Northwestern Melanesia.* London: Routledge and Kegan Paul.

———. [1948] 1954. *Magic, Science, and Religion.* New York: Doubleday Anchor Books.

Martin, Emily. 1991. The Egg and the Sperm: How Science Has Constructed a Romance Based on Stereotypical Male-Female Roles. *Signs* 16, no. 3:485–501.

McLennan, John Ferguson. 1896. *Studies in Ancient History.* London: Macmillan.

Morgan, Lewis Henry. 1871. *Systems of Consanguinity and Affinity of the Human Family.* Washington, D.C.: Smithsonian Contributions to Knowledge.

———. [1877] 1974. *Ancient Society: Or Researches in the Lines of Human Progress from Savagery through Barbarism to Civilization.* Gloucester, Mass.: Meridian Books.

Nasr, Seyyed Hossein. [1966] 1985. *Ideals and Realities of Islam.* London: George Allen and Unwin.

O'Brien, Conor Cruise. 1988. *God Land: Reflections on Religion and Nationalism.* Cambridge: Harvard University Press.

Paul, Robert. 1996. *Moses and Civilization: The Meaning behind Freud's Myth.* New Haven, Conn.: Yale University Press.

Pomata, Gianna. 1996. Blood Ties and Semen Ties: Consanguinity and Agnation. In *Gender, Kinship, Power: A Comparative and Interdisciplinary History,* edited by Mary Jo Maynes, Ann Waltner, Birgitte Soland, and Ulrike Strasser. New York: Routledge.

Pritchard, James B., ed. 1950. *Ancient Near Eastern Texts Relating to the Old Testament.* Princeton, N.J.: Princeton University Press.

Quell, Gottfried. 1967. Entry on "Pater" in the Old Testament. In *Theological Dictionary of the New Testament,* edited by Geoffrey W. Bromiley. Grand Rapids, Mich.: William B. Eerdmans Publishers.

Sandmel, Samuel. 1956. *Philo's Place in Judaism: A Study of the Conceptions of Abraham in Jewish Literature.* Cincinnati, Ohio: Hebrew Union College Press.

Sarna, Nahum M. 1966. *Understanding Genesis: The Heritage of Biblical Israel.* New York: Schocken Books.

Schneider, David M. 1968. Virgin Birth. *Man* 3, no. 1:126–29.

———. 1972. What Is Kinship All About? In *Studies in the Morgan Centennial Year,* edited by Priscilla Reining. Washington, D.C.: Anthropological Society of Washington.

———. 1977. Kinship, Nationality, and Religion in American Culture: Toward a Definition of Kinship. In *Symbolic Anthropology,* edited by Janet Dolgin, David Kemnitzer, and David Schneider. New York: Columbia University Press.

Schwartz, Regina. 1997. *The Curse of Cain: The Violent Legacy of Monotheism.* Chicago: University of Chicago Press.

Segal, Alan F. 1987. *The Other Judaisms of Late Antiquity.* Atlanta, Ga.: Scholars Press.

Soler, Jean. 1977. Dietary Prohibitions of the Hebrews. Translated by Elborg Forster. *New York Review of Books* 26:24–30.

Speiser, Ephraim Avigdor. 1963. The Wife-Sister Motif in the Patriarchal Narratives. In *Biblical and Other Studies,* edited by Alexander Altmann. Cambridge: Harvard University Press.

———. 1964. *Genesis.* New York: Doubleday and Co.

Spiegel, Shalom. 1969. *The Last Trial.* Translated by Judah Goldin. New York: Schocken Books.

Spiro, Melford. 1968. Virgin Birth, Parthenogenesis, and Physiological Paternity: An Essay in Cultural Interpretation. *Man,* no. 3:242–61.

Stocking, George. 1987. *Victorian Anthropology.* New York: Free Press.

Strathern, Marilyn. 1980. No Nature, No Culture: The Hagen Case. In *Nature, Culture, and Gender,* edited by Carol MacCormack and Marilyn Strathern. Cambridge: Cambridge University Press.

———. 1992. *Reproducing the Future: Essays on Anthropology, Kinship, and the New Reproductive Technologies.* New York: Routledge.

Swetnam, James. 1981. *Isaac and Jesus.* Rome: Biblical Institute Press.

Trautman, Thomas. 1987. *Lewis Henry Morgan and the Invention of Kinship*. Berkeley: University of California Press.

Yanagisako, Sylvia J., and Carol Delaney, eds. 1995. *Naturalizing Power: Essays in Feminist Cultural Analysis*. New York: Routledge.

CHAPTER 17

To Forget Their Tongue, Their Name, and Their
Whole Relation: Captivity, Extra-Tribal Adoption,
and the Indian Child Welfare Act
Pauline Turner Strong

The invitation to participate in a Wenner-Gren symposium on new directions in kinship study arrived as I was completing *Captive Selves, Captivating Others,* a book on colonial narratives of captivity among North American Indians (Strong 1999). Most famously expressed in the story of John
Smith's capture by Powhatan and rescue by Powhatan's daughter Pocahontas,
who adopted Smith as her brother, captivity has served in the United States
as a "foundational fiction" (Sommer 1991) that legitimates (as revenge) or
naturalizes (through kinship ties) the European appropriation of the North
American landscape. If John Smith is the most famous of colonial captives,
an equally compelling typification of captivity for successive generations of
Euro-Americans has been the woman or child who is adopted into an Indian
family and refuses to return to colonial or frontier society. Such "White
Indians" have fascinated Euro-Americans since at least the early eighteenth
century, when Puritan minister John Williams recounted his failure to "redeem" his daughter, Eunice, from the Mohawk family who had abducted and
adopted her. Whether in the form of historical and fictional narratives, paintings and sculptures, or dramas and films, representations of White Indians
have long reminded Euro-Americans of the enticing if threatening possibilities of cross-cultural kinship ties.

At the time of the invitation, I had also recently coauthored an article on
the trope of "Indian blood," arguing that the reckoning of identity through
"blood quanta" (that is, percentages or "degrees" of Indian blood) is at once
a "tragic absurdity" and a "tragic necessity" for many contemporary Native
Americans in the United States (Strong and Van Winkle 1996, 554–55). An
absurdity because of its grounding in an outmoded and racist biology, and
a tragedy because of its erasure of more flexible indigenous modes of kin-

ship, the discourse of blood quanta necessarily remains central to many Native American struggles for recognition, rights, and resources. This is due to federal policies — and in some cases, tribal ones — that have defined individual and community identities through what the "crossblood" author Gerald Vizenor calls the "perverse arithmetics" of blood mixture (1990, 12).

The contrast between the differentiating, essentializing trope of Indian blood and hybridizing trope of the White Indian was on my mind as I thought about a new direction I might take in a symposium on contemporary kinship studies. So, too, was the twentieth anniversary of the Indian Child Welfare Act (ICWA), which was enacted in 1978 after more than a decade of intensive work by the Association on American Indian Affairs, Inc. (AAIA) and other Indian rights organizations. Prior to the passage of the ICWA, generations of Native American children had been removed from their relatives and communities by governmental officials, missionaries, and social workers convinced that assimilation into the dominant society through adoption, foster care, or education in off-reservation boarding schools was in the Indian child's best interests (see Adams 1995). The use of boarding schools had decreased by the mid-1970s, but not the widespread practice of placing Indian children in non-Indian foster and adoptive families. According to an AAIA study (see Unger 1977), 25 to 35 percent of all Native American children were separated from their families, the adoption rate for Native American children was twenty times the national rate, and adoptive and foster families for Indian children were largely non-Indian.[1] Following U.S. Senate and congressional hearings reporting these statistics and demonstrating the deceptive, coercive, and discriminatory practices through which Native American children were often separated from their families, as well as the extent to which indigenous patterns of kinship and child rearing were disregarded in judgments concerning neglect, abuse, and abandonment, ICWA was enacted to restore tribal jurisdiction over the adoption of Indian children and prevent the decimation of Indian communities.[2]

The Native American anthropologist Alfonso Ortiz presided over the Association on American Indian Affairs when the ICWA was passed, and he considered the legislation one of his most significant accomplishments.[3] But the discipline of anthropology can take little credit for the passage of the act. The "destruction of Native American families," as an AAIA publication put it (Unger 1977), has received surprisingly little attention in anthropology, despite a long-standing disciplinary concern with Native American kinship that extends back to Lewis Henry Morgan's *League of the Iroquois* ([1851] 1962). To

be sure, scholars such as Fred Eggan (1966) and Eleanor Leacock (1980) investigated the impact of European colonization on indigenous kinship patterns,
and feminist anthropologists and ethnohistorians followed their lead in the
1980s and 1990s (see DeMallie 1994; Shoemaker 1995; Strong 1996). Nevertheless, compared to historians, legal scholars, sociologists, social workers, journalists, and novelists, anthropologists have contributed little to the literature
on the Euro-American assault on Native American families.[4]

Given the importance of Native American kinship in the development of
anthropology, together with the discipline's relative neglect of the politics
of Native American kinship, the discourses and practices surrounding the
ICWA offer a significant arena for reconfiguring and revitalizing anthropological studies of kinship. As we will see, the act rests less on the trope of
blood quanta ("substance," in David Schneider's [1980] formulation) than on
the political discourse of tribal sovereignty.[5] While "tribe" carries both the
romantic and disparaging connotations of primitivism, as a political designation it is fundamental to Native American claims to sovereignty over persons,
lands, and resources. As I have argued elsewhere (Strong and Van Winkle
1993), the continued existence of Native American tribes within the borders
of the United States poses distinct challenges to hegemonic conceptions of
U.S. nationalism and possessive individualism. Here, I consider how Native
American tribalism as codified in the ICWA specifically challenges (and is challenged by) hegemonic conceptions of kinship grounded in Euro-American
ideologies of individualism and the nuclear family (see Schneider 1984; Carriere 1994).

In keeping with the centrality of tribal sovereignty in the formulation, interpretation, and implementation of the ICWA, I have coined the term "extra-
tribal adoption" to refer to the placement of an Indian child with adoptive
parents who are not members of a tribe to which the child belongs (or is entitled to belong). This term serves to distinguish the issues involved in the
adoption of Indian children from those involved in the equally contested field
of transracial adoption.[6] The legal status of Indian tribes as "domestic dependent nations" brings the issues involved in extra-tribal adoption closer to
those encountered in transnational than transracial adoption. While cultural
identity and cultural survival are at stake in both extra-tribal and transracial
adoption, extra-tribal adoption shares the additional issues of sovereignty and
citizenship with transnational adoption.

Unlike many of the other authors in this volume, I focus not so much on
surprising and disorienting new constructions and experiences of kinship as

on subaltern constructions and experiences that were previously obscured by the prevailing analytic models within anthropology. In a commentary at the symposium, I noted that contemporary kinship studies depart from many of their predecessors by attending as much to violence and ambivalence as to solidarity, as much to erasure and exclusion as to inscription and inclusion, as much to contestation and transgression as to prohibition, and as much to property as to reproduction.[7] Adoption across political and cultural borders may simultaneously be an act of violence and an act of love, an excruciating rupture and a generous incorporation, an appropriation of valued resources and a constitution of personal ties. While at a later stage of my research I hope to be able to demonstrate these complexities and ambiguities through ethnographic examples, I am here more concerned with public discourses concerning extratribal adoption before and after the passage of the ICWA. I rely on a variety of sources, but am particularly interested in the treatment of extra-tribal adoption in two important contemporary novels: Sherman Alexie's *Indian Killer* (1996) and Barbara Kingsolver's *Pigs in Heaven* (1993). Together, these novels crystallize and illuminate the often polarized positions found in public and legal discourses.[8]

First, however, I consider several earlier narratives of captivity, adoption, and transculturation in order to underscore the historical context in which extra-tribal adoptions are situated. I begin with a discussion of *The Unredeemed Captive: A Family Story from Early America* (1994), a prizewinning work by social historian John Demos. This "family story" offers a multivocal rendering of Eunice Williams's captivity and adoption, with multiple beginnings (in England, Spain, Massachusetts, and Iroquoia), a multicultural cast (English, French, Mohawk), multiple endings (Catholic, Puritan, Mohawk), and a speculative epilogue that echoes a forward-looking eighteenth-century Puritan sermon in envisioning reconciliation through the blending of English and Mohawk blood. In his polyphonic retelling of Williams's captivity and adoption, Demos suggests how the violence of abduction and the intimacy of adoption are implicated in the uneasy relations that obtain between Indians and other North Americans.

CAPTIVITY AND ADOPTION IN IROQUOIA

Eunice Williams was seven years of age when she was abducted, in 1704, from Deerfield, Massachusetts by Catholic Mohawks—whose clans were accustomed to "requicken" the name of a deceased relative through adopting a captive enemy to take the relative's place (see Richter 1983). She remained a resident of the Canadian mission town of Kahnawake (or Caughnawaga) for the remaining eighty years of her life. As the daughter of Puritan minister John Williams, who recounted his own captivity in a widely read spiritual autobiography, *The Redeemed Captive Returning to Zion* ([1707] 1976), Eunice is among the most well-known of the colonial children who were adopted into Indian families and assimilated into their societies.[9]

On the basis of Jesuit and Puritan accounts, Demos has reconstructed the complicated course of Eunice's life. Shortly after her captivity, Eunice was adopted into a Mohawk matriclan as A'ongote ("she has been planted as a person"). Living with her adoptive mother's extended family, A'ongote would have experienced the dispersed mothering of a Mohawk matriclan as well as child-rearing practices that the English considered overindulgent. She had forgotten English within two years and refused to return to her English family when offered the opportunity. On her baptism as a Catholic, she was given a new Christian name, Marguerite. At sixteen, she married a Catholic Mohawk named Arosen, and they had several children, including a daughter who came to marry a prominent chief, Onnasategen. At some point, she acquired a new Mohawk name, Gannenstenhawi ("she brings in corn"), probably marking her status as a mature woman or clan matron. As a clan matron and the mother-in-law of a chief, Gannenstenhawi exercised a degree of authority unknown to women in New England. Although Gannenstenhawi, clad in buckskin and moccasins, paid a visit with her husband to her New England family (reportedly camping in her brother's apple orchard), she could not be persuaded to remain. Unable to "redeem" his daughter in either the material or spiritual sense, John Williams died with a profound sense of loss.

Speaking of similar captives in a 1698 sermon, Eunice's cousin Cotton Mather likened them to

> little chickens . . . seized by the Indian vultures, . . . little birds . . . spirited away by the Indian devourers, and brought up, in a vile slavery, 'til some of them have quite forgot their English tongue, and their Christian name, and their whole relation. ([1699] 1978, 222)

Half a century later, Titus King would echo Mather in his own unpublished captivity narrative, describing such an existence as

> an awful school for children when we see how quick they will fall in with the Indians' ways. Nothing seems to be more taking. In six months time

they forsake father and mother, forget their own land, refuse to speak their own tongue and seemingly be wholly swallowed up with the Indians. (Axtell 1985, 322; also Demos 1994, vii)

For John Williams, Mather, and King, the captivity of children among Indians constituted a profound threat because they were so readily "devoured" or "swallowed up" into a life of savagery and slavery to the Devil. Children, already so close to a wild state, easily "fell in with the Indians' ways," forgetting their language, family, country, religion, and even their English name. Vulnerable fledglings who were "seized" and "spirited away" by "Indian vultures," adopted captives were altogether lost to their natal family and society.

So it appeared to many colonists. But Gannenstenhawi's visit to Deerfield indicates that she and her Kahnawake Mohawk relatives viewed her adoption differently. Gannenstenhawi wished to maintain ties with her English family, viewing adoption as a way of gaining new relatives without severing her ties to the old. Likewise her Mohawk descendants: in 1837, nearly fifty years after Gannenstenhawi's death, two dozen of her descendants visited their ancestral town of Deerfield for about a week. Deerfield's minister was so affected by the visit that he welcomed the Mohawk with a sermon that asserted "a common origin for all the differing tribes and races of men [*sic*]," and praised "the workings of that mysterious Providence which has mingled your blood with ours" (Demos 1994, 247, 252). One and a half centuries previously, the inhabitants of Deerfield had recognized providence's work in the destruction of the Indian villages that preceded the establishment of Deerfield in the Pocumtuck Valley. Now the colonists' descendants were asked to recognize their membership in a "common family" with Indians, their sharing of the "same life-blood," and their living under "one hospitable roof" as "brethren of a single, united, harmonious household" (249, 251). In the minister's sermon, the Christian rhetoric of universal kinship was strongly inflected by Deerfield's kinship relations with their former enemies. The Mohawk pattern of "extending the rafters" through alliances based on kinship (Foster, Campisi, and Mithun 1984) had shown its remarkable power.

CAPTIVITY AND LOSS IN BOARDING SCHOOL NARRATIVES

Read against the grain, Mather's words evoke not only the little English chicks who were seized, spirited away, and brought up by their Indian captors but also the generations of Native American children, sometimes called Lost

Birds, who were removed from their families and devoured, as it were, by the dominant society.[10] Although it is the colonial captive who is repeatedly represented in the historical narratives and monuments of the dominant society, the captivity of Native Americans among Europeans dates to Columbus's first voyage, and Indian captives were sold into both domestic and foreign slavery during Mather's time (see Strong 1999, 2002). Closer to the present, a common sense of violence and loss unites Mather with another religious leader, the Hopi priest Don Talayesva. *Sun Chief,* Talayesva's life history, tells of U.S. troops coming to the town of Oraibi at the turn of the twentieth century "to take the children by force and carry them off in wagons" to the boarding school at the Keams Canyon Agency. He remarks that "the people said that it was a terrible sight to see Negro soldiers come and tear children from their parents" (Simmons 1942, 89). Later, Talayesva's sister went to the day school at New Oraibi, where "the teacher cut her hair, burned all her clothes, and gave her a new outfit and a new name, Nellie" (89). The unhappy girl managed to stay away for about a year by hiding, but when she went to the spring to fetch water for a religious ceremony she was "captured by the school principal, who permitted her to take the water up to the village, but compelled her to return to school after the ceremony was over. The teachers had then forgotten her old name, Nellie, and called her Gladys" (89).

Unlike his sister and a brother, Talayesva chose to enter day school on his own terms: he arrived unaccompanied, thus avoiding the humiliation of being ushered to school by the police, and he wore only a Navajo blanket so that his shirt would not be ripped from his back and burned. Later, he attended two separate boarding schools, where like most students he suffered homesickness, illness, and physical punishment, and was required to engage in such seasonal labor as picking sugar beets in Colorado, pitching hay on a California ranch, and picking cantaloupes in the Imperial Valley. At boarding school he learned, he reports sardonically, "that a person thinks with his head instead of his heart" (99). After a near-death experience and spiritual vision, Talayesva finally returned home, "to become a real Hopi again, to sing the good old Katcina songs, and to feel free to make love without fear of sin or a rawhide" (134).

Talayesva's tale is repeated, in essence, in many other autobiographical accounts. Indeed, abduction, captivity, and resistance narratives can be read as the counterhegemonic version of what I have called, following Raymond Williams (1977), the selective tradition of captivity in the dominant society

(Strong 1999). Zitkala Sa (Gertrude Bonnin), who chose to leave the Yankton Sioux reservation in 1884 at the age of eight to attend a Quaker boarding school, wrote in the *Atlantic Monthly* of crying herself to sleep; having her braids cut off while she was tied to a chair, struggling all the while; and finally, losing her health and her spirit. When she was grown, she taught at the Carlisle Indian School, which sent her on a recruiting mission; she was searching, as she put it, for "overconfident parents who would entrust their children to strangers" (Zitkala Sa [1900] 1976, 85). Looking back on her own schooling, Zitkala Sa likened herself to an uprooted tree:

> For the white man's papers I had given up my faith in the Great Spirit. For these same papers I had forgotten the healing in trees and brooks. On account of my mother's simple view of life, and my lack of any, I gave her up, also. I made no friends among the race of people I loathed. Like a slender tree, I had been uprooted from my mother, nature, and God. (97)

Talayesva and Zitkala Sa were to take opposite paths—he returning to his village "to become a real Hopi again," she taking a prominent role in the nascent Indian rights movement—but boarding school was, for both, profoundly alienating and disorienting. Talayesva's sense of being unreal, Zitkala Sa's sense of being uprooted, and their relatives' sense of powerlessness, sorrow, and loss as their children were captured, whether by force or promises, are frequently echoed in the narratives of Indians removed from their families and placed in institutions, foster families, or adoptive families. While some narratives recount the kindness of adoptive and foster families as well as the camaraderie and broadened horizons of boarding school, many tell of violent separation from family, harsh discipline, forced labor, and prohibitions against any manifestations of Indian language, religion, or culture.[11] That Euro-Americans fail to appreciate the strength of these historical memories, even while repeatedly reproducing the somewhat analogous experiences of colonial captives such as John Smith and Eunice Williams, is one measure of their estrangement from the experiences and perspectives of indigenous people.

CAPTIVITY, ADOPTION, AND LOSS IN *INDIAN KILLER*

"We are what/We have lost" (Alex Kuo) is the epigraph to *Indian Killer*, a complex and hard-hitting novel by the Spokane/Coeur d'Alene author Sherman

Alexie. Treated by critics as an angry revelation of racial hatred, *Indian Killer* is more precisely a novel about the loss of self generated by extra-tribal adoption—and by the more general losses and dislocations that extra-tribal adoption represents. An inversion of Euro-American captivity or "Indian hater" narratives (see Slotkin 1973), *Indian Killer* tells of an adopted Indian's search to become "a real person" (Alexie 1996, 19). Alexie's novel develops skillfully, if elliptically, many of the themes commonly found in the narratives of displaced and adopted Indians, including that of captivity. In order to elucidate these themes I have selected, subtitled, and occasionally rearranged a number of passages concerning crucial moments in the life of the protagonist, who is named John Smith by his adoptive father—and ultimately, of course, by Alexie, whose characters, including a Professor Mather, bear names revealing the parodic relationship of *Indian Killer* to the Euro-American captivity genre.

Let us begin, as does Alexie, with John Smith's "mythology":

The Birth Story

> The sheets are dirty. An Indian Health Service hospital in the mid-sixties. On this reservation or that reservation. Any reservation, a particular reservation. . . .
>
> The Indian woman on the table in the delivery room is very young, just a child herself. She is beautiful, even in the pain of labor, the contractions, the sudden tearing. When John imagines his birth, his mother is sometimes Navajo. Other times she is Lakota. Often, she is from the same tribe as the last Indian woman he has seen on television. . . .
>
> The doctor cuts the umbilical cord quickly. There is no time to waste. . . . His mother is crying.
>
> *I want my baby. Give me my baby. I want to see my baby. Let me hold my baby.*
>
> The doctor tries to comfort John's mother. The nurse swaddles John in blankets and . . . carries John outside. . . . Inside the hospital, John's mother has fainted. The doctor holds her hand, as if he were the loving husband and father. (3–6)

The Captivity

> With John in her arms, the nurse stands in the parking lot. She is white or Indian. She watches the horizon. Blue sky, white clouds, bright sun.

The slight whine of a helicopter in the distance. Then the violent whomp-whomp of its blades as it passes overhead, hovers, and lands a hundred feet away. . . .

A man in a white jumpsuit steps from the helicopter. . . . The nurse meets him halfway and hands him the baby John. . . . The sky is very blue. Specific birds hurl away from the flying machine. These birds are indigenous to this reservation. They do not live anywhere else. They have purple-tipped wings and tremendous eyes, or red bellies and small eyes. . . .

Suddenly this is a war. The jumpsuit man holds John close to his chest as the helicopter rises. The helicopter gunman locks and loads, strafes the reservation with explosive shells. . . . Back at the clinic his mother has been sedated. . . . Gunfire in the distance. Nobody, not even the white doctor, is surprised by this. . . .

The pilot searches for the landing area. Five acres of green, green grass. A large house. Swimming pool. A man and woman waving energetically. Home. . . .

John cries as the jumpsuit man hands him to the white woman, Olivia Smith. She unbuttons the top of her dress, opens her bra, and offers John her large, pale breasts with pink nipples. John's birth mother had small, brown breasts and brown nipples, though he never suckled at them. Still, he knows there is a difference, and as John takes the white woman's right nipple into his mouth and pulls at her breast, he discovers it is empty. (6–8)

The Best Thing

"Indian?" asked Daniel. "As in American Indian?"

"Yes," said the agent. . . . "Now, ideally, we'd place this baby with Indian parents, right? But that just isn't going to happen. The best place for this baby is with a white family. This child will be saved a lot of pain by growing up in a white family. It's the best thing, really." (10)

Sealed Records

The adoption agency refused to divulge John's tribal affiliation and sealed all of his birth records, revealing only that John's birth mother was fourteen years old. Olivia spent hours looking through books, searching the photographs for any face like her son's face. (12)

The Difference

John was five years old when he first realized his parents were white and he was brown, and understood that the difference in skin color was important. . . .

He did not look like his parents, especially when they were naked. . . . He wanted to look like his parents. He rubbed at his face, wanting to wipe the brown away. (305–6)

The Movies

"Smith," Michael said, because white boys always called each other by their last names. "I was just wondering. I mean, you're adopted, right? I mean, she's not even your real mother. Not really." . . .

"She's a gorgeous white woman and you're an Indian, right? Don't you watch the movies? Don't Indians always want to fuck white women?" (77)

Generic Indians

"What's your name?"

"John."

"What tribe you are?"

He could not, would not, tell her he had been adopted as a newborn by a white couple who could not have children of their own. . . .

His adopted parents had never told him what kind of Indian he was. They did not know. . . . John only knew that he was Indian in the most generic sense. . . . When asked by white people, he said he was Sioux, because that was what they wanted him to be. When asked by Indian people, he said he was Navajo, because that was what he wanted to be.

"I'm Navajo," he said to Marie. (31–32)

Real Indians

"So," the foreman had said. "Why do you want to work construction?"

"I read about it," John had said. "In a magazine. Indians like to work construction. Mohawks. In New York City." (132)

To Kill a White Man

"Hey, chief, what you doing? Trying to land a plane?" . . .

John knew if he were a real Indian, he could have called the wind. He could have called a crosscutting wind that would've sliced through the fortieth floor, pulled the foreman out of the elevator, and sent him over the edge of the building. . . .

John needed to kill a white man. (24–25)

His Real Name

He was not afraid of falling. John stepped off the last skyscraper in Seattle.

John fell. . . . Falling. Because he finally and completely understood the voices in his head. . . .

He stood above his body embedded in the pavement. . . . John looked at himself and saw he was naked. Brown skin. . . . John stood, stepped over that body, and strode into the desert. . . . An Indian father was out there beyond the horizon. And maybe an Indian mother with a scar on her belly from a Cesarean birth. She could know John's real name. (411–13)

Coercion, displacement, secrecy, anonymity, rootlessness, emptiness, alienation, inauthenticity, fantasy, rage, despair: John Smith's experience of adoption mirrors that described in Judith Modell's (1994, 115–68) ethnography of the experience of adoptive kinship in the United States. The particular intensity with which these experiences are expressed in *Indian Killer* is not only due to Alexie's fictional treatment. Rather, each aspect of the adopted child's experience is intensified by John Smith's identity as a generic Indian. He envisions his displacement as an extension of the Indian wars and removals — that is, as a physical and psychological assault on his ability to survive. Sealed records hide not only his name but also his tribal affiliation, without which he has no hope of being a "real Indian." Even among other Indians he does not belong: the only place he belongs is that singular reservation where birds have "purple-tipped wings and tremendous eyes, or red bellies and small eyes." Like the birds, John Smith is "indigenous to this reservation," and he can live nowhere else. His experience of emptiness and his sense of estrangement are heightened by the physical difference between himself and his adoptive parents. His sense of inauthenticity is intensified by the simulations of authentic Indianness with which he is surrounded (see Vizenor 1994). In search of the "real," he mimics these simulations, only to become increasingly more "generic." In the end, John Smith identifies with the stereotypical savage. Then, like seven out of every ten thousand Indians placed in non-Indian homes, he commits suicide.[12] In death, he hopes to fulfill his search for his Indian parents and his real name. An inversion of the stereotypical Indian hater, John Smith imagines himself as not only born in violence but also "regenerated through violence" (Slotkin 1973).

Both the historical John Smith and Alexie's character are captive to a family seeking to transform him into a relative. But unlike the historical character, Alexie's has no past and no future — only brown skin that marks his difference. "It's the best thing, really," said the "agent" who arranged the adoption, just as Indian agents for generations thought it best to send children to boarding school and foster families, utilizing violence when necessary. "Nobody, not even the white doctor, is surprised by this," for in the mid-1960s, when John Smith was born, the "best interests" of an Indian child were routinely thought to be placement off the reservation, with a white family. Such a placement signified escape, opportunity, and advancement. As the agent put it, "This child will be saved a lot of pain."

THE BEST INTERESTS OF THE INDIAN CHILD

The guiding principle of legal adoption in the United States is "the best interests of the child."[13] Adoption is viewed as moving a child from "unfit" parents to "fit" ones, and from an "unstable" to a "stable" home (Modell 1994, 28–29, 41–42). High levels of intervention in Indian families, as in Native Hawaiian ones (Modell 1998), reflect the imposition of hegemonic principles of fitness and stability on families organized according to alternative principles. As Steven Unger of the Association of Indian Affairs argued in advocating passage of the ICWA:

> The continuing bias of government policy is to coerce Indian families to conform to non-Indian child-rearing standards. Indian tribes are asking state and federal governments to stop "saving" Indian families in this way and, instead, recognize and respect the rights and traditional strengths of Indian children, families and tribes. (1977, iii)

Interpreting extra-tribal adoption as a threat to tribal sovereignty and survival, Unger called governmental interference with family life "perhaps the most flagrant infringement of the rights of Indian tribes to govern themselves in our time and the most tragic aspect of contemporary Indian life" (iii).

During the legislative hearings, advocates of the ICWA pointed out not only the disproportionate percentage of Indian children separated from their natal families but also that many of these separations were effected without regard to the rights of either birth parents or tribes. Often the birth parents did not understand the documents or proceedings, were threatened with the loss of welfare benefits, and were neither represented by counsel nor advised of their rights. Tribal authorities and community agencies were rarely consulted. Nor were "Indian children's rights to live with their families," as Laguna-Yaqui social worker Evelyn Blanchard put it, taken into account (Unger 1997, 59). Children were removed for conditions that were not demonstrably harmful or before supportive services were extended to families experiencing problems. Few children were removed from their families because of physical abuse. Most often they were removed for "neglect," "abandonment," or "social deprivation." These might consist of simply living on a poverty-stricken reservation; being under the care of grandparents, siblings, or other members of an extended family; or being raised under less restrictive conditions than were tolerated in the dominant society (iii, 4). Likening the "epidemic" of extra-tribal adoptions to a "modern Trail of Tears" (a reference to the removal of the "Five Civilized Tribes" from the Southeast in the 1830s), psychiatrist Joseph Westermeyer noted "a social imperative operating against Indian families in our institutions. The result is a de facto ethnocide of values, attitudes, and customs" (cited in Unger 1977, 54–55).

Blanchard, who became known as the "mother of the Indian Child Welfare Act" (Johnson 1991, 149), criticized "culture of poverty" theories for ignoring the U.S. government's role in destroying Indian family life:

> Indian families are continually subjected to theories of child abuse and neglect that have been developed in the non-Indian community. The basis for those positions is that people who abuse and neglect their children are people who themselves have been abused and neglected. We do not deny that there are many Indian parents who lived in neglectful situations. However, we do contest the interpretation and the application of that theory . . . [because] we can clearly demonstrate that the circumstances in our lives that have contributed to the presence of abuse and neglect in our communities have been directly caused by activities, poli-

cies, and regulations of the federal government. It has consistently sought to destroy the Indian family. (cited in Myers 1981, 87)

Acknowledging abusive situations on reservations, Blanchard argued for providing Indian tribes the power and resources to address the abuses, rather than continuing with destructive policies destined to compound them.[14] She and other proponents of the ICWA also offered a cogent and far-reaching critique of a universalizing and ethnocentric interpretation of the principle of best interests. As Navajo legal specialist Leonard B. Jimson put it:

> A judge who thinks in terms of the comfort and stability of a middle-class Anglo home may unconsciously think about this when he looks at a Navajo hogan where people do not have these same comforts. He may not see the importance of raising children to speak Navajo or to know their own culture and religion, because he assumes that all Navajos want to speak and think like Anglos, and this is best for them. In short, the way that the caseworker and judge look at family life may be so different that Navajo people cannot ever satisfy them, even though they also want to do what is in "the best interests" of the children. (cited in Unger 1977, 69)

Senator James Abourezk of South Dakota (who chaired the Subcommittee on Indian Affairs and ran the Senate hearings on the ICWA) made a similar point, observing that "public and private welfare agencies seem to have operated on the premise that most Indian children would really be better off growing up non-Indian" (cited in Unger 1977, 12). Indeed, they did: off-reservation placements were one of the main ways of implementing governmental policies of "terminating" Indian tribes and assimilating Indian children to the Euro-American value of possessive individualism (see Adams 1995; Strong and Van Winkle 1993). The most dramatic example of this is the American Indian Adoption Project, initiated in 1958 as a joint program of the Bureau of Indian Affairs and the Child Welfare League of America. During the ten years in which this experiment in "transracial adoption" was in effect, 395 Indian children were placed in non-Indian families, generally in the East and Midwest. On the basis of interviews with the adoptive parents, the project was declared a success, in large part because Indian children were relatively easy to place due to Euro-Americans' idealization of the country's original inhabitants. Researchers did not interview the children's Indian families, nor follow the development of the children beyond the first five years (see Fanshel 1972; Johnson 1991, 22).

Blanchard went beyond the notion of culturally determined best interests in asserting that "the question of best interest is much broader in Indian country than it is elsewhere. Termination hearings sever not only rights of parents but rights of children and rights of tribes" (cited in Unger 1977, 60). She is referring here, like Jimson above, to the right of parents to follow culturally specific child-rearing practices, but also to the right of children to be affiliated with their tribes and to the right of tribes to ensure their cultural and demographic survival. In all these ways, the spirit of the ICWA is to broaden the principle of best interests beyond its individualistic basis, and to establish that the balancing act entailed in any determination of best interests should be the responsibility of Indian tribes.[15]

Blanchard, Jimson, Abourezk, and others contended that the best interests of the Indian child could only be ascertained in tribal terms, not in the individualistic terms of the dominant society. While arguments for the passage of the ICWA were grounded in empirical observations about the destructive consequences of extensive extra-tribal adoptions on children, the devastating impact of these adoptions on families and tribes was also emphasized. Building on well-established principles of tribal sovereignty, the act offered a radical challenge to the principle of best interests by recognizing the interest of tribes in their children and the interest of children in their tribes. In order to underscore the political significance of the reconceptualization of best interests embodied in the ICWA, it is useful to employ models formulated by feminist anthropologists for analyzing the politics of kinship (see Franklin and Ragoné 1998; Ginsburg and Rapp 1995; Strathern 1992). In these terms, the ICWA can be seen to establish:

(a) the right of Native American children to have their best interests understood *relationally, or in terms of culturally-constructed personhood;*

(b) the right of Native American parents and families to have the *dispersed nature of their modes of social and cultural reproduction* taken into account; and

(c) the right of Indian tribes as quasi-sovereign nations to *control their social and cultural reproduction.*

This formulation makes evident the counterhegemonic nature of the ICWA. Like the concept of tribal sovereignty itself, the ICWA sets out collective rights that are in considerable tension with hegemonic constructions of possessive individualism and the liberal state. In the twenty years since its passage, however, the act has successfully withstood several constitutional challenges based on claims that it legislated "disparate treatment of parties in state courts based on the parties' race" (Jones 1995, 8). The failure of these challenges is largely because courts have found that the classification "Indian child" is "not based upon race but upon the unique legal status of Indians and the political relationship between the quasi-sovereign tribes and the federal government" (Myers 1981, 53; also Hager 1997, 1–7). In other words, for the purposes of the act an "Indian child" is any child who is potentially a member of any federally recognized Indian tribe — a designation that varies from tribe to tribe, but that has a legal and political rather than a purely biological basis.

The Indian Child Welfare Act is far from being fully implemented, especially in urban areas (largely because of inadequate resources and expertise), and it continues to be challenged in state and federal courts, the federal legislature, and the court of public opinion. A handbook published by the American Bar Association remarks that "the custodial fight between biological parents as opposed to psychological parents is a common thread woven through many of the ICWA cases involving adoption and foster placement" (Jones 1995, viii). Such disputes occur in a small minority of cases, generally in voluntary adoptions that are completed without the timely involvement of the tribe in question (either due to negligence, misrepresentation, or because the child had not been identified as a tribal member or potential member). But these rare instances, which pit a tribe's interest in a child against the emotional bond between the child and his or her adoptive parents, are most prominent in public discourse and the developing case law.[16]

CONTESTED KINSHIP IN *PIGS IN HEAVEN* AND THE COURTS

In *Pigs in Heaven* Barbara Kingsolver imagines a fictional dispute of this kind, one based on extensive research into the intent, interpretation, and implementation of the ICWA.[17] Kingsolver has described *Pigs in Heaven* as an exploration of the "tension between individualism and community" through a reexamination of the relationship between Taylor and her adopted daughter Turtle, the two central characters of a previous novel, *The Bean Trees* (1988). Realizing she "hadn't even touched on the political ramifications of taking a Cherokee baby away from her tribe," Kingsolver "felt an obligation to pick up those characters and address that part of the story" (cited in Fleischner 1994, 14–15). As we have seen in the case of *Indian Killer*, extra-tribal adoption offers a productive context for the exploration of the construction, contestation, and negotiation of individual and social identities as well as individual and collective rights. Indeed, Kingsolver's original neglect of the impact of Turtle's loss to her Cherokee family and tribe is itself indicative of the individualistic assumptions underlying extra-tribal adoption. Also indicative of underlying hegemonic assumptions is Kingsolver's characterization of Turtle in *The Bean Trees* as an abused orphan left in Taylor's car by her maternal aunt. This plus the abrasive nature of the Cherokee lawyer Annawake Fourkiller, who labels herself a "hawk" and seeks to restore Turtle to tribal control, reproduces the hegemonic "structure of feeling" (R. Williams 1977) in which the bond between adoptive parent and child is far more emotionally compelling than any tribal interest in the child.

The deck is completely stacked against a tribally based interpretation of the best interests of the Indian child until the reader becomes familiar with Fourkiller's own loss of a twin brother to adoption and, eventually, the many tragedies suffered by Turtle's Cherokee grandfather, Cash. Kingsolver has said she conceived of Cash after an attorney whose practice is devoted to ICWA cases pointed out "that no child would simply vanish from a tribe without leaving a hole. There would be someone there who needed her back" (cited in Fleischner 1994, 15). Kingsolver has Fourkiller use similar words in trying to convince her Cherokee boss, Franklin, that she should pursue the case. "Don't you think there's a hole in somebody's heart because that child is gone? Did you ever hear about a Cherokee child that nobody cared about?" Franklin replies, "But somebody cares about her now, too. That mother who found her." He adds, "No matter what her story is, a lot of hearts are involved" (Kingsolver 1993, 66–67).

As the story proceeds, Fourkiller learns to appreciate the strength of Taylor and Turtle's attachment to each other, while Taylor comes to understand the importance of Turtle and her grandfather to each other. In exploring Taylor's and Fourkiller's learning curve, Kingsolver educates her readers in the experiences and perspectives underlying the ICWA, as well as its amenability to flexible and humane application in tribal courts. In the kind of magical ending possible in fiction, Turtle's two families are blended through the marriage of Cash to Taylor's mother.

Alexie has criticized Kingsolver, a non-Indian, for writing on Indian themes (see Egan 1998), and his dark treatment of extra-tribal adoption might be read as a response to hers. But I would argue that the issue of extra-tribal adoption is not solely an Indian theme but a transcultural one that, like the captivity of Eunice Williams, benefits from multiple tellings. *Indian Killer* is a tale of the kind of estrangement that ICWA was enacted to prevent, just as *Pigs in Heaven* imagines the kind of reconciliation that the sensitive implementation of the act can effect. Several centuries of extra-tribal adoption and two decades under the Indian Child Welfare Act have generated a host of stories that are only beginning to be told. Alexie's and Kingsolver's novels are valuable not only as works of fiction but also as indications of the rich narratives of captivity, loss, conflict, and reconciliation that further historical and ethnographic studies of extra-tribal adoption will undoubtedly reveal.

NOTES

I am grateful to Sarah Franklin, Susan McKinnon, and Sydel Silverman for inviting me to participate in a most stimulating and enjoyable symposium. I also appreciate Jean Jackson's invitation to present a version of this essay at the MIT Peoples and States Lecture Series, and Barbara Burton's collaboration on the version of this essay that we presented at the 1998 annual meetings of the American Anthropological Association. I benefited greatly from the comments, suggestions, and encouragement I received in all of these settings, especially from the organizers as well as discussants Daniel Segal and Thomas Buckley. Above all, I am indebted to Betsy Mennell Putnam for bibliographic assistance, to Kortney Kloppe-Orton for legal research, and as always, to Barrik Van Winkle for advice and support.

    My interest in the ICWA dates to my work as a research assistant for Alfonso Ortiz in the mid-1970s. More recently, I have been inspired by the work of Sharon Stephens on behalf of Sami children. This essay is dedicated to the memory of their strong commitment to indigenous children and families.

1 See also Mannes 1995; Simon, Altstein, and Melli 1994. Margaret Ward (1984) surveys the Canadian situation, which offers interesting contrasts to that in the United States.

2 For the text of the ICWA (PL 95–608, 92 Stat. 3069, 8 November 1978), see Myers 1981, 177–86); National Indian Child Welfare Association's Web site (www.nicwa.org/ policy).

3 Personal communication, 1978. *Indian Affairs* and *Indian Family Defense,* published by the Association of American Indian Affairs, Inc. (New York City), document AAIA activities in support of ICWA; see also Carriere 1994; Mannes 1995; Unger 1977.

4 Notable exceptions to the anthropological neglect of contemporary Indian families include works by Margaret Mead ([1932] 1966), M. Inez Hilger ([1939] 1998), and more recently, Theresa Deleane O'Nell (1996).

5 For a penetrating critique of Schneider's (1980) distinction between relatedness based on shared substance and relatedness based on codes for conduct, see Carsten, this volume. While I agree that the distinction between substance and code for conduct should by no means be taken as universal, they are undoubtedly opposed in debates about adoption in the United States (see Modell 1994). Nevertheless, con-

flicts among various codes for conduct (for example, rights of natal families versus rights of adoptive families, versus rights of tribes, versus rights of state courts and agencies, versus rights of the federal government) are at least as significant in extra-tribal adoption controversies as those between substance and code for conduct. Just as our understanding of substance needs to be complicated, as Janet Carsten and other contributors to this volume do so well, so too does our notion of code for conduct.

6 In contrast to my approach, David Fanshel (1972), Rita Simon, Howard Altstein, and Marygold Melli (1994), and Margaret Ward (1984) all consider the adoption of Native American children by whites as transracial or interracial adoptions. Unlike American Indians, African Americans have been unable to claim sovereignty over African American children, a point emphasized at the conference by Christine Ward Gailey (see Gailey 2000a, 2000b, in press; see also Simon, Altstein, and Melli 1994). Signe Howell (this volume) discusses transnational adoption.

7 These trends are amply illustrated in the essays in this volume. On violence, see also Burton (1999) and Haraway (1997); on ambivalence, see also Peletz (1995); on exclusion, see also Stolcke (1995), Tapper (1999), and B. Williams (1995); on contestation and transgression, see also Burton (1999), Ginsburg (1989), and Weston (1991); on property, see also Marcus and Hall (1992).

8 In offering an anthropological analysis of fictional portrayals of kinship, I am following the lead of Richard Handler and Daniel Segal (1990). See also Weston, this volume.

9 James Axtell (1985) and Richard Slotkin (1973) are two important contributions to the extensive literature on white Indians; for others, see Strong 2002.

10 The Lost Bird Society, founded by Marie Not Help Him, an Oglala woman from Pine Ridge, is named after a Lakota baby adopted by a U.S. cavalry officer after the massacre at Wounded Knee in 1890 (see Flood 1995). Yvette Melanson (1999) offers the personal account of an adopted Jewish woman who discovers that she was stolen from her Navajo family in 1953, shortly after her birth. Melanson's description of her birth mother's heartbreak, her Navajo family's unrelenting search for their stolen child, her search for her birth family through the Internet, and her decision to join her Navajo family on the reservation is, like *Indian Killer* and *Pigs in Heaven,* a counterhegemonic captivity tale. The book appeared after this essay was written, as did *The Return of Navajo Boy* (2000), a remarkable documentary film about the restoration of another stolen child, John Wayne Cly, to his Navajo family.

11 Many foster or adoptive families have been Mormons; see, for instance, the works by Louise Udall (1969) and Emily Benedek (1995). The latter also provides an example of the informal adoption practices (in this case, by a Navajo clan mother) that off-reservation placements ignored or disrupted. For boarding school narratives, see Child 1998; Lomawaima 1994. For autobiographical narratives more generally, see Bataille and Sand 1984; Krupat 1994. Leslie Marmon Silko's *Gardens in the Dunes* (1999), is a compelling account of an Indian child who is forced to attend a California boarding school, runs away, is taken to Europe under an informal fostering arrangement, and eventually manages to rejoin her sister. The novel appeared after

this essay was written, but its fictional rendering of the sufferings and losses that resulted from the removal of Indian children from their families as well as the empathy some foster and adoptive parents develop for the child's dilemma is well worth comparing to Alexie's and Kingsolver's accounts.

12 This is six times the suicide rate of the general population, and four times the rate of the most suicide-prone tribe (see Johnson 1991, vi, 153). See also O'Nell 1996; Shkilnyk 1985.

13 A classic discussion of "best interests" is by Hillary Rodham (1973). For critiques, see the works by Joseph Goldstein, Anna Freud, and Albert Solnit (1973), and specifically in relation to the ICWA, Jeanne Louise Carriere (1994).

14 Other notable accounts of the genealogy and consequences of abuse on reservations are Theresa Deleane O'Nell (1996), Anastasia Shkilnyk (1985), and Michael Dorris (1989), which recounts the adoption of a child with fetal alcohol syndrome.

15 Arguments regarding the right of Indian children to be affiliated with their tribes were influenced by the children's rights movement of the 1970s (see Minow 1997; Rodham 1973) and anticipated the United Nations Convention on the Rights of the Child (see Stephens 1995, 335–52; see esp. Articles 5, 8, 20, and 30). For a critical discussion of the convention's framing of a child's right to a cultural identity, see Stephens 1995, 37–39.

16 The most significant court cases to date are *Mississippi Band of Choctaw Indians v. Holyfield,* 490 US 30, 36 (1989), in which the U.S. Supreme Court affirmed the jurisdiction of a tribal court over a child who had never lived on a reservation (see Carriere 1994; Monsivais 1997); and *In re: Bridget R.,* 49 Cal Rptr 2d 507 (Cal App 2, Dist 1996), in which a California appellate court ruled in favor of a child's non-Indian parents (the Rosts) because the child and her Indian nuclear family were found not to be "socially or culturally connected with an Indian community" (*In re: Bridget R.,* 522, 526). This judicially created exception to the ICWA, called the "significant ties exception" or "existing Indian family exception," threatens tribal sovereignty, limits the applicability of the act, and ultimately questions its constitutionality (see Metteer 1996; Monsivais 1997; Myers, Thorington, and Myers 1998; Philips 1997). The exception was embodied in a bill introduced in the House by Representative Deborah Pryce, the Rost's representative, in 1995 (H.R. 1448), and in the Adoption Promotion and Stability Act of the following year (H.R. 3286). The Adoption Promotion and Stability Act passed the House (but not the Senate), and compromise amendments were proposed, with the involvement of the National Congress of American Indians, in 1997 (H.R. 1082, S. 569). These amendments did not pass, but debates continue; for current developments, see the National Indian Child Welfare Association's Web site (www.nicwa.org/policy).

17 Christine Metteer (1996) offers a detailed reading of Kingsolver's book as a parable expressing the legal issues involved in extra-tribal adoption.

REFERENCES

Adams, David Wallace. 1995. *Education for Extinction: American Indians and the Boarding School Experience, 1875–1928.* Lawrence: University Press of Kansas.

Alexie, Sherman. 1996. *Indian Killer.* New York: Atlantic Monthly Press.

Axtell, James. 1985. *The Invasion Within: The Contest of Cultures in Colonial North America.* Oxford: Oxford University Press.

Bataille, Gretchen M., and Kathleen Mullen Sands. 1984. *American Indian Women, Telling Their Lives.* Lincoln: University of Nebraska Press.

Benedek, Emily. 1995. *Beyond the Four Corners of the World: A Navajo Woman's Journey.* Norman: University of Oklahoma Press.

Burton, Barbara Ann. 1999. *Telling Survival Stories: Trauma, Family, Violence, and Everyday Life in an American Community.* Ph.D. diss., University of Texas at Austin.

Carriere, Jeanne Louise. 1994. Representing the Native American: Culture, Jurisdiction, and the Indian Child Welfare Act. *Iowa Law Review* 79:587–652.

Child, Brenda. 1998. *Boarding School Seasons: American Indian Families, 1900–1949.* Lincoln: University of Nebraska Press.

DeMallie, Raymond J. 1994. Fred Eggan and American Indian Anthropology. In *North American Indian Anthropology: Essays on Society and Culture,* edited by Raymond J. DeMallie and Alfonso Ortiz. Norman: University of Oklahoma Press.

Demos, John. 1994. *The Unredeemed Captive: A Family Story from Early America.* New York: Alfred A. Knopf.

Dorris, Michael. 1989. *The Broken Cord.* New York: HarperCollins.

Egan, Timothy. 1998. An Indian without Reservations. *New York Times Magazine,* 18 January, 16–19.

Eggan, Fred. 1966. *The American Indian: Perspectives for the Study of Social Change.* Chicago: Aldine Publishing Company.

Fanshel, David. 1972. *Far from the Reservation: The Transracial Adoption of American Indian Children.* Metuchen, N.J.: Scarecrow Press.

Fleischner, Jennifer. 1994. A Conversation with Barbara Kingsolver. In *A Reader's Guide to the Fiction of Barbara Kingsolver.* New York: HarperCollins.

Flood, Renee S. 1995. *Lost Bird of Wounded Knee: Spirit of the Lakota.* New York: Scribner.

Foster, Michael K., Jack Campisi, and Marianne Mithun, eds. 1984. *Extending the Rafters: Interdisciplinary Approaches to Iroquoian Studies.* Albany: State University of New York Press.

Franklin, Sarah, and Helena Ragoné, eds. 1998. *Reproducing Reproduction: Kinship, Power, and Technological Innovation.* Philadelphia: University of Pennsylvania Press.

Gailey, Christine Ward. In press. *"Blue Ribbon Babies" and "Labors of Love": Race, Class, and Gender in United States Adoption Practice.* Austin: University of Texas Press.

———. 2000a. Ideologies of Motherhood and Kinship in U.S. Adoption. In *Ideologies and Technologies of Motherhood: Race, Class, Sexuality, Nationalism,* edited by Helena Ragoné and Frances Winddance Twine. New York: Routledge.

———. 2000b. Race, Class, and Gender in Intercountry Adoption in the U.S. In *Inter-*

country Adoption: Developments, Trends and Perspectives, edited by Peter Selman. London: Skyline House/British Agencies for Adoption and Fostering.

Ginsburg, Faye D. 1989. *Contested Lives: The Abortion Debate in an American Community.* Berkeley: University of California Press.

Ginsburg, Faye D., and Rayna Rapp, eds. 1995. *Conceiving the New World Order: The Global Politics of Reproduction.* Berkeley: University of California Press.

Goldstein, Joseph, Anna Freud, and Albert J. Solnit. 1973. *Beyond the Best Interest of the Child.* New York: Free Press.

Hager, C. Steven, with Tina Law. 1997. *Handbook on the Indian Child Welfare Act.* Edited by Colline Meek and Michael Snyder. Oklahoma City: Oklahoma Indian Legal Services.

Handler, Richard, and Daniel A. Segal. 1990. *Jane Austen and the Fiction of Culture: An Essay on the Narration of Social Realities.* Tucson: University of Arizona Press.

Haraway, Donna J. 1997. *Modest_Witness@Second_Millennium.FemaleMan©_Meets_ OncoMouse.*™ New York: Routledge.

Hilger, M. Inez. [1939] 1998. *Chippewa Families: A Social Study of White Earth Reservation, 1938.* Introduction by Brenda J. Child and Kimberly M. Blaeser. St. Paul: Minnesota Historical Society Press.

Johnson, Troy R., ed. 1991. *The Indian Child Welfare Act: Indian Homes for Indian Children.* Los Angeles: American Indian Studies Center, University of California at Los Angeles.

Jones, B. J. 1995. *The Indian Child Welfare Act Handbook: A Legal Guide to the Custody and Adoption of Native American Children.* Chicago: Section of Family Law, American Bar Association.

Kingsolver, Barbara. 1988. *The Bean Trees.* New York: HarperCollins.

———. 1993. *Pigs in Heaven.* New York: HarperCollins.

Krupat, Arnold, ed. 1994. *Native American Autobiography: An Anthology.* Madison: University of Wisconsin Press.

Leacock, Eleanor. 1980. Montagnais Women and the Jesuit Program for Colonization. In *Women and Colonization: Anthropological Perspectives,* edited by Mona Etienne and Eleanor Leacock. New York: Praeger.

Lomawaima, K. Tsianina. 1994. *They Called It Prairie Light: The Story of Chilocco Indian School.* Lincoln: University of Nebraska Press.

Mannes, Marc. 1995. Factors and Events Leading to the Passage of the Indian Child Welfare Act. *Child Welfare* 74, no. 1:264–82.

Marcus, George E., with Peter Dobkin Hall. 1992. *Lives in Trust: The Fortunes of Dynastic Families in Late Twentieth Century America.* Boulder, Colo.: Westview Press.

Mather, Cotton. [1699] 1978. *Decennium Luctuosum.* Vol. 3 of *Narratives of North American Indian Captivities,* edited by Wilcomb Washburn. New York: Garland.

Mead, Margaret. [1932] 1966. *The Changing Culture of an Indian Tribe.* Rev. ed. New York: Capricorn.

Melanson, Yvette, with Claire Safran. 1999. *Looking for Lost Bird: A Jewish Woman Discovers Her Navajo Roots.* New York: Avon.

Metteer, Christine. 1996. *Pigs in Heaven:* A Parable of Native American Adoption under the Indian Child Welfare Act. *Arizona State Law Journal* 28, no. 2:589–628.

Minow, Martha. 1997. Whatever Happened to Children's Rights? In *Reassessing the Sixties: Debating the Political and Cultural Legacy,* edited by Stephen Macedo. New York: W. W. Norton.

Modell, Judith S. 1994. *Kinship with Strangers: Adoption and Interpretations of Kinship in American Culture.* Berkeley: University of California Press.

———. 1998. Rights to the Children: Foster Care and Social Reproduction in Hawai'i. In *Reproducing Reproduction: Kinship, Power, and Technological Innovation,* edited by Sarah Franklin and Helena Ragoné. Philadelphia: University of Pennsylvania Press.

Monsivais, Jose. 1997. A Glimmer of Hope: A Proposal to Keep the Indian Child Welfare Act of 1978 Intact. *American Indian Law Review* 22, no. 1:1–36.

Morgan, Lewis Henry. [1851] 1962. *League of the Ho-dé-no-sau-nee or Iroquois.* New York: Corinth.

Myers, Joseph A., ed. 1981. *They're Young Once but Indian Forever: A Summary and Analysis of Investigative Hearings on Indian Child Welfare.* Oakland, Calif.: American Indian Lawyer Training Program.

Myers, Raquelle, Nancy Thorington, and Joseph Myers, eds. 1998. *Significant Ties Exception to the ICWA: Judicial Decision-Making or Incorporating Bias into Law?* Petaluma, Calif.: National Indian Justice Center.

O'Nell, Theresa Deleane. 1996. *Disciplined Hearts: History, Identity, and Depression in an American Indian Community.* Berkeley: University of California Press.

Peletz, Michael G. 1995. "Kinship Studies in Late Twentieth Century Anthropology." *Annual Review of Anthropology* 24:343–72.

Philips, Sloan. 1997. The Indian Child Welfare Act in the Face of Extinction. *American Indian Law Review* 20, no. 2:351–64.

The Return of Navajo Boy. 2000. Directed by Jeff Spitz. Coproduced by Jeff Spitz and Bennie Klain. Chicago: Amdur Spitz and Associates/New York: Public Broadcasting Service.

Richter, Daniel K. 1983. War and Culture: The Iroquois Experience. *William and Mary Quarterly* 40, no. 4:528–59.

Rodham, Hillary. 1973. Children under the Law. *Harvard Educational Review* 43, no. 4: 487–514.

Schneider, David M. 1980. *American Kinship: A Cultural Account.* 2d ed. Chicago: University of Chicago Press.

———. 1984. *A Critique of the Study of Kinship.* Ann Arbor: University of Michigan Press.

Shkilnyk, Anastasia M. 1985. *A Poison Stronger than Love: The Destruction of an Ojibwa Community.* New Haven, Conn.: Yale University Press.

Shoemaker, Nancy, ed. 1995. *Negotiators of Change: Historical Perspectives on Native American Women.* New York: Routledge.

Silko, Leslie Marmon. 1999. *Gardens in the Dunes.* New York: Simon and Schuster.

Simmons, Leo W., ed. 1942. *Sun Chief: The Autobiography of a Hopi Indian.* New Haven, Conn.: Yale University Press.

Simon, Rita J., Howard Altstein, and Marygold S. Melli. 1994. *The Case for Transracial Adoption*. Washington, D.C.: American University Press.

Slotkin, Richard. 1973. *Regeneration through Violence: The Mythology of the American Frontier, 1600–1860*. Middletown, Conn.: Wesleyan University Press.

Sommer, Doris. 1991. *Foundational Fictions: The National Romances of Latin America*. Berkeley: University of California Press.

Stephens, Sharon, ed. 1995. *Children and the Politics of Culture*. Princeton, N.J.: Princeton University Press.

Stolcke, Verena. 1995. Talking Culture: New Boundaries, New Rhetorics of Exclusion in Europe. *Current Anthropology* 36:1–24.

Strathern, Marilyn. 1992. *After Nature: English Kinship in the Late Twentieth Century*. Cambridge: Cambridge University Press.

Strong, Pauline Turner. 1996. Feminist Theory and the Invasion of the Heart in North America. *Ethnohistory* 43, no. 4:683–712.

———. 1999. *Captive Selves, Captivating Others: The Politics and Poetics of Colonial American Captivity Narratives*. Boulder, Colo.: Westview Press.

———. 2002. Transforming Outsiders: Captivity, Adoption, and Slavery Reconsidered. In *A Companion to American Indian History*, edited by Philip J. Deloria and Neal Salisbury. Oxford: Blackwell Publishers.

Strong, Pauline Turner, and Barrik Van Winkle. 1993. Tribe and Nation: American Indians and American Nationalism. *Social Analysis* 33:9–26.

———. 1996. "Indian Blood": Reflections on the Reckoning and Refiguring of Native North American Identity. *Cultural Anthropology* 11, no. 4:547–76.

Tapper, Melbourne. 1999. *In the Blood: Sickle Cell Anemia and the Politics of Race*. Philadelphia: University of Pennsylvania Press.

Udall, Louise, ed. 1969. *Me and Mine: The Life Story of Helen Sekaquaptewa, as Told to Louise Udall*. Tucson: University of Arizona Press.

Unger, Steven, ed. 1977. *The Destruction of American Indian Families*. New York: Association on American Indian Affairs, Inc.

Vizenor, Gerald. 1990. *Crossbloods: Bone Courts, Bingo, and Other Reports*. Minneapolis: University of Minnesota Press.

———. 1994. *Manifest Manners: Narratives on Postindian Survivance*. Lincoln: University of Nebraska Press.

Ward, Margaret. 1984. *The Adoption of Native Canadian Children*. Cobalt, Ontario: Highway Book Shop.

Weston, Kath. 1991. *Families We Choose: Lesbians, Gays, Kinship*. New York: Columbia University Press.

Williams, Brackette F. 1995. Classification Systems Revisited: Kinship, Caste, Race, and Nationality as the Flow of Blood and the Spread of Rights. In *Naturalizing Power: Essays in Feminist Cultural Analysis*, edited by Sylvia J. Yanagisako and Carol Delaney. New York: Routledge.

Williams, John. [1707] 1976. *The Redeemed Captive Returning to Zion*. Edited by Edward W. Clark. Amherst: University of Massachusetts Press.

Williams, Raymond. 1977. *Marxism and Literature.* Oxford: Oxford University Press.

Zitkala Sa (Gertrude Bonnin). [1900] 1976. The School Days of an Indian Girl, and An American Teacher among the Indians. In *American Indian Stories.* Reprint, Glorieta, N.Mex.: Rio Grande Press.

CONTRIBUTORS

MARY BOUQUET studied social anthropology at Cambridge University, where she first developed an interest in kinship. She left Britain in 1983 and has worked in Portugal, Norway, and the Netherlands, where she is currently working at the Tropenmuseum of the Royal Tropical Institute in Amsterdam. She has published on the cultural specificity of English notions of genealogy in British kinship theory, the diagrammatic visualization of genealogy, photography, and exhibition making. Her publications include *Reclaiming English Kinship: Portuguese Refractions on English Kinship Theory* (1993).

JANET CARSTEN is Senior Lecturer in Social Anthropology at the University of Edinburgh. Her research interests include kinship, gender, the house, and historical migration. She has carried out fieldwork in Langkawi, Malaysia, and has recently worked on reunions between adult adoptees and their birth kin in Britain. She is author of *The Heat of the Hearth: The Process of Kinship in a Malay Fishing Community* (1997) and has edited *Cultures of Relatedness: New Approaches to the Study of Kinship* (2000).

CAROL DELANEY is Associate Professor in the Department of Cultural and Social Anthropology at Stanford University. Her primary interests have been the conjunction of gender and religion and origin stories. These have been explored in *The Seed and the Soil: Gender and Cosmology in Turkish Village Society* (1991) and *Abraham on Trial: The Social Legacy of Biblical Myth* (1998). Current research focuses on the strand of millennial thinking in American history.

GILLIAN FEELEY-HARNIK is Professor of Anthropology at the University of Michigan, Ann Arbor. Her areas of ethnographic and archival research include Madagascar (since 1971) and the United States (since 1994). She is also interested in the history and anthropology of the Bible and biblically inspired religions in the Jewish and

Christian diasporas and beyond. Her research in these areas has been published in several articles and books, including *A Green Estate: Restoring Independence in Madagascar* (1991), *The Lord's Table: The Meaning of Food in Early Judaism and Christianity* (1994), and a third book in progress, *The Ethnography of Creation,* a comparative study of Charles Darwin and Lewis Henry Morgan that focuses on popular ideas and practices concerning religion, science, kinship, and ecology.

SARAH FRANKLIN is Professor of Anthropology of Science at Lancaster University, where she has taught since 1990. She is the author of *Embodied Progress: A Cultural Account of Assisted Conception* (1997) and coauthor of *Technologies of Procreation: Kinship in the Age of Assisted Conception* (1998) and *Global Nature, Global Culture* (2000). She is currently completing a book on cloning titled *Dolly Mixtures.*

DEBORAH HEATH is Associate Professor at Lewis and Clark College, where she teaches anthropology. Her publications on scientists, genetic disease research, and patient activism have appeared in the journals *Science, Technology and Human Values* and *Culture, Medicine, and Psychiatry,* and in several edited volumes. She is a coeditor of the forthcoming *Anthropology in the Age of Molecular Genetics* and author of the forthcoming *Travels with Science.*

STEFAN HELMREICH is Assistant Professor in Science Studies in the Draper Program at New York University. He is interested in changing conceptions of "life" in the age of genomics and informatics. His book, *Silicon Second Nature: Culturing Artificial Life in a Digital World* (1998), is based on fieldwork with computer scientists and biologists at the Santa Fe Institute for the Sciences of Complexity in New Mexico. He is at the beginning of a research project on marine biology, biotechnology, and ocean politics.

SIGNE HOWELL is Professor of Social Anthropology at the University of Oslo, Norway. She is currently engaged in research on transnational adoption in Norway and is extending this to include a comparative investigation of kinship values and practices in some of the countries from which children are adopted into the West. Her previous research has been with hunter-gatherers in Malaysia and on Flores in Indonesia. Her books include *Society and Cosmos: Chewong of Peninsular Malaysia* (1989) and the edited volumes *For the Sake of Our Futures: Sacrificing in Eastern Indonesia* (1996) and *The Ethnography of Mortalities* (1997).

JONATHAN MARKS is a biological anthropologist at the University of North Carolina at Charlotte, having formerly taught at Yale and Berkeley. His primary area of research is molecular anthropology—the application of genetic data to illuminate our place in the natural order—or more broadly, the area of overlap between (scientific) genetic data and (humanistic) self-comprehension. He is the author of *Human Biodiversity* (1995) and *What It Means to Be 98% Chimpanzee* (in press).

SUSAN McKINNON teaches at the University of Virginia, where she is Associate Professor of Anthropology. Her research on kinship and gender in Eastern Indonesia resulted in a book titled *From a Shattered Sun: Hierarchy, Gender, and Alliance in the Tanimbar Islands* (1991) and a number of articles that challenge anthropological models of kinship and marriage. Her teaching focuses on the intersection of kinship, gender, science studies, and transnationalism. She is currently working on a book of essays, *The Culture of Kinship Theory,* which critically assesses the cultural understandings that have shaped kinship theory in anthropology.

MICHAEL G. PELETZ is W. S. Schupf Professor of Far Eastern Studies and Professor of Anthropology at Colgate University. His research focuses on kinship, gender, sexuality, religion, law, social and cultural theory, and Southeast Asia. He is author of *A Share of the Harvest: Kinship, Property, and Social History among the Malays of Rembau* (1988); "Kinship Studies in Late Twentieth-Century Anthropology" (*Annual Review of Anthropology,* 1995); *Reason and Passion: Representations of Gender in a Malay Society* (1996); and *Islamic Courts and Modernity in Malaysia* (2002). He is currently working on a book on transgendered practices and identities in Southeast Asia from 1500 to the present.

RAYNA RAPP teaches anthropology at New York University. She edited or coedited *Toward an Anthropology of Women* (1975); *Promissory Notes: Women in the Transition to Socialism* (1989); *Articulating Hidden Histories: Exploring the Influence of Eric R. Wolf* (1995); and *Conceiving the New World Order: The Global Politics of Reproduction* (1995). Her recent book, *Testing Women, Testing the Fetus: The Social Impact of Amniocentesis in America* (1999), won the Basker Prize, the Forsythe Prize, and the American Ethnological Society Senior Book Prize in 1999.

MARTINE SEGALEN is Professor of Sociology at the Universite de Paris X-Nanterre. She has conducted extensive research on kinship in peasant societies and on contemporary transformations in kinship formations in France. Her publications include *Fifteen Generations of Bretons: Kinship and Society in Lower Brittany* (1991) and the coedited (with Marianne Gullestad) volume, *Family and Kinship in Europe* (1997). She is in the process of completing two more works on grandparenting: One compares the phenomenon across European and North American countries, and the other questions the forms and causes of the enduring *esprit de famille* in France.

POLLY TURNER STRONG is Associate Professor of Anthropology at the University of Texas at Austin, where she is also affiliated with the Cultural Studies and Women's

Studies programs. She is author of *Captive Selves, Captivating Others: The Politics and Poetics of Colonial American Captivity Narratives* (1999), and coeditor of *Theorizing the Hybrid,* a special issue of the *Journal of American Folklore* (1999). Her current research concerns historical and contemporary representations of Native Americans in a variety of cultural, political, and scholarly venues.

MELBOURNE TAPPER is author of *In the Blood: Sickle Cell Anemia and the Politics of Race* (1999). He currently lives in Denmark, where he is working as an independent scholar on two new projects. One concerns the integration of doctors from outside the European Union — specifically those coming to Denmark as refugees. The other focuses on the question of multiculturalism in Danish society.

KAREN-SUE TAUSSIG is Assistant Professor of Anthropology and Medicine at the University of Minnesota. Her research has focused on the relationships between the explosion of knowledge about molecular biology and identity in the Netherlands and on the production and circulation of genetic knowledge in the United States. Her book, *Just Be Ordinary: Normalizing the Future Through Genetic Research and Practice,* is in press.

CHARIS THOMPSON is Assistant Professor of the History of Science at Harvard University. She works on selective pronatalism in the life and environmental sciences. She has a forthcoming book, *Charismatic Megafauna and Miracle Babies: Essays in Selective Pronatalism,* and is working on another, *I Am Become Life: Technologies and the Self.*

KATH WESTON is Director of Studies for the Committee on Degrees in Women's Studies at Harvard University. She is the author of several books, including *Families We Choose: Lesbians, Gays, Kinship* (1991), *Render Me, Gender Me: Lesbians Talk Sex, Class, Color, Nation, Studmuffins* (1996), and *Long Slow Burn: Sexuality and Social Science* (1998). Her work in progress examines the effects of globalization on living poor in the United States and the consequences of commodification for gender theory.

YUNXIANG YAN is Associate Professor of Anthropology at the University of California, Los Angeles. He has carried out research in Beijing and rural north China on topics relating to social change and development, family and kinship, exchange, and cultural globalization. He is author of *The Flow of Gifts: Reciprocity and Social Networks in a Chinese Village* (1996) and *Private Life under Socialism: Love, Intimacy, and Family Change in a Chinese Village, 1949–1999* (in press).

INDEX

AAIA (Association on American Indian Affairs, Inc.), 469, 480
Ablon, Joan, 399
Abourezk, James, 482
Abraham story. *See* Genesis
Abstraction, 93–94, 98, 111–12, 127
Academia, 148
Achondrodysplasias. *See* Dwarfing conditions; Marfan's syndrome
Adoption, 6; France, 261–62; little people children, 393–94; substance and, 470, 486–87 n.5; transracial, 196–97, 470, 482, 487 n.6. *See also* Extra-tribal adoption; Native Americans; Transnational adoption
Adoption Act (1986), 207
Adoption Promotion and Stability Act, 488 n.16
Affinity, 56, 279–80, 385
Affirmative action, 171 n.21
Africa, 269. *See also* Colonialism; Sickling
African-Eurasian split, 359–61, 366–67
Africanist school, 248, 258
After Nature (Strathern), 5, 302
Agency, 12, 226–27, 239, 242, 243 n.2, 307; ambivalence and, 430–31
Agnatic kin, 100–101, 228, 231, 233, 283–84, 286
Agriculture, 78–79, 281, 283, 285–86
Agriculture of New-York (Emmons), 78

AIDS, 152, 161–63, 170 n.12
Alchemical Informatics, 138
Alcoholics Anonymous, 397
Alcott, William Andrus, 77
Alexie, Sherman, 471, 475–80, 485–86
Algorithms, 129–30, 132–33
Alliance, 159–61, 248, 256; elementary structures, 294–95; uncertainty of, 231–33
Alliance of Genetic Support Groups, 393
Altruism, 154, 165
Ambiguity, 415
Ambivalence, 18–19, 216, 413–15, 471; agency, 430–31; British studies, 415–20; class issues, 433–34; crises in filiation, 425–26; diasporic contexts, 426; domaining and, 419, 435; evaluative frameworks, 431–32; feminist studies, 420–21; friendship, 429; gender-based struggles, 426–27, 432–33; idealized viewpoints, 435–36; love, 429–30; political and economic contexts, 427–29, 433–34; production of, 430–34; psychological perspectives, 432–34; social dramas, 421–22; sociocultural anthropology and, 424–25; studies, 1940s–1970s, 415–22, 437–38 n.2; studies, 1980s–1990s, 422–30; tasks for researchers, 434–36; terminology, 414–15, 437

Library of Congress Cataloging-in-Publication Data

Relative values : reconfiguring kinship studies / edited
by Sarah Franklin and Susan McKinnon.

p. cm.

Includes bibliographical references and index.

ISBN 0-8223-2786-4 (cloth : alk. paper)

ISBN 0-8223-2796-1 (pbk. : alk. paper)

1. Kinship.   I. Franklin, Sarah   II. McKinnon, Susan

GN487 .R45 2001

306.83—dc21   2001040472